International Handbook of Intelligence

This book is the first international handbook of intelligence ever published. It is intended to provide a truly international perspective on the nature of intelligence. It covers intelligence theory, research, and practice from all over the globe. Areas covered include Great Britain, Australia, French-speaking countries, German-speaking countries, Spanish-speaking countries, India, Japan, Israel, Turkey, and China. Each author is an internationally recognized expert in the field of intelligence. Authors represent not just their own viewpoints but also the full variety of viewpoints indigenous to the areas about which they write. Each chapter deals with, for its area, definitions and theories of intelligence, history of research, current research, assessment techniques, and comparison across geographical areas. An integrative final chapter synthesizes the diverse international viewpoints.

Robert J. Sternberg is IBM Professor of Psychology and Education and Director of the Center for the Psychology of Abilities, Competencies, and Expertise at Yale University. He is also 2003 President of the American Psychological Association.

International Handbook of Intelligence

Edited by

ROBERT J. STERNBERG

Yale University, PACE Center

Editorial Board

Paul Baltes
Berit Carlstedt
Ian J. Deary
Jan-Eric Gustafsson
Elias Mpofu
Ricardo Rosas
Lazar Stankov

CAMBRIDGE
UNIVERSITY PRESS

PUBLISHED BY THE PRESS SYNDICATE OF THE UNIVERSITY OF CAMBRIDGE
The Pitt Building, Trumpington Street, Cambridge, United Kingdom

CAMBRIDGE UNIVERSITY PRESS
The Edinburgh Building, Cambridge CB2 2RU, UK
40 West 20th Street, New York, NY 10011-4211, USA
477 Williamstown Road, Port Melbourne, VIC 3207, Australia
Ruiz de Alarcón 13, 28014 Madrid, Spain
Dock House, The Waterfront, Cape Town 8001, South Africa

http://www.cambridge.org

First published 2004

Printed in the United States of America

Typeface Palatino 10/13 pt.   *System* LATEX 2ε [TB]

A catalog record for this book is available from the British Library.

Library of Congress Cataloging in Publication data

International handbook of intelligence / Robert J. Sternberg, editor.
    p. cm.
Includes bibliographical references and index.
ISBN 0-521-80815-4 – ISBN 0-521-00402-0 (pbk.)
1. Intellect.   I. Sternberg, Robert J.
BF431.I59   2003
153.9–dc21   2003048462

ISBN 0 521 80815 4 hardback
ISBN 0 521 00402 0 paperback

Contents

Contributors

Juko Ando, Keio University, Tokyo

Bibhu D. Baral, University of Alberta

Berit Carlstedt, National Defence College, Sweden

Roberto Colom, Autonoma University of Madrid

J. P. Das, University of Alberta

Ian J. Deary, University of Edinburgh

Andreas Demetriou, University of Cyprus

Rocío Fernández-Ballesteros, Autonoma University of Madrid

Elena L. Grigorenko, Yale University

Sami Gulgoz, Koc University, Istanbul

Jan-Eric Gustafsson, Göteborg University, Sweden

Giyoo Hatano, The University of the Air, Chiba, Japan

Jarkko Hautamäki, Helsinki University

Cigdem Kagitcibasi, Koc University, Istanbul

Ute Kunzmann, Max Planck Institute for Human Development, Berlin

Jacques Lautrey, Université René Descartes, Paris

Shu-Chen Li, Max Planck Institute for Human Development, Berlin

Gerald Matthews, University of Cincinnati

Elias Mpofu, Pennsylvania State University

Hiroshi Namiki, Waseda University, Tokyo

Timothy C. Papadopoulos, University of Cyprus

Anik de Ribaupierre, Université de Genève

Richard D. Roberts, University of Sydney

Ricardo Rosas, Universidad Católica de Chile

Tatsuya Sato, Ritsumeikan University, Kyoto, Japan

Jiannong Shi, Institute of Psychology, Chinese Academy of Sciences

Pauline Smith, NFER-Nelson, London

Lazar Stankov, University of Sydney

Robert J. Sternberg, Yale University

Moshe Zeidner, University of Haifa

Preface

A school psychologist in the United States who was seeking to assess the source of difficulties of a child with learning problems would be very likely to give the child a conventional intelligence test, such as the Stanford-Binet; a French psychologist would be unlikely to use such a test. The reason for the difference is that the two countries have different histories and current traditions with regard to the study and understanding of human intelligence. This particular pair of countries illustrates an especial irony because intelligence testing as we know it began at the turn of the twentieth century in France with a Frenchman, Alfred Binet, whereas widespread use of intelligence testing in the United States did not begin until World War I.

Some fields in psychology and other sciences have a unified history; others do not. Intelligence is one of those fields that does not. For example, French-speaking countries have traditions emanating from Binet and Piaget. English-speaking countries have traditions emanating from Spearman and Thomson (United Kingdom) and Thurstone and Thorndike (United States). German-speaking countries have traditions emanating from Wundt and later, the Gestalt psychologists. Chinese work on intelligence goes back even to before the Common Era, when ability tests were used for selection for jobs. Work in several countries in Africa reveals very different conceptions of intelligence than in Western countries.

As a result of these varied traditions, histories of the field, textbook citations to the field, and current practices in the field vary fairly widely across different national and language borders. As an example, two widely cited recent reference works on intelligence (Sternberg, 1994,

2000) both contain an overwhelming majority of their contributions from American contributors, whose points of view on intelligence are likely quite different from points of view of researchers from other cultures.

The goal of this volume is to present a truly international and unique set of perspectives on the psychology of human intelligence. This goal has been accomplished by asking authors from around the world who are distinguished scholars to write chapters of the volume that speak to the history and current state of intelligence research in their respective parts of the world. This book thereby becomes a unique source of information that is systematically international in its perspectives.

It is not possible in a book of this kind to cover every area in the world. For example, there is only one chapter from Africa and only one from each of South America and North America. The decisions about which areas to represent were complex ones. For example, with regard to the United States and Canada, although both have excellent scholars studying intelligence, it is not clear that the U.S. and Canadian traditions are sufficiently different to justify separate chapters. We were unable to find a strong enough tradition of psychological research on intelligence in Mexico and other countries in North America (e.g., Bermuda or the Bahamas) to justify separate chapters. With regard to South America, Ricardo Rosas was asked to cover as much of South America as he could, but he had difficulty finding large volumes of research to cover from the full complement of South American countries. Europe and Asia have greater representation in the book in terms of separate chapters, simply because there are more countries in which there are active and distinctive research programs.

The book is written for scholars and students with an interest of any kind in the psychology of human intelligence. Among psychologists, this includes differential, clinical, cognitive, school, educational, developmental, counseling, personality, and industrial-organizational psychologists, among others. But the book may also be of interest to audiences in education and business. The chapters are written at a level comprehensible to upper-level undergraduate students.

The book is organized by national or language areas. Each chapter author was expected to cover:

1. Definitions and theories of intelligence within the area
2. History of research within the area
3. Current research within the area
4. Current techniques of assessment within the area

5. Comparisons to theory, research, and assessment in other geographical areas, when possible

The book was written to serve several purposes:

1. It uniquely provides an international perspective on theory, research, and assessment of intelligence.
2. Each chapter has been written by an investigator from the area of interest.
3. It deals both with the history and current state of work in the section.
4. Intelligence is by its nature cultural, at least in part. What constitutes adaptive behavior in one culture may constitute irrelevant or even maladaptive behavior in another country. This book therefore seeks to understand intelligence from diverse points of view.

I am grateful to the editorial board of the *Handbook* for their efforts in bringing this book to fruition. The editorial board included Paul Baltes, Berit Carlstedt, Ian J. Deary, Jan-Eric Gustafsson, Elias Mpofu, Ricardo Rosas, and Lazar Stankov. I also thank Alex Isgut for his help in preparing the manuscript.

Robert J. Sternberg

References

Sternberg, R. J. (Ed.). (1994). *Encyclopedia of human intelligence*. New York: Macmillan.
Sternberg, R. J. (Ed.). (2000). *Handbook of intelligence*. New York: Cambridge University Press.

Intelligence Research and Assessment in the United Kingdom

Ian J. Deary and Pauline Smith

OVERVIEW

British contributions to research and practice in human intelligence are described and discussed. The emphasis on individual differences in humans' cognitive abilities and the search for the origins of human intelligence differences are British contributions. Some applications of intelligence testing are described in education, in the workplace, and in clinical settings. In theory and research, British contributors commune with those from other countries, especially the United States and, therefore, their contributions are not distinctly different. In the application of intelligence testing there is more United Kingdom-specific practice, with tests and procedures that are specific to the United Kingdom. There are differences in practice even within the United Kingdom's nations.

DISSEMINATING AND CRITICIZING RESEARCH ON INTELLIGENCE: U.K. CONTRIBUTIONS

There are several U.K. academic psychologists who have written books on the research surrounding psychometric intelligence-in-the-round. These include introductory books and higher-level monographs.

Among the entry-level, introductory books – intended for lay people, junior students, and other non-experts – there is a range of opinions. Some are critical appraisals of the field but are from researchers

Some of the material preceding the section titled "Recent Developments in Intelligence Testing in the UK" first appeared in Deary (2001a). Reproduced with permission from *The British Journal of Psychology*, © The British Psychological Society.

whose work is within the psychometric tradition (e.g., Cooper, 1999; Deary, 2001b; Kline, 1991). Included in this group is Brand's (1996) *The g Factor*, which was withdrawn by the publisher soon after publication despite positive critical evaluations (e.g., Mackintosh, 1996a). Other books at this level are highly critical of the concept of intelligence and the psychometric approach more generally. For example, Richardson's (1999) book concludes by arguing that intelligence testing should be banned as a social evil. This is congruent with Richardson's (e.g., Richardson & Webster, 1996) research commentaries, which argue that reasoning cannot be assessed in a context-free manner, a view contested by Roberts and Stevenson (1996). Another very negative assessment of psychometric intelligence research was one of a number of books by Howe (1997). This accords with Howe's research into high-level skill acquisition, which tended to emphasize factors other than innate talents, such as experience and practice (Howe, Davidson, & Sloboda, 1998).

Higher-level books included Mackintosh's (1998) well-received critical appraisal of research on psychometric intelligence. This had special impact because of his disinterestedness: Mackintosh is an expert in animal learning. His other valued services to intelligence research included assessments of sex differences (Mackintosh, 1996b), an edited volume assessing the nature of Cyril Burt's alleged misdemeanors (Mackintosh, 1995), and his many expert commentaries in the field of intelligence research (e.g., Mackintosh, 1981, 1996a, 2000). Anderson's (1992) book was an original fusion of neuropsychological and developmental psychology with the psychometrics of intelligence, producing a novel account of the origins, structure, and cognitive bases of intelligence differences. Deary's (2000a) monograph was a critical appraisal of the success of reductionistic research into individual differences in psychometric intelligence.

UNDERSTANDING INTELLIGENCE: U.K. CONTRIBUTIONS

There continues to be discussion and some incomprehension between those who emphasize the usefulness of experimental versus individual differences approaches to human cognitive functions, between those who sought the structure of modal cognitive function in humans and those who were interested in how and why people differed in these functions (Novartis Foundation, 2000). Historically, these complementary points of view were represented in Britain by the difference between the Cambridge (Bartlett, 1932) and London (Spearman, 1927) schools of psychology, respectively. Bartlett paid tribute to the London school's forerunner Galton as "a brilliant and original investigator," dubbing him "the father of experimental psychology in England" (p. 7). He further lauded the contribution made by differential psychologists, "as all the psychological world knows, in the extremely important work of Prof. C. E. Spearman" (p. 7). But Bartlett worried that

Such statistical treatment gives, not, indeed, the mode of determination of the individual reaction, but a picture of trends of response and their interrelations. . . . Largely by direct influence, but probably also because Galton's outlook contains something that is peculiarly attractive to the English temperament, the methods initiated by him have become very widely used in English psychology, and have been greatly developed by his successors. (p. 7)

Some commentators bemoaned the separation of differential and experimental psychology, insisting that it is important to know both the modal structure and function of cognition as well as the parameters governing individual differences. Thus, Spearman (1904, 1923) insisted that the understanding of human ability differences must be founded upon valid variables delivered by experimental psychologists, and that the study of intelligence differences must be preceded by an understanding of the "principles of cognition." To bridge the gap, Spearman, prior to writing his statistics-strewn *The Abilities of Man* (1927), wrote *The Nature of Intelligence and the Principles of Cognition* (1923), which was deemed the first textbook of cognitive psychology (Gustafsson, 1992). Sporadically, as the 20th century matured, the calls to combine experimental (or cognitive) and differential approaches to human ability and its differences have echoed more or less strongly back and forth across the Atlantic (Cronbach, 1957; Eysenck, 1967; Sternberg, 1978; Eysenck, 1995), with the result being an intermittently satisfying but rather desultory affair (Deary, 1997, 2000a, 2000b).

A related disagreement was between the British, London-school approach to intelligence differences and that of Binet and Simon. The former aimed to "understand" intelligence differences in terms of elementary psychological processes, such as sensory discrimination and reaction times (Deary, 1994a, 1994b Galton, 1883; Johnson et al., 1985; Spearman, 1904), whereas Binet's approach was to construct a "hotchpot" (Spearman's 1927 epithet) of higher-level tasks to gain a "measurement" of ability (Binet, 1905).

The contrast between Spearman's and Binet's approaches is often portrayed as a disagreement about the best way to measure human mental abilities (see Deary, 1994a, for an historical review and discussion). That is incorrect: They agreed on the matter of how to measure. They parted on two other matters. Binet, according to Spearman, preferred a faculty (modular) structure for mental abilities, whereas Spearman sought a structure that could incorporate *g*. Second, Spearman worried that proceeding with measurement prior to any theory of, or explanation for, intelligence differences would curtail the necessary work of understanding the general factor. Though Binet's test might measure the general factor, its nature was still mysterious:

> But notice must be taken that this general factor *g*, like all measurements anywhere, is primarily not any concrete thing but only a value or magnitude. Further, that which this magnitude measures has not been defined by declaring what it is like, but only by pointing out where it can be found. (Spearman, 1927, p. 75)

It was these British concerns about the nature of intelligence differences that would be taken up seriously over half a century later with the "information processing approach" to intelligence differences (e.g., Hunt, 1980; Deary, 2000a, 2000b).

U.K. CONTRIBUTIONS TO UNDERSTANDING THE STRUCTURE OF HUMAN INTELLIGENCE DIFFERENCES

Academic argument about the structure of human intelligence differences continues (e.g., Mackintosh, 1998; Gardner, 1999; Deary, 2000a). The central issues of the argument are the best way to construe the associations among those correlations that occur between psychometric test scores, and whether such psychometric tests omit important aspects of human ability. British psychologists made a large contribution to the partial consensus that emerged in the mid-1980s and early 1990s concerning the structure of psychometric intelligence.

Five of the greatest books in the history of psychometric intelligence and mental measurement were written by Britons in the first half of the 20th century: Spearman (1923, 1927), Thomson (1939), Burt (1940), and Vernon (1950). The authors impress the reader on a number of fronts: their erudition and knowledge of disparate research literature, their ability to devise complex novel statistical methods, their empirical contribution (this must be qualified for Burt; Mackintosh, 1995), and their contribution to theory. Moreover, they lasted the course. Among them, they emphasized the facts about psychometric intelligence that emerged in the next 50 years: that mental ability differences may be described as a hierarchy of more or less specific packets of variance with g on top; that psychometrics will never explain intelligence differences; and that ability factors, especially g, should be treated as discoveries to be explained rather than things in the brain.

Though there seemed to be a U.K.–U.S. argument about the existence of a general factor for a sizeable portion of the 20th century, the cognoscenti knew very early on that there was no substantial difference in results obtained across the Atlantic; it was one of emphasis rather than substance. Those who – for example, Gould (1981, 1997) – retained the erroneous notion that Thurstone (1938) rid the scene of g, or that g is an arbitrary artifact of statistical whim, should note two things. First, even Thurstone was aware very early on that his data contained a g factor (Eysenck, 1939). Second, Gould's (1981) incorrect comments on the psychometric nature of abilities have been corrected (Carroll, 1995). Gustafsson (1984) explained clearly why g does not go away with different factor analytic approaches, and Humphreys (1979) commented:

The neglect in the United States of the general factor in human abilities has arisen from the popularity of the group factor model and the almost universal restriction of that model to factors in the first order only. (p. 107)

Today the converging consensus about mental ability differences incorporates ideas from Thurstone (concerning primary-level mental abilities), Burt and Vernon (concerning a hierarchy of intelligence factors ranging from specific abilities to g with group factors in between) and Spearman (concerning specific factors and g; in his 1927 book he was rather dismissive about group factors). Whether one examines the analyses of diverse mental test batteries given to large, discrete samples of subjects (Undheim, 1981a, 1981b; Gustafsson, 1984; Carretta & Ree, 1995; Bickley, Keith, & Wolfle, 1995), or considers Carroll's (1993) standardized re-analyses of hundreds of mental test data sets gathered throughout the 20th century, the result is similar: Human mental ability differences show near universal positive correlations; the packets of covariance in a heterogeneous mental test battery given to a broad sample of adults or children can be arranged into correlated group factors; and a g factor can be extracted that accounts for around 50% of the variance among individuals. Gustafsson referred to "this unifying model" of mental abilities (p. 193) and summarized its characteristics as follows,

The Spearman, Thurstone, and Cattell-Horn models may, in a structural sense at least, be viewed as subsets of the HILI [Hierarchical, LISREL (Linear Structural RELations)-based] model: the Spearman model takes into account variance from the third-order factor; The Thurstone model takes into account first-order variance; and the Cattell-Horn model takes into account both first- and second-order variance. The Vernon model comes close to the proposed model: The *g*-factor is included in both models, and at the second-order level v:ed [Vernon's (1950) verbal-educational factor)] closely corresponds to G_c [crystallised intelligence], and k:m [Vernon's spatial-mechanical factor] corresponds to G_v [general visualization].

The "three-stratum" (Carroll, 1993) account of human ability differences is sometimes nowadays referred to as a "theory" (Bickley et al., 1995; Bouchard, 1998). It is, rather, a taxonomy that construes covariance into different-sized packages that serve the purposes of providing predictive validity and the substrate for explanatory science. Burt (1940) warned,

So far as it seeks to be strictly scientific, psychology must beware of supposing that these principles of classification can forthwith be treated as "factors in the mind," e.g., as 'primary abilities' or as "mental powers" or "energies." (p. 251)

It is interesting to see equal criticism thus aimed specifically at both Thurstone and Burt's London-school forerunner Spearman.

Similarly, Vernon (1961) was concerned that

the best-established factors, such as Thurstone's, represent the external qualities or materials of the tests – verbal, numerical, spatial, etc. – rather than central mental functions. It may be that statistical analysis alone is incapable of yielding these more fundamental functional components of the mind. (pp. 138–139)

The exact same factors do not appear from every analysis, nor would one expect that, given the variation in test batteries, and the possibility – first suggested by Spearman and Burt – that human abilities might be structured slightly differently at different levels of ability (Deary et al., 1996).

Burt's (1940) mid-century "four factor" (the three strata model plus error variance, essentially) solution to human ability differences was very similar to, perhaps even more general than, the model that attracted some consensus half a century later,

Four kinds of factors may be formally distinguished – (i) general, (ii) group or bipolar, (iii) specific, and (iv) error factors, that is, those possessed by all the traits, by some of the traits, by one trait always, or by one trait on the occasion of its measurement only. . . .

From the four-factor theorem (as it may be termed) all the familiar factor theories may be derived. (p. 249–250)

The diamond jubilee of Burt's (1940) suggestion witnessed many psychometricians unwittingly re-converging on his conclusion. Others continued to differ to some degree (see Neisser et al., 1996). Among these was the quondam Briton Raymond Cattell whose influential theory of fluid and crystallized intelligences recognized correlated general factors in human ability but, by way of diktat rather than data, never quite accommodated Spearman's *g* (Horn & Cattell, 1966; Cattell, 1998; Horn, 1998).

Godfrey Thomson (1939) was famous within intelligence research for his statistical innovations and debates with Spearman about the interpretation of the general factor in mental ability. However, whereas his "anarchic" theory of intelligence differences is largely absent from mainstream intelligence research worldwide, his lasting contribution might be the part he played in the Scottish Council for Research in Education's (1933) national surveys of psychometric intelligence. In the first of these surveys, in 1932, almost the entire nation of Scottish children born in 1921 took a version of the Moray House Test on June 1. This test was like the general reasoning section of the "eleven-plus" tests, which were used in the United Kingdom between about the 1930s and the 1960s to select children for different types of secondary school education. Small pockets of eleven-plus testing remain in the United Kingdom today. The number of children tested in the 1932 survey was 87,498, representing well over 90% of the population. As it turned out at the time, this proved mostly to be a descriptive achievement. However, the data were retained and, therefore, within Scotland there are high-quality mental test data for an entire birth cohort. Our research team followed up on 101 of the Scottish cohort 66 years to the day after the original test. They took the same test using the same instructions and the same time limit. Comparing the 1932 and the 1998 results on the Moray House Test gave a correlation of 0.63 (0.73 when corrected for attenuation) (Deary et al., 2000). Two better-established British contributions to aging-related studies of intelligence should be noted. Among other cohort studies worldwide the United Kingdom has contributed some large scale studies of cognition and aging (e.g., Rabbitt et al., 1993). On the theoretical side, Cattell's (e.g., 1998) ideas of fluid and crystallized intelligence find much application in the contemporary study of aging and intelligence differences.

SOME CAUSES OF HUMAN INTELLIGENCE DIFFERENCES

Spearman's (1904) first investigations examined the association between psychometric intelligence and sensory discrimination, an idea that had been suggested and tried by others, Galton (1883) among them. Review and re-analyses of largely British studies before and during World War I showed that there was a small, significant correlation between visual and auditory discrimination and mental test scores (Deary, 1994a). These hold up in more recent investigations, and Raz, Willerman, and Yama (1987) commented that

no matter what the exact mechanisms of information processing underlying intelligence, Galton's (1883) suggestion of an important link between "the avenues of the senses" and good sense may not be as far-fetched as previously supposed. (p. 209)

However, correlations between any one information-processing index and psychometric intelligence are not large, and there are few current researchers who search after the Holy Grail (Hunt, 1980) of a single information-processing index that will explain g or other abilities in the psychometric hierarchy.

Currently, the lively but heterogeneous research activity that seeks the causes of psychometric intelligence has the following agenda. It examines associations between psychometric test scores and indices of brain function at putatively lower levels of reduction than the test scores themselves. When correlations are obtained and replicated, it then considers the possible mechanisms of the associations and the validity and tractability of the brain indices. Properly self-critical investigators consider the possibility that, in some cases, the cause of any correlation might be the reverse of that which is supposed, that is, better performance on supposedly lower-level brain indices might be caused by, rather than be the cause of, psychometric intelligence differences. Collections of this type of research may be found in Eysenck (1982), Vernon (1987, 1993), and Deary (2000a). For the purposes of a resumé, it is convenient to describe the state of this area by descending through different levels of reduction. Thus, brain indices have been sought at, arguably, psychometric, cognitive, psychophysical, psychophysiological, physiological, and biological levels. The focus of this area is the continuity that recent research shows with ideas contributed by British psychologists. Though his most prominent contributions were to the science of personality, the British psychologist H. J. Eysenck championed and supported the experimental study of intelligence from the 1960s onward, several years before such a movement really took off in the United States (Eysenck, 1967; see also 1982 and 1995).

R. J. Sternberg (1977, 1985) executed inventive experiments using psychometric tasks. Developing a legacy from Spearman, Sternberg dissected, using a partial cueing technique and regression models, analogical reasoning performance into "mental components." He chose analogical reasoning because so many past researchers on psychometric intelligence had placed this type of reasoning near to the center of their thinking about psychometric intelligence differences. Sternberg's models of component function accounted successfully for performance differences on reasoning tasks. Sternberg's components of reasoning bore strong resemblances to Spearman's "principles of cognition" (1923), especially the eduction of relations and correlates. And they also suffered the same problems as Spearman's principles and components: They were brought into being from the armchair and not the lab; they were never validated outside the rarefied world of the mental test item; and it was never finally established whether they were components of mind or merely components of mental test items (Deary, 1997, 2000a).

Successors to Sternberg have also concentrated on reasoning ability and have applied newer analytic techniques. Carpenter, Just, and Shell's (1990) analysis of performance success on Raven's matrices used subjects' verbal reports and eye tracking information to construct computer models of average and good performers on the task. Raven's (1938) Matrices, a British-built task based on Spearman's (1923) principles of cognition, is widely acknowledged as just about the best single group test of *g* (Westby, 1953; Marshalek, Lohman, & Snow, 1983). It is not easy to decide whether Carpenter and colleagues got beneath the psychometric skin of performance of the Raven task or just elaborately redescribed Raven's own task building principles, but the key processes involved in task success were rule-finding (like Spearman's eductions of relations and correlates) and keeping track of multiple goals in working memory (like Spearman's [1927] mental span).

Working Memory

Accounts of reasoning performance frequently appeal to the British construct of working memory (Baddeley, 1986, 1992a) as a basis for individual differences. Working memory is "a limited capacity system allowing the temporary storage and manipulation of information

necessary for such complex tasks as comprehension, learning and reasoning" (Baddeley, 2000, p. 418). Baddeley's articulation of the construct
of working memory arose from the growing problems with the notion
of a single short-term memory store. A key observation was that reasoning, comprehension and learning could still take place in patients
whose short-term memory was damaged or in healthy people who
had to remember digits while performing a dual task. Baddeley (1992a)
replaced the single short-term memory notion with a tripartite working
memory model with

an attentional controller and the central executive, supplemented by two subsidiary slave systems. The articulatory or phonological loop was assumed to be
responsible for maintaining speech-based information, including digits in the
digit span test, whereas the visuospatial sketch pad was assumed to perform a
similar function in setting up and manipulating visuospatial imagery. (p. 556)

Baddeley (1992a) described two complementary types of research on
working memory. The first, more British-based, used dual-task methodology to examine neuropsychological cases and thereby explore the
modal structure of working memory in humans. This approach dominated Baddeley's own research. He continued to explore the structure
and function of working memory in humans and, in response to limitations in the original model, added a fourth component. This "episodic
buffer" is

a limited capacity system that provides temporary storage of information held in
a multimodal code, which is capable of binding information from the subsidiary
systems, and from long-term memory, into a unitary episodic representation.
(Baddeley, 2000, p. 417)

The second, more common in North America, devised tests of working
memory to discover whether this construct could account for variance in
related cognitive tasks, including the reasoning tasks that are common
in tests of psychometric intelligence. It is the second approach that has
had such a large influence on intelligence theory. Baddeley (1992b) stated
that

An emphasis on individual differences has the further advantage of linking up
with more traditional psychometric approaches. This appears to be meeting
with some success, since working memory measures appear to correlate very
highly with performance on a range of reasoning tasks that have traditionally
been used for measuring intelligence. (p. 287)

Using Baddeley's ideas to construct psychometric tests of working memory, Kyllonen and Christal's (1990) structural equation models of thousands of U.S. armed forces applicants' test scores found reasoning and working memory to be highly correlated constructs. They were not able to decide which of the two had causal precedence over the other (see also Kyllonen, 1996), but they suggested they were not synonymous. Working memory, in Kyllonen's Cognitive Abilities Measurement (CAM) test battery, loads .95 on the CAM general factor and this factor correlated .994 from the Armed Services Vocational Aptitude Battery (ASVAB) test battery (Stauffer, Ree, & Carretta, 1996). Engle et al. (1999), using a latent trait approach, found individual differences in working memory highly related to short-term memory ($r = .68$) and to general fluid intelligence ($r = .59$) but short-term memory was not significantly correlated with fluid intelligence.

If working memory is so closely related to psychometric intelligence, then researchers in the latter field would be well-advised to make use of the extensive neuropsychological, cognitive, and biological information about working memory in thinking about the elements of mental ability differences. This would make a nice meeting ground for a proper reconciliation of the Cambridge and London school approaches to cognition.

g and Frontal Lobe Function

Working memory is, therefore, a strong British contender as an explanatory factor for *g*. Another British contender is frontal lobe function, as suggested by Duncan and colleagues (Duncan, Emslie, & Williams, 1996; Duncan et al., 2000). Duncan argued that low intelligence bears resemblances to frontal lobe dysfunction (Duncan et al., 1996). He devised a task that is performed poorly by people with frontal lobe lesions when compared with healthy subjects. This involved reading letters from a temporal stream of stimuli that appear on a computer screen as horizontal pairs of letters or numbers. Every so often a + or – sign appears, which indicates whether or not the subject should change the stream (left or right) of stimuli to which they must attend. Duncan et al. (1996) found people with frontal lobe damage often failed to implement this instruction, despite being aware of what they should have done. Among healthy subjects, this failure to implement this so-called second side instruction correlated –.52 with scores on Cattell's Culture-Fair test.

This evidence for a frontal lobe seat for differences in g was supplemented by evidence from positron emission tomography (Duncan et al., 2000). Verbal, spatial and numerical tasks were devised in similar-looking versions that were either low or high on g-loading. In each type of task the differences in brain metabolism between the high and low g-loading versions of the task were examined. Common to all three high g-loaded tasks was activation of an area in the lateral frontal lobes. Duncan and Owen (2000) reviewed a number of functional neuroimaging studies and concluded that there is a "specific frontal-lobe network that is consistently recruited for solution of diverse cognitive problems" (p. 475). The evidence was a pattern of recruitment of the mid-dorsolateral, mid-ventrolateral and dorsal anterior cingulate cortex areas in the frontal lobes.

Therefore, whereas Baddeley has produced a single cognitive function (central executive of the working memory system) that relates highly to g differences, Duncan has located g in a single cerebral location, associated with "goal activation" (Duncan et al., 1996, p. 293). These two concepts see application in others' models of intelligence differences. Also in the mode of Sternberg's componential approach, Embretson (1995) used multicomponent latent trait models to decompose reasoning performance. She found that reasoning performance differences were well accounted for by two latent traits derived from the psychometric tests she had devised: general control processing and working memory. Her opinion was that this modern methodology was rediscovering some of Spearman's ideas: "General control processing, Spearman's mental energy, is the conative directing of attention, whereas working memory capacity parallels Spearman's mental span concept" (p. 184).

Reaction Time

Appeals to cognitive variables in an attempt to account for variance in human ability differences have leaned heavily on various reaction time procedures. Buried within Galton's unanalyzed data from his anthropometric laboratory in South Kensington was some indirect evidence to link faster reactions with higher mental ability (Johnson et al., 1985). In recent research on intelligence differences the most researched of the reaction time procedures is that first described by the British psychologist Hick (1952). He modeled the linear increase in reaction times as a function of the log of the number of stimulus alternatives in a choice reaction time procedure. His epithet for the slope's psychological importance was that it might represent the "rate of gain of information" of the subject. Beginning with the German psychologist Roth (1964), differential psychologists alighted on the possibility that individual differences in this slope parameter might account for some of the individual differences in psychometric intelligence. However, three decades on from Roth's pioneering study something rather surprising has emerged. Along with other favored reaction time procedures, especially the S. Sternberg (1966) memory scanning task and the Posner (Posner & Mitchell, 1967) letter-matching task, the Hick task does indeed throw up significant correlations with psychometric intelligence differences (for reviews, see Vernon, 1987; Jensen, 1987; Neubauer, 1997). Galton was correct, higher test scorers do have faster reactions. They also have less variable reactions. In all three procedures the effect sizes are small-to-medium, that is, enough to be interesting but not enough to "explain" what it is to have high psychometric intelligence. But in all three procedures the elementary processing stage that attracted the differential psychologists failed to have any special association with psychometric intelligence. Thus, the slope in the Hick task, the speed of memory scanning in the Sternberg task and the speed of access to long-term memory in the Posner task are outshone by the prosaic indices assessed in the intercept and variability of the reaction times (Neubauer, 1997; Deary, 2000a). It was also British psychologists Barrett, Eysenck, and Lucking (1986) who showed that not all subject's reaction time data agree with Hick's law.

Much of the research into intelligence and speed of information processing is conducted on biased samples, often college and university students. There has been a lack of studies based on representative samples. The first large, representative study of reaction time and psychometric intelligence was a result of the West of Scotland Twenty-07 Study. Among 900 representative 55-year-olds the correlation between scores on the Alice Heim 4 test and simple and choice reaction times was −.31 and −.49, respectively (Deary, Der, & Ford, 2001). The correlation between psychometric intelligence and intraindividual variability was −.26 for both simple and choice reaction times. These estimates of effect size are larger than previously reported on more attenuated samples. These and other results might herald a change in research focus, away from the supposed processing components that are manufactured from differences between one reaction time condition and another, to the basic reaction times and variabilities themselves. Against this trend, some

British psychologists found an interest in complicating the choice reaction time procedure by adding an element of discrimination, which
increases the correlation with intelligence (Frearson & Eysenck, 1986).

Inspection Time

At what seems to common sense like a lower level of reduction, still,
than reaction times comes the study between psychometric intelligence
and indices related to sensory processing. Galton (1883) hypothesized
that people with higher levels of mental ability had finer powers of discrimination. But a more prescient lead was McKeen Cattell's (1886a,
1886b) discovery, in Wundt's lab, that the minimum stimulus duration required to make an accurate discrimination might be related to
ability level (Deary, 1986). Also, Burt (1909–10), in his first empirical
study, found a strong association between tachistoscopic recognition
and imputed intelligence level. In the modern era, a mass of research
has accumulated around a procedure termed "inspection time," and
this research suggests that the efficiency of the early stages of sensory processing have a moderate association with psychometric intelligence. Inspection time was developed in Australia by Vickers, a student of the British psychologist Welford (Vickers, Nettelbeck, & Willson,
1972). This task involves a forced-choice, two-alternative discrimination.
Typically, the subject views two parallel lines, one much longer than
the other. Without any pressure to respond quickly, they indicate to
the experimenter which line is longer. The task is made challenging by
exposing the stimulus lines for varying durations, some of them very
brief. Also, the stimulus lines are replaced by a backward mask immediately after exposure. In essence, the task appears to measure the duration needed by a subject to inspect a stimulus before making a simple
decision.

In 1976, Nettelbeck and Lally reported that individual differences in
this simple task correlated substantially with individual differences in
psychometric intelligence. The 25th anniversary of this report was cel-
ebrated by a special issue of the journal *Intelligence* in 2001 that was
co-edited by the British psychologist Deary (Petrill & Deary, 2001), who
has contributed to the empirical study of inspection time and critically appraised its place in the theory of intelligence differences (Deary,
2000a, chap. 7). The British psychologist Brand was a major influence
in the spread of influence of inspection time as a theoretically interesting correlate of psychometric intelligence (Brand, 1979, 1987; Brand &

Deary, 1982). Qualitative reviews, meta-analyses and single large studies agree that there is a correlation of about .4 between inspection times and psychometric intelligence (Nettelbeck, 1987; Kranzler & Jensen, 1989; Deary & Stough, 1996; Crawford et al., 1998).

British contributions to the data and theory concerning the association between inspection time and intelligence have been substantial. These have been reviewed by Deary (Deary & Stough, 1996; Deary, 1996, 1997, 1999, 2000a, 2000b). The historical precedents of inspection time were first reviewed by Deary (1986), and the first substantial theoretical critique of inspection time was by Levy (1992). Some of the early inspection time studies came from U.K. laboratories (Brand, 1979; Brand & Deary, 1982). Later, some of the larger and more representative samples studying the relationship between intelligence and inspection time were British (Crawford et al., 1998; Deary, 1993; McGeorge, Crawford, & Kelly, 1996). These tended to find that inspection time had a higher association with performance scores on the Wechsler Adult Intelligence Scale-Revised (WAIS-R) battery than with verbal scores, and that inspection time was associated with g but more strongly with the perceptual-organizational aspect of the WAIS-R.

Mechanisms to explain this association between inspection time – a psychophysical task – and psychometric intelligence test scores have yet to be uncovered; however, British work has made strong contributions on many fronts. Among the very few studies to include inspection- and reaction-time measures in the same study was that by Eysenck (Bates & Eysenck, 1993a). The attempts to explore possible inspection time phenomena in other sensory modalities was led by British research. Deary, using a task based on pitch discrimination, found that speed of processing in the auditory modality was associated with psychometric intelligence (Brand & Deary, 1982; Deary et al., 1989; Deary, Head, & Egan, 1989; Deary, 1994b, 1995). Scottish psychologists Parker, Crawford, and Stephen (1999) used an auditory task based on spatial localization and found a similar association, with the advantage that a higher proportion of people could complete their task compared with pitch discrimination.

The possible biological bases of the association between inspection time and intelligence have been pursued prominently in the United Kingdom. Studies that examined event related brain electrical potentials concurrently with inspection time performance were first performed in the United Kingdom (Zhang, Caryl, & Deary, 1989a, 1989b; Caryl, 1994; Caryl, Golding, & Hall, 1995; Caryl & Harper, 1996). These studies produced convincing links with the gradient of the excursion between the N140 and the P200 wave of the event related response: People with faster inspection time and higher psychometric intelligence have steeper gradients. The first psychopharmacological study of inspection time showed no effect of smoking (Petrie & Deary, 1989), though later studies reported that nicotine improved inspection times (Stough et al., 1995). Clinical applications of inspection time were pioneered in the United Kingdom: Deary et al. (1991) found slower inspection times in Alzheimer's disease but not in Korsakoff's psychosis, and Shipley et al. (2002) showed slower inspection time in people with Parkinson's disease versus matched controls. Deary and colleagues have explored the effect of hypoglycemia on inspection time, demonstrating that low levels of blood glucose slow visual inspection time and low-level auditory processing at the same time as they affect higher cognitive functions (McCrimmon et al., 1996; McCrimmon et al., 1997; Ewing et al., 1998; Strachan, et al., 2001). The first study to explore the brain activation–deactivation patterns associated with inspection time was conducted by Deary, Simonotto, et al. (2001). Using functional magnetic resonance imaging they showed that performing inspection time was associated with activation in the cingulate gyrus and some temporal, and parietal lobe areas. There were also areas of deactivation in some frontal, temporal, and parietal areas. There were similarities between the areas active during inspection time and those areas active during higher tasks of psychometric intelligence.

British psychologists have been prominent in the developmental study of inspection time. Anderson has promulgated a theory that humans' "basic processing mechanism" is central to intelligence differences, can be indexed by inspection time, and does not change its speed and efficiency with development (Anderson, 1992). Anderson, Reid, and Nelson (2001) have supported this idea by showing that task familiarity can explain some apparent developmental changes in inspection time in children. Deary (1995) showed that individual differences in auditory processing efficiency were causally related to intelligence differences in schoolchildren tested at age 12 and followed up at 14 years. At the other end of the age spectrum, the British psychologist Rabbitt worked with Nettelbeck on the role of inspection time in cognitive aging. They found that inspection time could account for much of the variance in the aging of higher cognitive functions, but that initial recall was an exception (Nettelbeck & Rabbitt, 1992; Nettelbeck et al., 1996; and see the re-analyses of these data by Deary, 2000a, p. 245).

Balancing the view that inspection time might be a lower-level processing index responsible for some of the variance in intelligence differences is an idea that inspection time might be the result of higher-level processes, that is, a consequence rather than a cause of intelligence differences. Theoretically, among the first to articulate this idea were the British psychologists Mackintosh (1981) and Howe (1988), and among the first theoretically to refute it was Brand (1987). British research on the idea that cognitive strategies might account for the association between inspection time and intelligence have tended to refute rather than support the idea (Egan, 1994; Simpson & Deary, 1997). Supporting this, Deary, McCrimmon, and Bradshaw (1997) showed that a latent trait from three different visual processing tasks, rather than the strategies associated with any one task, related to intelligence differences.

Brain Size

The idea that bigger brains might be found in cleverer people goes back to antiquity (the Spanish writer Huarte, 1575, provided an early review), though the British writer Fuller (1648) wrote equivocally about mental ability and brain size. Early research on the hypothesis was carried out in Britain by Galton (1888) and Pearson (1906–1907), who examined head size and academic achievement. Pearson concluded that there is a slight correlation between size of head and general intelligence and that measuring head size would never be a useful contribution to estimating cognitive function. The advance in this area since the 1980s has been the opportunity to measure brain size in vivo using magnetic resonance imaging. Several studies now more or less agree that there is a correlation up to about 0.4 between brain size and mental ability test scores (Rushton & Ankney, 1996). Among the studies contributing to this consensus was the sample studied by the British psychologist Egan (Egan et al., 1994; Egan et al., 1995). Newer studies concentrate on those areas of the brain whose volumes correlate most highly with ability test scores (Flashman et al., 1998).

Evoked Potentials

The issue of whether there are aspects of brain electrical activity that associate reliably with intelligence differences is not settled. Nevertheless, British psychologists have contributed prominently to this area of research. Two of the most comprehensive reviews of the field were British, by

Barrett and Eysenck (1992a) and Deary and Caryl (1993). An influential idea from the United Kingdom was that the "string length" of the evoked potential was related to intelligence differences (A. E. Hendrickson, 1982; D. E. Hendrickson, 1982). This string length was based on the idea that people with higher ability had more reliable brain-electrical responses to stimuli. A study by Blinkhorn and Hendrickson (1982) did show the expected associations, but further research from Eysenck's laboratory failed to replicate the effect, and even reversed it at times (Barrett & Eysenck, 1992b, 1994). The string length measure of individual differences in evoked potentials remains as one candidate measure in a relatively confused area of research (Deary, 2000a, chap. 9).

Genetics

One of Britain's best-known, and regrettable, contributions to the question of the environmental and genetic contributions to intelligence was Burt's dubious twin data (Hearnshaw, 1979; Mackintosh, 1995). Striking them from the experimental canon was the only prudent option.

Burt's results aside, the accumulated family, adoption, and twin (reared together and apart) data allow the following conclusions: The heritability of psychometric intelligence is moderately high, as is the environmental contribution; the heritability is probably higher in adulthood and even more so in old age; non-shared environment makes a larger contribution than family upbringing; much of the heritability of psychometric intelligence is via Spearman's g; and some group factors of ability are more heritable than others (Bouchard, 1998; Devlin, Daniels, & Roeder, 1997; McClearn et al., 1997; Petrill et al., 1998; Plomin et al., 2001; Plomin & Petrill, 1997).

The United Kingdom now has, in Robert Plomin, one of the most effective researchers and communicators in the environmental and genetic aspect of intelligence. His and his coworkers' voices are effective over at least three aspects of genetic-environmental research on intelligence. First, Plomin has proved a reasonable and clear communicator of genetic findings and trends in intelligence research. His reviews and essays appear regularly in general journals and successful books (Plomin, 2003; Plomin et al., 2001; Plomin & Petrill, 1997; Plomin & Crabbe, 2000; Plomin, 2001a, 2001b; McGuffin, Riley, & Plomin, 2001). Second, Plomin has employed classical behavior genetic methods such as twin studies and applied them to answer new questions, such as aspects of developmental change in intelligence and molarity versus modularity of cognitive functions. This multivariate genetic research has shown, for example, that much of the high heritability of specific cognitive functions in old age arises primarily from the high heritability of g at that age (Petrill et al., 1998). However, Plomin's research demonstrated the relative independence of mental abilities and their genetic influence in the first few years of life, and that there is a developmental trend from modularity to molarity in early childhood (Price et al., 2000; Petrill et al., 2001).

Third, Plomin is among the world leaders in the application of molecular genetics techniques to the study of intelligence differences. Classical behavior genetic studies' findings point to sources of variance in ability test scores. They do not offer tractable accounts of the biological mechanisms of ability differences. A start on this longer and more interesting road is being made by the application of molecular genetic research to psychometric intelligence differences (McGuffin & Martin, 1999; Plomin & Crabbe, 2000). British research features prominently, because of Plomin and his team's IQ QTL (quantitative trait loci) project at the Institute of Psychiatry in London and collaborating institutions. Though mental handicaps were previously the focus of genetic research into ability levels, this has shifted to include normal and exceptional ability (Daniels et al., 1998). The aim of the IQ QTL project is to search for associations using over 3000 genetic markers and to replicate any findings in other samples (Plomin et al., 1995; Petrill et al., 1996; Plomin & Craig, 2001; Plomin, 2000; Hill et al., 2001). No one should doubt the difficulties of such a project: There are an unknown number of genetic influences on different abilities; some smaller or greater proportion of these might have effect sizes too small feasibly to be detected; even finding an association just announces the start of a tortuous job of unraveling the route between gene effect and ability level; there are so many loci to investigate that Type 1 errors will be common (Petrill et al., 1998; Wahlsten, 1999). Already, the IQ QTL project has thrown up some non-associations (e.g., with polymorphisms of the Apolipoprotien E gene; Turic et al., 2001) and some possible associations (e.g., with polymorphisms of the cystathionine beta-synthase gene; Barbaux, Plomin, & Whitehead, 2000). Commentators agree that progress in this field will include cognitive constructs related to information processing at some level of explanation between psychometric phenotypes and biology as revealed (if it is) by molecular genetic associations (Gottesman, 1997). Plomin and Crabbe (2000) call this process of investigation "behavioural genomics." Another hopeful sign is that research focus is on understanding human differences in cognitive aging, rather than on brave new world scenarios of increasing mental ability in normal people (MacLullich et al., 1998).

Group Differences

The now-retired-but-still-active British psychologist Richard Lynn has contributed prominently to several issues in human intelligence research. For example, he contributed information to the differentiation hypothesis of intelligence, which suggests that there is a stronger g factor at lower levels of intelligence (Lynn, 1992; and see Deary & Pagliari, 1991; Deary et al., 1996), and he contributed an hypothesis to explain the Flynn effect of increasing IQ scores by suggesting that nutritional improvements might explain the effect to some extent (Lynn, 1990). Among his best-known contributions are those on group differences in cognitive abilities, including sex and ethnic differences. Against much prevailing opinion (including that from the United Kingdom; Mackintosh, 1996b), Lynn used European and American standardization samples to argue that there are sex differences in intelligence, with men scoring higher on verbal IQ on the Wechsler tests (Lynn, 1998; Lynn & Mulhearn, 1991). Lynn, Irwing, and Cammock (2002) studied undergraduates and found that males had higher scores on a test of general knowledge. They used this to argue that the Wechsler results were not due to test bias. Another consistent topic addressed by Lynn is ethnic group differences, where he has especially addressed the issue of relatively high scores among Japanese people (Lynn, 1982; Lynn, 1991; Lynn, 1994; Lynn, 1996a). In particular, he has argued that Asian people have higher scores on nonverbal reasoning and spatial ability, but less of a mean advantage on verbal ability (Lynn, 1987). Work on sex and ethnic differences in intelligence is inherently controversial, and Lynn's work especially so. The controversy has been increased with Lynn's spate of books that appeared in his years of retirement. He set out his arguments concerning dysgenic trends – with an emphasis on intelligence and personality – in modern populations (Lynn, 1996b) and a companion volume conducted a reassessment of eugenics (Lynn, 2001a). These books recall Galton's original interests in the late 19th century, and it will surprise many that books with such titles appear in the 21st century. Lynn also echoed another centuries-old British (Scottish, cf. Adam Smith) interest by addressing IQ as a cause of differences in the relative "wealth of nations" (Lynn & Vanhanen, 2002). Lynn also wrote a history of the Pioneer

Fund, the organization that funds, for the most part, research into the genetic and ethnic bases of intelligence differences (Lynn, 2001b).

RECENT DEVELOPMENTS IN INTELLIGENCE TESTING
IN THE UNITED KINGDOM

Ability testing in the United Kingdom proceeds within several separate domains, with surprisingly little interaction between them. The education system provides the most widespread use of cognitive testing in the United Kingdom though, even here, cognitive assessments are conducted within either a pedagogical context or a clinical context. The first type of testing, usually of whole classes or cohorts, is done by teachers or administrators. The second type, of individual children, is done by educational psychologists. The occupational world also engages in considerable cognitive testing. Finally, what can loosely be termed "clinical testing" takes place within the mental health domain. It overlaps to some extent with the educational and occupational contexts, but involves clinical psychologists or neuropsychologists, rather than teachers and human resources professionals or occupational psychologists. Even academic psychologists, who are best placed to integrate the three areas, generally work within one of the three domains, with the exception of those few U.K. researchers working on theoretical studies of "intelligence," whose work has relevance across all domains (e.g., see Cooper, 1999; Deary, 2000a; Mackintosh, 1998). The separation of these forms of testing is perpetuated by the organizational structure of education, employment, and healthcare in the United Kingdom, and by the separate training and professional associations of the individuals concerned. Regulation of testing has developed within the different contexts, with occupational testing standards being in place for many years, while educational standards, encompassing the work of teachers and educational psychologists, are being developed at the present time.

Educational Testing

Pedagogical/Group Testing
Educational ability testing in the United Kingdom has evolved from the middle of the 20th century, when it was dominated by the so-called eleven-plus test (11+) mentioned earlier. This was a group-administered test, typically of verbal reasoning, given to pupils during the year in which they became 11 years old. The results were

used to select who would go on to academically elite grammar schools and who would go to "secondary modern schools."[1] This system of selection was widely vilified by academics, teachers, and educational psychologists, perhaps most notably by Brian Simon (1953, republished 1971). Simon noted that the system created great inequalities in educational opportunities for those who did and did not obtain grammar school places. For example, he claimed that in 1952 only one child in 22,000 went directly from a secondary modern school to a university.

Much of the concern about the inequities of the 11+ subsided in the light of widespread introduction of non-selective "comprehensive" schools from the 1960s onward. However, in a few regions of the United Kingdom, state-funded selective schooling persists, with what are now termed "transfer procedures" still involving the use of cognitive ability testing, alongside tests of English and mathematics in some cases. In the past 15 to 20 years, there has been a marked shift to a use of non-verbal reasoning tests in addition to or instead of verbal reasoning tests for such selection purposes. This has been motivated partly by a desire to broaden the cognitive basis of the assessment but mainly by concerns about fairness. There is a belief that non-verbal tests are less likely than verbal ones to favor the white, middle-class children whose cultural and educational background is thought to be best reflected in the subject matter of the verbal tests. The tests used are compiled from item banks held by NFER-Nelson, which were originally created in the light of theoretical developments in cognitive and differential psychology (see Smith, 1986). The increased preference for non-verbal reasoning tests is also reflected in voluntary testing programs carried out by head-teachers, with the NFER-Nelson Non-Verbal Reasoning test series outselling the equivalent verbal series to a substantial degree.

Another minor but interesting use of cognitive testing at age 11 is that for City Technology Colleges (CTCs). These are 15 secondary schools that are funded partly by private sources and partly by direct grants from the government. They aim to provide children with a technology-based general curriculum, and are charged with taking in a comprehensive ability range, reflecting the local communities that they serve. They ensure this by testing all applicants and then selecting a normal distribution of children from across the score range, rather than taking the highest scorers. In the past few years, 14 of the CTCs have

---

[1] In a few areas of the country, a tripartite scheme of secondary education existed, with technical schools also being available for the education of children.

co-ordinated their entry procedures and are currently using a non-verbal reasoning test as the basis of their pupil selection.[2]

By far the most widespread use of cognitive testing in U.K. schools takes place within the non-selective, comprehensive schools. This is for the purposes of gaining indications of the likely academic achievement of pupils and for providing a baseline against which to judge the "value added" by the schools. Much of this testing takes place when pupils enter the schools at age 11 years, though some schools test or retest two years after, in order to contribute information about relative cognitive strengths to decisions that are then made about subject choices for examination courses. The most widely used test for these purposes is the Cognitive Abilities Test or CAT, published by NFER-Nelson and adapted from the CogAT^{TM} series (Thorndike, Hagen & Lorge, 1954–1993; Lohman, Thorndike & Hagen, 2001), with around 800,000 answer sheets being sold in 2000. The CAT consists of three batteries: verbal, quantitative, and non-verbal, measuring reasoning processes using words, numbers, and shapes, respectively. Overlapping levels serve ages 9 to 14 years.

The theoretical framework underlying CogAT^{TM} is based upon two models of human abilities: Vernon's (1961) hierarchical model and Cattell and Horn's fluid- and crystallized-abilities model (Cattell, 1987; Horn,1988). Vernon's model provided the concept of a three-level structure with g at the apex, major group factors below this and more specific factors at the lowest level. Cattell and Horn's model has been used more directly, to determine the nature of the batteries and the tasks represented within them. All the batteries measure fluid reasoning (G_f), the verbal and quantitative batteries also measure crystallized abilities (G_c) and the non-verbal battery also measures general visualization (G_v). The mean CAT score gives a measure of overall general reasoning ability, or g. From this, it seems that CogAT^{TM} and CAT constitute an embodiment of the drawing together of the Vernon and Cattell-Horn models discussed earlier (e.g., Gustafsson, 1984).

The "indicator" service uses the mean CAT score, based on the three standardized battery scores, since this yields the closest relationship with subsequent academic achievement, except for English, where the verbal battery alone is slightly better. The Pearson correlations between test scores at age 11 or 12 and different school examinations at age

---

[2] The 15th CTC specializes in the performing arts and so bases its selection on other methods.

16 years are between 0.45 (with art and design) and 0.76 (with mathematics). The correlation with summary scores for overall General Certificate of Secondary Education (GCSE) performance are all over 0.7. Similar indicators for national assessments in English, mathematics and science at 14 years and at 11 years (based on the easier levels of CAT given in primary schools) show correlations as high as 0.87 and 0.83, respectively, with average marks (Fernandes & Strand, 2000; Strand, 2001).

These remarkably high levels of predictive validity may to some extent reflect the fact that group tests of verbal reasoning necessarily involve basic reading skills and general knowledge and those of quantitative reasoning involve some simple arithmetic. However, it is noteworthy that the non-verbal battery alone, which uses only shapes as content, achieves high correlations with future achievement (e.g., 0.64 with GCSE mathematics, 0.72 with national tests at age 14 and 0.69 at age 11). This degree of association is not limited to CAT scores: the NFER-Nelson Non-Verbal Reasoning 8/9 test has been found to correlate 0.66 with marks in national tests at age 11 (Strand, 1999). The newest version of the CAT, CAT3, has been designed to reduce as far as possible the extent to which it assesses prior learning rather than reasoning and also to minimize any "middle-class" bias in the item content. It will be interesting to discover in due course if these changes reduce the correlations with future achievement to any substantive degree.

While mean CAT scores provide the best predictors for examination performance, schools are strongly encouraged to look at the separate battery scores in order to gain valuable diagnostic information about the strengths and weaknesses of individual children. As Carroll (1993) concluded after a discussion of the CogAT™ and other batteries, there is no "universally valid resolution" of the controversy about the relative worth of single index g versus multiple abilities. It is necessary to evaluate and choose the best approach for each situation. In this setting, the g score provides the best prediction of overall performance in almost all school subjects, but the group factors yield information of pedagogical value.

Finally, some cognitive testing takes place in schools as part of the process of career guidance for pupils aged 14 and above. Test batteries typically used for this purpose include the Morrisby Battery (Fox & Morrisby, 1991) and the Differential Aptitude Tests for Schools (Bennett, Seashore, & Wesman, 1997).

It is worth noting that the cognitive testing that now takes place in U.K. schools does so within a context of vastly increased use of standardized achievement testing over the past 10 to 15 years. The introduction of national curricula within each of the U.K. countries and associated methods of assessment has led to pupils and teachers having far greater familiarity with the mechanics of standardized assessment than used to be the case.

Individual Educational Testing

Educational psychologists in the United Kingdom, as in many countries, are divided as to the value of psychometric testing. A few local authority services do not use such tests at all on principle but the majority of public sector educational psychologists, and most "independents" (who do private assessments for a fee) make pragmatic use of individually administered cognitive tests as part of their assessment of children. The increasing number of legal cases concerning educational provision for children with special needs is adding to the pressure to provide "objective" evidence of cognitive abilities. Educational psychologists tend to use one of two instruments: the Wechsler tests, the Wechsler Preschool and Primary Scale for Intelligence (WPPSI) and the Wechsler Intelligence Scale for Children (WISC) III[UK] (Wechsler, 1989; Wechsler, 1992); or the British Ability Scales, BAS II (Elliott with Smith & McCulloch, 1996).

The Wechsler tests are widely used because they are well established and accepted internationally and because most educational psychologists have been introduced to them during their training. The 1992 U.K. norms for WISC III[UK] have made the test even more attractive to U.K. users, as has the provision of associated achievement batteries for reading, language, and numeracy (WORD, WOLD, and WOND, combined into the Wechsler Individual Achievement Test, or WIAT[UK] (Rust, 1995) and a software package to facilitate scoring and interpretation (Wechsler Scorer Version 2.1, The Psychological Corporation, 1997). Although some users are content to report the established IQ composites of Full-Scale, Verbal and Performance, the more psychometrically sophisticated make use of the four-factor solution, which provides index scores for verbal comprehension, perceptual organization, processing speed, and freedom from distractibility. The processing speed index, composed of Coding and Symbol Search, seems to be of diagnostic value when assessing children for dyslexia (see Turner, 1997).

The other battery commonly used in the United Kingdom is the BAS II, the most recent U.K. version of the series of batteries that began with development work in the 1960s and 1970s leading to the BAS

(Elliott, Murray, & Pearson, 1979) and progressed through a U.S. version, the Differential Ability Scales or DAS (Elliott, 1990) to its current form. Although the original plans for this battery were for a U.K. intelligence test – the original name was the British Intelligence Scale – it had as a primary focus from the outset "special abilities" to be measured by the many component scales. Elliott (1975) explained that the research team aimed to provide practitioners with a flexible tool that could be used to test hypotheses about the source of difficulties experienced by particular children. It was never intended that the full battery would be given to each child routinely.

The BAS did provide IQs – termed General, Verbal, Visual, and Short-Form – but by the time DAS and BAS II were created, Elliott had removed all reference to IQ and provided composites that were more narrowly defined in relation to psychometric g. In BAS II, these consist of three composite or cluster scores, comprising two scales each, which together combine to create a six-scale measure of general conceptual ability (GCA). The Technical Manual for the BAS II (Elliott with Smith & McCulloch, 1997) reports the results of both confirmatory and exploratory factor analyses of the component scales. The confirmatory analyses for both the Early Years Upper Level and School Age Batteries showed that three-factor models fitted the data better than either one- or two-factor models (see Table 1.1). The data for the Early Years Lower Level, covering ages 2.6 to 3.5 years, was best fitted by a one-factor model. Elliott et al. (1997) advocate interpreting BAS II by working from the top down. That is, the GCA will be the best summary of a child's abilities unless there are significant differences between the component clusters, in which case the group factor level will provide the most meaningful summary. The cluster scores have actually proven to be a more fruitful level of analysis than the GCA, assessing as they do a child's verbal, spatial, and non-verbal ("pictorial" in the Early Years Battery) reasoning abilities.

The distinction between the spatial and non-verbal clusters is an important one. The spatial cluster assesses the ability to perceive, analyze, and remember spatial relationships, and gives little scope for obtaining high scores by using verbal mediation strategies. In other words, it represents the broad visualization factor (G_v) in the Horn-Cattell-Carroll model (Cattell, 1971; Horn, 1985, 1988; see discussion in Elliott et. al, 1997). The non-verbal cluster represents the fluid intelligence factor (G_f), assessing the ability to formulate and test hypotheses, identify relationships and apply these to new information. To

TABLE 1.1. *Confirmatory Factor Analyses of the British Ability Scales II*

a. Early Years Battery. Scale Loadings for the one-, two-, and three-factor models. Ages 3.6–5.11 (N = 241).

	Factor Loadings					
		Two-factor		Three-factor		
Scale	One-factor	Verbal	Non-verbal	Verbal	Pictorial Reasoning	Spatial
Verbal Comprehension	.67	.70		.78		
Naming Vocabulary	.66	.69		.75		
Picture Similarities	.49		.53		.79	
Early Number Concepts	.80	.79			.50	
Pattern Construction	.55		.62			.62
Copying	.59		.67			.69

b. School Age Battery. Scale Loadings for the one-, two-, and three-factor models. Ages 6.0–17.11 (N = 1133).

	Factor Loadings					
		Two-factor		Three-factor		
Scale	One-factor	Verbal	Non-verbal	Verbal	Pictorial Reasoning	Spatial
Word Definitions	.77	.83		.83		
Verbal Similarities	.79	.86		.86		
Matrices	.64		.72		.73	
Quantitative Reasoning	.67		.74		.75	
Recall of Designs	.56		.61			.66
Pattern Construction	.55		.60			.65

perform effectively in the non-verbal scales, the test-taker has to use visual and verbal information and to engage in higher level executive processing in order to co-ordinate and integrate them effectively. The tasks involved, matrices and numerical analogy completion, thereby constitute good measures of "working memory" (Baddeley, 1986). It is therefore not surprising that the non-verbal cluster yields the highest loading on g since, as noted earlier, academic research has concluded that g and working memory are often factorially near-identical (Kyllonen & Christal, 1990; Stauffer, Ree, & Carretta, 1996). Factor analyses of the U.S. standardization data for DAS, reported by Elliott (1997), also support the equivalence of the non-verbal reasoning factor, G_f and the higher order g.

In addition to the clusters, BAS II provides several "diagnostic scales," which load less highly on g but supply information on specific areas of strength or difficulty such as information processing speed and short-term auditory memory. Finally, three brief achievement scales are included, which can be used with the GCA to perform discrepancy analyses. This approach to identifying dyslexia is controversial but nonetheless much used in the United Kingdom, where some local authorities limit provision of additional support to those in the most extreme 1%, 2%, or even 1.5% of children, as far as IQ/GCA – achievement discrepancies are concerned. The more psychometrically sophisticated go beyond the mere assessment of underachievement, as defined by a regression analysis linking achievement and ability, to look for additional evidence of information processing deficits, since underachievement can have social, personal, and motivational causes as well as intellectual ones. Recall of Digits and Speed of Information Processing are particularly valuable in the diagnosis of dyslexia (see Turner, 1997).

Educational testing in the United Kingdom can therefore be characterized as un-self-conscious use by educators of dazzlingly effective g-based group tests of academic potential and self-conscious but pragmatic use by educational psychologists of individually administered ability tests, with both types of test gradually evolving toward a closer fit with recent academic research into cognitive abilities.

Occupational Testing

Occupational testing in the United Kingdom encompasses a far wider variety of instruments and suppliers than the other domains. Also, this domain is currently marked by much more regulation, training, and advice than the others in the United Kingdom. The British Psychological Society (BPsS), working with major test publishers, developed Levels A and B as qualifications in the use of ability and personality assessments, respectively. These were intended for anyone using tests and questionnaires, such as human resource professionals, not just for psychologists. Publishers use the possession of these qualifications as part of their criteria for access to their assessments. Additionally, the BPsS publishes compendia of test reviews by experts as guides in choosing appropriate instruments (Bartram & Lindley, 1997; Lindley, 2000).

There is widespread application of traditional paper-and-pencil tests of reasoning, which are used in many large organizations as part of a selection or development process (the latter generally meaning selection of current employees for new, more-demanding responsibilities). Examples of graduate level tests are the Graduate and Managerial Ability Tests (GMA, Psychometric Research and Development Ltd, 1985) and the Critical Reasoning Test Battery (CRTB, SHL, 1982–1991). Traditional reasoning tests are also used in Further Education settings as initial assessments, to help in the context of career guidance or course selection. At least some of the traditional types of reasoning batteries have been designed with reference to the relevant research in cognitive psychology (e.g., General Ability Tests Two, GAT2, Smith, Whetton, & Caspall, 1999).

The exact nature of such batteries depends upon the educational level of the candidates for whom they were designed, but they usually involve separate assessments of verbal, numerical, and sometimes non-verbal/abstract reasoning, with the users able to pick whichever combination best suits their assessment purposes. Tests intended for graduates or for selecting people for graduate-level posts typically include verbal items embedded in text; either discrete blocks of text with several items attached (e.g., GMA or SHL Critical Reasoning Test Battery) or a textually presented scenario linking all the items in the test (e.g., ASE Critical Reasoning Tests, CRT, Smith & Whetton, 1992). Numerical items at this occupational level are also textually presented, though a wide variety of commonly used graphical elements are also used, e.g., pie charts, graphs. Tests intended for lower levels of educational achievement avoid the use of text, except when reading comprehension is deliberately being assessed. Instead, verbal reasoning tends to be assessed via analogical reasoning or classification, since these tasks require only single-word reading. Text-free formats are also used for numerical reasoning assessment, e.g., GAT2 Numerical uses a variety of grids in which numbers are entered via some underlying rule. Using different grids enables many items to be devised without involving mathematical attainment beyond an elementary level. A similar approach has been taken in GAT2 Non-Verbal, a matrices-type test that increases the "eduction of relations" element of reasoning by using grids that permit a wider range of possible relationships than traditional 3-by-3 matrices. A different approach to ensuring that task difficulty lies mainly in the relationship-seeking aspect of the task is used in GMA Abstract, a test intended for high level assessment. It uses a classification task in which the test-taker has to identify the rules underlying membership of groups of figures and then assign new figures. The task is based upon the "Bongard problems" described by Hofstadter (1979), and requires flexibility in identifying classes at differing levels of analysis.

The considerations outlined above highlight one of the major themes behind current occupational testing in the United Kingdom, namely, the concern for fairness. Although developing later than in the United States, since the late 1980s, there has been an increasing awareness among most corporate test users of the need to avoid any unfair adverse impact on one or another sex or ethnic group. Publishers have addressed this need at the stages of test use and test design. For test users, they have provided guidance in the form of training courses (e.g., SHL's Fair Selection course) and in published materials (e.g., ASE's Testing People Fairly; see Mathews, 1999), to encourage users to take steps such as conducting job analyses and validity studies so as to ensure that the tests used are appropriate and effective.

At the design stage, publishers have considered sex and ethnic fairness throughout the development process, by choosing test formats carefully, reviewing trial items, conducting item bias analyses, reporting group scores differences and offering advice in the test manuals on how to use tests fairly (see Feltham & Smith, 1993; Feltham, Baron, & Smith, 1994). *Item bias analyses* are statistical procedures that are carried out to identify any items that are disproportionately difficult for one sex or ethnic group, once their overall performance is taken into account. One difficulty faced by U.K. test developers is that it is very difficult to obtain sufficiently large samples of ethnic minority groups[3] to enable the most powerful, Item Response Theory (IRT)-based methods of item bias analysis to be conducted at the item-trialing stage. However, it has proven possible to achieve worthwhile results by substituting the Mantel-Haenszel procedure, which provides a good approximation to IRT-based analyses, though with much smaller groups (Hills, 1989).

A different approach taken by some test authors and publishers is to develop new types of cognitive assessment that may prove less likely to show adverse impact. It is claimed that the job-related Aptitude for Business Learning Exercises, or ABLE series of assessments (Blinkhorn

---

[3] Not only are ethnic minority populations in the United Kingdom fairly small, but they consist of several groups whose socio-economic and cultural backgrounds differ significantly, so they cannot be pooled to increase numbers without obscuring effects upon one or other of them. For example, people of Indian origins cannot be pooled with people of Pakistani or Bangladeshi origins because those of Indian descent will, on average, be more advantaged in their socio-economic and educational backgrounds than the other two groups.

& Johnson, 1996–2002), are fairer than more traditional reasoning tests. These assessments are scenario-embedded, cover a range of contexts from finance to customer service and legal specialists, and are suitable for any job level from helpline operatives to senior managers and professionals. Each test includes a learning, and then an applying, element, requiring candidates to employ reasoning processes to glean underlying rules or valid conclusions from data.

Another major theme in U.K. occupational testing is the wish to expand the types of intellectual measures available, taking account of conceptualizations like the "multiple intelligences" of Gardner (1983, 1999). In particular, there is much corporate interest in being able to assess "emotional intelligence," defined by the work of Salovey & Meyer (1990) and Goleman (1995, 1998) to encompass self-awareness, motivation, empathy, and social skills. Although most publishers still cover these elements within their personality assessment instruments, an instrument has been developed in the United Kingdom that is specifically focused on emotional intelligence, as conceptualized by Goleman and others (EIQ, Dulewicz & Higgs, 1999).

Finally, occupational testing is at the forefront of moves towards embracing new technology as a means of delivering assessments. Most U.K. publishers have been offering scoring and assessment management systems in software form for many years. This is also the case to some extent in other domains of U.K. test use, particularly educational psychology. Increasingly, occupational test suppliers are now providing assessments in CD-Rom form and are working toward on-line delivery of assessments.

However, there is an increasing awareness, as in other countries, that on-screen delivery, especially in an on-line environment, presents a whole range of new concerns about practical matters like security and wider issues regarding validity. This is more worrying in relation to ability testing than for personality assessment, and various parties are beginning to conduct equivalence studies and develop guidance information for users. The United Kingdom hosted an International Test Commission conference on computer-based testing and the Internet in June 2002. The mission of this conference was to generate outcomes that would aid the development of international good practice guidelines. It considered the use and misuse of electronically transmitted assessments and addressed the methodological, technical, professional, and ethical issues that arise from the use of new technology within testing. The resulting draft guidelines are currently being considered and revised with the aim of producing the final version by August 2004.

Clinical Testing

Clinical psychologists in the United Kingdom tend to be the most conservative in their use of ability tests. The Wechsler series are by far the most commonly used, and the provision of U.K. validation samples and promise of "increased clinical utility" in the new Wechsler Adult Intelligence Scale (WAIS)-III[UK] and Wechsler Memory Scale (WMS)-III[UK] (Wechsler, 1997) will doubtless help to consolidate this tendency. This is hardly surprising, given that the Wechsler batteries were originally intended as clinical instruments and have been extensively used in clinical research.

Clinical psychologists also make use of the National Adult Reading Test (NART-2, Nelson & Willison, 1991). This test assesses the ability to read non-phonetic words, which is unaffected by dementia and brain injuries. The scores have then been co-normed with WAIS-R, to allow estimation of the test-taker's premorbid intelligence level.

Aside from Wechsler-linked instruments, clinicians use the British Picture Vocabulary Scale II (Dunn et al., 1997) in assessing the receptive language ability of younger clients. This is a U.K. version of the Peabody Picture Vocabulary Scale (Dunn & Dunn, 1997), which simply requires the test-taker to point to one of four line-drawings in response to a spoken word. Clinical use is also made of Raven's Matrices, a Scottish assessment of non-verbal reasoning (see later). The United Kingdom's enviable system of national mortality and morbidity records allows associations to be computed between intelligence and health. For example, data from the Scottish Mental Survey of 1932 were matched with records of death and National Health Service records of allocations of people to general medical practitioners. This exercise provided the first evidence that childhood IQ is related to longevity (Whalley & Deary, 2001).

Cross-Domain Assessments

While the vast majority of tests used in the United Kingdom are specific to one or other domain, as described above, there are two exceptions that have played an important role across all areas of U.K. psychology, most notably in academic research. These are the AH tests developed by the late Alice Heim and the Progressive Matrices tests developed by J. C. Raven.

The AH series was developed between 1947 and the late 1970s, by Alice Heim and colleagues (Heim, 1947; Heim, Watts & Simmonds, 1956–1983) at the Psychological Laboratory, Cambridge. They cover six difficulty levels, suitable for ages from 5 years to managerial level graduates. The parallel tests for youngest children, AH1X and AH1Y, are entirely non-verbal, consisting of line drawings of people, birds, animals, and shapes. There are four subtests, covering: series, classes-alike, analogies, and classes-unlike. The next level are AH2 and AH3, which are parallel in content and difficulty and suitable for ages 10 and above.

The AH4 test, for assessing school-leavers and the general adult population, and AH5, for assessing higher ability adults, were the earliest tests devised by the Heim team, originating in the 1940s and 1950s. As Heim notes in her introduction to the later AH6, these tests were devised when psychometricians believed that g equalled non-verbal reasoning, so they consisted of two parts, one with verbal and numerical items and one with non-verbal items. In so doing, the tests reflected Vernon's (1950, 1961) hierarchical model of g with major group factors v:ed and k:m, especially since some of the non-verbal items clearly required spatial visualization in addition to reasoning.

By the time that AH6 was being developed in 1970, Heim had come to believe that this structure over-emphasized non-verbal reasoning, because high-level tests were primarily used as measures of scholastic aptitude, which was not best predicted by non-verbal tests. Consequently, the two versions of AH6 have a reduced proportion of non-verbal items. The AH6 SEM, intended for scientists, mathematicians, and engineers, has equal proportions of verbal, numerical, and diagrammatic items, whereas the AH6 AG (Arts and General), intended for everyone without a science background, comprises a half verbal, a quarter numerical, and a quarter diagrammatic items. The AH2 and AH3 tests, devised after the AH6, share the AH6 SEM structure.

Ironically, recent research findings have returned to the belief that non-verbal reasoning may be the best indicator of overall g (e.g., Gustafsson, 1984), suggesting that perhaps Heim's earlier AH4 and AH5 might prove the better assessments of g. However, for the purposes of predicting future performance in traditional academic courses, the reduced non-verbal content may be advantageous. It is interesting to note that the CAT, described earlier as a good indicator of future school performance, also has the AH2/AH3/AH6 SEM balance of item types.

In their early days, the AH series were widely used. They were appreciated for their wide range of item types, presented within the separately timed sections in a spiral omnibus – which rotated the item types while increasing the difficulty. They also provided excellent guidance to test administrators and introduced more thorough example and practice sections than other tests available in that era. In recent decades, they have been largely superseded in the occupational domain by the wide range of modern tests, but they still occupy a favored position among U.K. academics.

The earliest forms of the Progressive Matrices Series predate the AH series somewhat, with the RECI Series of Perceptual Tests (Raven, 1938, 1939) being adopted in 1941 by the U.K. military as the primary general intelligence test, to counteract the fears of educational bias in verbal tests (see Vernon & Parry, 1949). An initial version of the Advanced Progressive Matrices (APM) was created by Raven in 1943 for selecting officer candidates. In the decades since, the tests have undergone some content revisions and re-ordering but retain their basic nature. The items in them consist of figures set out in a 3-by-3 layout, with one cell missing. The test-taker has to select the missing piece from eight options. The first few items in the Standard Progressive Matrices (SPM) and the APM consist of continuous wallpaper patterns over the same 3-by-3 area, with one piece missing. Later developments include the Coloured Progressive Matrices (CPM), for younger children or people with intellectual impairments of one or other type (e.g., learning difficulties, dementia), as well as parallel forms of the three levels and a plus version of SPM, to cope with the increase in test-takers who score near the top of the SPM range, as highlighted in the IQ drift research of Flynn (1987).

The tests are based on Spearman's (1923, 1927) two-factor theory of g, and are designed to assess eductive ability, one of the two components of g. Raven and his colleagues also developed a series of vocabulary scales (Mill Hill and Crichton Vocabulary Scales) to assess the second component, reproductive ability.

The factorial structure of Raven's Matrices has long been the subject of investigation and debate (e.g., Vernon & Parry, 1949 to Carroll, 1993), with most researchers concluding, as noted earlier, that the SPM are a fairly pure measure of g possibly with some element of visualization. An in-depth analysis by Carpenter, Just, and Shell (1990) concluded that the SPM measured the ability to "induce abstract relations and the ability to dynamically manage a large set of problem-solving goals in working memory." This is in accord with the analysis of the BAS II Matrices test outlined earlier, and it may explain the conflicting views about the suitability of matrices-type tests for assessing dyslexics. The manual for the SPM states that the test "has found application in the diagnosis and handling of various forms of dyslexia," and that some of those children having great difficulty in school work obtain high scores on the SPM. However, doubts have been expressed about its suitability for assessing all dyslexics (Turner, 1997), and results discussed by Elliott (1997) indicate that the DAS and BAS II Matrices and Quantitative Reasoning scales can be especially difficult for some dyslexic children. Elliott interprets this as evidence of a "weakness in the integration and processing of complex information from the verbal and visual systems." Given the earlier discussion of the role of working memory in Matrices, it seems it might equally well be characterized as a working memory deficit, particularly in the use of verbal processing to support a visual task.

The reputation that the Raven series has for being a pure measure of g and its use in over 100 countries may explain why such a vast research literature has been amassed using the test. The research supplements published with the series list many hundreds of studies, providing normative reliability and validity information.

Clinical psychologists, and those with a medical background, will know that mental tests find huge and growing application as indicators of brain integrity in uncountable medical conditions. To end this section, however, two British contributions are recorded. The age pattern of industrialized countries has shifted to containing more old people. Short of frank dementia, the issue of cognitive decline has become a major medical research topic since it is known that retention of cognitive function predicts quality of life and survival (Korten et al., 1999). In addition to testing current cognitive function, it is important to know the relative level of people's previous mental ability. This is almost never available. In cases where early life mental ability differences have been retrieved, even though the estimates are poor and the population sample rather unusual, they have proved invaluable (e.g., in the Nun study; Snowdon et al., 1996). Therefore, the British innovation of estimating premorbid ability levels by assessing the ability to read words that do not comply with normal phonological rules stands as a major achievement in mental testing (Nelson, 1982; O'Carroll, 1995). Nelson's National Adult Reading Test combines the simplicity of conception and widespread application that put it on a par with Binet's original test in providing a quick-and-dirty answer to a pressing practical need. Recently it was shown that the NART scores of healthy people aged 78 years correlated .69 with their IQ scores at age 11 (Crawford et al., 2001).

CONCLUSION

The main foci of concern about the structure of psychometric intelligence – namely, the general factor and the hierarchy of more specific abilities – are, in large part, British-originated contributions to the international research effort. Similarly, searches for explanations of intelligence differences among genes, reaction times, brain size, and so forth were ideas and efforts that began with British scientists. More recently, British scientists have contributed alongside others to these research topics. The most recent original British conceptual contribution to intelligence research is Baddeley's construct of working memory. The application of psychometric ability tests is more U.K.-specific than the research. Some occupational and educational tests and their large-scale use in the respective settings have been described. In the clinical sphere a notable British contribution has been the articulation and measurement of the concept of premorbid IQ, using the National Adult Reading Test.

References

Anderson, M. (1992). *Intelligence and development: A cognitive theory*. Oxford: Blackwell.

Anderson, M., Reid, C., & Nelson, J. (2001). Developmental changes in inspection time: What a difference a year makes. *Intelligence, 29*, 475–486.

Baddeley, A. D. (1986). *Working memory*. Oxford: Clarendon.

Baddeley, A. (1992a). Working memory. *Science, 255*, 556–559.

Baddeley, A. (1992b). Working memory: The interface between memory and cognition. *Journal of Cognitive Neuroscience, 4*, 281–288.

Baddeley, A. (2000). The episodic buffer: A new component of working memory? *Trends in Cognitive Sciences, 4*, 417–423.

Barbaux, S., Plomin, R., & Whitehead, A. S. (2000). Polymorphisms of genes controlling homocysteine/folate metabolism and cognitive function. *Neuroreport, 11*, 1133–1136.

Barrett, P. T., & Eysenck, H. J. (1992a). Brain electrical potentials and intelligence. In A. Gale & H. J. Eysenck (Eds.), *Handbook of individual differences: Biological perspectives*. New York: Wiley.

Barrett, P. T., & Eysenck, H. J. (1992b). Brain-evoked potentials and intelligence: The Hendrickson paradigm. *Intelligence, 16*, 361–381.

Barrett, P. T., & Eysenck, H. J. (1994). The relationship between evoked potential component amplitude, latency, contour length, variability, zero-crossings, and psychometric intelligence. *Personality and Individual Differences, 16*, 3–32.

Barrett, P., Eysenck, H. J., & Lucking, S. (1986). Reaction time and intelligence: A replicated study. *Intelligence, 10*, 9–40.

Bartlett, F. C. (1932). *Remembering: A study in experimental and social psychology*. Cambridge: Cambridge University Press.

Bartram, D. J., & Lindley, P. A. (1997). *Review of ability & aptitude tests (level A).* Leicester, UK: British Psychological Society.

Bates, T. C., & Eysenck, H. J. (1993a). Intelligence, inspection time, and decision time. *Intelligence, 17,* 523–531.

Bennett, G. K., Seashore, H. G., & Wesman, A. G. (1997). *Differential ability tests for schools.* London: The Psychological Corporation.

Bickley, P. G., Keith, T. Z., & Wolfle, L. M. (1995). The three-stratum theory of cognitive abilities: Test of the structure of intelligence across the life span. *Intelligence, 20,* 309–328.

Binet, A. (1905). New methods for the diagnosis of the intellectual level of sub-normals. *L'Annee Psychologique, 12,* 191–244. (Translated in 1916 by E. S. Kite in *The development of intelligence in children.* Vineland, NJ: Publications of the Training School at Vineland.)

Blinkhorn, S., & Johnson, C. (1996–2002). *The ABLE series.* Oxford: Oxford Psychologists Press.

Blinkhorn, S. F., & Hendrickson, D. E. (1982). Average evoked responses and psychometric intelligence. *Nature, 195,* 596–597.

Bouchard, T. J. (1998). Genetic and environmental influences on adult intelligence and special mental abilities. *Human Biology, 70,* 257–279.

Brand, C. R. (1979). General intelligence and mental speed: Their relationship and development. In J. P. Das & N. O'Connor (Eds.), *Intelligence and learning* (pp. 589–593). New York: Plenum.

Brand, C. R. (1987). A rejoinder to Pellegrino. In S. Modgil & C. Modgil (Eds.), *Arthur Jensen: Consensus and controversy.* Brighton, UK: Falmer.

Brand, C. R. (1996). *The g factor.* Chichester, UK: Wiley. (This book was withdrawn by the publisher shortly after publication, making it difficult to obtain.)

Brand, C., & Deary, I. J. (1982). Intelligence and "inspection time." In H. J. Eysenck (Ed.), *A model for intelligence* (pp. 133–148). Berlin: Springer-Verlag.

Burt, C. (1909–1910). Experimental tests of general intelligence. *British Journal of Psychology, 3,* 94–177.

Burt, C. (1940). *The factors of the mind.* London: University of London Press.

Carpenter, P. A., Just, M. A., & Shell, P. (1990). What one intelligence test measures: A theoretical account of processing in the Raven's Progressive Matrices Test. *Psychological Review, 97,* 404–431.

Carretta, T. R., & Ree, M. J. (1995). Near identity of cognitive structure in sex and ethnic groups. *Personality and Individual Differences, 19,* 149–155.

Carroll, J. B. (1993). *Human cognitive abilities: A survey of factor analytic studies.* Cambridge: Cambridge University Press.

Carroll, J. B. (1995). Reflections on Stephen Jay Gould's *The mismeasure of man* (1981): A retrospective review. *Intelligence, 21,* 121–134.

Caryl, P. G. (1994). Event-related potentials correlate with inspection time and intelligence. *Intelligence, 18,* 15–46.

Caryl, P. G., Golding, S. J. J., & Hall, B. J. D. (1995). Interrelationships among auditory and visual cognitive tasks: An event-related potential (ERP) study. *Intelligence, 21,* 297–326.

Caryl, P. G., & Harper, A. (1996). Event related potentials (ERPs) in elementary cognitive tasks reflect task difficulty and task threshold. *Intelligence, 22,* 1–22.

Cattell, J. McK . (1886a). The inertia of eye and brain. *Brain, 8,* 295–381.

Cattell, J. McK . (1886b). The time taken up by cerebral operations. *Mind, 11,* 220–242, 377–392, 524–538.

Cattell, R. B. (1971). *Abilities: Their structure, growth and action.* Boston: Houghton Mifflin.

Cattell, R. B. (1987). *Intelligence: Its structure, growth and action.* Amsterdam: North Holland.

Cattell, R. B. (1998). Where is intelligence? Some answers from the triadic theory. In J. J. McArdle & R. W. Woodcock (Eds.), *Human cognitive abilities in theory and practice.* London: Lawrence Erlbaum Associates.

Cooper, C. (1999). *Intelligence and abilities.* London: Routledge.

Crawford, J. R., Deary, I. J., Allan, K. M., & Gustafsson, J.-E. (1998). Evaluating competing models of the relationship between inspection time and psychometric intelligence. *Intelligence, 26,* 27–42.

Crawford, J. R., Deary, I. J., Starr, J., & Whalley, L. J. (2001). The NART as an index of prior intellectual functioning: A retrospective validity study covering a 66 year interval. *Psychological Medicine, 31,* 451–458.

Cronbach, L. J. (1957). The two disciplines of scientific psychology. *American Psychologist, 12,* 671–684.

Daniels, J., McGuffin, P., Owen, M. J., & Plomin, R. (1998). Molecular genetic studies of cognitive ability. *Human Biology, 70,* 281–296.

Deary, I. J. (1986). Inspection time: Discovery or rediscovery? *Personality and Individual Differences, 7,* 625–631.

Deary, I. J. (1993). Inspection time and WAIS-R IQ subtypes: A confirmatory factor analysis study. *Intelligence, 17,* 223–236.

Deary, I. J. (1994a). Sensory discrimination and intelligence: Postmortem or resurrection? *American Journal of Psychology, 107,* 95–115.

Deary, I. J. (1994b). Intelligence and auditory discrimination: Separating processing speed and fidelity of stimulus representation. *Intelligence, 18,* 189–213.

Deary, I. J. (1995). Auditory inspection time and intelligence: What is the direction of causation? *Developmental Psychology, 31,* 237–250.

Deary, I. J. (1996). Reductionism and intelligence: The case of inspection time. *Journal of Biosocial Science, 28,* 405–423.

Deary, I. J. (1997). Intelligence and information processing. In H. Nyborg (Ed.), *The scientific study of human nature: Tribute to Hans Eysenck at eighty* (pp. 282–310). Oxford: Elsevier.

Deary, I. J. (1999). Intelligence and visual and auditory information processing. In P. L. Ackerman, P. C. Kyllonen, & R. D. Roberts (Eds.), *Learning and individual differences: Process, trait, and content determinants* (pp. 111–133). Washington, DC: American Psychological Association.

Deary, I. J. (2000a). *Looking down on human intelligence.* Oxford: Oxford University Press.

Deary, I. J. (2000b). Simple information processing and intelligence. In R. J. Sternberg (Ed.), *Handbook of intelligence* (pp. 267–284). Cambridge: Cambridge University Press.

Deary, I. J. (2001a). Individual differences in cognition: British contributions over a century. *British Journal of Psychology, 92*, 217–237.

Deary, I. J. (2001b). *Intelligence: A very short introduction.* Oxford: Oxford University Press.

Deary, I. J., & Caryl, P. G. (1993). Intelligence, EEG, and evoked potentials (pp. 259–315). In P. A. Vernon (Ed.), *Biological approaches to the study of human intelligence.* Norwood, NJ: Ablex.

Deary, I. J., Caryl, P. G., Egan, V., & Wight, D. (1989). Visual and auditory inspection times: Their interrelationship and correlations with IQ in high ability subjects. *Personality and Individual Differences, 10*, 525–533.

Deary, I. J., Der, G., & Ford, G. (2001). Reaction times and intelligence differences: A population-based cohort study. *Intelligence, 29*, 389–399.

Deary, I. J., Egan, V., Gibson, G. J., Brand, C. R., Austin, E., & Kellaghan, T. (1996). Intelligence and the differentiation hypothesis. *Intelligence, 23*, 105–132.

Deary, I. J., Head, B., & Egan, V. (1989). Auditory inspection time, intelligence and pitch discrimination. *Intelligence, 13*, 135–147.

Deary, I. J., Hunter, R., Langan, S. J., & Goodwin, G. M. (1991) Inspection time, psychometric intelligence and clinical estimates of cognitive ability in presenile Alzheimer's disease and Korsakoff's psychosis. *Brain, 114*, 2543–2554.

Deary, I. J., McCrimmon, R. J., & Bradshaw, J. (1997). Visual information processing and intelligence. *Intelligence, 24*, 461–479.

Deary, I. J., & Pagliari, C. (1991). The strength of *g* at different levels of ability: Have Detterman and Daniel rediscovered Spearman's "Law of Diminishing Returns." *Intelligence, 15*, 247–250.

Deary, I. J., Simonotto, E., Marshall, A., Marshall, I., Goddard, N., & Wardlaw, J. M. (2001). The functional anatomy of inspection time: A pilot fMRI study. *Intelligence, 29*, 497–510.

Deary, I. J., & Stough, C. (1996). Intelligence and inspection time: Achievements, prospects, and problems. *American Psychologist, 51*, 599–608.

Deary, I. J., Whalley, L. J., Lemmon, H., Crawford, J. R., & Starr, J. M. (2000). The stability of individual differences in mental ability from childhood to old age: Follow-up of the 1932 Scottish Mental Survey. *Intelligence, 28*, 49–55.

Devlin, B., Daniels, M., & Roeder, K. (1997). The heritability of IQ. *Nature, 388*, 468–471.

Dulewicz, V., & Higgs, M. (1999). *Emotional intelligence questionnaire: General.* Windsor, UK: ASE.

Duncan, J., Emslie, H., & Williams, P. (1996). Intelligence and the frontal lobe: The organisation of goal-directed behavior. *Cognitive Psychology, 30*, 257–303.

Duncan, J., & Owen, A. M. (2000). Common regions of the human frontal lobe recruited by diverse cognitive demands. *Trends in Neurosciences, 23*, 475–483.

Duncan, J., Seitz, J., Kolodny, J., Bor, D., Herzog, H., Ahmed, A., Newell, F. N., & Emslie, H. (2000). A neural basis for general intelligence. *Science, 289*, 457–460.

Dunn, L. M., & Dunn, L. M. (1997). *Peabody picture vocabulary test* (3rd ed.). Circle Pines, MN: AGS.

Dunn, L. M., Dunn, L. M., Whetton, C. & Burley, J. (1997). *British picture vocabulary scale* (2nd ed.). Windsor, UK: NFER-Nelson.

Egan, V. (1994). Intelligence, inspection time, and cognitive strategies. *British Journal of Psychology, 85,* 305–316.

Egan, V., Chiswick, A., Santosh, C., Naidu, K., Rimmington, J. E., & Best, J. J. K. (1994). Size isn't everything: A study of brain volume, intelligence, and auditory evoked potentials. *Personality and Individual Differences, 17,* 357–367.

Egan, V., Wickett, J. C., & Vernon, P. A. (1995). Brain size and intelligence: Erratum, addendum, and correction. *Personality and Individual Differences, 19,* 113–115.

Elliott, C. D. (1975). British Intelligence Scale takes shape. *Education, 25,* 460–461.

Elliott, C. D. (1990). *Differential ability scales.* San Antonio, TX: The Psychological Corporation.

Elliott, C. D. (1997). The differential ability scales. In D. P. Flanagan, J. L. Genshaft, & P. L. Harrison (Eds.), *Contemporary intellectual assessment: Theories, tests, and issues.* New York: Guilford Press.

Elliott, C. D., Murray, D. J., & Pearson, L. S. (1979). *British Ability Scales.* Slough, UK: NFER.

Elliott, C. D., with Smith, P., & McCulloch, K. (1996). *British Ability Scales* (2nd ed.). Windsor, UK: NFER-Nelson.

Elliott, C. D., with Smith, P., & McCulloch, K. (1997). *British Ability Scales* (2nd ed.). *Technical Manual.* Windsor, UK: NFER-Nelson.

Embretson, S. E. (1995). The role of working memory capacity and general control processes in intelligence. *Intelligence, 20,* 169–189.

Engle, R. W., Tuholski, S. W., Laughlin, J. E., & Conway, A. R. A. (1999). Working memory, short-term memory, and general fluid intelligence: A latent-variable approach. *Journal of Experimental Psychology: General, 128,* 309–331.

Ewing, F. M. E., Deary, I. J., McCrimmon, R. J., Strachan, M. W. J., & Frier, B. M. (1998). Effect of acute hypoglycemia on visual information processing in adults with Type 1 diabetes mellitus. *Physiology and Behavior, 64,* 653–660.

Eysenck, H. J. (1939). Primary mental abilities. *British Journal of Educational Psychology, 9,* 270–275.

Eysenck, H. J. (1967). Intelligence assessment: A theoretical and experimental approach. *British Journal of Educational Psychology, 37,* 81–97.

Eysenck, H. J. (Ed.). (1982). *A model for intelligence.* Berlin: Springer.

Eysenck, H. J. (1995). Can we study intelligence using the experimental method? *Intelligence, 20,* 217–228.

Feltham, R. T., Baron, H., & Smith, P. (1994). Developing fair tests. *The Psychologist, 7,* 23–25.

Feltham, R. T., & Smith, P. (1993). Psychometric test bias: How to avoid it. *International Journal of Selection and Assessment, 1,* 117–122.

Fernandes, C., & Strand, S. (2000). *CAT and KS3/GCSE indicators: Technical report.* Windor, UK: NFER-Nelson.

Flashman, L. A., Andreasen, N. C., Flaum, M., & Swayze, V. W. (1998). Intelligence and regional brain volumes in normal controls. *Intelligence, 25,* 149–160.

Flynn, J. R. (1987). Massive IQ gains in 14 nations: What IQ tests really measure. *Psychological Bulletin, 101,* 171–191.

Fox, G., & Morrisby, M. J. (1991). *Morrisby profile.* Hemel Hempstead, UK: EITS.

Frearson, W., & Eysenck, H. J. (1986). Intelligence, reaction time (RT) and a new "odd-man-out" RT paradigm. *Personality and Individual Differences, 7*, 807–817.

Fuller, T. (1648, reprinted 1936). Of natural fools. In R. Vallance (Ed.), *A hundred english essays*. London: Nelson.

Galton, F. (1883). *Inquiries into human faculty*. London: Dent.

Galton, F. (1888). Head growth in students at the University of Cambridge. *Nature, 38*, 14–15.

Gardner, H. (1983). *Frames of mind: The theory of multiple intelligences*. New York: Basic Books.

Gardner, H. (1999). *Intelligence reframed: Multiple intelligences for the 21st century*. New York: Basic Books.

Goleman, D. (1995). *Emotional intelligence: Why it can matter more than IQ*. New York: Bantam.

Goleman, D. (1998). *Working with emotional intelligence*. London: Bloomsbury.

Gottesman, I. I. (1997). Twins: En route to QTLs for cognition. *Science, 276*, 1522–1523.

Gould, S. J. (1981, 2nd ed. 1997). *The mismeasure of man*. Harmondsworth, UK: Penguin.

Gustafsson, J.-E. (1984). A unifying model for the structure of mental abilities. *Intelligence, 8*, 179–203.

Gustafsson, J.-E. (1992). The relevance of factor analysis for the study of group differences. *Multivariate Behavioral Research, 27*, 239–247.

Hearnshaw, L. S. (1979). *Cyril Burt: Psychologist*. London: Hodder and Stoughton.

Heim, A. W. (1947). An attempt to test high grade intelligence. *British Journal of Psychology, 37*, 70–80.

Heim, A. W., Watts, K. P., & Simmonds, V. (1956 to 1983; Dates follow tests). *AH1X/Y* (1977), *AH2/3* (1974, 1978), *AH4* (1967, 1975), *AH5* (1956, 1975), *AH6AG & AH6SEM* (1970, 1983). Windsor, UK: NFER-Nelson.

Hendrickson, A. E. (1982). The biological basis of intelligence. Part 1: Theory. In H. J. Eysenck (Ed.), *A model for intelligence*. Berlin: Springer.

Hendrickson, D. E. (1982). The biological basis of intelligence. Part II: Measurement. In H. J. Eysenck (Ed.), *A model for intelligence*. Berlin: Springer.

Hick, W. E. (1952). On the rate of gain of information. *Quarterly Journal of Experimental Psychology, 4*, 11–26.

Hill, L., Craig, I. W., McGuffin, P., Lubinski, D., Thompson, L. A., Owen, M. J., & Plomin, R. (2001). A genome-wide allelic association scan of 1847 DNA markers for general cognitive ability: A five-stage design using DNA pooling. *American Journal of Medical Genetics, 105*, 586.

Hills, J. R. (1989). Screening for potentially biased items in testing programs. *Educational Measurement: Issues and Practice, 8*, 5–11.

Hofstadter, D. R. (1979). *Godel, Escher, Bach: An eternal golden braid*. New York: Basic Books.

Horn, J. L. (1985) Remodelling old models of intelligence. In B. B. Wolman (Ed.), *Handbook of intelligence: Theories, measurements, and applications*. New York: Wiley.

Horn, J. L. (1988). Thinking about human abilities. In J. R. Nesselroade & R. B. Cattell (Eds.), _Handbook of multivariate experimental psychology_ (2nd ed.). New York: Plenum.

Horn, J. L. (1998). A basis for research on age differences in cognitive capabilities. In J. J. McArdle & R. W. Woodcock (Eds.), _Human cognitive abilities in theory and practice_. London: Erlbaum.

Horn, J. L., & Cattell, R. B. (1966). Refinement and test of the theory of fluid and crystallised general intelligences. _Journal of Educational Psychology, 57_, 253–270.

Howe, M. J. A. (1988). Intelligence as an explanation. _British Journal of Psychology, 79_, 349–360.

Howe, M. J. A. (1997). _IQ in question: The truth about intelligence_. London: Sage.

Howe, M. J. A., Davidson, J. W., & Sloboda, J. A. (1998). Innate talents: Reality or myth? _Behavioral and Brain Sciences, 21_, 399–407.

Huarte, J. de San Juan. (1969, originally published 1575, originally translated 1594). _Examen de ingenios, or, A triall of wits (The examination of mens wits)_. Amsterdam: Da Capo Press, Theatrum Orbis Terrarum. (This facsimile edition from a copy held in the Bodleian Library, Oxford, is an English translation [by R. Carew] from an Italian translation [by M. Camilio Camiili] of the original Spanish. Published by Richard Watkins, London, 1594.)

Humphreys, L. G. (1979). The construct of general intelligence. _Intelligence, 3_, 105–120.

Hunt, E. (1980). Intelligence as an information processing concept. _British Journal of Psychology, 71_, 449–474.

Jensen, A. R. (1987). Individual differences in the Hick paradigm. In P. A. Vernon (Ed.), _Speed of information processing and intelligence_ (pp. 101–175). Norwood, NJ: Ablex.

Johnson, R. C., McClearn, G. E., Yuen, S., Nagoshi, C. T., Ahern, F. M., & Cole, R. E. (1985). Galton's data a century later. _American Psychologist, 40_, 875–892.

Kline, P. (1991). _Intelligence: The psychometric view_. London: Routledge.

Korten, A. E., Jorm, A. F., Jiao, Z., Letenneur, L., Jacomb, P. A., Henderson, A. S., Christensen, H., & Rogers, B. (1999). Health, cognitive, and psychosocial factors as predictors of mortality in an elderly community sample. _Journal of Epidemiology and Community Health, 53_, 83–88.

Kranzler, J. H., & Jensen, A. R. (1989). Inspection time and intelligence: A meta-analysis. _Intelligence, 13_, 329–347.

Kyllonen, P. C. (1996). Is working memory capacity Spearman's g? In I. Dennis & P. Tapsfield (Eds.), _Human abilities: Their nature and measurement_ (pp. 77–96). Hillsdale, NJ: Erlbaum.

Kyllonen, P. C., & Christal, R. E. (1990). Reasoning ability is (little more than) working memory capacity?! _Intelligence, 14_, 389–433.

Levy, P. (1992). Inspection time and its relation to intelligence: Issues of measurement and meaning. _Personality and Individual Differences 13_, 987–1002.

Lindley, P. A. (2000). _Review of personality assessment instruments (level B) for use in occupational settings_. Leicester: British Psychological Society.

Lohman, D. F., Thorndike, R. L., & Hagen, E. P. (2001). _Cognitive Abilities Test. Form 6_. Chicago: Riverside.

Lynn, R. (1982). IQ in Japan and the United States shows a growing disparity. *Nature, 297,* 222–223.

Lynn, R. (1987). The intelligence of the Mongoloids: A psychometric, evolutionary, and neurological theory. *Personality and Individual Differences, 8,* 813–844.

Lynn, R. (1990). The role of nutrition in secular increases in intelligence. *Personality and Individual Differences, 11,* 273–285.

Lynn, R. (1991). Race differences in intelligence: A global perspective. *Mankind Quarterly, 31,* 255–296.

Lynn, R. (1992). Does Spearman's *g* decline at high IQ levels? Some evidence from Scotland. *Journal of Genetic Psychology, 153,* 229–230.

Lynn, R. (1994). Some reinterpretations of the Minnesota transracial adoption study. *Intelligence, 19,* 21–27.

Lynn, R. (1996a). Racial and ethnic differences in intelligence in the United States on the Differential Ability Scale. *Personality and Individual Differences, 20,* 271–273.

Lynn, R. (1996b). *Dysgenics: Genetic deterioration in modern populations.* Westport, CT: Praeger.

Lynn, R. (1998). Sex differences in intelligence: Data from a Scottish standardization of the WAIS-R. *Personality and Individual Differences, 24,* 289–290.

Lynn, R. (2001a). *Eugenics.* Westport, CT: Praeger.

Lynn, R. (2001b). *The science of human diversity: A history of the pioneer fund.* Lanham, MD: University Press of America.

Lynn, R., Irwing, P., & Cammock, T. (2002). Sex differences in general knowledge. *Intelligence, 30,* 27–39.

Lynn, R., & Mulhearn, G. (1991). A comparison of sex differences on the Scottish and American standardization samples of the WISC-R. *Personality and Individual Differences, 12,* 1179–1182.

Lynn, R., & Vanhanen, T. (2002). *IQ and the wealth of nations.* Westport, CT: Praeger.

Mackintosh, N. J. (1981). A new measure of intelligence? *Nature, 289,* 529–530.

Mackintosh, N. J. (1995). *Cyril Burt: Fraud or framed?* Oxford: Oxford University Press.

Mackintosh, N. J. (1996a). *The g factor* (book review). *Nature, 381,* 33.

Mackintosh, N. J. (1996b). Sex differences and IQ. *Journal of Biosocial Science, 28,* 559–571.

Mackintosh, N. J. (1998). *IQ and human intelligence.* Oxford: Oxford University Press.

Mackintosh, N. J. (2000). Intelligence: Evolutionary psychology meets g. *Nature, 403,* 378–379.

MacLullich, A. M. J., Seckl, J. R., Starr, J. M., & Deary, I. J. (1998). The biology of intelligence: From association to mechanism. *Intelligence, 26,* 63–73.

Marshalek, B., Lohman, D. F., & Snow, R. E. (1983). The complexity continuum in the radex and hierarchical models of intelligence. *Intelligence, 7,* 107–127.

Mathews, S. (1999). *Testing people fairly: The best practice handbook.* Windsor, UK: ASE.

McClearn, G. E., Johansson, B., Berg, S., Pedersen, N. L., Ahern, F., Petrill, S. A., & Plomin, R. (1997). Substantial genetic influence on cognitive abilities in twins 80 or more years old. *Science, 276,* 1560–1563.

McCrimmon, R. J., Deary, I. J., & Frier, B. M. (1997). Auditory information processing during acute insulin-induced hypoglycaemia in non-diabetic human subjects. *Neuropsychologia, 35,* 1547–1553.

McCrimmon, R. J., Deary, I. J., Huntly, B. J. P., MacLeod, K. J., Frier, B. M., (1996). Visual information processing during controlled hypoglycaemia in humans. *Brain, 119,* 1277–1287.

McGeorge, P., Crawford, J., & Kelly, S. W. (1996). The relationship between WAIS-R abilities and speed of processing in a word identification task. *Intelligence, 23,* 175–190.

McGuffin, P., & Martin N. (1999). Behaviour and genes. *British Medical Journal, 319,* 37–40.

McGuffin, P., Riley, B., & Plomin, R. (2001). Genomics and behavior: Toward behavioral genomics. *Science, 291,* 1232.

Neisser, U., Boodoo, G., Bouchard, T. J., Boykin, A. W., Brody, N., Ceci, S. J., Halpern, D. F., Loehlin, J. C., Perloff, R., Sternberg, R. J., & Urbina, S. (1996). Intelligence: knowns and unknowns. *American Psychologist, 51,* 77–101.

Nelson, H. E. (1982). *National Adult Reading Test (NART): Test manual.* Windsor, UK: NFER: Nelson.

Nelson, H. E., & Willison, J. (1991). *National Adult Reading Test (NART) (2nd ed.): Test manual.* Windsor, UK: NFER: Nelson.

Nettelbeck, T. (1987). Intelligence and inspection time. In P. A. Vernon (Ed.), *Speed of information processing and intelligence.* Norwood, NJ: Ablex.

Nettelbeck, T., & Lally, M. (1976). Inspection time and measured intelligence. *British Journal of Psychology, 67,* 17–22.

Nettelbeck, T., Rabbitt, P. M. A. (1992). Age, intelligence, and speed. *Intelligence, 16,* 189–205.

Nettelbeck, T., Rabbitt, P. M. A., Wilson, C., & Batt, R. (1996). Uncoupling learning from initial recall: The relationship between speed and memory deficits in old age. *British Journal of Psychology, 87,* 593–607.

Neubauer, A. C. (1997). The mental speed approach to the assessment of intelligence. In J. Kingma & W. Tomic (Eds.), *Advances in cognition and education: Reflections on the concept of intelligence.* Greenwich, Connecticut: JAI.

Novartis Foundation. (2000). *The nature of intelligence.* Chichester, UK: Wiley.

O'Carroll, R. (1995). The assessment of premorbid ability: A critical review. *Neurocase, 1,* 83–89.

Parker, D. M., Crawford, J. R., & Stephen, E. (1999). Auditory inspection time and intelligence: A new spatial localization task. *Intelligence, 27,* 131–139.

Pearson, K. (1906–1907). On the relationship of intelligence to size and shape of head, and to other physical and mental characters. *Biometrika, 5,* 105–146.

Petrie, R. X. A., & Deary, I. J. (1989). Smoking and human information processing. *Psychopharmacology, 99,* 393–396.

Petrill, S. A., Ball, D., Eley, T., Hill, L., Plomin, R., McClearn, G., Smith, D. L., Chorney, K., Chorney, K., Hershz, M. S., Detterman, D. K., Thompson, L. A.,

Benbow, C., Lubinski, D., Daniels, J., Owen, M. J., & McGuffin, P. (1998). Failure to replicate a QTL association between a DNA marker identified by ESToo083 and IQ. *Intelligence, 25,* 179–184.

Petrill, S. A., & Deary, I. J. (2001). Inspection time and intelligence: Celebrating 25 years of research. *Intelligence, 29,* 441–442.

Petrill, S. A., Plomin, R., Berg, S., Johansson, B., Pedersen, N. L., Ahern, F., & McClearn, G. E. (1998). The genetic and environmental relationship between general and specific cognitive abilities in twins age 80 and older. *Psychological Science, 9,* 183–189.

Petrill, S. A., Plomin, R., McClearn, G. E., Smith, D. L., Vignetti, S., Chorney, M. J., Thompson, L. A., Detterman, D. K., Benbow, C., Lubinski, D., Daniels, J., Owen, M. J., & McGuffin, P. (1996). DNA markers associated with general and specific cognitive abilities. *Intelligence, 23,* 191–203.

Petrill, S. A., Saudino, K. S., Wilkerson, B., & Plomin, R. (2001). Genetic and environmental molarity and modularity of cognitive functioning in 2-year-old twins. *Intelligence, 29,* 31–43.

Plomin, R. (2000). A genome scan for QTLs associated with general cognitive ability ("g"). *Behavior Genetics, 30,* 414–415.

Plomin, R. (2001a). The genetics of *g* in human and mouse. *Nature Reviews Neuroscience, 2,* 136–141.

Plomin, R. (2001b). Genetics and behaviour. *The Psychologist, 14,* 134–139.

Plomin, R. (2003). Genetics, genes, genomics, and g. *Molecular Psychiatry, 8,* 1–5.

Plomin, R., & Crabbe, J. (2000). DNA. *Psychological Bulletin, 126,* 806–828.

Plomin, R., & Craig, I. (2001). Genetics, environment and cognitive abilities: Review and work in progress towards a genome scan for quantitative trait locus associations using DNA pooling. *British Journal of Psychiatry, 178,* S41–S48.

Plomin, R., DeFries, J. C., McClearn, G. E., & McGuffin, P. (2001). *Behavioral Genetics* (4th ed.). New York: Worth.

Plomin, R., McClearn, G. E., Smith, D. L., Skuder, P., Vignetti, S., Chorney, M. J., Kasarda, S., Thompson, L. A., Detterman, D. K., Petrill, S. A., Daniels, J., Owen, M., & McGuffin, P. (1995). Allelic associations between 100 DNA markers and high versus low IQ. *Intelligence, 21,* 31–48.

Plomin, R., & Petrill, S. (1997). Genetics and intelligence: What's new? *Intelligence, 24,* 53–77.

Posner, M. I., & Mitchell, R. F. (1967). Chronometric analysis of classification. *Psychological Review, 74,* 392–409.

Price, T. S., Eley, T. C., Dale, P. S., Stevenson, J., Saudino, K., & Plomin, R. (2000). Genetic and environmental covariation between verbal and nonverbal cognitive development in infancy. *Child Development, 71,* 948–959.

Psychological Corporation, The. (1997). *Wechsler Scorer Version 2.1.* The Psychological Corporation.

Psychometric Research and Development Ltd (1985). *Graduate and Managerial Assessment.* Windsor, UK: ASE.

Rabbitt, P., Donlan, C., Bent, N., McInnes, L., & Abson, V. (1993). The University of Manchester Age and Cognitive Performance Research Centre and

North-east Age Research longitudinal programs 1982 to 1987. *Zeitschrift fur Gerontologie, 26*, 176–183.

Raven, J. C. (1938). *Progressive Matrices*. London: Lewis.

Raven, J. C. (1939). The RECI series of perceptual tests: An experimental survey. *British Journal of Medical Psychology, 18*, 16–34.

Raz, N., Willerman, L., & Yama, M. (1987). On sense and senses: Intelligence and auditory information processing. *Personality and Individual Differences, 8*, 201–210.

Richardson, K. (1999). *The making of intelligence*. London: Weidenfeld and Nicolson.

Richardson, K., & Webster, D. S. (1996). Analogical reasoning and the nature of context: A research note. *British Journal of Educational Psychology, 66*, 23–32.

Roberts, M. J., & Stevenson, N. J. (1996). Reasoning with Raven: With and without help. *British Journal of Educational Psychology, 66*, 519–532.

Roth, E. (1964). Die geschwindigkeit der verabeitung von information and ihr zusammenhang mit intelligenz. *Zeitschrift fur Experimentelle und Angewandte Psychologie, 11*, 616–622.

Rushton, J. P., & Ankney, C. D. (1996). Brain size and cognitive ability: Correlations with age, sex, social class, and race. *Psychonomic Bulletin and Review, 3*, 21–36.

Rust, J. (1995). *Wechsler Individual Achievement Test™*. London: The Psychological Corporation.

Salovey, P., & Meyer, J. D. (1990). Emotional intelligence. *Imagination, Cognition, and Personality, 9*, 185–211.

Scottish Council for Research in Education. (1933). *The intelligence of Scottish children: A national survey of an age group*. London: University of London Press.

SHL (1982–1991). *Critical reasoning test battery*. Thames Ditton, Surrey: SHL.

Shipley, B. A., Deary, I. J., Tan, J., Christie, G., & Starr, J. M. (2002). Efficiency of temporal order discrimination as an indicator of bradyphrenia in Parkinson's disease: The inspection time loop task. *Neuropsychologia, 40*, 1488–1493.

Simon, B. (1953/1971). *Intelligence testing and the comprehensive school*. Republished in *Intelligence, Psychology, and Education: A Marxist critique*. London: Lawrence & Wishart.

Simpson, C. R., & Deary, I. J. (1997). Strategy use and feedback in inspection time. *Personality and Individual Differences, 23*, 787–797.

Smith, P. (1986). Application of the information processing approach to the design of a non-verbal reasoning test. *British Journal of Educational Psychology, 56*, 119–137.

Smith, P., & Whetton, C. (1992). *Critical reasoning tests*. Windsor, UK: NFER-Nelson.

Smith, P., Whetton, C., & Caspall, L. (1999). *General ability tests – 2*. Windsor, UK: NFER-Nelson.

Snowdon, D. A., Kemper, S. J., Mortimer, J. A., Greiner, L. H., Wekstein, D. R., & Markesbery, W. R. (1996). Linguistic ability in early life and cognitive function and Alzheimer's disease in late life: Findings from the Nun Study. *Journal of the American Medical Association, 275*, 528–532.

Spearman, C. (1904). "General intelligence" objectively determined and measured. *American Journal of Psychology, 15*, 201–293.

Spearman, C. (1923). *The nature of intelligence and the principles of cognition.* London: Macmillan.

Spearman, C. (1927). *The abilities of man.* London: Macmillan.

Stauffer, J. M., Ree, M. J., & Carretta, T. R. (1996). Cognitive-components tests are not much more than *g*: An extension of Kyllonen's analyses. *Journal of General Psychology, 123*, 193–205.

Sternberg, R. J. (1977). *Intelligence, information processing, and analogical reasoning: The componential analysis of human abilities.* Hillsdale, NJ: Erlbaum.

Sternberg, R. J. (1978). Intelligence research at the interface between differential and cognitive psychology. *Intelligence, 2*, 195–222.

Sternberg, R. J. (1985). *Beyond IQ: A triarchic theory of human intelligence.* Cambridge: Cambridge University Press.

Sternberg, S. (1966). High speed scanning in human memory. *Science, 153*, 652–654.

Stough, C., Mangan, G., Bates, T., Frank, N., Kerkin, B., & Pellett, O. (1995). Effects of nicotine on perceptual speed. *Psychopharmacology, 119*, 305–310.

Strachan, M. W. J., Deary, I. J., Ewing, F. M. E., Ferguson, S. S. C., Young, M. J., & Frier, B. M. (2001). Acute hypoglycaemia impairs functions of the central but not the peripheral nervous system. *Physiology and Behavior, 72*, 83–92.

Strand, S. (1999). *NFER-NELSON non-verbal reasoning 8/9 and KS2 chances tables: Autumn 1999.* Windsor, UK: NFER-Nelson.

Strand, S. (2001). *CAT and KS2 indicators: Technical report.* Windsor, UK: NFER-Nelson.

Thomson, G. H. (1939). *The factorial analysis of human ability.* London: University of London Press.

Thorndike, R. L., Hagen, E. P., & Lorge, I. (1954–1993). *Cognitive abilities test. Forms 1 to 5.* Chicago: Riverside.

Thurstone, L. L. (1938). Primary mental abilities. *Psychometric Monographs,* No. 1.

Turic, D., Fisher, P. J., Plomin, R., & Owen, M. J. (2001). No association between apolipoprotein E polymorphisms and general cognitive ability in children. *Neuroscience Letters, 299*, 97–100.

Turner, M. (1997). *Psychological assessment of dyslexia.* London: Whurr.

Undheim, J. O. (1981a). On intelligence II: A neo-Spearmanian model to replace Cattell's theory of fluid and crystallised intelligence. *Scandinavian Journal of Psychology, 22*, 181–187.

Undheim, J. O. (1981b). On intelligence IV: Toward a restoration of general intelligence. *Scandinavian Journal of Psychology, 22*, 251–265.

Vernon, P. A., (Ed.). (1987). *Speed of information processing and intelligence.* Norwood, NJ: Ablex.

Vernon, P. A., (Ed.). (1993). *Biological approaches to the study of human intelligence.* Norwood, NJ: Ablex.

Vernon, P. E. (1950). *The structure of human abilities.* London: Methuen.

Vernon, P. E., (1961). *The structure of human abilities* (2nd ed.). London: Methuen.

Vernon, P. E., and Parry, J. B. (1949). *Personnel selection in the armed forces*. London: University of London Press.

Vickers, D., Nettelbeck, T., & Willson, R. J. (1972). Perceptual indices of performance: The measurement of "inspection time" and "noise" in the visual system. *Perception, 1*, 263–295.

Wahlsten, D. (1999). Single-gene influences on behavior. *Annual Review of Psychology, 50*, 599–624.

Wechsler, D. (1989). *Wechsler preschool and primary scale of intelligence (rev.)*. San Antonio, TX: The Psychological Corporation.

Wechsler, D. (1992). *Wechsler intelligence scale for children (3rd ed.)[UK]*. London: Psychological Corporation.

Wechsler, D. (1997). *Wechsler adult intelligence scale (3rd ed.)*. San Antonio, TX: Psychological Corporation.

Westby, G. (1953). Review of the Raven Progressive Matrices. In O. K. Buros (Ed.), *The fourth mental measurements yearbook*. Highland Park, NJ: Gryphon.

Whalley, L. J., & Deary, I. J. (2001). Longitudinal cohort study of childhood IQ and survival up to age 76. *British Medical Journal, 322*, 1–5.

Zhang, Y., Caryl, P., & Deary, I. J. (1989a). Evoked potential correlates of inspection time. *Personality and Individual Differences, 10*, 379–384.

Zhang, Y., Caryl, P., & Deary, I. J. (1989b). Evoked potentials, inspection time, and intelligence. *Personality and Individual Differences, 10*, 1079–1094.

2

Intelligence

Theory, Research, and Testing in the Nordic Countries

Berit Carlstedt, Jan-Eric Gustafsson,
and Jarkko Hautamäki

INTRODUCTION

This chapter describes research on intelligence and practices of assessment in the Nordic countries. For the purposes of this chapter, the Nordic group of countries is taken to comprise Denmark, Finland, Norway and Sweden. These four small (between 4 and 9 million persons) countries, share many characteristics. Three of the countries (Denmark, Norway, and Sweden) have highly similar languages, which are typically understood across countries. The fourth country (Finland) has a Swedish-speaking minority, while the main language (Finnish) is a quite different language than the other languages. All countries also have a high standard of living and are what is often referred to as "welfare states," with societal solutions to problems such as medicine, health care, unemployment, and education. From a cultural point of view, there are also are many similarities among the four countries, which go far back in history.

DEFINITIONS AND MEASUREMENT OF INTELLIGENCE IN THE NORDIC COUNTRIES

Conceptions of intelligence in the Nordic countries have been very strongly influenced by the psychometric research traditions that were developed in Britain, the United States, and elsewhere. There has, thus, been a strong focus on development and adaptation of tools for measuring intelligence and on empirical approaches in research on intelligence.

DEVELOPMENT OF TESTING

As was observed by Carroll (1982), the fundamental principles of the technology of intelligence testing were well established by the 1930s, whereas the development after this time may be described as elaborations, extensions, and refinements of these basic principles. Before World War II the Nordic countries tended to be more oriented toward, and influenced by, continental Europe (primarily Germany and France), whereas after World War II, English-speaking countries, and primarily the United States, exerted the strongest influence.

The Early Decades

Use of ability tests in Norway dates back to the first decades of the 20th century. Typically, test instruments were imported from other countries, performance tests being used in their original versions and language tests after translation (Hagtvet & Undheim, 1988). As early as 1913, Looft (1913) used the Binet test in Norway to test school children. A Norwegian adaptation and standardization of the 1916 Stanford-Binet test was published by Lofthus (1931), and the Norwegian version of the 1937 Terman-Merrill revision of the Stanford-Binet test was published by Sandven (1954).

In Sweden, intelligence testing was introduced by Jaederholm (1914), who in his doctoral dissertation translated the Binet and Simon (1905, 1908) test into Swedish and reported results from several empirical studies comprising fairly large groups of school children at different age levels. One of the questions studied by Jaederholm was whether the quite heterogeneous test items included in the Binet test measure a general factor of intelligence, as would be hypothesized from the Spearman (1904b) two-factor theory. Jaederholm concluded from an analysis of correlations among test items that these supported the existence of a general factor, even though he hesitated to conclude that the results supported Spearman's view that general intelligence is a unitary factor.

In Finland, too, the Binet-Simon scales were introduced early by Lilius (1913). Lilius (1916) presented the Binet-Simon 1911 scales, the Meumann 1914 scales, and the Jaederholm 1914 scales. There were also some other early applications of the Binet scales (e.g., Rosenqvist, 1919) and analyses of the educational implications of differences in intelligence (Ensiö, 1917). The major issue was the question of basic intellectual requirements for selection to higher levels of education from compulsory school.

Denmark had an early translation of the Stanford-Binet test in the 1930s. It was standardized for children and used by school psychologists. For a long time this was the only test that was available, and it was often used for adults as well. However, the test produced misleading results for adults.

To summarize, in Finland, Norway, and Sweden there was early, direct contact with the French research, but the strong influence on actual test use came via Lewis Terman at Stanford University in the United States and particularly through the 1916 Stanford-Binet test and the 1937 Terman-Merrill revision. The death of Alfred Binet in 1911 is one possible reason why the ground-breaking work done in France did not have a stronger influence on early use of intelligence tests in the Nordic countries.

Development from the 1930s

In Norway tests have continued to be imported, particularly so after World War II. Among individual tests, the Wechsler family of tests has had the strongest impact. Beverfelt, Nordvik, and Nygård (1967) standardized the Wechsler Adult Intelligence Scale (WAIS), and new norms for young adults were established by Engvik, Hjerkin, and Seim (1980). The revised version of the Wechsler Intelligence Scale for Children (WISC-R) was standardized on a large nationwide sample by Undheim (1978a), and the Wechsler Preschool and Primary Intelligence Scales (WPPSI) were published in a Norwegian edition by Langset (1984).

Several group tests have been translated from English and standardized for use in Norway, such as the Kuhlman-Anderson Test by Ribsskog (1941), the Illinois Test of Psycholinguistic Abilities by Gjessing, Nygaard, and Solheim (1975), and the Raven Progressive Matrices test by Eckhoff (1978). A Norwegian test based on Thurstone's model was published in 1948 by Mønnesland (1948; see Hagtvet & Undheim, 1988, for further information).

In comparison with the other Nordic countries, Danish psychological research has been more influenced by European continental lines of thought than by Anglo-American approaches. Thus, during the 1930s and 1940s Danish research was strongly influenced by the psychology of perception and by Gestalt psychology in particular. One example of a researcher contributing to Gestalt psychology is Edgar Rubin, who has become immortalized through his figure-ground picture, the Vase, presented in most textbooks on psychology.

However, in Denmark, too, the Wechsler tests have been made available. WAIS was introduced in the late 1950s and has been standardized for the age groups 20–30 and 40–50 years when Mortensen, Reinisch, and Teasdale (1989) in a research project related it to the military draft board test. The performance tests of WISC were initially used with U.S. norms but since 1975 Danish norms have been available. In 1996 a test named DEP (short for Dansk Evneprøve) built on the British Ability Scales and Differential Ability Scales was standardized in Denmark and used for the testing of school children (Spelling, 1999). Currently, psychologists in Denmark have access to the WAIS-R, WISC-III, and WPPSI. The Wechsler scales are the ones most commonly used in both research and in clinical settings. The Dansk Psykologisk Forlag, which publishes tests for the Danish market, offers in its catalogue two cognitive tests besides the Wechsler tests: the Raven Progressive Matrices and a Dutch non-verbal intelligence test for children (Snijders-Oomen).

In Sweden, too, psychologists rely on imported and translated tests to a rather large extent. The Terman-Merrill test was translated into Swedish in 1960 from the 1937 version of Stanford-Binet Intelligence Scale (Hellström, 1960). Recently, the WISC III and the WPPSI-R tests have been translated and normed for the Swedish population, and the WAIS-R test is also available.

However, in Sweden test constructors have been quite prolific in developing their own intelligence tests, and there has been less of a reliance on translated tests than in the other Nordic countries. This development goes back to the 1940s, and the influence that Thurstone's (1931, 1947) method of multiple factor analysis achieved toward the end of that decade. Siegvald (1944) published a major study on intellectual differences between the sexes. The 600-page book provides a thorough summary of intelligence theory and research at that time. The Spearman, Thorndike, and Burt views on the structure of intelligence are described, but it also refers to many German researchers and to Binet, which indicates that up to the start of World War II there were strong influences from the European continent on Swedish research on intelligence. However, after World War II Thurstone's factor analytic methods and the Primary Mental Abilities (PMA) model (Thurstone, 1938) were introduced and had considerable impact, which possibly partly is due to the fact that Thurstone was of Swedish origin. For example, Husén (1948) applied Thurstone's method of multiple factor analysis in the analysis of test data and observed that "test construction has been released from the subjective judgments of the meaning of the tests, and from the one-sided dependence of the external, and in most cases very unreliable, validity criteria" (p. 7). At Göteborg University, a series of doctoral dissertations were completed in which different domains of intelligence, such as spatial abilities, were investigated with the Thurstonian methodology (Björsjö, 1951).

On the basis of such research, several group test batteries were published for different purposes, in most cases before 1970. The batteries were, among other things, constructed for testing of conscripts (see section on Military Test Development), to help young students make their way through comprehensive school (Härnqvist, 1960), and for testing of feebleminded subjects (Kebbon, 1968). Other test batteries were developed or adapted for the measurement of aptitude for different educations and occupations (Westrin, 1967; Psykotekniska Institutet, 1970) but also for the assessment of cognitive ability in clinical applications (Dureman & Sälde, 1959). All these tests had the Thurstone (1938) model of primary mental abilities as the theoretical starting point, even if sometimes the full score was used as a measure of general cognitive ability.

In the late 1960s a project was started under the leadership of Sten Henrysson to develop a test to be used as an instrument for selection of students to higher education. The resulting instrument (Högskoleprovet, or Swedish Scholastic Aptitude Test, SweSAT) was to some extent modeled after the Scholastic Aptitude Test (SAT) published by the College Board in the United States. The first version of the test, which was published in 1977, consisted of six subtests: two reasoning subtests with mainly mathematical content and four verbal subtests (vocabulary, general information, reading comprehension, and study techniques). The scores on the six subtests were summed into a total score on the basis of which the applicants were rank ordered. Originally, only applicants who had not obtained grades from upper secondary school could take the test, which meant that the number of persons taking the test each year was limited. However, starting in 1991 everyone who filed an application to higher education could be admitted either on the basis of grades from upper secondary school or on the basis of the SweSAT score. This has caused the number of test takers to increase dramatically. The increased importance of the test also has prompted research to be conducted on different aspects of the test, to which we return in a later section.

In Finland the development has been quite similar to that in Sweden, with an emphasis on test development along with adaptation of tests developed in other countries. During the 1930s Koskenniemi (e.g., 1938) contributed several pieces of work on intelligence and on issues of measurement. Among other things he analyzed the intellectual requirements for the upper secondary school, and he also analyzed the role of the test situation in the estimation of intelligence (Koskenniemi, 1938). There were close relations to Torsten Husén, in Sweden. These relations were important in forming the Finnish version of educational psychology.

The Salomaa Scales, the first standardized scales for children and adults, were made of adapted Binet-Simon items (Salomaa, 1938) and were used in practical psychological applications, for example, family counseling offices, and in research. The 1937 version of the Terman-Merrill adaptation of the Binet-Simon Scales was the basis for the Finnish translation and adaptation (Lehtovaara, 1960). This version has been widely used under the label the TML Scales (Terman-Merrill-Lehtovaara).

Just as was the case in Sweden, factor analysis exerted a strong influence on psychological research in Finland from the late 1940s into the 1960s (Korkiakangas, 1977), and this held true particularly for the field of intelligence. Major contributions using factor analysis were made by Takala (e.g., 1953) and his students in studies on different aspects of abilities and skills, with a focus on visualization and psychomotor aspects of personality. Ahmavaara (1954) presented an important extension of the factor analytic method, *the transformation analysis of factorial data,* to compare the outcomes of factor analyses in different studies, which was also applied in a series of substantive contributions (e.g., Ahmavaraa, 1957a, 1957b, 1963).

In 1948 a study designed to test Thurstone's model was conducted under the name "The Great Study on Mental Abilities" (see AVO, 1981). In the study 62 paper-and-pencil scales for the estimation of primary abilities were given to 311 university students. The by-hand-calculated factor analysis yielded a nine-factor solution, and after repeating the analyses by genders, there were three more factors. The interpretation was made that the *g*-factor existed but at the same level as the primary factors.

In Finland several test batteries designed to measure narrow abilities have been published. The KTK-Performance Scales (Elonen, Takala, & Ruoppila, 1963) include several performance measures, among others a psychometric adaptation of Vygotsky Blocks. The Finnish vocational guidance office also has designed several factor tests. Because of the national coverage of the offices, it was possible to produce national norms for the reliable scales. The scales are used both as reference tests in various studies and still, to some extent, in vocational guidance. They were also used recently as the criteria in an intervention study on cognitive education (Scheinin & Mehtäläinen, 1999).

The Illinois Test of Psycholinguistic Abilities (ITPA) was standardized in 1972 (Kuusinen & Blåfield, 1972). The standardization sample also has been followed up in a longitudinal study that has shown the power of intelligence measures to predict later school achievement and also the stability of school careers as these are reflected in grade piont averages (Kuusinen & Leskinen, 1988).

In Finland, as well as in other countries, a separation of the lines of intelligence research slowly took place. The academic institutions ceased being active in research on intelligence. Applied psychologists, however, still needed the intelligence scales. The publishing house of psychologists was founded in 1970 to serve the need for psychological tools. The TML test, for example, became outdated but was still in use in the late 1970s. But the practical needs required new solutions, which were provided by the introduction of standardized tests, most notably WPPSI, WAIS and WISC.

The first translation of WAIS was made in 1971, but the norms applied still were the U.S. norms. The first standardized WAIS scales were published in 1992. The WAIS-III reference data have just recently been collected, and it is expected that the new version will be published in 2004. The WISC translation was first published in 1984, and these scales have been in extensive use in educational psychology and in other psychological services for children.

In the new standardizations it was found that either the old norms were simply old and the tests too easy, or that the new norms were based on items that were too difficult. The discussions in professional circles ended with the revelation that, indeed, the norms have to be renewed frequently and that the standardization has to be based on representative samples.

Military Test Development

Clinical applications and psychological counseling in schools, and particularly in special education, have been major areas of application of ability tests in the Nordic countries. Another important area in which tests have been used in the Nordic countries is in screening for enlistment in military service. Since this has involved test development, there is reason to describe the trends in and influences on this development.

During World War II the Norwegian defense collaborated with psychological institutions in Canada, Great Britain, and the United States and observed the investments in development of psychological tests and what could be gained in using systematic assessment of intelligence in selection (Riis, 1988; Torjussen & Hansen, 1999). Applicants to the Norwegian defense schools had to pass psycho-technical tests beginning in 1946, and at the same time it was decided that tests were to be used for the classification of soldiers. The so-called U-battery was published in its first edition in 1949. Three tests (Mathematical Problems; Figure Rules, which was similar to the Raven Matrices; and Synonyms) yielded a measure of general ability (Rist, 1982). The current version of the battery includes four tests: Figure Rules, Number Series, Technical Comprehension, and Verbal Items. It is evaluated as a composite score, reflecting general ability, and as scores on each test.

In Denmark the Draft Board Screening Test (DBST) was developed in the late 1950s, based on ideas contributed by the Danish statistician Georg Rasch. Rasch outlined the principles for the test construction, and his son-in-law, Børge Prien, a psychologist, constructed the tests. Within eight months Prien created the four tests of cognitive ability that since 1957 have been used for testing young men at military draft boards. The tests – Letter Matrices, Verbal Analogies, Number Series, and Geometric Figures Test – are constructed so as to make guessing impossible, by requiring the respondents to produce the answers. A sum of the correct responses on all four tests is computed, and the score level is used to decide whether the conscript is suitable for duty. A contemporary Danish psychologist at the University of Copenhagen (E. L. Mortensen, personal communication, November 8, 2001) regards the DBST as one of the best cognitive ability tests ever constructed. It has never been changed, and it is still used. The full population of young men, except for approximately 5–10%, is tested every year.

In Sweden, the Enlistment Battery was developed in its first form in 1944 by Torsten Husén, who because of Swedish neutrality had to wait until the end of the war to get information about the American military testing experiences. As mentioned earlier, Norway could get access to this knowledge during the war, because Norwegian pilots got their training in Canada, and some Norwegian officers worked in Britain during the war. From 1944 until today, nine versions of the Enlistment Battery have been developed (Carlstedt, 2000). The first version included eight subtests of varying content and emphasized the measurement of the general factor. Group test batteries used in the military in the United States from World War I onward were sources of inspiration. Theoretically, the work was strongly influenced by Spearman and his concept of general ability. The test constructors evidently strived to measure g with the first batteries. The 1947 version made an even better g test, in that three new inductive tests were included. In 1948 the test was improved in a number of ways to increase the reliability of the test: Items of the same type were administered together; the test instructions were separated from the problems of the tests; time limits were not as tight; multiple choice responses were given, and so forth (Husén, 1948). At this time Thurstone's multiple factor analysis was used in the analysis of data, and for more than 30 years Thurstone's primary factor model had a very powerful influence on the view of individual differences and on test development. This influence was also obvious in the Enlistment Test Batteries used up to 1994 (see Carlstedt, 2000).

The Enlistment Battery of 1994 meant a break with the former tradition in that it was strongly influenced by the hierarchical model of Undheim and Gustafsson (see below), and also by development in item response theory (IRT) and adaptive computer-administered testing. The computer-administered battery of 10 tests is evaluated according to a hierarchical model in which all tests contribute to the G factor, but the inductive tests do so most strongly. The remaining variance is captured in two factors orthogonal to G named $G_c{}'$ and $G_v{}'$. $G_c{}'$ captures residual variance of the verbal tests and $G_v{}'$ residual variance of the spatial tests.

In 2000 the Enlistment Battery was transformed into a semi-adaptive version. According to IRT-based parameters of the difficulty of the items, each test was divided into three shorter tests of three difficulty levels. Based on the results of an initial test common to all subjects, the difficulty level of the next subtest is chosen. The difficulty level of the next test is determined on the basis of all earlier test results achieved. One aim of the semi-adaptive testing is to improve the efficiency of the measurement by letting each subject solve the items that discriminate best at his level of performance, and another aim is to reduce testing time.

Psychological selection and testing started in 1947 in the Finnish Defense Forces. The first test battery employed tests similar to those of the

Americans and was used for selection of fighter pilots in the Finnish Air Force. Thurstone's structure of intelligence factors and the theory of multiple aptitudes guided the design of this first test battery and several other test batteries in the Finnish Defense Forces.

The enlistment test battery for screening and classifying of conscripts was taken in use in 1955. In 1981, the old tests were replaced with new ones with new norms and higher validity. The new tests were Matrices, Verbal Relations, and Arithmetic Problems. These tests are still used for screening and classifying conscripts (Vainikainen, 1998).

Sinivuo (1977) conducted a validity study of the Air Force psychological test battery. Based on data from 10 years, he developed a regression model for the military pilot selection. The measured abilities in the Air Force test battery were reasoning (induction), verbal ability, spatial ability, numeric ability, mathematics, mechanical knowledge and skill, visualization, memory, restructured closure, reaction time, processing speed, timesharing, psychomotor skill, and personality traits. In the very homogeneous group of reserve officers ($N = 151$), the multiple correlation between the psychological tests and the criterion of flying skills varied from .35 to .55. General intelligence (g) and the mathematical-logical reasoning test predicted success in theoretical subjects.

In 1996, it was unclear if those tests earlier included in the Air Force psychological test battery were measuring all the critical abilities needed in modern fighters and in other man–machine environments. New theories of modern cognitive psychology have guided the ability test development. When the Finnish Air Force purchased new modern F/A 18 fighters in mid 1990s, there were several signs that the work of the pilot was dramatically changed. According to a task analysis of F/A 18 radar attack missions (Haavisto & Oksama, 1997), the abilities that needed to be measured were defined.

The following cognitive abilities (and psychometric abilities) are measured and studied in the new Air Force ability test battery: fluid intelligence, crystallized intelligence, working memory (WM) (visuospatial and verbal WM), short-term memory (STM) (visuospatial and verbal STM), information processing speed, simple and choice reaction time, visual tracking, vigilance, two-hand coordination, multilimb-coordination, multiple-task performance, coordination, and attention switching. Experimental and correlational studies for validating the new cognitive measures are being conducted (Haavisto & Lehto, 2003).

Trends and Problems in the Development of Testing

From the short review of the development of testing and of test development in the Nordic countries presented here we can identify commonalities as well as differences among the countries. First, it may be concluded that in all countries tests have been imported, translated, and supplied with local norms. The Binet tests and, more recently, the Wechsler tests thus have exerted considerable influence in practical applications of individual testing, and even though these tests are essentially atheoretical, they certainly have had an impact on conceptions of the nature of intelligence. As was observed by Hagtvet and Undheim (1988) this strong influence from human ability research conducted in the United States "mirrors the cultural stream of technological influence generally and the direction of research more specifically" (p. 263).

In Sweden and Finland the ambition to adopt such standard measures has been somewhat less marked than in the other countries, and instead there has been a stronger emphasis on development of new tests, with the Thurstone model as the primary source of inspiration. These developmental efforts mainly took place in the 1950s and the 1960s, but since 1970 there have been few new tests or updates of previously published tests. This is a source of great concern, because not only is the test material growing obsolete, but so are the norms. The phenomenon of rising test scores in the population over time (the so called "Flynn effect," after Flynn, 1984), which in particular has been observed for tests of non-verbal problem-solving ability, makes this a very serious problem indeed.

The problem of norms also affects the imported tests. In several instances, it has not been possible to secure data from sufficiently large and representative samples for purposes of establishing the norm tables. This may be one reason why both in Sweden and Denmark the recently completed standardizations of WISC III have been regarded with some doubt, since the norms by the users of the tests are viewed as being too harsh for certain age groups. The problem keeping the norm tables of the tests current also has been strongly felt in all the countries, and there is an almost constant need to renorm all the major tests.

The technology of intelligence testing is a complex one, even though it is impossible to tell just by looking at a test (see Carroll, 1982, for a more elaborate discussion of what is involved in the technology of testing). In particular, it requires vast amounts of data, which are difficult and expensive to collect. Given that the Nordic-language populations are small, the potential market for each edition of a test is limited, which makes norming and renorming of tests economically risky projects. This harsh economical reality exerts a serious threat to the quality of intelligence testing in any country with a language that is spoken by a limited number of people.

METHODOLOGICAL DEVELOPMENTS

Psychometrically oriented intelligence research relies on advanced statistical methods, and ever since the days of Spearman (1904a, 1904b) there has been an interplay between development in the substantive and the methodological areas. Nordic researchers have contributed some methodological innovations that have influenced research on intelligence and practices of assessment both locally and elsewhere.

One of the central assumptions in research on intelligence is that the distribution of scores is approximately normal. This issue was empirically investigated by Jaederholm (1914), to whom we have already referred. He investigated the distributions of test scores within and across age groups and arrived at the conclusion that they closely approximate a normal distribution within age groups. A similar investigation was done concerning the grading practices of school teachers. Here, too, Jaederholm concluded that the grades assigned followed the normal distribution, even though differences in harshness and leniency of grading between teachers could also be observed. These results were later to be taken as a basis for the construction of a new grading system, which was based on the idea that the grades should be normally distributed in the population. Common achievement tests were to be used to ascertain the level of performance of the class in relation to other classes in the country.

A very different position was taken by the Danish statistician Georg Rasch. He found it difficult to accept the assumption about normally distributed test scores, and he was skeptical about factor analysis. Proposing an alternative methodology that did not require any distributional assumptions but instead invoked assumptions about unidimensionality and item homogeneity, Rasch (1960, 1966) developed a measurement model that made it possible to determine the difficulty of items, irrespective of the distribution of ability in the group of persons taking the test, and to determine the ability of persons irrespective of the difficulty of the items included in the test. This so-called Rasch model is now recognized as one member of the family of test-theoretic models referred to as *latent-trait* models, or *item-response theory* models, which form the core of modern test theory.

Rasch trained most of the Danish statisticians and psychologists with an interest in psychometrics, so his standpoint and own methodological contributions exerted a strong influence on the education of Danish psychologists and their way of regarding the measurement of intelligence. In certain areas, like clinical neuropsychology, this influence has been weaker, but the negative attitude toward factor analysis and the normality assumption has been a strong influence on approaches to analysis of tests in Danish educational psychology (Mortensen, 2001).

Although factor analysis has never been a popular method in Denmark, it has attracted quite a lot of attention among Swedish and Finnish researchers. As has already been mentioned, Thurstonian multiple factor analysis came to significantly influence test devlopment in Sweden and Finland, and Ahmavaraa's (1954) contributions have already been described. Interest in factor analysis developed among statisticians as well, and Jöreskog published a dissertation on statistical estimation in factor analysis (see Jöreskog, 1967). After the dissertation, Jöreskog continued his work on multivariate statistical methods. This resulted in a wide array of new techniques, such as a method for confirmatory factor analysis (Jöreskog 1969, 1970), techniques for factor analysis in multiple populations (Jöreskog, 1971), and a general method for analyzing relations among sets of variables, some of which could be unobserved (Jöreskog, 1973). This general method was implemented in a series of computer programs referred to as LISREL (Linear Structural RELations), of which the first more generally useful version (LISREL III) was published in 1973 (Jöreskog and Sörbom, 1973), and the most recent version (LISREL 8.50) was published in 2001 (Jöreskog et al. 2001). This methodology, which is now generally referred to as structural equation modeling, has been extended in a large number of different ways by Jöreskog himself, and by his students and colleagues, and it is now widely applied in research on intelligence. In Nordic research in this field the technique has been used by, among others, Gustafsson (1984) and by Undheim and Gustafsson (1987).

Not only statisticians made methodological contributions. During the 1960s and early 1970s several pieces of work on methodological problems in factor analysis and test theory were published (e.g., Henrysson, 1962; Werdelin & Stjernberg, 1971), as well as textbooks (e.g., Magnusson, 1961), and the level of competence in quantitative

methods and differential psychology generally was high in the departments of psychology and education. These departments shared, at this
time, responsibility for the education of psychologists, and psychometrics and test theory were given a rather strong emphasis in the training
programs. However, in the late 1960s and during the 1970s the strong
emphasis on testing both in the professional practice of psychologists
and in the education of psychologists was challenged. As a consequence,
test theory, differential psychology, and practical training in testing more
or less disappeared from the education of psychologists in Sweden.

RESEARCH ON INTELLIGENCE

It is quite impossible to review the history of research on intelligence in
the Nordic countries in a few pages, so here we restrict the presentation
to some of the main lines of research.

Test Validity

One of the most essential characteristics of a test is its validity
(Messick, 1989). Hagtvet and Undheim (1988) observed that the common
practice of importing tests from one cultural context (e.g., the United
States) to another cultural context (e.g., one of the Nordic countries)
is implicitly based on an assumption of universal (or at least Western)
validity. They also observed that this assumption is probably based (or
can be based) on the presence of certain common cultural factors, such
as a literate population, and compulsory schooling based on a common
core of content. For transfer of tests between the United States and the
Nordic countries, there probably is sufficient overlap of such cultural
factors for the assumption of validity to be reasonable, but Hagtvet and
Undheim (1988) nevertheless reviewed the empirical evidence pertinent
to the correctness of the assumption of validity.

One category of studies compared results from criterion-related validity studies across countries, and Hagtvet and Undheim (1988) concluded that the correlations among intelligence test scores, achievement
test results, and teacher-assigned grades generally are quite similar
when Norway is compared with other countries. This conclusion may
be safely generalized to apply to the other Nordic countries as well. It
is also interesting to observe that the strength of these relations seems
to be stable over time. Jaederholm (1914) studied the relation between
intelligence test scores and school achievement as reflected in grades

and found high correlations, close to those found in current studies (0.50–0.60; see Gustafsson & Balke, 1993).

The seemingly simple problem of estimating the predictive power of the SweSAT offers special methodological problems, which are caused by the fact that acceptance to higher education can be made on the basis either of school marks or test scores. This procedure may cause the correlation betweeen the SweSAT score and achievement to appear to be zero or even negative, when in fact there is a fairly strong positive correlation. These problems are discussed and solved by Gustafsson and Reuterberg (2000).

Hagtvet and Undheim (1988) also observed that correlations between intelligence test scores and socio-economic background factors in Norwegian studies are highly similar to those obtained in research in the United States. Gustafsson and Westerlund (1994) found in a Swedish study that socio-economic background accounts for about 10% of the variance in intelligence test scores, which is close to the estimate found by White (1982) in a meta-analytic study that primarily included empirical results from the United States.

Information about the construct validity of tests also has been obtained more or less routinely in factor analyses conducted on the standardization samples (e.g., Undheim, 1978a). Results from such studies "indicate a close correspondence to the structural relations of the performances as obtained in the original standardization samples" (Hagtvet & Undheim, 1988, p. 265), which lends credence to the conclusion that tests may have the same measurement properties after translation.

Studies investigating the construct validity of tests developed in the Nordic countries and other tests have also been published. For example, the relation between the individually administered WAIS test and the group administered DBST was investigated by Mortensen, Reinisch, and Teasdale (1989), and it was concluded that both tests measure the same factor of general intelligence.

The Structure of Intelligence

In the Nordic countries there is also a line of research that has given much information about the construct validity of tests, but where the major purpose has been to investigate theoretical questions concerning the structure of human intelligence. The late J. O. Undheim investigated, in a series of studies, alternative models of the structure of intelligence (e.g., the Guilford model, Undheim, 1979; Undheim & Horn, 1977; and the Cattell and Horn model, Undheim, 1981a, 1981b, Undheim & Gustafsson, 1987). The major conclusion from this work is that there is empirical support for the restoration of Spearman's factor of general intelligence, which is also reflected in the title of one of Undheim's papers: "A neo-Spearman model to replace Cattell's theory of fluid and crystallized intelligence" (Undheim, 1981a). The differentiation of cognitive abilities as a function of age also was studied by Undheim, mainly because of the theoretical relevance of this issue (Gustafsson & Undheim, 1992; Undheim, 1978b).

Originally independent of the work of Undheim, but later in collaboration with him, J. E. Gustafsson in Sweden pursued a similar line of research and arrived at the same conclusions. Empirical support was found for a model with factors at three levels: a level of first-order factors corresponding to the primary mental abilities introduced by Thurstone (1938), a level of second-order factors corresponding to the broad abilities of the Cattell–Horn model, and a single third-order general factor that is identical to the second-order factor of Fluid Intelligence (Gustafsson, 1984, 1988; Gustafsson & Undheim, 1996; Undheim & Gustafsson, 1987). This hierarchical model thus has a similar structure to the "Three-Stratum Model" proposed by Carroll (1993), even though Carroll could not find any perfect equivalence between G_f and g. However, in a recent study using confirmatory factor analysis, Carroll (2003) also arrived at the conclusion that G_f and g are one and the same.

The hierarchical model has been the basis for several test development projects in Sweden, such as the Swedish Enlistment Battery from 1994 (Mårdberg & Carlstedt, 1998), the Officer School Admission Battery (Carlstedt & Widén, 1999), and for a recently published test battery for intelligence assessment (BasIQ) for use in vocational guidance and selection (Mårdberg, Sjöberg, & Henrysson Eidvall, 2000). From batteries of reasoning tests, spatial tests and verbal tests (and in BasIQ numerical ability) the g factor is extracted, typically with the largest weights for the reasoning tests. There also are residual factors, orthogonal to g, which account for the additional covariance among groups of tests (e.g., verbal and spatial groups). However, since the g factor accounts for all the covariance among the reasoning tests there typically is no residual factor for this group of tests.

Validation studies have shown good predictive validity for the general factor estimated from the hierarchical model, with some additional variance accounted for by the residual factors (Gustafsson, 2001; Gustafsson & Balke, 1993). However, for practical applications it must be remembered that the residual factor scores must be interpreted given the level of G. This makes the residual factor scores useful for intraindividual comparisons, but when comparing individuals, results are more meaningful when factor scores are estimated from a model with correlated factors. These factors thus combine variance from the general factor and the residual factors.

The hierarchical model has proven to be a useful tool for test development both when it comes to investigations of construct validity (Gustafsson, Wedman, & Westerlund, 1992; Mårdberg & Carlstedt, 1998) and item analysis (Ullstadius, Gustafsson, & Carlstedt, 2002). The model has been used for the test development in the projects mentioned here, and also for the test batteries that are used at the National Labour Market Board (Gagnerud & Haglund, 2000). Hypotheses about the factor structure of a test or of a test item are typically formulated, and structural equation modeling is used to test the hypotheses. The model also has been used in basic research concerning the definition of g and fluid intelligence (Carlstedt, Gustafsson, & Ullstadius, 2000), the differentiation hypothesis (Carlstedt, 2001), gender differences in cognitive abilities (Rosén, 1998), and development of cognitive abilities as a function of education (Gustafsson, 2001).

In Finland research on the structure of intelligence has partly been conducted along other lines. Hautamäki (1989) applied Rasch modeling in a study on Piagetian measurements and showed that the idea of formal operational thinking provided a good interpretation of the unidimensionality of Piagetian scales. Hautamäki later used the Piagetian scales together with a set of other scales for measuring learning aptitudes, or learning-to-learn competencies, in three studies (Hautamäki, 1999; Hautamäki et al., 1999; Hautamäki et al., 2000). The new data indicate that measures of formal operational thinking also partly measure fluid intelligence.

The study also included Sternberg's Triarchic Ability Test, on which the Finnish team has collected what seems to be the largest data set with this test in the world. A paper by Sternberg et al. (2001) argues that the data provide evidence in support of the triarchic model. However, an interpretation in terms of one single higher-level construct seems equally plausible because the triarchic measures (analytical, practical, and creative) correlate strongly with each other, and in a structural equation model the loadings on the higher-order factor are all close to one.

Behavioral Genetics

Another line of basic research in the Nordic countries has concerned the relative importance of genetic and environmental sources of variance in explaining individual differences in intelligence.

Sundet, Tambs, & Magnus (1981) analyzed twin data to investigate the hypothesis that equalization of social and economic conditions in the population has caused the contribution of environmental sources of variance to decrease and the contribution of genetic sources of variance to increase. In the analysis, they divided a sample of 40 monozygotic and 40 dizygotic twin pairs into one group born before 1940 and another group born after 1940. The results indicated that within-family variance increased over time, which supports the hypothesis. However, the small sample size and some other problems with the analysis (see Hagtvet & Undheim, 1988, p. 271) imply that the results should be viewed with caution until replicated in other studies.

In Sweden a considerable number of studies have been conducted on the basis of the Swedish Twin Registry, which was established in the late 1950s. The Swedish Twin Registry is the largest in the world and includes register information about all twin births in Sweden, along with information from follow-up studies of subsets of the twins (see Pedersen & Lichtenstein, 2000, for an overview). These data have been used as a basis for a large number of studies on genetic determination of human characteristics, including cognitive abilities.

The Swedish Adoption/Twin Study of Aging (SATSA) is an ongoing longitudinal study, which started in 1984, and in which there have been new waves of measurement every third year. Among other things, changes in the relative contribution of genetic and environmental factors over the life span, with a focus on age groups over 50 years of age, have been studied in this project. Pedersen et al. (1992) found that about 80% of the differences in intellectual ability in these age groups are due to genetic factors, which is a higher estimate than what is typically obtained in young age groups. However, a further analysis of differences among different age groups (Finkel et al. 1995) showed that Swedish twins over 65 years of age demonstrated a lower heritability for general cognitive ability, which suggests that environmental influences become increasingly important for individual differences in cognitive ability late in life.

The OCTO-Twin project has a similar design as has the SATSA project, but it has its focus on the oldest old (80 years and older). Results from this study (McClearn et al., 1997) confirm the trend for the heritabilities to be somewhat lower among the oldest old.

Thomas Teasdale, a British psychologist living in Denmark for many years, also has done research on the heredity of intelligence (e.g., Teasdale & Owen, 1984). Data from the Danish draft board screening test (DBST) have been used in these studies. Opportunities to link the results of siblings, fathers and sons, and adopted sons and adopting fathers have provided favorable conditions for such research.

In Finland, too, research on the inheritance of intelligence has been conducted. Partanen, Bruun, and Markkanen (1966) used a set of tests designed to measure Thurstonian abilities to study heritability. The set included two tests for the Verbal factor, two tests for the Spatial factor, two tests for the Number factor, and two tests for Memory. The study showed that heritabilities for the primary factors were all considerable (for older subjects h's varied from .40 to .57, and for younger subjects from .30 to .60). There was no evidence for the existence of different heritability levels for different primary abilities, and rather the results suggest that the heritability of intelligence can be explained in terms of one single strongly heritable general ability.

Group Differences

A considerable amount of research has been done in the Nordic countries on group differences in test performance, for example, between genders, cohorts, and social and demographic groups. One reason for this is the ready availablility of good data. As has already been mentioned, the DBST has been a useful source of information for behavior genetic studies, and the good coverage of the population with a test that has been unchanged for a long time has provided an excellent basis for studying the continuing secular changes in intelligence in Denmark (see Teasdale & Owen, 1987, 1989, 1994, 2000).

The extensive population registration in Sweden also has provided a good basis for longitudinal studies, which have been an important source of information on group differences, among other things. Jansson (2000) describes seven large and long-lasting studies, of which one in particular ("Evaluation through follow-up," Härnqvist, 2000) has included intelligence measures as variables. In this project, several cohorts – the oldest one born in 1948 and the youngest (so far) born in 1982 – have been followed from age 13 (in some cases from age 10) and onward. Among other things, these data have been used to investigate secular changes in intelligence between cohorts. Both the Danish and the Swedish studies support the Flynn (1984) results of major increases in performance, even though the results of the most recent Swedish study (Emanuelsson, Reuterberg, & Svensson, 1993) indicate that the increases may have started to level off.

In the Swedish studies both males and females have been included, which has made it possible to investigate gender differences, and changing patterns of gender differences over time. One interesting finding is that in early studies on samples born in 1948 and 1953, there was a difference in favor of males with respect to spatial visualization ability (see also Werdelin, 1961), as measured by a test called "mental folding," but not for samples born later (e.g., 1972, 1977, 1982). Hagtvet and Undheim (1988, p. 269) report that a similar trend toward vanishing gender differences in spatial visualization ability can be observed in Norwegian studies. Härnqvist and Stahle (1977) found in the Swedish data for the sample born in 1948 that the gender difference in spatial visualization ability was smaller for students attending the new comprehensive school, which had been introduced in certain parts of the country, than it was for students attending the traditional school. One of the differences between the curricula for the new and the old school systems is that the curriculum for the comprehensive school stressed equality between males and females, as was shown, for example, in a common curriculum for handicraft instruction. This equalization of the treatment of males and females in school may thus, at least partly, explain the vanishing gender differences in spatial visualization ability.

Gender differences in performance on the SweSAT also have been observed, which are similar to those observed for the SAT (Willingham & Cole, 1997). Females perform at a lower level than do males on the two reasoning subtests. Åberg-Bengtsson (1999) has shown the performance difference to be particularly strong for reasoning items that involve numerical content. As has been shown by Reuterberg (1998), the gender difference is, however, not only due to characteristics of the test but also to the fact that the subgroup of males that actually takes the SweSAT is a more strongly positively selected group than is the subgroup of females taking the test.

Schooling and Intelligence

The oldest Swedish longitudinal study is the Malmo Study, which included 1,540 children born in 1928 who have been followed from age 10 until their retirement in 1993. A number of intelligence tests were administered when the subjects were about 10 years old, and the subjects have then been followed in four questionnaire surveys and in repeated collections of register-data to trace the development of the individuals in a life-course perspective (Furu, 2000). Husén (1950, 1951; see also Husén & Tuijnman, 1991) analyzed the relations between the test results at the age of 10 and the results achieved in the military enlistment test at the age of 18, to study effects of schooling on intelligence. He found substantial enhancements in IQ scores as a function of schooling and concluded that the reserves of ability for higher education were substantial at the time.

Härnqvist (1968a, 1968b) used the males in the sample born in 1948 to investigate effects of amount of schooling on intelligence changes from the age of 13 until the age of 18, when a military enlistment test was taken. Intelligence test scores at age 13 were used to control for selection into educational programs of different lengths. In that study too substantial enhancements in intelligence were found as a function of amount of schooling. Balke-Aurell (1982) replicated the Härnqvist findings on a sample born in 1953 and extended the findings by demonstrating that the relative strength of verbal and spatial abilities is related to whether the educational and occupational experiences had a verbal or a technical orientation.

In a Norwegian study, Lund and Thrane (1983) gave a large sample ($N = 7,703$) of Norwegian school children in grade 7 a set of military enlistment tests. Five years later the boys got the same tests at military enlistment, leaving a sample of 2,485 individuals who had test results at both testing occasions. Lund and Thrane arrived at a similar estimate of the effect of schooling on intelligence as was obtained by Härnqvist.

As has already been mentioned, Gustafsson (2001) has continued the research on effects of schooling on intelligence by relying on structural equation modeling techniques applied to large-scale data bases. The results from this study agree with those obtained in the previous studies.

In Finland Räty et al. (1995; Räty & Snellman 1992, 1998) has conducted a set of interesting studies on the social representations of intelligence and educability in relation to schooling. They have applied the Sternberg paradigm of implicit intelligence but have also developed their own approach based on the concept of educability. They also have analyzed the relations of schooling and intelligence.

Problem Solving and Intelligence

Kjell Raaheim has published a large number of papers during a period of almost 35 years on the relation between intelligence and problem solving. Aspects like novelty and complexity of the tasks, past experience, and convergent or divergent production have been studied for the understanding of intelligence (Raaheim, 1988; Hellesnes, Raaheim, & Bengtsson, 1982). He has also especially studied the highly intelligent problem solver (Raaheim, 1991).

CONCLUSIONS

The Nordic countries have experienced differences in their political situation during periods of the 20th century that have been important for the development of psychological testing and intelligence research, but the outcome is in many ways similar. The theoretical influences and the actual tests have come from Britain and the United States, first from Spearman and later from the Thurstone and Guilford multiple factor tests or from the Wechsler school of intelligence. Binet had an early direct influence in Finland, Sweden, and Norway, but the strongest impact came via the United States.

The most striking difference is that there has been much more of actual test development in Finland and Sweden than in the other countries, which has also been associated with a stronger orientation toward methodological issues in Finland and Sweden than in the other countries. It may also be noted that the test batteries used in enlistment testing in Norway and Denmark have changed very little during the decades they have been used. In Sweden, however, the periods under which the same test has been used are shorter, which indicates a willingness on the part of the authorities to gradually improve measurement and to try to benefit by contemporaneous theoretical and technical development.

Much of the test development in Finland and Sweden was, however, done during the 1950s and the 1960s, and since that time not much new work, or maintenance of existing tests, has been done. There are several reasons for this decline in interest in the technological aspects of the field of intelligence. One is that test development and maintenance are highly demanding in terms of empirical data, which also make them expensive activities. When these projects had scientific interest, funding was less of a problem than when they were mainly seen as refinements of an already developed basis of knowledge and intruments. Because of a diminishing scientific interest, it also has proven difficult to publish reports on test development in scientific journals. Many of the reports on test development in the Nordic countries have therefore been reported in the native language only, in internal reports with limited circulation. Even in writing this chapter we have experienced difficulties getting access to information, which has caused us in some cases to use interviews to gather information.

References

Åberg-Bengtsson, L. (1999). Dimensions of performance in the interpretation of diagrams, tables, and maps: Some gender differences in the Swedish Scholastic Aptitude Test. *Journal of Research in Science Teaching, 36*, 565–582.

Ahmavaara, Y. (1954). *Transformation analysis of factorial data and other new analytical methods of differential psychology with their application to Thurstone's basic studies.* Annales Academiae Scientiarum Fennicae, B 88.2.

Ahmavaava, Y. (1957a). *On the unified factor theory of mind.* Annales Academiae Scientiarum Fennicae, B 106.

Ahmavaara, Y. (1957b). *The structure of mental abilities.* Helsinki: WSOY (In Finnish).

Ahmavaara, Y. (1963). *On the mathematical theory of transformation analysis.* Publication of the Finnish Foundation of Alcohol Studies, No. 1/63.

AVO (1981). *The Great Study 1948.* Publication of the Office of Vocational Guidance, No. 33. Helsinki: Office of Vocational Guidance.

Balke-Aurell, G. (1982). *Changes in ability as related to educational and occupational experience.* Göteborg, Sweden: Acta Universitatis Gothoburgensis.

Beverfelt, E., Nordvik, H., & Nygård, A. (1967). *WAIS håndbog, Wechsler Adult Intelligence Scale.* [WAIS handbook, Wechsler Adult Intelligence Scale]. Oslo: Norsk Psykologforening.

Binet, A., & Simon, T. (1905). Méthodes nouvelles pour le diagnostic du niveau intellectuel des anormaux [New methods for diagnosing the intellectual level of abnormals]. *L' Année Psychologique, 11*, 191–336.

Binet, A., & Simon, T. (1908). Le développment de l'intelligence chez les enfants [The development of intelligence in children]. *Année Psychologique, 14*, 1–94.

Björsjö, M. (1951). *Om spatial, teknisk och praktisk begåvning.* [On spatial, technical, and practical abilities]. Göteborg: Elanders.

Carlstedt, B. (2000). *Cognitive abilities – aspects of structure, process, and measurement.* Göteborg, Sweden: Acta Universitatis Gothoburgensis.

Carlstedt, B. (2001). Differentiation of cognitive abilities as a function of level of general intelligence: A latent variable approach. *Multivariate Behavioral Research, 36*(4), 589–609.

Carlstedt, B., Gustafsson, J.-E., & Ullstadius, E. (2000). Item sequencing effects on the measurement of fluid intelligence. *Intelligence, 28*(2), 145–160.

72 *B. Carlstedt, J.-E. Gustafsson, and J. Hautamäki*

2

2

Carlstedt, L., & Widén, H. (1999). Militärhögskoleprovet – manual [The officer selection test – manual]. Report LI-T:22. Karlstad, Sweden: National Defence College.

Carroll, J. B. (1982). The measurement of intelligence. In R. J. Sternberg (Ed.), *Handbook of human intelligence* (pp. 29–120). New York: Cambridge University Press.

Carroll, J. B. (1993). *Human cognitive abilities. A survey of factor-analytic studies.* Cambridge: Cambridge University Press.

Carroll, J. B. (2003). The higher-stratum structure of cognitive abilities: There is a G, but no Gf. In H. Nyborg (Ed.) *The scientific study of general intelligence: Tribute to Arthur R. Jensen.* Elsevier Science/Pergamon Press.

Dureman, I., & Sälde, H. (1959). Psykometriska och experientalpsykologiska metoder för klinisk tillämpning [Psychometric and experimental methods for the clinical evaluation of mental functioning]. Stockholm, Sweden: Almqvist & Wiksell.

Eckhoff, R. (1978). Raven's Standard Progressive Matrices. Rapport fra Normeringsarbeid. Unpublished manuscript. Arbeidspsykologisk Institutt, Oslo.

Elonen, A. S., Takala, M., & Ruoppila, I. (1963). *A study of intellectual functions in children by means of the KTK performance scales.* Jyväskylä studies in Education, Psychology, and Social research, 3.

Emanuelsson, I., Reuterberg, S.-E., & Svensson, A. (1993). Changing differences in intelligence. Comparisons between groups of 13-year-olds tested from 1960 to 1990. *Scandinavian Journal of Educational Research, 37,* 259–277.

Engvik, H., Hjerkin, O., & Seim, S. (1980). *Håndbog WAIS. Norsk utgave.* [WAIS handbook. Norwegian edition]. Oslo: Norsk Psykologförening.

Ensiö, A. (1917). *Oppikoulujen pohjakoulukysymys Suomessa [The Basic Educational Requirements for Gymnasia].* Turku: Author.

Finkel, D., Pedersen, N. L., McGue, M., & McClearn, G. E. (1995). Heritability of cognitive abilities in adult twins: Comparison of Minnesota and Swedish data. *Behavior Genetics, 25,* 421–431.

Flynn, J. R. (1984). The mean IQ of Americans: Massive gains 1932 to 1978. *Psychological Bulletin, 95,* 29–51.

Furu, M. (2000). The Malmo Study. In C.-G. Jansson (Ed.), *Seven Swedish longitudinal studies in the behavioral sciences.* Stockhom, Sweden: Swedish Council for Planning and Coordination of Research.

Gagnerud, S., & Haglund, B. (2000). Begåvningsstruktur och prognosvärde. [Structure of abilities and predictive validity]. Rapport till Styrgruppen för APU, National Labour Market Board.

Gjessing, H. J., Nygaard, H. D., & Solheim, R. (1975). *Illinois Test of Psycholinguistic Abilities. Handbok med instruktioner og normer* [Illinois Test of Psycholinguistic Abilities. Handbook with instructions and norms] Oslo, Norway: Universitetsforlaget.

Gustafsson, J.-E. (1984). A unifying model for the structure of intellectual abilities. *Intelligence, 8,* 179–203.

Gustafsson, J.-E. (1988). Hierarchical models of individual differences in cognitive abilities. In R. J. Sternberg (Ed.), *Advances in the psychology of human intelligence* (Vol. 4, pp. 35–71). Hillsdale, NJ: Erlbaum.

Gustafsson, J.-E. (2001). Schooling and intelligence: Effects of track of study on level and profile of cognitive abilities. Paper presented at the Spearman Conference, Sydney, Nov 28–30, 2001.

Gustafsson, J.-E., & Balke, G. (1993). General and specific abilities as predictors of school achievement. *Multivariate Behavioral Research, 28*(4), 407–434.

Gustafsson, J.-E., & Westerlund, A. (1994). Socialgruppsskillnader i prestationer på Högskoleprovet [Differences between socio-economic groups in performance on the Swedish Scholastic Aptitude Test]. In R. Eriksson & J. O. Jonsson (Eds.), Sorteringen i skolan. Studier av snedrekrytering och utbildningens konsekvenser. Stockholm, Sweden: Carlsson Bokförlag.

Gustafsson, J.-E., & Reuterberg, S.-E. (2000). Metodproblem vid studier av Högskoleprovets prognosförmåga – och deras lösning! [Methodological problems when studying the predictive validity of the SWE-SAT – and the solution!] *Pedagogisk Forskning i Sverige, 5*(4), 273–283.

Gustafsson, J.-E., & Undheim, J. O. (1992). Stability and change in broad and narrow factors of intelligence from ages 12 to 15 years. *Journal of Educational Psychology, 84*(2), 141–149.

Gustafsson, J.-E., & Undheim, J. O. (1996). Individual differences in cognitive functions. In D. C. Berliner & R. C. Calfee (Eds.), *Handbook of educational psychology* (pp. 186–242). New York: Macmillan.

Gustafsson, J.-E., Wedman, I., & Westerlund, A. (1992). The dimensionality of the Swedish Scholastic Aptitude Test. *Scandinavian Journal of Educational Research, 36*(1), 21–39.

Haavisto, M.-L., & Oksama, L. (1997). F/A 18 tutkatorjuntatehtävän *tehtäväanalyysi* [The task analysis of F/A 18 radar attack missions]. Unpublished manuscript.

Haavisto, M.-L., & Lehto, J. (2003). Fluid and crystallized intelligence in relation to domain-specific Working Memory: A latent-variable approach. Submitted.

Hagtvet, K. A., & Undheim, J.-O. (1988). The Norwegian experience of test use: A selective review of Norwegian tests and measurements in cultural context. In S. H. Irvine & J. W. Berry (Eds.), *Human abilities in cultural context*. New York: Cambridge University Press.

Härnqvist, K. (1960). Manual till DBA – differentiell begåvningsanalys [Manual for DBA – Differential Aptitudes Battery]. Stockholm, Sweden: Skandinaviska Testförlaget.

Härnqvist, K. (1968a). Relative changes in intelligence from 13–18. I. Background and methodology. *Scandinavian Journal of Psychology, 9*, 50–64.

Härnqvist, K. (1968b). Relative changes in intelligence from 13–18. II. Results. *Scandinavian Journal of Psychology, 9*, 65–82.

Härnqvist, K. (2000). Evaluation through follow-up: A longitudinal program for studying education and career development. In C.-G. Jansson (Ed.), *Seven Swedish longitudinal studies in the behavioral sciences*. Stockhom, Sweden: Swedish Council for Planning and Coordination of Research.

Härnqvist, K., & Stahle, G. (1977). An ecological analysis of test score changes over time. Institute of Education, University of Gothenburg, Report No. 64.

Hautamäki, J. (1989). The application of a Rasch model on Piagetian measures of thinking. In P. Adey, J. Bliss, J. Head, & M. Shayer (Eds.), *Adolescent development and school science*. London: Falmers.

Hautamäki, J. (1999). Epidemiology of Excellence – an assessment of the commitment to thinking with Sternberg triarchic ability test. In *Potential intó performance*, (pp. 20–23). QCA Ref: QCA/99/400. London: Qualifications and Curriculum Authority (QCA).

Hautamäki, J. Arinen, P., Bergholm, B., Hautamäki, A., Kupiainen, S., Kuusela, J., Lehto, J., Niemivirta, M., & Scheinin, P. (1999). *Learning-to-learn: The 6th graders* (in Finnish). Publications 3/1999. Helsinki: National Board of Education.

Hautamäki, J. Arinen, P., Hautamäki, A., Ikonen-Varila, M., Kupiainen, S., Lindblom, B., Niemivirta, M., Rantanen, P., Ruuth, M., & Scheinin, P. (2000). *Learning-to-learn: The 9th graders* (in Finnish). Publications 7/2000. Helsinki: National Board of Education.

Hellesnes, T., Raaheim, K., & Bengtsson, G. (1982). Attempts to predict intelligent behavior: III. The relative importance of divergent and convergent production. *Scandinavian Journal of Psychology, 23*(4), 263–266.

Hellström, A. (1960). *Intelligensmätning (Lewis M. Terman and Maud A. Merrill)*. Stockholm, Sweden: Föreningen Sävstaholmsskolorna.

Henrysson, S. (1962). The relation between factor loadings and biserial correlations in item analysis. *Psychometrika, 27*, 419–424.

Husén, T. (1948). *Konstruktion och standardisering av svenska krigsmaktens inskrivningsprov. 1948 års version* [Construction and standardization of the Swedish Armed Forces' Enlistment battery, 1948 version]. Lund, Sweden: Håkan Ohlssons Boktryckeri.

Husén, T. (1950). *Testresultatens prognosvärde* [The predictive validity of test results]. Stockholm: Almqvist & Wiksell.

Husén, T. (1951). The influence of schooling upon IQ. *Theoria, 17*, 61–88.

Husén, T., & Tuijnman, A. (1991). The contribution of formal schooling to the increase in intellectual capital. *Educational Researcher, 20*(1), 17–25.

Jaederholm, G. (1914). *Undersökningar över intelligensmätningarnas teori och praxis* [Investigations concerning the theory and practice of measurement of intelligence]. Stockholm, Sweden: Almqvist & Wikzell.

Jansson, C.-G. (2000). *Seven Swedish longitudinal studies in the behavioral sciences*. Stockholm, Sweden: Swedish Council for Planning and Coordination of Research.

Jöreskog, K. G. (1967). Some contributions to maximum likelihood factor analysis. *Psychometrika, 32*(4), 443–482.

Jöreskog, K. G. (1969). A general approach to confirmatory maximum likelihood factor analysis. *Psychometrika, 34*(2), 183–202.

Jöreskog, K. G. (1970). A general method for analysis of covariance structures. *Biometrika, 57*, 239–251.

Jöreskog, K. G. (1971). Simulatenous factor analysis in several populations. *Psychometrika, 36*, 409–426.

Jöreskog, K. G. (1973). A general method for estimating a linear structural equation system. In: O. D. Duncan & A. S. Goldberger (Eds.), *Structural equation models in the social sciences* (pp. 85–112). New York: Seminar Press.

Jöreskog, K. G., & Sörbom, D. (1973). *LISREL III – Estimation of linear structural equation systems by maximum likelihood methods. A FORTRAN IV program.*

Jöreskog, K. G., Sörbom, D., Du Toit, S., & Du Toit, M. (2001). *LISREL 8: New statistical features* (Third printing with revisions). Chicago: Scientific Software International.

Kebbon, L. (1968). *Manual till US-batteriet* [Manual for the US-battery]. Stockholm: Skandinaviska Testförlaget.

Korkiakangas, M. (1977). Factor analytic methodology in Finnish psychological studies in the 40's and 50's. *Psykologia, 12*(1), 3–12.

Koskenniemi, M. (1938). *Älykkyystutkimuksen menetelmät* [Methods of Intelligence Research]. Porvoo: WSOY.

Kuusinen, J., & Blåfield, L. (1972). *ITPA – theory, characteristics, and use* (in Finnish). Publications 156/72. Institute for Educational Research, University of Jyväskylä.

Kuusinen, J., & Leskinen, E. (1988). Latent structure analysis of longitudinal data on relations between intellectual abilities and school achievement. *Multivariate Behavioral Research, 23*, 103–188.

Langset, M. (1984). *Håndbok for WPPSI. Norsk utgave.* [WPPSI handbook. Norwegian edition]. Oslo, Norway: Norsk Psykologforening.

Lehtovaara, A. (1960). *Stanford-Binet type of tests for the assessment of intelligence of children and adults (standardized for Finnish circumstances).* Publications 7/1960. The Central Union for the Protection of Children.

Lilius, A. (1913). Något om intelligensundersökningar [Measuring intelligence]. Tidskrift utg. Af Pedagogiska föreningen i Finland.

Lilius, A. (1916). *Skolålderns själsliv* [The intellectual life of school-aged children]. Borgå: Holger Schildts Förlag.

Lofthus, J. (1931). *Intelligensmåling* [Measurement of intelligence]. Oslo.

Looft, C. (1913). Intelligensundersökelser av skolbarn [Investigations of intelligence among school children]. *Medicinsk Revue, 569–585.*

Lund, T., & Thrane, V. C. (1983). Schooling and intelligence: A methodological and longitudinal study. *Scandinavian Journal of Psychology, 24*, 161–173.

Magnusson, D. (1961). Testteori [Test theory]. Stockholm, Sweden: Almqvist och Wiksell/Gebers Förlag.

Mårdberg, B., & Carlstedt, B. (1998). Swedish Enlistment Battery (SEB): Construct validity and latent variable estimation of cognitive abilities by the CAT-SEB. *International Journal of Selection and Assessment, 6*(2), 107–114.

Mårdberg, B., Sjöberg, A., & Henrysson Eidvall, S. (2000). *BasIQ begåvningstest. Manual* [BasIQ test of cognitive abilities. Manual]. Stockholm: Psykologiförlaget AB.

McClearn, G. E., Johansson, B., Berg, S., Pedersen, N. L., Ahern, F., Perrill, S. A., & Plomin, R. (1997). Substantial genetic influence on cognitive abilities in twins 80 or more years old. *Science, 276*, 1560–1563.

Messick, S. (1989). Validity. In R. L. Linn (Ed.), *Educational measurement* (pp. 13–103). New York: MacMillan.

Mönnesland, K. (1948). *Intelligensprøver for voksne.* [Intelligence tests for adults]. Oslo, Norway: Norli.

Mortensen, E. L., Reinisch, J. M., & Teasdale, T. W. (1989). Intelligence as measured by the WAIS and a military draft board group test. *Scandinavian Journal of Psychology, 30*, 315–318.

Partanen, J., Bruun, K., & Markkanen, T. (1966). *Inheritance of drinking behavior. A study on intelligence, personality, and use of alcohol of adult twins.* Alcohol research in the Northern countries, Studies 14. Helsinki: The Finnish Foundation for Alcohol Studies.

Pedersen, N. L., Plomin, R., Nesselroade, J. R., & McClearn, G. E. (1992). A quantitative genetic analysis of cognitive abilities during the second half of the life span. *Psychological Science, 3*, 346–353.

Pedersen, N., & Lichtenstein, P. (2000). The Swedish Twin Registry. A presentation. In B. Smedby, I. Lundberg, & T. Sörensen (Eds.) *Scientific evaluation of the Swedish Twin Registry.* Stockholm: Swedish Council for Planning and Coordination of Research, report 2000:10.

Psykotekniska Institutet (1970). DELTA batteriet [The DELTA-battery]. Stockholm, Sweden: Psykologiförlaget.

Raaheim, K. (1988). Intelligence and task novelty. In R. J. Sternberg (Ed.), *Advances in the psychology of human intelligence,* (Vol. 4, pp. 73–97). Hillsdale, NJ: Erlbaum.

Raaheim, K. (1991). Is the high IQ person really in trouble? Why? In H. A. H. Rowe (Ed.), *Intelligence, reconceptualization and measurement* (pp. 35–46). Camberwell, Australia: Australian Council for Educational Research, Ltd.

Rasch, G. (1960). *Probabilistic models for some intelligence and attainment tests.* Copenhagen, Denmark: Danish Institute for Educational Research.

Rasch, G. (1966). An item analysis which takes individual differences into account. *British Journal of Mathematical and Statistical Psychology, 19*, 49–57.

Räty, H., Pölönen, K., Pölönen, P., & Snellman, L. (1995). Student assessment and definition of intelligence: A historical perspective. *Psykologia, 30*, 179–185.

Räty, H., & Snellman, L. (1992). Does gender make any difference? Common sense conceptions of intelligence. *Social Behavior and Personality, 20*, 23–34.

Räty, H., & Snellman, L. (1998). Social representation of educability. *Social Psychology of Education, 1*, 359–373.

Reuterberg, S.-E. (1998). On differential selection in the Swedish Scholastic Aptitude test. *Scandinavian Journal of Educational Research, 41*(2), 81–92.

Ribsskog, B. (1941). *Evneprøver for 1. klasse i folkeskolen. Standardisert på grunnlag av Kuhlmann-Andersons gruppeprøver* [Ability tests for grade 1 of compulsory school. Standardized on the basis of the Kuhlmann-Anderson group test]. Oslo.

Riis, E. (1988). Militaerpsykologin I Norge [Military psychology in Norway]. *Tidsskrift for Norsk psykologforening, 23*, 21–37.

Rist, T. (1982). *Det intellektuelle prestationsnivået I befolkningen sett i lys av den samfunnsmessiga utvecklinga. En undersøkelse av norske rekrutters prestationer på psykologiske sesjonsprøver* [The intellectual level in the population seen in the light of the development of society. Norwegian recruits' results on the draft board tests]. Forsvarets Psykologitjeneste, Oslo.

Rosén, M. (1998). *Gender differences in patterns of knowledge.* Göteborg, Sweden: Acta Universitatis Gothoburgensis.

Rosenqvist, A. (1919). Kasvatus ja koulu [How to take into account the giftedness of pupils at school.] *Education and School* (in Finnish), *5*, 56–65.

Sandven, J. (1954). *Norsk standard av Terman-Merrill Stanford-revisjon av Binet-prövene* [Norwegian standardization of the Terman-Merrill revision of the Binet tests]. Oslo, Norway: Cappelen.

Salomaa, J. E. (1938). *Älykkyyden mittaaminen [The measurement of intelligence].* Porvoo: WSOY.

Scheinin, P., & Mehtäläinen, J. (1999). Applying the theory of knowledge to teaching thinking. In J. H. M. Hamers, J. E. H. van Luit, & B. Csapo, (Eds.), *Teaching and learning thinking skills.* Lisse: Swets & Zeitlinger.

Siegvald, H. (1944). *Experimentella undersökningar rörande intellektuella könsdifferenser* [Experimental investigations concerning intellectual sex differences]. Lund, Sweden: Håkan Olssons Boktryckeri.

Sinivou, J. (1977). *Ilmavoimien varusmiesohjaaja- ja lentokadettikurssilla men-estymisen ennustamisesta: Sotilasohjaajan ammattianalyysi ja valintajärjestelmän kehittämismahdollisuudet [The predictors of success in the training of Finnish Air Force conscripts and cadets: The occupational analysis and the future scenarios of developing the selection system].* Military Psychological Series of Publications, 9/A/77. Helsinki: Pääesikunta.

Spearman, C. (1904a). The proof and measurement of association between two things. *American Journal of Psychology, 15,* 72–101.

Spearman, C. (1904b). "General intelligence," objectively determined and measured. *American Journal of Psychology, 15,* 201–293.

Spelling, K. (1999). Danish Ability Test. *Psykologisk paedagogisk Radgivning, 29*(2), 127–132.

Sternberg, R. J., Castejon, J. L., Prieto, M. D., Hautamäki, J., & Grigorenko, E. (2001). Confirmatory factor analysis of the Sternberg Triarchic Ability Test (multiple-choice items) in three international samples: An empirical test of the triarchic theory of intelligence. *European Journal of Psychological Assessment, 17*(1), 1–16.

Sundet, J. M., Tambs, K., & Magnus, P. (1981). Heritability analysis as a means of analyzing the effects of social changes on psychological variables. An empirical study of IQ-scores. *Psychiatry and Social Sciences, 1,* 241–248.

Takala, M. (1953). *Studies of psychomotor personality tests.* Helsinki: Institute of Occupational Health.

Teasdale, T. W., & Owen, D. R. (1984). Heredity and familial environment in intelligence and educational level: A sibling study. *Nature, 309,* 620–622.

Teasdale, T. W., & Owen, D. R. (1987). National secular trends in intelligence and education: A 20-year cross sectional study. *Nature, 325,* 119–121.

Teasdale, T. W., & Owen, D. R. (1989). Continuing secular increases in intelligence and a stable prevalence of high intelligence levels. *Intelligence, 13,* 255–262.

Teasdale, T. W., & Owen, D. R. (1994). Thirty-year secular trends in the cognitive abilities of Danish male school leavers at a high educational level. *Scandinavian Journal of Psychology, 35,* 328–335.

Teasdale, T. W., & Owen, D. R. (2000). Forty-year secular trends in cognitive abilities. *Intelligence, 28,* 115–120.

Thurstone, L. L. (1931). Multiple factor analysis. *Psychological Review, 38,* 406–427.

Thurstone, L. L. (1938). Primary mental abilities. *Psychometric Monographs, No. 1.*

Thurstone, L. L. (1947). *Multiple factor analysis.* Chicago: University of Chicago Press.

Torjussen, T. M., & Hansen, I. (1999). Forsvaret best i test? Bruk av psykologiske tester i forsvaret, med speciell vekt på flygerseleksjon [Is the Defense best in test? Use of psychological tests in the Defense with special weight on pilot selection.] *Tidsskrift for Norsk Psykologförening, 36*(8), 772–779.

Ullstadius, E., Gustafsson, J.-E., & Carlstedt, B. (2002). Influence of general and crystallized intelligence on vocabulary test performance. *European Journal of Psychological Assessment, 18*(1), 78–84.

Undheim, J. O. (1978a). *WISC-R håndbog. Norsk utgave* [WISC-R handbook. Norwegian edition]. Oslo, Norway: Norsk Psykologforening.

Undheim, J. O. (1978b). Broad ability factors in 12- to 13-year-old children, the theory of fluid and crystallized intelligence and the differentiation hypothesis. *Journal of Educational Psychology, 70*(3), 433–443.

Undheim, J. O. (1979). Capitalization on chance: The case of Guilford's memory abilities. *Scandinavian Journal of Psychology, 20,* 71–76.

Undheim, J. O. (1981a). On intelligence: II. A neo-Spearman model to replace Cattell's theory of fluid and crystallized intelligence. *Scandinavian Journal of Psychology, 22*(3), 181–187.

Undheim, J. O. (1981b). On intelligence IV: Toward a restoration of general intelligence. *Scandinavian Journal of Psychology, 22,* 251–265.

Undheim, J. O., & Gustafsson, J.-E. (1987). The hierarchical organization of cognitive abilities: Restoring general intelligence through the use of linear structural relations (LISREL). *Multivariate Behavioral Research, 22,* 149–171.

Undheim, J. O., & Horn, J. L. (1977). Critical evaluation of Guilford's structure-of-intellect theory. *Intelligence, 1,* 65–81.

Vainikainen, A. (1998). *Varusmiesten johtajavalintatutkimus 1995. [Study of leader selection (among conscripts) in 1995].* Finnish Defence Forces, Education Development Centre, Separate Reports, 1/1998. Pieksämäki, Finland: RT-Print OY.

Werdelin, I. (1961). *Geometrical ability and the space factors in boys and girls.* Lund: Gleerups.

Werdelin, I., & Stjernberg, G. (1971). The relationship between difficulty and factor loadings of some visual-perceptual tests. *Scandinavian Journal of Psychology, 12,* 21–28.

Westrin, P. A. (1967). *WIT III Manual* [Manual of WIT III]. Stockholm, Sweden: Psykologiförlaget.

White, K. R. (1982). The relation between socioeconomic status and academic achievement. *Psychological Bulletin, 91,* 461–481.

Willingham, W. W., & Cole, N. S. (1997). *Gender and fair assessment.* Mahwah, NJ: Erlbaum.

3

The Psychology of Human Intelligence in Spain

Rocío Fernández-Ballesteros and Roberto Colom

The scientific study of human intelligence is a relatively recent development in Spain. Its study began early in the twentieth century with a strong influence from psychometrics (Yela, 1956). Nevertheless, current Spanish research on human intelligence covers the main topics within the field, from the structure of human intelligence to its biological correlates.

This chapter begins with a brief review of the history of human intelligence and of the most important databases in psychology, to identify content domains. Second, current research programs are discussed within the context of the international literature. Finally, assessment instruments for the measurement of intelligence are summarized, and data related to their use for practical purposes are presented.

THE HISTORY OF HUMAN INTELLIGENCE IN SPAIN

Human intelligence has a long history as a philosophical issue,[1] but a short one as the subject of scientific inquiry. Therefore, before describing contemporary research in Spain, we should consider some representative thoughts of a sixteenth-century physician-philosopher, Juan Huarte de San Juan, as well as some more modern pioneers in the area.

---

[1] The terms used (intellect, mind, understanding) and the conceptualizations (as a soul, "potentia": as a mind, function, etc.), have changed over the course of history (for a review, see McReynolds, 1986).

Main Antecedents

As is widely recognized,[2] Juan Huarte de San Juan (1526–1588?) was a pioneer of experimental and differential psychology, as well as of the study of personality and intelligence. Huarte published the *Exam of the Talents for Sciences*[3] in 1575. This book presents a quite modern concept of intelligence as a set of mental abilities. The book deals not only with types of intelligence, but also with their application to counseling and personnel selection. The main issues explored by Huarte were (1) the characteristics that make human beings capable or incapable of science, (2) the differential characteristics of human beings, (3) which characteristics are more appropriate for arts and for sciences, and (4) how these characteristics can be assessed.

Huarte can be considered as the first author to make serious progress in the study of primary mental abilities and their application to personnel selection and counseling. His ideas became familiar to several leading scholars and philosophers, such as Bacon, Descartes, Pascal, and Montesquieu.

However, Huarte's work is mainly philosophical. Psychology as a science was not founded until the end of the nineteenth century. In Spain, the first important figures in the field were Ramon y Cajal, Lafora, Turró and Mira (Carpintero, 1982; Prieto et al., 1994). The Nobel laureate Ramon y Cajal was a pioneer of neuroscience and biological research on intelligence. Lafora worked on mental retardation, founding programs for training intelligence and developing and adapting instruments for assessing retardation (Lafora, 1919). Turró worked in the field of personnel selection, doing important work in psychometrics. The so-called first measure of intelligence, in its first American edition, the Terman-Binet Test, was published in the first third of the twentieth century (Germain & Rodrigo, 1930).

---

[2] As the *Encyclopedia Britannica* notes, Juan Huarte de San Juan was one of the pioneers of experimental psychology, and of the field of individual differences. Also, among other North American authors, McReynolds (1986) considers Huarte as one of the most important antecedents in the study of assessment, intelligence, and personality.

[3] The title in Spanish is "Examen de los ingenios para las ciencias," translated into the English as "The tryal of wits" (translator: E. Bellamy. London: Richard Sare at Grays-Inn Gate in Holborn, 1698). This translation can be considered inappropriate, because "examen" in English is without doubt "exam," and "ingenios" cannot be translated as "wits" but rather as "talents" and in current psychological language, taking into consideration Huarte's work proposals, as skills, abilities or aptitudes.

From a theoretical perspective, Spanish pioneers maintained regular contact with European psychologists, mainly from France, Switzerland, and Germany. Spanish psychology reflects the influence of structuralism and phenomenology (Carpintero, 1994). However, the main characteristic of the first Spanish psychology was its applied perspective. A sign of the vitality of applied psychology in Spain was the organization, on two occasions, of the International Congress on Psychotechnics, in Barcelona (in 1921 and 1930).

In summary, psychology in Spain began as an applied field with two main orientations: educational or clinical psychology, with Luis Simarro, in Madrid, as the leading figure, and professional psychology, with Ramón Turró working in Barcelona.

The parenthesis of the Spanish Civil War (1936–39) and all its consequences for scientific activity meant that Spanish psychology did not restart until the end of the 1950s. Yela was the leading figure in the study of human intelligence in the second half of the twentieth century. He introduced a research program on intelligence, verbal abilities, and psychomotor abilities, which has extended up to recent times (Yela, 1956, 1987; Martínez-Arias & Yela, 1991). His work was strongly influenced by his mentor Thurstone and the Chicago school (like other psychologists, such as Pinillos in the field of personality or Siguan in that of language), beginning a new period of Spanish psychology mainly influenced by functionalism, and with a strong experimental and mathematical methodological basis.

The Study of Human Intelligence in Spain From Publication Databases

How can we summarize the evolution of research on human intelligence in Spain? One way of evaluating the state of the art in research is to examine publication databases. Following this avenue of inquiry, two databases were examined; (1) the most commonly used database in the Spanish language, ISOC, and (2) the most widely used international database, PsychInfo.

ISOC is a Spanish publication database of psychology and education, founded in 1976. The sources of information are scientific journals, doctoral dissertations, reports, and congress presentations. At the end of 2001 it included 40,600 records, with a growth rate of 3,000 references per year. A search for the word *intelligence* in titles and abstracts, from 1976 to 2000, yielded 790 references. The evolution of articles referring

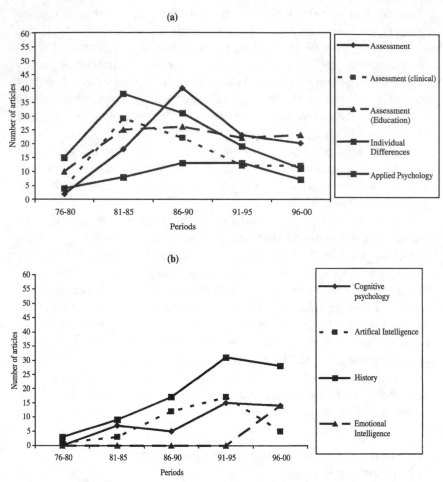

FIGURE 3.1. (a & b) Evolution of intelligence literature by content (ISOC)

to intelligence as the main topic goes from 3 articles in 1976 to 25 in the year 2000. Figure 3.1 shows the evolution of intelligence literature over five-year periods in the ISOC database.

There is a variety of content under the keyword *intelligence*. Therefore, a content analysis was performed: Two independent judges classified the 790 articles (with the available abstracts), with an inter-rater agreement of 91% (García & Escorial, 2001). Eleven categories were selected: individual differences ($N = 114$), assessment (general) ($N = 103$), educational assessment ($N = 107$), clinical assessment ($N = 80$), history ($N = 88$), practical applications ($N = 46$), cognitive psychology (N=46), artificial intelligence ($N = 39$), emotional intelligence ($N = 14$), creativity ($N = 13$), and others[4] ($N = 113$).

Figure 3.1 (a & b) shows the evolution of these categories over five-year periods. Two patterns are observed: Five categories – assessment (all types: general, educational, and clinical), individual differences and practical applications – increased from the 1970s to the 1980s and showed a sharp decrease in the 1990s, whereas the remaining five – history, cognitive psychology, artificial intelligence, emotional intelligence and creativity – increased in the 1990s.

These changes can be explained by two interactive events: paradigmatic changes and/or socio-political local shifts. Let us briefly consider the types of events that could justify these two patterns. It is well known that at the beginning of the 1960s, cognitive psychology became the dominant paradigm in psychology. Research from the "cognitive psychology" and "artificial intelligence" perspectives increased during the 1970s. However the study of intelligence has been linked in Spain to the psychology of individual differences as an academic subject. In 1984, a new law relating to university studies was published and was subsequently modified and implemented at the end of the 1980s. As a result of this law, the psychology of individual differences was deleted from psychology curricula. This change (possibly linked to the previously mentioned paradigmatic shift) could help to explain a certain reduction in research on individual differences in intelligence and cognitive abilities. Furthermore, this "political" decision led to the study of human intelligence becoming spread out across academic subjects.

PsychInfo is a well-known database of psychology dating back to 1887; it includes more than one and a half million documents (1,720,551 in 2000), with an increase per year of approximately 60,000. The literature on intelligence increased dramatically from 1887 to 2000: from 13 entries for the period 1887–1900 to 10,706 in 1991–00. From 1887 to 2000 there are 43,437 documents on intelligence, which is 2.52% of the total literature in PsychInfo. We also searched for articles written by Spaniards, finding no articles until the 1920s and 8,433 articles in the 1990s; from 1887 to 2000, there are 15,123 documents (0.88% of the total). Finally, with regard to articles written by Spaniards on intelligence, no articles were found before the 1930s, but in the 1990s, 215 articles were written by researchers in Spanish institutions. From 1887 to 2000 there are 527

---

4 The category "Others" includes non-scientific articles.

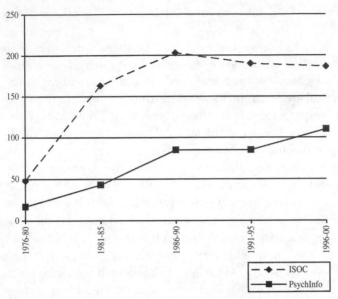

FIGURE 3.2. Evolution of the literature on intelligence in ISOC and PsychInfo from 1976 by five-year periods

documents on intelligence written by Spaniards. That is, the proportion of intelligence literature is 3.48%, which is higher than the figure for articles in general. In an attempt to make comparisons between ISOC and PsychInfo, Figure 3.2 displays the evolution of publications on "intelligence."

In summary, it can be concluded that the literature on intelligence from Spanish authors has increased during the last three decades. Over the last five years, while it has slightly decreased in Spanish databases, it has increased its presence on the international literature scene.

CURRENT RESEARCH ON HUMAN INTELLIGENCE IN SPAIN

There are several identifiable areas in Spanish research. Most of the central topics considered in the *Handbook of Intelligence*, edited by R. J. Sternberg (2000), are studied: the structure of human intelligence, human information processing, biological correlates, genes and environment, practical validity, population differences, emotional intelligence, and cognitive training. It should be made clear in advance that not all of these areas show equal research efforts.

The Structure of Human Intelligence

It is recognized that human intelligence has a hierarchical structure (Burt, 1940). The seminal work by Carroll (1993) demonstrated this beyond any reasonable doubt. More than 60 cognitive abilities are identified in a first stratum, and eight broad abilities in a second stratum; finally, g (general intelligence) was located at the apex of the hierarchy.

A broad cognitive ability widely investigated in Spain is spatial ability. This is partly due to the work done by Yela (1956). The group coordinated by G. Prieto at the *Universidad de Salamanca* has developed a long-term research project on this topic. The group designed several computerized tests to measure spatial aspects such as visualization or spatial relations. A summary of research findings can be found in Prieto et al. (1996). The group also studied related topics that will be mentioned subsequently.

Juan-Espinosa coordinated a group at the *Universidad Autónoma de Madrid* that investigated large-scale spatial orientation. The group developed a battery of tasks that closely resemble real-life situations. Virtual reality programs were employed for this purpose. In addition, they measured spatial orientation in real situations and several cognitive abilities through standardized printed tests. Juan-Espinosa, Abad et al. (2000) published the main findings. Confirmatory factor analyses showed that a general factor identified with g predicted individual differences in large-scale spatial orientation.

Colom, Contreras, et al. (2002) developed several computerized measures of dynamic spatial performance. "Dynamic" refers to the prediction of *where* a moving object is going and *when* it will arrive at its predicted destination. Their study suggests that there is no clear separation among markers of some core spatial factors (spatial relations or visualization are some examples). They re-analyzed a seminal study by Hunt et al. (1988) on dynamic spatial performance: The results support the view that there is a single powerful source of variance underlying several diverse spatial ability measures. Moreover, the factor representing general spatial ability strongly correlated with G_f or g. The latter result agrees with Juan-Espinosa, Abad, et al. (2000).

An issue particularly relevant to the analysis of the structure of human intelligence is the differentiation of cognitive abilities across ability levels and over the life span. Detterman and Daniels (1989) found that intelligence is less differentiated for less intelligent people; Deary et al. (1996) obtained similar findings with a finer-grained methodology.

However, Abad et al. (2003) have shown that the differentiation phenomenon may not be genuine, but rather a by-product of differences in academic level. These Spanish researchers analyzed a crystallized and a fluid battery. Crystallized intelligence is more sensitive to education than fluid intelligence. Differentiation was much higher in the *Wechsler Adult Intelligence Scale* (WAIS)-III than in a fluid battery containing mostly reasoning tests.

Juan-Espinosa, García, et al. (2000), and Juan-Espinosa et al. (2002) have questioned the differentiation of cognitive abilities over the life span. Instead of supporting the *investment theory* originally proposed by Cattell (1987) and later endorsed by Ackerman (1996), these researchers proposed the *anatomic metaphor*: Like the human skeleton, the structure of human intelligence remains invariant throughout the life span.

In sum, spatial ability is the aspect most studied by Spanish researchers, who have also shown considerable interest in the differentiation of cognitive abilities across ability levels and over the life span.

Human Information Processing

Intelligence as a set of mental abilities has been related to performance in several laboratory tasks. Research efforts began with the seminal work by Hunt, Frost, and Lunneborg (1973).

Vigil-Colet, Pérez-Olle, and Fernández (1997) investigated the relationship between BIP (Basic Information Processing) measures and crystallized intelligence (G_c). They confirmed the findings of Draycott and Kline (1994): BIP measures are related to G_c. Moreover, their findings suggest that elementary measures related to initial stages of information processing such as inspection time are more related to fluid intelligence than measures involving response processes such as BIP parameters. The group coordinated by Vigil-Colet at the *Universidad de Tarragona* has designed paper-and-pencil measures of processing speed (Vigil-Colet & Cordorniu-Raga (2002). These measures correlated with crystallized intelligence and scholastic performance.

Colom, Palacios, et al. (2003) expanded the seminal research by Kyllonen and Christal (1990) – *Reasoning is little more than working memory capacity*. In three separate studies carried out at the *Universidad Autónoma de Madrid* (Spain) and at the Armstrong Laboratory (United States), Colom, Palacios, et al. (2003) demonstrated that a second-order factor representing *g* predicts fairly well a first-order factor representing working memory. In fact, the studies have shown that working memory is not distinguishable from *g*. This finding suggests that we can learn about the nature of *g* by looking at the widely researched properties of working memory (Baddeley, 1996).

Colom, Flores-Mendoza, and Rebollo (2003) found that working memory can be considered as a general cognitive resource, irrespective of content domain or type of processing. Studying two samples from different countries (Spain and Brazil), these researchers found a correlation of +.70 between working memory capacity and measures of G_f. These findings support the main result of Colom, Palacios, et al. (2003): There is something underlying several diverse measures of working memory, in the same way that there is something underlying several diverse measures of psychometric *g* (Jensen, 1998).

Prieto et al. (1993) have been working on spatial ability within the framework of human information processing. In fact, these researchers based their entire research program on this framework. The measures of spatial ability derived from a cognitive analysis of spatial performance. They identified several cognitive processes responsible for spatial performance. The findings strongly agree with the research results derived from Lohman and his group (see Lohman, 2000).

Biological Correlates

There have been several attempts to find the biological roots of intelligence differences (see Vernon et al., 2000, for a review).

Within this area, Vigil-Colet, Ferrando, and Andrés-Pueyo (1993) published a study in which they explored the relationships between inspection time (IT) and the latency of some components of ERP (event-related potential). The results show that IT is more related to the speed of stimulus input processing than to later stages of information processing.

Andrés-Pueyo and Bonastre (1999) studied a group of university undergraduates to test the "neural efficiency hypothesis": High intelligence is related to high neural efficiency (Haier et al., 1992). Nerve conduction velocity (NCV) was taken as a measure of neural efficiency (Vernon et al., 2000). NCV was assessed at the visual pathway. Magnetic resonance imaging served to measure the length of the visual pathway for each participant, and ERPs were used to measure speed of transmission. The NCV measure resulted from both the ERP and the length of the visual pathway. Participants were also measured by means of the Advanced Progressive Matrices (APM) and the WAIS. The correlation between performance in the WAIS and NCV was 0.047, while the correlation between APM and NCV was 0.40. The latter result replicated previous findings reported by Reed and Jensen (1992).

Colom, Bonastre, and Andrés-Pueyo (2000) re-analyzed the database of Andrés-Pueyo and Bonastre (1999). They used a procedure designed by Jensen (1998), called the *method of correlated vectors*. Jensen (1998) summarized results showing that g is responsible for the observed correlation among a variety of cognitive tests on scholastic achievement, work-place performance, brain size, brain glucose metabolic rate, average evoked potential, reaction time, and so forth. The effect can be seen whenever there is a significant correlation between the vector of tests' g loadings (obtained from a hierarchical factor analysis) and the vector of the same tests' loadings in variable X. Colom, Bonastre, et al. (2000) obtained a g factor from the WAIS and a column vector from the correlation between NCV and performance in the WAIS subtest. A positive correlation between the two vectors implies that g is responsible for the observed correlation, but the correlation was not significant $r = 0.4$, $p > .05$). However, it is well recognized that the Wechsler has a crystallized bias (Lynn, 1994). Thus, following a suggestion by Flynn (1999), the column vector corresponding to the correlation between APM and performance in every WAIS subtest was obtained. This produced what can be called as a "fluid intelligence vector." This vector was correlated with the vector representing the correlation NCV × WAIS performance. The correlation was highly significant this time: $r = +0.724$ ($p < .01$). In sum, the findings support the statement that nerve conduction velocity is related to fluid intelligence (G_f), but not to crystallized intelligence (G_c).

Genes and Environment

Genes are not on the research agenda of Spanish psychologists. There is no research program like the SATSA or the CAP (see Plomin et al., 2001). However, there are some studies developed by Spaniards that can be linked to the general research program of the behavioral geneticists.

Colom, Aluja-Fabregat, and García-López (2002) studied 342 married couples (age range 34–77). They found a correlation of +.492 (p < .01) between couples. The result suggests strong assortative mating for intelligence in Spain. However, the correlation changed when couples were divided into older and younger ones. For older couples the correlation was +.578, whereas for younger couples the correlation was +.496. The latter result suggests slightly lower level of assortative mating for recent generations. This, presumably, may have some impact on the "genetic pool" of the population (Plomin et al., 2001).

On the side of environmental effects on intelligence, one intriguing phenomenon widely investigated by Spanish researchers is the so-called Flynn Effect (Neisser et al., 1996; Neisser, 1998). Colom, Andrés-Pueyo, and Juan-Espinosa (1998) demonstrated that the Spanish population gained almost 20 IQ points between the 1960s and the 1990s. Intelligence was measured through the Progressive Matrices Test. Colom, Quiroga, and Juan-Espinosa (1999) have shown that the gains are greater for fluid than for crystallized intelligence. Replying to a study published by Rushton (1999), Colom, Juan-Espinosa, and García (2001) demonstrated that the secular increase in test scores is genuine. This means that higher test scores reflect higher intelligence. Colom & García-López 2003 found a gain of 3 IQ points per decade in the Culture-Fair Intelligence Test. This test is considered as one of the best measures of general intelligence (Cattell, 1980; Jensen, 1980).

Fernández-Ballesteros and Juan-Espinosa (2001) reviewed socio-historical evidence about gains in intelligence test scores over the twentieth century. Their review emphasized the importance of including longitudinal intelligence measures in the international data set as markers of human development.

Practical Validity

There are no large-scale studies in Spain about the predictive validity of standardized measures of intelligence. Most studies are performed within private companies. Thus, the results are not easily available. However, there are some studies that support the published literature. The largest body of evidence can be found in test manuals. A couple of examples may serve our present purposes.

The Spanish adaptation of the Primary Mental Abilities (PMA) measured the academic achievement of a sample of students. The obtained correlation between intelligence and academic performance was +.54.

Chico (1997) assessed 400 army recruits and 942 prison inmates through the Raven Matrices Test. The mean scores were 46.83 and 39.26, respectively. The recruits and inmates had the same academic level. Thus, prison inmates were found to be less intelligent than the recruits.

The reported values are not far from those obtained in hundreds of studies found in the literature (Neisser et al., 1996). However, it seems desirable to study other social correlates of intelligence. Although there are several Spanish studies, all of them are small scale. Studies like the well-known *National Longitudinal Study on Youth* (NLSY) are strongly suggested.

Population Differences

The term *population differences* refers to the study of representative samples of human groups such as males and females. Likewise, we can identify groups such as old and young people.

Colom, Juan-Espinosa, Abad, and García (2000) found a negligible sex difference in g using the largest sample in which sex differences in g have ever been tested ($N = 10,475$). Colom, García, Abad, and Juan-Espinosa (2002) found a null correlation between g and sex differences in the Spanish standardization sample of the WAIS-III. Colom and García-López (2002) found a null sex difference in Cattell's Culture-Fair Intelligence Test. These studies support Jensen's (1998) statement: "in no case is there a correlation between subtests' g-loadings and the mean sex differences in the various subtests . . . the g-loadings of the sex differences are all quite small" (p. 540). This means that cognitive sex differences result from differences in specific cognitive abilities, but not from differences in the core of intelligence, namely, g. These results strongly disagree with the view of Lynn (1994, 1999), according to which there is a small but consistent sex difference in general intelligence favoring males.

Although there is no sex difference in general intelligence (g), the research literature supports the statement that there is a sex difference in some specific cognitive abilities (Hedges & Nowell, 1995). The Spanish data support the accuracy of this statement.

Colom et al. (1999) studied the Spanish standardization samples of the DAT and the PMA. Males scored higher in verbal, quantitative, and spatial measures. There were null sex differences in reasoning and processing speed. An interesting finding was that females outperformed males in the PMA reasoning test, whereas males outperformed females in the DAT reasoning test. Note that the PMA reasoning test is based on *letters*, whereas the DAT reasoning test is based on *figures*. This supports the findings of Colom and García-López (2002), that the content domain is germane for testing a sex difference in reasoning or fluid intelligence. Their conclusions are noteworthy: "researchers must be careful in selecting the markers – measures – of central abilities like fluid intelligence, which is supposed to be the core of intelligent behaviour (Carroll, 1993). A 'gross' selection can lead to confusing results and misleading conclusions."

Sex differences in spatial ability have been investigated to some extent by Spanish researchers. Delgado & Prieto (1996, 1997) found that mental rotation processes contributed to sex differences in visualization tasks. Although there is a stable sex difference in this ability, not every spatial facet contributed to the same extent to the overall difference.

Contreras et al. (2001) found that males outperform females in dynamic spatial tests. Their findings suggest that (a) males have an overall better dynamic spatial performance than females, and (b) neither males' nor females' type of education makes any difference to their dynamic spatial performance. When males and females have the same type of education, dynamic spatial performance is still superior in males.

Age differences are another important aspect explored in population studies. Although there are no longitudinal studies in Spain that include intelligence measures (Fernández-Ballesteros, Diez-Nicolás, & Ruiz-Torres, 1999), Fernández-Ballesteros and her group are working on a European longitudinal study on aging (EXCELSA), with the main purpose of investigating "competence." Until now only one pilot cross-sectional study conducted in seven European countries (including Spain) has yielded interesting results: Intelligence (measures by digit symbol and digit span) is strongly associated with bio-behavioral measures (vital capacity and speed), loading in a factor that could be interpreted as "competence" and explained (through structural equation modeling) by other external and personal characteristics. Even more important, this model received cross-European validation. Subsequent steps of EXCELSA will allow the replication of this model, as well as the study of age differences across Europe (Fernández-Ballesteros et al., 2001).

Emotional Intelligence

As interest in the concept of emotional intelligence increases in general, Spain is no exception. Particular interest has been shown by a research team from the *Universidad de Málaga*, which has published work carried out with one of the most important researchers in the field: Peter Salovey (see Fernández-Berrocal et al., 2001).

Emotional intelligence is seen as a component of intelligence, according to the theory proposed by Mayer and Salovey (1993), and is a component related to classical cognitive abilities, such as verbal ability.

Cognitive Training

Three research areas can be identified in Spain: learning potential, philosophy for children, and the Sternberg triarchic theory of intelligence.

The so-called cognitive training approach to intelligence (Sternberg, 1981) has been a fruitful research area. Fernández-Ballesteros at the *Universidad Autónoma de Madrid* and Calero at the *Universidad de Granada* have developed a research program on learning potential. They designed assessment instruments that have been administered to children (normal and with brain damage), adolescents (normal and educable mentally retarded) and elders (normal and demented). They emphasize the "modifiability of intelligence" through two mechanisms: neural plasticity and cognitive learning strategies leading subjects' executive control (see Fernández-Ballesteros et al., 1997; Fernández-Ballesteros et al., 2003).

Another important aspect is the study of the impact of *Philosophy for Children* (P4C), a program designed by Lipman in the United States that was introduced into Spain by the philosopher García-Moriyón. P4C is based on several narratives adapted to different scholastic periods. The narrations touch on the main philosophical topics, and pupils discuss these topics within so-called research communities. Some research findings support the prediction that P4C increases general cognitive ability (García-Moriyón et al., 2000), but the results are far from conclusive. Moreover, P4C does not appear to increase scholastic achievement (García-Moriyón Colom et al., 2002). However, the findings should be considered with caution, since the assessment of academic achievement carried out in the Spanish educational system has recently been called into question. Some researchers have claimed that academic performance is evaluated ignoring the cognitive components usually demanded by educators.

The third line of research follows Sternberg's *Triarchic Theory of Intelligence* (Sternberg, 1988). A group from the *Universidad de Murcia* coordinated by Mª. Dolores Prieto is responsible for the Spanish adaptation of the Sternberg Triarchic Abilities Test (STAT) and the corresponding training program. Some research findings have already been published (Sternberg et al., 2000).

CURRENT ASSESSMENT TECHNIQUES

As previously mentioned, assessment techniques have been a central issue in Spain. Two types of measure have been developed: Those for research purposes and those published as standardized tests within testing corporations. Let us examine the latter type.

Intelligence and Ability Tests Published

Table 3.1 shows those tests translated and adapted for Spanish populations. The most international intelligence tests – the Weschler Scales, the Raven Matrices Test, and the Primary Mental Abilities Test – have been translated, adapted, and standardized for use with Spanish populations. Most of these tests have also been used in basic research, as mentioned above.

Table 3.2 shows tests developed by Spaniards. An analysis of the content of these tests shows three main characteristics: (1) a core interest in the measurement of abilities more than in general intelligence, (2) personnel selection and education, and (3) numerous spatial orientation tests.

The Use of Intelligence Tests in Spain

A final issue that should be briefly presented concerns the extent to which these tests are used. Several surveys were carried out among Spanish psychologists to find out details of their practices in psychological assessment (Fernández-Ballesteros, 1992). The data that follow, taken from the 1987 survey, are not representative, but rather merely illustrative of some aspects of the work of Spanish psychologists using psychological assessment. Of the intelligence tests most frequently used by those who answered the survey, 83% said that they used some of the Wechsler Scales of Intelligence, whereas 90% used some of the factorial tests (mainly Raven's Progressive Matrices and Thurstone's PMA).

Under the auspices of the International Test Commission (ITC), the European Federation of Professional Psychologists Associations

TABLE 3.1. *Tests and Other Assessment Methodologies Translated and Adapted into Spanish (Adapted from Fernández-Ballesteros, 1992; Pawlik et al., 2000)*

Name of test	Author
Intelligence and aptitudes	
Alexander Scale	W. P. Alexander
APT, Academic Promise Tests	M. G. Bennet, G. K. Bennet, & D. M. Clendenen et al.
Beta, Revised Beta Examination	C.-E. Kellog & N. W. Morton
Cognitive Ability Tests, Primary I & II	R. C. Throndike, E. Hagen & I. Lorge
DAT, Differential Aptitudes Tests	M. G. Bennett, H. G. Seashore & A. G. Wesman
D-48, Dominoes Test	P. Pichot
D-70, Dominoes Test	F. Kowrousky & P. Rennes
GCT, General Clerical Test	The Psychological Corporation Staff
g factor Culture-Fair Intelligence Tests 1/2/3	R. B. Cattell & A. K. S. Cattell
GMA, Graduate & Managerial Assessment	S. F. Blinkhorn
K-ABC, Kaufman Assessment Battery for Children	A. S. Kaufman & N. L. Kaufman
K-BIT, Kaufman Brief Intelligence Test	A. S. Kaufman & N. L. Kaufman
MacQuarrie for Mechanical Ability	T. W. MacQuarrie
Otis Self-Administering Test of Mental Ability	A. S. Otis
Progressive Matrices Tests (CPM, SPM, APM)	J. C. Raven
Primary Mental Aptitudes (PMA)	L. L. Thurstone
Seashore Measures of Musical Talents	C. E. Seashore, J. C. Saetvit & D. Lewis
SET, Short employment Test	G. K. Bennet & M. Gelink
TEA, SRATest of Educational Ability	L. L. Thurstone & T. G. Thurstone
Toni-2, Test of Non-verbal Intelligence	L. Brown, J. Sherbenou & S. K. Johnsen
TP, Toulouse-Piéron	E. Toulouse & H. Piéron
WAIS-III, WISC-R, WPPSI, Intelligence Scales	D. Wechsler

TABLE 3.2. *Tests and Other Assessment Methods Developed in Spanish (Adapted from Fernández-Ballesteros, 1992; Pawlik et al., 2000)*

Name of test	Author
General Intelligence	
Cards "G"	N. García Nieto & C. Yuste
CC-78, Complex Questions	J. Crespo Vázquez
CHANGES, Test of Cognitive Flexibility	N. Seisdedos
CM-76, General Intelligence Test	J. García Yagüe
General Aptitudes, Lower Level	J. García Yagüe
IG-2, General Intelligence	TEA Publishers
TIG-1, Dominoes Test	TEA Publishers
TIG-2. Dominoes Test	TEA Publishers
TISD, Test of Data Selective Interpretation	N. Seisdedos
TEI, A & B	M. Yela
Aptitudes Tests	
Battery of General Aptitudes	J. García Yagüe
ABI, Basic Aptitudes of Computer Science	M. V. de la Cruz López
ABG-1 & 2, General Basic Aptitudes	TEA Publishers
AMD-77, Differentiated Mental Aptitudes	J. García Yagüe
AMDI, Differentiated Mental Aptitudes, Lower	J. García Yagüe
Elementary AMPE	F. Secadas
AMPE, Factorial	F. Secadas
BAC, Commercial Activity Battery	N. Seisdedos
BADYG, Battery of Differential and General Aptitudes	C. Yuste
BC, Battery for Drivers	TEA Publishers & J. L. Fernández Seara
BO, Battery of workers	TEA Publishers
BPA, Batteries of Admission Tests (Levels 1 & 2)	N. Seisdedos
BPA, Admission Test Battery	N. Seisdedos
BS, Battery for Subordinates	TEA Publishers
Differential Battery of Intelligence	J. García Yagüe
De-catest	F. Secadas
SAE, Aptitude Test for Studying	F. Secadas
Verbal Aptitudes Tests	
COE, Comprehension of Written Orders (1 & 2)	TEA Publishers
TCV, Verbal Culture Test	TEA Publishers

(continued)

TABLE 3.2 *(continued)*

Name of test	Author
Numerical Aptitudes Tests	
COINS, Numerical Aptitudes (Levels 1 & 2)	N. Seisdedos
Spatial and Mechanical Aptitudes Tests	
Development of Surfaces	M. Yela
Levers	M. Yela
Mechanics	M. Yela
Printed Puzzles	M. Yela
Solid Figure Rotation	M. Yela
Vocation Tests	F. Secadas
Others	
Learning Potential Assessment test	R. Fernández-Ballesteros, M. D. Calero, J. M. Campllonch & J. Belchí

(EFPPA) and the *Colegio Oficial de Psicólogos* (Spanish Psychological Association), a survey on the use of tests in several countries around the world was carried out. Results from Spain have been reported by Muñiz and Fernández-Hermida (2000), and results from Spain, Portugal and Latin America by Prieto et al. (1999). Reported results from experts in the field show that the use of tests is not as frequent and appropriate as it might be, and that there is a need for the involvement of national professional psychological associations and universities to improve testing and increase its use. The most important conclusion is that the most frequently used tests (among all categories) in Spain are intelligence tests, specifically the Wechsler tests.

In sum, Spain has available a broad spectrum of intelligence and cognitive ability tests. However, Spanish-speaking psychologists generally use tests developed in other countries, which have an international reputation.

FUTURE PERSPECTIVES AND CONCLUSIONS

This chapter has reviewed the history of human intelligence in Spain, the principal current research areas, and several assessment techniques. From the first naïve efforts made by Huarte, Spaniards have developed numerous scientific studies on human intelligence. Research results have had a more international projection in recent times (see Figure 3.1), and this can be attributed to the development of research within "universal" areas, such as the structure of human intelligence or its biological roots.

Spatial ability has been widely investigated by Spanish researchers. New measures of spatial performance have been designed, taking advantage of so-called new technologies, such as virtual reality programs. Some researchers have explored differences in cognitive abilities across ability levels and over the life span.

The relations between abilities and human information processing are also analyzed. Research findings have shown that it is possible to measure processing speed with paper-and-pencil tests, or that working memory capacity can be considered as a general cognitive resource not distinguishable from g.

Biological correlates have also been studied; for example, nerve conduction velocity would appear to be related to fluid intelligence. The Flynn Effect has been widely studied, and it can be said that Spaniards have contributed to advancement in this area.

Population differences have also been explored. Researchers have found a negligible difference in g between the sexes. However, sex differences in some specific cognitive abilities are found, especially in spatial ability. Age differences have begun to be investigated within large-scale programs such as EXCELSA. This program is currently in progress in Europe.

Research programs related to cognitive training are frequently used by Spaniards. Some examples are the learning potential approach, learning-to-think programs, such as P4C, or the framework derived from Sternberg's Triarchic Theory of Intelligence. Finally, it must be remembered that we have a broad variety of instruments designed to measure intelligence and cognitive abilities; it can be also concluded that intelligence tests are the most frequently employed assessment instruments by Spanish psychologists. This may result from the previously mentioned *applied flavor* of Spanish psychology.

However, it is important to emphasize what human intelligence research requires in the future. Long-term research programs are necessary; let us consider three examples in this regard. First, there are no programs investigating the relationships between brain and intelligence in a systematic way. Second, there are no longitudinal studies such as the well-known NLSY. Third, it is difficult to understand why there are no research programs within the field of behavior genetics. These are research programs that must be developed in the future if Spanish research in human intelligence is to be in the mainstream of human intelligence investigation.

In summary, research on human intelligence in Spain is alive and healthy. Apart from some important omissions, the evidence in general encourages optimism for the future.

References

Abad, F. J., Colom, R., Juan-Espinosa, M., & García, L. F. (2003). Intelligence differentiation in adult samples. *Intelligence, 31*, 157–166.

Ackerman, P. L. (1996). A theory of adult intellectual development: Process, personality, interests, and knowledge. *Intelligence, 22*, 227–257.

Andrés-Pueyo, A., & Bonastre, R. (1999). Nerve conduction velocity, MRI, and intelligence: Presented at the 9th Biennial Meeting of the ISSID Vancouver.

Baddeley, A. (1996). Exploring the central executive. *The Quarterly Journal of Experimental Psychology, 49A(1)*, 5–28.

Burt, C. (1940). *The factors of the mind*. London: University of London Press.

Carpintero, H. (1982). The introduction of scientific psychology in Spain. In W. Woodward & M. Ash (Eds.), *Psychology in XIX century thoughts* (pp. 255–275). New York: Praeger.

Carpintero, H. (1994). *Historia de la Psicología en España*. Madrid: Eudema.

Carroll, J. B. (1993). *Human cognitive abilities*. Cambridge: Cambridge University Press.

Cattell, R. B. (1980). They talk of some strict testing of us–Pish. *Behavioral and Brain Sciences, 3*, 336–337.

Cattell, R. B. (1987). *Intelligence: Its structure, growth, and action*. Amsterdam: North-Holland.

Chico, E. (1997). La invarianza de la estructura factorial del Raven en grupos de delincuentes y no delincuentes [The invariant factor structure of the Raven Matrices on delinquent and nondelinquent groups]. *Psicothema, 9, 1*, 47–55.

Colom, R., Aluja-Fabregat, A., & García-López, O. (2002). Tendencias de emparejamiento selectivo en inteligencia, dureza de carácter, extraversión e inestabilidad emocional [Assortative mating on intelligence, psychoticism, extraversion, and neuroticism]. *Psicothema, 14, 1*, 154–158.

Colom, R., Andrés-Pueyo, A., & Juan-Espinosa, M. (1998). Generational IQ gains: Spanish data. *Personality and Individual Differences, 25, 5*, 927– 935.

Colom, R., Bonastre R., & Andrés Pueyo, A. (2000). *Velocidad de conducción nerviosa, Cociente Intelectual y factor g* [Nerve conduction velocity, IQ, and g]. Paper presented to the V Meeting of the Spanish Society for the Study of Individual Differences. Universidad de Barcelona.

Colom, R., Contreras, Mª. J., Botella, J. & Santacreu, J., (2002). Vehicles of spatial ability. *Personality and Individual Differences, 32*, 903–912.

Colom, R., Flores-Mendoza, C., & Rebollo, I. (2003). Working memory and intelligence. *Personality and Individual Differences, 34*, 33–39.

Colom, R., García, L. F., Abad, F. J., & Juan-Espinosa, M. (2002). Null sex differences in general intelligence: Evidence from the WAIS-III. *Spanish Journal of Psychology, 5*, 1, 29–35.

Colom, R., & García-López, O. (2002). Sex differences in fluid intelligence among high-school graduates. *Personality and Individual Differences, 32*, 445–451.

Colom, R., & García-López, O. (2003). Secular increase in fluid intelligence: Evidence from the Culture-Fair Intelligence Test. *Journal of Biosocial Science, 35*, 33–39.

Colom, R., Juan-Espinosa, M., Abad, F., García, L. F. (2000). Negligible sex differences in general intelligence. *Intelligence, 28*, 1, 57–68.

Colom, R., Juan-Espinosa, M., & García, L. F. (2001). The secular increase in test scores is a "Jensen effect". *Personality and Individual Differences, 30*, 553– 559.

Colom, R., Palacios, A., Rebollo, I. & Kyllonen, P. (2003). Working memory is (almost) perfectly predicted by *g*. Paper submitted for publication.

Colom, R., Quiroga, Mª. A., & Juan-Espinosa, M. (1999). Are cognitive sex differences disappearing? Evidence from Spanish populations. *Personality and Individual Differences, 27*, 6, 1189–1196.

Contreras, Mª. J., Colom, R., Shih, P., Alava, Mª. J., & Santacreu, J. (2001). Dynamic spatial performance: Sex and educational differences. *Personality and Individual Differences, 30*, 1, 117–126.

Deary, I. J., Egan, V., Gibson, G. J., Austin, E. J. Brand, C. R., Kellaghan, T. (1996). Intelligence and the differentiation hypothesis. *Intelligence, 23*, 105– 132.

Delgado, A., & Prieto, G. (1996). Sex differences in visual-spatial ability: Do performance factors play such an important role? *Memory & Cognition, 24*, 504–510.

Delgado, A., & Prieto, G. (1997). Mental rotation as a mediator for sex-related differences invisualization. *Intelligence, 24*, 405–416.

Detterman, D. K., & Daniels, M. H. (1989). Correlations of mental tests with each other and with cognitive abilities are highest for low IQ groups. *Intelligence, 13*, 349–359.

Draycott, S. G., & Kline, P. (1994). Further investigation into nature of the BIP: A factor analysis of the BIP with primary abilities. *Personality and Individual Differences, 17*, 2, 201–210.

Fernández-Ballesteros, R. (1992). Psychological assessment. *Applied Psychology. An International Review, 43*, 157–174.

Fernández-Ballesteros, R., & Calero, M. D. (2000). The assessment of learning potential: The EPA instrument. In C. S. Lidz & J. G. Elliot (Eds.), *Dynamic assessment: Prevailing models and applications*. Amsterdam: JAI.

Fernández-Ballesteros, R., Diez-Nicolás, J., & Ruiz-Torres, A. (1999). Spain. In J. J. F. Scroots, R. Fernández-Ballesteros, & G. Rudinger (Eds.), *Aging in Europe*. Amsterdam: IOS Press.

Fernández-Ballesteros, R., & de Juan-Espinosa, M. (2001). Sociohistorical changes and intelligence gains. In R. J. Sternberg & E. L. Grigorenko (Eds.), *Environmental effects on cognitive abilities*. Mahwah, NJ: LEA.

Fernández-Ballesteros, R., de Juan-Espinosa, M., Colom, R., & Calero, M. D. (1997). Contextual and personal sources of individual differences in intelligence: Empirical results. In J. S. Carlson, J. Kingman, & W. Tomic (Eds.), *Advances in cognition and educational practice. Reflexion on the concept of intelligence.* London: JAI Press.

Fernández-Ballesteros, R., Zamarrón, M. D., Tarraga, L., Moya, R. & Iniguez (2003): Cognitive plasticity in Healthy, Mild Cognitive Impairment (MCI) subjects and Alzheimer's disease patients. *European Psychologist*, in press.

Fernández-Ballesteros, R., Zamarrón, M. D., et al. (2001). The European research protocol on aging: Assessing competence. *International Congress of Gerontology Proceedings*. Vancouver: IAG.

Fernández-Berrocal, P., Alcaide, R., & Ramos, N. (1999). The influence of emotional intelligence on the emotional adjustment in high-school students. *Bulletin of Kharkov State University, N. 439 "Personality and transformational processes in the society. Psychological and pedagogical problems of the modern education,"* 1–2, 119–123.

Fernández-Berrocal, P., Salovey, P., Vera, A., Ramos, N., & Extremera, N. (2001). Cultura, inteligencia emocional percibida y ajuste emocional: un estudio preliminar [Culture, perceived emotional intelligence, and emotional adjustment: A preliminaty study]. *Revista Española de Motivación y Emoción, 4*, 8.

Flynn, J. (1999). Evidence against Rushton: The genetic loading of WISC-R subtests and the causes of between-group IQ differences. *Personality and Individual Differences, 26*, 373–379.

García, L. F., & Escorial, S. (2001). Búsqueda bibliográfica de "inteligencia" en ISOC. Unpublished manuscript. Madrid: Autónoma University of Madrid.

García-Moriyón, F., Colom, R., Lora, S., Rivas, M., & Traver, V. (2000). Valoración de "Filosofía para Niños": Un programa de enseñar a pensar [Evaluation of "Philosophy for Children": A program of learning to think]. *Psicothema, 12, 2*, 207–211.

García-Moriyón, F., Colom, R., Lora, S., Rivas, Mª., & Traver, V. (2002). *La estimulación de la inteligencia racional y la inteligencia emocional* [Stimulating analytic and emotional intelligence]. Madrid: Ediciones de la Torre.

Germain, J., & Rodrigo, M. (1930). *Pruebas de inteligencia Revisión española y adaptación, práctica del método de L. M. Terman.* Madrid: Espasa Calpe.

Haier, R., Siegel, B., Tang, C., Abel, L., & Buchsbaum, M. (1992). Intelligence and changes in regional cerebral glucose metabolic rate following learning. *Intelligence, 16*, 415–426.

Hedges, L., & Nowell, A. (1995). Sex differences in mental test scores, variability and numbers of high scoring individuals. *Science, 269*, 41–45.

Huarte de San Juan, J. (1575). *Examen de los ingenios para las ciencias*. Baeza.

Hunt, E. B., Frost, N., & Lunneborg, C. (1973). Individual differences in cognition: A new approach to intelligence. In C. Bower (Ed.), *Advances in learning and motivation, Vol. 7*. New York: Academic Press.

Hunt, E., Pellegrino, J. W., Frick. R. W., Farr, S. A., & Alderton, D. (1988). The ability to reason about movement in the visual field. *Intelligence, 12*, 77–100.

Jensen, A. R. (1980). Author's response. Précis of *Bias in Mental Testing. Behavioral and Brain Sciences, 3*, 359–368.

Jensen, A. (1998).*The g factor*. London: Praeger.

Juan-Espinosa, M., Abad, F. J., Colom, R., & Fernández-Truchaud, M. (2000). Individual differences in large-spaces orientation: *g* and beyond? *Personality and Individual Differences, 29*, 1, 85–98.

Juan-Espinosa, M., García, L. F., Colom, R., & Abad, F. J. (2000). Testing the age differentiation hypothesis through the Wechsler's scales. *Personality and Individual Differences, 29*, 6, 1069–1075.

Juan-Espinosa, M., García, L. F., Rebollo, I., Colom, R., & Abad, F. J. (2002). Age differentiation hypothesis: Evidence from the WAIS III. *Intelligence, 30, 5*, 395–408.

Kyllonen, P., & Christal, R. (1990). Reasoning ability is (little more than) working memory capacity?! *Intelligence, 14*, 389–433.

Lafora, G. R. (1919). Los niños mentalmente anormales [Mentally abnormal Children]. Madrid: Espasa Calpe.

Lohman, D. (2000). Complex information processing. In R. J. Sternberg (Ed.), *Handbook of intelligence*. Cambridge: Cambridge University Press.

Lynn, R. (1994). Sex differences in intelligence and brain size: A paradox resolved. *Personality and individual differences, 17*, 2, 257–271.

Lynn, R. (1999). Sex differences in intelligence and brain size: A developmental theory. *Intelligence, 27*, 1, 1–12.

Malcom, K. R. (1958). *Juan Huarte de San Juan*. Boston: Twayne.

Martínez-Arias, R., & Yela, M. (1991). *Pensamiento e inteligencia* [Thinking and intelligence]. Madrid: Alianza.

McReynolds, P. (1986). History of assessment in clinical and educational settings. In R. O. Nelson & S. C. Hayes (Eds.), *Conceptual foundations of behavioral assessment*. New York: Guilford.

Mayer, J., & Salovey, P. (1993). The intelligence of emotional intelligence. *Intelligence, 17*, 433–442.

Muñiz, J., & Fernández-Hermida, J. R. (2000). La utilizaciónde los tests en España [The use of tests in Spain]. *Papeles del Psicólogo, 76*, 41–49.

Neisser, U. (1998). *The rising curve*. Washington, DC: American Psychological Association.

Neisser, U., Boodoo, G., Bouchard, T., Boykin, A., Brody, N., Ceci, S., Halpern, D., Loehlin, J., Perloff, R., Sternberg, R., & Urbina, S. (1996). Intelligence: Knowns and unkowns. *American Psychologist, 51*, 2, 77–101.

Pawlik, K., Zhan, H., Vrignau, P., Roussalov, V., & Fernández-Ballesteros, R. (2000). Psychological assessment & techniques. In K. Pawlik & M. R. Rosenzweig (Eds.), *The international handbook of psychology*. (pp. 365–406). London: Sage.

Plomin, R., Defries, John, C., McClearn, Gerald E., & McGuffin, P. (2000). *Behavior genetics*. New York: W. H. Freeman & Co.

Prieto, G., Carro, J., Pulido, R., Orgaz, B., Delgado, A., & Loro, P. (1996). Medición de la visualización espacial mediante tests informatizados [Measurement of spatial visualization through computerized tests]. *Estudios de Psicología, 55,* 41–59.

Prieto, G., Carro, J., Orgaz, B., & Pulido, R. (1993). Análisis cognitivo de un test informatizado de visualización espacial [A cognitive análisis of a computerized test for the measurement of spatial visualization]. *Picothema, 5, 2,* 293–301.

Prieto, J. M., Fernández-Ballesteros, R., & Carpintero, H. (1994). Contemporary Psychology in Spain. In L. W. Porter & M. R. Rosenzweig (Eds.), *Annual Review of Psychology, 45:* 51–78.

Prieto, G., Muñiz, J., Almeida, L., & Bartram, D. (1999). Uso de los tests psicológicos en España, Portugal e Iberoamérica [The usage of psychological tests on Spain, Portugal, and Latin-America]. *Revista Iberoamericana de Diagnóstico y Evaluación Psicológica, 8,* 67–82.

Reed, T. E., & Jensen, A. R. (1992). Conduction velocity in a brain nerve pathway of normal adults correlates with intelligence level. *Intelligence, 16,* 259–272.

Rushton, J. P. (1999). Secular gains in IQ not related to the *g* factor and inbreeding depression – unlike Black-White differences: A reply to Flynn. *Personality and Individual Differences, 26,* 381–389.

Sternberg, R. J. (1981). Testing and cognitive psychology. *American Psychologist, 36,* 1181–1189.

Sternberg, R. J. (1988). *The triarchic mind*. London: Penguin.

Sternberg, R. J. (2000). *Handbook of intelligence*. Cambridge: Cambridge University Press.

Sternberg, R. J., Prieto, M. D., & Castejón, J. (2000). Análisis factorial confirmatorio del Sternberg Triarchic Abilities Test (nivel-H) en una muestra española: resultados preliminares [Confirmatory factor analysis of the Sternberg Triarchic Abilities Test (level-H) on a Spanish sample: Preliminary results]. *Psicothema, 12, 4,* 642–647.

Vernon, P. A., Wickett, J. C., Bazana, G., & Stelmack, R. (2000). The neuropsychology and psychophysiology of human intelligence. In R. J. Sternberg (Ed.), *Handbook of intelligence* (pp. 245–264). Cambridge: Cambridge University Press.

Vigil-Colet, A., & Cordorniu-Raga, M. (2002): How inspection time and paper-and-pencil measures of processing speed are related to intelligence. *Personality and Individual Differences, 33,* 1149–1162.

Vigil-Colet, A., Ferrando, P., Andrés-Pueyo, A. (1993). Initial stages of information processing and inspection time: Electrophysiological correlates. *Personality and Individual Differences, 14, 5,* 733–738.

Vigil-Colet, A., Pérez-Olle, J., Fernández, M. (1997). The relationships of basic information processing measures with fluid and crystallized intelligence. *Personality and Individual Differences, 23, 1,* 55–65.

Yela, M. (1956). *Psicología de las aptitudes* [Psychology of abilities]. Madrid: Gredos.

Yela, M. (1987). Psicología de la inteligencia: un ensayo de síntesis [Psychology of intelligence: A synthesis essay]. In M. Yela (Ed.), *Estudios sobre inteligencia y lenguaje.* [Research on intelligence and language.] Madrid: Pirámide.

4

Psychology of Human Intelligence in France and French-Speaking Switzerland

Jacques Lautrey and Anik de Ribaupierre

INTRODUCTION

In France and in French-speaking Switzerland, research on intelligence has traditionally referred to a relatively wide range of studies. On the one hand, intelligence is studied by differentialists – differential psychology, in the Francophone tradition, refers to both psychometrics and to the study of individual differences, the latter referring both to fundamental and to applied issues – who devise and use tests of intelligence. On the other hand, because Piaget referred to the "development of intelligence," it also includes developmental studies of cognition, in particular, the Piagetian studies. Currently, researchers working in the Piagetian tradition no longer consider that they work on intelligence, but this is a relatively recent shift. Thus, the study of intelligence is not restricted to the use of standardized tests of intelligence scales nor to interest in individual differences. For example, the *Traité de Psychologie Expérimentale*, first edited in 1963, devoted a whole volume to the study of intelligence (Oléron et al., 1963), three chapters of which consisted essentially of the presentation of the Piagetian theory by Piaget and collaborators. As in many other countries, experimental psychologists working with adults on reasoning, problem solving, language, or other cognitive functions do not consider that they are working on intelligence.

This chapter therefore reflects these fuzzy frontiers including the differential and the Piagetian traditions but not the other types of cognitive studies. The choice to present the situation in France and in the French-speaking part of Switzerland is justified by the geographical and linguistic proximity of these two countries and also by the existence of numerous interactions between the researchers interested in intelligence in these two countries, including those due to the influence of Piaget's theory in France.

The first part of the chapter provides some elements of the history of research on intelligence in these two countries; the second deals with applications, in particular, techniques of assessment; and the third is devoted to contemporary research. Except for history, we do not introduce subparts specifically devoted to France and Switzerland, but the country in question is specified each time the point discussed is specific to this country.

SOME ELEMENTS OF HISTORY

France

In France, the psychology of human intelligence began with the development by Alfred Binet (1857–1911) and Théodore Simon (1873–1960) of the first measurement scale (Binet & Simon, 1905, 1908; Binet, 1911b). The Binet–Simon test was immediately recognized as a major contribution to the assessment of intelligence in Europe and the United States, where it was promptly translated and adapted. However, it did not have the same success in France. We will not dwell at length on the history of this discovery, which is now well known, but rather we seek to understand why this discovery occurred in France at this particular moment, and why, nevertheless, it did not attract followers in France.

Why in France and Why Binet?

At the turn of the 19th century, Binet was not the only psychologist seeking to devise an objective assessment of intelligence. But he was the first to free himself from the prevailing ideas on this issue. The leading approach at the time was associationism, a theory proposing that complex psychic phenomena such as images, ideas, and conscious thoughts were formed through associations of elementary sensations. Wundt, who in 1879 created the first laboratory of experimental psychology in Leipzig, had an associationist approach and popularized the idea that to study complex psychic phenomena, experimental psychology had first to break down these phenomena into their elements, that is sensations. Thus, the methods developed in Wundt's laboratory to implement this research program consisted essentially of measuring sensations: perceptive thresholds, sensory discrimination, and reaction times. The early psychologists who sought to measure intelligence operated naturally within this theoretical framework, and the tests they designed were in fact simplified versions of these new experimental paradigms (Cattell, 1890).

Binet broke the deadlock on this line of research by relying on two ideas that were quite original in the historical context. First, he proposed that the study of elementary processes was not a necessary step for research on intelligence. Binet argued that measures of intelligence should focus directly on individual differences in higher processes such as memory, imagination, judgment, and comprehension (Binet & Henri, 1895). Thus, this program broke with associationism, but came up against a major obstacle: Experimental psychology had made it possible at the time to measure sensations but not higher processes. Binet's second idea allowed him to overcome this obstacle. His approach was to use development to rank tasks according to their cognitive complexity. Ranking the test items according to ages at which they were successfully completed defined, in an indirect way, their rank of cognitive complexity. This made it possible to rank children as well, depending on the level reached on this scale. Binet was well aware of the ordinal nature of this assessment procedure: "The word measure is not used here in its mathematical sense: It does not mean the number of times a quantity is contained in another. To us, the idea of measurement is one of hierarchical ranking"(Binet, 1911a, p. 135).

Why was this breakthrough achieved by Binet rather than by one of the other psychologists seeking to measure intelligence at the same period? Part of the answer lies perhaps in the specificity of French psychology, which, at the time, was oriented mainly toward psychopathology. Ribot (1839–1916), who can be considered as the founder of scientific psychology in France, defended the idea that pathological phenomena provided a privileged method for studying the mind, as this method provides a dissociation of processes that are usually integrated in non-pathological individuals. Binet came to psychology through Ribot's influence and collaborated for seven years – from 1882 – with Charcot at La Salpêtrière Hospital, where he practiced hypnosis and observed hysterical patients. Through this experience, Binet became familiar with the clinical method of observation, which allowed him to observe some of the deteriorations that pathology inflicts on higher processes. He could also observe that in psychiatric institutions, the diagnosis of mental retardation and the distinctions between different degrees of mental retardation were very subjective. This is the reason why he began, with the help of a young psychiatrist, Dr. Simon, to seek an objective method of assessment of mental retardation by comparing retarded and non-retarded subjects. Thus, the psychopathological orientation of French psychology at the turn of the 19th century could have been a facilitating factor in the sense that this approach was relatively focused on higher processes and that the comparison between normal and pathological cases offered an alternative to the experimental approach.

These facilitating factors are of course not sufficient to explain why Binet freed himself more easily than others from the associationnist approach. His discovery may also be explained in terms of personal characteristics. Those who met Binet described him as an independent person, not very driven toward social contacts, more at the fringe of psychology's institutional circle. He was not a follower of any particular theoretical or methodological approach, and he more or less practiced them all.

Why Was the Line of Work of Binet Abandoned in France?

The development of the psychology of intelligence in France between the world wars occurred in fact within another trend of research. While Binet designed his intelligence scale, another French psychologist, Edouard Toulouse (1865–1947), worked toward the same objective. The work of Toulouse is less well known than Binet's, but thanks to recent research (Huteau, 2002a, 2002b) – on which we draw in this chapter – the complex relationships between Binet and Toulouse are better known today.

Toulouse, trained as a psychiatrist, became the head of a department at Villejuif's psychiatric hospital in 1898. Toulouse thought that psychiatry should be based on psychology. Accordingly, as soon as he arrived in Villejuif, he created a laboratory of experimental psychology and asked two assistants, Nicolas Vaschide and Henri Piéron, to design rigorous observational techniques for psychological processes. Here we have to point out that both of them previously had been Binet's assistants at the Sorbonne's experimental psychology laboratory, which Binet headed from 1894. As Binet neglected this laboratory to observe children in schools, Vaschide first, and Piéron later, joined Toulouse's new laboratory. Their work led to the publication of the *Technique de Psychologie Expérimentale* (Toulouse, Vaschide, & Piéron, 1904), a collection of tests designed within the associationist framework, with its main part devoted to the measurement of sensations. The second edition (Toulouse & Piéron, 1911) shows a slight evolution by integrating a few tasks designed to assess higher processes (comprehension, judgment, memory, and reasoning). It is worth noting that even in this second edition, Binet's scale is not mentioned. This omission cannot be attributed to ignorance but rather to a deep disagreement between the two laboratories. Toulouse and his collaborators believed firmly that experimental psychology was now being studied in their own laboratory, and they accused Binet of having given up experimental psychology in favor of a kind of psychopathology based on observation. They criticized the concept of intellectual level, as assessed by Binet's scale, as being too global and unable to distinguish nature and nurture influences. Binet for his part said little about the *Technique de Psychologie Expérimentale* but found it vague and outdated when he reviewed it (Huteau, 2002a).

Binet died in 1911 at 54 years of age, the same year the last version of his intelligence scale was published. The Sorbonne's laboratory of experimental psychology had been more or less deserted, and he had no followers, which can probably be related to his personal characteristics, as mentioned here. Henri Piéron, one of the assistants who had left Binet to join Toulouse, took over in 1912 as the head of the Sorbonne's laboratory. Deeply at odds with Binet's global approach of intelligence, Piéron never extended this line of work but reoriented the laboratory's activity toward the kind of analytical experimental psychology Binet had practiced for some time, then abandoned.

Piéron played a key role in the institutionalization of psychology in France. Most of his scientific work was in fact devoted to psychophysiology, but he was also important in the development of the psychometric approach (called *psychotechnique* at the time). Like his mentor Toulouse, Piéron was a positivist and believed that society should be reformed on a more rational and fair basis by drawing on a scientific approach. More specifically, he believed that students' academic and professional orientations should be chosen according to their aptitudes – objectively measured by means of a scientific psychology – rather than based on their social origins. He considered that these aptitudes were innate and independent from one another. Thus, within a same individual, these aptitudes could be of varying levels, depending on the domains.

This conception ruled out the idea of a global hierarchy of intellectual levels. In some sense, Piéron's "theory of aptitudes" can be considered as a precursor to Gardner's (1983) theory of multiple intelligences. Within the framework of Piéron's theory, the goal of a scientifically based program of vocational guidance was to match the aptitudes profile of each individual with the aptitudes profile required for a given occupation.

In 1928 Piéron was able to give substance to this social program by participating in the creation of the *Institut d'Orientation Professionnelle* (Institute for Vocational Guidance) for training vocational advisers using the psychometric approach. This institute, which Piéron headed from 1928 to 1963, included a research department whose first assignment was to design a battery of aptitudes tests, called the *Fiche d'Orientation Professionnelle* (Piéron, 1930). This battery was mainly composed of tasks drawn from the second version of the *Technique de Psychologie Expérimentale*; however, only tests assessing higher processes had been retained (4 attention tasks, 6 memory tasks, 2 verbal tasks, 1 task of imagination, and 6 concerning intelligence). The battery comprised a total of 21 tasks supposed to tap independent aptitudes (this independence was more postulated than demonstrated). Each one of these tasks was normed in percentiles, and the results obtained were reported on a form as a scatterplot representing the profile of aptitudes of each individual.

The development of the psychology of intelligence at the beginning of the 20th century in France was thus influenced by the conflicting relation between two approaches to individual differences in terms of intelligence (Huteau, 2002a). The first one, developed by Binet, was both global and oriented toward higher processes. The second one, supported by Toulouse and Piéron, was both analytical and oriented toward elementary processes. A sort of compromise finally took over. Toulouse and Piéron themselves evolved – more slowly than Binet – toward a measure of individual differences in higher processes, but Piéron remained opposed to a global measure of intelligence and tried to develop an analytical evaluation of higher processes. In the meantime, the Binet–Simon scale was somewhat forgotten in French psychology, and its use was restricted to the field of education for the diagnosis of mental retardation. It was not until 1949 that revised norms were established; in 1966 a revised version appeared called the *Nouvelle Echelle Métrique de l'Intelligence* (NEMI) (Zazzo, Gilly, & Verba-Read 1966). In the meantime, since the beginning of the 1950s, the French versions of Wechsler's scales became more popular than the Binet-Simon scale among French psychologists.

French Switzerland

The French Swiss tradition has been very strongly marked by the work of Piaget and his collaborators, and interest was essentially placed on the theoretical aspects of the development of intelligence in children. Piaget himself was certainly influenced by Baldwin (e.g., Case, 1985) and by both Edouard Claparède and Alfred Binet (or more exactly, by Simon, the collaborator of Binet) in whose laboratory he spent some time. Edouard Claparède (1873–1940) was a precursor in proposing to link experimental pedagogy and the psychology of the child. He adopted a "genetico-functional" point of view, arguing that for child study to be useful for educators, it was necessary to go beyond simple normative description. It was necessary to determine the role played by a given process in the individual's development, identify factors that favor or hinder development, and discover how and why, at a given period, one process is succeeded by another (e.g., Claparède, 1905). These principles are indeed very close to those adopted and defended later by Piaget.

The Underrecognized Contribution of André Rey

The empirical practices and methods, if perhaps not the theoretical approach, of the psychologists interested in assessing intellectual functions have been strongly influenced by the work of André Rey, who would certainly have been much better known internationally, had he not been in the same institute as Piaget. André Rey (1906–1965) was indeed a "universal psychologist" in that he was interested in many facets of behavior, as well as in the combination of many different approaches, ranging from clinical and school psychology to vocational guidance to neuropsychology (as a young researcher, he collaborated with Lashley) and general and animal psychology. He wrote a number of books and papers on the clinical methods of psychological assessment, which very strongly contributed to the establishment of scientific foundations of psychometric assessment (e.g., Rey, 1958, 1963). He pleaded for the use, in psychological assessment, of a "hypothetico-deductive method" and considered that a psychological examination should consist in a "progressive experimental analysis of individual behavior." That is, he argued for the necessity to adopt a flexible battery of tests, adapted to the hypotheses progressively set with respect to the individual's difficulties as they progressively unfold in the course of a psychological examination.

Rey developed numerous, very ingenious psychometric tests, many of which unfortunately were not published. The best known, not only because they were commercially published, but probably also because they crossed the Atlantic, are the "Fifteen Words" test and the "Complex

Figure" (respectively translated as the Rey Auditory-Verbal Learning test and the Rey-Osterrieth Complex Figure test; see Lezak, 1995). However, many other tasks were developed. Rey did not propose a theoretical model of intelligence; this is probably another reason why he is relatively little known despite his very abundant production. In fact, rather than speaking of intelligence, he preferred stressing the necessity of assessing learning competencies. Thus he emphasized the necessity of assessing the capacity to learn and systematically suggested differentiating the results of past learning experience – nowadays one would probably speak of the knowledge base – from the present learning potential of an individual, and he used this distinction to propose and classify a very wide variety of tests. In this context, it should be stressed that Rey's work was a very important source of Feuerstein's work (1979), all the more so because Feuerstein spent some time working in Geneva with Rey. More generally, Rey can also be considered to be, at least in the French-speaking countries, a precursor of the present cognitive neuropsychological approach (e.g., Seron, 1993).

The Contribution of Piaget
Geneva remains best recognized in the field of research on intelligence because of Piaget's school. It is well known that Piaget, who trained as a biologist, had a primary objective to understand the development of knowledge in the human species rather than to describe and understand how children develop; that is, his ultimate goal was epistemological in nature. Nonetheless, it is Piaget's psychology of intelligence that is the most universally known (and disputed) facet of his work, even though he himself did not consider it to be the main part (e.g., Piaget, 1947, 1970; Piaget & Inhelder, 1966). His theory transformed the field of developmental psychology by providing it with a new vision of the development of the child. With his collaborators, he developed many test situations to understand the construction of cognitive operations, addressing a very wide range of domains and using a quasi-standardized method of interview, initially labeled the *clinical method* and later, the *critical method*. Intelligence is defined as the most general form of coordination of the actions and operations that characterize the various developmental levels, not as a mental faculty or an entity in itself; it develops through a succession of general stages, defined by overall structures ("structures d'ensemble").

The focus of Piagetian theory was always placed on the *epistemic*, or ideal subject, to unravel universal laws of development. Piaget was not interested in individual or task-specific performances, even though he acknowledged the existence of temporal lags between different notions supposed to pertain to a same general structure (horizontal decalages). For example, he stated, addressing the issue of the use of data obtained through the clinical method for diagnostic purposes:

"We are no longer dealing with a problem of general psychology, but of differential psychology, of psychology of the individual – of each individual. This, I must confess, is a problem I have unfortunately never studied, because I have no interest whatsoever in the individual. I am very interested in general mechanisms, intelligence and cognitive functions, but what makes one individual different from another seems to me far less instructive as regards the study of the human mind in general" (Inhelder & Piaget, 1971, p. 211).

The closest Piaget came to recognizing the potential theoretical relevance of individual differences and the possibility of different developmental pathways was in an article about the attainment of formal operations (Piaget, 1972); he then acknowledged the possibility that not all adolescents reach the stage of formal operations and suggested that they might acquire formal thinking in different content domains depending on their specific aptitudes and professional expertise. However, he did not pursue further this line of exploration, nor did he attempt to envisage the possible implications of such a hypothesis for his general model.

Piagetian Theory and Intelligence Assessment

There were, nevertheless, two lines of work in Geneva that opened the way to the study of individual differences; they were concerned with applications of Piagetian theory and the clinical method to atypical populations, on the one hand, and standardization, on the other hand. Barbel Inhelder (1943) was the first to use operational tasks with clinical populations. She argued that Piagetian theory offered more information and was more adapted than traditional tests to understanding the cognitive processes involved in mental retardation; she also emphasized the interest of using a flexible method of interviewing the child (critical method) rather than a fixed set of questions. She offered empirical evidence that mentally retarded children, while following apparently the same developmental path as normal children in terms of cognitive operations, did not reach formal operations or the later substage of concrete operations. Inhelder nevertheless also stressed that mentally retarded children presented functional specificities, such as oscillations or perseverations, that were larger than those observed in normal children. Her work opened the way to a number of studies, particularly in Geneva but also abroad, that applied the Piagetian method to a variety of cognitive disorders (Ajuriaguerra & Tissot, 1966). The argument was then that it was more promising to use theory-based tasks, firmly grounded in a developmental model, rather than tasks such as IQ tests that were atheoretical and had only empirical norms to offer.

However, these Genevan studies faced a major problem: They usually compared clinical populations with the epistemic subject and often concluded that there are disharmonies in the face of large horizontal decalages, whereas the amplitude of such decalages in a normal population was not known. Yet, it has been shown since then that intraindividual decalages can also be very large in a normal population (see section on Piagetian Theory and Individual Differences.). As a result, and because of both the scarcity of normative data and the difficulty of the critical method, Piagetian tasks have never become a major tool of psychological assessment for the French Swiss clinical or educational psychologists. They have, nevertheless, remained in the toolbox of the psychologists, particularly those interested in understanding the cognitive functioning of the primary school-aged child.

In the early 1960s, a second line of approach to the study of individual differences began in Geneva, initiated in particular by Inhelder and Vinh Bang (cited in Inhelder, 1963; see also Bang, 1988). It consisted of standardizing the tasks to establish valid evaluation and scoring criteria. Approximately at the same time, longitudinal studies were launched. Unfortunately, none of these studies were published. Nassefat (1963) standardized a number of formal operational tasks, to offer norms to the psychologist interested in the cognitive functioning of adolescents and to be used in the context of vocational guidance. There was also a Genevan project, in the 1970s, to assemble a standard battery of Piagetian tasks, which led to the confection of two or three dozen standard sets of material. These sets remained, however, used within academic settings only and were never produced at a commercial level. To our knowledge, only the battery assembled by Longeot (*Echelle de la Pensée Logique*) was produced on a relatively large scale by a test publisher. Most standardization work was accomplished outside of Geneva, both in Canada by Laurendeau and Pinard (1968) and in France, in particular, by Longeot (see Piagetian Theory and Individual Differences). The initial objective of Rieben and de Ribaupierre's work (describing Piagetian theory and individual differences) was in direct continuation of these first attempts toward standardization. In view of the large inter- and intraindividual variability that was observed, however, they soon became more interested, with Jacques Lautrey, in understanding the processes underlying such variability rather than pursuing strict standardization.

APPLICATIONS OF INTELLIGENCE TESTS

In France, intelligence tests were rather widely used in the period following World War II. Since the end of the 1960s, however, their use has declined, partly because of criticisms of these tests, but mainly because the social demands concerning intelligence tests evolved.

The Criticisms

Before describing the various applications of intelligence tests, we will briefly summarize the main criticisms that were raised, restricting ourselves to the ones that were specific to the French and Francophone regions.

We already mentioned, when we discussed the contributions of Toulouse and Piéron, that one of the specificities of the development of psychometric tests in France was that this development was supported by left-wing intellectuals, convinced that society could be reformed by relying on science. For this group, the use of aptitude tests seemed to be a means to correct social inequalities concerning access to education and thus to promote greater justice in the society. During the period between the two world wars, this social project and psychometrics were criticized by right-wing parties.

The situation changed after World War II, when the use of intelligence tests was criticized by intellectuals and psychologists associated with the Communist Party. It should be noted that a resolution adopted in 1936 by the central committee of the Communist Party in the Soviet Union had forbidden the use of tests, psychometrics being considered "bourgeois" and "anti-scientific." In France, intellectuals close to the French Communist Party accused intelligence tests of confirming, legitimating, and even inducing the acceptance of social inequalities (*La Raison*, 1952). At the time, the criticisms remained in the realm of intellectual debates and did not have any major influence on the use of intelligence tests because their use was increasing in any case. After May 1968, however, these criticisms were revived by extreme-left movements (see, e.g., Tort, 1974). They were then more influential and contributed to a certain dismissal of tests and, more globally, of any type of assessment.

In French-speaking Switzerland, the criticisms were of a rather different nature and came from within the psychological community. As already mentioned, the Piagetian school, and more particularly Inhelder, criticized intelligence tests for totally lacking a theoretical basis and for being too static. In the 1960s, together with psychiatrists such as Ajuriaguerra and Tissot, Inhelder therefore tried to encourage the use of Piagetian tasks in educational as well as in clinical psychology. However, the lack of proper standardization, the intensive training required by the Piagetian critical type of questioning, and the absence of norms restricted the use of these tasks. In parallel, Rey was also showing the way to using a more adaptive and more analytical type of testing.

Returning now to the applications of tests, we will examine the three main domains in which they have been employed: education, health, and work.

The Domain of Education

In the French educational system, the use of intelligence tests has differed between elementary and secondary schooling. The problems are different at each of these two levels, and the psychologists involved at each level have different training.

At the elementary level, the main goal of the *psychologues scolaires* (school psychologists), whose training is mainly oriented toward clinical psychology, consists of preventing school failure. These psychologists practice individual check-ups requested by parents or teachers when children are facing major difficulties. At times they include an intelligence test to determine whether the problems may be due to intellectual retardation. The tests most commonly employed are the Wechsler Preschool and Primary Intelligence Scales (WPPSI) and the Wechsler Intelligence Scale for Children (WISC) or, less frequently, the NEMI (i.e., the revised version of the Binet-Simon) or the Kaufmann Assessment Battery for Children (K-ABC).

Cases of mental retardation requiring special education are not very common (currently less than 5% of the school population). Admission to special classes or institutions is subject to the decision of a commission. Intelligence test scores, interpreted by the school psychologist, are one of the major elements on which the decision is based. Thus, at the elementary level, the function of intelligence scales remains the same as in Binet's era when he created his first test.

Psychologists involved in the secondary school system are referred to as *conseillers d'orientation–psychologues* (COP) (guidance counselors–psychologists); their main function consists of guiding students in career and course choices made during schooling. The training of the COPs – there are currently about 4,000 in France – has been oriented for a long time toward differential psychology and psychometrics, following the tradition established by Piéron when he created the Institut d'Orientation Professionnelle. Between the 1950s and the 1980s, these psychologists administered factorial tests of aptitudes in a rather systematic fashion. The aim was to detect "aptitudes reserves," in other words, to detect in the group of children not admitted into secondary school those who performed well according to intelligence tests. It should be noted that in the 1950s, only children from upper-class families had access to the secondary school system. The aptitude tests were administered at the end of the elementary school (5th grade) with the goal of encouraging pupils who performed well on these tests to be candidates for the admission exam for secondary schools.

At the end of the 1950s, a reform of the educational system created the *collège unique* (unique junior high school), corresponding to the first part of secondary school (grades 6 to 9) and making schooling mandatory for all children up to grade 9. This reform eliminated the need to identify children having aptitudes for secondary school.

The testing activity of the COP moved then to grade 9, corresponding to the end of junior high school. Factorial intelligence tests were administered systematically. The objective was then to take both school performance and test results into account for guidance decisions. In this way students who showed good levels of intellectual aptitudes in the tests, even if their school results were not completely satisfactory, could have a chance to enter into high school (grades 10, 11, and 12). This practice of aptitude testing declined rapidly in the 1970s and has now disappeared. The criticism of tests that developed after May 1968 in France probably played a part in the discontent with the evaluation of aptitudes, but the main reason for the decline is the progressive generalization of the high school education, which made the identification of aptitudes reserves unnecessary at the end of 9th grade.

It must be stressed that in France, diplomas are national, which means that students who earn a given diploma, for example, the *baccalaureat* (the diploma obtained at the end of the high school that is required to enter a university), have followed exactly the same curriculum, with the same program, and passed the same national examination, whatever the area of France or the school in which they studied. The use of standardized tests for entry to a university, such as the Scholastic Aptitude Test (SAT) in the United States (where the diplomas and programs can be very different), is therefore not necessary in France. The homogeneity of programs and diplomas in the French system probably explains why, compared to the American system, the use of collective tests has now practically disappeared.

In French Switzerland, the situation was roughly similar with respect to intelligence testing. It should be stressed, however, that the educational system is different from France's, and, more importantly, that it differs within the different *cantons*, or provinces. Also, school psychologists do not exist in each canton, but are sometimes integrated within clinical guidance institutions, at least as concerns the primary school age range. As a result of this diversity, and also due to the small size of each region, there have never been general recommendations with respect to testing or national (or regional) norms, and the choice of psychological tools is left to the individual psychologists or to the institutions in which they are hired. The only generalized practice was to administer intelligence scales to youngsters who had to enter special education programs, because social insurance at the federal level was assuming school costs for those who presented an IQ lower than 75; by now, this rule has been changed, and psychologists show a renewed interest for both intelligence tests (such as the WISC or the K-ABC) and analytical testing.

The Health Care Domain

Several thousands of clinical psychologists are involved in the health care system. They practice psychological examinations in psychiatric hospitals or other institutions and in private practice. The situation is roughly identical in both countries. Since the 1960s, clinical training has been strongly influenced by the psychoanalytic approach, with a clear neglect of the psychometric approach. This evolution led to a decreased use of tests, specifically intelligence tests. Lately, this situation seems to have changed and, as a recent survey (Castro, Meljac, & Joubert, 1996) shows, clinical psychologists are reintroducing intelligence tests as one of their assessment tools. According to this survey, the most widely used tests are Wechsler's WPPSI, WISC, and Wechsler Adult Intelligence Scale (WAIS); Kaufman's K-ABC; and the Brunet-Lézine (a developmental scale for infants, based on Piaget's work on the sensori-motor stage).

The Work Domain

In the occupational field, intelligence tests are not widely used. A few companies use factorial batteries of aptitudes tests, for example, some companies in the transportation sector. Given the importance of the security issues in this field, there is a long tradition of psychometrics in this branch of industry, and these companies have often their own psychological testing service. This is the case for the French railway company (SNCF), the Parisian transportation company (RATP), and major French airlines. Private recruitment agencies, which many companies hire, use intelligence tests (in general, factorial tests of aptitude) only in approximately 30% of the cases. The majority of the recruitment procedures are limited to examining curricula vita, an interview, and often a graphological analysis – a curious French and French-Swiss specificity (Bruchon-Schweitzer & Ferrieux, 1991).

The French army administered aptitude tests to its recruits for a long time. These tests were systematically administered to the 400,000 young recruits enrolled each year, and the results were taken into account in their assignments. This passage is written in the past tense because mandatory military service was eliminated in 2001 and replaced by a professional army. The use of collective tests is thus also disappearing in the army.

In summary, the use of intelligence tests in social applications in France has experienced highs and lows. During the period between the 1950s and 1970s, rather massive applications of collective tests occurred in the education system, the army, and, more rarely, in industry. In French Switzerland the use of tests was never so massive, however. Because of criticism concerning these tests and the evolution of social institutions, the systematic use of collective tests has practically disappeared. On the contrary, the use of intelligence scales in individual psychological examinations for guidance and therapeutic goals has been maintained. After a period of relative disinterest in the 1970s and 1980s, intelligence tests have seen a renewed interest in the fields of education and health.

CONTEMPORARY RESEARCH ON INTELLIGENCE IN FRANCE
AND SWITZERLAND

Concerning the present state of research on intelligence in France and French Switzerland, we will distinguish three relatively original streams of studies. First, we will briefly describe developmental studies of intelligence or of cognitive development that can be qualified as post-Piagetian or neo-Piagetian. These are studies that extended Piaget's general theory of intellectual development to areas that he already pointed to but ignored or treated only in passing (e.g., language or time, or the role of the social context) or studies that combined the Piagetian theory (at least some of the Piagetian principles) with a very different approach (generally cognitive psychology), resting on different epistemological and psychological traditions. As Case (1992) already noted, the latter approaches cannot be considered simple extensions of the Piagetian theory or revisions along lines that Piaget might have followed himself. A second stream includes researchers who attempted to combine the Piagetian method with the differential or psychometric approach to intelligence. Third, there are a number of studies centered on the study of intelligence from an individual differences perspective, usually in adults. There is almost no research on new tests of intelligence, but there are a number of studies, particularly in France, that focus on the use of strategies in existent tests of intelligence and their link to individual differences.

Developmental Perspectives

Most of developmental research has retained Piaget's fundamentalist option, with little interest granted to individual differences, while, nevertheless, opening the way to the study of variability. Pierre Mounoud, a student of Piaget, conducted and initiated a large number of studies on infant and child development, basically related to motor and perceptual development (e.g., Mounoud & Hauert, 1982). Very early, he proposed a relatively radical departure from Piaget's model, particularly by suggesting the central role of representations during infancy and proposing cyclical recursion through substages at each level of development. Mounoud was always more interested, like most Piagetians and neo-Piagetians, in the development of central systems, and he defended the idea that action and thought (or procedural and declarative knowledge) entertain dialectic instead of unidirectional relationships in the course of development, considering that action is as much a product as a previous condition for thought (Mounoud, 1993; 1995). In his empirical research (in collaboration with Hauert, Vinter, Zesiger, and Badan, in particular), he has mainly studied the elaboration of "motor" invariants by children, in a similar way as Piaget investigated the "conceptual" ones (e.g., Badan, Hauert, & Mounoud, 1985; Mounoud et al., 1985; Zesiger, Mounoud, & Hauert, 1993). He has also studied the development of selective attention in the Stroop task and in pointing tasks, in collaboration with Koenig, Badan, and Pegoraro, in particular. Currently, he is studying, in collaboration with Moy, Perraudin, and Peyer, the role of perceived and evoked action on object recognition, by means of the semantic priming paradigm, to understand the structuration of semantic networks for manufactured objects.

Another direction, which was initiated in Geneva by Willem Doise under the inspiration of Piaget, was sociocognitive. Doise was a pioneer in empirically demonstrating the role of sociocognitive conflict in the development of intelligence and in promoting a strong research stream in developmental social psychology in Europe (e.g., Doise & Mugny, 1984). Although Doise himself more recently orientated his research toward the domains of social representations and of human rights, the line of research that he initiated with respect to the influence of social interactions on intelligence has been continued by Mugny and his students in Geneva, whose studies currently focus essentially on the themes of social marking and social influences (Doise, Mugny, & Perez, 1998; Mugny & Carugati, 1989), and by Perret-Clermont and her collaborators in Neuchâtel, mainly in educational psychology. Perret-Clermont conducted numerous studies on the role of peer interactions in cognitive development, most often with Piagetian tasks such as the conservation paradigm, showing that a child can take advantage of interactions with more advanced peers to restructure his or her answer and give a logically more complex response (e.g., Perret-Clermont, 1980). Such interactions create a sociocognitive conflict, which in turn accounts for the positive effect of social influence. A more recent line of studies consists of analyzing the social context itself, focusing on interactional patterns (e.g., Grossen & Perret-Clermont, 1994; Schubauer-Leoni & Perret-Clermont, 1997) finely observed in the context of tests (e.g., conservation or mathematical tasks) or didactic situations, and showing that children's cognitive abilities are the fruit of a social co-construction whose result does not depend solely on the child or the experimenter (teacher). These latter studies lead to conclusions that converge with propositions issued in a more Vygotskian perspective such as that adopted by a number of North American researchers.

Montangero (e.g., 1984) extended Piaget's theory to the domain of the development of the concept of time. He recently developed studies on the development of diachronic thinking, that is, on how one understands changes in a given situation taking into account past and future, possible changes, in relation with reasoning and problem solving abilities (Montangero, 1996a; 1996b).

In France, Lécuyer and Streri's research on infant development critically addressed the exclusive role attributed by Piaget to action in the structuration of cognition during the sensori-motor period. For Piaget, it is through motor activity that babies structure their environment, via the transformations that such activity makes possible. Piaget thought, for example, that intermodal transfer between vision and touch is only possible when vision and touch are coordinated by the activity of prehension. Lécuyer and Streri argue that motricity is too immature during the first months of life for the babies' action to play this structuring role; it does not allow an efficient transformation of their environment. In contrast, perceptual activity – which, however, does not impose a transformation on the environment – would already be sufficiently functional to play this structuring role (Lécuyer & Streri, 1992). This hypothesis about developmental processes at work in the sensori-motor period is tested by studies showing that capacities of transfer from touch to vision and from vision to touch develop between 2 and 4 months of age, that is, before vision and prehension are coordinated (Streri & Molina, 1993). Along the same line, Lécuyer and colleagues also consider that perceptual activity is sufficient to explain early abstract categorization – 3 versus 4 objects – observed in 3- and 5-month-old infants (Poirier, Lécuyer, & Cybula (2000).

As concerns the age period corresponding to concrete operations, studies conducted by Bideaud help to demonstrate that, besides action, various representational systems that Piaget considered to be only secondary (language, mental imagery, socially transmitted knowledge, etc.) play an important role in the development of logical operations. Operations of classification, seriation, and numeration were studied (Bideaud, 1988; Lautrey & Bideaud, 1985; Lautrey, Bideaud, & Puysegur, 1986). A review of the French language research on the developmental studies of numeration was recently published (Bideaud & Lehalle, 2002).

Concerning mental retardation, the line of work opened by Inhelder has been extended by Paour; he abandoned Inhelder's structural approach but pursued functional analyses that she had also conducted (Paour, 2001). Paour's research stresses the fact that several levels of processing co-exist in retarded children – that their responses are fragile and that non-cognitive factors (emotional, motivational) determine this fragility. This functional approach led Paour to develop a procedure of cognitive remediation that consists of training mentally retarded children to deal with abstract arbitrary relations as well as to defend, anticipate, and apply their inferences. Training thus results in improved comparison, classification, and even conservation skills, and ultimately in greater interest and more efficient performance in academic learning (Paour, 1992; Paour & Soavi, 1992; Paour, Cèbe, & Haywood, 2000).[1]

Within a neo-Piagetian framework (e.g., Demetriou, 1988), and in parallel with her work in collaboration with Lautrey and Rieben on individual differences and cognitive development (see section on Piagetian Theory and Individual Differences), de Ribaupierre pursued studies on the development of working memory or attentional capacity, considering that working memory tasks tap central resources in terms of activation and inhibition (e.g., de Ribaupierre, 2000; de Ribaupierre & Bailleux, 1995). These central or attentional resources develop with age and set upper limits on cognitive development as assessed by logical or reasoning tasks. In line also with approaches such as Engle's (Engle, Kane, & Tuholski, 1999) or Miyake's (Miyake & Shah, 1999), her hypothesis is that individual and developmental differences in working memory tasks reflect the interplay of underlying processes that are the same as those at work in fluid intelligence tasks. Her work has extended to a lifespan perspective, to understand the relationships among working memory, inhibition, and processing speed, assuming that the latter two constructs might account for age differences in working memory, whereas working memory in turn accounts for age differences in fluid intelligence tasks, both during childhood and during older adulthood (de Ribaupierre, 2002).

Another neo-Piagetian line of work considers limitations in inhibitory capacities as being the major constraint shaping cognitive development (Houdé, 2000). Following Dempster (1992) and Pascual-Leone (1987), Houdé considers that many Piagetian tasks are misleading situations, in which the correct answer implies the inhibition of a more primitive but salient response scheme. The assumption underlying this line of work is that development cannot be reduced to the coordination–activation of structural units, but that it also requires learning to inhibit a competing structure or scheme. This approach has been applied to the study of number (Houdé & Guichart, 2001), categorization, and reasoning. Concerning the role of inhibition in reasoning tasks, functional imagery

[1] For other, non–post-Piagetian, research on cognitive remediation in this part of the world, see Loarer (2003) and Büchel (2000, 2001).

techniques used during a Wason-like reasoning task have shown that, after a bias-inhibition training, a shift is observed in cortical activations from the posterior part of the brain to a left prefrontal network (Houdé et al., 2000).

Piagetian Theory and Individual Differences

The so-called French connection (Larivée, Normandeau, & Parent, 2000) is based on Reuchlin's (1964) proposal to articulate the developmental Piagetian and the factorial psychometric approaches. This proposal was in line with Cronbach's (1957) address to the APA meeting in which he argued for the unification of general and differential psychology. Reuchlin suggested that Piaget's notion of an overall structure could provide a theoretical explanation of the *g* factor of intelligence, on the one hand, and that the "horizontal decalage" well known in Piagetian studies could be linked to the existence of group factors in factorial approaches, on the other hand. These hypotheses proved to be very fruitful, because Reuchlin provided both a theoretical framework and some methodological avenues; they generated a host of empirical studies, among which the most extensive were those by Longeot and by Rieben, de Ribaupierre, and Lautrey.

Later on, Reuchlin (1978) developed another productive hypothesis, that of the existence of vicarious or equifunctional processes. The idea underlying the notion of vicariance is that, in many situations, every individual has in his or her repertoire several processes available to elaborate an adaptive response. The processes that are likely to fulfill the same function are considered vicarious because they can substitute for each other in cognitive functioning. This kind of redundancy is a fundamental property that offers the cognitive system its reliability and resistance to local impairments. These possibilities of substitution can also explain the various forms of intra- and interindividual variability, observed in cognitive strategies (Lautrey, 2003).

Longeot's first set of studies (Longeot, 1969) confirmed the existence of a general factor in formal operational tasks, observing not only that the Piagetian tasks tended to load on the same factor, but also that subjects at the formal operational level succeeded better than the others in all kinds of psychometric tests. Factor analyses also showed the existence of two group factors that were defined by Longeot as combinatorial and INRC group (Identity, Negation, Reciprocity, Correlation) (e.g., proportionality), corresponding to the two main structures defined by Piaget at this stage. Based on a second set of studies, Longeot (1978) proposed some years later a model of development in which several routes are possible within the same stage.

At the beginning of the 1980s, Rieben, de Ribaupierre, and Lautrey launched a set of studies to investigate inter- and intraindividual variability in Piagetian tasks in school-age children (de Ribaupierre & Rieben, 1995; de Ribaupierre, Rieben, & Lautrey, 1991; Rieben, de Ribaupierre, & Lautrey, 1983, 1990). Using several tasks representative of different domains, they proposed a qualitative type of analysis in terms of dimensions of transformation, which made it possible to conduct cross-domain comparisons; they also resorted to correspondence analyses and other, more quantitative techniques (Lautrey, de Ribaupierre, & Rieben, 1986). A quasi-longitudinal design was adopted, with two points of measurement, separated by a three-year interval. All analyses pointed to a large individual variability that is not compatible with a unidimensional model of development. Although a general factor was obtained, it was largely insufficient to account for all the variance. The analysis of the form of intraindividual variability and, in particular, the decalages that were termed "individual," as well as the observation of group factors in correspondence analyses, led these researchers to propose that there are different developmental pathways for different types of children; such a proposition was backed up by the variability observed in intraindividual change over the three-year interval. Combining these results with Reuchlin's model of vicarious processes led to a pluralistic model of development, in which several processes are likely to fulfill the same cognitive function; these processes would be present across all subjects, but their relative weight and their interplay might vary between individuals, these variations accounting then for variations in the developmental trajectories (Lautrey, 1993, 2002; Lautrey, & Caroff, 1996; de Ribaupierre, 1993).

Rieben et al. also studied severely learning disabled children and preadolescents with the same set of tasks, showing once again that inter- and intraindividual variability was very large (but not larger) in such a population (de Ribaupierre, & Rieben, 1987; Rieben, de Ribaupierre, & Lautrey, 1985; see also Doudin, 1992). Grégoire (1992) partly replicated these results in other types of learning disabled children. Rieben et al. resorted to the concept of executive control to account for the fact that these learning disabled children displayed discordant performances between Piagetian tasks in which they did not present a large developmental lag, on the one hand, and school performance, on the other hand. In particular, they suggested that, due to the Piagetian method of critical questioning that was used, the experimenter provided executive processes that children could not use spontaneously. Their conclusions thus converged with those of North American researchers involved in so-called metacognitive studies (e.g., Brown et al., 1983; Campione, & Brown, 1977).

The Differential Perspective

Research aiming at developing new tests of intelligence is currently practically nonexistent in this part of the world. The differential approach to intelligence tests seeks rather to reinterpret the behaviors observed in the existing tests within the framework of cognitive psychology. This approach can be illustrated by three examples of research on individual differences in the strategies used when taking intelligence tests. The first and the second studies are inspired by the vicariance model proposed by Reuchlin (see section on Piagetian Theory and Individual Differences), whereas the third study relies on a model of problem solving.

The first example is Rozencwajg's work on strategies in the Kohs Block design task. In a first phase of the research, video recordings of 17-year-old subjects were analyzed, and three different strategies were observed: a global and an analytic strategy (i.e., the two classically observed strategies) and a third strategy labeled "synthetic" (Rozencwajg, 1991), according to which subjects place the blocks in an order that conforms to the gestalt in the test design (for example, triangles, diamond, stripes). These strategies were related to the cognitive style of field dependence or independence: Field-independent subjects adopted more frequently the analytic and the synthetic strategies, whereas field-dependent subjects more often used global strategies. In the second phase of the research, the Kohs blocks task was computerized to facilitate the automatic collection of the behavioral indices characterizing the strategy of subjects (inspection time of the design, placement order of the cubes, anticipation, etc.). Software was devised to assess the subject's strategy by comparing its profile with a theoretical profile characterizing each strategy. This computerized version of the task is published (Corroyer & Rozencwajg, 1995). It has been used to study the developmental evolution of strategies from age 12 to adulthood. The results showed that the frequency of the global strategy decreases regularly with age, whereas the frequencies of the analytic and the synthetic strategies increase (Rozencwajg & Corroyer, 2002).

Another example is the research on the processes used for solving the D70, a *g* factor test used in France (Dickes & Martin, 1998). Each item of this test is made of a series of dominoes. Each domino has a given number of dots on each of its two faces. The configuration of the series of dominoes varies with items: They can form a line, a circle, a cross, and the like. One of the dominoes in the series is empty, and the task is to infer the rule of the series in order to find the number of dots that should be put on each face of this domino. A factorial analysis of the items showed that some of them load on a numerical factor, and others, on a spatial factor (Dickes & Martin, 1998). In a subsequent study, the strategies used by subjects to solve the D70 items were studied by relying on verbalizations and on reaction times (Rémy & Gilles, 1999). Two main strategies were found: The numerical strategy consists in counting the number of dots on each face of each domino and in searching for the underlying rule; the spatial strategy consists in relying on the symmetries present in the set of dominoes of a series. Some items can only be solved by using a numerical strategy; others are easily solved by a spatial strategy; and there are "equipotent" items, lending themselves to either strategy. In these equipotent items, subjects show a relatively stable preference for one of these two strategies. A clever and economic method for diagnosing the strategies was designed, using items with two possible correct answers, one for each strategy. This device is used to study the stability of strategies and their relations to aptitudes (Rémy, 2001).

Individual differences in strategy use in intelligence tests are also studied within the framework of problem solving. Richard and Zamani (2003) proposed a model in which the representation of the situation is formalized as an ordered list of constraints, a constraint being defined as a restriction on the set of a priori possible responses. Three types of constraints are distinguished: those relative to the interpretation of instructions, which may be correct or not; those relative to heuristics; and those relative to goals. The method of individual protocol analysis is used to identify the set of constraints that is sufficient to simulate the solving procedure adopted by a given individual. Within this approach, individual differences are accounted for by differences in the constraints underlying the representation (differences in either the list of constraints and/or their order of priority). This approach has been applied to the stategies used when solving a computerized version of the Passalong test. Results have shown that differences in the ability to discover and learn useful information from failures and impasses account for a large part of the individual differences observed in strategy and performance in this test (Richard & Zamani, 2002; Zamani & Richard, 2000).

CONCLUSION

How specific is the French and French–Swiss research on human intelligence? Two major contributions emanated from this part of the world: that of Binet, who proposed the first test of intelligence, and that of Piaget, who proposed the first developmental theory of intelligence. Both propositions were made outside, if not in rupture with, the mainstream of the time: associationism in the case of Binet and behaviorism in the case of Piaget. In both cases, too, the focus was placed on intelligence as a general characteristic of behavior: an undifferentiated product of a variety of performances as concerns Binet, an overall structure of behaviors as concerns Piaget. Both contributions also were perhaps too general.

Another characteristic of the French and French–Swiss research on intelligence is that they addressed fundamental rather than applied issues. Binet's test was adapted, improved, and disseminated in other regions than France, and the Piagetian theory has rarely been used to build techniques for assessing intelligence. The latter theory inspired more tentatives in educational psychology (but again more so in other countries), where it has been used to stress the role of action in the construction of knowledge; it also helped educators to draw attention to the limits that a developmental stage imposes on learning. This fundamental orientation of research still prevails today, and very few studies are devoted to the elaboration of new diagnostic tools.

Finally, and as a result, there is also a certain French and French–Swiss specificity in the theoretical orientations of the contemporary research on intelligence. From a developmental perspective, the influence of the Piagetian theory remains strong. Even though several features of the original theory have been disregarded or adapted, such as the purely structural approach that was only a part of Piaget's work, many facets of the theory were retained and often combined with other perspectives. This is the case, for example, of Piaget's constructivist option, of the structuring role of action or of decentration mechanisms. The objects of study often remain those that Piaget identified as particularly heuristic for a developmental study of intelligence. This is, for example, the case of the child's naive ideas, of the coordination of perspectives, of the permanence of objects and of number; even theories of mind, which are often considered a new field of study, is a concept very close to the Piagetian theory. From the standpoint of differential psychology, the influence of Reuchlin is obvious in the development of a fundamental approach, within which the different forms of inter- and intraindividual variability are studied from a theoretical point of view rather than from a psychometric and applied perspective; the objective is to integrate the study of variability within the general theories of cognition, to better understand the individuality as well as the universality of human intelligence.

References

Ajuriaguerra, J., & Tissot, R. (1966). Application clinique de la psychologie génétique [Clinical application of genetic psychology]. In *Psychologie et épistémologie génétiques. Thèmes piagétiens. [Genetic psychology and epistemology. Piagetian topics]* (pp. 333–338). Paris: Dunod.

Badan, M., Hauert, C.-A., & Mounoud, P. (2000). Sequential pointing in children and adults. *Journal of Experimental Child Psychology, 75*, 43–69.

Bang, V. (1988). *Textes choisis* [Selected texts]. Genève: Université de Genève.

Bideaud, J. (1988). *Logique et bricolage* [Logic and "handy doing"]. Lille: Presses Universitaires de Lille.

Bideaud, J., & Lehalle, H. (Eds.). (2002). *Le développement des activités numériques chez l'enfant* [The development of numerical activities in children]. Paris: Hermès Science Publications.

Binet, A. (1911a). *Les idées modernes sur les enfants* [The modern ideas on children]. Paris: Flammarion.

Binet, A. (1911b). Nouvelles recherches sur la mesure du niveau intellectuel chez les enfants des écoles [New studies on the measurement of the intellectual level of children in schools]. *L'Année Psychologique, 17*, 145–201.

Binet, A., & Henri, V. (1895). La psychologie individuelle [Individual psychology]. *L'Année Psychologique, 2*, 415–465.

Binet, A., & Simon, T. (1905). Méthodes nouvelles pour le diagnostic du niveau intellectuel des anormaux [New methods for the diagnostic of the intellectual level of abnormal persons]. *L'Année Psychologique, 11*, 191–244.

Binet, A., & Simon, T. (1908). Le développement de l'intelligence chez les enfants [The development of intelligence in children]. *L'Année Psychologique, 14*, 1–94.

Brown, A. L., Bransford, J., Ferrara, R. A., & Campione, J. C. (1983). Learning, remembering and understanding. In P. H. Mussen (Ed.), *Handbook of child psychology* (pp. 77–166). New York: Wiley.

Bruchon-Schweitzer, M., & Ferrieux, D. (1991). Une enquête sur le recrutement en France [A survey on recruitment in France]. *European Review of Applied Psychology, 41*, 9–17.

Büchel, F. P. (2000). Metacognitive control in analogical reasoning. In W. J. Perrig & A. Grob (Eds.), *Control of human behavior. Mental processes and consciousness* (pp. 203–224). New York: Wiley.

Büchel, F. P. (2001). DELF: Un programme métacognitif pour adolescents en formation professionnelle [A metacognitive program for adolescents in occupational training]. In P.-A. Doudin, D. Martin, & O. Albanese (Eds.), *Métacognition et éducation* [Metacognition and education] (2ᵉ éd., pp. 141–162). Berne: P. Lang.

Campione, J. C., & Brown, A. L. (1977). Memory and metamemory development in educable retarded children. In R. V. Kail & J. W. Hagen (Eds.), *Perspectives on the development of memory and cognition* (pp. 367–406). Hillsdale, NJ: Erlbaum.

Case, R. (1985). *Intellectual development. Birth to adulthood.* New York: Academic Press.

Case, R. (1992). Neo-Piagetian theories of intellectual development. In H. Beilin & P. B. Pufall (Eds.), *Piaget's theory: Prospects and possibilities* (pp. 61–104). Hillsdale, NJ: Erlbaum.

Castro, D., Meljac, C., & Joubert, B. (1996). Pratiques et outils des cliniciens français. Les enseignements d'une enquête [Practices and tools of the French clinicians. The lessons of a survey]. *Pratiques Psychologiques, 4*, 73–80.

Cattell, J. M. (1890). Mental tests and their measurement. *Mind, 15*, 373–380.

Claparède, E. (1905). *Psychologie de l'enfant et pédagogie expérimentale: Aperçu des problèmes et des méthodes de la nouvelle pédagogie* [Child psychology and experimental pedagogy: An overview of the problems and methods of the new pedagogy]. Genève: H. Kündig.

Corroyer, D., & Rozencwajg, P. (1995). *"Samuel," un outil de diagnostic automatique des stratégies dans la tâche des cubes de Kohs* ["Samuel," a tool for automatic diagnostic of strategies in the Kohs block-design task]. (Windows software for compatible PC, written in Pascal-Delphi). Cergy, France: Delta-Expert. Available from: http://www.delta.expert.com

Cronbach, L. J. (1957). The two disciplines of scientific psychology. *American Psychologist, 12*, 671–684.

Demetriou, A. (Ed.). (1988). *The Neo-Piagetian theories of cognitive development: Toward an integration.* Amsterdam: North Holland.

Dempster, F. N. (1992). The rise and fall of the inhibitory mechanism: Toward a unified theory of cognitive development and aging. *Developmental Review, 12*, 45–75.

Dickes, P., & Martin, R. (1998). Les composantes de l'intelligence générale du D70 [Components of the general intelligence in the D70 test]. *Psychologie et Psychométrie, 19*, 27–51.

Doise, W., & Mugny, G. (1984). *The social development of the intellect.* Oxford: Pergamon.

Doise, W., Mugny, G., & Perez, J. A. (1998). The social construction of knowledge: Social marking and socio-cognitive conflict. In U. Flick (Ed.), *The psychology of the social* (pp. 77–90). Cambridge: Cambridge University Press.

Doudin, P. A. (1992). Une comparaison de sujets de 11–13 ans avec et sans difficultés scolaires: Variabilité intra et inter-individuelle du niveau d'acquisition opératoire [A comparison of 11–13 year-old children with and without school problems: Intra- and interindividual variability of the operational level]. *Bulletin de Psychologie, 44*, 47–55.

Engle, R. W., Kane, M. J., & Tuholski, S. W. (1999). Individual differences in working memory capacity and what they tell us about controlled attention, general fluid intelligence, and functions of the prefrontal cortex. In A. Miyake & P. Shah (Eds.), *Models of working memory. Mechanisms of active maintenance and executive control.* (pp. 102–134). Cambridge: Cambridge University Press.

Feuerstein, R. (1979). *The dynamic assessment of retarded performers.* Baltimore: University Park Press.

Gardner, H. (1983). *Frames of mind: The theory of multiple intelligences.* New York: Basic Books.

Grégoire, J. (1992). *Evaluer l'intelligence de l'enfant. Echelle de Wechsler pour enfants* [Assessment of the child's intelligence. The Wechsler scale for children]. Liège: Margada.

Grossen, M., & Perret-Clermont, A. N. (1994). Psychosocial perspective on cognitive development: Construction of adult-child intersubjectivity in logic tasks. In W. De Graaf & R. Maier (Eds.), *Sociogenesis reexamined* (pp. 243–260). New York: Springer.

Houdé, O. (2000). Inhibition and cognitive development: Object, number, categorization, and reasoning. *Cognitive Development, 15*, 63–73.

Houdé, O., & Guichart, E. (2001). Negative priming effect after inhibition of number/length interference in a Piaget-like task. *Developmental Science, 4*, 119–123.

Houdé, O., Zago, L., Mellet, E., Moutier, S., Pineau, A., Mazoyer, B., & Tzourio-Mazoyer, N. (2000). Shifting from the perceptual brain to the logical brain: The neural impact of cognitive inhibition training. *Journal of Cognitive Neuroscience, 12*, 721–728.

Huteau, M. (2002a). Le débat Binet-Toulouse et les débuts de la psychologie différentielle en France [The Binet-Toulouse debate and the beginnings of differential psychology in France]. In A. Flieller, C. Bocéréan, J.-L. Kop, E. Thiébaut, A.-M. Toniolo, & J. Tournois (Eds.), *Questions de Psychologie Différentielle* [*Questions of differential psychology*]. Rennes: Presses Universitaires de Rennes.

Huteau, M. (2002b). *Psychologie, psychiatrie et société sous la Troisième République. La biocratie d'Edouard Toulouse (1865–1947)* [Psychology, psychiatry, and society under the third republic. The biocraty of Edouard Toulouse (1865–1947)]. Paris: L'Harmattan.

Inhelder, B., & Piaget, J. (1971). Closing remarks. In D. R. Green, M. P. Ford, & G. B. Flammer (Eds.), *Measurement and Piaget* (pp. 210–213). New York: McGraw Hill.

Inhelder, B. (1943/1963). *Le diagnostic du raisonnement chez les débiles mentaux.* [The diagnosis of reasoning in the mentally retarded]. Neuchâtel: Delachaux et Niestlé.

Larivée, S., Normandeau, S., & Parent, S. (2000). The French connection: Some contributions of French-language research in the post-Piagetian era. *Child Development, 71*, 823–839.

Laurendeau, M., & Pinard, A. (1968). *Les premières notions spatiales de l'enfant* [The first spatial notions of the child]. Neuchâtel: Delachaux et Niestlé.

Lautrey, J. (1993). Structure and variability: A plea for a pluralistic approach to cognitive development. In R. Case & W. Edelstein (Eds.), *The new structuralism in cognitive development: Theory and research on individual pathways* (pp. 101–114). Basel: Karger.

Lautrey, J. (2003). A pluralistic approach to cognitive differenciation and development. In R. J. Sternberg, J. Lautrey, & T. Lubart (Eds.), *Models of intelligence. International perspectives*. Washington, DC: American Psychological Association.

Lautrey, J., & Bideaud, J. (1985). Issues raised by training procedures in the study of cognitive development: The example of reasoning in inclusion tasks. In C. J. Brainerd & V. F. Reyna (Eds.), *Developmental psychology* (pp. 209–226). Amsterdam: North Holland.

Lautrey, J., Bideaud, J., & Pierre-Puységur, M. A. (1986). Aspects génétiques et différentiels du fonctionnement cognitif lors des tâches de sériation [Genetic and differential aspects of cognitive functioning in seriation tasks]. *L'Année Psychologique, 86*, 489–526.

Lautrey, J., & Caroff, X. (1996). Variability and cognitive development. *Polish Quarterly of Developmental Psychology, 2*, 71–89.

Lautrey, J., de Ribaupierre, A., & Rieben, L. (1986). Les différences dans la forme du développement cognitif évalué avec des épreuves piagétiennes: Une application de l'analyse des correspondances [Differences in the form of cognitive development assessed with Piagetian tasks: An application of correspondence analysis]. *Cahiers de Psychologie Cognitive, 6*, 575–613.

Lécuyer, R., & Streri, A. (1994). How should intelligence be characterized in the infant ? In A. Vyt, H. Bloch, & M. H. Bornstein (Eds.), *Francophone perspectives in mental development*. Hillsdale, NJ: Erlbaum.

Lezak, M. D. (1995). *Neuropsychological assessment* (3rd ed.). New York: Oxford University Press.

Loarer, E. (2003). Cognitive training for individuals with deficits. In R. J. Sternberg, J. Lautrey, & T. Lubart (Eds.), *Models of intelligence. International perspectives*. Washington, DC: American Psychological Association.

Longeot, F. (1969). *Psychologie différentielle et théorie opératoire de l'intelligence* [Differential psychology and operatory theory of intelligence]. Paris: Dunod.

Longeot, F. (1978). *Les stades opératoires de Piaget et les facteurs de l'intelligence* [Piaget's operatory stages and the factors of intelligence]. Grenoble: Presses Universitaires de France.

Miyake, A., & Shah, P. (Eds.). (1999). *Models of working memory. Mechanisms of active maintenance and executive control*. Cambridge: Cambridge University Press.

Montangero, J. (1984). Perspectives actuelles sur la psychogenèse du temps [Current perspectives on the psychogenesis of time]. *L'Année Psychologique, 84*, 433–460.

Montangero, J. (1996a). *Understanding changes in time*. London: Taylor & Francis.

Montangero, J. (1996b). Understanding things along the time dimension: An adequate developmental approach can provide partial explanations of behavior. *Swiss Journal of Psychology, 55*, 104–111.

Mounoud, P. (1993). The emergence of new skills: Dialectic relations between knowledge systems. In G. J. P. Savelsbergh (Ed.), *The development of coordination in infancy* (pp. 13–46). Amsterdam: North Holland.

Mounoud, P. (1995). From direct to reflexive (self-)knowledge: A recursive model. About (self-produced) actions considered as transformations. In P. Rochat (Ed.), *The self in early infancy: Theory and research* (pp. 141–160). Amsterdam: Elsevier Science Publishers.

Mounoud, P., & Hauert, C. A. (1982). Sensorimotor and postural behaviors: Their relation to cognitive development. In W. H. Hartup (Ed.), *Review of child development* (pp. 101–132). Chicago: The University of Chicago Press.

Mounoud, P., Viviani, P., Hauert, C.-A., & Guyon, J. (1985). Development of visuo-manual tracking in the 5- to 9 year-old child and the adult. *Journal of Experimental Child Psychology, 40*, 115–132.

Mugny, G., & Carugati, F. (1989). *Social representations of intelligence.* New York.

Nassefat, M. (1963). *Etude quantitative sur l'évolution des opérations intellectuelles* [Quantitative study of the evolution of intellectual operations]. Neuchâtel: Delachaux & Niestlé.

Oléron, P., Piaget, J., Inhelder, B., & Gréco, P. (1963). *Traité de psychologie expérimentale* (Vol. 7). *L'intelligence.* [Experimental psychology, its scope and method (Vol. 7). Intelligence]. Paris: Presses Universitaires de France [(1969).

Paour, J.-L. (1992). Induction of logic structures in the mentally retarded: An assessment and intervention instrument. In H. C. Haywood & D. Tzuriel (Eds.), *Interactive assessment.* New York: Springer.

Paour, J.-L. (2001). From structural diagnosis to functional diagnosis of reasoning: A dynamic conception of mental retardation. In A. Tryphon & J. Vonèche (Eds.), *Working with Piaget. Essays in honour of Bärbel Inhelder.* London: Psychology Press.

Paour, J.-L., Cèbe, S., & Haywood, H. C. (2000). Learning to learn in preschool education: Effect on later school achievement. *Journal of Cognitive Education and Psychology, 1*, 3–25.

Paour, J.-L., & Soavi, G. (1992). A case study in the induction of logic structures. In H. C. Haywood & D. Tzuriel (Eds.), *Interactive assessment.* New York: Springer.

Pascual-Leone, J. (1987). Organismic processes for neo-Piagetian theories: A dialectical causal account of cognitive development. *International Journal of Psychology, 22*, 531–570.

Perret-Clermont, A. N. (1980). *Social interaction and cognitive development in children.* London: Academic Press.

Piaget, J. (1947). *La psychologie de l'intelligence* [The psychology of intelligence]. Paris: Armand Colin.

Piaget, J. (1970). Piaget's theory. In P. H. Mussen (Ed.), *Carmichael's manual of child psychology (3rd ed., Vol. 1).* London: Wiley.

Piaget, J. (1972). Intellectual evolution from adolescence to adulthood. *Human Development, 15*, 1–12.

Piaget, J., & Inhelder, B. (1966). *La psychologie de l'enfant* [The psychology of the child]. Paris: Presses Universitaires de France.

Piéron, H., & Piéron, M. (1930). Instructions pour la fiche psychologique d'orientation professionnelle [Instructions for the psychological form of vocational guidance]. *Bulletin de l'Institut National d'Orientation, 2,* 197–206.

Poirier, C., Lécuyer, R., & Cybula, C. (2000). Categorization of geometric figures composed of three or four elements by 3-month-old infants. *Cahiers de Psychologie cognitive, 19,* 221–244.

Raison (La). (1952). Cahiers de psychopathologie scientifique. Numéro spécial consacré à la psychologie [Scientific psychopathology. Special issue devoted to psychology], n°4, 3–27.

Rémy, L. (2001). *Etude des stratégies de résolution d'une épreuve d'intelligence générale: Variabilité intra-individuelle et différences interindividuelles* [Study of the strategies of resolution in a task of general intelligence: Intraindividual variability and individual differences]. Unpublished doctoral dissertation, Université de Provence, Aix-en-Provence, France.

Rémy, L., & Gilles, P.-Y. (1999). Stratégies de résolution spatiale et numérique du D70 [Spatial and numerical strategies of resolution in the D70 test]. In M. Huteau & J. Lautrey (Eds.), *Approches différentielles en psychologie* [Differential perspectives in psychology]. Rennes: Presses Universitaires de Rennes.

Reuchlin, M. (1964). L'intelligence: Conception génétique opératoire et conception factorielle [Intelligence: Genetic, operatory, and factorial approaches]. *Revue Suisse de Psychologie Pure et Appliquée, 23,* 113–134.

Reuchlin, M. (1978). Processus vicariants et différences individuelles [Vicarious processes and individual differences]. *Journal de Psychologie, 2,* 133–145.

Rey, A. (1958). *L'examen clinique en psychologie* [The clinical assessment in psychology]. Paris: Presses Universitaires de France.

Rey, A. (1963). *Connaissance de l'individu par les tests* [The knowledge of the individual by the tests]. Bruxelles: Charles Dessart.

de Ribaupierre, A. (1993). Structural and individual differences: On the difficulty of dissociating developmental and differential processes. In R. Case & W. Edelstein (Eds.), *The new structuralism in cognitive development: Theory and research on individual pathways* (pp. 11–32). Basel: Karger.

de Ribaupierre, A. (2000). Working memory and attentional control. In W. Perrig & A. Grob (Eds.), *Control of human behavior, mental processes, and consciousness* (pp. 147–164). Mahwah, NJ: Erlbaum.

de Ribaupierre, A. (2002). Working memory and attentional processes across the lifespan. In P. Graf & N. Ohta (Eds.), *Lifespan development of human memory* (pp. 59–80). Cambridge, MA: The MIT Press.

de Ribaupierre, A., & Bailleux, C. (1995). Development of attentional capacity in childhood: A longitudinal study. In F. E.Weinert & W. Schneider (Eds.), *Memory performance and competencies: Issues in growth and development* (pp. 45–70). Hillsdale, NJ: Erlbaum.

de Ribaupierre, A., & Rieben, L. (1987). Investigation psychologique et épreuves piagétiennes: Des aspects structuraux aux contrôles exécutifs [Psychological examination and Piagetian tasks: From structural aspects to executive controls]. *Revue Suisse de Psychologie, 46,* 41–54.

de Ribaupierre, A., & Rieben, L. (1995). Individual and situational variability in cognitive development. *Educational Psychologist, 30,* 5–14.

de Ribaupierre, A., Rieben, L., & Lautrey, J. (1991). Developmental change and individual differences. A longitudinal study using Piagetian tasks. *Genetic, Social, and General Psychology Monographs, 117,* 285–311.

Richard, J.-F., & Zamani, M. (2003). A problem-solving model as a tool for analyzing adaptive behavior. In R. J. Sternberg, J. Lautrey, & T. Lubart (Eds.), *Models of intelligence. International perspectives.* Washington, DC: American Psychological Association.

Rieben, L., de Ribaupierre, A., & Lautrey, J. (1983). *Le développement opératoire de l'enfant entre 6 et 12 ans. Elaboration d'un instrument d'évaluation* [The operational development of the 6- to 12-year-old child. Development of an assessment tool]. Paris: Editions du CNRS.

Rieben, L., de Ribaupierre, A., & Lautrey, J. (1985). Le fonctionnement cognitif d'adolescents fréquentant des écoles de formation préprofessionnelle [The cognitive functioning of adolescents attending pre-occupational training schools]. *Revue Suisse de Psychologie, 44,* 119–133.

Rieben, L., de Ribaupierre, A., & Lautrey, J. (1990). Structural invariants and individual modes of processing: On the necessity of a minimally structuralist approach of development for education. *Archives de Psychologie, 58,* 29–53.

Rozencwajg, P. (1991). Analysis of problem solving strategies on the Kohs block design test. *European Journal of Psychology of Education, 1,* 73–88.

Rozencwajg, P., & Corroyer, D. (2002). Strategy development in a block design task. *Intelligence, 30,* 1–25

Schubauer-Leoni, M. L., & Perret-Clermont, A. N. (1997). Social interactions and mathematics learning. In T. Nunes & P. Bryant (Eds.), *Learning and teaching mathematics. An international perspective* (pp. 265–283). Hove: Psychology Press.

Seron, X. (1993). *La neuropsychologie cognitive* [Cognitive neuropsychology]. (2nd. ed.) Paris: Presses Universitaires de France.

Streri, A., & Molina, M. (1993). Visual-tactual and tactual-visual transfer between objects and pictures in 2-month-old infants. *Perception, 22,* 1299–1318.

Tort, M. (1974). *Le quotient intellectuel* [The intellectual quotient]. Paris: Maspero.

Toulouse, E., & Piéron, H. (1911). *Technique de Psychologie Expérimentale de Toulouse, Piéron et Vaschide* [Techniques of experimental psychology of Toulouse, Piéron, and Vaschide]. Paris: Douin.

Toulouse, E., Vaschide, N., & Piéron, H. (1904). *Technique de Psychologie Expérimentale [Techniques of Experimental Psychology].* Paris: Douin

Zamani, M., & Richard, J. F. (2000). Object encoding, goal similarity, and analogical transfer. *Memory and Cognition, 28,* 873–886.

Zazzo, R., Gilly, M., & Verba-Read (1966). *Nouvelle échelle métrique de l'intelligence* [New metric scale of intelligence]. Paris: Colin.

Zesiger, P., Mounoud, P., & Hauert, C.-A. (1993). Effects of lexicality and trigram frequency on handwriting production in children and adults. *Acta Psychologica, 82,* 353–365.

5

Research on Intelligence in German-Speaking Countries

Shu-Chen Li and Ute Kunzmann

RESEARCH ON INTELLIGENCE IN GERMAN-SPEAKING
COUNTRIES

Philosophical and scientific traditions of a given region shape a re-searcher's conception of intelligence and the methods he or she em-ploys to study mental abilities. In this chapter, we highlight an arguably unique aspect of intelligence research in German-speaking countries, namely, the emphasis on investigations of intellectual abilities from a contextual and/or lifespan perspective. In this research tradition, intel-lectual development has been considered as a dynamic lifelong process that involves a continual interplay between individuals' biological and sociocultural inheritances. Considering intellectual abilities from such a perspective goes hand in hand with a research focus on the processes and functions of intelligent behavior rather than with a focus on mea-suring and predicting the product of intelligence per se.

This chapter is divided into four sections. First, we review the historical tradition of lifespan developmental conceptions developed in German-speaking countries since the 18th century. Second, we introduce a modern dual-process model of lifespan intellectual devel-opment that emphasizes two distinct but interactive aspects of intelli-gence (i.e., the mechanics and pragmatics of the mind). Although many researchers in this region do not explicitly focus on developmental aspects, in our view, components and processes of intelligence stud-ied can be related to the dual-process model. Hence, we use this model as an organizational framework to help structure the review of contem-porary research on intelligence in the third part of the chapter. As will become evident, the goals of past investigations of intelligence have been diverse and ranged from understanding information-processing, sensory, and neurobiological correlates of academic intellectual abilities to studying higher-order reasoning, complex problem solving, giftedness, and the regulation of intelligent behavior in everyday life. In the final section of this chapter, we offer a summary of past research on intelligence in German-speaking countries and discuss possible future investigations.

THE HISTORICAL TRADITION OF LIFESPAN DEVELOPMENTAL CONCEPTIONS

The origins of modern systematic research on lifespan developmental psychology can be traced back to 18th century philosophical and scientific work from Germany and neighboring countries. We will discuss some of the major historical contributions that seem to have shaped contemporary lifespan conceptions of intelligence with their focus on systemic and dynamic processes (i.e., in these conceptions, intelligence is thought to result from a continuing exchange between biological and cultural factors; for more comprehensive historical reviews, see also Groffmann, 1970, or Reinert, 1979).

The Notion of Lifespan Development in the 18th Century

Johann Nicolaus Tetens (1736–1807) was one of the first scholars to consider human development as a lifelong process starting with an individual's conception and ending with his or her death. At least two aspects of Tetens's work have had important implications for modern lifespan approaches to intelligence.

First, Tetens directed his attention to developmental processes as they unfold over the entire lifespan rather than as they occur in specific periods of life such as infancy or childhood. He described "developmental courses" of "mental powers" or "mental capacities" (e.g., intellectual achievement, reasoning ability, memory, or self-determination) as consisting of three phases characterized by (a) growth or increases in performance level, (b) temporal stability at maximum performance levels, and (c) decline or decreases in performance.

Second, Tetens assigned extraordinary plasticity to human nature and, thus, discussed multiple opportunities for environmental, cultural, and individual factors to jointly affect an individual's intellectual development. On a more general level, Tetens stated that the development of intellectual abilities is shaped by two broad and heterogeneous sets of variables – an individual's biological dispositions and his or her sociocultural context.

Friedrich August Carus (1770–1808) was born when Tetens published his book on human nature and development. The concept of psychophysical parallelism was important in Carus's work as well. Similar to Tetens, he discussed biological and sociocultural forces of intellectual development and considered their interplay as a co-constructive process.

Building on these ideas, Carus (1808) developed a "general age-oriented science," which he took to be an ideal description of human ontogenetic lifespan development. With his psychological description of four life periods – childhood, youth, adulthood, and old age – Carus emphasized that chronological age itself is a carrier variable rather than a psychological determinant. For this reason, he considered life periods or chronological stages as continuous and not clearly separable. In his conceptualization, each life period is thought to be a preparation for the next, and life periods are not sharply divided; rather, they flow gradually into one another. In addition to this lifespan orientation, Carus also discussed an individual's gender, temperament, or nationality as factors that can have important influences on intellectual development.

Successions in the 19th and Early 20th Century

Adolphe Quetelet (1796–874) was a Belgian who published some of his work in German. Similar to Tetens and Carus, Quetelet was interested in individual development over the entire lifespan rather than in specific life periods. What was new in Quetelet's approach was his effort to study age differences in intellectual performances (e.g., in memory performance) empirically. He studied individuals of different ages and related their performance levels to the statistical "average performance." Put in modern terms, Quetelet conducted cross-sectional studies that were often based on lifespan samples. With the assessment methods available to him at his time, Quetelet acknowledged all human characteristics and investigated not only intellectual but also physical and moral development. He was able to report developmental curves for a diverse set of characteristics, with each curve demonstrating a maximal performance level at a certain time in the lifespan and minimal magnitudes at the beginning and the end of life.

Given his empirical findings, Quetelet was aware of the complex structure of mental abilities. He completed his writing about intellectual abilities and their developmental curves in 1838 with a visionary view: "Our intellectual abilities have their origin, growth, and decline, each of them reaching its maximum at a certain age. It would be important to know which of them matures first and which one last" (p. 424). The essence of this notion continues to play a major role in modern theories on intelligence. For example, Cattell (1971) states in his investment theory that more biologically driven fluid abilities mature first and are invested into the acquisition of crystallized abilities involving culture-based knowledge and skills (see also Horn, 1982).

Moving into the early 20th century, Charlotte Bühler (1933), at the University of Vienna, published a series of books on developmental psychology that clearly cover a lifespan orientation. In line with Carus's psychophysical parallelism, she emphasized the usefulness of establishing a psychological analog to biological life curves. Bühler predicted that life curves of psychological characteristics, such as intellectual abilities, show growth in childhood and youth, relative stability in adulthood, and regression in old age.

Together, the historical work on lifespan development just reviewed here has had important influences on modern lifespan conceptions of intellectual development in German-speaking countries. As will become evident in the remainder of this chapter, modern lifespan conceptions of intelligence have directed researchers' attention to the study of the processes and contexts that shape the development and plasticity of human intellectual abilities. One consequence of this orientation might be that many researchers in German-speaking countries have considered laboratory or experimental studies as complementary approaches to understanding developmental and individual differences in intelligence (e.g., Baltes, 1987; Klix, 1985; Weinert, Schneider, & Knopf, 1988).

Two Domains of Intellectual Functioning: Cognitive Mechanics and Pragmatics

The dual-process theory of lifespan intellectual development (Baltes, 1987; Baltes, Staudinger, & Lindenberger, 1999) is consistent with many elements of the historical approaches to intelligence reviewed above and is in some aspects similar to the theory of fluid-crystallized intelligence developed in North America (Cattell, 1971; Horn, 1982).

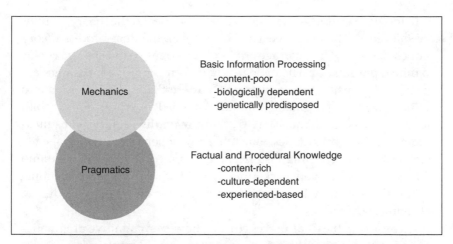

FIGURE 5.1. The dual-process model of lifespan intellectual development distinguishes between cognitive mechanics and pragmatics of intellectual functioning (adapted from Baltes, Staudinger, & Lindenberger, 1999, with permission from the Annual Review of Psychology, Vol. 50 © 1999 by Annual Reviews www.annualreviews.org).

The model distinguishes between two interacting aspects of intellectual functioning: the mechanics and pragmatics of the mind (for a graphical representation, see Figure 5.1). The biology-based *cognitive mechanics* refer to basic information-processing primitives for memorizing and learning. These primitives are implemented by the neurophysiological architecture of the mind as it evolved during biological evolution and unfolds during individual ontogenesis. Although akin to the notion of fluid intelligence, the concept of cognitive mechanics emphasizes more explicitly relationships between psychometrically defined fluid abilities and the speed, accuracy, and coordination of elementary information-processing mechanisms.

The primary constituent of the *cognitive pragmatics* is culture-based knowledge that individuals acquire through lifelong learning and engagement in their social and physical environment. Although similar to the notion of crystallized intelligence, the concept of cognitive pragmatics covers a more heterogeneous set of specific abilities ranging from verbal-based knowledge (closer to the core of crystallized intelligence) to practical, social, or emotional competencies. Being able to speak and to understand the social implications of language or to acquire the knowledge and skills related to professional expertise are two examples of cognitive pragmatics.

In line with Cattell's (1971) investment theory and the theory of fluid-crystallized intelligence (see also Horn, 1982), the dual-process theory proposes different lifespan age gradients for cognitive mechanics versus cognitive pragmatics: The biologically driven cognitive mechanics are postulated to display an early growth pattern that is then invested into the acquisition of pragmatic skills and knowledge. Whereas most abilities of cognitive mechanics start to decline in midlife, abilities subsumed under cognitive pragmatics, which heavily depend on individuals' life experiences and learning histories, are assumed to remain stable into old age. In a related vein, Ackerman (1996) has stated that occupational and avocational knowledge can be maintained or even improved during late adulthood.

According to the dual-process theory, however, cognitive pragmatics show declines in old age as soon as the efficiency of cognitive mechanics falls below a certain threshold. Predictions of late-life declines in cognitive pragmatics are even more reasonable considering that the role of the biology-based cognitive mechanics in regulating the culture-based cognitive pragmatics increases with age, whereas the efficacy of cultural or contextual supports decreases (Baltes, 1997).

Proponents of lifespan developmental conceptions of intelligence have emphasized the causes, contexts, and processes of intellectual development over the lifespan. In contrast to the psychometric tradition of intelligence testing pioneered by Binet (1890), intelligence is not thought to be a static entity that results from basic information-processing mechanisms, matures in childhood, and manifests itself in adolescence or early adulthood. From the perspective of lifespan psychology, intelligence reflects a dynamic system of contextualized and adaptive functions that individuals continue to acquire throughout the entire lifespan. There has been a similar emphasis on contextual contingencies operating in an individual's physical and social environment as sources of individual differences in North America. The main focus of North American bio-ecological theories, however, has been on child development (e.g., Bronfenbrenner, 1979; Bronfenbrenner & Ceci, 1994).

For the remainder of this chapter, we use the dual-process theory as an organizational framework for our review of contemporary research on intelligence in German-speaking countries. We start with a line of research that has focused on various substrates of the cognitive mechanics, in particular, information-processing mechanisms and neurobiological processes. We then review a second line of research that has investigated the sub-components and processes of cognitive pragmatics.

After reviewing research on cognitive mechanics and pragmatics separately, we review empirical studies on the interplay between these two domains.

THE MECHANICS OF THE MIND

Over the last two decades a growing number of researchers in Europe and North America have been exploring information-processing mechanisms, along with their neurobiological substrates, that may underlie individual differences in intelligence. As discussed previously, the dual-process theory of intellectual development states that cognitive mechanics are more directly subserved by information-processing mechanisms and their neurobiological substrates than cognitive pragmatics.

Traditionally, cognitive mechanics (or fluid-type cognitive abilities) have been measured by psychometric tests indicating perceptual speed (e.g., digit-symbol substitution), memory (e.g., paired-associate recall), or reasoning (e.g., Raven Progressive Matrices). In this section, we discuss research conducted in the German language area that explored the relations between cognitive mechanics and its elementary information-processing and neurobiological correlates.

Cognitive Mechanics and Elementary Information Processing

Speed of Information Processing
The speed with which information can be processed is a basic constituent of cognitive mechanics. Reaction time (RT) derived either from choice reaction tasks along the line of the Hick paradigm (Hick, 1952) or from performance in discrimination tasks using the inspection time (IT) paradigm (Vickers, Nettelbeck, & Wilson, 1972) has consistently been found to correlate with abilities indicating cognitive mechanics. The correlations usually range from $r = .20$ to $r = .70$ (for a review, see Neubauer, 1997).

In their study with adults (age range from 18 to 53 years), for example, Neubauer and Bucik (1996) reported correlations of $r = .19$ to $r = .27$ between individual differences in Raven's test and individual differences in the speed of accessing short-term and long-term memory as measured by the Sternberg and the Posner tests.

In a second study with a lifespan sample (age range from 6 to 89 years), overall processing speed, measured by a variety of elementary information-processing tasks, correlated positively with a composite measure of cognitive mechanics, indicated by perceptual speed, memory, and reasoning. The correlations were of moderate size and ranged from $r = .40$ to $r = .70$ (S.-C. Li et al., in press). Interestingly, the association between processing speed and cognitive mechanics was significantly stronger in the youngest and oldest age groups than in age groups falling in between (S.-C. Li et al., in press). This finding supports the so-called differentiation–dedifferentiation hypothesis of intellectual abilities (e.g., Baltes et al., 1980; Lienert & Crott, 1964).

Past studies have also investigated intraindividual variability in processing speed as indicating a lack of processing robustness (e.g., Hultsch et al., 2000; S.-C. Li et al., in press; Rabbitt, Osman, & Moore, 2001). For example, in their study of children aged between 11 and 15 years, Neubauer, Bauer, and Hoeller (1992) have reported that variability of RT derived from the Hick paradigm correlated negatively ($r = -.25$) with individual differences in reasoning ability as assessed by Raven's test. In the study by S.-C. Li et al. (in press), overall processing robustness (i.e., low intraindividual variability in processing speed) was related to measures of individual differences in cognitive mechanics and to measures of individual differences in processing speed, whereby correlations were of equal size. In addition, processing robustness had unique predictive validity beyond processing speed in the aging portion of the lifespan (S.-C. Li et al., in press). These findings underscore the importance of considering the lifespan dynamics of intellectual development. It might well be that the relations between sub-domains of intelligence and their substrates change as a function of lifespan development itself.

In order to facilitate research on processing speed, researchers in German-speaking countries have developed several paper-and-pencil tests to assess this ability. For instance, Oswald and Roth (1987) developed the Zahlen-Verbindungs-Test (ZVT). The ZVT is a variant of the trail-making test with matrices of randomly arranged numbers from 1 to 90. Individuals are asked to connect the numbers in an ascending order by drawing lines. Lehrl and Fischer (1990) developed a short general intelligence test (Kurztest für Allgemeine Intelligenz; KAI), which measures the minimum amount of time that an individual requires to process one bit of information when reading series of letters. Given that the alphabet contains 26 letters, the reading of a single letter involves 4.7 bits of information ($26 = 2^{4.7}$).

In past research, the ZVT showed moderately high and positive correlations with other general intelligence measures (correlations were in the range of $r = .70$), whereas the KAI showed somewhat weaker correlations to these other measures (i.e., correlations were $r = .40$ and lower). More recently, Neubauer and Knorr (1998) developed a comprehensive paper-and-pencil test battery to assess information processing speed. This battery includes memory-scanning tests, letter-matching tests, and coding tests that correlate with the Raven's test and other measures of general intelligence (e.g., the Berlin Model of Intelligence Structure, Jäger, 1982, 1984; Jäger, Süß, & Beauducel, 1997) in the 0.3 to 0.5 range. When all subtests were taken into consideration, the entire test battery accounted for about 60% of the variance in individual differences in general intelligence.

Akin to the general emphasis on understanding intellectual functioning both as process and product that permeates intelligence research in this region, the Berlin Model of Intelligence Structure (BIS) cross-classifies each cognitive test with respect to (1) an operation and (2) a content facet. Operation is further categorized into four ability groups (reasoning, memory, creativity, and speed), whereas content is divided into three groups (figural, numerical, and verbal). Taken as a whole, the 12 "operation by content" combinations (4×3) are thought to represent general intelligence. It is also possible to average test scores across either content domains or operations to consider individual differences in certain operations (e.g., reasoning) or individual differences in certain content domains (e.g., verbal intelligence). In other words, by factoring groups of variables that are homogeneous within one of the two facets but are heterogeneous in the other facet, one can either extract the four operational or the three content factors. According to BIS, any given mental ability is a linear combination of two factors. Put in conceptual terms, mental abilities are thought to encompass a process and a content aspect.

Memory

Working memory capacity – an individual's ability to simultaneously hold information in immediate memory while transforming the same or other information (Baddeley, 1986) – has been thought to be a basic constituent of cognitive mechanics. Researchers in German-speaking countries have developed comprehensive computerized tests for working memory capacity that include the assessment of processing aspects (e.g., simultaneous storage, coordination, and supervision) and content aspects of working memory. The processing aspects are measured by reading span, short-term memory, memory updating, and spatial coordination. The content aspects are measured in terms of verbal, numerical, and spatial tasks (e.g., Oberauer et al., 2000). Past research with adult samples has shown that individual differences in reasoning ability were positively correlated with three factors of working memory, namely, spatial, verbal-numerical, and processing-speed factors (e.g., Süß et al., 2002; Wittmann & Süß, 1999).

A growing number of studies in German-speaking countries have taken an integrated approach involving both psychometric measures of intelligence and cognitive experimental tasks to understand the relation between intellectual competencies and memory development during childhood (e.g., the Munich Longitudinal Study, see Weinert & Schneider, 1999, for overview). In the context of the Munich Longitudinal Study, a large battery of verbal memory tasks (i.e., memory span, text recall, and recall in a sort-recall task) was employed to assess non-strategic (e.g., short-term memory span) and strategic (e.g., recall in a sort-recall task) memory performance. Analyzing the data of about 200 children initially aged between 3 and 4 years and followed up longitudinally over 9 years, Weinert and Schneider (1995) found that short-term memory span (e.g., non-strategic memory) correlated moderately with verbal and non-verbal intelligence (correlations ranged from $r = .19$ to $r = .50$).

Neurobiological Correlates of Cognitive Mechanics and Information Processing

Recent developments in cognitive neuroscience have motivated researchers to investigate functional relationships between information-processing primitives and their neurobiological substrates subserving the cognitive mechanics of intellectual functioning. With the development of neuroimaging techniques, it is now possible to examine relations between individual differences in intelligence and patterns of topographical distribution of cortical activation. For example, EEG (electroencephalogram) mapping methods can be used to measure short-lasting variations in electrophysiological background activity in response to elementary cognitive processing. It has been demonstrated in young adult samples that individuals who performed better on Raven's test showed more focused and specific patterns of cortical activation (indication of more efficient neuronal information processing) than individuals who performed worse on the Raven test (Neubauer, Freudenthaler, & Pfurtscheller, 1995; Neubauer, Sange, & Pfurtscheller, 1999).

Although functional relationships between individual differences in intelligence and the topographical distribution of cortical activation have been observed, questions as to how these functional relations arise await further empirical and theoretical explication. Recently, a cross-level integrative neurocomputational framework was developed to investigate neurobiological substrates of cognitive mechanics in terms of neuromodulation of cortical representations. Specifically, individual differences in the efficacy of neuromodulation can be modeled by a network parameter regulating the signal-to-noise ratio of information processing. Simulation studies have suggested that individuals with less efficient neuromodulation (e.g., older adults) exhibit noisy neural information processing, which in turn leads to less distinctive cortical representations. These less distinctive representations might be implicated in elementary cognitive processes, such as processing speed, working memory, and attention, which underlie intellectual development and aging (S.-C. Li, Lindenberger, & Frensch, 2000; S.-C. Li, Lindenberger, & Sikström, 2001; S.-C. Li & Sikström, 2002).

THE PRAGMATICS OF THE MIND

A second main focus of intelligence research conducted in German-speaking countries has been on identifying the bodies of pragmatic knowledge and skills that help individuals to adapt to changes in biological and contextual conditions inevitably taking place throughout the lifespan. For example, knowledge about complex life problems, abilities related to a person's social and emotional functioning, or motivational competencies have been investigated as the pragmatic aspects of intelligence that play an important role for the lives of adults in today's world. In contrast to cognitive mechanics, pragmatic forms of intelligence heavily depend on an individual's social and cultural context and deal with problems of everyday life. These problems are by definition poorly defined and are characterized by multiple acceptable solutions. As discussed previously, abilities subsumed under the heading of cognitive mechanics are relatively more biology based and are most helpful when people deal with intellectual or academic problems that typically represent parts of reality in a highly specific and compartmentalized way.

In the next section, we discuss work on pragmatic forms of intelligence such as high-order reasoning, complex problem solving, giftedness, motivational competencies, and wisdom-related knowledge. As will be evident, these research fields have focused on different phases of the lifespan and are based on rather different theoretical models and empirical paradigms. What proponents of these rather disparate research fields have in common, however, is the belief that intelligence and intelligent behavior encompasses more than scholastic abilities.

Higher-Order Reasoning

Higher-order reasoning involves relatively complex conceptual and semantic knowledge rather than the more basic perceptual based analogies as assessed by Raven's Progressive Matrices or related tests designed to measure components of cognitive mechanics. Past studies on cognitive development during childhood demonstrated that verbal and non-verbal psychometric tests of intelligence show meaningful and consistent correlations with non-psychometric measures of higher-order reasoning and thinking abilities (e.g., false beliefs as measured by the theory of mind task, or logical and scientific reasoning; e.g., Schneider et al., 1999). Specifically, during the preschool years, relatively weak correlations ranging from $r = .18$ to $r = .35$ were found between performance on the theory of mind task and two psychometric intelligence tests, namely, the German versions of the Wechsler Intelligence Scale and the Culture Fair Test. Psychometric measures of intelligence were also weakly correlated with the traditional Piagetian Number Conservation task (correlations were $r = .24$ or lower). The correlations between psychometric "test" intelligence and non-psychometric measures of formal operation, logical reasoning, and scientific reasoning seem to become stronger in later childhood and adolescence (in school-aged children, correlations were moderate to high and ranged from $r = .45$ to $r = .60$). As for research into the component processes of analogical reasoning involving complex conceptual knowledge, Klix and Bachmann (1998) found that semantic similarities among concepts play an important role in analogy construction.

Complex Problem Solving

Cognitive pragmatics also involve solving problems as they occur in everyday life. Since about 1975, research on problem solving in German-speaking countries has shifted its attention from simple to complex problems due to ideas developed by Dietrich Dörner (e.g., Dörner et al., 1983). In this region, research on complex problem solving has emphasized that efficient or good solutions to complex problems require the simultaneous activation and synchronization of cognitive, motivational, and social competencies. Summarizing German and European approaches, Frensch and Funke (1995, p. 18) defined complex problem solving in the following way:

Complex problem solving occurs to overcome barriers between a given state and a desired goal state by means of behavioral and/or cognitive, multistep activities. The given state, goal state, and barriers between given state and goal state are complex, change dynamically during problem solving, and are intransparent. The exact properties of the given state, goal state, and the barriers are unknown to the solver at the outset, complex problem solving implies the efficient interaction between a solver and the situational requirements of the task and involves a solver's cognitive, emotional, personal, and social abilities and knowledge.

To study people's problem-solving abilities, complex computerized scenarios with varying degrees of complexity and domain reality, such as the problem of managing a small town or of using complex technical equipment have been utilized (e.g., the LOHHAUSEN project, Dörner et al., 1983). These scenarios have a number of characteristics in common: (1) they contain a large number of interconnected variables to be influenced by the problem solver, (2) the nature of the interconnections among variables is unknown and can take all kinds of functions implemented in dynamic systems (e.g., linear, curve-linear, exponential), (3) variables can change autonomously, and (4) the problem solver has to pursue multiple and sometimes contradictory goals simultaneously (e.g., managing labor market, tax regulation, housing policy). Using these computerized scenarios, Dörner and associates have provided support for the view that complex problem solving requires cognitive as well as motivational and emotional skills (Dörner, 1986; Dörner & Wearing, 1995).

Over the last two decades, two different schools or traditions have emerged in research on complex problem solving. As Buchner (1995) reviewed, the first tradition (Bamberg School, for example, Dietrich Dörner, Harald Schaub, Stefan Strohschneider) continues to be interested in predicting complex problem solving abilities by variables such as intelligence, self-esteem, or social-emotional skills. The second tradition (Bonn School, for example, Axel Buchner, Joachim Funke, Horst Müller) has focused on system attributes of complex problems (e.g., degree of time delay, number of side effects) and their influences on the solving of complex problems (e.g., the DYNAMIS project, Funke 1986; see also Funke, 2001, for review of other formal frameworks).

Decision Making: A Domain of Complex Problem Solving
Real-life complex problem solving often involves decision making that requires individuals to consider arrays of information and choose among alternatives under the constraints of limited time, money, knowledge, and other resources. Decision-making researchers in this region have argued that adaptive thinking and rationality is regulated and bounded by ecological, social, and emotional contingencies (e.g., Gigerenzer, Todd, & the ABC Research Group, 1999; Gigerenzer & Selten, 2001; Todd & Gigerenzer, 2000). Viewed from the framework of adaptive behavior and cognition, when confronted with complex decision making, individuals tend to exploit the way information is structured in the particular environments and social contexts, thus extracting simple heuristics to aid reasoning and decision making. For example, with limited knowledge individuals could still make rather accurate inferences about cities in foreign countries (e.g., population and size) by basing their judgments and decisions on how well they recognize the names of these cities (Goldstein & Gigerenzer, 2002).

"Test" Intelligence and Complex Problem Solving
Empirical evidence for the correlation between measures of complex problem solving and intelligence is not unequivocal. In some studies, subcomponents of intelligence correlated substantially with the ability to solve complex problems. For example, the processing capacity factor as measured by the BIS (Jäger, 1982), which encompasses the ability to recognize relations among variables and to construct formal logical inferences, showed a substantial correlation with complex problem solving ability (e.g. Süß, Kersting, & Oberauer, 1991). Other studies, however, have yielded nonsignificant or low correlations (for reviews see Beckmann & Guthke, 1995; Kluwe et al., 1991).

Beyond Traditional Conceptions: Dynamic Assessment, Expertise, and Giftedness

The lack of correspondence between traditional intelligence measures and complex problem-solving tests has motivated alternative conceptions that focus on the contextual and cumulative developmental aspects of intelligence. For example, the so-called operative intelligence tests (e.g., Dörner, 1986) are designed to measure more complex and hence ecologically more valid processes that may be affected by non-cognitive personal characteristics, such as emotional reactions or assertive behavior.

Dynamic Assessment and Testing-the-Limit Procedure

The concept of learning test (Lerntest) focuses on the progressive developmental aspect and stresses that measures of intelligence should not only assess an individual's momentary intellectual performance in a one-time administration of the usual static test procedure. Rather, dynamic assessments and repeated measures should be taken to assess the individual's learning potential as well (e.g., Guthke, 1972, 1992; Guthke & Stein, 1996). More specifically, according to Guthke (1993), the validity of intelligence tests can be increased if they involve multiple sessions so that individuals have the opportunity to practice test items in several trials and get feedback on their performance. With this procedure, individual differences in familiarity with a test are minimized. The concept of learning tests is closely related to the "testing-the-limit" experimental procedure adopted in research on lifespan cognitive development (e.g., Baltes & Kliegl, 1992; Kliegl, Smith, & Baltes, 1990) and in clinical research (e.g., Schmidt, 1971).

Practice and Expertise

In a related vein, given the lack of success of traditional measures of intelligence in predicting exceptional achievements and professional success in several domains (Ericsson & Smith, 1991), some researchers have turned their attention to studying the processes and contexts of expertise skill acquisition, instead of searching for basic innate abilities. This line of research has shown that the amount of practice (e.g., deliberate practice, Ericsson, Krampe, & Tesch-Römer, 1993; Krampe & Ericsson, 1996) as well as the quality of practice (e.g., strategy acquisition, Kliegl et al., 1989) both contribute to expertise performance.

Giftedness

The research focusing on the assessment and education of gifted individuals also inclines more toward contextualized multidimensional typographical models of giftedness that emphasize both biological and non-biological influences. Giftedness is considered as an individual's cognitive and motivational potential for achieving excellence in one or more areas, such as mathematics, language, art, and music (e.g., Heller,

1991; Heller et al., 2000; Klix, 1983). In a large longitudinal study involving six cohorts of children and adolescents, researchers of the Munich Longitudinal Studies of Giftedness assessed a wide variety of cognitive, personality, and achievement measures. Overall, results from these studies supported the multidimensional topographical conception of giftedness. Achievements in specific domains were best predicted by domain-specific tests. Personality factors such as motivation played a mediating role in achievement, and traditional IQ measures alone were not enough to predict developments in specific talents (Heller, 1991; Perleth & Heller, 1994; Trost, 1993).

In summary, research on complex problem solving, expertise, and gifted performance all point to the usefulness of expanding the traditional concepts of intelligence. Specifically, researchers have emphasized the importance of taking the contextual constraints and opportunities as well as the individual's learning potential and motivation into consideration.

Life Management: Motivational Competencies

Most recently, researchers have also been focusing more specifically on component processes of the cognitive pragmatics, such as motivational and emotional competencies that are involved in solving problems of everyday life. In the following, we review three overarching theories that have focused on the motivational competencies assumed to play an important role in developmental regulation and positive developmental outcomes (e.g., high life satisfaction, good physical health, professional success, or life insight). These models have emphasized the active role that individuals play in shaping their own development and that of others. Although the models describe and explain motivational processes involved in life management from a lifespan perspective, most of the empirical studies have focused on the life period of adulthood and old age.

The Model of Selection, Optimization, and Compensation (SOC)
The SOC model states that three cognitive-motivational processes, selection, optimization, and compensation, play a major role in achieving successful development, defined as the simultaneous maximization of gains and minimization of losses over time (Baltes & Baltes, 1990; Freund & Baltes 2000; Freund, K. Z. H. Li, & Baltes, 1999; Marsiske et al., 1995).

The SOC model is a general model of development and applies to various domains of functioning (e.g., identity formation, social relations, academic achievement) and to different levels of analysis (e.g., societal, group, or individual level). Much of the past work on SOC has been based on an action-theoretical formulation of this model. In this approach, processes of selection, optimization, and compensation have been studied in the context of personal goals (e.g., Freund & Baltes, 2000; Freund et al., 1999). The action-theoretical framework of SOC states that a person actively shapes his or her development through (1) the selection of personal goals, (2) the optimization of functioning in selected goal domains, and (3) the compensation of losses in goal-relevant means.

Two paradigms were developed to assess the three processes of selection, optimization, and compensation. First, a self-report questionnaire asks study participants to indicate whether they engage in behaviors that were categorized as selection, optimization, and compensation or in alternative, that is, non-SOC behaviors. Past work on the basis of this questionnaire has suggested that adults who reported making greater use of the three SOC processes also reported higher subjective well-being as, for example, indicated by high levels of positive affect or life satisfaction. Furthermore, during midlife, individuals express the strongest preference for SOC-related behaviors whereas older adults report less engagement in the strategies of goal pursuit (Freund & Baltes, 1998).

Second, SOC was studied from a process-oriented perspective. The purpose of this line of research was to investigate the mechanisms and functions of setting, pursuing, and maintaining personal goals. For example, one study has examined how young adults manage two central developmental tasks of their age – establishing themselves in their work life and founding a family (Wiese & Freund, 2000). As one would predict on the basis of the SOC model, selecting and optimizing the two goals sequentially rather than simultaneously turned out to be the more adaptive strategy. Other studies have investigated the effects of framing goals either in terms of achieving maximum gains (optimization) or in terms of counteracting a loss in goal-relevant means (compensation) on individuals' motivation. These studies have shown that younger adults are more persistent in their goal-pursuit when trying to achieve higher levels of performance (optimization) than when trying to counteract a loss (compensation). In contrast, older adults show higher persistence when engaged in compensation of a loss than when aiming at maximum performance (Freund, submitted).

Taken together, work on the SOC model strongly suggests that goal selection, optimization, and compensation are essential for a successful individual development over the adult lifespan. Interesting avenues for future studies will be to investigate the interplay of these three processes (e.g., selection might only be adaptive when a person has the means to achieve the selected goals) and to explore contextual opportunities or constraints as moderators of the relations between SOC processes and successful development (e.g., pursuing a subjectively important goal might be maladaptive in a non-supportive environment).

The Model of Primary and Secondary Control (OPS)

In the context of a second theoretical model on motivational competencies as co-producers of a successful lifespan development, J. Heckhausen and Schulz (1999) have delineated three principles that people must consider when selecting and optimizing personal goals. The first one is age-appropriateness, that is, goal selection and pursuit should be in accordance with biological and societal opportunity structures. A second principle refers to the balancing of positive and negative trade-offs for other life domains and future life course (e.g., pursuing a career as a world-class athlete may be devastating for other important life goals that compete for resources such as education or friendships). The third principle pertains to the maintaining of a reasonable degree of diversity and the avoidance of dead ends (e.g., although selectivity in resource investment is necessary for a successful development, it potentially becomes dysfunctional if pushed to the extreme).

J. Heckhausen and her colleagues have provided consistent evidence that adults tend to regulate their development in accordance with these three principles and that considering these principles when selecting and pursuing certain life goals goes hand in hand with higher levels of self-esteem and subjective well-being. For example, attempts to change the environment so that it fits the goals of an individual (primary control) have been shown to be most adaptive when the goals are actually reachable. In contrast, attempts to fit in with the environment by revisiting one's goals and downscaling one's internal standards (secondary control) seem to be adaptive when an individual's goals have become unrealistic and inappropriate because of biological and/or societal constraints in a given life situation (e.g., J. Heckhausen, Wrosch, & Fleeson, 2001; Wrosch & Heckhausen, 1999; Wrosch, Heckhausen, & Lachman, 2000). In their research, J. Heckhausen and her colleagues have used a questionnaire that assesses people's general and domain-specific strategies of primary and secondary control.

The Model of Assimilation and Accommodation

There is a third cognitive-motivational model on successful development that has instigated a great number of empirical studies in German-speaking countries, namely, the model of assimilative and acommodative coping with discrepancies between desired and actual self-states proposed by Brandtstädter and his colleagues (e.g., Brandtstädter & Greve, 1994; Brandtstädter & Rothermund, 1994; Brandtstädter, Wentura, & Rothermund, 1999). In contrast to the two cognitive-motivational models reviewed previously, this model focuses primarily on old age and an individual's ability to age successfully. The model of assimilation and accommodation was originally developed to explain a widely known paradox, namely, that subjective indicators of personal well-being (e.g., life satisfaction, self-esteem) remain more or less stable into old age – despite the increase in physical, social, and cognitive losses in this life period (e.g., Kunzmann, Little, & Smith, 2000; Staudinger, 2000).

According to Brandtstädter and his colleagues, adults basically have two different ways of achieving a match between actual and desired developmental outcomes. In the assimilative mode, a person actively tries to change an unsatisfying situation so that it becomes compatible with a desired self-definition. In the accommodative mode of coping, a person tries to eliminate discrepancies between actual and desired self by adjusting personal goals and preferences. Thus, accommodative processes deactivate goals and projects that turned out to be unreachable (e.g., Brandtstädter et al., 1999).

Brandtstädter and his colleagues have developed a trait questionnaire to assess assimilative and accommodative strategies of coping. Their empirical research with this questionnaire suggests that these two strategies form two highly distinct coping competencies. Individual differences in assimilative and accommodative coping are stable and are generally related to differences in various indicators of subjective well-being. Past research suggests that both coping competencies play an important role in subjective indicators of successful aging. This research has also shown that the adaptivity of assimilative and accommodative coping strategies depends on a person's actual control potential. Specifically, under limited potentials accommodative coping becomes more adaptive, whereas assimilative coping becomes more and more dysfunctional (for an overview of this research, see Brandtstädter et al., 1999).

Wisdom: Expert Knowledge about Life Meaning and Conduct

During the last decade, a number of promising wisdom models have been proposed in psychological research both in North America and Germany (e.g., Baltes & Staudinger, 2000; Kramer, 2000; Sternberg, 1990, 1998). Although these models slightly differ in what aspects of wisdom they highlight, each model emphasizes wisdom's potential in contributing to a good life on both the individual and societal level. In the following, we will present the model of wisdom that was developed by Paul Baltes and his colleagues (for recent overviews, see Baltes & Staudinger, 2000; Baltes, Glück, & Kunzmann, 2002).

The Berlin Wisdom Model

Baltes and his colleagues have considered wisdom as a prototype of cognitive pragmatics. Informed by the dual-process model of intelligence introduced previously, wisdom has been defined as an expert *knowledge* about the fundamental pragmatics of life (e.g., Baltes & Smith, 1990; Baltes & Staudinger, 2000). The term "fundamental pragmatics of life" refers to knowledge about important and difficult aspects of life meaning and conduct and includes knowledge about life planning, life management, and life review. Wisdom involves both general knowledge about human nature that transcends a given cultural context and historical period and specific knowledge about the variations in life meaning and conduct.

In their empirical paradigm, the Berlin group instructs participants to read short vignettes about difficult and uncertain life problems and to think aloud about these problems (e.g., Baltes & Smith, 1990; Baltes & Staudinger, 2000). For example, a problem concerning life review reads: "In reflecting upon their lives, people sometimes realize that they have not achieved what they had once planned to achieve. What could they do and consider?" Participants' transcribed responses are evaluated by trained raters using five criteria that, according to the theory, indicate wisdom-related knowledge: rich factual knowledge in the fundamental pragmatics of life, rich procedural knowledge in the fundamental pragmatics of life, lifespan contextualism, value relativism and tolerance, and awareness and management of uncertainty. Past empirical research has shown that the assessment of wisdom-related knowledge on the basis of these five criteria exhibits satisfactory reliability and validity (for an overview, see Baltes & Staudinger, 2000).

As this theoretical and empirical definition of wisdom signals, the bodies of factual and procedural knowledge typical of wisdom clearly go beyond those included in traditional conceptions of intelligence (e.g., logical reasoning or abstraction). Wisdom also differs from other pragmatic abilities (e.g., practical or motivational skills). There is certainly conceptual overlap. Similar to wisdom, these abilities refer to our everyday lives rather than to content-free laboratory tasks. They are, however, tailored to relatively specific problems. For example, creativity can help people in dealing with a problem that requires a particular invention or social intelligence can help in getting along with others well. But how can a person coordinate his or her behavior so that it is appropriate from a broader viewpoint extending over time and a given context? It is here that wisdom-related knowledge comes into play. Wisdom can help individuals place a situation into a broader context, to acknowledge the triangulation of the past, present, and future, to consider not only their own needs but also those of the people around them, and to deal with life's uncertainties constructively (Baltes & Staudinger, 2000; Kunzmann & Baltes, 2003; see also Sternberg, 1998).

Past research in the Berlin Wisdom Project has focused on the development of wisdom-related knowledge during adulthood. Age-comparative studies suggest that wisdom-related knowledge, as one aspect of cognitive pragmatics, remains fairly stable during most of adulthood (Pasupathi, Staudinger, & Baltes, 2001, Staudinger, 1999). The stability of wisdom-related knowledge is good news when one considers the relatively early decline in many other cognitive abilities, especially in cognitive mechanics. However, the stability also suggests that age is not a sufficient condition for wisdom-related knowledge to develop.

The ontogenetic model of wisdom developed by Baltes and his colleagues (e.g., Baltes & Staudinger, 2000) states that multiple individual and social resources need to interact to ensure age-related improvement in wisdom-related knowledge. As to individual resources, Staudinger, Lopez, and Baltes (1997) provided evidence that a person's test intelligence, temperament, and lifestyle play an important role in wisdom-related knowledge. In addition, we know from other studies that certain life experiences contribute considerably to wisdom-related knowledge. People with higher levels of wisdom-related knowledge appear to have been exposed to existentially critical life events or to work in professions that provide contact with others grappling with serious problems (Staudinger et al., 1998). A recent study suggests that people's emotional lives, values, and interpersonal behavior also play a significant role in wisdom-related knowledge (Kunzmann & Baltes, 2002).

Together, findings from the Berlin Wisdom Project suggest that there is not an easy road to wisdom. Rather, acquiring higher levels of wisdom might at times be cumbersome; multiple facilitative conditions and factors need to interact for wisdom to develop. Importantly, however, it has been shown in intervention studies that many people have the capacity to enhance their wisdom-related knowledge. Staudinger and Baltes (1996) found, for example, that adults could improve their wisdom-related performance when they had the opportunity for social discourse.

INTERPLAY BETWEEN COGNITIVE MECHANICS AND PRAGMATICS

Thus far we have reviewed studies that have addressed cognitive mechanics and cognitive pragmatics separately. In the following, we will review work that has considered the two broad categories of intellectual functioning simultaneously. The main purpose of this work was to investigate whether cognitive mechanics versus pragmatics relate to different classes of variables and show different lifespan trajectories.

Considering cognitive mechanics and pragmatics as two highly distinct factors does not mean to imply that these two aspects of intellectual functioning are independent or mutually exclusive. On the contrary, in everyday life, many intellectual tasks simultaneously require mechanic and pragmatic abilities. According to the dual-process model of intellectual functioning, the cognitive pragmatics and mechanics represent an interactive and collaborative system. Only recently, some research efforts have been devoted to exploring the interplay between the mechanic and pragmatic aspects of intelligence. In the following section, we will review a recent study on the interaction between culture-based mnemonic skills and cognitive mechanics in old and very old age.

Cognitive Mechanics and Pragmatics: Differential Biological and Cultural Influences

To test predictions derived from the dual-process model of intelligence, past studies have examined the relations of cognitive pragmatics and mechanics to biological and cultural factors. For example, using data from the Berlin Aging Study (age range 70 to 100 years), Baltes and Lindenberger (1997) have shown that basic sensory processing (visual and auditory acuity) is more highly correlated with cognitive mechanics, as assessed by tests of perceptual speed, memory, and reasoning, than cognitive pragmatics as assessed by tests of verbal and practical knowledge. In contrast, socio-biographical characteristics showed stronger correlations with the cognitive pragmatics than cognitive mechanics (see Figure 5.2). Notably, the correlation between sensory functioning and

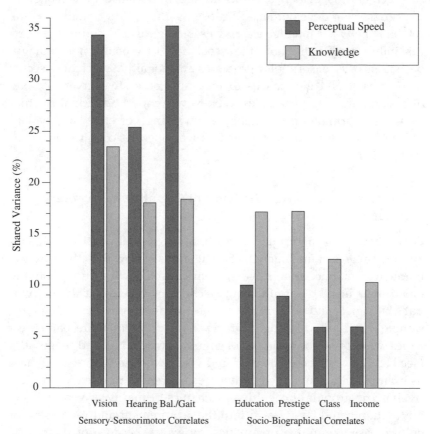

FIGURE 5.2. Differential associations of perceptual speed (a marker of cognitive mechanics) and verbal knowledge (a marker of cognitive pragmatics) with biological and socio-biographical indicator (adapted with permission from Lindenberger & Baltes, 1997, © 1997 by the American Psychological Association).

overall intellectual functioning was significantly stronger in a younger sample (age range 25 to 69 years) than in the sample of older people ($r_{young} = .37$ vs. $r_{old} = .71$). Similar evidence has been found in a different study. S.-C. Li, Jordanova, and Lindenberger (1998) showed that individual differences in tactile sensory discrimination ability is predictive of intelligence even in a younger sample. Subdividing the sample into two age groups revealed, however, that this relation was stronger in the older group (age range 41 to 50 years; $r = .49$) than in the younger group (age range 30 to 40 years; $r = .23$).

Together this evidence points to the importance of considering the progressive developmental history as a factor that modulates the relations between intelligence and its biological and cultural contextual influences. Furthermore, the association between the more biology-based sensory–sensorimotor processes and cognitive mechanics seems to be robust and generalizes to measures other than average level of performance. For example, week-to-week intraindividual fluctuations in sensorimotor performance (i.e., walking) correlated highly with episodic and special memory performance, aspects of cognitive mechanics (S.-C. Li, Aggen, et al., 2001).

Differential Lifespan Age Gradients of Cognitive Mechanics and Pragmatics

Given that biology and culture contribute differentially to the mechanics and pragmatics of intelligence, investigations of how these two aspects of intellectual functioning develop, remain, and decline throughout life could offer insights into the complex interplay between the individual's biological and cultural inheritances in development. In a lifespan sample with individuals aged 6 to 89 years, differential lifespan trajectories were found for measures of cognitive mechanics and pragmatics (see Figure 5.3; perceptual speed and verbal knowledge are given here as example indicators of cognitive mechanics and pragmatics, respectively). The growth of cognitive mechanics primarily driven by brain maturation could be invested into the acquirement and refinement of culture-based cognitive pragmatics. However, because of their close ties to biology and thus to genome-based processes, continuous loss of cognitive mechanics starts early in adulthood. In contrast, the decline in culture-based pragmatics, represented by knowledge and language, has a later onset, and it is less pronounced (S.-C. Li et al., in press).

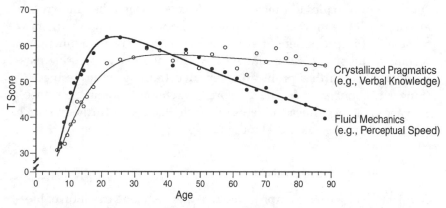

FIGURE 5.3. Differential lifespan age gradients of cognitive mechanics and pragmatics. Plotted are means of 31 age groups (on average $n = 10$ per group). T-scores are computed based unit-weight composite of 9 and 6 indicator variables for cognitive mechanics and pragmatics, respectively.

Culture-Based Mnemonics and Cognitive Mechanics in Old and Very Old Age

The testing-the-limits paradigm has been developed to allow individual differences in intellectual functioning to be measured independently of age-related declines in biology-based cognitive mechanics. It assesses the amount of reserved cognitive plasticity by training people with adaptive training procedures and testing them at their optimal performance level (e.g., Kliegl, Smith, & Baltes, 1990). For example, old people in their 60s to 80s can still improve their memory recall up to 10 words by using a culture-based mnemonic technique, although cognitive mechanics at this stage of life usually do not yield recall of more than 5 words (Baltes & Kliegl, 1992).

Notably, however, although the need for culture increases during the aging process, the efficacy of culture decreases with age (Baltes, 1997). This is because the continual declines in cognitive mechanics predominately driven by brain aging leave the older individuals decreasing pools of information-processing resources for the maintenance and further refinement of culture-based cognitive pragmatics. The aging-related decline of cognitive mechanics limits the maximum performance level. Specifically, older adults can benefit from the culture-based mnemonics to a certain degree; however, even after 38 sessions of training, they do not reach the young adults' level of performance. Thus finally, in very old age, cognitive mechanics may fall below the limit required for cognitive pragmatics to function well. Recent research has shown that although people in their fourth age (i.e., 80 years and onward) show some initial improvement after being instructed to use the mnemonic technique, most of them no longer have the necessary cognitive plasticity to allow further profit from repeated training with the method (Singer, Lindenberger & Baltes, in press; Singer & Lindenberger, 2000). Advanced old age thus represents major challenges for further research on lifespan intellectual development.

CONCLUSION AND OUTLOOK

In this chapter we have emphasized that there is a long tradition of lifespan psychology in German-speaking countries that has affected current intelligence research conducted in this region. Much of the research reviewed above has considered intellectual functioning from a contextual and/or lifespan developmental perspective (e.g., Baltes, 1987; Weinert et al., 1988). Besides the lifespan developmental context, a main goal of past work on intelligence in this region has been to understand the causes, processes, and functions of intelligent behavior (e.g., Dörner & Wearing, 1995; Guthke, 1992; Klix, 1985; Jäger, 1982).

The distinction of the more biology/information-processing based and the more culture/life-experience based aspects of intelligence has motivated a number of researchers to investigate the components involved in these two broad domains of intelligence and their interrelations in more detail. For example, the research on sensorimotor processes involved in supporting the cognitive mechanics has recently extended the scope of intelligence to seemingly non-intellectual tasks such as the coordination of sensorimotor behavior. This line of research suggests that as people grow older, they allocate an increasingly larger amount of cognitive resources to tasks that require maintaining balance in an upright posture or walking. Similar findings exist for other domains of locomotion and motor behavior (K. Z. H. Li et al., 2001; Lindenberger, Marsiske, & Baltes, 2000). Past research on cognitive pragmatics has extended research on intelligence to abilities that are highly relevant to individuals' everyday life and involve an integration of intellectual, motivational, and emotional competencies (e.g., Baltes, et al., 1999; Baltes & Staudinger, 2000; Kunzmann & Baltes, 2002). Furthermore, the emphasis on lifespan intellectual development has extended intelligence research in this region from studies on child cognitive development and educational application to research on adult life management in many practical life domains and issues of cognitive aging. Taken together, studies reviewed in this chapter are one indication that intelligence and cognitive processes encompass many facets and multiple levels and may manifest differently depending on an individual's age and the associated biological and socio-cultural constraints at different life periods.

Given that both biology and culture are involved in constituting intelligent behavior, one line of future research needs to outline interactive processes at different levels contributing to an integrated whole of biocultural influences on intellectual development across the lifespan. As a first attempt, a recent meta-theoretical framework relates the co-evolution of cognition and culture on the human phylogenetic time scale with the co-construction of neurobiological and socio-cultural processes in shaping intellectual development on the individual ontogenetic scale. It helps to bring to the foreground the interconnections between interactive processes currently studied at different levels (S.-C. Li, 2003). Research questions of cultural influences on self construal, parental style, schooling, and language development that subsequently affect the development of different aspects of cognitive mechanics and pragmatics would further our understanding of the dynamic interplay between these two aspects of intelligence.

Regarding further investigation on how individuals allocate their cognitive resources to achieve "intelligent" adaptive behavior in different contexts, Krampe and Baltes (in press) have proposed a general theoretical framework that delineates the wide range of everyday contexts to which people of different ages can allocate their intellectual resources. A fascinating topic for future research will be the systematic investigation of differences in resource allocation across a wide range of life contexts that involve individuals at different life periods.

References

Ackerman, P. L. (1996). A theory of adult intellectual development: Process, personality, interests, and knowledge. *Intelligence, 22*, 227–257.

Baddeley, A. D. (1986). *Working memory*. Oxford, England: Clarendon Press.

Baltes, P. B. (1987). Theoretical propositions of life-span developmental psychology: On the dynamics between growth and decline. *Developmental Psychology, 23*, 611–626.

Baltes, P. B. (1997). On the incomplete architecture of human ontogeny: Selection, optimization, and compensation as foundation of developmental theory. *American Psychologist, 52*, 366–380.

Baltes, P. B., & Baltes, M. M. (1990). Psychological perspectives on successful aging: The model of selective optimization with compensation. In P. B. Baltes

& M. M. Baltes (Eds.), *Successful aging: Perspectives from the behavioral science* (pp. 1–34). New York: Cambridge University Press.

Baltes, P. B., Cornelius, S. W., Spiro, A., Nesselroade, J. R., & Willis, S. L. (1980). Integration versus differentiation of fluid/crystallized intelligence in old age. *Developmental Psychology, 16,* 625–635.

Baltes, P. B., Glück, J., & Kunzmann, U. (2002). Wisdom: Its structure and function in successful lifespan development. In C. R. Snyder & S. J. Lopez (Eds.), *Handbook of positive psychology* (pp. 327–350). New York: Oxford University Press.

Baltes, P. B., & Kliegl, R. (1992). Further testing of limits of cognitive plasticity: Negative age differences in a mnemonic skill are robust. *Developmental Psychology, 28,* 121–125.

Baltes, P. B., & Lindenberger, U. (1997). Emergence of a powerful connection between sensory and cognitive functions across adult life span: A new window to the study of cognitive aging? *Psychology and Aging, 12,* 12–21.

Baltes, P. B., & Smith, J. (1990). Toward a psychology of wisdom and its ontogenesis. In R. J. Sternberg (Ed.), *Wisdom: Its nature, origins, and development* (pp. 87–120). New York: Cambridge University Press.

Baltes, P. B., & Staudinger, U. M. (2000). A metaheuristic (pragmatic) to orchestrate mind and virtue toward excellence. *American Psychologist, 55,* 122–136.

Baltes, P. B., Staudinger, U., and Lindenberger, U. (1999). Lifespan psychology: Theory and application to intellectual functioning. *Annual Review of Psychology, 50,* 471–507.

Beckmann, J. F., & Guthke, J. (1995). Complex problem solving, intelligence, and learning ability. In P. A. Frensch and A. Fink (Eds.), *Complex problem solving: The European perspective* (pp. 178–195). Hillsdale, NJ: Erlbaum.

Binet, A. (1890). Perceptions d'enfants [Children's perceptions]. *Revue Philosophique, 30,* 582–611.

Birren, J. E. (1964). *Relations of development and aging.* Springfield: Thomas.

Brandtstädter, J., & Greve, W. (1994). The aging self: Stabilizing and protective processes. *Developmental Review, 14,* 52–80.

Brandtstädter, J., & Rothermund, K. (1994). Self-percepts of control in middle and late adulthood: Buffering losses by rescaling goals. *Psychology and Aging, 9,* 265–273.

Brandtstädter, J., Wentura, D., & Rothermund, K. (1999). Intentional self-development through adulthood and later life: Tenacious pursuit and flexible adjustment of goals. In J. Brandtstädter & R. M. Lerner (Eds.), *Action and self-development: Theory and research through the life span* (pp. 373–400). Thousand Oaks, CA: Sage.

Bronfenbrenner, U. (1979). *The ecology of human development.* Cambridge, MA: Harvard University Press.

Bronfenbrenner, U., & Ceci, S. J. (1994). Nature-nurture reconceptualized in developmental perspective: A bioecological model. *Psychological Review, 101,* 568–589.

Buchner, A. (1995). Basic topics and approaches to the study of complex problem solving. In P. A. Frensch & J. Funke, (Eds.), *Complex problem solving: The European perspective* (pp. 27–63). Hillsdale, NJ: Erlbaum.

Bühler, C. (1933). *Der menschliche Lebenslauf als psychologisches problem* [The human life course as a psychological concept] Leipzig: Hirzel.

Carus, F. A. (1808). *Geschichte der psychologie* [The history of psychology] Leipzig: Barth & Kummer.

Cattell, R. B. (1971). *Abilities: Their structure, growth, and action.* Boston: Houghton Mifflin.

Dörner, D. (1986). Diagnostik der operativen intelligenz [Diagnosis of operative intelligence]. *Diagnostica, 32,* 290–308.

Dörner, D., Kreuzig, H. W., Reither, F., & Stäudel, T. (1983). *Lohhausen. Vom umgang mit unbestimmtheit und komplexität* [Lohhausen. On dealing with uncertainty and complexity]. Bern, Switerland: Hans Huber.

Dörner, D., & Wearing, A. J. (1995). Complex problem solving: Toward a theory. In P. A. Frensch and A. Fink (Eds.), *Complex problem solving: The European perspective* (pp. 65–99). Hillsdale, NJ: Erlbaum.

Ericsson, K. A., & Smith, J. (Eds.). (1991). *Toward a general theory of expertise – Prospects and limits.* Cambridge: Cambridge University Press.

Ericsson, K. A., Krampe, R. Th., & Tesch-Römer, C. (1993). The role of deliberate practice in the acquisition of expert performance. *Psychological Review, 100,* 363–406.

Frensch, P. A., & Funke, J. (1995). Definitions, traditions, and a general framework for understanding complex problem solving. In P. A. Frensch and J. Funke (Eds.), *Complex problem solving: The European perspective* (pp. 3–25). Hillsdale, NJ: Erlbaum.

Freund, A. M., *Striving for more or maintaining what you have: Age-differential motivational effects of optimization and compensation.* Manuscript submitted.

Freund, A. M., & Baltes, P. B. (1998). Selection, optimization, and compensation as strategies of life management: Correlations with subjective indicators of successful aging. *Psychology and Aging, 13,* 531–543.

Freund, A. M., Li, K. Z. H., & Baltes, P. B. (1999). Successful development and aging: The role of selection, optimization, and compensation. In J. Brandtstädter & R. M. Lerner (Eds.), *Action and self-development: Theory and research through the life span* (pp. 401–434). Thousand Oaks, CA: Sage.

Funke, J. (1986). *Komplexes problemlösen. Bestandsaufnahme und perspektiven* [Complex problem solving. State of the art and perspectives]. Heidelberg: Springer.

Funke, J. (2001). Dynamic systems as tools for analyzing human judgement. *Thinking and Reasoning, 7,* 69–89.

Gigerenzer, G., Todd, P. M., & the ABC Research Group (1999). *Simple heuristics that make us smart.* New York: Oxford University Press.

Gigerenzer, G., & Selten, R. (2001). (Eds.). *Bounded rationality: The adaptive toolbox.* Cambridge, MA: MIT Press.

Goldstein, D. G., & Gigerenzer, G. (2002). Models of ecological rationality: The recognition heuristic. *Psychological Review, 109,* 75–90.

Groffman K. I. (1970). Life-span developmental psychology in Europe. In L. R. Goulet & P. B. Baltes (Eds.), *Life-span developmental psychology. Research and theory* (pp. 54–67). New York: Academic Press.

Guthke, J. (1972). *Zur Diagnostik der intellektuellen Lernfähigkeit* [On the measurement of intellectual learnning ability]. Berlin: Deutscher Verlag der Wissenschaften.

Guthke, J. (1992). Learning tests – The concept, main research findings, problems, and trends. *Learning and Individual Differences, 4*, 137–152.

Guthke, J. (1993). Development in learning potential assessment. In J. H. M. Hamers, K. Sijtsma, & A. J. M. Ruijssenaars (Eds.), *Learning potential assessment* (pp. 43–67). Amsterdam: Swets & Zeitlinger.

Guthke, J., & Stein, H. (1996). Are learning tests the better version of intelligence tests? *European Journal of Psychological Assessment, 12*, 1–13.

Heckhausen, J., & Schulz, R. (1999). Selectivity in life-span development. Biological and societal canalizations and individuals' developmental goals. In J. Brandtstädter & R. M. Lerner (Eds.), *Action and self-development: Theory and research through the life span* (pp. 67–103). Thousand Oaks, CA: Sage.

Heckhausen, J., Wrosch, C., & Fleeson, W. (2001). Developmental regulation before and after a developmental deadline: The sample case of "biological clock" for childbearing. *Psychology and Aging, 16*, 400–413.

Heller, K. A. (1991). The nature and development of giftedness: A longitudinal study. *European Journal for High Ability, 2*, 174–188.

Heller, K. A., Moenks, F. J. Sternberg, R. J., & Subotnik, R. F. (Eds.). (2000). *International handbook of giftedness and talent* (2nd ed.). New York: Elsevier Applied Science.

Hick, W. E. (1952). On the rate of gain of information. *Quarterly Journal of Experimental Psychology, 4*, 11–26.

Hofstaetter, P. R. (1990). The tradition of cognitive psychology. *Psychologishe Rundschau, 41*, 46–49.

Horn, J. L. (1982). The theory of fluid and crystallized intelligence in relation to concepts of cognitive psychology and aging in adulthood. In F. I. M. Craik & S. Trehub (Eds.), *Aging and cognitive processes* (pp. 237–278). New York: Plenum Press.

Hultsch, D., F., MacDonald, S. W. S., Hunter, M. A., Levy-Bencheton, J., & Strauss, E. (2000). Intraindividual variability in cognitive performance in older adults: Comparison of adults with mild dementia, adults with arthritis, and healthy adults. *Neuropsychology, 14*, 588–598.

Jäger, A. O. (1982). Mehrmodale klassifikation von intelligenzleistungen: Experimentell kontrollierte weiterentwicklung eines deskriptiven intelligenzstrukturmodells [Multimodal classification of intellectual performance: experimentally controlled further development of a descriptive model of the structure of intelligence]. *Diagnostica, 28*, 195–226.

Jäger, A. O. (1984). Intelligenzstrukturforschung: Konkurrierende modelle, neue entwicklungen, perspektiven [Research on the structure of intelligence: Rivaling models, new developments and perspectives]. *Psychologische Rundschau, 35*, 21–35.

Jäger, A. O., Süß, H.-M., & Beauducel, A. (1997). *Berliner Intelligenzstruktur-Test: BIS-Test, Form 4*. Göttingen, Germany: Hogrefe.

Kliegl, R., Smith, J., Baltes, P. B. (1989). Testing-the-limits and the study of adult age differences in cognitive plasticity of a mnemonic skill. *Developmental Psychology. 25*, 247–256.

Kliegl, R., Smith, J., & Baltes, P. B. (1990). On the locus and process of magnification of age differences during a mnemonic training. *Developmental Psychology, 26*, 894–904.

Klix, F. (1983). Begabungsforschung – ein neuer Weg in der kognitiven Intelligenzdiagnostik? [Research on giftedness – A new approach to cognitive intelligence measurement] *Zeitschrift für Psychologie, 191*, 360–387.

Klix, F. (1985). Basic processes of mental dispositions. *Zeitschrift für Psychologie. 193*, 27– 50.

Klix, F., & Bachmann, T. (1998). Analogy detection – analogy construction: An approach to similarity in higher order reasoning. *Zeitschrift für Psychologie, 206*, 125–143.

Kluwe, R. H., Schilde, A., Fischer, C., & Oellerer, N. (1991). Problemlöseleistungen beim umgang mit komplexen systemen und intelligenz [Problem solving in complex systems and intelligence]. *Diagnostica, 37*, 291–313.

Kramer, D. A. (2000). Wisdom as a classical source of human strength: Conceptualizing and empirical inquiry. *Journal of Social and Clinical Psychology, 19*, 83–101.

Krampe, R. T., & Baltes, P. B. (in press). Intelligence as adaptive resource development and resource allocation: A new look through the lenses of SOC and expertise. In R. J. Sternberg & E. L. Grigorenko (Eds.), *Perspectives on the psychology of abilities, competencies, and expertise* (pp. in press). New York: Cambridge University Press.

Krampe, R. T., & Ericsson, K. A. (1996). Maintaining excellence: Deliberate practice and elite performance in young and older pianists. *Journal of Experimental Psychology: General, 125*, 331–359.

Kunzmann, U., & Baltes, P. B. (2003). Beyond the traditional scope of intelligence: Wisdom in action. In R. J. Sternberg, J. Lautry, & T. I. Lubart (Eds.), *Models of intelligence for the next millennium* (pp. 329–343). Washington, DC: American Psychological Association.

Kunzmann, U., & Baltes, P. B. (in press). *Wisdom-related knowledge: Emotional, motivational, and interpersonal correlates. Personality and Social Psychology Bulletin.*

Kunzmann, U., Little, T. D., & Smith, J. (2000). Is age-related stability of subjective well-being a paradox? Cross-sectional and longitudinal evidence from the Berlin Aging Study. *Psychology and Aging, 15*, 511–526.

Lehrl, S., & Fischer, B. (1990). A basic information psychological parameter (BIP) for the reconstruction of concepts of intelligence. *European Journal of Personality, 4*, 259–286.

Li, K. Z. H; Lindenberger, U., Freund, A. M., & Baltes, P. B. (2001). Walking while memorizing: Age-related differences in compensatory behavior. *Psychological Science, 12*, 230–237.

Li, S.-C. (2003). Biocultural orchestration of developmental plasticity across levels: The interplay of biology and culture in shaping the mind and behavior across the lifespan. *Psychological Bulletin, 129*, 171–194.

Li, S.-C., Aggen, S. H., Nesselroade, J. R., & Baltes, P. B. (2001). Short-term fluctuations in elderly people's sensorimotor functioning predict text and spatial
memory performance: The MacArthur Successful Aging Studies. *Gerontology,*
47, 100–116.

Li, S.-C., Jordanova, M., & Lindenberger, U. (1998). From good senses to good
sense: A link between tactile information processing and intelligence. *Intelli-*
gence, 26, 99–122.

Li, S.-C. Lindenberger, U., & Frensch, P. A. (2000). Unifying cognitive aging:
From neuromodulation to representation to cognition. *Neurocomputing, 32–*
33, 879–890.

Li, S.-C., Lindenberger, U., & Sikström, S. (2001). Aging cognition: from neuromodulation to representation. *Trends in Cognitive Sciences, 5,* 479–486.

Li, S.-C., Lindenberger, U., Hommel, B., Aschersleben, G., Prinz, W., & Baltes,
P. B. (in press). Lifespan ontogenetic transformations in the couplings among
intellectual abilities and underlying cognitive processes. *Psychological Science.*

Li, S.-C., & Sikström, S. (2002). *Integrative neurocomputational perspectives on cog-*
nitive aging, neuromodulation, and representation. Neuroscience and Biobehavioral
Reviews, 26, 795–808.

Lindenberger, U., & Baltes, P. B. (1997). Intellectual functioning in old and very
old age: Cross-sectional results from the Berlin Aging Study. *Psychology and*
Aging, 12, 410–432.

Lindenberger, U., Marsiske, M., & Baltes, P. B. (2000). Memorizing while walking: Increase in dual-task costs from young adulthood to old age. *Psychology*
& Aging, 15, 417–436.

Lienert, G. A., & Crott, H. W. (1964). Studies on the factor structure of intelligence
in children, adolescents, and adults. *Vita Humana, 7,* 147–163.

Marsiske, M., Lang, F. R., Baltes, P. B., & Baltes, M. M. (1995). Selective optimization with compensation: Life-span perspectives on successful human development. In R. A. Dixon & L. Bäckman (Eds.), *Compensating for psychological*
deficits and declines: Managing losses and promoting gains (pp. 55–79). Mahwah,
NJ: Erlbaum.

Neubauer, A. C. (1997). The mental speed approach to the assessment of intelligence. In J. Kingma & W. Tomic (Eds.), *Advances in cognition and educational*
practice: Reflections on the concept of intelligence (pp. 149–174). Greenwich, CT:
JAI Press.

Neubauer, A. C., Bauer, C., Hoeller, G. (1992). Intelligence, attention, motivation, and speed-accuracy trade-off in the HICK paradigm. *Personality and*
Individual Differences, 13, 1325–1332.

Neubauer, A. C., & Bucik, V. (1996). The mental speed-IQ relationship: Unitary
or modular? *Intelligence, 22,* 23–48.

Neubauer, A. C., Freudenthaler, H. H., & Pfurtscheller, G. (1995). Intelligence
and spatiotemporal patterns of event-related desynchronization (ERD). *Intel-*
ligence, 20, 249–266.

Neubauer, A. C., & Knorr, E. (1998). Three paper-pencil tests for speed of information processing: Psychometric properties and correlations with intelligence. *Intelligence, 26,* 123–151.

Neubauer, A. C., Sange, G., & Pfurtscheller, G. (1999). Psychometric intelligence and event-related desynchronization during performance of a letter matching task. In G. Pfurtscheller and F. H. Lopes da Silva (Eds.), *Event-related Desynchronization and related oscillatory EEG phenomena of the awake brain. Handbook of EEG and Clinical Neurophysiology*, Revised Series (Vol. 6, pp. 219–231). Amsterdam: Elsevier.

Oberauer, K., Süß, H.-M., Schulze, R., Wilhelm, O., Wittmann, W. W. (2000). Working memory capacity-facets of a cognitive ability construct. *Personality & Individual Differences, 29,* 1017–1045.

Oswald, W. D., & Roth, E. (1987). *Der Zahlen-Verbindungs-Test* (ZVT). Göttingen: Hogrefe.

Pasupathi, M., Staudinger, U. M., & Baltes, P. B. (2001). Seeds of wisdom: Adolescents' knowledge and judgment about difficult life problems. *Developmental Psychology, 37,* 351–361.

Perleth, Ch., & Heller, K. A. (1994). The Munich Longitudinal Study of Giftedness. In R. F. Subotnik and K. D. Arnold (Eds.), Beyond Terman: Longitudinal studies in contemporary gifted education (pp. 77–114). Stamford, CT: Ablex Publishing.

Quetelet, A. (1838). *Über den menschen und die entwicklung seiner fähigkeiten* [A treatise on man and the development of his faculties]. Stuttgart: Schweizerbarts Verlagshandlung.

Rabbitt, P., Osman, P., & Moore, B. (2001). There are stable individual differences in performance variability, both from moment to moment and from day to day. *Quarterly Journal of Experimental Psychology, 54,* 981–1003.

Reinert, G. (1979). Prolegomena to a history of life-span developmental psychology. In P. B. Baltes and O. G. Brim (Eds.), *Life-span development and behavior* (Vol. 2, pp. 205–243). New York: Academic Press.

Rott, C. (1999). Cognitive appraisal, coping behavior, and social integration of centenarians. *Zeitschrift für Gerontologie und Geriatrie, 32,* 246–254.

Rott, C. (1993). Three components of intellectual development in old age: Results from the Bonn longitudinal study on aging. *Zeitschrift für Gerontologie, 26,* 184–190.

Rott, C. (1991). Development of intelligence in old age. *Zeitschrift für Gerontologie, 23,* 252–261.

Schaarschmidt, U., & Schmidt-Atzert, L. (1997). A review of the Intelligence Structure Test (IST 70). *Zeitschrift für Differentielle und Diagnostische Psychologie, 18,* 106–112.

Schmidt, L. R. (1971). Testing the limits im leistungsverhalten: Möglichkeiten und grenzen [Testing the limits in performance test: Potential and limits]. In E. Duhm (Ed.), *Praxis der klinischen Psychologie* (pp. 2–29). Göttingen, Germay: Hogrefe.

Schneider, W., Perner, J., Bullock, M., Stefanek, J., & Ziegler, A. (1999). Development of intelligence and thinking. In F. E. Weinert and W. Schneide. (Eds.), *Individual development from 3 to 12: Findings from the Munich Longitudinal Study* (pp. 9–28). Cambridge: Cambridge University Press.

Schweizer, K. (2000). Cognitive mechanisms at the core of success and failure of intelligence. *Psychologische Beitrage, 42,* 190–200.

Singer, T., & Lindenberger, U. (2000). Plastizität [Plasticity]. In H.-W. Wahl & C. Tesch-Römer (Eds.), *Angewandte gerontologie in schlüsselbegriffen* [Key concepts in applied gerontology]. (pp. 39–43). Stuttgart: Kohlhammer.

Singer, T., Lindenberger, U., & Baltes, P. B. (in press). Plasticity of memory for new learning in very old age: A story of major loss? *Psychology and Aging*.

Staudinger, U. M. (1999). Older and wiser? Integrating results on the relationship between age and wisdom-related performance. *International Journal of Behavioral Development*, *23*, 641–664.

Staudinger, U. M. (2000). Many reasons speak against it, yet many people feel good: The paradox of subjective well-being. *Psychologische Rundschau*, *51*, 185–197.

Staudinger, U. M., & Baltes, P. B. (1996). Interactive minds: A facilitative setting for wisdom-related performance? *Journal of Personality and Social Psychology*, *71*, 746–762.

Staudinger, U. M., Lopez, D. F., & Baltes, P. B. (1997). The psychometric location of wisdom-related performance. *Personality and Social Bulletin*, *23*, 1200–1214.

Staudinger, U. M., Maciel, A. G., Smith, J., & Baltes, P. B. (1998). What predicts wisdom-related performance? A first look at personality, intelligence, and facilitative experiential contexts. *European Journal of Personality*, *12*, 1–17.

Stern, E. (2001). Intelligence, prior knowledge, and learning. In N. J. Smelser and P. B. Baltes (Eds.), *International encyclopedia of the social and behavioral sciences* (Vol. 11. pp. 7670–7674). Oxford: Elsevier.

Sternberg, R. J. (Ed.). (1990). *Wisdom: Its nature, origins, and development*. New York: Cambridge University Press.

Sternberg, R. J. (1998). A balance theory of wisdom. *Review of General Psychology*, *2*, 347–365.

Süß, H.-M., Kersting, M., & Oberauer, K. (1991). Intelligenz und wissen als prädikotoren für leistungen bei computersimulierten komplexen problemen [Intelligence and knowledge as predictors of performance in computer simulated complex problems]. *Diagnostica*, *37*, 334–352.

Süß. H.-M., Oberauer, K., Wittmann, W. W., Wilhelm O., & Schulze, R. (2002). Working-memory capacity explains reasoning ability – and a little bit more. *Intelligence*, *30*, 261–288.

Tetens, J. N. (1777). *Philosophische versuche über die menschliche natur und ihre entwicklung* [Philosophical considerations about human nature and development]. Leipzig: Weidmanns Erben und Reich.

Wiese, B. S., & Freund, A. M. (2000). The interplay of work and family in young and middle adulthood. In J. Heckhausen (Ed.), *Motivational psychology of human development: Developing motivation and motivating development. Advances in psychology*, *131* (pp. 233–249). New York: Elsevier Science.

Todd, P. M., & Gigerenzer, G. (2000). Précis of simple heuristics that make us smart. *Behavioral and Brain Sciences*, *23*, 727–780.

Trost, G. (1993). Prediction of excellence in school, university, and work. In K. A. Heller, F. J. Mönks, and A. H. Passow (Eds.), *International handbook of research and development of giftedness and talent* (pp. 325–338). Oxford: Pergamon.

Wittmann, W. W; Süß, H.-M. (1999). Investigating the paths between working memory, intelligence, knowledge, and complex problem-solving performances via Brunswik symmetry. In P. L. Ackerman and P. C. Kyllonen (Eds.), *Learning and individual differences: Process, trait, and content determinants* (pp. 77–108). Washington, DC: American Psychological Association.

Vickers, D., Nettelbeck, T., & Wilson, R. J. (1972). Perceptual indices of performance, the measurement of inspection time and noise in the visual system. *Perception, 1,* 263–295.

Weinert, F. E., Schneider, W., & Knopf. M. (1988). Individual differences in memory development across the life span. In P. B. Baltes, D. L. Featherman, & R. M. Lerner (Eds.), *Life-span Development and Behavior* (Vol. 9, pp. 40–86). Hillsdale, NJ: Erlbaum.

Weinert, F. E., & Schneider, W. (1999). (Eds.). *Individual development from 3 to 12: Findings from the Munich Longitudinal Study.* Cambridge: Cambridge University Press.

Weinert, F. E., & Schneider, W. (1995). Memory development during early and middle childhood: Findings from the Munich Longitudinal Study. In F. E. Weinert and W. Schneider (Eds.), *Memory performance and competence: Issues in growth and development* (pp. 263–282). Mahwah, NJ: Erlbaum.

Wrosch, C., & Heckhausen, J. (1999). Control processes before and after passing a developmental deadline: Activation and deactivation of intimate relationship goals. *Journal of Personality and Social Psychology, 77,* 415–427.

Wrosch, C., Heckhausen, J., & Lachman, M. E. (2000). Primary and secondary control strategies for managing health and financial stress across adulthood. *Psychology and Aging, 15,* 387–399.

6

Is It Possible to Study Intelligence Without Using the Concept of Intelligence?

An Example from Soviet/Russian Psychology

Elena L. Grigorenko

In his insightful exploration of the history of the emergence and establishment of the conceptual apparatus of psychology, Danziger (1997) stated a number of dimensions on which the concept of *intelligence* differs from the concepts of *intellect* and *reason*. First, although synonymous (*The American Heritage Dictionary of the English Language*, 1992), *intellect* and *intelligence* have different time trajectories: The concept of *intelligence* emerged much later, only at the end of the nineteenth century, while the concept of *intellect* was introduced at least as long ago as the appearance of Aristotelian writings.[1] Second, the very surfacing of the concept of *intelligence* in psychological literature was deeply rooted in the discourse of the biological foundation of the human mind and its evolutionary development. The introduction of this concept led to the idea that stages of evolution somehow coincide with the amount of

---

[1] Aristotle had introduced the idea of clear separation between those aspects of the human *psyche* that it had in common with the *psyche* of other living organisms and those that were absolutely specific to humanity. It is the latter that had been translated from Aristotle's scripts as *intellectus* and remained that through centuries of scholastic writings. In English, *intellectus* was expressed as "intellect," which remained a specific human attribute that made humans distinctly different from anything else, anything non-human. This gap between humans and non-humans was deepened even further by the introduction of Descartes's "pure intellect," which emphasized the irreducibility of intellect to anything like sensory experience of gradual learning. Clearly, the new biological conception of intelligence that emerged during the late nineteenth century was incompatible with ancient usage.

This chapter utilizes portions of previously published material (see Grigorenko & Kornilova, 1997). The materials are reproduced with permission from Cambridge University Press.

intelligence – the lower the evolutionary position, the less intelligence; the higher the position, the more intelligence. Third, the concept of *intelligence* has an embedded connotation of a quantitative distribution (one can have more or less intelligence compared to the other), whereas the concepts of *intellect* and *reason* appear to be dichotomous (one either has it or does not). Fourth, the concept of *intelligence* emerged in a time when school as a societal institution had started to become much more accessible to large masses of people; if previously the lack of education was primarily explained by one's social class, in the late nineteenth to the early twentieth century, the variation in educational achievement within social background groups was much larger than across social background groups, calling for a new (compared with social background) explanatory variable for educational failure. Since the mission of schooling was to teach reasoning, the concept of *intellect*, intimately related to philosophical reasoning, did not provide any new insight in understanding why some children did better in reasoning than others. Fifth, *intelligence* was the first concept on which the notion of heritability was exercised, establishing the tendency of associating the traditional social label of "brightness" with the ideas of biological superiority and inferiority. Once again, by its very nature, *intellect* denoted social mind, that is, the impact of a society on an individual, something that cannot be heritable by definition.

In short, Danziger (1997), similar to many other historians of science, stressed the importance of understanding the emergence and utilization of scientific concepts within a broader cultural, historical, and social context. Specifically, the combination of cultural, societal, educational, and scientific factors in France, Great Britain, and the United States created a need for the emergence of a specific psychological concept that could explain the observed variability in intellectual performance of these societies' members to a higher degree than that of the concepts of *intelligence* and *reason*. The concept of *intelligence* appeared to be such a variable.

However, while the concept of *intelligence* had been winning the minds of British and American psychologists, it did not produce nearly as much enthusiasm in Russia. In fact, as if to show total lack of interest, Russian psychology has not come up with a word to signify *intelligence* specifically: Both the words *intellect* and *intelligence* are translated into a single word, *интеллект*, meaning that the concept of *intelligence* has been merged with the concept of *intellect*. This chapter addresses the question of why Soviet/Russian psychology did not adopt (and still has not adopted) the concept of *intelligence* in its conceptual apparatus and what other concepts it used to react to cultural, historical, social, and educational needs addressed by the concept of *intelligence* elsewhere. The main argument of the chapter is that studying intelligence without using the concept of *intelligence* is possible – Soviet/Russian psychology has contributed valuable thoughts to the development of the field of intelligence without incorporating the term *intelligence* in its conceptual apparatus.

THINKING AS GENERALIZED AND MEDIATED COGNITION
OF REALITY: MAJOR CONCEPTS AND GENERAL
IDEOLOGICAL-PHILOSOPHICAL BASES FOR RESEARCH
ON THINKING IN RUSSIAN/SOVIET PSYCHOLOGY

The Historical Circumstances of the Development of the Soviet Psychology of Thinking and Intelligence

Soviet psychology, as well as many other sciences in the former Soviet Union, developed under a heavy load of ideological attitudes and requirements. Scientific programs quite often were evaluated and redirected through discussions in the mass media and at different Communist Party meetings, or by state decrees and resolutions. This "tradition" was established soon after the Civil War of 1918–1922. In 1922–1923, a large group of Russian intellectuals, among whom were the famous psychologists and philosophers Nikolai Berdiev, Sergei Bulgakov, Nikolai Lossky, Ivan Lapshin, and Semen Frank, were briefly imprisoned and subsequently exiled to the West. They were charged with opposing the dominant ideology based on Marxism–Leninism by their "idealistic" theories. Former colleagues of the exiled scholars did not raise any question concerning their fate; it was as if they had never existed.[2] As Kozulin wrote, "The exile of the psychologists was in some sense just one more act of the "class struggle," but it provided a clear sign of the erosion of scientific ethics. While their colleagues were exiled, the rest of the psychological community remained silent" (Kozulin, 1984, p. 13).

This silence had a compelling cause: By the early 1920s a psychologist could either follow the Marxist orientation or be exiled or subdued

---

[2] Most of the exiled scientists continued working abroad and developed original philosophical and psychological theories (e.g., Berdiev, Frank).

(Etkind, 1990). Remember, though, that the spirit of time was such that Marxist ideas were everywhere; they were easy to learn and accept. To paraphrase Karl Popper's words about Marx, one cannot do justice to young Soviet psychologists without recognizing their sincerity. Driven by the Marxist idea of creating a new type of a person – the liberated proletarian, with new morals, culture, and rules of conduct – Soviet psychologists stormed old bourgeois ideological and philosophical barricades on their way to building a new type of a human being, a Soviet human being.

No scientific struggle existed between Marxist and non-Marxist psychological theories: No philosopher–psychologists remained in the country who could argue with enthusiasts of Marxist approaches (or if they did, they changed their professions). As Kozulin has pointed out (1984, p. 14), "The new Soviet psychology from its very beginning abandoned dialogue and therefore lost the invigoration that comes with pluralism. Later on it started to 'discover' idealists within its own number and treated them accordingly."

In the early years, struggles were waged between rival groups of Soviet psychologists. Each of these groups claimed that its methodology was the most scientific and most purely Marxist, as compared to other groups' methodologies. Because of the ideological importance of psychology as a science for raising a new type of human being, the party was closely involved in these debates. However, the discussions did not last long. In 1930, Boris Ananiev gave a talk at the Congress on Human Behavior that essentially ended these discussions. In closing his presentation, Ananiev made a statement that became the basis of the meta-theoretical and theoretical work of Soviet psychologists for the next half-century: "The real founders of Soviet psychology as a dialectical–materialist discipline are neither schools nor trends...but the founders of Marxism–Leninism" (cited from Kozulin, 1984, p. 21). This statement corresponded to the party line, and from that time until recent years it was accepted that Soviet psychology was to derive the categories of consciousness and behavior directly from the works of Marx, Engels, and Lenin. Marxism, as interpreted by Soviet psychologists, was a deterministic social doctrine that alone was "correct" as a philosophy of the proletariat. Psychologists who deviated from the party line were forced to admit their "mistakes" in the early 1930s. And, for some of them, these mistakes were costly – they paid for them with their lives. What is remarkable, however, is that, although forced into a limited framework, post-revolutionary psychology in the Soviet Union flourished and produced many interesting theoretical ideas and empirical findings (see Brushlinsky, 1997; Etkind, 1990; Joravsky, 1987; Kozulin, 1984).

In 1936, educational psychologists' work came under fire. A decree by the Central Committee of All-Russia Communist Party (Bol'shevikov), known as the Decree of Pedology,[3] criticized the social impact of their work, condemning those psychologists who had been engaged in pedological studies. Given that almost all work in educational psychology in the 1920s was called "pedology," one can imagine the consequences of this decree. All forms of intelligence testing were forbidden. Numerous trumped-up charges, including cosmopolitism (a tendency to analyze and refer to Western theories), idealism, and being an enemy of the Soviet people, complicated or even interrupted the lives of some psychologists and geneticists who had high official positions.[4] Along with pedology, social psychology, psychotherapy, and behavioral genetic research were prohibited in the Soviet Union for more than 40 years. Marxism was imposed on all research as the only possible philosophical underpinning for any science, including the study of thinking.

A Mosaic of Approaches

Although the majority of researchers accepted the Marxist approach, emphasizing the social determination of the development of the psyche in general, and thinking in particular, their positions varied significantly. It would be wrong to state that this strong philosophical inclination could be explained only by ideological pressure from the state. In philosophical debates on the bases of Soviet psychology, one can see a

[3] *Pedology* was the term used in the 1920s for research and testing in child and educational psychology.
[4] For example, Sergei L. Rubinstein, one of the most famous figures in Soviet psychology, was awarded the State Premium of the Soviet Union in 1941, but was fired in 1951 from his position as chair of the division of psychology in the philosophy department of Moscow State University. He was charged with cosmopolitism and was forced to defend his research in front of various party and state committees (Zhdan, 1993).

The fate of Dr. Levit is an even more unfortunate example. As director of the Medical Biological Institute in Moscow, he was severely criticized in 1936 in the first round of Vavilov–Lysenko discussions. (This meeting was an example of ideologically driven struggle against "cosmopolitism," where genetics was announced to be a bourgeois science and prohibited). Levit was subjected to repression in 1937 and imprisoned. He died there in prison.

spectrum of different explanatory principles and ideas related to mechanisms of social determination.

There are several good reasons for the variation of ideas and opinions in Soviet/Russian psychology, which existed regardless of state and party attempts to unify all approaches and merge them into one easily controllable theory.

First, Soviet psychology incorporated various ideas developed in Russian philosophy, characterized by its humanistic ideals (for example, Losev's ideas of the role of sign, symbol, and myth in development, 1991, the philosophical and religious ideas of Berdiaev, 1990, and Florensky, 1991) and scientific findings (the scientific ideas of Pavlov, 1953, and Sechenov, 1952), despite the exile of pre-Revolutionary Russian psychologists and philosophers. Vygotsky's theory, for example, appeared at the close of the Silver century of Russian culture (i.e., the beginning of the twentieth century), when there were no strict borders between the sciences, arts, philosophy, and theology.[5] Vygotsky, a true man of his time, was a philosopher, literary critic, meta-theoretician, scientist, and psychologist. All of these aspects of Vygotsky's professionalism were expressed in his cultural-historical theory (discussion to follow). The most important characteristic of his theory was its integration of knowledge about man with different approaches and methods of understanding human development.[6]

Second, traditionally, the Russian intelligentsia was very open to foreign ideas, and Russian scientists themselves never divided science into "ours" and "theirs." Even though a concept of "bourgeois science" appeared in the late 1920s, many Soviet psychologists who were forced to

[5] There are many examples of scientists' interest in humanities and philosophers' interest in science. Even the great "anti-psychologist" Pavlov wrote to Chelpanov when the latter opened the first Russian psychological institute: "I, who have always excluded in my laboratory work on the brain any mention of subjective conditions, congratulate your psychological institute and you as its creator and leader, from my heart and wish you full success" (Pavlov, 1953, p. 92).

[6] As time progressed, Vygotsky, and later his students, thoroughly developed some aspects of the cultural-historical theory, while others were left sketchy (e.g., the concepts of symbol and myth were hardly touched by either Vygotsky or his colleagues). However, the initial image of the theory, reflecting Russian spirituality and a humanistic interest in mankind, often referred to as the Russian tradition, was present even in the darkest days of its development. A similar evaluation could be made of many other Soviet/Russian psychological theories (e.g., Bernstein, 1966; Rubinstein, 1957, 1958). The Russian philosophical and scientific traditions, in which the majority of Soviet psychological theories were rooted, served as a vaccine against the ideological epidemics of the regime, providing the basis for varying approaches.

contrast their work to this "false bourgeois science" did so with scientific sensitivity, rigor, and tact.[7] Such constant attention to psychological developments and events abroad also guaranteed variability in opinions among Soviet psychologists.

Third, differences among theoretical approaches were also due to the "implicit" division of psychological research into periods: (1) 1917–1936, the period prior to the 1936 State Decree on Pedology; (2) 1936–1950 (Dubinin, 1988), the period ending with Pavlov's session, where many Soviet psychologists were charged with cosmopolitism and a tendency to depart from Marxism; (3) the early 1950s–late 1980s, a relatively quiet and stable period in which Marxist-oriented mainstream psychology was still dominant, but connections were established with Western psychology,[8] and some approaches deviating from Marxism began to develop; and, finally, (4) the current period, in which no ideological limitations exist, and Soviet/Russian theories and ideas can be compared with foreign approaches without fear of recrimination. These historical stages of Soviet/Russian psychology determined the nature of the theories. Thus, in the late 1950s, when the atmosphere in the country changed dramatically with Stalin's death, many psychologists digressed from the required earlier crass meta-theoretical principles (e.g., Zinchenko & Morgunov, 1994). For example, Rubinstein not only deviated from the principle of the unity of consciousness and activity and the principle of determinism (Rubinstein, 1957), but also inverted his own formula

---

[7] An example of the nature and style of such critical evaluation is given in an article on the crisis in psychology written in 1927 by the young Vygotsky (1982a). Analyzing in detail schools of foreign psychological thought, the author pointed to philosophical and methodological dead ends and suggested new principles of accumulating psychological knowledge. Vygotsky's idea was to build psychology using the example of hard-core experimental sciences and to use "psychopractice" as a way for the "creation of a man by himself." According to modern historians of psychology, Vygotsky himself did not accomplish these goals (Vygotsky died when he was 38); it was done instead by his students (in particularly, Leont'ev, *Psikhologiya i novye idealy nauchnosti*, 1993). In addition, due to his interest in testing, his name was put on a black list in 1936 after the State decree on pedology. His work was not published until the 1960s. However, Vygotsky's influence was tremendous. He created a humanistically oriented psychological school, which survived the 1930s and early 1940s and served as the basis for Leont'ev's theory of the psychology of activity, which, in its turn, was recognized in the 1960s as an official Soviet psychological doctrine. Moreover, Vygotsky's ideas acted as a fulcrum for the work of Soviet philosophers Zinov'ev (1954) and Mamardashvili (1968, 1984).

[8] A turning point in the history of Soviet psychology's attitudes toward foreign psychology was the publication of Tikhomirov's book (1969), in which the researcher suggested an approach based on Bruner's theory and data (Bruner, 1977), but providing a completely different interpretation of the results.

"the external through the internal," arguing the internal to be dominant (Rubinstein, 1958). Thus, scientists tended to evaluate critically their own theories and to modify them, deviating from the official dogmas, thereby adding to the variability in positions.

Fourth, experimental results obtained in studies implementing traditional methods in the psychology of thinking – such as concurrent verbal report, establishing physiological correlates of thinking processes, and concept formation – "accidentally" led to the discovery of unconscious determinants of thinking (e.g., insight). Findings in this area disturbed the clear theoretical pictures based on social determination of thinking, because researchers' interpretations did not always correspond to the widely accepted psychological theories. As previously discussed, these "official" theories were often forced to flirt with Marxism (e.g., Leont'ev, 1975).[9] It became obvious that other theoretical schemes were necessary to incorporate these newly obtained experimental results in the body of psychological theory, once again, bringing variability.

In sum, certain historical and political circumstances surrounding the development of psychology in Russia, in particular the victory of Marxism-oriented psychology and the Decree on Pedology, led to many consequences, some of which are relevant to the subject of this chapter. First, IQ tests were prohibited, that is, intelligence, in its Western-like definition, was not present in psychological research. Second, it led to the appearance of the psychology of thinking – which defined thinking accordingly to Marxist philosophy, that is, as the highest form of mental reflection – to be its main object of research. And, finally, the majority of Soviet/Russian psychologists recognized an unquestionable dominance of the social in the development of thinking. As a result, the concepts of intelligence and thinking have been studied in different theoretical and empirical contexts that were quite incomparable to the Western tradition. However, regardless of the heavy ideological pressure, Soviet/Russian psychology remained a rich scientific field, integrating many different approaches. A precise overview of the study of thinking in Soviet/Russian psychology would take a great many pages. Moreover, such attempts have already been made (e.g., Mattaeus, 1988).

---

[9] For example, Leont'ev's theory was criticized for its non-psychological nature because, according to Marx, the outer determines the inner, but in Leont'ev's theory, activity plays a major role and consciousness "is held in leash activity" (*Psikhologiya i novye idealy nauchnosti*, 1993, p. 7), that is, it is always secondary. Thus, Leont'ev "directly" applied Marx's philosophical concepts to psychological reality, for which was often objected to criticism.

Thus, for the sake of capturing the richness of the existing approaches, various theoretical and experimental traditions are sketched here rather briefly, with the accentuation on their conceptual frameworks rather than on detailed empirical data. It is worth noting that this overview is selective and reflects the author's priorities, which have themselves been shaped by various factors.[10]

The Concepts of Intelligence and Thinking in Soviet/Russian Psychology

In this section the concepts of *thinking* and *intelligence* as they were used in Soviet/Russian psychology are briefly defined. The term *intelligence* (translated as интеллект, as already mentioned) was introduced to Soviet psychology in the early 1920s and attracted considerable attention from professionals. A decade later, by will of the state and the Communist Party, this concept was no longer mentioned or studied in mainstream psychology. Due to the official prohibition of intelligence testing, announced in 1936, the term *intelligence* was excised from the official psychology. As a result, until the late 1970s, the concept of intelligence was used mostly in two contexts: (1) research and theories on the development of the psyche in phylogenesis (mostly in relation to animal intelligence) and (2) in condemnations of Western tests of intelligence.

However, some related concepts remained in the terminology of Soviet/Russian psychologists. For example, Vygotsky[11] (1984) used the terms *intellectual development* and *cognitive development* interchangeably in his theory of higher mental functions. It was, in part, due to such terminology that Vygotsky was criticized for the "intellectualism" of his theory (Brushlinsky, 1968). Another psychological tradition uses the concept of *intellectual strategy* (Gurova, 1976; Kornilova & Tikhomirov, 1990). The broad meaning of this term includes a reference to the

[10] This selection was influenced, no doubt, by the fact that the author is a graduate of Moscow State University and belongs to what is known as the "Moscow Psychological School." (Zhdan & Martsinovskaia, 2000). If a similar analysis were performed by psychologists affiliated with Sanct-Petersburg State University, it would have included Wekker's (1970) work, for example, which is not presented here due to its lack of connection to the major figures of the Moscow Psychological School (Vygotsky, Leont'ev, Luria, Gal'perin, and others).

[11] Unfortunately, in many cases the dates associated with a particular author refer to the data of publication, sometimes many years after the text was written.

regulating role of an individual in his cognitive efforts and actions. Mostly, the researchers using this concept allude to: (1) the selective direction of problem solving and decision making and (2) the goal-oriented nature of thinking activity and the correction of subjective plans in the process of problem solving. The concept of the *intellectual solution* is used to refer to a type of decision making that is mediated by thinking, in contrast to other forms of decision making (Kornilova, Grigorenko, & Kuznetsova, 1991; Kornilova & Tikhomirov, 1990).

Intelligence testing was also implicitly present in clinical psychology. Clinical psychologists in their diagnostic practice always used "experimental methods," which, in reality, were analogous to subtests of intellectual assessments (classification, analogies, vocabulary, etc.). The interpretation of these results, however, was done in the context of understanding generalization and categorization processes, and motivational and goal-oriented regulation of activity (Rubinstein, 1970; Zeigarnik, 1962).

The prohibition on intelligence testing did not mean that Soviet psychologists did not use diagnostic tasks of children's intellectual development. These tasks, however, were designed as criterion tasks or educational tasks, not as level-oriented tests (Gurevich & Gorbacheva, 1992; Podgoretskaya, 1980; Talyzina, 1981; Zaporozhets, 1986).

The term *intelligence* reappeared in Soviet/Russian psychology in the 1960s and 1970s, when the first study using tests of intelligence was performed at Sanct-Petersburg State University (Palei, 1974). In the late 1960s and 1970s, a number of Soviet/Russian psychologists used tests of intelligence in their research studies (e.g., Ananiev, Pansiuk, Iliasheva – as cited in Burlachuk & Morozov, 2000). Since then, Soviet/Russian psychologists have adapted and created many psychological tests of intelligence, and this concept is widely used in experimental psychological research.[12] Intelligence, however, has not yet become popular as a theoretical construct. Its previous cultural image has not yet been restored, and the concept has not been integrated in the current conceptual apparatus (Zinchenko & Morgunov, 1994). In other words, currently Russian

---

[12] Although there are many translated tests of intelligence, there is only one test (WISC) that was properly adapted to and standardized for the Russian population. The standardization of the WISC took place in 1973 (Panasiuk, 1973) and was carried out to make available a reliable and valid instrument for diagnostic tasks. It is important to know that, although the test itself has been re-printed multiple times (by a company called IMATON), it has not been re-standardized since the early 1970s.

psychologists use tests of intelligence, but there are no original theories of intelligence in Russian psychology.

The term *thinking* was defined on the basis of Engels's and Marx's work as the highest level of human cognition. In response to the demands of the party and state officials regarding the "true Soviet psychology," a number of Soviet psychologists (e.g., Rubinstein and Leont'ev) ventured to derive psychological categories directly from the works of Marx and Lenin. Although sensations were considered the sole source for thinking, according to Leont'ev (1972), thinking transcended the limitation of direct sensory reflection and enabled the human being to receive knowledge about objects, qualities, and relations of the real world that cannot be sensed directly. *Thinking*, in its broad philosophical definition, was viewed as the subject matter of logic, psychology, and neurophysiology. In the context of experimental research, psychologists developed a narrower definition of thinking as a process of problem solving.

The following meta-theoretical ideas, formulated in the context of studying thinking, were regarded as the basis of any theoretical or experimental study of thinking in Soviet psychology.

Soviet psychologists stressed the primary role of *external* (social) sources and activity in mediating individual thinking schemes (Zinchenko & Smirnov, 1983). The principle of *historicism* (the principle of non-interrupting change in the societal conditions of development) was treated as one of the most important philosophical ideas in Soviet psychology. Based on this principle, psychologists criticized the "mistaken nature" (Smirnov, 1975, p. 253) of naturalistic and sociological theories.

In addition, when elaborating ideas regarding the social determination of thinking and its development, researchers stated that individual *mastery* of social historical experience could not be explained only by the accumulation of individual experience. Such processes as "interiorization," "translation of activities," "internalization," and others were suggested to explain how thinking develops. The idea that mental formations evolve as individuals develop and have a material basis was represented by the concept of *functional systems of brain processes*.

Determinants of thinking were perceived to vary for: (1) phylogenesis, (2) the cultural and historical development of the human psyche, (3) ontogenesis, and (4) the functional unfolding of an individual's thinking. Soviet psychologists studying phylogenesis treated the mediated nature of thought by sign (or, more precisely, by the meaning of words) as the most crucial factor in the "humanization" of behavior. The process of mastering signs was included in the context of the analysis of human activity and consciousness (Leont'ev, 1975; Vygotsky, 1982b; Zaporozhets, 1986). Psychologists studying ontogenesis sought the *impetus* of development in the contradictions of a child's life, in a child's activity. Examples were contradictions between new tasks and old ways of thinking, and between what a child is allowed to do and a child wants to do. Genetic factors were treated as prerequisites, limiting the possibilities for managing and manipulating the development of children's thinking through ontogenesis. Even though the limiting nature of genetically imposed individual characteristics was acknowledged by Soviet psychologists, the genetic basis of behavior was treated as something unfortunate, something necessarily negative and restrictive of positive cultural and societal influences. The link among different theories such as those of Leont'ev (1975), Rubinstein (1958), Kostiuk (1969), Zaporozhets (1986), and Luria (1969) was the statement that child *activity*, that is, the way in which a child interacts with the environment, circumscribes the conversion of external and inner determinants into psychological regulators. The physical maturation of the organism and its neural system is absolutely necessary for mental development, but this maturation is dependent upon the child's relation to the environment. In turn, a child's relation to the environment is *mediated by the world of adults*, that is, social determination is characteristic of all forms of human activity in ontogenesis.

Even though modern readers of many of the classical pieces on the mechanisms of *socialization* written by Soviet psychologists note the lack of experimental support for some conclusions, few would question the originality of their ideas. In terms of the conceptual apparatus of Soviet psychology, its research on the sources of individual variability in thinking cannot be classified into neat dichotomies of "social" versus "biological" or "genetic" versus "environmental." The vast majority of research on thinking was done in the context of looking for social determinants of thinking, while ignoring the biological ones. Given that the body of research assuming the social nature of thinking is much larger in Soviet/Russian psychology compared to research on biological determinants of thinking, this chapter will focus primarily on the former; the readers who are interested in the latter are referred to other sources (e.g., Grigorenko & Ravich-Scherbo, 1997; Segal, 2002).

SEARCHING FOR SOCIAL DETERMINANTS OF THINKING

As stated previously, the assumption that thinking is a social phenomenon and the development of thinking is socially determined underlies virtually all Russian research on thinking. The concept of the social was divided into two main components (Burmenskaya, 1997): (1) social-historical experience, meaning culture as a source of reproduction of human abilities, and (2) aspects of specific microsocial environments (e.g., school, familial, situational). Correspondingly, studies of thinking and the mechanisms of social determination of thinking can be classified into three groups: (1) theories dealing with the means and mechanisms of social-historical and social-cultural determinations of thinking; (2) theories of environmental conditioning of the development of thinking; and (3) approaches to applying these various theoretical ideas in educational practice.

The Social-Historical and Social-Cultural Determinations of Thinking

As examples of theoretical studies exploring the social-historical and social-cultural mechanisms underlying the development of thinking, I will consider: (1) the theory of practical thinking (Teplov, 1990); (2) studies of the inner and outer determination of scientific thinking and scientific creativity (Yaroshevsky, 1971, 1981); (3) ideas on the "raising" of thinking (Zinchenko & Mamardashvili, 1977; Mamardashvili, 1992a, 1992b); and (4) research on the active nature of thinking (Smirnov, 1985, 1994).

Teplov's paper, written in 1943 during World War II, is an interesting representative paper to investigate issues regarding the social-historical determination of thinking. The paper was devoted to understanding practical thinking in military leaders in critical situations. To reconstruct the peculiarities of thinking in situations of extreme difficulty and high levels of responsibility, Teplov relied on military historical materials, military commanders' autobiographies, and literary pieces. Stressing the most remarkable traits of military commanders and the historical and cultural determination of their thinking, Teplov considered a number of personalities and historical and geographical events, describing such different military commanders as Alexander of Macedonia, Julius Caesar, Hannibal, Napoleon, Suvorov, and Kutuzov. Teplov first analyzed the situations that military commanders face and described their activities and the tasks these activities should accomplish. Then the author analyzed the psychological characteristics of military commanders, as demonstrated in their professional activities. Third, Teplov considered the relations between these characteristics, attempting to draw a complete psychological portrait of a military commander. In addition, in the paper, Teplov treated the social-historical situations in which every military commander acted as initial determinants and stimuli for commanders' intellectual activity.

It is also important to note that Teplov compared the intellectual, emotional, and self-regulatory characteristics of military commanders. It is trivial to say that a distinctive military commander can be characterized by a remarkable intelligence and a strong will. The question, however, is, which is more advantageous and crucial for a talented commander? Discussing this issue, Teplov wrote: "I have never seen any discussion in which this question was ever resolved in intelligence's benefit. Usually the question itself is formulated in order to state the dominance of strong will in a military commander's activity" (Teplov, 1985, vol. 1, p. 288). Teplov himself, however, disagreed with the emphasis on the dominance of will, stating that practical intelligence is a unity of intellectual and volitional components. Knowing that his interpretation was contrary to most widespread ones, Teplov supported it with a citation from Klauzevits: "Resoluteness is obliged by its existence to a special type of mind" (Teplov, 1985, vol. 1, p. 251).

This paper established a whole school of the study of thinking devoted to the issues of how personality, reacting to a particular social-historical situation, regulates processes of thinking. However, the experimental realization of these ideas had not reached in originality, deepness, and novelty the level of generalization established by Teplov.

One of the most interesting concepts developed by Yaroshevsky (1981) in the context of his work on the mechanisms of social determination in scientific thinking is the concept of the *categorical regulation* of scientific thinking. According to this theory, with a change of paradigms in any system of knowledge, the greatest shift is observed in the categorical apparatus used rather than in the logical basis of knowledge. Using as a basis for his studies the development of psychological science worldwide, Yaroshevsky showed how a shift in scientific interpretations leads to a change at the level of formal logical operations, that is, in the objective logical structure of scientists' thoughts. In this sense, the individual creativity of scientists is inevitably heavily influenced by shared, historically developing categorical networks. Consequently, individual perceptions of reality are objectively determined, independent of the originality of the ideas developed by a creative personality (Yaroshevsky, 1971, 1981).

Merab Mamardashvili, one of the most interesting Georgian/Soviet philosophers, theorized about mechanisms for the social/cultural determination of thinking. He wrote on the objective method in psychology (Zinchenko & Mamardashvili, 1977), the content and forms of thinking (Mamardashvili, 1968), and on the importance of the raising of (improving) thinking (Mamardashvili, 1992a, 1992b). Among the extremely rich psychological ideas he left behind, only two are discussed here. One is related to the role of science and culture in the development of thinking, and the second deals with issues of the "precision of thinking" in intellectually developed people. Science, as well as culture, is normative (Mamardashvili, 1992b). Both ideas embed a possibility of mastering knowledge, that is, they are connected not to a person, but to a "possible person," one who can potentially develop from a given person. Mamardashvili related a person's mastering scientific thinking to this person's overcoming his innate propensities at the moment of his "second birth" (Mamardashvili, 1992b). Scientific activity involves oscillating movements in two different directions: toward new possible structures (mastering the norms of cultures and science), and, in the opposite direction, toward destroying these structures for the sake of creating new ones. Cognition in this sense is experimenting with forms, not the forms themselves. When a person defines himself in an action of thought while she is dependent on cultural and scientific norms of thinking, she is simultaneously free to choose or reject those norms.

Not every individual "producing thoughts" demonstrates relative freedom of individual thought from societally habitual "laws of ideas or moral structures." The first instance of modern intellectual work, according to Mamardashvili, was that of the Russian classical writer Fedor Dostoyevsky. Dostoyevsky allowed himself to think about a number of issues in a way that was not typical of the public consciousness at his time (for example, his views on the oppressed and abused in society).

"Precision of thinking" refers to an ability to think an issue or a problem through, from all possible angles, realizing the complete responsibility of a thinker for the level and products of his thinking. An individual, when thinking responsibly, cannot use excuses such as "I did not think," "I did not mean," "I could have not guessed" (Mamardashvili,

1992a, p. 130). When the Russian intelligentsia capitulated in the face of evil at the beginning of this century, its true betrayal was not its social sin, but its "slovenliness of thinking" (Mamardashvili, 1992a, p. 132). Russian intelligentsia failed to "create a sphere of autonomous thought, autonomous spiritual life, behind the back of which there is tradition . . . in which you immerse yourself and for which you feel personal and professional responsibility" (Mamardashvili, 1992a, p. 132).

In this sense, precision of thinking can be interpreted as the moral obligation to finish thoughts, to think everything through. Consequently, social factors determining thinking in the context of this framework are themselves shaped by cultural traditions' ways of reproducing thought. In addition, the standards of thinking defined by culture and science imply that a person perceives them as something more highly ordered and superior to his own ways of thinking. Therefore, a thinking person develops from a person with spontaneous attitudes toward himself and others into a "possible person," that is, a person mastering his second nature via the qualities of his thinking.

These ideas on fusing the artificial and the natural in individual thinking and on the roles of cultural systems in the social determination of thinking have not been transformed into experimental tasks. Remaining a philosopher, Mamardashvili, with his unique personality and strength and depth of thought, himself became the ideal "possible person." Mamardashvili's work is an alternative understanding of the social nature of thinking in Soviet philosophy and psychology that is receiving much attention in the current circuit in the search for criteria for rationality of human knowledge and cognition (Mamardashvili, 1984).

Other theorists studied the societal-historical and cultural determinations of thinking by focusing on the active nature of thinking (Smirnov, 1985, 1994). According to Leont'ev and his students and colleagues (e.g., Leont'ev, 1972; Smirnov, 1985), the dualism of environment and heredity, inevitably occurring in studying human development, can be avoided by introducing the concept of activity, which takes into account both the psychophysiological particulars of the child (determined primarily genetically) and unlimited environmental variation. Both of these factors influence, rather than determine, development, because the positive or negative constitutional qualities are mediated by the child's social environment from the very moment of birth. The reason activity holds such a central position is that, within this theory, activity is viewed not simply as a combination of various physical actions mediated by mental processes. Rather, object-oriented activity forms the connection between the individual and the world, and this connection is bidirectional. That is, the individual acts on and changes the environment through activity, but, as a result, the individual herself is also changed as she absorbs a wider range of experiences from the environment. According to the theory of activity, it is necessary to study neural-physiological aspects of the ontogenetic development of thinking; however, the main area of psychological research remains the content and conditions of a child's optimal interactions with the world.

The Environmental Determination of Thinking

Social Environment as a Determinant of the Development of Thinking

Following chronological order, this review of Soviet psychological theories that view the social environment as a determinant of the development of thinking will begin with an analysis of Kornilov's work, because Kornilov was the first psychologist to develop a theory of the interaction of heredity and environment as a basis for "Marxist differential psychology" (Kornilov, 1980). He also introduced the *biosociological concept* of reaction[13] that supposedly differed in various societies, and could be developed in its "correct" form in members of a socialist society. However, Kornilov's "reactology" was so mechanistic that even historians of psychology do not treat it as an original interpretational scheme.

A more concrete and well-developed attempt not only to build an "objective psychology," but also to study mechanisms for the social determination of thinking, was Blonsky's theory, developed in the 1920s and 1930s (Blonsky, 1935a, 1935b). According to Blonsky, the mind has an ability to gain successful individual experience, that is, the ability to learn: The mind is seen as non-emotional and non-instinctive; practical interest is its main engine. Thinking is a process, and the way one thinks shows one's mental level. Thinking as "something developing" can be represented by three stages: imaginative (primitive), visual, and systematic. According to Blonsky, during secondary school education, only memory reaches its developmental summit. Thinking remains immature and can be fully developed only at higher levels of education.

---

[13] In contrast to the concept of reflex, Kornilov's reaction contained "a wealth of ideological content, which was not characteristic of a reflex" (Smirnov, 1975, p. 146).

Blonsky interpreted changes in thinking caused by learning and school experience as an increase in the "volume" of thinking and a shift from visual to abstract (systematic) thinking occurs. Formal logic creates the necessary background for mastering dialectics. Consequently, school systems directly influence the psychological characteristics of pupils' minds. Such a simplified interpretation of the mechanisms for the social determination of thinking evolved in the context of challenging Vygotsky's approach, in which Blonsky tried to criticize the distinction between natural and higher mental functions.[14]

Vygotsky, called the "Mozart of psychology" (Tulmen, 1981), created a cultural-historical theory, which, on a surface level, did not appear to have been influenced by the forces of Soviet or worldwide psychological thought or the methods of his time. However, this level of analysis is mistaken – Soviet ideology was deeply rooted into the writings of Vygotsky, and his very views of psychology were resonant to philosophical theories of his time (Brushlinsky, 1996). As a Russian psychologist wrote: "similar to *Don Quixote*, cultural-historical psychology was possible but not inevitable" (Puzyrei, 1986, p. 10). In Vygotsky's work, thinking itself is regarded as possible but not inevitable. Thinking is not simply one of the functions of the human mind, but is a process related to mastering sign and its function.

Vygotsky worked as a professional psychologist for only 10 years.[15] However, his writing does not seem either unprofessional or archaic and remains a focus of active debate. His ideas have influenced many modern theories to an extent frequently unrecognized by their authors, because of the high degree to which Soviet/Russian psychology emerged from Vygotsky's theory[16] (Asmolov, 1996; Kondakov, 1996; Leont'ev, 1996; Yaroshevsky, 1996; Zinchenko, 1996).

Vygotsky's scientific path was quite unusual. In 1925 he began to try to develop a concrete psychological study of consciousness. This idea seemed extremely brave and challenging in the context of the struggle

[14] Blonsky's objections to Vygotsky's theory were published only after Vygotsky's death, and a public debate did not take place.

[15] Before the Revolution of 1917, Vygotsky was a student in the Law School and in the history and philology departments of Moscow State University. Then he worked in Homel (Belorussia) as a schoolteacher. In 1924, after his presentation at the Second Russian Psychoneurological Congress, Vygotsky was invited by Kornilov to return to Moscow, where Vygotsky accepted a position as an assistant research fellow at the Psychological Institute.

[16] Here I draw an analogy to a famous statement that all Russian literature emerged from Gogol's *Greatcoat*.

between the old subjective-empirical psychology, the main object of which was consciousness, and the "objective" orientation of "new" psychology (behaviorism and reactology). As has been mentioned, with the ongoing debates on the appropriate objects of study in Marxist psychology, scientists of the 1920s and 1930s had only two options if they were to survive – to choose to study the materialistic basis of mind and thinking, or to recognize the dominance of social (cultural) mechanisms in determining cognitive development. Given those options, Vygotsky chose culture (Etkind, 1993).

Vygotsky was the first Russian scientist to develop a complete Marxist-oriented psychological theory. In studying thinking and development, Vygotsky created an approach that became the basis for 50 years of experimental research. Vygotsky's theory has attracted attention because it provides an alternative to classic psychological approaches with regard to the role of social factors in the development of thinking and the role of tools and signs (especially human language) in the formation of human psychological processes. Vygotsky's writings on thinking emphasized the use of developmental analysis and made the claim that higher (that is, uniquely human) mental functions[17] have their origin in social life and are heavily shaped by the historically evolved tools and sign systems (especially human language) that mediate them. No attempt is made to summarize Vygotsky's theory, which is presented in six volumes of his writings; instead, this chapter will briefly touch upon the aspects of his writing on thinking already mentioned (Vygotsky, 1982b).

Preoccupied with the idea of developmental analysis of higher mental functions, Vygotsky developed the historical-genetic[18] method (Vygotsky, 1982b, 1984), which allowed him to obtain results that would be non-obtainable using the regular cross-sectional method. Along with this method, Vygotsky developed a new psychological hypothesis regarding the mediated nature of higher, "cultural," mental functions in contrast to "natural" functions that differ in their structure, nature, and control mechanisms. The concept of *mediation* implied mastering "psychological tools" as means to mastering psyche. The tools are initially

---

[17] There is a distinct tradition in the Soviet/Russian psychological literature, established in the 1920s (Krogius, 1980), of using the term *mental/intellectual functions* in its broadest sense, that is, applying it to all cognitive processes – perception, thinking, attention, memory, etc.

[18] Here *genetic* means developmental. Using this word, Vygotsky *never* referred to genetic in the biological sense.

connected to a situation involving communicative social interaction with a partner but are then turned by the child into a means of self-regulation. In regard to thinking, an example of such means is a word used as a sign. The process of mastering of such means is, in its essence, the development of self-regulation, a transition from external signs to inner signs. Such widely different things as "making a knot in order to remember something" and a word meaning are both artificial things intentionally created by man, and are both cultural elements and have dialogical natures in the sense that they can originate only in human communicative interactions.

A child does not invent, but she also does not simply learn to manipulate signs. Learning and intellectual discoveries are embedded in the history of the development of a child's operations on signs. The development of verbal thought takes place at the intersection of two roads: The speech becomes intellectualized and intelligence becomes verbalized (after age two). Mastering words, a child discovers new ways of manipulating and dealing with objects. The inner formation of sign relations occurs over a long period of time, that is, a child's thought develops through understanding the relationships between a sign and its meaning. The particular way in which a child uses a word is determined by the level of generalization and conceptualization: Initially concepts are syncretic concepts, then complexes, then pseudo-concepts, then functional concepts, and – only finally, much later – true concepts. Scientific concepts, reflecting essential qualities of objects and learned systematically at school, outstrip everyday concepts, which develop as empirical generalizations of individual experience. This finding, that the understanding of scientific concepts developed more quickly than everyday ones, led Vygotsky to formulate the concept of the zone of proximal development (Vygotsky, 1982b), a zone in which the actual level of intellectual development can be changed. Learning in this sense is ahead of development because it stimulates psychological functions (e.g., memory) that are still at the stage of maturing, that is, in the zone of proximal development. Accordingly, in the zone of proximal development, a child can change his level of his achievement with a teacher's help, that is, he can do with help what he cannot do alone. This potential level of mental development reflects the change of systemic connections in consciousness, which is a result of the stage development of consciousness.

Wertsch and Youniss (1987) saw the historical-cultural theory as primarily applicable to the formal school setting. According to these authors, to the extent that Vygotsky was trying to outline a psychology of pedagogy, his tendency to focus on the skills required in formal schooling contexts was legitimate. However, Vygotsky, his colleagues, and his students viewed their overall enterprise as one of constructing a theoretical approach that had broader applications than merely education. For example, Smirnov (1975), the author of a classic book on the history of theoretical discussions in Soviet psychology, wrote that the concept of the meaning of a word as the unit of analysis in thinking, developed by Vygotsky, is the key to understanding the nature of human consciousness as a whole. In this context, verbal thought is "a social-historical form of behavior" (Smirnov, 1975, p. 175). That is why the issue of the relationship between scientific and everyday concepts cannot be simplified to the issue of child-developed individual generalization versus socially given concepts, because both types of concepts are learned in a social situation involving communication with adults. The difference between scientific and everyday concepts lies in the degree of one's awareness and systematization of them. The system of mental functions, developing in a child's consciousness along with the mastery of scientific concepts, changes everyday concepts as well.

Vygotsky and his associates lived at a time when the major scientific myth shared by Soviet scientists was that they could overwrite human nature and create a system of upbringing that would result in a new type of a man exemplifying only the best of humanity. This ethno- and historicocentrism resulted in the use of socio-historically specific concepts in an attempt to examine the development of human consciousness in general. Vygotsky, his colleagues, and his students, viewed themselves as creating a general theory of development, with the leading role belonging to culture and society.

Two circumstances led to the wide acceptance and use of Vygotsky's methodological and theoretical approach. Vygotsky's group in Kharkov survived the repression in the 1930s and, upon their return to Moscow, had no serious theoretical or experimental competition in the field. Their theoretical approach corresponded to the overall Marxist dogma of the dominance of social influences in development. Hence, ideas formulated by Vygotsky and his methodological approaches[19] were successfully

---

[19] In addition to introducing Piaget's clinical method, the method of dual stimulation, the method of completing unfinished sentences, and the method of analyzing children's explanations, Vygotsky introduced a number of other methodological approaches. For example, in his scientific writing he used an analysis of literary dialogues, and he

developed in a variety of different theories. His ideas on the mediated nature of psyche were developed by Leont'ev in his theory of activity (Leont'ev, 1975; Voiskunsky, Zhdan, & Tikhomirov, 1999), his semiotic ideas were used by the famous Russian producer Sergei Eisenstein (Leont'ev, 1982), and his thoughts on the systemic structure of consciousness, functional organs, the localization of higher mental functions, and the disintegration of consciousness, were cultivated by Zeigarnik (1962), Luria (1969, 1979), and Rubinstein (1970).

It is important to note that even though higher mental functions in Vygotsky's theory were contrasted with natural mental functions, his approach focuses on the opposition of "social and individual," rather than "social and biological." The "higher-natural" dichotomy was criticized by Rubinstein and his students (Brushlinsky, 1968; Gurevich & Gorbacheva, 1992; Rubinstein, 1958), when they pointed out that in this interpretation, social could be equated with external. This, according to the critics, was an incorrect interpretation, because, according to Marx, inner conditions could not be limited to pure biological conditions, because "human nature itself is a product of social history" (Brushlinsky, 1968, p. 97).

A reinterpretation of the concepts of "higher" and "natural" functions is suggested by Puzyrei, a representative of the third generation of Vygotsky's students (Puzyrei, 1986). Puzyrei treats the act of mastering a sign as creating that sign based on its particular meaning and uses to the individual. He stresses the manipulative nature of culture and of culturally determined mediating tools (symbols and signs). When mastering a stimulus, "an action occurs that is organized in a special form, the performance of which alone allows development to happen" (Puzyrei, 1986, p. 85). These actions allow the transformation of one's innate natural functions into higher ones, and they are the means by which humans regulate behavior and the human psyche is reorganized. Such an understanding of the "higher-lower" or "cultural-natural" contradiction suggests a change in our understanding of the mechanisms of higher mental functions: The objects of study are not the natural processes of mental functioning but rather systems of actions targeted toward the transformation of mental functioning. Puzyrei's interpretation of the concept of "individual" in Vygotsky's theory assumes the dialogical nature of human consciousness: It is possible for a man to

suggested a method of placing a child in a group of children speaking foreign languages to study changes in the egocentric speech of this child.

relate to himself, as to another person, and in this process to change his self-regulation of mental functioning.

Social Situations Involving Communication with Others as a Determinant of the Development of Thinking

Vygotsky's idea that thought is born not from a word or another thought, but from the "motivating sphere" of our consciousness, has been the source of many different approaches to understanding the motivation for thinking and the relations between the mental processes of a subject as an individual and as a bearer of socially determined forms of thinking.

In Russian, the notion of consciousness might be translated as "co- (or shared) knowledge," determined by the "coexistence" of an individual and human culture. This notion was widely accepted among Marxist psychologists. On the way to mastering one's culture (or societal historical experience), human thinking develops. Within the inner activity of thinking, an individual forms inner schemata that, even though they do not correspond exactly to "external" activity, link individual thoughts to forms of thinking developed by humanity. The transition between these forms, according to Vygotsky, is a shift from "shared" thinking to individual thinking but is mediated by social structures of thoughts through the semantic function of a word as a sign.

It is important to note that the most frequent criticism of Vygotsky's theory was complexity of the mediated nature of an individual's thought by systems of signs, that is, the difficulty in finding a correspondence between mediation by activity and mediation by sign in a single process of the development of individual consciousness. Brushlinsky (1968) wrote that the Achilles' heel of cultural-historical theory was the idea that signs transform interpersonal interaction into individual spiritual life. According to this author, Vygotsky's interpretation of signs led to intellectualism (the assumption that consciousness is prior in its development to activity) and, consequently, to idealism[20] (Brushlinsky, 1968).

In the context of a concrete psychological study, however, the question of the mediated nature of an individual's thought can be reformulated

---

[20] This argument was addressed by Smirnov (1975). According to Smirnov, it is wrong to mix the cultural-historical context of the development of consciousness, which Vygotsky considered in talking about the development of higher mental functions, and the context of individual development in a society that (via child–adult interactions) guides the self-directed activity of a child on his way to mastering a sign and its relations.

into a study of the internal dialogue of thinking and into a study of internal modification of thinking through mastering higher-order psychological tools (e.g., informational technologies). Kuchinsky, a Belorussian psychologist, was one of the first to explore the dialogical nature of thinking (Kuchinsky, 1983). He attempted a holistic analysis of the structural involvement of speech in pure thinking activity. It is important to note that the author did not formulate the task as one of describing the structural-functional peculiarities of thinking in communication situations, that is, the structure of thinking as a goal-directed activity. Rather, his analysis focused on the formal characteristics of dialogues between partners attempting to solve problems and in finding analogous formal structures in individual problem solving.

Kuchinsky based his analysis on ideas coming from linguistics, especially on the concept of sign in Bakhtin's theory (Bakhtin, 1979). Bakhtin analyzed the dialogical position of different meanings using literary characters (e.g., Dostoyevsky's characters). Kuchinsky (1988), using experimental data from dialogues between partners, attempting to solve problems, separated speech components into different clusters – a cluster related to finding a solution and a cluster related to planning steps of thinking. However, Kuchinsky focused only on studying the exteriorized (e.g., translated from the inner to the external), as expressed in speech actions, ignoring purely mental actions as components of the goal-directed activity of thinking. In this sense, Kuchinsky's theory appears to be limited.

Soviet psychologists also developed a variety of other approaches, including studies of the internal content of an action, reflection, goal-creation, and the correspondence between the orientation and performance of an action (e.g., Gal'perin, 1959, 1981; Davydov, 1986). Many authors studied how problem solving is influenced by communicating information at various times and in various ways. Sources of additional knowledge in these studies were other people and different technological systems (e.g., Brushlinsky, 1982; Kornilova, 1986; Kornilova & Tikhomirov, 1990; Urvantsev, 1974).

Mechanisms of Social Determination Conceptualized in Terms of "External" and "Inner" Conditions of Thinking

The methods used in Soviet/Russian psychology were determined by the shared understanding of thinking as the process or activity of solving particular problems. Different theoretical schools used a variety of methods, including, for example, having the subject perform creative tasks that required no special knowledge; studying concept development (methods of Vygotsky-Sakharov, see Vygotsky, 1982b; Bruner, 1977, and Tikhomirov, 1969); organizing help for a subject in the form of ordered clues; and associative experiments. These shared methods made the findings obtained in different schools of thought comparable. However, the broad Marxist definition of thinking as a generalized and mediated type of cognition of reality allowed enough freedom for variability in theories of thinking.

One theory of thinking, developed by Rubinstein and recognized as the official approach to the study of thinking, overshadowed Vygotsky's and Leont'ev's theories in the period between the 1930s and the 1960s (Lomov, 1989; Zinchenko, 1999). Rubinstein's theory was based on the assumption that the mechanism of "analysis through synthesis" was the main mechanism of regulation of human thinking (Rubinstein, 1958). The mechanism of "analysis through synthesis" determines the "productivity" of thinking. The object of thinking is incorporated into new connections and relations with other objects, allowing the individual to learn new sides of the object and to reflect on new characteristics of this object in new concepts. According to Rubinstein, the principle means of thinking are analysis, synthesis, abstraction, and generalization (Rubinstein, 1958).

Tikhomirov (Luria's student) criticized this approach, pointing to the lack of a psychological "flavor" and the too-general nature of these concepts. According to Tikhomirov, these concepts could easily be included in a variety of different frameworks and theoretical approaches, some of which would result in contradictory arguments and predictions. He also pointed to the fact that Rubinstein's students' favorite experiments, using the method of "reasoning out loud," failed to address the causal mechanisms of thinking (Tikhomirov, 1975).

Rubinstein's line of research was continued by his students, Abul'khanova (1968), Antsyferova (1988), and Brushlinsky (1979) (for a review, see Brushlinsky, 1997; Lomov, 1989). These scientists experimentally developed one of Rubinstein's general ideas: the idea of "the external through the inner" as the mechanism that determines thinking (Rubinstein, 1958).[21] The importance of inner conditions of

[21] These experiments were mostly performed with so-called small creative tasks. An example of such a task is the question, "Will a candle light up on a space ship (under conditions of weightlessness)?" At different stages in a subject's thinking, an experimenter gives the subject different specially formulated clues. The way in which a subject uses or ignores different clues provides information on the mediated nature of external influences via inner conditions.

thinking has been recognized in many theories. The question is, however, what aspects of thinking are considered to be these inner conditions? In Rubinstein's tradition, inner conditions were perceived as different stages in the process of thinking. For example, to be ready to accept a clue and to progress in finding a solution, a subject must reach a certain stage in his thinking; for example, he must have completed his analysis of the task and be ready to synthesize the information it provides. That is, for Rubinstein, the inner conditions of thinking are determined by characteristics of the process of thinking itself. In addition, the advocates of this theory assume that these inner conditions can be influenced by the external conditions of the problem-solving situation. In other words, a subject can be led from one stage to another stage in his thinking under the guidance of an experimenter. Inner conditions have been treated differently in more recent experimental work by Kornilova (Kornilova et al., 1991; Kornilova & Tikhomirov, 1990). In her research, such formal-dynamic constructs as cognitive styles, cognitive risk, situational and personal anxiety, and success motivation were regarded as inner conditions.

Obviously, the way in which inner conditions of thinking are understood in different theoretical frameworks determines how issues regarding the determination of thinking can be addressed. If inner conditions are defined as types and levels of generalization, manipulable by external influences, then it seems logical to search for social causes of interindividual variability on these characteristics. Then researchers can describe more or less successful clues and other pedagogical or experimental tricks and observe their manipulative role in subjects' searches for solutions. In contrast, in defining formal-dynamic stylistic characteristics as inner conditions, researchers make a reasonable case for formulating questions about social as well as non-social causes of individual differences in stylistic traits. They state, for example, that a subject's cognitive style is a fundamental inner condition of his thinking that mediates the effect of a clue. Thus, in order to understand the clue's influence on the process of thinking, the researcher should understand the structure of the subject's cognitive style, which may be of a social, as well as a non-social, nature.

In any discussion of the inner determinants of thinking, research into the motivational aspects of thinking cannot be ignored. These aspects were addressed in analyses of the subjective regulation of thinking developed in the school of Tikhomirov (1969, 1975, 1977). He accepted Leont'ev's theory of activity and concentrated his attention on studying the structure of thinking activity, focusing on the process of goal development. Tikhomirov viewed intermediate goals that arise during problem solving as new products of thinking activity; as long as the task has not been accepted by a subject, he will not attempt to solve it. The act of accepting a task consists of connecting the task to a motivational structure that is active in the specific situation. Tikhomirov separated external and inner (purely cognitive) motivations, but he also noted that this separation on its own does not completely resolve issues regarding the emotional-motivational regulation of thinking.

The originality of this approach was in pointing out the regulating aspects of goals and emotions in the activity of thinking. "The goal-making process is one of the most essential components of thinking activity, and concentrates in itself connections between thinking and other mental processes – memory, imagination, emotional-volitional and motivational aspects of personality" (*Psikhologicheskie mekhanismy tseleobrazovaniya*, 1977, p. 24). This theoretical idea was realized in experiments investigating associations between aspects of final and intermediate goals of thinking (e.g., their trivial or original nature, their concrete or general character, their hierarchy) and characteristics of thinking activity and its productivity, as well as exploring the influence of shifts in emotional-motivation evaluations on changes in characteristics of thinking activity.

A separate line of studies was devoted to research on the regulatory influence of motives on thinking activity. Researchers, working in the framework of Tikhomirov's approach (Berezanskaya, 1977; Kornilova, 1994; Kornilova & Chudina, 1990; Vasiliev, Popluzhnyi, & Tikhomirov, 1980), developed the concept of a structural function of a motive. The authors argue that thinking as an activity has its own motive, which structures thinking, that is, defines a set of actions constituting the activity and determines a set of goals and operations or strategies leading to these the realization of these goals. These studies, combining experimental and clinical methods, investigate different types of motives and their influences on subjects' thinking. The researchers show that different motives and motivational shifts dramatically influence the structure of thinking, as well as lead to changes in subjects' plans and goals and in types of intellectual strategies.

The most important idea in Tikhomirov's approach is that goal-making processes and motivation are directly related to the management of cognitive activity (Tikhomirov, 1977). Tikhomirov argues that thinkers are active, that they themselves produce the motivational and regulating mechanisms of their thinking activity, and that motivations in thinking are not completely determined by external influences. This active nature of the thinker was a point of contention between Tikhomirov's school and Gal'perin and Talyzina's theory of stage formation (Gal'perin, 1959, 1981; Talyzina, 1981, 1984). Gal'perin's approach (see next section) treats thinking as a form of orientation, which, according to Tikhomirov, restricts thinking to very limited forms from the start. The active nature of a subject (in terms of goal-making) is suppressed under conditions in which he is required to follow an explicitly formulated scheme of mental activity.

Understanding thinking as a high-level self-regulatory process, Tikhomirov objects to Gal'perin's contention that thinking can be formed through a system of direct "manipulating" influences. He proposes a less direct management of thinking that involves changing a thinker's motivation by providing motivational and emotional support to problem solving (Tikhomirov, 1984).

Theories of the Social Determination of Thinking as Applied and Implemented in Educational Practice

The belief that the development of thinking is entirely socially determined,[22] both functionally and developmentally, had been the basis of Soviet education throughout its 70-year history. Thus, it was assumed that all children attending regular Soviet schools could be taught to do virtually anything. According to the official belief, education plays an extremely important role in development. Next, I will briefly present three psychological educational theories as examples of how the notion of the social determination of thinking was applied to pedagogy: (1) Gal'perin's theory of planned formation, (2) Shchedrovitsky's approach to education, and (3) Davydov's theory of the content and structure of learning activity (the theory of developing education).

---

[22] One exception to this belief existed in work done with handicapped children. The importance of biological determination was fully recognized. Handicapped children were placed in special educational institutions where they were trained more or less successfully to overcome their deficits. However, such "exceptions" existed outside of the psychology of thinking and were not incorporated into the theories discussed here. Moreover, a specific area of science, independent of psychology and pedagogy, existed, called *defectologiya*, defined as an integrated scientific discipline that embraces the study and education of all handicapped children and adults. It is in the framework of this science that issues regarding the development of abnormal thinking are studied.

The development of thinking in a child is closely related to his education. Influential situations range from spontaneous practical interactions such as game playing, to goal-directed, controlled interactions, such as classroom lessons. Each of these types of interaction contributes to a child's development in its own way. In his theory of the zone of proximal development, Vygotsky showed that every step in development depends upon the previous steps. However, the child himself does not determine these steps. The child's education is the result of child–adult cooperation that borders her "zone of proximal development."

Even though the mastery of thinking and, therefore, its development, takes place only through the child's own activity, this activity itself should be directed and organized (Gal'perin, 1985) to achieve maximum impact on development. The forms and organization of activity are not arbitrary but are determined by certain conditions.

In an attempt to find an alternative to a traditional type of schooling, Gal'perin developed a method[23] that allows any action in any given child to be formed with minimum energy and maximum efficiency (Liders & Frolov, 1991). This method is based on the principle that "an action is not formed in parts, but rather as a complete and correct structure containing all necessary components in their proper relation to other concepts" (Gal'perin, 1978, p. 102). Gal'perin's theory of staged and planned formation of actions and concepts suggested that the critical, and purely psychological, aspect of an individual's activity is its orientational aspect (Gal'perin, 1976). That is why one of the main components of this method is the process of building an orientational scheme, that is, a scheme containing all of the relevant information needed to create a plan of action and all the information needed to master an action faultlessly on the very first attempt. Thus, the orientation scheme is a special type of instruction, characterized by the completeness and clarity with which it describes an action. Moreover, this instruction is created in a way that permits the transfer of a mastered action to completely different situations.

Gal'perin showed experimentally that both the process and results of education depend upon the nature and efficiency of an individual's orientation, and upon how well this orientation reflects the aspects of objects and environments needed for successful action. The concept of

---

[23] It is important to note that in this school "planned formation" is understood not only as a method of teaching, but also as a "method of forming new concrete mental processes and phenomena, that is as a method of psychological research" (Gal'perin, 1978, p. 93).

orientational activity provides a key to understanding the mechanisms of learning and to the quality of new knowledge. In addition, orientational activity makes complicated connections between learning and natural, spontaneous ontogenetic processes more concrete. From this point of view, the traditional form of education, widely found in schools today and embedded in many experiments, can be classified as based on the first type of orientation. This type of orientation does not provide a differentiated understanding of the full system of conditions necessary for the successful outcome of an action. In the context of such an orientation, a student is forced to search for missing information himself. Thus, learning is performed via trial and error, with a student finally (usually only partially) discovering the products of his activity through blind groping. The efficiency of this type of education is mostly determined by a child's previously formed systems of orientation. Hence, this type of learning is subordinated to the level of mental development of the child. Piaget was, no doubt, right in his evaluation of the weak developmental potential of traditional education. However, this is not the only type of education. According to Gal'perin, education can be built on a completely different foundation.

In a second type of education, based on the second type of orientation, a student's activity is organized in a special way: She is given all of the directions necessary for successful completion of a given task from the very beginning. This leads to the disappearance of a lengthy and psychologically unjustifiable period of trial and error. A child, according to Gal'perin, obtains valuable knowledge and masters actions consciously, based on common sense and her sense of reality. However, researchers have found that this type of education does not have any direct influence on a child's general level of cognitive activity, because it does not guarantee the wide applicability of the mastered knowledge to other situations, and does not require students to develop the ability to establish a system of orientations for new tasks in the same knowledge domain.

These limitations can be overcome if a child masters not actions and concepts (or their systems), but methods of analyzing objects and developing orientations. This constitutes a third type of education, with a corresponding orientation, that is, when a child can build an orienting basis for each concrete situation based on general principles. When a child masters a method of creating orientational bases for his actions he then has a real means for independent and rational research. In this process the child learns to select the main qualities, units, and

connections among studied materials, revealing their underlying structure. As a result, general orientational schemes for a wide range of activities are formed, constituting, according to Gal'perin, the main condition for development. During the 1960s and 1980s, a set of studies was
conducted that showed a close connection between the third type of orientation and the development of thinking. In particular, the third type of
orientation was applied in teaching scientific concepts to preschoolers
(Obukhova, 1981), and in the development of complex graphical skills
(Gal'perin, 1985).

Thus, unlike many other types of education, Gal'perin's method of
planned formation of actions and concepts, which models various frag-
ments of children's general mental and cognitive development in experimental conditions, is not limited to "problematic representations" of the
learning material. This method assumes that a full system of conditions
is completely established, guaranteeing that a child can successfully
perform new actions, that this action can be correctly transferred to a
new context, and that, step by step, the child will master and learn the
desired qualities of these actions. Mastery of the objective means that
analyzing objects constitutes the basis for organizing a child's rational
search for a problem solution. Thus, in contrast to widespread traditional types of education that vary only at the surface level, this third
type of education, based on the third type of orientation, addresses the
internal mechanisms of children's cognitive development. According to
Gal'perin, "the heart" of developmental education is teaching a child to
be able to establish the third type of orientation independently in any
new situation.

Another major practical application of the principle of social determination of thinking was developed in the framework of the activity
of Moscow Meta-theoretical Circle (MMC).[24] These scientists believed
that it was necessary to study the educational process holistically as a
system and restructure it accordingly. This approach rests on the following epistemological premises. First is a distinction between naturalistic
and activity approaches to human behavior. The naturalistic view assumes that objects in the surrounding world are independent entities
with which humans interact. The principal theoretical categories of the

---

[24] This circle was formed on the basis of the Moscow logical circle, which appeared in
1952 in the department of philosophy at Moscow State University. The founder and the
real leader of this circle was Alexander Zinoviev, but in the fall of 1954, when Zinoviev
was exiled from the country, the leadership switched to Georgy Shchedrovitsky.

naturalistic approach are subjects and objects, where subjects are always human beings. The activity approach starts with human activity as an all-embracing principle within which objects and relations are revealed as embodiments of the activity itself. Objects in the external world now appear as secondary constructions dependent for their existence on the activity that is applied to them. As for the subject, the concept of activity is more important than the humans involved in it. This is Shchedrovitsky's major thesis: Activity should not be regarded as an attribute of the individual but rather as an all-embracing system that "captures" individuals and "forces" them to behave in a certain way.

Activity thus appears as a complex system whose structure can be viewed from different perspectives and grasped by different means of analysis. What follows from this is the third of Shchedrovitsky's theses, namely, that an essential distinction exists between an object of study and its presentation in a particular scientific domain. A single complex object (e.g., behavior) might be analyzed in a number of different scientific domains, depending on the epistemological and methodological positions chosen. The scientist's task therefore includes not only the study of the object within a chosen scientific framework, but also the choice of theoretical procedures that mark this subject as a distinct component of scientific knowledge.

In 1957, Shchedrovitsky and Alekseev published an article about the study of thinking, in which they argued that thinking should not be viewed as only fixed knowledge, but also as a process and an activity in which knowledge about objects is formed and used. Such a formulation of the main research task implies both (1) a separation and description of the structure of processes of thinking and the creation of an "alphabet" of elementary thinking operations, and (2) a study of laws, based on which complex combinations of ways and types of thinking can be created from existing thinking operations. This approach had more than theoretical significance: The scientists involved always stressed its practical orientation. They stated that this research would "allow them to improve education in such a way that a teacher would not only translate certain types of knowledge for his students, but also would be able to consciously shape certain actions and ways of thinking in his pupils" (Shchedrovitsky & Alekseev, 1957, p. 46). Based on this approach, a new activity- and content-oriented type of education was developed – one impossible to realize in the context of regular school subjects (physics, math, chemistry, history, etc.). School subjects only provide material in a form of prepackaged knowledge from which the content of education (e.g., those ways and tricks of thinking used to obtain this knowledge) has yet to be extracted through special logical analysis (Shchedrovitsky, 1964).

That is why this group of scientists perceived education as "a complex structural whole, containing a number of heterogeneous parts: along with what children should study there are also pupils' learning activities and teachers' activities, organizing this process" (Shchedrovitsky, 1963, p. 162). Therefore, along with logical and meta-theoretical studies that allowed researchers to examine the content of education (i.e., the types of thinking and the activities to be mastered), two other types of studies were designed and undertaken. The first type included psychological studies of how children master the content of education (e.g., the activity that students must perform to master a new type of activity). In this context, special attention was given to the problem of the ontogenetic development of thinking in learning settings (Shchedrovitsky & Alekseev, 1957). The second group of studies involved purely pedagogical research that was designed to explore the types of teacher activity required for children to master new content.

Such a complex and simultaneously clear-cut formulation of the program of studies was possible in the MMC because the object of research was not an abstract process of learning or an isolated, decontextualized educational situation, but rather a holistic system of education in its social environment. Education was perceived as a special social institution that had its own history and functional role in society. Its historical function was to provide an uninterrupted process of societal reproduction by means of "implementing" in new generations the abilities and types of thinking needed to perform socially significant activities (Shchedrovitsky, 1966). This approach not only provided a certain framework for educational research (including educational psychological research), but it also allowed the formulation of a much broader circle of research tasks related to the reorganization of the education system based on the activity principle.

Finally, Davydov's pedagogical theory (for a review, see Zhdan, 2000) was founded on his criticism of traditional Soviet educational psychology, which, he argued, was based on an empiricist doctrine of concept formation that prevented students from acquiring a broad-scale theoretical foundation in science and the humanities. Using Shchedrovitsky's distinction between the object of study and the scientific subject, Davydov argued that the only coherent way to acquire new knowledge is through theoretically constructed scientific concepts. Educational psychology must therefore revise the methodological apparatus that focused on the gradual development of quasi-scientific concepts, based in the everyday experience of the child.

In the 1960s, Davydov and El'konin, inspired by Vygotsky's work (Vygotsky, 1982b, 1983), conducted a series of studies directed toward creating new forms of education. The main premise was that the role of pedagogy and of pedagogical psychology is not to search for effective new ways of schooling (as was required by traditional pedagogy), but rather to concentrate on the content of mastered knowledge. Vygotsky viewed ways of teaching as derived from the content of mastered knowledge and stressed that the content of knowledge has a leading influence on a child's mental development. That is why it is necessary in school settings to introduce a child to a system of scientific (theoretical) concepts. These concepts cannot be mastered independently by a child simply through his personal experience. Vygotsky argued that a teacher should not simply be an organizer of a child's personal experience or a translator of his or her own experience, but rather a representative of science and cultural knowledge, the mastery of which requires special settings. The traditional methods of teaching theoretical concepts in Soviet schools did not make theoretical knowledge the content of education, but instead resembled the process of mastering primitive "everyday" (empirical) concepts (Davydov, 1972). Davydov designed a special curriculum for primary schools in which scientific subjects were presented in a way that provided students with a basis for mastering scientific concepts that meet the epistemological standards of modern science and the humanities. The special curriculum in grammar and mathematics designed by Davydov and his collaborators have shown that a seven-year-old child can, in fact, handle highly abstract concepts.

In addition, it has been shown that theoretical knowledge cannot be mastered if memorization and recall are the only means by which the child studies material. The mastery of theoretical concepts requires special types of activity, "learning activity," that must be intentionally encouraged and developed in a child. That is why, along with developing new curricula and new ways of teaching, psychologists working within this theoretical framework conducted a series of theoretical and experimental studies aimed at exploring the process by which learning activity develops in young school-age children. Later, the results of these studies were assembled into the "theory of the content and structure of learning activity" (Davydov, 1972; Davydov & Vardanian, 1981; El'konin, 1974).

In sum, in this section an attempt has been made to present a complex and elaborate picture of Russian/Soviet theories on mechanisms and the development of thinking and their practical applications. The approaches reflect not only the complexity of the existence of Russian/Soviet psychology within a strong ideological system of Marxism–Leninism, but also a wide range of creativity and novelty of Soviet/Russian theoretical and experimental ideas.

One might wonder whether the change of political scenery in Russia which took place in the early 1990s has re-shaped the field. The answer to this question is yes, but not much: the schools that have been described here are still active and productive, but their development is incremental now – although there are many interesting experimental studies, no distinctly new directions have originated within the last 10 years (for review, see Druzhinin, 1999; Kholodnaia, 1997). One possible explanation for this is that the cultural atmosphere in Russian society now is such that the society looks to psychology for new developments in (1) social psychology due to the emergence of large immigrant populations and the dramatic diversifications of ethnic background in major cities, (2) the psychology of aging, (3) industrial and organizational psychology, (4) gender psychology, (5) educational psychology, and (6) clinical psychology and psychotherapy. The survey of Russian psychological periodicals within the last five years resulted in the identification of a rather limited number of articles on the psychology of thinking and reasoning. As is true of any social science, Russian psychology is vulnerable to fads and the study of thinking is not very fashionable today.

Is it possible to study intelligence without using the Western concept of intelligence?

This chapter aimed to provide a brief summary of the contribution of Russian/Soviet psychology to the field of intelligence and thinking. Having described the historical background and major assumptions underlying studies of intelligence and thinking in Russian/Soviet psychology, I attempted to bring the reader's attention to the fact that even though significant ideological pressure existed, Soviet/Russian psychology was never made uniform and flat. Certainly, the idea of the dominance of social determination in cognition did correspond in its basic form to the ideological pressures of Marxism–Leninism. But, even such a generic statement is a simplification. Russian/Soviet psychology is characterized by a variety of approaches and ideas that contributed, individually and collectively, to what we currently refer to as the field of intelligence. Yet, it has managed to contribute to this field without using the concept of intelligence, and it still is rather cautious in using it.

References

Abul'khanova, K. A. (1968). *Mysl' v deistvii (Psikhologiya myshleniya)* [Thought in action (Psychology of thinking)]. Moscow: Politizdat.

American Heritage Dictionary of the English Language, The (1992). (3rd ed.). New York: Houghton Mifflin Company.

Antsyferova, L. I. (Ed.). (1988). *Kategorii materialisticheskoi dialektiki v psikhologii* [Categories of materialistic dialectics in psychology]. Moscow: Nauka.

Asmolov, A. G. (1996). Ot kul'tury poleznosti – k culture dostoinstva: sotsial'naia biographia kul'turno-istoricheskoi psikhologii. *Izvestia Academii Pedagogicheskikh i Sotsial'nykh Nauk, 1,* 39–43.

Bakhtin, M. M. (1979). *Estetika slovesnogo tvorchestva* [Esthetics of verbal creativity]. Moscow: Arts.

Berdiaev, N. A. (1990). *Samopoznanie (opyt philosophskoi biographii)* [Self-cognition (philosophical autobiography)]. Moscow: International Affairs.

Berezanskaya, N. V. (1977). K analizy kritichnosti i vnushaemosti v intellektual'noi deyatel'nosti [Toward an analysis of critical ability versus suggestibility in intellectual activity]. In A. N. Leont'ev & E. D. Khomskaya (Eds.), *Psikhologicheskie issledovaniya* (pp. 50–57). Moscow: Moscow State University.

Bernstein, N. A. (1966). *Ocherki po phisiologii dvizhenii i phisiologii activnosti* [Essays on the physiology of movements and the physiology of activity]. Moscow: Nauka.

Blonsky, P. P. (1935a). *Pamyat' i myshlenie* [Memory and thinking]. Moscow: Sotsekgiz.

Blonsky, P. P. (1935b). *Razvitie myshleniya shkol'nika* [The development of thinking in preschoolers]. Moscow: Uchpedgiz.

Bruner, J. (1977). *Psikhologiya poznaniya. Za predelami neposredstvennoi informatsii* [The psychology of cognition. Beyond the limits of immediate information]. Moscow: Progress.

Brushlinsky, A. V. (1968). *Kul'turno-istoricheskaya teoriya myshleniya* [Cultural-historical theory of thinking]. Moscow: Higher School.

Brushkinsky, A. V. (1979). *Myshlenie i prognozirovanie* [Thinking and prognosis]. Moscow: Thought.

Brushkinsky, A. V. (Ed.). (1982). *Myshlenie: protsess, deyatel'nost', obshchenie* [Thinking: Process, activity, communication]. Moscow: Nauka.

Brushkinsky, A. V. (1996). Teoria L. S. Vygotskogo i ideologia [The theory of L. S. Vygostky and ideology]. *Izvestia Academii Pedagogicheskikh i Sotsial'nykh Nauk, 1,* 52–58.

Brushkinsky, A. V. (Ed.). (1997). *Psikhologicheskaia nauka v Rossii XX stoletia: Problemy teorii i istorii* [Psychological science in Russia in the 20th century: Issues of theory and history]. Moscow: Institut Psikhologii RAN.

Burlachuk, L. F., & Morozov, S. N. (2000). *Slovar'-spravochnik po psikhodiagnostike* [Psychometric dictionary]. Sanct-Petersburg: Psychologia.

Burmenskaya, G. V. (1997). The psychology of development. In E. L. Grigorenko, P. Ruzgis, & R. J. Sternberg (Eds.), *Continuing the tradition: Russian psychology today* (pp. 215–249). Commack, NJ: Nova.

Danziger, K. (1997). *Naming the mind.* Thousand Oaks, CA: Sage.

Davydov, V. V. (1972). *Vidy obobshcheniya v obuchenii (logiko-psikhologicheskie problemy postroeniya uchebnykh predmetov* [Types of generalizations in learning (Logic-psychological issues of school subjects' curriculum]. Mosocow: Pedagogika.

Davydov, V. V. (1986). *Problemy razvivauyshchego obucheniya: opyt teoreticheskogo i eksperiental'nogo issledovaniya* [Issues of developing learning: Results of theoretical and experimental psychological research]. Moscow: Pedagogy

Davydov, V. V., & Vardanian, A. U. (1981). *Uchebnaya deyatel'nost' i modelirovanie* [Learning activity and modeling]. Erevan: Luis.

Druzhinin, V. N. (Ed.). (1999). *Sovremennaia psikhologia: Spravochnoe rukovostvo* [Modern psychology: Handbook]. Moscow: INFRA-M.

Dubinin, N. P. (1988). *Genetika – stranitsy istorii* [Genetics – pages of history]. Kishenev: Shtiinitsa.

El'konin, D. B. (1974). *Psikhologiya obucheniya mladshego shkol'nika* [The psychology of primary school students]. Moscow: Znanie.

Etkind, A. M. (1990). Obschestvennaya atmosphera I individual'nyi put' uchenogo: Opyt prikladnoi psikhologii 20-kh godov [The societal atmosphere and a scientist's individual path: An overview of applied psychology in the 1920s].*Voprosy psikhologii, 5*, 13–22.

Etkind, A. M. (1993). Eshche o Vygotskom: zabytye teksty i nendidennye konteksty [Again on Vygotsky: forgotten texts and undiscovered contexts]. *Voprosy Psikhologii, 3*, 37–54.

Florensky, P. (1991). *Vodorazdely mysli* [Paths of thought]. Novosibirsk: Shol'nye biblioteki.

Gal'perin, P. Ya. (1959). Razvities issledovanii po formirovaniya umstvennykh deistvii [Research on the formation of mental actions]. In *Psychological Science in the USSR* (pp. 441–461). Moscow: USSR Academy of Sciences.

Gal'perin, P. Ya. (1976). *Vvedenie v psikhologiyu* [Introduction to psychology]. Moscow: MGU.

Gal'perin, P. Ya. (1978). Poetapnoe formirovanie kak metod psikhologicheskogo issledovaniya [The method of stage formation as a method of psychological research]. In P. Ya. Gal'perin, A. V. Zaporozhetst, & S. N. Karpova (Eds.), *Current issues in developmental psychology* (pp. 93–110). Moscow: MGU.

Gal'perin, P. Ya. (1981). K Issledovaniyu intellektual'nogo razvitiya rebenka [Toward research on children's intellectual development]. In I. I. Il'yasov & V. Ya. Lyaudis (Eds.), *Textbook on developmental psychology. Soviet psychologists' papers in 1946–1980* (pp. 198–203). Moscow: MGU.

Gal'perin, P. Ya. (1985). *Metody obucheniya i ymstvennoe razvitie rebenka* [Methods of learning and child intellectual development]. Moscow: MGU.

Grigorenko, E. L., & Kornilova, T. V. (1997). The resolution of the nature–nurture controversy by Russian psychology: Culturally biased or culturally specific?

In R. J. Sternberg & E. L. Grigorenko (Eds.) *Intelligence, heredity, and environment* (pp. 393–493). New York: Cambridge University Press.

Grigorenko, E. L., Ravich-Scherbo, I. V. (1997). Behavior genetics and general psychological theory. In M. L. LaBuda & E. L. Grigorenko, *On the way to individuality: Behavior genetics today* (pp. 83–121). Commack, NJ: Nova.

Gurevich, K. M., & Gorbacheva, E. I. (1992). *Umstvennoe razvitie shkol'nikov: Kriterii i normy* [School students' cognitive development: Criteria and norms]. Moscow: Znanie.

Gurova, L. L. (1976). *Psikhologicheskii analiz resheniya zadach* [A psychological analysis of problem solving]. Voronezh: VGU.

Joravsky, D. (1987). L. S. Vygotskii: The muffled deity of Soviet psychology. In M. G. Ash & W. R. Woodward (Eds.), *Psychology in twentieth-century thought and society* (pp. 189–211). New York: Cambridge University Press.

Kholodnaia, M. A. (1997). *Psikhologia intellekta: Paradoksy issledovania* [Psychology of intelligence: Research paradoxes]. Moscow-Tomsk: Psikhologia.

Kondakov, M. I. (1996). L. S. Vygotsky i pedagogika [L. S. Vygotsky and pedagogical sciences]. *Izvestia Academii Pedagogicheskikh i Sotsial'nykh Nauk, 1,* 59–64.

Kornilov, K. N. (1980). Biogenetichesky printsip i ego znachenie v pedagogike [Biogenetic principle and its significance for pedagogy]. In I. I. Il'yasov & V. Ya. Lyaudis (Eds.), *Textbook on developmental and pedagogical psychology. Soviet psychologists' papers in 1918–1945* (pp. 12–17). Moscow: MGU.

Kornilova, T. V. (1986). Myshlenie, oposredovannoe dannymi EVM [Thinking mediated by a computer]. *Voprosy psikhologii, 6,* 123–130.

Kornilova, T. V. (1994). Risk i myshlenie [Risk and thinking]. *Psikhologicheskii zhurnal, 4,* 20–32.

Kornilova, T. V., & Chudina, T. V. (1990). Personality and situational factors influencing decision-making in dialogues with a computer. *Mind, Culture, Activity. An International Journal, 4,* 25–32.

Kornilova, T. V., Grigorenko, E. L., & Kuznetsova, O. G. (1991). Pozanavatl'-naya activnost' i individual'no-stilevye osobennosti intellektual'noi deya-tel'nosti [Cognitive activity and individual-stylistic characteristics of problem solving]. *Vestnik MGU, 1,* 16–26.

Kornilova, T. V., & Tikhomirov, O. K. (1990). *Prinyatie intellectual'nykh reshenii v dialoge s komp'uterom* [Intellectual decision-making in dialogues with a computer]. Moscow: MGU.

Kostiuk, G. S. (1969). Printsip razvitiya v psikhologii [The principle of development in psychology]. In E. V. Shorokhova (Ed.), *Metodologicheskie i teoreticheskie problemy psikhologii* (pp. 118–152). Moscow: Nauka.

Kozulin, A. (1984). *Psychology in utopia. Toward a social history of Soviet psychology.* Cambridge, MA: MIT Press.

Krogius, A. A. (1980). Eksperimental'noe issledovanie intellectual'nykh functsii studentov [Experimental studies of students' intellectual functions]. In I. I. Il'yasov & V. Ya. Lyaudis (Eds.), *Textbook on developmental and pedagogical psychology. Soviet psychologists' papers in 1918–1945* (pp. 38–43). Moscow: MGU.

Kuchinsky, G. M. (1983) *Dialog i myshlenie* [Dialogues and thinking]. Minsk: Belorussian University.

Kuchinsky, G. M. (1988). *Psikhologiya vnutrennego dialoga* [The psychology of inner dialogues]. Minsk: Universitetskoe.

Leont'ev, A. A. (1996). Lev Semenovich Vygotsky kak pervyi psikholingvist [Lev Semenovich Vygotsky as a first psycholinguist]. *Izvestia Academii Pedagogicheskikh i Sotsial'nykh Nauk*, 1, 65–73.

Leont'ev, A. N. (1972). *Problemy razvitiya psikhiki* [Issues in the development of the psyche]. Moscow: MGU.

Leont'ev, A. N. (1975). *Deyatel'nost'. Soznanie. Lichnost'* [Activity. Consciousness. Personality.]. Moscow: Politizdat.

Leont'ev, A. N. (1982). O tvorcheskom puti L. S. Vygotskogo [On Vygotsky's creativity]. In *Selected works by Vygotsky* (vol. 1, pp. 9–41). Moscow: Pedagogika.

Liders, A. G., & Frolov, Yu. I. (1991). *Formirovanie psikhicheskikh processov kak metod issledovania v psikhologii* [The formation of mental processes as a method of research in psychology]. Moscow: MGU.

Lomov, B. F. (Ed). (1989). *Sergei Leonidovich Rubinshtein* [Sergei Leonidovich Rubinstein]. Moscow: Nauka.

Losev, A. F. (1991). *Philosophiya. Miphologiya. Kul'tura* [Philosophy. Mythology. Culture]. Moscow: Politizdat.

Luria, A. R. (1969). *Vyshie korkovye funcstii cheloveka I ikh nerusheniya pri lokal'nykh porazheniyakh mozga* [Higher cortical functions in man and their disturbance by local brain damage]. Moscow: MGU.

Luria, A. R. (1979). *Yazyk i soznanie* [Language and consciousness]. Moscow: MGU.

Mamardashvili, M. K. (1968). *Soderzhanie i formy myshleniya* [Content and forms of thinking]. Moscow: Vyshaya Shkola.

Mamardashvili, M. K. (1984). *Klassichesky i neklassichesky idealy ratsional'nosti* [Classical and nonclassical ideals of rationality]. Tbilisi: Metsniereba.

Mamardashvili, M. K. (1992a). D'yavol igraet s nami kogda my myslim ne tochno . . . [The evil plays with us when our thinking is not precise . . .]. In M. K. Mamardashvili (Ed.), *Kak ya ponimau philosophiyu* (pp. 126–142). Moscow: Progress.

Mamardashvili, M. K. (1992b). Nauka i kyl'tura [Science and culture]. In M. K. Mamardashvili (Ed.), *Kak ya ponimau philosophiyu* (pp. 291–310). Moscow: Progress.

Mattaeus, W. (1988). *Die sowietische Denkpsychologie* [Soviet psychology of thinking]. Goettingen: Hogrefe.

Obukhova, L. F. (1981). *Kontseptsiya Zhana Piazhe: za i protiv* [Pros and conts of Piaget's theory]. Moscow: MGU.

Palei, I. M. (1974). K differentsial'no-psikhologicheskomu issledovaniyu studentov v svyazi s zadachami izucheniya potentsialov razvitiya vzroslogo cheloveka [Toward differential-psychological studies of students in the context of adult development]. *Sovremennye psikhologo-pedagogicheskie problemy vyshei shkoly*, 2, 133–143.

Panasiuk, A. Yu. (1973). *Adaptirovannyi variant metodiki D. Vekslera* [A Russian adaptation of the WISC by D. Wechsler]. Moscow: NII Psikhiatrii MZ RSFSR.

Pavlov, I. P. (1953). *Issledovanie vyshei nervnoi deyatel'nosti* [Research on higher nervous activity]. Kiev: Gosmedizdat USSR.

Pavlov, I. P. (1993). Pis'mo Chelpanovy [A letter to Chelpanov] *Voprosy Psikhologii*, 2.

Podgoretskaya, N. A. (1980). *Izuchenie priemov logicheskogo myshleniya u vzroslych* [Studying strategies of logical thinking in adults]. Moscow: MGU.

Puzyrei, A. A. (1986). *Kul'turno-istoricheskaya teoriya Vygotskogo i sovremennaya psikhologiya* [Vygotsky's cultural-historical theory and modern psychology]. Moscow: MGU.

Rubinstein, S. L. (1957). *Bytie i soznanie* [Being and consciousness]. Moscow: Nauka.

Rubinstein, S. L. (1958). *O myshlenii i putyakh ego razvitiya* [On thinking and methods of studying thinking]. Moscow: AN SSSR.

Rubinstein, S. Ya. (1970). *Eksperimental'nye metodiki patopsikhologii I opyt ikh primeneniya v klinike* [Experimental methods in psychopathology and their applications in clinics]. Moscow: Meditsyna.

Sechenov, I. M. (1952). *Refleksy golovnogo mozga [Brain reflexes]*. Moscow: AMN SSSR.

Segal, N. L. (2002). Twins: Not just in science, but in society. *Twin Research*, 5, 139–140.

Shchedrovitsky, P. G. (1963). Mesto logiki v psikhologo-pedagogicheskikh issledovaniyakh [The place of logic in psychological-pedagogical research]. *Detskaya I pedagogicheskaya psikhologiya* (pp. 162–164). Moscow: Izdatel'stvo APN RSFSR.

Shchedrovitsky, P. G. (1964). O printsipakh analiza ob'ectivnoi struktury myslitel'noi deyatel'nosti na osnove ponyatii soderzhatel'no-geneticheskoi logiki [On the principles of the analysis of objective structure of thinking activity on the basis of concepts of content-genetic logic]. *Voporsy psikhologii*, 2, 125–131.

Shchedrovitsky, P. G. (1966). Ob iskhodnykh printsipakh abaliza problemy obucheniya I razvitiya v ramkakh teorii deyatel'nosti [On basic principles of the analysis of learning and development in the context of the theory of activity]. In *Obuchenie i razvitie* (pp. 89–119). Moscow: Prosveshchenie.

Shchedrovitsky, P. G., & Alekseev, N. G. (1957). O vozmozhnykh putyakh issledovaniya myshleniya kak deyatel'nosti [On possibilies of studying thinking as an activity]. *Doklady APN RSFSR*, 3, 41–46.

Smirnov, A. A. (1975). *Razvitie i sovremennoe sostoyanie psikhologicheskoi nauki v SSSR* [History and the modern situation of psychological science in the USSR]. Moscow: Pedagogika.

Smirnov, S. D. (1985). *Psikhologiya obraza: Problema aktivnosti psikhicheskogo otrazheniya* [Psychology of image: The active nature of mental reflection]. Moscow: MGU.

Smirnov, S. D. (1994). Intelligence and personality in the psychological theory of activity. In R. J. Sternberg, & P. Ruzgis (Eds.), *Personality and Intelligence* (pp. 221–247). New York: Cambridge University Press.

Talyzina, N. F. (1981). Printsipy sovetskoi psikhologii i problema psikhodiagnostiki poznavatel'noi deyatel'nosti [Principles of Soviet psychology and issues concerning the assessment of cognitive activity]. In I. I. Il'yasov & V. Ya. Lyaudis (Eds.), *Textbook on developmental and pedagogical psychology. Soviet psychologists' papers in 1918–1945* (pp. 38–43). Moscow: MGU.

Talyzina, N. F. (1984). *Upravlenie protsessom usvoeniya znanii* [Managing the process of mastering knowledge]. Moscow: MGU.

Teplov, B. M. (1985). *Izbrannye trudy (t. 1,2)* [Selected works (Vols. 1–2)]. Moscow: Pedagogika.

Teplov, B. M. (1990). *Um polkovodtsa* [A military commander's mind]. Moscow: Pedagogika.

Tikhomirov, O. K. (1969). *Stuktura myslitel'noi deyatel'nosti* [The structure of thinking activity]. Moscow: MGU.

Tikhomirov, O. K. (1975). Aktual'nye problemy razvitiya psikhologicheskoi teorii myshleniya [Current problems in the psychological theory of thinking]. In O. K. Tikhomirov (Ed.), *Psukhologicheskie issledovaniya tvorcheskoi deyatel'nosti* (pp. 5–22). Moscow: Nauka.

Tikhomirov, O. K. (Ed.). (1977). *Psikhologicheskie mechanismy tseleobrazovaniya* [Psychological mechanisms of goal formation]. Moscow: Nauka.

Tikhomirov, O. K. (1984). *Psikhologiya myshlenia* [The psychology of thinking]. Moscow: MGU.

Tulmen, C. (1981). Mostart v psikhologii [Mozart in psychology]. *Voprosy philosophii, 10,* 129.

Urvantsev, L. P. (1974). *Formirovanie suzhdenii v usloviyakh neopredelennosti visual'noi stimulyatsii* [The formation of reasoning across conditions that vary the certainty of visual information]. Unpublished doctoral dissertation, MGPI, Moscow.

Vasil'ev, I. A., Popluzhnyi, V. L., & Tikhomirov, O. K. (1980). *Emotsii i myshlenie* [Emotions and thinking]. Moscow: MGU.

Voiskunsky, A. E., Zhdan, A. N., & Tikhomirov, O. K. (Eds.). (1999). *Traditstii i perspectivy deiatel'nostnogo podkhoda v psikhologii* [The past and the future of the activity theory in psychology]. Moscow: Smysl.

Vygotsky, L. S. (1982a). *Istorichesky smysl psikhologicheskogo krizisa* [The historical meaning of psychological crises]. Moscow: Pedagogy.

Vygotsky, L. S. (1982b). *Myshlenie i rech'* [Thinking and speech]. Moscow: Pedagogika.

Vygotsky, L. S. (1983). *Istoriya razvitiya vyshikh psukhicheskikh phunktsii* [The history of development of higher mental functions]. Moscow: Pedagogika.

Vygotsky, L. S. (1984). *Razvitie myshlenia podrostka I obrazovanie ponyatii* [The development of thinking in adolescents and concept formation]. Moscow: Pedagogika.

Wekker, L. M. (1970). *Psikhicheskie protsessy. Myshlenie i intellekt* [Mental processes. Thinking and intelligence]. Sanct-Petersburg: S-PGU.

Wertsch, J. V., & Youniss, J. (1987). Contextualizing the investigator: The case of developmental psychology. *Human Development, 30,* 18–31.

Yaroshevsky, M. G. (Ed.). (1971). *Problemy nauchnogo tvorchestva v sovremennoi psikhologii* [Modern psychological research on scientific creativity]. Moscow: Nauka.

Yaroshevsky, M. G. (1981). Katerogial'nyi apparat psikhologii [Categorical apparatus of psychology]. In *Sechenov i mirovaya psikhologicheskaya mysl'* (pp. 139–152). Moscow: Nauka.

Yaroshevsky, M. G. (1996). Integratsia 'dvukh psikhologii' kak zaviaz' shkoly Vygotskogo [The integration of "two psychologies" as the source of Bygotsky's school]. *Izvestia Academii Pedagogicheskikh i Sotsial'nykh Nauk, 1,* 44–51.

Zaporozhets, A. V. (1986). *Izbrannye psikhologicheskie trudy (v dvykh tomakh)* [Selected psychological writings (Vols. 1–2)]. Moscow: Pedagogika.

Zeigarnik, B. V. (1962). *Patologiya myshleniya* [Thinking pathologies]. Moscow: MGU.

Zhdan, A. N. (1993). Prepodavanie psikhologii v Moscovskom universitete [Teaching psychology in Moscow State University]. *Voprosy Psikhologii, 4,* 80–93.

Zhdan, A. N. (2000). K istoricheskoi rekonstruktsii psikhologicheskikh osnov razvivaiushchego obuchenia [Toward a reconstruction of psychological bases of the developing education]. *Voprosy Psikhologii, 6,* 76–90.

Zhdan, A. N., & Marstinkovskaia, T. D. (2000). Mosckovskaia psikhologicheskaia schola [Moscow Psychological School]. *Voprosy Psikhologii, 3,* 117–127.

Zinchenko, V. P. (1996). Ot klassicheskoi k organicheskoi psikhologii [From classical to organic psychology]. *Izvestia Academii Pedagogicheskikh i Sotsial' nykh Nauk, 1,* 8–38.

Zinchenko, V. P. (1999). Slovo o Rubinshteine [A word about Rubinstein]. *Voprosy Psikhologii, 5,* 107–109.

Zinchenko, V. P., & Mamardashvili, M. K. (1977). Ob ob'ektivnom metode v psikhologii [On objective method in psychology]. *Voprosy philosophii, 7,* 109–125.

Zinchenko, V. P., & Morgunov, E. B. (1994). *Chelovek razvivaushchiisya: Osherki rossiiskoi psikhologii* [A developing person: Essays on Russian psychology]. Moscow: Trivola.

Zinchenko, V. P., & Smirnov, S. D. (1983). *Metodologicheskie voprosy psikhologii* [Meta-theoretical issues in psychology]. Moscow: MGU.

Zinov'ev, A. A. (1954). *Voskhozhdenie ot abstractnogo k konkretnomu* [A rise from the abstract to the concrete]. Unpublished doctoral dissertation, MGU, Moscow.

7

Intelligence Theory, Assessment, and Research

The Israeli Experience

Moshe Zeidner, Gerald Matthews,
and Richard D. Roberts

OVERVIEW

Modern-day Israel, much like the United States, may aptly be described as a test-oriented and test-consumed society. During the first few decades of its existence, Israeli society almost miraculously managed to come to grips with a multitude of pressing social problems, including helping large numbers of immigrant children to assimilate into Israeli society. This process demanded a concerted effort at raising the standards of the educational system as a whole. Standardized aptitude and intelligence tests have a particularly formidable presence in the Israeli school system. These tests are primarily employed to serve the following functions: screening and diagnosis, student selection, classification, and placement (e.g., streaming). They have also been used to identify and select children for special programs, research and program evaluation, and vocational guidance and counseling (Zeidner, 1990b). In addition, scholastic aptitude tests are employed in the Israeli university system for purposes of student selection, classification, and placement (Beller, 1992, 1993; Zeidner, 1987b).

Generally, intelligence and ability assessments have important pedagogical, social, and economic implications for social systems. Because of the heterogeneous nature of the Israeli population, hosting more than

We thank the following individuals for providing us with materials, preprints, publications, and references for preparing this chapter: Prof. Surel Cahan and Prof. Gershon Ben-Shahar, Hebrew University of Jerusalem; Prof. Reuven Feuerstein, Bar-Ilan University; Prof. Baruch Nevo, University of Haifa; and Dr. Yoav Cohen, National Institute for Testing and Evaluation.

212

100 linguistic subcultures, Israeli researchers have understandably been concerned with group differences in ability and achievement, and in developing equitable methods of testing. Furthermore, given that Israel is severely deficient in natural resources, policy makers have realized that the development of its human intellectual resources is not only an economic vital investment, but is perhaps the only road to Israel's survival. Thus, the importance of valid intellectual assessment for modern-day Israel appears to go beyond sheer utility to critical consequences for the future social and economic development, and very survival, of Israel as a nation in the years to come.

With these few brief observations in mind, this chapter surveys a number of important trends in intelligence theory, research, and assessment that have been conducted by Israeli psychologists over the past five decades. This chapter focuses primarily on the educational arena (i.e., the pre-school, school, and university contexts), where copious published data are available. A wide array of intelligence and ability tests are currently used by the military, industry, and government, but much of this material is disparate, fragmentary, or confidential. This chapter begins with a survey of intelligence and aptitude assessment in different populations, including studies of sociocultural group differences. The second part of the chapter highlights three, among many possible, seminal contributions made by Israeli psychologists to intelligence research – facet theory, dynamic assessment and cognitive modifiability, and the personality–intelligence interface. This chapter concludes by reviewing existing accomplishments and directions for future research.

INTELLIGENCE ASSESSMENT IN ISRAEL

Overview

Over the centuries, Jewish culture has held learning, scholarship, and intellectual pursuit, particularly in the religious domain, in the highest regard (Alexander, 1999). This is personified in the writing of the famous medieval Jewish philosopher, Maimonides: "Every Jew . . . is under an obligation to study Torah, whether he is poor or rich, in sound health or ailing, in the vigor of youth or very old and feeble" (Mishneh Torah, 1:8). Moreover, Maimonides advocated that each sage be obliged to teach every willing student, for "those who are obliged to study are also obligated to teach" (1:2). Based on this cultural heritage, the

Israeli educational system puts much emphasis on cultivating students' learning competencies, aptitudes, and cognitive abilities.

The goal of providing various ethnic, social, and linguistic subgroups in Israeli society with rich opportunities for learning and educational progress has become exceedingly complicated. Prior to the establishment of the State of Israel in 1948, school and university student populations were relatively homogeneous, being composed mainly of children from Jewish middle-class families of European origin (about 90%), who typically fared well academically. Since the inception of the State of Israel, the student body has changed radically in content and scope, with the school student population growing over seven-fold since 1943. Mass immigration from over 70 countries doubled the population over the first 3 years of statehood and tripled it over the first 12 (Zeidner, 1990b). During the early years of statehood, the educational system in Israel was charged with accommodating an increasing percentage of Jewish children from Eastern cultures (e.g., Morocco, Algeria, Yemen), many of whom presented the classical symptoms of cultural deprivation (Raviv, 1989). Consequently, the student body became increasingly heterogeneous in family structure and cultural-educational orientation, traditional customs, and behavior patterns. Whereas immigrant students of European extraction adapted quite readily to modern Israeli society (and its Western-oriented school system), students of Eastern background evidenced considerable difficulty in the school acculturation process. These students may tend to regard attainment of education in a more instrumental way, being prepared to invest less in education as a means of acquiring status (Kfir, 1988). Because students of Eastern origin had lower levels of achievement aspiration compared with their Western counterparts, they were also destined to be less mobile within a society that holds modern status-attainment norms (Adler, 1984).

The educational system assumed the main burden and responsibility for equalizing opportunities and integrating culturally different groups into Israeli society. School and educational psychologists have been charged with assessing and placing the masses of immigrant children, requiring a move away from their traditional role of assessing and diagnosing failing students. Only in the past three decades have standardized, culturally appropriate instruments for the assessment of intelligence and cognate measures been developed to support these efforts. At the level of higher education, a common scholastic aptitude test is taken by applicants to Israel's research universities. Each university independently determines its own admission policies (Beller, 1993), but, typically, candidates are rank-ordered using composite scores, derived from a combination of high school matriculation certificate grades and scholastic aptitude exam scores. In this section, we first describe the principal measures constructed for Israeli populations and then review studies of group differences.

Intelligence Measures: Brief Description

Leading Individual Tests

Individual assessment is generally performed with the aid of a conventional test battery. Sampling of students, much like in the United States and other Western industrialized nations, uses stratified random cluster sampling procedures, with schools serving as clusters, and strata defined by socially significant variables (i.e., geographic region, social class, ethnic composition, etc.). Properties of four leading tests are summarized in Table 7.1. The major scale for pre-school children is the Hebrew version of the Wechsler Preschool and Primary Scale for Intelligence (WPPSI; Lieblich, 1973). The standardization of the Hebrew version of the Wechsler Intelligence Scale for Children–Revised (WISC-R; Lieblich, Ben-Shachar, & Ninio, 1976), initiated by the Psychoeducational Service in 1972, was conducted on a nationwide representative sample of both the Jewish and Arab populations. The Hebrew version of the WISC-R has since been used for diagnostic, guidance, and school classification purposes among normal, gifted, and retarded Israeli populations. The recently published WISC-R95 (Cahan, 1998), intended for children aged 6 to 14, is the latest Hebrew adaptation of the WISC, developed in the early 1990s. The Hebrew adaptation of the Kaufmann Assessment Battery for Children (K-ABC; Kaufman & Kaufman, 1996) was published in 1996 by the Israeli Ministry of Education (Cahn, 1998). Like the original K-ABC, the test aims to assess children's intellectual abilities based on a solid theoretical and empirical framework and to differentiate between factual knowledge (Achievement) and the ability to solve problems (Cognitive Processing).

For college-aged populations, the principal test of cognitive and scholastic aptitude is the Israeli Psychometric Entrance Exam (PET), which is centrally constructed and administered by the National Institute for Testing and Evaluation. The test battery comprises three subtests, which bear some resemblance to the Verbal and Quantitative sections of the Scholastic Aptitude Test (SAT). The Verbal Reasoning

TABLE 7.1. *Summary of Four Intelligence Tests Used in Israel, with Illustrative Psychometric Data.*

	TEST			
	Wechsler Preschool and Primary Scale for Intelligence (WPPSI)	**Wechsler Intelligence Scale for Children–Revised (WISC-R)**	**Kaufmann Assessment Battery for Children (K-ABC)**	**Psychometric Entrance Exam (PET)**
Target population	Children aged 4–6.5 years	Children aged 6–16	Children aged 3–12	University applicants to 6 research universities and major colleges
Subscales	10 subtests: composite scores on Verbal and Performance abilities	10 subtests: composite scores on Verbal and Performance abilities	16 subtests: composite scores on Cognitive Processing and Achievement abilities	Originally consisted of 5 subtests: General Knowledge, Figures, Comprehension, Mathematical Reasoning, English. From October 1990, consists of the following 3 subtests: Verbal Reasoning, Quantitative Reasoning, and English.
Normative sample	1,072 children obtained from 192 preschool institutions in 3 major	1,100 children: 100 children from each of 11 age groups (6–16)	1,984 children, aged 3–12: sampled from 59 elementary schools and	24,146 (47% male) applicants to institutions of higher

216

Israeli cities		35 junior high schools	education in Israel. Scores were calculated for each of the 5 original subtests, and average scores for subtests were standardized to a mean of 500 and SD of 100. Later versions of PET, based on 3 rather than 5 subtests, were calibrated to 1984 scores, also Standardized to mean of 500 and SD of 100.
Internal consistency	0.91 (split-half)	0.96 (α)	0.97 for both age groups (ages 3–4 and 5–16) – *rxx* for total based on Guilford's formula for reliability of composite based on subtest split-half *rxx*	0.97 (KR-20 estimate)
Test-retest stability	0.79: 6–7 weeks	0.90+ (15 days)	Test-retest data not available for Israeli version (as noted in the manual)	0.85–0.90

Note. Test–retest stabilities vary with retest lag. Data sources: WPSSI: (Lieblich 1973), WISC-R: (Lieblich et al., 1976), K-ABC: (Cahan, 1998), PET: (Beller 1992).

(PET-V) subtest (60 items) focuses on verbal skills and abilities needed for academic studies, including (1) the ability to analyze and comprehend complex written materials, (2) the ability to think systematically and logically, and (3) the ability to perceive fine distinctions in meaning among words and concepts. The Quantitative Reasoning (PET-Q) subtest (50 items) focuses on the ability to use numbers and mathematical concepts, such as solving quantitative problems and analysis of graphical and tabular information. Only basic knowledge of math is required. The English (PET-E) subtest (54 items) is a foreign language subtest that serves the additional purpose of indicating whether a student should be placed in a remedial English class. It tests command of the English language in the academic context and contains three types of questions: sentence completion, restatements, and reading comprehension. Each subtest is scored separately and then standardized. The total PET is a weighted average of the scores on the three subtests (40%, PET-V; 40%, PET-Q; 20%, PET-E), transformed onto a scale with a mean of 500 and a standard deviation (SD) of 100 (range 200–800). Currently, the test is translated into Arabic, English, French, Spanish, and Russian.

Psychometric Properties of Tests

Overall, the psychometric properties of the Hebrew versions of the major intelligence tests just described are highly similar to those reported for the original versions. Table 7.1 summarizes some illustrative data on internal consistency and test–retest reliability for the tests highlighted here. These are generally very high in most cases for subtests as well as for total scores. Construct validity, as evidenced by correlations with other intelligence tests, is also very good. For example, the WPSSI showed a correlation of .84 for total Stanford-Binet score in a sample of 100 Israeli children. In the English version, the equivalent correlation is about .76. Nevo and Oren (1986) report a correlation of .85 between PET and SAT total scores, in a sample of English-speaking Israeli college students. The different tests also show good convergent validity. The K-ABC is associated with the following WPPSI scores: Verbal, $r = .73$; Performance, $r = .67$; and Full Scale IQ, $r = .80$. Similarly, its correlations with the WISC-R95 were substantial: K-ABC total score correlated at .79, .73, and .83 with Verbal, Performance, and Total scores, respectively. Conversely, WISC total score was strongly related to the K-ABC subtests of Cognitive Processing ($r = .77$), Achievement, ($r = .85$), and Total scores ($r = .83$). At the subtest level, the K-ABC Achievement scale correlated higher with WISC Verbal than with WISC Performance scores

(.86 > .68). In addition, Cognitive Processing correlated about equally with Verbal ($r = .69$) and Performance scores ($r = .72$). Similarly, for the PET, the median inter-correlation between verbal and quantitative subtests ($r = .68$) is very similar to that between the respective sections of the SAT (Donlon, 1984).

The tests also appear to have similar diagnostic and predictive validity to the original versions. Various studies provide evidence for the diagnostic validity of the WISC-R profile in differentiating learning disabled from normal children aged 8 to 12 years (e.g., Raviv et al., 1981). Achievement subtests of the K-ABC were more highly correlated with school grades (GPA) than Cognitive Ability subtests. For example, median correlations of $r = .38$ and $r = .68$ were reported for Arithmetic and Verbal Analogy. The predictive validity of the PET, with first year GPA as criterion, shows striking resemblance to the psychometric data reported for the SAT, as evidenced by a meta-analytic study of the predictive validity of the PET in Israeli universities (Kennet-Cohen, Bronner, & Oren, 1995). These findings are based on an analysis of the academic achievement at the end of the freshman year of almost all students (97,744) who began their studies at Israeli universities in the nine years between 1985 and 1993. The correlation (corrected for range of restriction) between the PET score and the criterion ranges, on average, between .33 and .51. Across all fields of study, except for medicine and engineering, the correlations of PET with the criterion were higher than for those between matriculation scores and the criterion (overall average validity of .44 and .37, respectively). Hence, the validities reported for the selection system used in Israel meet international standards and are similar to validities reported for other national selection systems, such as the SAT system used in the United States.

Group Tests of Ability

The two most popular group tests for the assessment of intelligence in the school system are the Milta Group Verbal Intelligence Test (Ortar, 1966) and Raven's Progressive Matrices (Raven, 1960). The Milta is modeled after the Lorge-Thorndike Intelligence Test and appears in parallel forms for three different grade categories (grades 4–6, 7–9, and 10–12). The Milta subtest composition and number of items vary from form to form. The Milta total score is reported to be of acceptable reliability (about $r_{xx} = .90$) and has satisfactory criterion validity, against school grades (r of about .60) (Ortar, 1966). Raven's Progressive Matrices, despite their lack of reliable Israeli norms, is probably the most widespread group measure of nonverbal ability used among Israeli children aged 8 to 13. The adequacy of the test's validity is generally deemed modest compared with verbal tests such as the Milta (Zeidner, 1985).

Group Differences in Test Scores

As in other multicultural nations, research has been directed toward sociocultural differences in test scores. Because the tests are translated from English, any comparison of groups rests on the assumption that test adaptation is "culture-fair." This section first reviews the principles of test adaptation to the Israeli setting, followed by an examination of sociocultural, gender, and age differences in intelligence test performance. Studies primarily sample school-aged populations, because there are scarce data from adult populations, reflecting the lack of standardized measures for Israeli adults, although some PET data are available.

Cultural Adaptation Principles and Procedures

The basic principal guiding the development of all major Hebrew standardized test versions was to stay as close to the English original as possible, unless items lacked compatibity with Israeli culture or the psychometric attributes of the items in Israeli samples needed upgrading. Consequently, the general framework and scoring system forming the adaptation of the WPPSI and WISC-R remained relatively unchanged. Changes in the WISC-R95 were designed to make the present version congenial to Israeli language and culture, largely by updating vocabulary items and concepts, simplifying administration and scoring, and improving standardization. Thus, while the Performance subtests remained relatively unchanged, a large number of items forming the Verbal subtests were revamped. These often reflected cultural differences between Israel and Western nations – for example, differences between Jewish and Gregorian calendars.

The Hebrew version of the K-ABC, however, required a large number of changes in the test content. Thus, some items were changed (or deleted) because they offended the sensibilities of students from traditional backgrounds. For example, to avoid negative reactions among children coming from religious background on the Gestalt Closure subtest, it was necessary to change the picture of a *pig* (a non-kosher animal, typically perceived as offensive by Jews and Muslims) as a figural stimulus. Other items were changed due to linguistic considerations. For example, in the Riddles subtest, the item, "What is made from beans, is brewed, and is often drunk by grownups for breakfast?", would elicit an inappropriate response because the word *brew* is typically used for tea in Israeli society. Furthermore, some items were found to be inappropriate following item analysis. For example, the word for *wristwatch* in Hebrew is more basic than in English and thus easier than intended by the original item. Finally, a Verbal Analogy subtest was added to the Achievement battery to enhance the representation of verbal abilities.

Sociocultural Differences: Jewish Sector

It is commonly held that those sociocultural subgroups closer to modern technological society score relatively high on standardized intelligence tests, partly because they are more readily socialized in the relevant concepts and skills (cf. Samuda, 1975). Indeed, numerous studies over the past 50 years report marked differences between Jewish examinees of Western and Eastern (i.e., Asian/African) background in intelligence test performance. The group disparities range anywhere from about one-half to one and a half standard deviations and are documented at the preschool (Lieblich, 1983), primary and secondary school (Lieblich, 1983; Minkowitch, Davis, & Bashi, 1982; Zeidner, 1985), and university levels (Zeidner, 1987b). Using the WPPSI, Lieblich (1983) found that children of European-American origin scored above children of Asian-African extraction by 13 to 15 points, on average. Furthermore, significant social class differences were evidenced in each ethnic group, with middle-class preschool children scoring above lower-class students by about 8 to 10 points. Children whose parents were born in Israel obtained the highest intelligence test scores. Research based on the WISC-R normative sample also shows that European students scored meaningfully above their Asian/African counterparts (Lieblich, 1983).

The pattern of group differences in Hebrew-speaking children supports the *cumulative deficit hypothesis*. Thus, there appears to be a cumulative increase in ethnic group differences on intelligence scores with age, rising from about .75 SD at ages 6 to 7 years to a discrepancy of about 2 SDs at age 15 to 16 years. Furthermore, middle-class children in each ethnic group are reported to outperform their lower-class counterparts in total WISC-R performance by about .5 sigma unit (Lieblich, 1983). Thus, the IQ difference among socioeconomic groups on the WISC-R starts out at about a .7 SD discrepancy at ages 6 to 7 years and increases to about a 1.1 SD discrepancy at ages 15 to 16 years. The students' ethnic group is reported to have a more sizable effect than socioeconomic status (SES) on Performance IQ, though there is a tendency for the ethnic gap to narrow among second-generation Israelis.

Lieblich (1983) also found a relative advantage of students of Western extraction on Verbal tests and an advantage for Asian students on the Performance tests, with the greatest ethnic group differences on the Information, Vocabulary, and Comprehension subtests. Other studies confirm that Eastern examinees generally score below their Western counterparts on verbal, relative to nonverbal, measures of ability (Minkowitch et al., 1982; Zeidner, 1985). At all ages, middle-class children showed advantages over lower-class children on Information and Vocabulary. A similar trend has been reported by Zeidner (1985, 1988b) for group verbal ability tests. Social class and ethnicity appear to have additive effects, that is, consistent social class differences across different ethnic groups. Zeidner (1985) also reported that sociocultural group differences, in favor of middle-class students, were more marked on a verbal test of intelligence than on a nonverbal test.

Zeidner (1987b) examined ethnic group differences in a sample of 1,538 Israeli student candidates applying for admission to a major university in Northern Israel for the academic year 1983–1984. Ethnicity had a highly significant effect on total test scores, accounting for about 7% of the composite test score variance. Israeli and European student candidates, who were not differentiated, scored significantly higher on average than did their Asian counterparts. Ethnicity had similar significant effects on two second-order factors – Verbal and General Reasoning – represented by a 0.78 SD difference between Israeli and Asian subgroup means on the Verbal factor, and a 0.38 SD difference on the General Reasoning factor. Again, ethnic group differences in mean ability test performance in Israel are linked primarily to the verbal dimension of the test battery, which is heavily influenced by the examinee's past learning experiences (cf. Jensen, 1980).

The observed group differences have been attributed mainly to sociocultural group differences in socialization patterns, home language, and differential schooling experiences. Studies of the PET suggest that effects of ethnic background (Western or Asian) are substantially linked to parental SES (Ben-Simon & Nevo, 1986) and education level (Kennet-Cohen, 2001). Furthermore, in view of the relatively more marked cultural group disparities commonly found on verbal (relative to nonverbal) tests, verbal deficit may be the main locus of the poor showing of minority groups on psychometric ability tests (Minkowitch et al., 1982).

Sociocultural Differences: Arab Sector

Research on cognitive abilities and achievements in the Arab sector has been relatively sparse over the years, due to lack of suitable tools. Thus, the WPPSI was translated into Arabic (rather than specifically adapted), such that culturally appropriate norms are not available even to the present point in time. Several studies have shown that Israeli Jewish preschool students outscore their Arab counterparts by about 1 SD on standardized tests of intelligence and scholastic ability (Kugelmass, Lieblich, & Bossik, 1974; Lieblich, 1983; Lieblich & Kugelmass, 1981). Kugelmass et al. (1974) investigated two samples of Israeli Arab village children tested with an Arabic translation of the WPPSI and compared scores with normative data for Jewish children. Arab rural children showed a different pattern of subscale scores, with a relative advantage in Verbal as compared with Performance IQ. Kugelmass and Lieblich (1975) obtained a similar result. A large-scale study of the WISC-R (which has been specifically adapted to the Arab culture and standardized on a representative group) also attests to a distinct profile among Arab students, who consistently score higher on Verbal IQ relative to the Performance composite (Lieblich & Kugelmass, 1981). Studies using the WISC-R, including one involving a representative sample of 639 Arab children aged 6 to 16 years (Lieblich, Ben-Shakhar-Segev, & Ninio, 1980) have confirmed that the superiority of the Verbal as compared with the Performance Scales is a consistent characteristic of Arab children up to the age of 12 years (see also Bashi, Cahan, & Davis, 1981).

Zeidner (1987a) compared the PET test scores for 1,778 Jewish and 1,017 Arab candidates for university admission. Culture was found to have a highly significant effect on scaled composite test scores, accounting for about 8% of the test score variance. Accordingly, Jewish student candidates outperformed their Arab counterparts by a margin of about 1 SD, with group differences largest on language but smallest in mathematics.

Overall, the few studies examining the effects of religious subgroup affiliation on intelligence test scores within the Arab population tend to suggest that Christian Arabs outscore their Muslim and Druze counterparts, whereas the latter two groups are not reliably differentiated in mean test performance (Bashi, 1976; Lieblich, 1983; Lieblich & Kugelmass, 1981). Christian students also outperformed students of Muslim or Druze background on Raven's Matrices group test (Bashi, 1976; cf. Bashi et al., 1981). However, much like in the Jewish sector, subgroup affiliation is correlated with social background, with most of the Muslims belonging to the lower class and the Christians to the upper class. Indeed, the rank order of groups by religion conforms to what would be expected on the basis of the respective groups' socioeconomic status. Overall, religious background in the Arab sector functions very similarly to social class in the Jewish sector.

The Arab culture and home environment may provide a clue toward the relative superiority of verbal versus nonverbal test performance. The central role of the Arabic language in both oral and written form may lead to disproportionate attention being paid to verbal skills at expense of other aspects of communication. Furthermore, the Muslim religion prohibits pictorial art and sculptures, perhaps limiting the experience of young Muslim children in this area. Informal observations also suggest that in the home environment of the Arab child there is much less opportunity, as well as demand, to carry out most of the depiction and construction activities that underlie the majority of the Performance subtests. Another relevant factor has to do with Arab attitudes toward time and speed. "Speed is from the devil" is a popular Arab saying, and Arab students may be accustomed to working in a relaxed, unhurried fashion, whereas the majority of the Performance subtests demand fast reactions and participants who take longer to carry out the instructions are penalized, even if they are correct.

Gender Differences

As Safir (1986) has pointed out, gender differences in IQ in Israel appear considerably greater than in the United States from an early age on. Such gender differences are evident on both verbal and analytical tests among both Jewish and Arab college candidates (Zeidner, 1986a, 1986b). In fact, gender is the third demographic factor in magnitude of effect on intelligence in both the Jewish (ethnicity > SES > gender) and Arab (religion > SES > gender) population. These data invariably have males outperforming females on the various cognitive tests. By contrast, Western studies find that adolescent boys are usually better in spatial and numerical abilities, whereas girls are superior in verbal abilities.

Gender differences in intelligence test scores are non-significant at the preschool level (Lieblich, 1983). However, data provided by Lieblich et al. (1976), involving 1,100 children aged 6 to 16 years given the Hebrew version of the WISC-R revealed significant gender differences in favor of boys, in the area of verbal intelligence. This effect appears initially at age 11. At age 13, significant differences appear in almost all subtests and all three IQ scores (Lieblich, 1983). The gender group differences grow through age 16, culminating in a .75 SD difference in overall IQ. Similar trends are observed for both the Verbal (.67 SD) and Performance composites (.75 SD). Findings reported for the Arab sector (Lieblich, 1985), reveal differences of about a third SD in favor of adolescent boys in total IQ. Cahan and Ganor (1995) conducted a more recent large-scale study that suggested fewer, and smaller magnitude, gender differences in cognitive ability. Data were collected from 11,000 schoolchildren in grades 4 to 6, drawn from 61 schools during the 1986–87 school year. Twelve tests were administered, covering a wide range of item content (classification, analogies, and series) and varying in item modality (verbal, numerical, and figural). Noticeable differences, at a magnitude of .20 SD, appeared in favor of boys for both Mathematical Reasoning and Verbal Oddities.

Zeidner (1986a) assessed SAT performance among Israeli college student candidates (1,088 female and 690 male), applying for admissions to a major Israeli campus. There was a small but consistent sex difference in favor of male examinees for the test as a whole and for the quantitative subscale, in particular. In a study by Gafni, Beller, and Bronner (2000), analysis of sociocultural group differences was based on all Israeli students in six universities who began their studies between 1985–86 and 1996–97. In the Hebrew-speaking groups, there was no meaningful difference between females and males in the admissions scores or in achievement at the end of the first year of studies. A different pattern was found for the Arabic-speaking students, where the admissions scores were higher for females, while academic performance was higher for males. Unlike the Hebrew-speaking group, the number of Arabic-speaking female applicants is about half that of Arabic-speaking males. Admission scores in this group may reflect self-selection of Arabic females; those who choose to apply to higher education tend to be of higher socioconomic status. In each group, the largest advantage for males was found for PET-Q. Much smaller differences were found for PET-V and PET-E, which favored men for the Hebrew-speaking group but women for the Arabic-speaking group.

The disparity between gender differences observed for the United States and Israel may be artifactual or real. Cahan and Ganor (1995) speculate that the content of their math items was not gender fair, dealing largely with types of vehicles, of more interest to boys. The higher male score may reflect also a greater tendency to guess among males than females, with boys observed to skip fewer items than girls do on all tests. Alternatively, the various data may reflect the cultural gap between North America and Israel regarding the issue of gender equality, expectation from boys and girls, and the opportunities offered to each gender, as reflected in the attitudes of various agencies (e.g., family, school, and media). Lieblich (1983) suggests that although males may fulfill their potential and progress according to abilities and have adequate role models, females have few models of high achievement and consequently do not meet their potential. Thus, the gender gap in math ability, in particular, may reflect the presence of more tradition-alist (i.e., deferential, sexist, and stereotyped) attitudes within Israeli society. In contrast to the realm of math, a virtual lack of gender differ-ences in verbal and spatial ability was found in the more recent study conducted by Cahan and Ganor (1995). This conforms to the trend in the United States that points to a clear tendency toward the disappearance of the gender gap for many cognitive abilities. Overall, observed gen-der differences may reflect the summation of a host of factors, including biological and constitutional gender differences, differential sex-typed expectations, and artifacts of some specific tests.

Age Differences (PET Studies)

A study by Kennet-Cohen and Oren (1993), based on 8,945 examinees who sat for the PET, compared scores for older (30 years old and above) versus younger (25 years and below) examinees in four universities. The mean score, across universities and departments, was $M = 529.62$ (SD $= 64.15$) for older and $M = 518.45$ (SD $= 68.09$) for younger ex-aminees, with older participants outperforming younger ones by about .17 SD. A small advantage was found for younger students on Figures ($d = 0.7$), Comprehension ($d = 0.5$), and Math ($d = 0.3$). By contrast, on General Information, older examinees outscored younger ones by .9 SD. However, Zeidner (1988a) showed that composite test scores correlate near zero with age. With respect to individual subtest scores, age was observed to correlate significantly with two out of three sub-tests designed to assess Verbal Ability, namely, General Information and Vocabulary. In addition, age correlates inversely with two out of the three subtests aimed at assessing General Reasoning Ability, namely, Figural Reasoning and Analytical Thinking. These results are what one might expect from the literature on cognitive aging, where fluid intelligence is thought to decline with age, while crystallized ability improves (see Matthews, Zeidner, & Roberts, 2002).

Test Bias and Equity in School-Based Intelligence Testing

The widespread reliance on measures of scholastic ability for assessment and placement of students from diverse cultural backgrounds in the

Israeli school system has raised serious concern regarding cultural test bias and fairness (Zeidner, 1987b, 1988b). The recent Israeli "anti-test movement" corresponds closely to criticisms voiced in the American educational system over the past 30 or so years. In Table 7.2, striking cross-cultural parallels in the Israeli and American anti-test movement are depicted. Rather than acknowledge the persistence of sociocultural group differences in test performance and focus on raising the level of minority group performance, many commentators have simply preferred to "kill the messenger" by attacking the validity and equity of the tests themselves. College admissions scholastic aptitude tests have been claimed to be political instruments used by the European Jewish majority groups to deny Arab and Jewish minority groups the prospects of higher education and high-status vocations, thus perpetuating ethnic segregation and ethnic social stratification in Israel.

The counterarguments raised by test proponents (Levinson, 1986) call to mind similar arguments found in the American litigation literature of the last three decades (cf. Jensen, 1980; Samuda, 1975). Among these are the satisfactory prediction, on basis of tests, of students' future achievement across ethnic groups; blindness of tests to various race, social class, and sex groupings; potential misuse of alternative assessment techniques; and the redeeming evidence of group aptitude test scores in protecting disadvantaged students from erroneous classification and special education classes. The PET has been a focus for empirical studies that have tested whether, according to accepted definitions of test bias (Jensen, 1980), it is equally fair to different groups of examinees, whether characterized by differences in ethnicity, social class, gender, or country of origin (Ben-Shakhar & Beller, 1983; Zeidner, 1986b, 1987b). In fact, a survey of the Israeli bias literature by Beller (1993) concluded that "Empirical evidence, gathered in studies conducted by Israeli universities and by the National Institute for Testing and Evaluation, indicates that, from a psychometric point of view, there is no problem of test bias in the selection process used by the universities" (p. 18).

One of the first studies of predictive bias in Israel (Zeidner, 1987b) analyzed the scholastic aptitude test scores of 1,538 Hebrew-speaking Israeli student candidates of varying ethnicity who were applying for admission to a major Israeli college campus. The psychometric properties of the test battery were compared by ethnic group via a variety of internal (factor structure, reliability, etc.) and external (predictive validity, homogeneity of regression, etc.) test bias criteria. Collectively, the data provided little evidence for differential construct or predictive

TABLE 7.2. *Antecedents, Manifestations, Consequences, and Empirical Research Emanating from the Anti-Test Movement in Israel*

Antecedents of Public Concern	Manifestations of *Anti-Test* Sentiments	Consequences of the *Anti-Test* Campaign	Results of Test-Bias Research
Sizable sociocultural differences in aptitude and achievement test scores	Vehement attack on scholastic aptitude tests in the media	A professional committee mandated to examine the goals, usages, problems, costs, and ethical implications of group ability test usage in the schools (Ministry of Education, 1985)	Empirical tests of cultural fairness in the predictive validity of both verbal and nonverbal tests for majority and minority group (Zeidner, 1986b)
Sequence of Israeli attempts to deal with ethnic and SES divergence in abilities and school performance at a structural level	Appeal to the courts by concerned parents to ban the usage of aptitude tests in elementary schools for student selection and classification purposes	Ban of widespread and massive administration of group ability tests for selection and placement purposes in elementary schools by the Ministry of Education as of January 1985	Evidence of intercept bias (scores overpredictive of minority group students) and little evidence in predictive slope bias by sociocultural group
Popularity of the cultural difference position in the mid-1970s	Development of an "anti-test syndrome" (cf. Jensen, 1980), characterized by intense emotional involvement in the test debate, contamination of reason by affect and ideology, and armchair speculation concerning the degree of bias and equity in testing (cf. Israeli Psychological Association Bulletin, 1986)		Tests of the "situational bias" hypothesis found sociocultural group membership does not interact with test atmosphere (Zeidner, 1985) or with examinees' test attitudes and dispositions (Zeidner, 1988a) in affecting ability test performance
Contentions of test bias and adverse impact for cultural minority groups in the population			
Severe overrepresentation of lower-class Eastern children in special education programs and low-status tracks			

validity of aptitude test scores as a function of ethnicity, thus negating the cultural bias hypothesis (see also Kennet & Oren, 1988). Large-scale studies examining gender (e.g., Gafni & Beller, 1989; Zeidner, 1987c) and age (Kennet-Cohen & Oren, 1993; Zeidner, 1988a) similarly find little support for test bias for college selection and admission. A recent large-scale study (Kennet-Cohen, 2001) found little evidence for predictive bias by socioeconomic group (based on parental education and income). No differences in validity were found for any components of the PET as a function of SES.

Findings from these many studies are consistent with most of the reviews of the literature examining sociocultural group differences in the predictive validity of aptitude test scores, providing little evidence for cultural bias in the prediction of scholastic performance (Jensen, 1980). When the regression equations do differ by culture, the difference is mainly in the intercept (Zeidner, 1987b). That is, the minority group is found to be significantly below the majority group intercept, resulting in the over-prediction of the former group's criterion performance when the common regression line is used (Jensen, 1980). These Israeli studies illustrate the ubiquity of the phenomenon of over-prediction of minority performance and underline the importance for educational psychologists to be fully cognizant of this phenomenon.

UNIQUE CONTRIBUTIONS FROM ISRAELI PSYCHOLOGY

Israeli researchers have made unique contributions to our understanding of a wide array of prominent issues in the domain of intelligence research. These include genetic and environmental determinants of intelligence (Elbedour, Bouchard & Mi Hur, 1997), birth order effects (Davis, Bashi, & Cahan, 1977), effects of schooling and age on intelligence (Cahan & Noyman, 2001); discovering affective (Zeidner, 1991) and cognitive (Ben-Shakhar & Sheffer, 2001) correlates of test performance; exploring the interface between personality and intelligence (Ganzach, Saporta, & Weber, 2000; Saklofske & Zeidner, 1995; Zeidner & Matthews, 2000); addressing both naïve theories (Zeidner, 1990a) and scientific conceptions (Zeidner & Feitelson, 1989) of intelligence; and both practical (Nevo & Chawarski, 1997) and emotional intelligence (Zeidner, Matthews, & Roberts, 2001; Zeidner, Roberts, & Matthews, 2002). Although there a good number of exemplary studies of Israeli psychologists we could showcase in this section, we present the work of two internationally acclaimed psychologists who have made seminal contributions to our understanding of various facets of intelligence – Louis Guttman and Reuven Feuerstein – together with research on the interrelationship of personality and ability.

Facet Theory: Research and Analysis

Conceptualization of the Intelligence Domain

Guttman's (1965a, 1965b, 1969) model of intelligence originates from his work on factor analysis, gaining its main thrust from developments in non-metric multidimensional scaling (in particular, Smallest Space Analysis). One of his insights is that, before developing a test of intelligence, one should explicitly express what one wants to test. Indeed, the persistence of uncertainty over the number of dimensions that constitute "intelligence" is a consequence of lack of clarity over the meaning of the construct (see Most & Zeidner, 1995).

Guttman observed that intelligence test items share two basic features. First, "questions are asked to which answers are given." Second, answers are scored as right or wrong (or from "very right" to "very wrong"). The first feature simply places intelligence tests in the context of stimulus and response, with the test stem (or question) serving as the stimulus. To characterize an intelligence test, therefore, first requires characterizing the test stimuli, in terms of facets such as language of test items (e.g., pictures) and test administration medium (e.g., auditory) (see Nevo, 1993a). Second, some notion of classifying answers as right versus wrong is required (Guttman, 1965b). Responses to intelligence tests should be interpreted against a veridical criterion, with the range being from perfectly true to not true at all. If behavior reflects a "true" intelligence, it may be judged on a continuum of correctness, objectively defined.

The criterion according to which the response is scored as correct can take many forms. These include: mathematical or logical relations (e.g., "What is 3×7?"), semantic ("How do you say hello in Hebrew?"), empirical ("Who discovered the laser?"), normative (What do you do if you find a stamped and addressed envelope in the street?), and authoritative ("To what extent do medical experts believe smoking increases your risk of lung cancer?"). Hence, intelligence test items typically require the deduction of an objective rule on tasks that are removed from specific instructional situations (e.g., "3, 7, 15, 31 – what comes next?"). A correct response is evidence that the examinee has deduced and used the rule appropriately.

According to facet theory (Guttman & Levy, 1991), an item belongs to the universe of intelligence test items if and only if its domain asks about a rule, be it logical, empirical, semantic, or normative, and the range is ordered from very right to very wrong with respect to that rule. The definitional commonality of the range of intelligence items provides part of the rationale for the well-replicated phenomenon of positive covariance among intelligence test items, item parcels, and tests. Based on this observation, Guttman formulated the "first law of intelligence" (Guttman & Levy, 1980), postulating that the population regression of any two test elements with similar ranges selected from the universe of intelligence items will be monotone with positive or zero signs (i.e., no negative correlations will be observed). This first law has been confirmed with respect to the WISC and WISC-R for children in Israel (Lieblich et al., 1976; Zeidner & Feitelson, 1989).

Sampling the Domain

Facet theory provides a method for systematically mapping out the domain of intelligence and sampling items, by contrast with the informal methods traditionally used in test construction. The first and crucial step in the facet approach is the specification of a theoretical framework and the a priori mapping out of the domain and universe of observation. That is, a definitional system for the content and observations forming the intelligence "universe" is, typically, formalized in the shape of a mapping sentence. Guttman and associates (Guttman, 1965b; Guttman & Levy, 1980, 1991; Schlesinger & Guttman, 1969) have subsequently identified three major dimensions or "facets" of the intelligence domain. These are: (1) language of test presentation or communication (e.g., verbal, numeric, figural), (2) mental or cognitive operation required by the test (e.g., rule inference, rule application, rule learning), and (3) modality of examinee expression (oral expression, manual manipulation of objects, and paper and pencil). The mapping sentence in Figure 7.1 delineates these three major facets and the specified observational domain of intelligence (Guttman & Levy, 1991).

The mapping sentence defines the test (or test battery) that can be developed by specifying the key facets and their constituent elements. In facet theory terminology (Schlesinger & Guttman, 1969), each of the elements in a facet (e.g., verbal, symbolic, figural) is termed a *struct*, whereas the facet profile of a given measure is termed a *structuple*. For example, a numerical item requiring rule application ($"x + 1 = 9$, $x = ?"$) would be designated by the structuple or profile a2b2, whereas a

The correct performance of subject (x) on an item:

Presented in the form of:	A. Language of Communication	Of an objective rule of:	B. Cognitive Operation	And requiring a response of:	C. Modality of Expression
	{a1. verbal}		{b1. inference}		{c1. oral}
	{a2. numerical}		{b2. application}		{c2. manual manipulation}
	{a3. figural}		{b3. learning}		{c3. paper & pencil}

↑

	According to that rule
{very right/high correctness of performance}	
to	
{very wrong/low correctness of performance}	

FIGURE 7.1. A mapping sentence of intelligence test items (based on the WISC–R items).

symbolic item requiring rule learning (e.g., digit-symbol task) would be designated as a2b3. Thus, any given intelligence task may be classified by the content facets of its structuple (or profile).

Assume we wish to sample items relating to the first two facets specified; that is, the language facet and the cognitive operation facet. (If we are developing a battery of paper-and-pencil tests, we can hold constant the third facet, modality). Since the language and cognitive operation facets each consists of three elements, we get a ninefold classification of test items by multiplication of the two facets (i.e., "$3 \times 3 = 9$"). We can then proceed to systematically develop items tapping each of the nine profiles (structuples). For example, using this specific table, verbal reasoning (a1b1) could be assessed by analogy type items (e.g., "cat : kitten :: cow :_ ?"}; numerical reasoning (a2b1) could be assessed by numerical progressions, such as: "2, 3, 5, 8, _ ?"; and so forth. Similarly, paired associate type items could systematically be constructed to assess learning and memory. Thus, participants could be presented with a series of paired associates in verbal ("boy-coat"), numerical ("34 − 16"), and figural ("○–♦") modes, and asked to provide the second element given the first (see Nevo, 1993b).

Geometical Presentation of Intelligence Test Data

Smallest Space Analysis (SSA) is one of a family of non-metric, multidimensional scaling procedures that Guttman and co-workers applied to study the dimensionality and structure of intelligence tests. In this procedure, tests are represented as a point in an n-dimensional space; the higher the correlation between the tests (or items), the greater their relative proximity in this Euclidean space. Guttman's SSA maps the points onto the smallest space that maintains an inverse relationship between the observed correlations and geometric distances. The spatial maps presented by the computer allow researchers to examine visually the spatial projection of the variables, thus facilitating interpretation.

The bulk of research using SSA has been conducted in Europe and Israel (Canter, 1985; Guttman & Guttman, 1974; Guttman & Levy, 1980; Koop, 1985; Levy, 1985). As Guttman (1967) has observed, much of current practice in factor analysis focuses on special forms of rotation of axis rather than on the general configurational problems of space. Because SSA looks at the space as a whole rather than at some coordinate system, it appears a more meaningful way for revealing lawfulness in the underlying structure than factor analysis (Guttman, 1967).

Furthermore, in SSA, an analysis of test content in terms of definitional facets is believed to lead to more fundamental insights into the structure of correlation matrices, given that the facet is intrinsically meaningful. Thus, a further advantage of SSA over factor analysis is in the ability to postulate laws of order among test variables, including circular order, that is, which points fall in (or around) a circle. Guttman observed that ability tests within a content area (spatial, verbal, or numerical) tend to form a *simplex*, a straight line array in scaling representation, on which tests are ordered from simple to complex. Test that are of comparable complexity sampled from separate content areas tend to form a *circumplex*, a circular array in scaling representation. For example, a study by Zeidner and Feitelson (1989) provides evidence for a circular (circumplex) ordering of variables, as specified by the language of communication facet, with points representing verbal, numeric, and geometric structs of language roughly in appointed place.

Guttman (1954, 1969) pointed out that if a battery of tests is constructed or selected according to two facets (i.e., language of communication and cognitive operation), the battery's intercorrelation matrix will tend to have a specific geometric structure, termed a *radex*. The radex is represented as a disc in two-dimensional space or a sphere in three dimensions, divided into verbal, numerical, and figural content areas, as shown in Figure 7.2. In this radex, the shorter the average distance of a test from all other tests in the universe, the higher its correlation with all other tests, and hence the higher its loading on the general factor, and the smaller its group factor and specific variance. The task facet assumes a modular role, representing the distance of the variables from the origin. Points within the inner circle around the origin are predicted to have the struct of "rule inference," whereas points in the outer bands are predicted to have the respective structs of "rule application" and "rule learning," respectively. Hence, all tests requiring rule inference tend to be highly correlated. However, correlations among rule applications may be low and vary according to differences in the specific language of test communication.

Empirical studies have provided evidence for a radex configuration in aptitude tests (Koop, 1985; Guttman, 1954; Levy, 1985; Schlesinger & Guttman, 1969; Snow, Kyllonen, & Marshalek, 1984; Tziner & Rimmer, 1984). Researchers at Stanford (Marshalek, Lohman, & Snow, 1983) reported that the radex model is a simple and objective scaling representation of the hierarchical organization of abilities. Specifically, if data conform to a radex structure, one finds that complex tests with

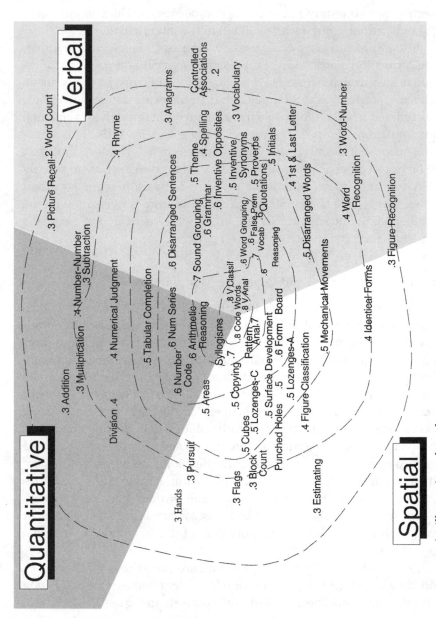

FIGURE 7.2. An illustration of a radex structure.

high loading on general intelligence (g) will scale in the center of the radex; simple tests reflecting mainly specific factors will scale in the periphery; and tests of intermediate complexity with high loading on a major or minor group factors will fall in the intermediate region.

If the third modality of expression facet (see Figure 7.1) is added, the correlation matrix may be represented as a cylinder, with the addition of a vertical dimension to the disk shown in Figure 7.2 (Levy, 1985). This axial facet indicates that elements in the three-dimensional space are ordered from (1) oral to (2) written expression through to (3) manual manipulations. Empirically, the SSA space for the WISC-R is three-dimensional and conforms to the lawfulness of a "cylinder" (Guttman & Levy, 1980; Lieblich et al., 1976). In view of the power of this approach, SSA appears a viable alternative to factor analysis. It is our hope that researchers in the United States will become more conversant with the methodology underlying SSA and employ this technique to assess the structure underlying intelligence test performance.

Dynamic Assessment and Cognitive Modifiability

Reuven Feuerstein, an internationally acclaimed professor of educational psychology at Bar-Ilan University in Israel, carried out groundbreaking work in the development of dynamic assessment procedures and systematic intervention materials for modifying the cognitive competencies of non-mainstream student populations (e.g., Feuerstein, Rand, & Hoffman, 1979; Feuerstein et al., 1980). Feuerstein's theory was developed after the establishment of the state of Israel, during times of massive immigration already alluded to in the opening of this chapter. The social pressures for integration and mainstreaming of these groups posed serious pressures for the development of new assessment methods that would take into account the immigrants' diverse cultures and allow the assessment and cultivation of their learning potential. Feuerstein found that standardized assessments did not reliably or validly assess the cognitive potential of these culturally different individuals.

Feuerstein et al. (1979) criticized standard procedures for their focus on static assessment and labeling and lack of guidelines for modification and remediation. The standard psychometric measures, he believed, did not provide relevant information on deficient cognitive functions responsible for learning difficulties or help in pointing to instructional strategies that would facilitate learning. According to Feuerstein and associates, the demonstration of *modifiability* is a prerequisite for intelligence assessment and should be the major goal of psychometric assessment of low performing students. Measuring intelligence without giving an examinee the opportunity to display change, learning, or modifiability is likened to measuring the volume of an iceberg by considering only its surface portion and not sounding its depth below sea level. As a result of the failure of static testing to provide specific descriptions of the cognitive processes involved in learning and recommendations for prescriptive teaching and remedial learning strategies, Feuerstein developed a novel mode of dynamic assessment, reconceptualizing the nature of intelligence by linking intervention with assessment.

Dynamic assessment is based on the theory of mediated learning experiences (MLE). MLE refers to an interactional process in which an adult interposes him- or herself between the child and a set of stimuli and modifies them by affecting their frequency, order, intensity, and context. The MLE processes are internalized and gradually become an integrated mechanism of change within the child. The acquired and internalized MLE processes allow the child to use them independently, to benefit from learning experiences and to modify his or her cognitive system. In the system Feuerstein developed, the Learning Propensity (Potential) Assessment Device (LPAD), the examiner intervenes during both the testing and teaching phase to assist the examinee to use effective cognitive strategies, rules, and behaviors to arrive at the correct response. The LPAD tasks do not tap specific contents but are constructed to be sensitive to change through variation of task complexity and abstractness. In a typical task, the examinee is taught how to solve a problem (categorization, analogies, progressions, matrices, dot patterns) using a mediational style. In the process, the application and transfer of learning of rules, principles, and strategies to other problems are examined (see e.g., Feuerstein, Feurstein, & Gross, 1997).

Tzuriel (2001) has summarized the most articulated characteristics of Feuerstein's dynamic assessment approach. These are as follows:

1. Assessment is targeted at learning processes.
2. The specific deficient cognitive functions serve as "keys" for understanding the examinee's learning difficulties.
3. The degree and type of modifiability of deficient cognitive functions during assessment provide strong indicators for future change.

4. The degree and type of mediation required for cognitive change, as well as the changes that take place during assessment in the mediational efforts, provide indicators for cognitive modifiability.
5. The role of the examiner-teacher in relation to both the examinee and the helping agents is of crucial importance.
6. The role of non-intellective factors as determinants of the individual's performance as well as their modifiability is important and integrated within the cognitive factors.

Feuerstein contends that the degree of modifiability displayed during the evaluation is highly indicative of actual propensity to learn and change. The LPAD is offered as a viable alternative to conventional testing practices, designed to assess the educability and modifiability of an examinee's cognitive ability through active learning of thinking and test-taking strategies. Rather than focus on total scores alone, this procedure uses the peaks in the pattern of results as indicators of cognitive potential. This method has been employed with varying degrees of success with a variety of low-performing populations, ranging from the culturally different to retarded, autistic, and learning-disabled individuals, and new immigrants. However, the LPAD procedures are currently less well known than Feuerstein's internationally disseminated instrumental enrichment program (Feuerstein et al., 1980; Kouzlin & Rand, 2000), and the procedure still has a number of unresolved psychometric issues (see Tzuriel, 2001).

Understanding the Interface between Intelligence and Personality

Israeli researchers have made important contributions in exploring the personality–intelligence interface. These conceptualizations suggest a rather complex reciprocal relationship between intelligence and a variety of personality factors, with cognitive and affective or motivational variables dynamically influencing each other in the course of development and day-to-day behavior (see Zeidner, 1995; Zeidner & Matthews, 2000). This work includes some studies with a clinical focus. For example, Kaplan et al. (2002) found that, in a sample of young men drafted into the Israeli army, intelligence measured prior to recruitment predicted reduced risk of future posttraumatic stress disorder. Interestingly – and in line with a dynamic perspective – the effect of intelligence appeared to be mediated by motivation to serve in the military. In this section, though, we confine ourselves to only two out of several active research fields: test anxiety and emotional intelligence.

Test Anxiety

Test anxiety figures prominently in the literature as a source of poor cognitive test performance, and a major confound surrounding intelligence testing (see Zeidner, 1998). Studies in Israel have addressed both psychometric issues in the assessment of test anxiety, and underlying psychological theory. The first task for test anxiety researchers has been to translate and validate test anxiety measures for use in Israeli populations. This enterprise recapitulates some of the issues in intelligence assessment previously discussed, such as checking that translations are reliable and investigating cross-cultural differences (see Zeidner, 1998, for a review). For example, Zeidner (1990c) used standard regression procedures to demonstrate that social class and gender differences in scholastic aptitude test performance were not a consequence of group differences in test anxiety. Anxiety research adopts a transactional perspective, such that individual differences in test anxiety are complemented by characteristics of the test situation that may exacerbate or soothe anxiety. Nevo (1995) has developed a useful addition to the researcher's toolkit, the Examinee Feedback Questionnaire, which assesses situational factors such as physical characteristics and examiner behavior.

At a theoretical level, studies have addressed how test characteristics may impact on anxiety, and how anxiety change is linked to test performance. A study of the PET confirmed that both personality and situational factors were implicated; anxiety relates to both traits, such as test anxiety and generalized efficacy, and to situation-specific expectancies (Zohar, 1998). Appraisals of task difficulty were most salient in provoking intense emotions, during performance of Raven's Matrices test (Zohar & Brandt, 2002). In general, Israeli research replicates the typical finding that test anxiety is inversely correlated with test performance (Zeidner & Nevo, 1992), but the transactional approach emphasizes interplay between person and situation over time. In line with this principle, Zeidner (1991) found that, whereas intelligence test performance is inversely related to test anxiety, this pattern of relationship is moderated by the time of anxiety assessment. Test anxiety was related to performance following, but not prior to aptitude testing, implying that anxiety reactions to failure are caused largely by a diminution in one's sense of competency induced by difficulties with the test.

Emotional Intelligence

Emotional intelligence (EI) is a new but controversial research field at the intersection of personality and intelligence. EI refers to abilities and dispositions that promote effective social functioning through skills for identifying, understanding and managing emotions (see Matthews et al., 2002, for a review). Israeli research offers contrasting perspectives. Bar-On (1997) has developed the most widely used questionnaire measure of emotional intelligence, the Emotional Quotient Inventory (EQ-i). It is available in an Israeli version, normed in a sample of 418 individuals (mean age: 23.4). Reliabilities and validities for this version appear to be similar to those for the North American version. Intriguingly, mean EQ in the Israeli sample exceeds the North American mean by about 1 SD, but Bar-On, probably wisely, cautions against making much of such cross-national comparisons.

Other research (Matthews et al., 2002; Zeidner, Roberts, & Matthews, 2002) takes issue with questionnaire assessment. These authors point out that the EQ-i is highly correlated with existing personality traits, such as low neuroticism, but not with cognitive abilities, rendering suspect the claim that the questionnaire assesses a distinct form of intelligence. Ability measures that seek to assess EI through items that may be objectively scored seem more promising. However, analysis of the psychometric properties of ability-like tests has identified difficulties in scoring them, according to Guttman's (1965) veridical criterion, and in the interpretation of test scores as ability measures (Roberts, Zeidner, & Matthews, 2001; Zeidner et al., 2001). In Israel, as in other countries, there is interest among educators in the enhancement of children's emotional competencies and skills. However, a recent review (Zeidner et al., 2002) concluded that existing intervention programs typically lack a coherent conceptual model of EI, and lead to rather mixed outcomes. Despite initial difficulties, it is likely that Israeli researchers will continue to contribute to this growing area of ability research.

CONCLUDING REMARKS

In this chapter, we have highlighted some prominent trends in the domain of intelligence theory, assessment, research, and practice occurring in Israel. Overall, researchers in Israel and the United States appear to share several common concerns. Encouragingly, strong resemblance was found between the psychometric features of key intelligence tests (specifically, the WPPSI, WISC, and K-ABC) and college entrance aptitude tests in Israel and the United States. In addition, general patterns of ethnic, social-class, and gender differences in tests are similar, despite differences between the United States and Israel in language, subpopulations, and educational practice. However, Israeli research has also addressed the unique features of intelligence assessment in that nation, reflecting its origins and history. For example, college admission data support the notion that ethnic group differences in mean ability test performance in Israel are largely accounted for by the verbal dimension of the test battery, which may reflect learning and socialization. In general, the social and educational environment throughout the school years appears to be more beneficial to the intellectual development of Western, middle-class, and male students compared to their respective Eastern, lower-class, and female student counterparts.

Additional striking parallels were found in the salient features of the anti-test controversy in the Israeli and U.S. scene. Curiously, the anti-test campaign in the Israeli arena suggests a cultural lag of about a decade vis-à-vis the American scene, with respect to the social and political currents and events impinging upon ability test policy and usage. This issue gains greater currency when coupled with the national goal of fully integrating culturally different groups in Israel by providing them with equal educational and social opportunities. Indeed, the documented differences in sociocultural and gender group attainment are in direct contrast to the basic values of Israeli society – first and foremost those of equality and national identity (Adler, 1984) and its common ideology, which views all children as having equal potential and deserving equal treatment (Blass & Amir, 1984). However, as in the United States, empirical evidence largely attests to fairness in test usage and prediction for different groups (sociocultural and gender). As a consequence, Israeli universities may justifiably continue to rely on conventional college admission indices as selection devices. Regrettably, the campaign to abolish testing in Israeli educational has become an escape from persevering in the effort to understand the reasons that the outcomes of educational policies have fallen short of social expectations of intellectual attainment. Rather than dismissing the empirical evidence, research should be directed toward understanding the origins of ethnic disparities in aptitude test performance within Israel and mitigating their impact on educational and occupational success.

Future developments in testing and assessment in Israel will most likely be accompanied by systematic research in a wide variety of areas, including the heritability and psychobiology of intelligence, influences on development of intelligence in different sociocultural groups, and increasingly sophisticated studies of multiple dimensions of intelligence (including practical, social, and emotional intelligence) and their cognitive bases. The innovative work of Guttman and Feuerstein suggests some promising avenues for the future. Possibly, work on test anxiety and emotional intelligence may prefigure a more broadly based approach to assessment that includes emotional as well as cognitive abilities. Intelligence assessment in Israel, as elsewhere, could profit from the application of recent advances in testing technologies: for example, item-banking of ability test items, computer adaptive testing programs (currently utilized on an experimental basis by the National Institute for Testing and Evaluation), and the use of modern test theory (e.g., item-response theory). Contemporary political events highlight the potential impact of chronic traumatic stress (terror, wars, missile attacks) and migration on cognitive performance. Finally, more attention needs to be given to the development of ethical standards for test administration and usage, credentials and licensure, implementing informed consent procedures, securing test data and storing test material, and confidentiality of test scores.

In sum, the first few decades of its existence, Israeli society has almost miraculously managed to come to grips with a host of pressing problems, one of the more serious being accommodating the waves of immigrants from developing countries and helping them raise their levels of achievement. The future demands a concerted effort at raising the level of functioning and standards of the educational system as a whole. A major effort directed at upgrading and improving school-based intelligence assessment procedures and university admissions tests may play a key role in helping to achieve this important national goal.

References

Adler, C. (1984). Social integration in the context of the development of Israel's educational system. In Y. Amir & S. Sharan (Eds.), *Social desegregation: Cross-cultural perspectives* (pp. 21–46). Hillsdale, NJ: Erlbaum.

Alexander, H. (1999). A Jewish view of human learning. *International Journal of Children's Spirituality, 4,* 155–164.

Bar-On, R. (1997). *The Emotional Intelligence Inventory (EQ-I): Technical manual.* Toronto, Canada: Multi-Health Systems.

Bashi, Y. (1976). *Verbal and nonverbal abilities of students in grades four, six and eight in the Arab sector.* Jerusalem: School of Education, Hebrew University.

Bashi, J., Cahan, S., & Davis, D. (1981). *An examination of academic achievement in Israeli Arabic-language elementary school.* Jerusalem: Hebrew University and Ministry of Education.

Beller, M. (1992). *Admissions procedures in Israeli Universities: Psychometric and social considerations.* Research report. Jerusalem: National Institute for Testing and Evaluation.

Beller, M. (1993). *Admission to higher education in Israel: Current dilemmas and proposed solutions.* Research report #178A. Jerusalem: National Institute for Testing and Evaluation.

Ben-Shakhar, G., & Beller, M. (1983). On the cultural fairness of psychological tests. *Megamot Behavioral Sciences Quarterly, 28,* 42–56.

Ben-Shakhar, G., & Sheffer, L. (2001). The relationship between the ability to divide attention and standard measures of general cognitive abilities. *Intelligence, 29,* 293–306.

Ben-Simon, A., & Nevo, B. (1986). *Differences in achievement on intercollegiate psychometric exam among different ethnic groups.* Research report # 50. Jerusalem: National Institute for Testing and Evaluation.

Blass, N., & Amir, B. (1984). Integration in education: The development of a policy. In Y. Amir & S. Sharan (Eds.), *Social desegregation: Cross-cultural perspectives* (pp. 63–98). Hillsdale, NJ: Erlbaum.

Cahan, S. (1998). *Intelligence scale for children. Revised Manual.* Hebrew Version of Wechsler's 1974 version. Jerusalem: Psychoeducational services and H. Szold institute.

Cahan, S., & Ganor, Y. (1995). Cognitive gender differences among Israeli children. *Sex Roles, 32,* 469–484.

Canter, D. (Ed.). (1985). *Facet theory: Approaches to social research.* New York: Springer.

Davis, D., Bashi, Y., & Cahan, S. (1977). Birth order and intellectual development: The confluence model in the light of cross-cultural evidence. *Science, 196,* 1470–1472.

Donlon, F. T. (Ed.). (1984). *The College Board technical handbook for the Scholastic Aptitude Test and Achievement tests.* New York: College Entrance Examinations Board.

Elbedour, S., Bouchard, J. T., & Mi Hur, Y. (1997). Similarity in general mental ability in Bedouin full and half siblings. *Intelligence, 25,* 71–82.

Feuerstein, R., Feuerstein, R., & Gross, S. (1997). The learning potential assessment device. In D. P. Flanagain, J. L. Genshaft, & P. L. Harrison (Eds.), *Contemporary intellectual assessment* (pp. 297–311). New York: Guilford Press.

Feuerstein, R., Rand, Y., & Hoffman, M. B. (1979). *The dynamic assessment of retarded performers.* Baltimore: University Park Press.

Feuerstein, R., Rand, Y., & Hoffman, M. B., & Miller, R. (1980). *Instrumental enrichment.* Baltimore: University Park Press.

Gafni, N., & Beller, M. (1989). *A test of the fairness in usage of psychometric exams for two gender groups.* Research report # 95. Jerusalem: National Institute for Testing and Evaluation.

Gafni, N., Beller, M., & Bronner, S. (2000). *A cross-cultural perspective on gender differences in higher education: Admissions and scholastic achievement.* Research report. Jerusalem: National Institute for Testing and Evaluation.

Ganzach, Y., Saporta, I., & Weber, Y. (2000). Interaction in linear versus logistic models: A substantive Illustration using the relationship between Motivation, ability and performance. *Organization research methods, 3,* 237–253.

Guttman, L. (1954). A new approach to factor analysis: The radex. In P. F. Lazarsfeld (Ed.), *Mathematical thinking in the social sciences* (pp. 258–348). New York: Free Press.

Guttman, L. (1965a). The structure of interrelations among intelligence tests. In *Proceedings of the 1964 invitational conference on testing problems.* Princeton, NJ: Educational Testing Service.

Guttman, L. A. (1965b). A faceted definition of intelligence. In R. Eiferman (Ed.), *Studies in psychology: Scripta Hierosolymita* (Vol. 14, 166–81). Jerusalem: Hebrew University Press.

Guttman, L. (1967). The development of nonmetric space analysis: A letter to Professor John Ross. *Multivariate Behavioral Research, 2,* 71–82. Princeton, NJ: Educational Testing Service.

Guttman, L. (1969). Integration of test design and analysis. In *Proceedings of the 1969 Invitational Conference on Testing Problems.* Princeton, NJ: Educational Testing Service.

Guttman, R., & Guttman, L. (1974). Cross-cultural stability of an intercorrelation pattern of abilities. *Human Biology, 35,* 53–59.

Guttman, L., & Levy, S. (1980). Two structural laws for intelligence. *Megamot, 25,* 421–438 (in Hebrew).

Guttman, L., & Levy, S. (1991). Two structural laws for intelligence. *Intelligence, 15,* 79–103.

Jensen, A. R. (1980). *Bias in mental testing.* New York: Free Press.

Kaplan, Z., Weiser, M., Reichenberg, A., Rabinowitz, J., Caspi, A., Bodner, E., & Zohar, J. (2002). Motivation to serve in the military influences vulnerability to future posttraumatic stress disorder. *Psychiatry Research, 109,* 45–49.

Kaufman, A. S., & Kaufman, N. L. (1996). *Kaufman Assessment Battery for Children* (K-ABC). Israeli version of interpretive manual. Jerusalem: Ministry of Education, Culture, and Sports.

Kennet-Cohen, T. (2001). *Differential prediction and validity of college entrance exams by candidates' socio-economic status* (in Hebrew). Jerusalem: National Institute for Testing and Evaluation.

Kennet, T., & Oren, C. (1988). *A test of the cultural fairness of the use of college entrance system in two universities.* Research report # 78. Jerusalem: National Institute for Testing and Evaluation.

Kennet-Cohen, T., Bronner, S., & Oren, C. (1995). *A meta-analysis of the predictive validity of the selection process to universities in Israel.* Jerusalem: National Institute for Testing and Evaluation.

Kennett-Cohen, T., & Oren, C. (1993). *Validity and fairness of psychometric exams and matriculation diploma in prediction of first year grades among elderly students* (in Hebrew). Research report. Jerusalem: National Institute for Testing and Evaluation.

Kfir, P. (1988). Achievements and aspirations among boys and girls in high school: A comparison of two Israeli ethnic groups. *American Educational Research Journal, 5,* 184–198.

Koop, T. (1985). Replication of Guttman's structure of intelligence. In D. Canter (Ed.), *Facet theory: Approaches to social research* (pp. 59–96). New York: Springer.

Kozulin, A., & Rand, Y. (2000). *Experience of mediated learning: An impact of Feuerstein's theory in education and psychology.* Oxford: Pergamon.

Kugelmass, S., & Lieblich, A. (1975). *A developmental study of the Arab child in Israel. Scientific Report.* Ford Foundation Grant 015.1261.

Kugelmass, S., Lieblich, A., & Bossik, D. (1974). Patterns of intellectual ability in Jewish and Arab children in Israel. *Journal of Cross-Cultural Psychology, 5,* 184–198.

Levinson, S. (1986). Psychological tests in the schools. *Ha'artez.* Tel-Aviv: Schoken.

Levy, S. (1985). Lawful roles of facets in social theories. In D. Canter (Ed.), *Facet theory: Approaches to social research* (pp. 59–96). New York: Springer.

Lieblich, A. (1973). *WPPSI-Wechsler Preschool and Primary Scale of Intelligence.* Jerusalem: Psychological Corporation and Hebrew University.

Lieblich, A., Ben-Shachar, S., &. Ninio, A (1976). *WISC-R Hebrew Manual* Psychological Corporation and Israeli Ministry of Education (in Hebrew).

Lieblich, A. (1983). Intelligence patterns among ethnic and minority groups in Israel. In M. Nisan & U. Last (Eds.), *Between education and psychology* (pp. 335–357). Jerusalem: Magnes Press (in Hebrew).

Lieblich, A. (1985). Sex differences in intelligence test performance of Jewish and Arab school children in Israel. In M. Safir, M. T. Mednick, D. Israeli, and J. Bernard (Eds.), *Women's worlds: From the new scholarship.* New York: Praeger.

Lieblich, A., Ben-Shahar-Segev, N., & Ninio, A. (1980). *WISC-R Manual for Arabic Examiner (in Arabic).* Jerusalem: Psycho-Counselling Services.

Lieblich, A., & Kugelmass, S. (1981). Patterns of intellectual ability of Arab school children in Israel. *Intelligence, 5,* 311–320.

Marshalek, B., Lohman, D. F., & Snow, E. R. (1983). The complexity continuum in the Radex and hierarchical model of intelligence. *Intelligence, 7,* 107–127.

Matthews, G., Zeidner, M., & Roberts, R. (2002). *Emotional intelligence: Science and myth.* Cambridge: MIT Press.

Minkowitch, A., Davis, D., & Bashi, Y. (1982). *Success and failure in Israeli elementary education.* New Brunswick: NJ: Translation Books.

Most, B., & Zeidner, M. (1995). Constructing personality and intelligence test instruments: Methods and issues. In D. Saklofske & M. Zeidner (Eds.), *International handbook of personality and intelligence* (pp. 475–503). New York: Plenum.

Nevo, B. (1993a). A multifaceted taxonomy of intelligence tests: A proposal. *Assessment Update, 5,* 14.

Nevo, B. (1993b). In search of correctness typology for intelligence. *New Ideas in Psychology, 11,* 391–397.

Nevo, B. (1995). Examinee Feedback Questionnaire: Reliability and validity measures. *Educational and Psychological Measurement, 55,* 499–504.

Nevo, B., & Chawarski, C. M. (1997). Individual differences in practical intelligence and success in immigration. *Intelligence, 25,* 83–92.

Nevo, B., & Oren, C. (1986). Concurrent validity of the American Scholastic Aptitude Test (SAT) and the Israeli Inter-University Psychometric Entrance Test (IUPET). *Educational & Psychological Measurement, 46,* 723–725.

Ortar, G. R. (1966). Milta Intelligence Test. Jerusalem: Hebrew University.

Raven, J. C. (1960). *Guide to using the Standard Progressive Matrices.* London: Lewis.

Raviv, A., Margalith, M., Raviv, A., & Sade, F. (1981). The cognitive patterns of Israeli learning disabled children as reflected in the Hebrew version of the WISC-R. *Journal of Learning Disabilities, 14,* 411–415.

Raviv, A. (1989). School psychology in Israel. In P. A. Saigh & T. Oakland (Eds.), *International perspectives on psychology in the schools* (pp. 11–124). Hillsdale, NJ: Erlbaum.

Roberts, R. D., Zeidner, M., & Matthews, G. (2001). Does emotional intelligence meet traditional standards for an intelligence? Some new data and conclusions. *Emotion, 1,* 196–231.

Safir, M. P. (1986). The effects of nature or of nurture on sex differences in intellectual functioning. *Sex Roles, 14,* 581–590.

Saklofske, D., & Zeidner, M. (Eds.). (1995). *International handbook of personality and intelligence.* New York: Plenum.

Samuda, R. J. (1975). *Psychological testing of American minorities.* New York: Harper & Row.

Schlesinger, I. M., & Guttman, L. (1969). Smallest space analysis of intelligence and achievement tests. *Psychological Bulletin, 71,* 95–100.

Snow, R. E., Kyllonen, P. C., & Marshalek, B. (1984). The topography of ability and learning correlations. In R. J. Sternberg (Ed.), *Advances in the psychology of human intelligence* (Vol. 2, pp. 48–103). Hillsdale, NJ: Erlbaum.

Tziner, A., & Rimmer, A. (1984). Examination of an extension of Guttman's model of ability tests. *Applied Psychological Measurement, 8,* 59–69.

Tzuriel, D. (2001). *Dynamic assessment of young children.* New York: Kluwer/ Plenum.

Zeidner, M. (1985). A cross-cultural test of the situational bias hypothesis – The Israeli scene. *Evaluation and Program Planning, 8,* 367–376.

Zeidner, M. (1986a). Sex differences in scholastic aptitude: The Israeli scene. *Personality and Individual Differences, 7,* 847–852.

Zeidner, M. (1986b). Are Scholastic Aptitude Tests in Israel biased towards Arab student candidates? Some Israeli findings. *Higher Education, 15,* 507–522.

Zeidner, M. (1987a). The validity of college admission indices for Jews and Arabs in Israel. *Personality and Individual Differences, 8,* 587–589.

Zeidner, M. (1987b). Test of the cultural bias hypothesis: Some Israeli findings. *Journal of Applied Psychology, 72,* 38–48.

Zeidner, M. (1987c). A cross-cultural test of sex bias in the predictive validity of scholastic aptitude examinations: Some Israeli findings. *Evaluation and Program Planning, 10,* 289–295.

Zeidner, M. (1988a). Age as a factor in scholastic aptitude test performance: The Israeli scene. *Journal of Applied Developmental Psychology, 9,* 139–149.

Zeidner, M. (1988b). Cultural fairness in aptitude testing revisited: A cross-cultural parallel. *Professional Psychology: Research and Practice, 19,* 257–262.

Zeidner, M. (1990a). Perceptions of ethnic group modal intelligence: Reflections of cultural stereotypes or intelligence test scores? *Journal of Cross-Cultural Psychology, 21,* 214–231.

Zeidner, M. (1990b). School-based assessment research in Israel: Current state and future directions. *McGill Journal of Education, 25,* 37–64.

Zeidner, M. (1990c). Does test anxiety bias scholastic aptitude test performance by gender and sociocultural group? *Journal of Personality and Personality Assessment, 55,* 145–160.

Zeidner, M. (1991). Test anxiety and aptitude test performance in an actual college admission testing situation: Temporal considerations. *Personality and Individual Differences, 12,* 101–109.

Zeidner, M. (1995). Personality trait correlates of intelligence. In D. Saklofske & M. Zeidner (Eds.), *International handbook of personality and intelligence* (pp. 299–319). New York: Plenum.

Zeidner, M. (1998). *Test anxiety: The state of the art.* New York: Plenum.

Zeidner, M., & Feitelson, D. (1989). Probing the validity of intelligence tests for preschool children: A smallest space analysis. *Journal of Psychoeducational Assessment, 7,* 175–193.

Zeidner, M., & Matthews, G. (2000). Intelligence and personality. In R. J. Sternberg (Ed.)., *Handbook of intelligence* (2nd ed., pp. 581–610.). NY: Cambridge University Press.

Zeidner, M., & Matthews, G., & Roberts, R. (2001). Slow down, you move too fast: Emotional intelligence remains an "elusive" intelligence. *Emotions, 1,* 265–275.

Zeidner, M., & Nevo, B. (1992). Test anxiety in examinees in a college admission testing situation: Incidence, dimensionality, and cognitive correlates. In K. A. Hagtvet & T. B. Johnsen (Eds.), *Advances in test anxiety research,* (Vol. 7, pp. 288–303). Bristol, PA: Zeitlinger Publishers.

Zeidner, M., Roberts, R., & Matthews, G. (2002). Can emotional intelligence be schooled? A critical review. *Educational Psychologist, 37,* 215–231.

Zohar, D. (1998). An additive model of test anxiety: Role of exam-specific expectations. *Journal of Educational Psychology, 90,* 330–340.

Zohar, D., & Brandt, Y. (2002). Relationships between appraisal factors during stressful encounters: A test of alternative models. *Anxiety, Stress, & Coping: An International Journal, 15,* 149–161.

8

Intelligence and Intelligence Testing in Turkey

Sami Gulgoz and Cigdem Kagitcibasi

At the beginning of the 21st century, looking back at the past century of psychological theory and practice, we observe what could probably be called a century of defining and redefining intelligence, as researchers across nations and disciplines addressed the commonalities and differences in cognitive skills of humans. Throughout this period, numerous approaches emerged to account for the variations in human abilities. The majority of these approaches have focused on individual differences. They set themselves apart from the theoretical streams focusing on the explanation of cognitive functioning. These different perspectives have found expression in the idiographic and nomothetic orientations, the so-called two disciplines of scientific psychology, put forth by Cronbach (1957) and before him, Allport (1937), who ascribed the distinction to the German philosopher Windelband. Only recently, we have begun to observe attempts at combining the two cultures of psychology to arrive at a unified approach to human intelligence, recognizing that the sources of differences were the exact same sources that gave humans the type of cognitive processing system shared by members of the same species.

The last century has also demonstrated a great shift from Europe to America of psychological inquiry into intelligence. From its modest beginnings in the attempt by Simon and Binet to address the practical need to establish which students would best benefit from education in France, the field moved in great strides to large-scale testing of thousands of children, adolescents and adults in the United States. Though applications and techniques developed somewhat before theoretical advances, the main theoretical contributions were also seen in American scholarship, with most of the rest of the world, even to a large extent Europe, following suit. This was particularly the case in the countries where psychology was imported from the West, such as Turkey.

The state of research on intelligence and of measurement of intelligence in Turkey has consisted of a series of disjointed standardization studies focusing on particular samples. It is rather difficult to speak of a concerted effort to build a research program on intelligence or a set of tests with solid psychometric qualities. The definition and conceptualization of intelligence has been imported from the West. Just as one cannot find an indigenous psychology in Turkey (Kagitcibasi, 1994), intelligence has also been associated with measures that are translations or adaptations of those developed elsewhere, particularly in the United States, with little concern for the theoretical or methodological underpinnings.

In this chapter, we attempt to introduce a perspective to understand the pattern of research on intelligence in Turkey. The chapter is on Turkey specifically, however, many of the distinctive characteristics of the field of intelligence and intelligence testing in Turkey show similarities to those in other societies in the region (see Kagitcibasi & Savasir, 1988). Thus what is covered here may serve as a hint about what one might expect to find in the larger Eastern Mediterranean–Middle Eastern region. At one level this has to do with rather similar levels of development in the more general disciplines of psychology and education, although Turkey, after Israel, tends to be more advanced in research and scholarship than the other countries in the region. At a higher level of abstraction, one could point to rather similar overall socio-economic development levels and similar cultural outlooks. This is not to say that there is uniformity in the region; indeed there is much diversity. Nevertheless, the differences from societies in other regions, and particularly from the Euro-American West, are more distinctive.

The chapter first presents the history and current state of research on intelligence and on the basis of this aims to analyze the overall picture. In particular, we focus on research in the past few decades and bring out the major foci of research in Turkey: adaptation studies, studies on socio-economic and sex differences, studies comparing Turkey with other countries, factor analytic studies, and studies focusing on cognitive processing and cognitive style. In the final part of the chapter, our focus shifts to intervention programs and research conducted on these programs.

HISTORY OF INTELLIGENCE TESTING IN TURKEY

Intelligence tests have a rather early beginning in Turkey. The Binet and Simon Test of Intelligence was translated into Turkish in 1915 (Tan, 1972), only one decade after the 1905 original test and before the American translation. The earliest article on intelligence originating from Turkey in an international journal appeared in 1929, six years after the fall of the Ottoman Empire and the establishment of the Turkish Republic. This study compared female students of different ethnic origins attending an American high school in Istanbul. The comparison included Bulgarians, Greeks, Armenians, and Turks, who were ranked according to their median intelligence score on the Otis test. The test was implemented in its original language, and the overall median was found to be 95 (Wood, 1929).

Between 1930 and 1945, eleven books on testing were published; eight of these were translations. In the 1950s, testing found acceptance at the state level with the Ministry of Education founding the Office of Testing and Research. The Office of Testing and Research invited a number of American experts for consulting and also sent Turkish experts, mainly teachers and education researchers, to the United States for further study. During the 1960s, the establishment of new psychology departments and schools of education in universities increased the interest in tests (Oner, 1994).

For the present review, we have conducted an extensive survey of tests of intelligence and cognitive skills. We have ascertained that the vast majority of tests currently available were developed or adapted after 1970. Our survey results are summarized here.

- 1 test before 1970 (Otis-Beta Quick Scoring Mental Ability Test)
- 13 tests between 1970 and 1979 (Basic Mental Aptitudes Test, Cattell Culture-Fair Intelligence Test, Coloured Progressive Matrices, D48 Test, Differential Aptitude Test, Draw-a-Man Test, Embedded Figures Test, Kahn Intelligence Test, Peabody Picture-Vocabulary Test, Porteus Mazes Test, Stanford-Binet Intelligence Scale, Wechsler Intelligence Scale for Children, Wechsler Adult Intelligence Scale)
- 9 tests in the 1980s (Alexander Practical Ability Test, Analytical Intelligence Test, General Aptitude Battery, General Aptitude Test, Healy Picture Completion Test, Logical Reasoning Test, Revised Visual Retention Test, Torrance Tests of Creative Thinking, Visual Motor Gestalt Test)

- 6 tests since 1990 (Gesell Development Test, Visual Auditory Digit Span, Wechsler Intelligence Scale for Children–Revised, Wechsler Memory Scale–Revised, Wechsler Preschool and Primary Scale of Intelligence–Revised, Wisconsin Card Sorting Test)

Most of these tests will be familiar to the reader because they were adaptations of tests developed abroad. Only two were original tests. Most of these tests were translated from English, but a few were translated from French and German. We obtained the information regarding these tests by scanning journal articles, conference proceedings, conference abstracts, unpublished master's theses, and doctoral dissertations. They were cross-checked with the most comprehensive cataloging of tests used in Turkey (Oner, 1994). There are probably some tests that were left out of this list, but it is clear that the tests listed here are the instruments used in the mainstream research in Turkey.

An interesting characteristic of these tests is that most of them are performance tests. There seems to be a clear preference for using performance-type tests. One possible reason for this preference is the ease of adaptation. Verbal tasks necessitate a considerably more complicated adaptation process, which is almost tantamount to constructing a new test. The adaptation of performance items is relatively simple in that the only requirement is obtaining the norms for the population at hand. Another possible reason for preferring performance tests may be to avoid getting tangled in the web of cultural equivalence of verbal tasks and items. Performance items are considered less prone to cultural differences and they are the types of items used in culture-fair tests.

AN OVERVIEW OF RESEARCH INVOLVING INTELLIGENCE

Our survey targeted all research conducted in Turkey that included measures of intelligence. The majority of studies we include in our review were reported in conferences, master's theses, doctoral dissertations, and national and university journals. There were very few publications that appeared in international journals or books. Our survey is limited by the accessibility of sources that were not indexed in any form. These sources reach as far back as the 1960s, but we did not survey earlier work. Our survey obtained information about 158 studies involving some measure of intelligence.

Among these studies, 62% were related to some form of pathology. These included a wide range of topics such as the diagnosis of brain disorders (Oktem, 1983), the study of child abuse cases (Selcuk, 1985), and the comparison of cognitive structures in children of various levels of mental retardation (Sezgin, 1987). About 12% of the research was related to education such as the relationship among creativity, intelligence, psychological disorders, and academic success (e.g., Tur, 1979; Ekberzade, 1982). Studies focusing on individual differences on the basis of sex, SES, parental attitudes, and similar factors composed approximately 10% of all the studies (e.g., Guray & Cokan, 1976; Davasligil, 1980; Kagitcibasi, 1979; Korkmazlar, 1980). About 7% of the studies were on biological and genetic factors (e.g., Tan, Akgun, & Telatar, 1993; Etaner, Kesemen, & Bakan, 1984) and 6% were on psychometric qualities (e.g., Togrol & Ozugurlu, 1973; Acikgoz, 1996). Finally, very few of the studies (3%) focused on the relationship between intelligence measures and cognitive tasks (e.g., Er & Karakas, 1992; Ozbaydar, 1971).

When we exclude those studies specifically devoted to the development or standardization of a particular test, we see that very few of the remaining work focuses on intelligence per se or the particular test of intelligence employed. Instead, intelligence tests are taken for granted as valid and reliable measures of cognitive abilities, and they are used as diagnostic tools. There is very little, if any, discussion of the underlying conceptualization of intelligence. Issues on the nature and origin of intelligence, such as unitary versus multifaceted or innate versus acquired, do not constitute a major concern in the literature of intelligence in Turkey.

Although not explicitly deliberated, these issues are inherent in the assumptions of researchers. The implicit assumption of a group of researchers is that intelligence is an inborn, biologically determined, and unchanging entity. For example, such an assumption is evident in the study of the relationship among handedness, testosterone levels, and intelligence (Tan, Akgun, Komsuoglu, & Telatar, 1993). Many other studies make similar assumptions, but they concentrate particularly on mental retardation or other mental disorders (e.g., Noyan, Yuksel, & Kucukyalcin, 1977). However, there are a number of studies with the clear but implicit assumption that intelligence level is primarily a function of the environment (e.g., Aydogmus, Gurkanlar, & Ezik, 1977; Guray & Cokan, 1977). Regardless of their views on the source of intelligence, all researchers seem to agree upon the unity of intelligence. Theories challenging the unitary perspective, such as Gardner's (1983) Multiple Intelligences or Sternberg's (1988) Triarchic Theory are not evident in the Turkish intelligence research literature. However, they have been influential in the design of a recent intervention program (Gulgoz et al., 2001).

In the next sections, we will group studies on intelligence and describe overall characteristics of the studies in each category, attempting a general profile of intelligence research in Turkey.

TEST DEVELOPMENT AND ADAPTATION STUDIES

Test adaptations in Turkey are generally directed toward use in a particular research question. Therefore, most adaptations are based on selected and limited populations, which are appropriate for research purposes but not sufficient to consider the work complete adaptations. There are also cases of tests that were adapted by two researchers using samples from different populations. For example, the Otis Beta Quick-Scoring Mental Ability Test has been adapted twice, first on a sample of 21,365 third, fourth, and fifth graders (Ozguven, 1961); and the second time, on a sample of 468 ninth graders (Turker, 1977). There are no norms available for other age groups.

In societies where there are vast differences between different social groups, standardization of tests is especially difficult because formation of representative normative samples is frequently problematic (Kagitcibasi & Savasir, 1988). Turkey is a case in point with important distinctions between rural and urban, and different ethnic and regional groups. Therefore, standardization based on samples restricted to a particular region suffers from lack of adequate representativeness. There have been efforts to address this problem by several test adapters. For example, the normative sample for the Wechsler Intelligence Scale for Children–Revised (WISC-R)'s Turkish version included children from 12 cities to assure the inclusion of different groups. However, it may still be considered not totally representative of the population because the sample was limited to the cities and excluded rural areas.

A recent preliminary study on the standardization of the Wechsler Preschool and Primary Scale of Intelligence–Revised (WPPSI-R) (Celik, 1998) was also quite limited in its sample in that it included 961 children between the ages of 6.6 and 6.9, which are the upper age limits in the original WPPSI-R. Test characteristics and specifically the inter-correlations among the subscales resembled the original test closely, supporting the validity of the test. High validity and reliability coefficients were also obtained in Wechsler Memory Scale–Revised (WMS-R; [Karakas, Kafadar, & Eski, 1996]), and Visual Auditory Digit

Span (Yalin & Karakas, 1994; Karakas & Yalin, 1995). The standardization samples of the Visual Auditory Digit Span test have consisted of
both a sample of young children (Yalin & Karakas, 1994) between the
ages of 6.6 and 12.11, and a sample of older children and adults (Karakas
& Yalin, 1995) between the ages of 13 and 54. The age differences in
short-term memory as shown by digit span have been in the expected
direction, increasing steeply from age 6.6 to 9.0 and continuing to increase afterwards with a lower slope. The increase continues until age 19,
and afterward a decline is observed. The standardization of the Visual
Auditory Digit Span test has been the most comprehensive in terms of
the age and education ranges of samples used in recent years. Cultural
and social changes are also implicative when we consider the adaptations of tests. The adaptations based on samples of the 1970s or 1980s
may no longer be appropriate for testing individuals today. For example, it is a common experience nowadays that the intelligence scores
of children seem inflated when tested with the Turkish WISC-R because the norm data was collected in 1978. Most urban children tested in
Istanbul achieve above-average IQ scores. They perform better than earlier generations, particularly on quantitative and verbal scores as a result
of higher standards in schools.

Overall, the standardization and adaptation studies are small in number and limited in their applicability because some of the restricted
normative samples are dated. Most researchers are satisfied with the
reliability of the tests for the particular sample appropriate for their
own research purposes, and other psychometric properties of the tests
are often neglected. The validation of most tests, however, requires that
anticipated age and sex differences be observed.

STUDIES ON COMPONENT STRUCTURES

Most of the measures discussed in this chapter have unitary factor structures. Therefore, investigation of the factor structure of these measures
is not common. Sahin (1983) analyzed the factor structure of the Turkish
standardization of WISC-R, and the factor analysis revealed a single factor that accounted for 66.4% of the variance. All of the subtests loaded
on this general factor, but this structure did not persist in age-based
analyses where a two-factor solution emerged.

More recently, two studies investigated the common factor structure
of a number of tests. Sahin (1996) investigated the component structure
of the WMS-R, the Wisconsin Card Sorting Test, the Line Direction Test,

and the WAIS. Factor analysis revealed three factors: a general factor consisting of all WAIS scores, logical memory in WMS-R and the Line Direction test; a mental flexibility factor including the subtests of the Wisconsin Card Sorting Test; and a figure memory factor including the shape memory, visual memory, and digit span subtests of the WMS-R, and performance score on the WAIS. In the second study, Acikgoz (1996) used the Auditory Verbal Learning Test, Wechsler Memory Scale–Revised, Visual Auditory Digit Span test, and Digit Sequence Learning Test. This analysis also revealed a three-factor solution with one factor including all subtests of the Visual Auditory Digit Span test and digit span tests of the WMS-R. The second factor included word association and logical memory subtests of the WMS-R and the interference subtest of the Auditory Verbal Learning Test. Finally, the third factor included the Digit Sequence Learning Test and the Free Recall, Delayed Recall, and Recognition subtests of the Auditory Verbal Learning Test.

These results do not readily lend themselves to a common interpretation because only one test, the WMS-R, is shared between the two studies. If we were to infer a general finding from these two studies, we might argue that one component has to do with working memory span because digit span, whether presented auditorily or visually, is a working memory task. In both of the studies just discussed, coherence was observed among digit span subtests, shape memory, visual memory, and performance scores on the WAIS, which are either direct measures or are affected by working memory span. Derivation of a factor represented by working memory span is in accordance with recent arguments that a major component of intelligence is the working memory span (Jurden, 1995; Kyllonen, 1996; Engle, Kane, & Tuholski, 1999).

The second factor in these studies, which contained the logical memory subtest of the WMS-R, also included word association, all of the WAIS scores, and the Line Direction Test. This factor is named as a general factor in one study and as associative memory in the other study. The myriad of tests loading on this factor conjures up the possibility of a general intelligence factor but at the same time the presence of a logical component. Judgment of line direction, logical memory subtest, and some WAIS subtests are obviously related to the ability for judgment, but logical strategies may also be effective in word associations and verbal tasks.

Our interpretation of the component structure in these studies is considerably speculative in nature. There is no doubt that it is premature to argue for the presence of a component structure with such limited evidence from Turkish samples. Future adaptations or construction of tests should allow for a more defensible component structure for intelligence in Turkey, and this may enable comparisons with other cultures. At this point, such comparisons would be unwarranted.

GROUP DIFFERENCES

A major focus of research regarding intelligence in Turkey has been on group differences, particularly regarding the socio-economic status (SES) of the participants. Additionally, group differences based on age, gender, and other characteristics have also been the focus of many studies. Although the first study that we encountered was a study on ethnic differences (Wood, 1929), that particular study seems to be the only example of its kind. Often, the emphasis has been on socio-economic differences based on urbanization. For example, Kagitcibasi (1979) sampled 218 children from three rural villages and one urban city and administered the Draw-A-Man test. Her results showed that children from the rural schools scored lower than children from urban schools, the difference increasing with the distance of the village from the urban center. Within the city, the lower SES group scored lower than the middle SES group but still above the rural groups, pointing to the greater environmental deprivation in rural areas. Epir et al. (1986) conducted a study where they administered the Stanford-Binet Intelligence Scale to 142 blind children. They observed an inclination for a difference between children of rural and urban backgrounds, but this difference was not large enough to be significant. Burkovik (2000) has recently investigated the intelligence scores, using the WISC-R, of 30 male children between the ages of 9 and 16 who had run away from their homes, lived in the streets, and who had been recently taken into the custody of the state. Among other comparisons, the study compared the children who had been inhabitants of the major cosmopolitan city of Istanbul with those who lived outside Istanbul. Children from Istanbul scored higher than those from outside the city on 11 of the subtests.

The definition of SES has shown variations in time and across studies. One approach to SES has been to identify it as the educational levels of the parents. Celik (1998) observed significant positive correlations between father's education and verbal, performance, and total scores as well as five of the subtests in the WPPSI-R. The correlations with mother's education were similar and significant in an even larger number of subtests. In the standardization study for the WISC-R (Savasir & Sahin, 1995), father's education was taken as an SES indicator and very large differences between different SES groups were observed. The authors note that the average score for the high SES group was almost twice the average for the low SES group on one of the subtests. Therefore, they include norm tables for different SES groups in the manual for the Turkish WISC-R. However, Davasligil (1994) failed to observe any correlations between family education and children's performance on the Standard Progressive Matrices test, although children of fathers with college educations performed better in a mathematics achievement test.

Another SES indicator is family income, but the reliability of income measures are often suspect. Because people are often hesitant in reporting their incomes, most surveys do not use direct self-report income measures. Nevertheless, Celik (1998) found significant positive correlations between family income and verbal, performance, and total scores as well as the scores on nine of the subtests of the WPPSI-R.

Gender differences is also a topic that has been investigated by researchers. Savasir and Sahin (1995) reported not finding any gender differences in verbal, performance, or total scores for any age group in the standardization of the WISC-R. Celik's (1998) research with the WPPSI-R included only a group of children between the ages of 6.6 and 6.9 and detected a gender difference in the subtest of mazes, with male children scoring higher than females. Ilhan (1993) compared 12- to 13- year-old male and female children using the Analytical Intelligence Test, and the only difference was that males performed better than females on one of the six subtests (missing parts subtest). However, Davasligil (1994) failed to find any gender differences in the scores of 8- and 11-year-old children on Standard Progressive Matrices test.

Based on the evidence just presented, we can conclude that group differences exist among children on the basis of SES, but there has been no evidence supporting consistent gender differences. Isolated cases of significant gender differences are limited to particular age groups and to a very small number of subtests that are hardly generalizable. Nevertheless, gender differences emerged in research demonstrating the relationship between serum testosterone levels and intelligence (Tan, 1990). The relationship between Cattell's Culture-Fair Intelligence test scores and serum testosterone levels was positive in right-handed males and negative in right-handed females. Thus the relationship between

IQ and serum testosterone levels was mediated by brain laterality (Tan, Akgun, & Telatar, 1993).

COMPARISONS ACROSS CULTURES

Comparison is inherent in all adaptations. For example, the standardization study for the WISC-R (Savasir & Sahin, 1995) indicated that there were no differences between the American normative sample and the Turkish normative sample in verbal components of the test, but there were differences in the performance subtests. When Turkish children were evaluated using the American norms, their performance was on the average 12 points less than the American sample. The difference is greater for Turkish children from smaller cities and lower socio-economic classes. It is notable, as Savasir and Sahin have observed, that the differences appear not on the verbal subtests, which are more commonly problematic, but on the performance subtests.

Other studies included comparisons of the developmental sequences in conservation tasks between children in England and Turkey (Lister, Leach, & Pain, 1993). Researchers tested both educable mentally retarded and non-retarded children and found a common developmental order for both cultures. Epir et al. (1986) tested blind children between the ages of 7 and 11, and found cross-cultural stability for Stanford-Binet Intelligence Scale. Karakas and Yalin (1995) and Karakas et al. (1996) reported that Visual Auditory Digit Span and Wechsler Memory Scale–Revised both demonstrated similar correlations to those reported for the original tests. However, Cantez and Girgin (1992) showed that the norms for the Gesell Development Schedules were not appropriate for most of the age groups in their Turkish sample. Except for 10-year-old female children, performance of male and female children between the ages of 3 and 11 was lower than indicated in the developmental norms of the test.

The presence of differences across cultures is open to multiple interpretations. The most straightforward, though often unwarranted, interpretation is that such differences reflect true differences between the individuals of two cultures. Several factors may play a role in bringing about cross-cultural diversity. A very important one has to do with differences between the socio-economic conditions prevalent in different cultures. For example, Savasir and Sahin (1995) reported larger gaps between the performance scores of American and Turkish children on the WISC-R when lower-SES children in Turkey were considered. The difference across nations or cultures may be solely a function of the significant discrepancies between social, educational, and economic circumstances of the individuals. In that respect, cross-cultural differences are just an extension of differences within a country arising from social class differences, access to education, environmental stimulation, and the like.

In understanding and interpreting group differences in intelligence, the distinction between capacity and performance needs to be stressed. This is of course a perennial problem in intelligence testing because capacity as a construct can only be inferred from performance. The distinction is only an academic one, however, for what really counts in real-life situations is performance. Still, in comparative testing of different social class, ethnic, national, rural–urban, and regional groups, the distinction has to figure importantly, so that unwarranted essentialist attributions to groups are avoided.

It is always possible that cultural differences are due to inappropriate translation or adaptation of the measure. Many of the tests we surveyed were not examined extensively for the adequateness of the items, although some did include validity measures, mostly in the form of correlations with measures that were adapted earlier. However, validation of new measures on the basis of existing measures may be a method that maintains earlier errors committed in test adaptation. Therefore, alternative methods are called for, especially to capture constructs that may show cultural variation. Of great importance here is the issue of equivalence of the underlying factor structures. Equivalence is often assumed but rarely established, resulting in problems in establishing validity and comparability.

Cultural variation in the construal of intelligence is another possible source of cultural differences in test scores. What is defined and demanded as intelligent behavior in one culture may be different from that in another culture. In particular, the cognitive skills reinforced in one culture because they make up the core of intelligence as understood in that culture may be less crucial, valuable, or useful in another culture. The history of cross-cultural research is replete with examples of different folk conceptions of intelligence. For example, Mundy-Castle (1974) first described "African social intelligence" to refer to the significance given to social sensitivity and responsibility as reflecting intelligence. This was supported by subsequent research in both Africa (Serpell, 1977; Harkness & Super, 1993) and other traditional rural populations with closely knit human relationships (for a review, see Kagitcibasi, 1996).

Given the research just described, the discrepancies must be more striking between rural and urban cultures than between two urban cultures within the same nation and across nations. Thus, the urban centers of the United States and Turkey may show smaller variations than the difference between rural and urban areas of Turkey. Indeed, Kagitcibasi (1979) has shown that there were very significant losses in intelligence scores as one moved away from urban centers and argued elsewhere that cultural patterns dictate the development of other skills in rural areas and among immigrant communities than those prescribed by urban middle-class educational system (e.g., Kagitcibasi, 1996; Kagitcibasi, Sunar, & Bekman, 2001). The same holds true for the differences between lower SES and middle SES cultures, as evidenced by the large differences found by Savasir and Sahin (1995), mentioned before.

Thus group differences in SES and cultural conceptions of intelligence impact intelligence. Here the proximal environment emerges as the key because it is through the mediation of the proximal environment, and especially the caretakers, that the distal environment leads to child outcomes. Children's cognitive competence in culturally valued domains gets promoted in childrearing, whereas development in other domains lags behind. For example, Harkness and Super (1993) contrasted the child outcomes deriving from different parental "ethnotheories" and their expression in daily life settings and childrearing in a traditional village in Africa and in an American city. While it was customary for the African children to take care of infants, look after cows, and cook dinner for the family, tasks in which the urban middle-class American children would fail badly, the African children did poorly on a simple cognitive task of retelling a story, which was easy for the American children. Such research provides insights into the differences found in the intelligence test scores of children from rural and urban contexts.

There are similar implications for differences in intellectual performance in contexts of migration and culture contact. Here parental ethnotheories, expectations, and values may conflict with mainstream institutional norms. For example, research in the United States showed that immigrant Mexican parents believe, erroneously, that if their children are quiet, obedient, and listen to the teacher, then they will succeed in school (Nunes, 1993). Similarly, Okagaki and Sternberg (1993) found that for immigrant parents from Cambodia, Mexico, the Philippines, and Vietnam, non-cognitive characteristics (social skills, practical skills, motivation) were as important as or more important than cognitive characteristics (problem solving ability, verbal ability, creativity) to their conceptions of an "intelligent first-grade child," but not for Anglo-American parents. Furthermore, parental beliefs regarding the importance of conformity correlated negatively with children's school performance, and American-born parents favored autonomy over conformity. Such misfits between parental beliefs and, therefore, parenting and changing environmental requirements may cause arrears in developmental outcomes.

Indeed, in an ongoing intervention program, we have developed a model to explain the adaptive difficulties of the rural and immigrant communities to urban life and to an education system based on an urban middle-class value system (Gulgoz et al., 2001). This model places the incompatibility of expectations by distinct cultures (traditional home culture versus urban and school culture) at the core of the explanation for lower levels of cognitive development.

EFFECTS OF INTERVENTION PROGRAMS

We present here three current intervention programs in Turkey and discuss the effects of these programs. Two of these programs were designed to improve cognitive skills of children, and one was designed to teach literacy to illiterate women. Although the latter program provides for a specific skill, there are indications that the effects of literacy acquisition may be more widespread than just obtaining the skills of reading and writing.

Mother-Child Education Program

Designed as an alternative to formal institutional early childhood education, the Mother-Child Education Program (MOCEP) aims to empower and train mothers of young children so that they can provide better care and enhanced stimulation for their children in their home environment (Kagitcibasi, 1997). The program has three components. One component emphasizes communication skills; health, nutrition, and care; discipline of children; and related issues. The second component aims to support the cognitive development of children with a number of activities to be conducted by the mothers with their children. It prepares five-year-old children for school. The final component is directed toward women's health and family planning.

MOCEP emerged from a longitudinal research study covering 10 years, involving a follow-up study (Kagitcibasi, Sunar, & Bekman, 2001).

With an experimental design involving 227 children from low-income areas in Istanbul, it was shown that the children whose mothers were trained, and who carried out the cognitive activities with their children, surpassed the control group on cognitive measures, achievement tests, and school performance. The results were sustained over time, reaching into adolescence, and were also reflected in higher educational attainment of the trained group. As a result, the Mother-Child Education Foundation was established to implement the program nationwide.

Bekman (1998) conducted an evaluation study of the large-scale MOCEP applications in four provinces in Turkey, in which 102 children who were trained by their mothers were compared with 115 matching children whose mothers were not participating in the MOCEP. The children were tested on pre-literacy and pre-numeracy skills both before and after their mothers' participation in the program. The results showed that children of participating mothers improved more than children of non-participating mothers on both pre-literacy and pre-numeracy measures. It was also reported that the gains of female children from this program were significantly higher than the gains of male children, due to the lower scores of female children before the program.

A follow-up study that was able to capture 85 of the trained children and 92 of the non-trained children investigated children's success at school and their performance at literacy and numeracy measures at school age. Those children who were trained by their mothers had significantly higher scores on the overall literacy and numeracy scores as well as higher grade averages at school than those whose mothers were not part of the MOCEP (Bekman, 1998).

Functional Adult Literacy Program

A large number of applicants to the MOCEP could not be accepted to the program because they were illiterate. The presence of such a high rate of illiterate women led the Mother-Child Education Foundation to establish a literacy program. The program developed by Durgunoglu, Oney, and Kuscul (1996) takes advantage of the phonological characteristics of the Turkish language and utilizes the regularity in the sound-letter correspondence as a means of teaching literacy effectively in a short period of time. The Functional Adult Literacy Program (FALP) is a 120-hour program conducted by volunteer educators. Recently, the second-phase literacy program of 80 hours (FALP II) was established to reinforce and boost the acquired literacy skills.

A comprehensive evaluation of the FALP is currently underway. This study assesses the changes in literacy skills and other cognitive abilities resulting from program participation. An initial evaluation study has also been conducted on the program. According to this study, which was based on the comparison of 59 FALP participants and 40 participants of the mainstream literacy program of the Ministry of Education, FALP participants completed the program with higher scores on literacy tests than the mainstream literacy program participants. This was the case despite the fact that FALP participants had started at a lower performance level at the beginning of the course.

A notable finding about the effects of FALP was obtained in another study on comprehension levels of the participants (Kagitcibasi, Goksen, & Gulgoz, 2003; Gulgoz, Goksen, & Kagitcibasi, 2000; Kagitcibasi, 2002). Participants of FALP were presented a fabricated televised news program, and they were later asked for recall of the news contents. The recall rates were higher at the testing after the completion of the program than at the testing at the beginning of the program. The literacy program had improved comprehension and recall abilities of the participants from spoken text. This was an indication that acquiring literacy had effects that propagated into the enhancement of various cognitive skills beyond the immediate effect.

Cognitive Capacity Development Program
Children from disadvantaged socio-economic backgrounds in Turkey have difficulty in optimally developing their critical thinking skills. Even though elementary education may equip them with basic cognitive skills, complex cognitive skills do not develop adequately for various reasons. These reasons include the inadequate quality of education in crowded public schools, the low value attached to cognitive skills in the traditional culture, the discrepancy between rural and urban cultures, and the ramifications of this discrepancy for the immigrant populations of former peasants without direct access to the urban culture although they reside in urban areas. These are global problems of human development (Kagitcibasi, 1996; 2002), which are also seen in Turkey.

Gulgoz et al. (2001) have proposed a model to explain the lower level of cognitive skills in disadvantaged groups and have developed a program to support the cognitive development of 11- to 13-year-old children, who are at the crossroads for such a development. The program consists of 130 modules, each of which lasts between 20 and 40 minutes, designed to last one school year with bi-weekly meetings of approximately one hour. Volunteer facilitators of the Turkish Educational Volunteers Foundation implemented the program after going through extensive training. The program is being implemented at the centers of the foundation, located in disadvantaged neighborhoods, without providing any extrinsic initiative for children. A comprehensive evaluation study for this program involving a control group is underway.

A pilot study to examine the influence of the program was conducted on a group of children who participated in a short-term trial version of the program (Gulgoz et al., 2000). The participants were 129 children who participated in the program, which lasted only six weeks (12 sessions with two modules implemented in each). The children were tested before and after participation in the program, using the Reading Test, the Whimbey Analytical Skills Inventory, and the Concrete Reasoning Test. The analyses showed significant improvement from pre- to post-tests in the Reading Test and Whimbey Analytical Skills Inventory. The scores on the Concrete Reasoning Test showed an interaction with the location of the program. The differences were significant and in the expected direction in four locations, significant and in the opposite direction in one location, and not significant in five locations. Although the results are encouraging, it is premature to arrive at a conclusion about the impact of the intervention. However, it was also observed that children with lower levels of performance at the beginning of the program improved the most. One would expect the gains to be much greater in response to a 65-hour program, given that even 12 hours of participation makes a change.

The concept of plasticity of intelligence is inherent in intervention work. The results obtained from the intervention research described here present a challenge to the commonly held assumptions in Turkey and elsewhere regarding intelligence as an innate and unchanging entity. They point to the potential of cognitively enriching experiences to support the development of human intelligence particularly in early ages and even in adulthood.

CONCLUSION

In this chapter, we have surveyed most of the limited number of studies on intelligence originating from Turkey. The most striking characteristic of these studies is that they are directed toward purposes other than understanding and investigating intelligence. Rather, intelligence is taken for granted, is not questioned, and is included in the studies as one of the variables that may be useful in explaining whatever the focus of the study may be. Many intelligence tests are used without proper cultural adaptations, but for the purposes of many studies, local norms are not a necessity. However, some studies do report that some items that are supposed to be more difficult are not as difficult, and some that are supposed to be solved with ease at a particular age are met with some difficulty. This may point to the unequivalence of the factor structures, a perennial problem in cross-cultural use of tests. The issue of difficulty is just one sign of the incompatibility of the test items. Thus, we may question the validity of many studies that employed a test without the process of adaptation, assuming this was not necessary because they were culture-fair tests.

Although the psychology of intelligence has a long history in Turkey, the early beginnings have not resulted in theoretical and methodological advances. The momentum behind the study of intelligence has waned or remained marginal to mainstream psychology dominated by clinical and social psychology. Experts in the field of education have also been laggard in producing sophisticated knowledge in this field. A recent promising development is seen in the intervention programs that should pave the way for increased research on intelligence and consequently help produce culturally valid conceptualizations and assessment of intelligence.

References

Acikgoz, D. (1996, September). *Bellek ve dikkat fonksiyonlarini olcen noropsikolojik testlerin faktor yapisi* [Factor structure of the neuropsychological tests measuring memory and attention functions]. Paper presented at the 9th Annual National Congress of Psychology, Istanbul, Turkey.

Allport, G. W. (1937). *Personality: A psychological interpretation.* New York: Holt.

Aydogmus, K., Gurkanlar, K., & Ezik, Z. (1977). Zeka geriligi duzeyleri ile sosyo-ekonomik kosullar arasindaki iliski konusunda bir calisma [A study on the relationship between levels of mental retardation and socio-economic conditions]. *Noro-Psikiyatri Arsivi, 14,* 39–44.

Bekman, S. (1998). *A fair chance: An evaluation of the Mother-Child Education Program.* Istanbul, Turkey: Mother-Child Education Foundation.

Burkovik, A. Y. (2000). *Sokakta yasayan evden kacmis cocuklarin WISC-R test sonuclarinin degerlendirilmesi* [Evaluation of WISC-R test results of runaway children living on the streets]. Unpublished master's thesis, Istanbul University, Istanbul, Turkey.

Cantez, E., & Girgin, Y. (1992). Istanbul'da yasayan 3–11 yas grubundaki kiz ve erkek cocuklara Gesell Gelisim Testi'nin uygulanmasindan elde edilen sonuclarin Gesell Gelisim Testi Normlari ile karsilastirilmasi ve normlara uygunlugunun arastirilmasi ile ilgili bir calisma [A study about the comparison of the results obtained from the application of Gesell Development Schedules to 3–11 year-old male and female children living in Istanbul with the norms of the Gesell Development Schedules]. In *VIII. Ulusal Psikoloji Kongresi Bilimsel Calismalari*. Ankara, Turkey: Turkish Psychological Association.

Celik, Z. (1998). *WPPSI-R zeka testi on uyarlama calismasi* [Preliminary adaptation study of WPPSI-R]. Unpublished master's thesis, Ege University, Izmir, Turkey.

Cronbach, L. J. (1957). The two disciplines of scientific psychology. *American Psychologist, 12*, 671–684.

Davasligil, U. (1980). Farkli sosyo-ekonomik ve kulturel cevreden gelen birinci sinif cocuklarinin dil gelisimine okulun etkisi [The influence of school on the language development of first grade children of different socio-economic and cultural backgrounds]. *Istanbul Universitesi Pedagoji Dergisi, 1*, 167–186.

Davasligil, U. (1994). Raven'in Progresif Matrisler Testi'nin normal ve normal ustu ogrencilerin ileriki matematik basarilarini kestirebilmesi [Prediction of future mathematics achievement of normal and above-normal students by Raven's Progressive Matrices Test]. In *VIII. Ulusal Psikoloji Kongresi Bilimsel Calismalari*. Ankara, Turkey: Turkish Psychological Association.

Durgunoglu, A., Oney, B., & Kuscul, H. (1996). Evaluation of an adult literacy program in Istanbul. Paper presented at the American Educational Research Association Meeting, New York.

Ekberzade, H. (1982). *Nevrotik cocuklarin okul basarisizliklarinda cevresel etkenler* [Environmental factors in the school failures of neurotic children]. Unpublished thesis, Istanbul University, Istanbul, Turkey.

Engle, R. W., Kane, M. J., & Tuholski, S. W. (1999). Individual differences in working memory capacity and what they tell us about controlled attention, general fluid intelligence, and functions of the prefrontal cortex. In A. Miyake & P. Shah (Eds.), *Models of working memory: Mechanisms of active maintenance and executive control* (pp. 102–134). New York: Cambridge University Press.

Epir, S., Biyikli, F. O., Gonul, M. F., & Sezgin, A. (1986). The Stanford-Binet Intelligence Test for Turkish primary school blind children: Variables related to IQ. *Journal of Visual Impairment and Blindness, 80*, 586–587.

Er, N., & Karakas, S. (1992). Cocuklarda Gorsel Isitsel Sayi Dizileri Testinden alinan puanlara mnemonik tekniklerin ve sunum hizinin etkisi [The effects of mnemonic tehniques and presentation speed on the Visual Auditory Digit Span Test scores of children]. In *VIII. Ulusal Psikoloji Kongresi Bilimsel Calismalari*. Ankara, Turkey: Turkish Psychological Association.

Etaner, U., Kesemen, A., & Bakan, G. (1984). Kalitsal ve cevresel etkenlerin tek ve cift yumurta ikizleri uzerinde kiyaslanmasi [The comparison of genetic and environmental factors on monozygotic and dizygotic twins]. In *XX. Norolojik Bilimler ve Psikiyatri Kongresi Calismalari* (pp. 97–98). Ankara.

Gardner, H. (1983). *Frames of mind, theory of multiple intelligences*. New York: Basic Books.

Gulgoz, S., Goksen, F., & Kagitcibasi, C. (2000). Literacy is more than learning to read: Information retention from TV news. *Proceedings of the Tenth*

Annual Meeting of the Society for Text and Discourse, 118–119, Université Lumiere Lyon 2.

Gulgoz, S., Erktin, E., Kagitcibasi, C., Cetinkaya, P., Ataibis, I., & Uzun-Sabol, A. E. (2001). *Zihinsel Kapasiteyi Gelistirme Programi Oku Dusun Yap Program Tanitim Kitabi* [Cognitive Capacity Improvement Program Read Think Do Program Handbook]. Istanbul: Turkiye Egitim Gonulluleri Vakfi.

Guray, O., & Cokan, Y. (1976). 8–12 yas grubu cocuklarda cevre, sosyo-ekonomik durum ve aile yapisinin zeka gelismesi uzerine etkisi [The effects of environment, socio-economic status, and family structure on the intelligence of 8–12-year-old children]. In *XII. Ulusal Psikiyatri ve Norolojik Bilimler Kongresi Calismalari* (pp. 449–455). Ankara.

Guray, O., & Cokan, Y. (1977). Cocuklarda zeka gelisiminde kirsal ve kentsel bolge etkinligi [Effect of rural or urban regions on the development of intelligence in children]. In *XIII. Ulusal Psikiyatri ve Norolojik Bilimler Kongresi Calismalari*. Ankara.

Harkness, S., & Super, C. (1993). The developmental niche: Implications for children's literacy development. In L. Eldering & P. Leseman (Eds.), *Early intervention and culture* (pp. 115–132). Paris: UNESCO.

Ilhan, U. (1993). *12–13 yas gruplarindaki cocuklarin Analitik Zeka Testi sonuclariyla Motor Beceri Testi sonuclari arasindaki iliskinin arastirilmasi* [The study of the relationship between the results of the Analytical Intelligence Test and Motor Skills Test in children between ages 12–13]. Unpublished master's thesis, Istanbul University, Istanbul, Turkey.

Jurden, F. H. (1995). Individual differences in working memory and complex cognition. *Journal of Educational Psychology, 87*, 93–102.

Kagitcibasi, C. (1979). The effects of socioeconomic development on Draw-a-Man scores in Turkey. *Journal of Social Psychology, 108*, 3–8.

Kagitcibasi, C. (1994). Psychology in Turkey. *International Journal of Psychology, 29*, 729–738.

Kagitcibasi, C. (1996). *Family and human development across cultures: A view from the other side.* Hillsdale, NJ: Erlbaum.

Kagitcibasi, C. (1997). Interactive mediated learning: The Turkish experience. *International Journal of Early Childhood, 29*, 22–32.

Kagitcibasi, C. (2002). Psychology and human competence development. *Applied Psychology: An International Review, 51*, 1, 5–22.

Kagitcibasi, C., Goksen, F., & Gulgoz, S. (2003). Functional adult literacy and empowerment of women: Impact of functional literacy in private and public lives of women.

Kagitcibasi, C., & Savasir, I. (1988). Human abilities in the Eastern Mediterranean. In S. H. Irvine & J. W. Berry (Eds.), *Human abilities in cultural context* (pp. 232–262). New York: Cambridge University Press.

Kagitcibasi, C., Sunar, D., & Bekman, S. (2001). Long-term effects of early intervention: Turkish low-income mothers and children. *Journal of Applied Developmental Psychology, 22*, 2, 333–361.

Karakas, S., Kafadar, H., & Eski, R. (1996). Wechsler Bellek Olcegi Gelistirilmis Formunun test-tekrar test guvenirligi [Test-retest reliability of Wechsler Memory Scale – Revised]. *Turk Psikoloji Dergisi, 11*, 46–52.

Karakas, S., & Yalin, A. (1995). Gorsel Isitsel Sayi Dizileri Testi B Formunun 13–54 yas grubu uzerindeki standardizasyon calismasi [The standardization study of the Visual Auditory Digit Span Test Form B on 13–54 age group]. *Turk Psikoloji Dergisi, 10,* 20–31.

Korkmazlar, U. (1980). *Relationship between parental child rearing attitudes and the cognitive styles of 5- to 6-year-old Turkish preschoolers.* Unpublished master's thesis, Bogazici University, Istanbul, Turkey.

Kyllonen, P. C. (1996). Is working memory capacity Spearman's *g*? In I. Dennis & P. Tapsfield (Eds.), *Human abilities: Their nature and measurement* (pp. 49–75). Hillsdale, NJ: Erlbaum.

Lister, C., Leach, C., & Pain, Y. (1993). The question of simlar sequence in development across cultures and the method of critical exploration. *Early Childhood Development and Care, 95,* 63–83.

Munday-Castle, A. (1974). Social and technological intelligence in Western and non-Western cultures. In S. Pilowsky (Ed.), *Cultures in collision.* Adelaide, Australian National Association of Mental Health.

Noyan, B., Yuksel, S., & Kucukyalcin, D. (1977). Iki kardeste zeka geriligi ile birlikte oculo-cutaneus albinismus [Oculo-cutaneus albinismus together with mental retardation in two siblings]. *Noro-Psikiyatri Arsivi, 14,* 7–13.

Nunes, T. (1993). Psychology in Latin America: The case of Brazil. *Psychology and Developing Societies, 5,* 123–134.

Okagaki, L., & Sternberg, R. J. (1993). Parental beliefs and children's school performance. *Child Development, 64,* 36–56.

Oktem, F. (1983). Asperger bozuklugu olan cocuklarda WCZO-R alt test orun-tuleri [WISC-R subtest patterns in children with Asperger disorder]. *Turk Psikoloji Dergisi, 13,* 1–12.

Oner, N. (1994). *Turkiye'de kullanilan psikolojik testler* [Psychological tests used in Turkey]. Istanbul, Turkey: Bogazici University Publications.

Ozbaydar, B. (1971). Verbal kabiliyet ve zeka [Verbal ability and intelligence]. *Istanbul Universitesi Tecrubi Psikoloji Calismalari, 9,* 1–7.

Ozguven, I. E. (1961). *Otis Beta Zihin Yetenegi Testleri Elkitabi* [Otis Beta Mental Ability Tests Manual]. Ankara, Turkey: Ministry of Education.

Sahin, A. (1996). *Bir grup universite ogrencisinde noropsikolojik testlerle zeka testi arasindaki iliskilerin incelenmesi* [The examination of the relationships between neuropsychological tests and an intelligence test on a group of university students]. Unpublished master's thesis, Hacettepe University, Ankara, Turkey.

Sahin, N. (1983). The factorial structure of the WISC-R in Turkish standardization. Unpublished paper, Middle East Technical University, Ankara, Turkey.

Savasir, I., & Sahin, N. (1995). *Wechsler Cocuklar icin Zeka Olcegi* [Wechsler Intelligence Scale for Children]. Ankara, Turkey: Turkish Psychological Association.

Selcuk, Z. (1985). *Turkiye'de cocuk istismari ve ihmali* [Child abuse and neglect in Turkey]. Unpublished master's thesis, Ankara University, Ankara, Turkey.

Serpell, R. (1977). Strategies for investigating intelligence in its cultural context. *Quarterly Newsletter, Institute of Comparative Human Development, 3,* 11–15.

Sezgin, N. (1987). *6–7.5 zeka yasindaki normal zekali, organik ve organik ol-mayan hafif derecede zihinsel ozurlu cocuklarin bilissel yapilarinin karsilastirilmasi*

[Comparison of the cognitive structures of 6- to 7.5-year-old normal intelligence children with children of minor mental disability of organic or non-organic causes]. Unpublished doctoral dissertation, Hacettepe University, Ankara, Turkey.

Sternberg, R. J. (1988). *The triarchic mind: A new theory of human intelligence.* New York: Viking.

Tan, H. (1972). Development of psychology and mental testing in Turkey. In L. J. Cronbach & P. J. D. Drenth (Eds.), *Mental tests and cultural adaptation* (pp. 3–12). The Hague: Mouton.

Tan, U. (1990). Relationship of testosterone and nonverbal intelligence to hand preference and hand skill in right-handed young adults. *International Journal of Neuroscience, 54,* 283–290.

Tan, U., Akgun, A., & Telatar, M. (1993). Relationships among nonverbal intelligence, hand speed, and serum testosterone level in left-handed male subjects. *International Journal of Neuroscience, 71,* 21–28.

Tan, U., Akgun, A., Komsuoglu, S., & Telatar, M. (1993). Inverse relationship between nonverbal intelligence and the parameters of pattern reversal visual evoked potentials in left-handed male subjects: Importance of right brain and testosterone. *International Journal of Neuroscience, 71,* 189–200.

Togrol, B., & Ozugurlu, K. (1973). Kulturden arinmis zeka testleri verilerinin istatistik degerlendirilmesi [Statistical evaluation of culture-free intelligence test data]. In *IX. Milli Psikiyatri ve Norolojik Bilimler Kongresi Calismalari* (pp. 293–296).

Tur, G. (1979). *Ilkokul ogrencilerinin yaraticilik, zeka, ve akademik basarilari arasindaki iliskiler* [The relationships between creativity, intelligence, and academic performance of primary school children]. Unpublished master's thesis, Ankara University, Ankara, Turkey.

Turker, V. (1977). *Ankara'da 3 lisede sosyo-ekonomik bakimdan avantajsiz ogrencilerin cesitli ozellikleri ve bellibasli egitim ve rehberlik sorunlari* [Various characteristics and primary educational and counseling problems of disadvantaged students in three high schools in Ankara]. Ankara, Turkey: Hacettepe University.

Wood, M. M. (1929). Mental test findings with Armenian, Turkish, Greek, and Bulgarian subjects. *Journal of Applied Psychology, 13,* 266–273.

Yalin, A., & Karakas, S. (1994). Gorsel Isitsel Sayi Dizisi A Formunun bir Turk cocuk ornekleminde guvenirlik, gecerlik ve standardizasyon calismasi [The reliability, validity, and standardization study of the Visual Auditory Digit Span Test Form A on a sample of Turkish children]. *Turk Psikoloji Dergisi, 9,* 6–14.

9

Intelligence

What Is Indigenous to India and What Is Shared?

Bibhu D. Baral and J. P. Das

The story is told of a discourse on mind, self, and intelligence that occurs in one of the seminal books of traditional knowledge, the *Upanishad* (Radhakrishnan, 1953). There is a learned man, Narada, who commutes between the land of gods and humans – he is dissatisfied in spite of his knowledge of books, which he teaches to humans; he wishes to know the nature of the self. He seeks out a wise man who is innocent of scriptural and book knowledge but is virtuous and practices love for all; this man is truly innocent like a five-year-old child. But he knows about the self. Narada asks him for lessons on self-knowledge, because he has heard that those who have such knowledge live beyond sorrow, and Narada says he is sad because he cannot cross over to the other side of sorrow! The wise man tells Narada to describe what knowledge he has already acquired, and then they can discuss how to go beyond it.

NAME, SPEECH, AND MIND

Narada's knowledge is vast – he knows the scriptures, mathematics and astronomy, medicine, warfare and weapons, the science of natural disasters, serpents, and the fine arts of dance and music. The boy-like wise man remarks that is good, you know the Name (declarative and procedural knowledge?), and as far as nomenclature goes, you should pursue it and be happy.

Narada asks, but is there not something beyond the knowledge of names?

Speech and language lie beyond Name. It is through speech and language that one can articulate the knowledge of the scriptures, the sciences, and the difference between good and bad. Without speech, one cannot even distinguish truth from falsehood and cannot articulate why something is pleasant or unpleasant.

But is there something greater than speech and language, Narada persists. Mind is certainly greater than both Name and Speech. It is like the closed fist, which holds, as it were, the two nuts of name and speech. It is the internal organ that makes choices and determines how to act to get what is in one's mind. If you have in mind to learn the scriptures and the sciences, you will find a way to learn them. When you have in mind to enjoy this world, you will then desire the pleasures of the world. Mind may thus appear like the self, because it acts like an agent, has authority for desired action. Greater than mind is *will*; without will, there is no action. However, greater than will is *thought*. An unthinking person may be learned, but would be ignored by others. When one thinks, one wills, then one reflects, and uses speech and speaks of what one knows. If one is thoughtful, people listen to him even if he does not have a vast knowledge. For if he speaks without thinking, people will say he must not be intelligent, for how can he speak like that! Know the nature of thought. One who knows the nature of thinking becomes endowed with intelligence and all the advantages of being intelligent. He wavers not and lives in an unwavering world; he becomes free of sorrow.

DEFINITIONS AND THEORIES

The major components of intelligence are found in the preceding discourse. It begins with the declaration that referential knowledge, a knowledge consisting of taxonomies, is not the essence of intelligence. Rather the ability for discriminating thinking is the hallmark of intelligence. The discourse describes a hierarchy. We know the name, but then we use speech and language to articulate exactly what we know. We can then put our mind to obtain what is known. We will, following what is in our mind, only upon thinking and reflection.

Definitions of Intelligence

Sternberg (1990) has proposed that the diverse theories of intelligence could be viewed within a taxonomy of metaphors. The top branch of the taxonomy distinguishes between inward-looking metaphors that focus on the mental capabilities of the individual without much concern for what this means for social interaction. In contrast, the outward-looking metaphors view intelligence as a set of behaviors to be evaluated within the context of an individual's society. The definition of intelligence in the preceding discussion is certainly *inward looking*, as is typical of the definitions from the classical literature of India written in Sanskrit. We will discuss the common concepts of intelligence found in the classical Indian philosophies (Zimmer, 1951).

Indian Philosophical – Psychological View of Intelligence

The notion of intelligence and its functioning in Indian tradition have been approached in different schools of philosophy in the context of discourse on knowledge. In an unbroken cultural tradition of some 3,000 years, one of the main topics of conceptual interest has been in philosophical psychology: how the mind is to be analyzed, trained, and developed to explain and obtain the religious goal of enlightenment and release from rebirth. The idea of intelligence (*buddhi* in Sanskrit) is an important epistemic concept in almost all philosophical systems. Here it is possible only to indicate some of the main structures and attitudes of Indian thought involving the concept of intelligence. *Buddhi* is the closest translation of *intelligence*. Etymologically, *buddhi* derives from *budh*, to be conscious (of), plus *ti*, a suffix indicating act, state, or fact. Its earliest meaning is evident as "awareness, consciousness." Intelligence in the Indian philosophical treatises has been treated as a state, a process, and an entity, the realization of which depends upon one's own effort, persistence, and motivations (Srivastava & Misra, 2000). Das (1994) has noted that the concept of intelligence in Indian philosophy refers to "waking up, noticing, recognizing, understanding, and comprehending. In contrast to the usual meaning of intelligence, as understood in the western literature, *Buddhi* includes such things as determination, mental effort, and even feelings and opinions in addition to such intellectual processes as knowledge, discrimination, and decision making" (p. 387). Thus, an intelligent person is thought to be capable of knowing the intention of others, is polite, and refrains from self-praise, shows initiative, interest in work, and lacks rigidity. Intelligence characterizes practical understanding situated in real life regarding self, others, objects, and the total habitat of a person (Srivastava & Misra, 1996). Like Western thought, the Indian view emphasizes the role of genetic and environmental factors in determining a person's intelligence. Persons reap the fruits of their own *karma* (deeds), and the *karma* passes through generations. Intelligence is seen as the result of one's own *karma*, and the child inherits it from his or her parents. However, the expression of this genetic endowment depends upon the child's own deeds and effort (Srivastava & Misra, 2000).

Intelligence and Consciousness

Enumerating the relationship between consciousness and the physical structure, Das (1994) has noted that according to the Eastern views, pure consciousness is at the top with no material basis. From consciousness evolves discriminative intelligence or *buddhi*. The consciousness of one's own identity as an individual emerges from discriminative and evaluative intelligence. Mental functions evolve secondarily out of intelligence and ego defense. Next to evolve are the five perceptual abilities (seeing, hearing, smelling, tasting, and kinesthetic) and five motor abilities (speech, grasping, locomotion, reproduction, and excretion). These abilities are then attached to the five basic elements or natural substances: earth, light, water, wind, and space. In the Indian view, motor organs, like sensory organs, contribute to one's experience and knowledge. A list of words commonly related to intelligence include *buddhi*, acquired knowledge (*vidya*), conscience (*vivek*) built on experiential knowledge, and knowledge through discourses (*jnana*) and their antonyms. *Buddhi* is achieved through *karma* or deeds and is characterized by a pragmatic understanding of the self and of the life situation. *Vidya* is acquired through the exercise of intelligence. *Vivek* refers to experiential intelligence derived from perceptual analysis, analogical reasoning, and materials learned from books and authorities (Das, 1994). *Jnana* is acquired through the discourses with a wise teacher (*guru*). Egotism is the greatest stumbling block in acquiring knowledge.

Buddhi is also considered within an "outward metaphor" as it includes the contextual aspects of intelligence comprising the appropriate situation (*desh*), time (*kala*), and the person (*patra*) for whom intelligent action is intended or directed. However, to acquire a pure form of intelligence, not only the context, but also the sources of knowledge have to be left behind. Why? Intelligence is not static; it evolves. Pure or discriminating intelligence has to rise above the activities of the mind (*manas*), as the mind is too close to the sources of knowledge and thus is likely to be contaminated and constrained by these and, consequently, becomes fickle and idiosyncratic. Therefore, discriminating intelligence needs to distance itself, taking on the role of a witness rather than a participant, witnessing the activities of the mind (Das & Thapa, 2000). Intelligence of the pure or discriminating kind is constantly evolving, getting closer to a state of "pure" knowledge by dint of an individual's efforts. These efforts are not only directed toward obtaining valid and appropriate knowledge as the Euro-American view confirms but are also directed at attempting to rise above the influences of desire and unfavorable temperament through right ideas, efforts, and reflections. Intelligence and wisdom can be had only when you are connected, united, or disciplined.

> The undisciplined have no wisdom,
> no one-pointed concentration;
> with no concentration, no peace;
> with no peace, where can joy be?

> When the mind constantly runs
> after the wandering senses,
> it drives away wisdom, like the wind
> blowing a ship off course.

(Mitchell, 1988, pp. 58–59)

In the case of human beings, ever higher states can be achieved until a stage is reached where the distinction between the knower and the object of knowledge becomes non-existent. Intelligence, then, takes on the form of the object, culminating in the process of knowing (Radhakrishnan, 1948; Zimmer, 1951). The preceding concepts of intelligence partly repeat the citation at the beginning of this chapter. These are also echoed in the widely read book of discourse that takes place between a uniquely revered teacher (Krishna) and his star pupil (Arjun); this discourse written in the *Bhagabad Gita* (Radhakrishnan, 1948) has influenced contemporary thinking in India, comparable to the influence of the Bible on Euro-American literature. Therefore, it is worthwhile to conclude the present section on the ancient concepts of intelligence in India by paraphrasing relevant parts of the *Bhagabad Gita* (Radhakrishnan, 1948)

1. *Buddhi* is above the mind, which is above the senses.
2. *Buddhi* is subject to confusion, error, and distortion, especially if it depends on the senses. It can know things as they truly are. Desire and lust, as well as anger, obscure knowledge.
3. *Buddhi* is something that some people have, while others do not (including wisdom and good judgment).
4. *Buddhi* is a cognitive entity, hence a mode of thought.
5. *Buddhi* is also affective and purposive. Reason, will, emotion, cognition, judgment, decision – all share in some parts the meaning of *buddhi*.

HISTORY OF RESEARCH

The Concept of Intelligence: Two Modern Philosophers

Intelligence in the Thought of Sri Aurobindo

For Sri Aurobindo (McDermott, 1988), *buddhi* can be translated as *understanding*. We paraphrase his views to show the continuity of the concept from ancient times. According to Sri Aurobindo, intelligence or understanding must be purified. The process of purification of intelligence consists of excluding from it the action of the mind, which is dominated by sensory experience and memory, since these merely consist of the recording of perceptions of all kinds without distinguishing between right and wrong, true and illusory. Such impure intelligence is without higher principles of judgment and discrimination. A proper perspective can be gained by overriding the constant play of habits of thought. These comprise desires, prejudices, and prejudgments. These have to be expunged and challenged by discriminating reasoning. This kind of "pure" understanding or intelligence separates animals from human beings. It has been useful in the development of man's intelligence as distinct from the intelligence of animals (Sri Aurobindo, 1922, p. 353). His conceptualization of intelligence closely reflects the same in Bahgabad Gita as summarized here; it is the whole action of the mind that decides, discriminates, and determines both the direction and use of our thoughts and actions.

The human mind engages in two kinds of intellectual activities, one lower than the other. The first obvious function of the mind is inference and reasoning based on sense experience. The senses sometimes mislead and, therefore, hinder the procurement of true knowledge – a theme that occurs in the Bhagabad Gita. But the yet higher function of intelligence is self-awareness, using the mind to know about oneself. According to Aurobindo, this is a unique characteristic of human intelligence that bypasses sense knowledge. The ultimate goal of intelligence is direct cognizance without the mediation of the senses, and hence without the distortions brought about by the ego (Sri Aurobindo, 1939) .

> If a man keeps dwelling on sense-objects,
> attachment to them arises;
> from attachment, desire flares up;
> from desire, anger is born;
>
> from anger, confusion follows;
> from confusion, weakness of memory;

weak memory – weak understanding
weak understanding – ruin.

(Mitchell, 1988, p. 58)

Intelligence in the Philosophy of J. Krishnamurti

As an original thinker Krishnamurti (1973) succeeds Aurobindo in the history of thought in India. His discussions and discourses have been carried out in several countries of Europe and in North America and recorded in print and conducted in television (Krishnamurti Foundation of America via Internet). Shringy (1976) also provides one of the contemporary reviews of his thoughts. Intelligence, to Krishnamurti, is the harmony of reason, emotion, and action. The intuitive rather than rational discernment of truth and falsehood is intelligence. Intelligence is the ability for knowing, reasoning and conceptualization without involving emotion. Intelligence is the inherent capacity to feel as well as to reason, and both capacities are equally represented (Shringy, 1976). It is the will of comprehension arising out of love that brings about intelligence. That is why he says that intelligence is the completeness of being, the fruition of the life processes.

Intelligence is total action that wipes out the sense of incompleteness entirely. Intelligence is the action of understanding. As Krishnamurti puts it, if we understand the functioning of our own thought and emotion, and thereby in that action become aware, then there is intelligence. To Krishnamurti, intelligence is truth, completeness, beauty, and love itself. These ideas are similar to Plato and Aristotle's truth, beauty, and goodness. To understand the environment, whatever it may be, is intelligence: The environment is the relationship of the individual with things, with people and with ideas. It is only when we fully understand the significance of environment and see its value that there is intelligence. These ideas seem to be an echo of Vygotsky (Vygotsky, 1978) in regard to the social–historical determinants of thought, language, and action. Krishnamurti's philosophical ideas have been reviewed in several sources including Shringy (1976) and the Krishnamurty Foundation of America (www.kfa.org).

CURRENT RESEARCH

In reviewing contemporary research on intelligence, first we select two studies that show the continuity of the concept from ancient times as these are reflected in prevalent proverbs and lay people's ideas of intelligence.

Proverbial Representation of Intelligence

Srivastava and Mishra (1999) made an analytical study of Hindi proverbs to understand the notion of intelligence as prevalent in the vernacular or folk tradition of north India. In this study 393 proverbs having a bearing on intelligence were collected and content analyzed. The analysis revealed that intelligence is characterized more as a valued procedural potentiality. It is classified into categories, that is, social competence, reasoning and problem solving, personality and motivation, and communication skills. About half of the proverbs stressed on the social competence of the individual, particularly one's sensitivity to the context and practical thinking. The analysis of proverbs revealed that the proverbs are largely concerned with three aspects of intelligence. First, there are proverbs focusing on the structure and determinants of intelligence. Second, a large chunk of proverbs describe the characteristics of an intelligent person or behavior. Third, the characteristics of an unintelligent person or behavior are also enumerated in these proverbs.

From the analysis of proverbs, it was revealed that intelligence is considered essential for acquiring knowledge. In fact, it has been treated synonymously with "knowledge." It is thought to be the supreme wealth and the greatest power. Intelligence is considered the real basis of discrimination among individuals. One is also judged intelligent on the basis of the outcome of one's actions. Practical intelligence is situated in the social context, and a limited number of individuals are fortunate enough to have both academic and practical types of intelligence. Exposure to varied environments is considered important for inculcating intelligence.

Proverbs reflect popular beliefs regarding intelligence; these are in agreement with the notions of the two popular philosophers, Sri Aurobindo and Krishnamurti. In turn, the essence of their views can be found in the ancient Indian history of thought. The analysis shows that Indian society accords high priority to intelligence and intelligent people (Srivastava & Mishra, 1999). The Western theories of intelligence are rooted in a positivist notion of knowledge and empiricist approach toward its understanding. Except Piaget and Vygotsky, who localized intelligence in action, the majority of researchers consider intelligence in terms of disposition, ability, or attribute of the person that is manifested in physiological, verbal, and behavioral forms. In contrast, the Indian conception of intelligence is process oriented and tied to the context. Intelligence in the Indian context stands for an adaptive potentiality of a person in different domains of life. It is not restricted to the cognitive domain alone. This adaptive potentiality consists of a range of skills that help one to overcome the life problems, to grow, and become what one wants to be. (Srivasta & Mishra, 1999)

Laypeople's Conception of Intelligence

Srivasta and Mishra (1999) also report a very interesting concept of intelligence among lay people. Participants ($n = 1,885$), varying along the dimensions of ecological context (rural or urban), schooling, age, and gender, from five localities volunteered for the study. Responding to an open-ended question, participants described the characteristics of an intelligent person. Analysis revealed four major dimensions of intelligence: cognitive competence, social competence, competence in action, and emotional competence.

The construal of intelligence in the Indian context is not limited to the cognitive domain alone. This is consistent with the ancient views and those of the two contemporary thinkers reviewed here. In addition to cognitive competence, Indians stress social and emotional competence as well as the modes of task accomplishment. Although about one-third of the laypeople's responses were related to the cognitive domain, two-thirds of responses referred to other domains. The main points are summarized here:

1. Cognitive competencies such as sensitivity to context, reflection, communication, and decision making
2. Social competencies such as helping the needy, obedience, service to elders, and following norms
3. Emotional competencies including control of emotions and patience
4. Action competencies such as commitment and efficiency were prominently reported by lay people

Some less frequently reported attributes included emotional competencies such as health consciousness, non-extravagance, honesty, good conduct, seriousness, religiousness, and empathy. Other attributes included qualities of task accomplishment such as working hard and being systematic.

Metacognition, or the ability to know one's strengths and weaknesses, was an important part of intelligence as conceived by lay people. We suggest that consistent with Krishnamurti's idea, one thing appears to emerge from a holistic view of both the layman's point of view as well as the previous study of common proverbs: The understanding of one's environment, whatever it may be, constitutes a major part of intelligence.

CURRENT TECHNIQUES OF ASSESSMENT

A Break With the Past: Contemporary Research in India is Mostly Euro-American

The majority of professors who taught me graduate courses in psychology at Patna University had degrees from Europe and the United States. One who influenced me the most and introduced me to intelligence and experimental methods earned his doctorate degree from the University of Edinburgh; he worked with Godfrey Thompson, a classic scholar in factor analysis. There were also two alumni of the University of London, and one of Cambridge University who took courses from students of Fredrick Bartlett. My professor with an American Ph.D. had graduated from the University of Michigan; he was taught by luminaries such as Theodore Newcomb. Even as an undergraduate at a different university in India, I had professors with degrees from universities of Oxford, London, Berlin, and the Teacher's College, Columbia University. My case was not unique – among my contemporaries most had professors who were similarly qualified. Many of my cohorts, after completing their M.A. degrees, became lecturers in psychology and eventually went to European and American universities for doctoral work. Many came back to work in India, and some of those who stayed outside India influenced Indian research through collaborative projects with former colleagues and students. It is then not surprising that contemporary Indian psychology is Euro-American, so much so that to correct the excessive influence of the West, a small group of those psychologists have started a movement for "indigenous psychology" and have begun to look at the ancient roots discussed in the earlier part of this chapter. However, Euro-American psychology prevails as the review of research given next will demonstrate. Some of that research, however, is not very good.

The Practice of Intelligence Testing in India

Intelligence testing in India, as Sinha (1983) has observed, remained for a long time one of the most popular academic pursuits for psychologists and educators. Harper (1960) observed that 40% of the test development work in India was related to intelligence. Kumar (1991) has reported that until 1988 about 43% of doctoral dissertations and institutional studies on test development were related to intelligence and about 2% to social intelligence.

The use of psychological tests in India was first initiated by Christian missionaries. It was Dr. Rice who first attempted the standardization of the Binet-Simon Test in India in Urdu and Punjabi (Sinha, 1983). In 1934, Mahalanobis for the first time attempted to devise and administer a group test of intelligence in Bengali (Mukherjee, 1993). In the opinion of several reviewers, psycho-educational assessment is weakened, a neglect of proper conceptualization, theoretical analysis and methodological rigor (see Kulkarni & Puhan, 1988; Mukherjee, 1993; Saraswathi & Dutta, 1987). Evaluating the quality of adapted tests, Sinha (1983) observed, "the so-called adaptations were no more than imperfect translations of some Western tests. Rarely was the exercise of back translation attempted, and even more rarely was the appropriateness of items for the changed socio-cultural context examined" (p. 19). A short review nevertheless is warranted.

The National Library of Educational and Psychological Tests (NLEPT) at the National Council of Educational Research and Training (NCERT) aims at collecting Indian and foreign tests and periodically brings out bulletins containing information about Indian tests in print. The NLEPT also brings out critical reviews on published tests in its bulletins (so far 29 bulletins have been published; Mohan, 1993) and has published Indian Mental Measurement Handbook; Intelligence and Aptitude Tests (Jain, 1991). The NLEPT has information on 43 published intelligence tests in India and five unpublished tests (Srivastava, Tripathi, & Misra, 1996). Out of these tests, the maximum number of tests (51%) was available in Hindi, followed by non-verbal (19%) and English (14%) tests. Only 5% of the tests were available in Gujurati and 2% each in Bengali, Marathi, and Tamil. Further, the majority of tests (81%) were administrable in group settings.

School counselors in India do the job of both school psychologists and vocational counselors. What are the tests of intelligence they use? Srivastava et al. (1996) in their report mention the following: with regard to the particulars of intelligence tests used in their day-to-day practice, the school counselors mentioned only four tests, that is, Raven's Standard Progressive Matrices (SPM) (96%), the test of General Mental Ability by Jalota (27%), Bhatia's Performance Battery (22%), and an Indian adaptation of the Stanford-Binet test by Kulshrestha (4%). Their overall satisfaction with the tests was not good. They made additional efforts to achieve a dependable measure of intelligence in varied ways, that is, use of more than one intelligence test (42%), scholastic achievement (27%), teacher's rating (11%), students' interview (9%), observation of students' behavior (7%), and parental interview (7%). On the meaning of intelligence, about one-third of school counselors conceptualized intelligence as one that enables the students to adjust to the environment. Some considered it a global capacity (15%), and others as a composite of different mental abilities (15%).

The psychometric tradition in India has not been as much concerned with the sociocultural milieu or ecology within which behaviors take place. Attending to the sociocultural characteristics requires focusing on those characteristics and traits or skills that are valued in a society. Apart from a few preliminary works (Das, 1994; Naglieri & Das, 1997), little systematic effort has so far been made in this direction.

Selected Studies on Intelligence as a General Ability (IQ)
General Intelligence

Kurian and associates (Kurian & Sharma, 1988) discuss a theoretical view of the concept of intelligence in terms of cognitive processes. They take a stand between heredity and environment in conceptualizing general intelligence, for their review suggests that a general developmental mechanism may show considerable flexibility and modifiability of intellectual ability. Language and thought were perceived as worthy of study using a general developmental mechanism. They believe that, whereas some areas of language development may be parallel to cognitive development, other specialized functions such as syntax may be autonomous in later adult life, that is, independent of general intelligence. An emphasis on the cognitive science perspective is also evident in the writings of Gupta (1991). The objective of cognitive science, according to him, is to discover the representational and computational capacities of the mind. Several other researchers have focused on the relationship between general intelligence and school achievement. For example, Pershad (1987) examined the Wechsler Adult Intelligence Scale–Revised

(WAIS-R) as it relates to a course in arithmetic and concluded that the arithmetic subtest in WAIS-R should not be timed for Indian subjects. The author argued that particularly in the case of older subjects, 50 years or above, speed was not an important consideration, but power was, as older subjects performed better than younger subjects when speed was not taken into account. Rani and Mehrotra (1991) used certain abilities from Guilford's structure of intellect model, which they believed would predict achievement in chemistry. They found that achievement in chemistry was significantly related to seven factors including convergent and divergent production of semantic relations, divergent production of symbolic units, and convergent production of symbolic transformations.

Gupta, Mukherjee, and Chatterjee (1993) examined factors affecting academic achievement of adolescents in West Bengal. Using a sample of 1,453 students from 64 urban and rural schools, they found wide variations in intellectual level (measured by the Standard Progressive Matrices) with the mean value being highest for urban boys and lowest for rural girls. Intelligence was found to be highly correlated with academic achievement. Sudhir and Muraleedharan-Pillai (1987) examined science achievement in relation to intelligence and socioeconomic status (SES) in a sample of secondary school students. The results thereby confirmed the earlier findings: Subjects from high SES and with high IQ obtained higher science achievement scores than subjects from lower SES and with lower IQ.

The personality correlates of intellectually superior and gifted students have been investigated with differing results. For example Chaudhari and Ray (1992) observed significant difference in the self-concept and locus of control of intellectually superior and normal students. However, Gautam and Singh (1992) did not find any difference in self-concept and academic motivation of gifted and average and low-ability students. Studying the consequences of consanguinity on cognitive ability, Afzal (1988) noted that inbred subjects obtained lower verbal and performance subtest scores on WISC-R. The effects were particularly pronounced if subjects lived in rural areas rather than in suburban areas. Although intelligence has been treated as an independent variable in a number of studies, the influence of intelligence on various psychological processes has been dealt with in a cursory and superficial manner, their selection often being random and at times logically untenable. This is best illustrated by a brief review of findings: Groups high and low on social intelligence differed in their interpersonal judgment

(Pandey, 1992); social and occupational class significantly influence subjects' intelligence (Srivastava, 1993); extroverted girls were more intelligent (Sharma & Bansal, 1991–1992); highly intelligent subjects scored higher on social, democratic, and knowledge values (Padhan, 1992) and were more creative (Gupta & Chandradash, 1994); and urban children obtained higher scores than rural children (Yenagi, 1993; see Das & Thapa, 2000). Some exceptions were also there. One such study is by Srivastava (1992), who examined the role and nature of intellectual processes in sex role adoption (SRA) and has meaningfully interpreted the results. A sample of 960 children studying in private, government, and corporation schools was studied, and it was observed that intelligence did not have any major effects on SRA. Focusing on cognitive factors, he argued that though intellectual growth may play a profound part in initiating gender role development, intellectual development itself was a product of social developmental forces and not influenced by purely intellectual types of stimulation. These views bear close correspondence with those of Piaget (Das & Thapa, 2000).

ASSESSMENT OF COGNITIVE ABILITIES

Piaget's Framework

Within the Piagetian framework, some studies have explored the field of cognitive development more or less on the lines of Piaget (Kulkarni & Puhan, 1988). One such attempt was made by the child study unit of NCERT (Kulkarni & Puhan, 1988). The team adapted cognitive tasks from the original Piagetian tasks for studying the levels of development of the concept of speed. It also collected data on children's intelligence as measured by Draw-A-Man test, SES, and the educational background of both parents. It was observed that the development of cognitive operations involved in the concept of speed among Indian children follows the same pattern as those of Genevan children studied by Piaget.

Information Processing

The cognitive revolution gave rise to an information processing approach to intelligence. This has not been ignored by contemporary researchers in India in the field of intelligence. Research in India has concerned itself with memory, reaction time, and speed, as well as cognitive information processing relating to reading, attention, aging, and

personality. Even the traditional yogic consciousness has been studied
using evoked potentials or event-related potentials (Das & Thapa, 2000).
Working memory and speed of processing are two of the major concepts
that have guided contemporary Indian research on intelligence. A sample of studies is summarized next. Agarwal and Kumar (1992) examined
aging in adults without dementia in terms of memory capacity and processing speed and concluded that the speed of processing was the most
important predictor of everyday memory. Speed as an index of intelligence, an influence from Jensen's attempt at defining g in terms of
speed, has been used by some researchers including Mohan and Jain
(1983). The aim of this study was to separate prior learning in school,
and speed as measured by reaction time as two predictors of school
achievement. Examining gifted and normal children, and children with
mental retardation, the authors noted that setting aside the influence
of prior learning, reaction time could be used as a measure of intellectual ability. However, although reaction time distinguished between the
three groups hierarchically placed on a scale of general intelligence, it
would be necessary to demonstrate within each group whether or not
reaction time was related to individual differences in intelligence (Das
& Thapa, 2000).

The relationship between indices of reaction time and crystallized
and fluid intelligence in different age groups was studied by Agarwal
and Kumar (1993). It was found that the nature of processing varied in
terms of the dimensions of intelligence, and the relationship between intelligence and reaction time was moderated by task variables. Another
study by Sen, Kurseja, and Chatterjee (1988) made a more sophisticated
use of reaction time by adopting a dual task performance paradigm. The
contrasting groups were proofreaders, telephone salesmen (telephone
advertising), and clerical workers in an office. As expected, proofreaders
processed visual messages better than auditory messages, whereas the
opposite was true of telephone salesmen. Clerical workers processed
visual messages only slightly better than auditory messages. In a theoretical essay, Anima Sen (1991) provided definitive support for using
information processing speed as an alternative measure of intelligence.
She argued that information processing speed as indexed through reaction time, inspection time, short-term memory, iconic image duration,
and the like, may be used for the diagnosis of functional psychoses, and
furthermore, assessment of personality in terms of signal detection parameters was a definite possibility. Unfortunately, however, empirical
research of sufficient weight is lacking in support of relating any of these

measures to personality and psychiatric conditions that cannot be detected by the various subtests of, for example, standardized intelligence
tests such as the WISC-R or WAIS-R.

Numerous other studies on memory did not yield any results
unique to Indian subjects. For example, Gupta (1985) demonstrated
that mnemonic devices facilitated recall of order in memory experiments. Gupta (1989) showed that when tasks were elaborated during
encoding, free recall and recognition of words were better and improved
significantly. However, these results were statistically significant only in
the case of recognition. Continuing in the same vein, Kurtz, Borkowski,
and Deshmukh (1988) related intelligence, metamemory, and memory
performance. However, the reach of this study was far wider; it included
a relationship between these cognitive abilities and the home environment. Based on their findings, the authors concluded that the home environment and the richness of children's metamemories must be taken
into account to explain performance on laboratory and academic tasks.
Some studies have used attention and arousal in relating these to measures of intelligence and information processing. For example, Mohan
and Bajaj (1983) demonstrated that fluctuation of attention as measured
by a classic Gestalt task involving a reversible figure was related to differences in intelligence represented by a sample of gifted children, children of normal intelligence, and mentally retarded children. Dwivedi,
Mishra, and Chaturvedi (1986) induced arousal by manipulating high-
or low-intensity white noise while the subjects processed 3-letter words.
It was seen that high noise was relatively detrimental as compared with
low noise.

Memory and personality research has been largely influenced by
Eysenck's extraversion and neuroticism dimensions. For example,
Helode and Sawade (1985); Helode (1985); Kumar, Malhotra, and Jerath
(1986); and Tanwar and Kumar (1986) used introversion–extraversion
versus neuroticism–stability as their major dimension. However, they
failed to add anything new. Helode and Sawade (1985) examined the relationships among verbal maze learning, general intelligence, extraversion, and neuroticism; they concluded that on verbal maze learning,
which was a timed test and scored as latency extroverts were faster,
neuroticism was related to slow learning time. Helode (1985) examined paired associate learning in terms of extraversion–introversion and
noted that there were stable relationships between extraversion on the
one hand, and verbal learning and the use of mnemonic strategies on
the other.

The Stroop test has been used in a few studies, less as a measure of attention than as a measure of verbal ability (Pati & Dash, 1990a), but in these studies memory impairment was complicated by anxiety and depression. However, the older subjects (all subjects were more than 60 years of age) showed deterioration in performance on tasks that required speed. It is a good sign that this study as well as other studies have obtained the same results with regard to aging as studies cited in the Euro-American literature. In another study, Pati and Dash (1990b) investigated whether intelligence and specific cognitive abilities were related to the academic achievement of grades 3 and 5 school children who were high and low achievers. They found that grade, gender, and achievement level had significant effects on Stroop scores. Negative correlations between Stroop scores and Progressive Matrices were obtained.

A related area is cognitive style. In their attempt to explore the relationship between cognitive style (field dependence/independence) and nonverbal intelligence, Biswas and De (1992) affirmed that cognitive style was positively and significantly correlated with nonverbal intelligence. Mukhopadhyay and Dash (1999) examined the change in cognitive style with age and its relationship with intelligence and locus of control in children. Results revealed progressive change in cognitive style from field dependence to field independence with age. A positive relationship between Raven's Colored Progressive Matrices and Field Independence was found.

Mathur and Das (1997) explored the use of an objective performance test and planned composition, two important aspects of conceptual planning in managerial work. To this end, two tests – planning composition (Das, 1980) and an objective performance Crack-the-Code test, which was like the game Master Mind (Das, Kar, & Parrila, 1996), were used in this study. The specific aim was to find out the connections between Crack-the-Code and planned composition. Their choice of strategies and justifications as written in their composition were then rated by three judges. The participants were engineering students in a course on management. The study confirmed the positive correlation between Crack-the-Code performance and planning strategies and justifications; when the participants were divided into low, medium, and high performers on Crack-the-Code, they could also be similarly arranged on composition. The authors comment that both tasks can be used for selection of potentially good managers.

We have encouraging evidence in these Indian studies for the application of information processing tasks to intelligent behavior.

CONTEMPORARY RESEARCH ON COGNITIVE ABILITIES
AND EFFECT OF SCHOOLING

PASS Theory of Intelligence and Cultural Universals

The Planning, Attention-Arousal, Simultaneous, and Successive (PASS) cognitive processing model is described as a modern theory of ability within the information-processing framework (Das, Naglieri & Kirby, 1994). It is based on Luria's analyses of brain structures (Luria, 1966). Luria described human cognitive processes within the framework of three functional units. The function of the first unit is cortical arousal and attention; the second unit codes information using simultaneous and successive processes; and the third unit provides for planning, self-monitoring, and structuring of cognitive activities. Luria's work on the functional aspects of brain structures formed the basis of the PASS model and was used as a blueprint for defining the important components of human intellectual competence. The Das-Naglieri Cognitive Assessment System provides the tests for PASS (Naglieri & Das, 1997). Thus, arising out of the clinical work of Luria that lead to the formulation of the three functionally organized blocks of the brain, research with the four PASS processes has integrated Luria's notions with cognitive psychology. The result is a model of cognitive processes that appears to have distinct advantages over standard IQ tests bereft of theory and implications for ameliorating cognitive deficits. The PASS theory in its present and earlier versions, and the tests that were derived from it, have been applied to different ethnic groups in several countries, and we have obtained the same results. When differences were observed, however, these could be explained meaningfully (Das, Kirby, & Jarman, 1975; Das, Naglieri, & Kirby, 1994). It provides an example of a cultural universal, which we discuss next.

In spite of the obvious differences in cultures of Indian and American children, and the warning that intelligence tests given to children in India must take into account the attitudes toward test-taking (see Sternberg, 1990), there is an equalizing agent, which is schooling. The effects of schooling act as levelers, allowing the schooled children to take on the attitudes of American school children while doing intelligence tests. Schooled children in Westernized schools seem to share the same set of core efficiencies in India as in Euro-American schools – attention to words and grammar, formalities of the writing system, and, above all, decontextualization of learned material. Both Olson and

Scribner caution us not to assume a general intellectual development due to schooling outside those that are connected to reading and writing (see Das & Dash, 1989). Test-taking attitude is an integral part of schooling. Therefore when language is not a barrier and the tester is of the same linguistic and cultural community as the student, there is little reason to expect that results of intelligence tests will not have cultural validity for children in school.

The following results of two recent studies using the Cognitive Assessment System (CAS; Naglieri & Das, 1997) for children in Bhubaneswar and Bombay proves the point. It should be noted that the two cities are located in culturally different parts of India, and yet that should not matter as both samples were school students. This will be further reinforced when we review the effect of schooling in a subsequent section.

In the Bhubaneswar study CAS data was obtained from 80 children 5 to 16 years of age. An important evidence that the test "works" is the normal distribution of the scores. The CAS has a "full score" equivalent to an IQ and scaled scores for its four processes; Planning, Attention, Simultaneous, and Successive. The full score distribution was normal – a mean of 98.9 and a standard deviation (SD) of 14.97, approximating the ideal of a mean of 100 and SD of 15. Further, the data provided support for the construct validity of the processing scores. Those with low scores in Simultaneous were poor in understanding problems in math and in comprehension of what they read; those with low scores in Attention were a bit hyperactive as distinct from those who could not manage their time and finish homework (poor in Planning) (Mishra, Mohanty, & Nanda, in preparation).

In a Bombay study by Mehta (2001), PASS processes of 100 low-achieving (LA) children and 100 high-achieving (HA) were assessed with the help of the CAS. The results indicated that the cognitive processes of PASS processes and the full-composite score of LA and HA groups of school children differed significantly, and the means indicated that the HA group was superior to the LA group. Their mean CAS full-scale scores were 88.69 (low) contrasted to 109.26 (high). The HA group was distinctly better in Simultaneous and Planning, and not so much better in Attention, as shown by discriminant function analyses that Mehta performed on the processing scales.

The sample consisted of male students from grades 5, 6, and 8 of six English medium schools of suburban Mumbai. The criterion for selecting the LA children was that their grand total for the previous year's final examination marks was 1 SD below the class mean. Likewise, the HA children had their grand total 1 SD above the class mean. The entire group of 200 children had scored above the 50th percentile on the Progressive Matrices (Standard and Color). Thus, according to that classification, they were all in the intellectually average to intellectually superior range.

Incidentally, Mehta's study used Progressive Matrices scores for ensuring that the groups had comparable intelligence. Thus the sensitivity of CAS to differences in school achievement is evident here, and the process differences can be meaningfully related to HA and LA results. Construct validity of CAS in these two samples of Indian school children is clearly supported.

Context of Schooling and Its Cognitive Consequences

In developmental literature, it is widely accepted that the "structure" of a child's intellect is shaped and nurtured by a variety of contexts and cultural milieu in which he or she grows up (Wagner & Spratt, 1987). Schooling provides one such manmade context, which is almost taken for granted for every child in the Western world; developmental inferences in respect of intellectual progression are confounded by factors of schooling at least beyond age 5 (Rogoff, 1981). Cross-cultural studies have demonstrated that schooling has a marked impact upon performance on a variety of classification, memory, and reasoning tasks (Cole & Scribner, 1977; Rogoff, 1981; Sharp, Cole, & Love, 1979). In summarizing their results on a wide variety of cognitive tasks, Sharp et al. (1979) reported strong education-related effects for tasks that were less structured and more hypothetical, or which required taxonomic principles as the correct basis of classification. However, education-related effects were greatly reduced and age-related effects were more prominent for tasks that were well structured or would be solved by taking recourse to real world knowledge. It will be apparent from the Indian studies described here later that just like the other studies, schooling does not influence performance on all tasks in an equal fashion. However, importantly, the schooling effect becomes less prominent, particularly when tasks are adapted to the cultural milieu of the subject populations (Das & Thapa, 2000).

Das and Dash (1989) compared the performance characteristics of schooled and unschooled children of Orissa, who were drawn from homogeneous sociodemographic backgrounds. The equal level of performance of schooled and unschooled children on a variety of Piagetian concrete operational, memory, and reasoning tasks was the same. Schooling played an influential role in the development of the coding processes, that is, simultaneous and successive processing in the theoretical framework of the PASS model. The initial years of schooling had a greater impact on successive than on simultaneous processing. The superiority of schooled children in the two processes of information coding was attributed to the teaching–learning conditions present in schools. Dash and Mishra (1989) examined the recall performance of schooled and unschooled children in a natural setting using a card game quite popular in rural Orissa. The card game allowed the experimenter to obtain estimates of immediate and delayed recall performance for each subject. There was practically no difference between grade 6 schooled children and their unschooled peers in respect of their overall memory competence including immediate and delayed recall. It was suggested that when unschooled children were faced with a task situation that spontaneously activated their memory potential, they performed as well as their school-going peers.

Mohanty (1992) examined the cognitive consequences of schooling in a tribal population in Orissa. Schooled and unschooled children were contrasted in the age groups of 6 to 8 and 10 to 12 years on a variety of classificatory, memory and reasoning tasks, which intended to assess their skills at different levels of cognitive representation. Schooling did not have an equal influence on performance on all tasks. The use of taxonomic principles in simpler classification tasks was influenced by chronological age; but schooling played a prominent role in taxonomic classification only when the task structure was more complex, abstract, or constrained. Schooling had a positive influence on the development of subjects' overall memory proficiency and their abstract and verbal–logical reasoning. In summary, education-related effects were more prominent for tasks that were abstract, required alternative strategies of solution, demanded responses within a given task structure or involved higher-order cognitive processing of information. Maturation was a necessary but not a sufficient condition for the development of these skills (Das & Thapa, 2000). Acculturation and its impact on intelligence and academic achievement were examined by Panda and Nath (1992). Two groups of least-acccultured (LA) and most-accultured (MA) Koya (one of the 16 primitive Oriya tribes) students were studied. In comparison to caste Hindu Oriya students, intelligence of the tribal groups showed an increment up to grade 8, a decrease at grade 10 and another incremental spurt at the college level. The authors explained that in college, Koya students were exposed to a diverse (enriched) accultured and academic environment, which contributed to intellectual and academic gains. The differences between the three groups at each grade level were attributed to acculturation to the dominant Oriya culture.

Agarwal and Mishra (1983) documented a significant effect of quality schooling even at the early age levels. The better quality schools in their study were those that had appreciable facilities in transportation, recreational activities, and physical space in addition to better methods of teaching and administrative policies. The findings revealed a significant effect of quality of schooling and age on category clustering as well as acquisition of memory items. The schooling effect was more pronounced for non-scheduled caste subjects than for scheduled caste subjects, who belonged to a relatively impoverished environment. Mishra and Gupta (1988) reported the significant role of better quality schooling on pictorial perception and comprehension skills. Children in better-quality schools were more able to attend to details in the pictures depicting some events, to narrate the possible links between two pictures, and to interpret the theme suggested by the picture as a whole. It may, however, be noted that the effect of better quality schooling may be confounded with many other sociodemographic factors that covary with it. As schools differ in terms of teaching-learning conditions, so do the sociodemographic characteristics of children who are enrolled in these institutions (Das & Thapa, 2000). RajaGopalan (1995) investigated the formal reasoning of school pupils and explored the relationships between formal reasoning and aspects like IQ, gender, SES, medium of instruction, age, and class. The finding reveals that formal reasoning is not unitary in nature, it is significantly correlated to IQ and academic achievement in mathematics and physical science, it is higher in boys than in girls, and a higher level of SES leads to a higher score in formal reasoning.

Singh, Siddiqui, and Srivastava (1995) have examined the development of the concept of intelligence among Indian children studying in grades 4 to 12. It was observed that children perceived the most intelligent child to be good at cognitive, behavioral, and interpersonal relationships. Developmental changes in the conception of intelligence were also observed, with older children placing more emphasis on success and academic achievement. It may be noted that in the Indian sociocultural context, academic achievement during grades 10 to 12 is highly valued as it is related to future career and success in life. It is clear that children do possess a conception of intelligence rooted in their specific ecocultural contexts (Das & Thapa, 2000).

INTELLIGENCE IN NEUROPSYCHOLOGICAL ASSESSMENT

Neuropsychological research has contributed significantly to the redefinition of the nature of intelligence. The aim of neuropsychological assessment is to chart a profile that reflects various higher mental functions. This would highlight the various signs, namely, particular dysfunction of the brain, along with symptoms reported by the patients about their dysfunction. Together they are classified as a syndrome. For example, sign (memory deficit, amnesia) + symptom (memory problem) = temporal lobe syndrome. Thus this would highlight the specific areas of dysfunction (Barnes, 1998).

To arrive at a profile that gives a comprehensive picture of cognitive and other sensory and motor functions, various neuropsychological test batteries have been used in the West as well as in India. Most popular batteries used in India have adopted, in whole or in parts, test items from the Halstead Reitan Neuropsychological Battery for Adults and Children and the Luria Nebraska Neuropsychological Battery (see Lezak, 1995). The two prominent Indian neuropsychological batteries are the National Institute of Mental Health and Neurosciences (NIMHANS) in Bangalore Neuropsychological Test Battery (1990) and the All India Institute of Medical Sciences (AIIMS) in Delhi Comprehensive Neuropsychological Test Battery in Hindi (1994). A description of the latter shows the seriousness of putting together a comprehensive set of neuropsychological tests adopted from Luria as described next.

AIIMS Comprehensive Neuropsychological Battery in Hindi (Adult Form)

With the emergence of advanced neuropsychological techniques abroad and the beginnings of psychiatry and neuroscience in India, an expert group of researchers in AIIMS has initiated the development and standardization of a comprehensive neuropsychological battery in Hindi (adult form) since 1986. The 160-item neuropsychological battery based upon Luria's functional approach had been suggested to be a useful investigatory procedure in the detection, lateralization, and localization of discrete brain lesions that are typically seen in the neurological setting.

Besides, the battery has implications for its application in neuropsycho-logical rehabilitation. It will thus help in opening avenues for demon-strating brain behavior relationships in addition to achieving self-reliance and advancing the practice of clinical neuropsychology in India and also expanding knowledge of the functioning of the human brain (Gupta et al., 2000). The following is a list of primary scales included in the neuropsychological battery:

1. The motor scale
2. The tactile scale
3. The visual scale
4. The receptive speech scale
5. The expressive speech scale
6. The reading scale
7. The writing scale
8. The arithmetic scale
9. Memory scale
10. The intellectual process scale
11. Pathogenic scale
12. Left hemisphere scale
13. Right hemisphere scale
14. Total score scale

The AIIMS Comprehensive Neuropsychological Battery is useful in the detection, lateralization, and localization of discrete brain lesions that are typically seen in neurological settings.

A Sample of Neuropsychological Studies

Research and clinical work in this field are relatively new but were in progress by the 1980s, a few years before the two neuropsychological batteries were available. A sample of these, presented next, are con-cerned with the typical cases studied both in the West and in India. These studies were selected from a review by Das and Thapa (2000) and Kulkarni and Puhan (1988).

Sampath presented a theory of spontaneous pattern generation as the basis of learning even though no stimuli are present to trigger neural activity. Spontaneous firing in neural nets can be processed and inter-preted as patterns of behavior. It has been suggested that if the spon-taneous rates in a neural net are sufficiently high, they can become the neurophysiological basis for self-generated habit formations.

Several clinical studies on impaired brain functions have been carried out. One examined the symptoms of confabulation. The subject of research was a 48-year-old patient suffering from subarachnoid hemorrhage. The finding suggests that frontal lobe dysfunction is a critical factor in confabulation. In another, it was shown that children suffering from temporal lobe epilepsy become schizophrenics, but those suffering from glandular epilepsy do not. This finding suggests that malfunctioning of the temporal lobe affects the functioning of the frontal lobe, which was considered to be the center of thought and intellective processes.

Addiction has recognized effects on neuropsychological functions, and this has not been overlooked by Indian researchers. For example, in the study by Ahmad, Ahmad, and Bindra (in Das & Thapa, 2000) heroin addicts and controls between 20 and 40 years of age were compared. It was observed that addicts had below average IQ, impaired memory, impaired attention and concentration, and greater psychomotor disturbance. Indian subjects manifested the same cognitive impairments as heroin addicts from other countries. A study by Nirmala and Swaminathan (Das & Thapa, 2000) examined the effect of nicotine consumption on performance in serial learning and retention tasks. It was reported that when smokers were given cigarettes during serial learning and retention, smoking facilitated serial learning but inhibited retention.

Head injury of both closed and open types are popular and important topics for neuropsychological studies both in the West as well as in India, and a sample of clinical cases show similar results.

Various types of neuropsychological testing along with visual information processing paradigms to examine the consequences of mild closed head injuries have been carried out. In one, it was found that deficits were significantly marked in those tasks that demanded attention and concentration. Another study reviewed the psychometric reports of 150 cases with a clear history of head injuries. It was reported that up to 80% of all cases had difficulty in performing psychometric tasks. Das & Thapa (2000) also review a study associated with occupational hazards including exposure to neurotoxic agents and their effect on neuropsychological functions. Indian research does not neglect this, as protection of workers from exposure to toxic agents is lax in India, and hence the incidence of cognitive and motor impairment is likely to be higher. Two examples of Indian studies are given next. Singh et al. (1986) reviewed the methodologies used in research on the effects of neurotoxic agents on occupationally related dysfunctions in behavior.

They recommended the use of tests of general intelligence, memory, and psychomotor abilities. Tripathi et al. (1989) reported an empirical study on the mental functions of workers in spray painting shops who were exposed to solvents. Their performance was examined in terms of reaction time, finger dexterity, hand precision, backward digit span, and word span. There was a significant deterioration in performance on choice reaction time, tweezer dexterity, hand precision and backward memory span among workers engaged in spray painting by the end of their work shift. Further, the extent of cognitive deterioration was proportionate to the length of the exposure. It appears that the clinical cases and the results of neuropsychological research in India are no different from those in the West (see Lezak, 1995).

COMPARISONS AND CONCLUSIONS

A sensitivity to cultural differences is a prerequisite for comparing research in cross-cultural contexts. Indeed the expected path for the researcher is to explore the vast differences in cultures of the West and the East, for example, describe such differences, and accept an obligation to say how these differences might have colored the results of psychological testing and experiments. Sometimes the differences cannot be predicted, and often the mode of interaction between cultural differences and cognitive performance must be imagined! Seldom does a preconceived theory predict the differences in the results. A sampling of research reviewed in this chapter instantiates some or all of those attitudes. Some other research that does not seriously take into account cultural differences simply "adapts" a Western test and applies it to samples of Indian participants; the reliabilities of these "adapted" tests are questionable, and their validities might remain undiscovered. Again, many examples of such studies are found in this chapter. Exceptions are research with cognitive processes such as PASS and neuropsychological processes. Paradoxically, the researchers, including the present writers, seldom explore the nominal differences between Western and Eastern participants. They assume that if differences in performance are observed, and these are reliable and unique characteristics obtained from test scores, then those differences are to be explained. De Vijver and Poortinga (1991) remark, and we agree, "The zeitgeist of cross-cultural psychology can be described as a difference climate, ... Cross-cultural psychologists should try to explain rather than explore cultural differences" (p. 304).

Exploring the arguments for and against "cultural universals" brings us to broader issues. An obvious one is the "emic" contrasted with the "etic" approach, or studying behavior within one culture versus studying it in many cultures for the purpose of comparison (see Berry & Dasen, 1974 for the origin of this distinction). Seeking universality is an associated product. The distinction is very similar to idiographic versus nomothetic approaches in psychology. These two, respectively, require paying attention to a single case as a unique event contrasted to placing the individual case in a field of coordinates defined by general laws of behavior and cognition.

So does the ancient and traditional view of intelligence fit the emic mode, whereas the later contemporary research on intelligence is clearly etic? One is sure of the latter classification – the roots of contemporary research on intelligence in India are obviously drawing their sustenance from Euro-American ground. If biology and physics are etic, why should the psychological study of intelligence depart from it?

The immediate or proximal cause of similarities in research methods followed in India and the West is the adoption of Euro-American curricula in psychology and testing in India. Similarly, the universality of results of research on assessment is also attributable to Western-type schooling. Because this chapter did not consider ethnographic approaches to intelligence, there was no chance of discovering emic-type differences.

Consider, though, the two basic sources of cognitive functions: the structure of our nervous system and the cultural milieu. The structure is universal and the milieu is often created by the structure, which in turn may be modified by the culture in a continuous dialectical progression. No duality can thus be detected between structure and its function in the individual's cultural milieu. In retrospect, it seems that the ancient conceptions of intelligence in India appear to be intuitively appealing to people from many different cultural backgrounds, distilled as they were from the sap of life through the ages by human minds that share a common structure.

References

Afzal, M. (1988). Consequences of consanguinity on cognitive behavior. *Behavior Genetics, 18*, 583–594.

Agarwal, R., & Kumar, A. (1992). Everyday memory in adulthood. *Psychological Studies, 37*, 161–172.

Agarwal, R., & Kumar, A. (1993). The relationship between intelligence and reaction time as a function of task and person variables. *Personality and Individual Differences, 14*, 287–268.

Agarwal, S. & Mishra, R. C. (1983). Disadvantages of caste and schooling and development of category organization skill. *Psychologia, 26,* 54–61.

Barnes, B. L. (1998). Cognitive functions in neuropsychological assessment. In A. K. Sen and P. Pandey (Eds.), *Current Issues in Cognitive Psychology* (pp. 29–40). New Delhi: Campus Publishers.

Berry, J. W., & Dasen, P. R. (Ed.). (1974). *Culture and cognition: Readings in cross-cultural psychology.* London: Methuen.

Biswas, P. C., & De, T. (1992). Relationship between cognitive style and non-verbal intelligence: An exploratory study. *Perspectives in Psychological Researches, 15,* 19–22.

Chaudhari, U. S., & Ray, S. (1992). A study of self-concept, locus of control, and adjustment of intellectually superior and normal students. *Indian Journal of Behavior, 16,* 24–29.

Cole, M., & Scribner, S. (1977). Cross-cultural studies of memory and cognition. In R. V. Kail Jr. & J. W. Hagen (Eds.), *Perspectives on development of memory and cognition* (pp. 239–271). Hillsdale, NJ: Erlbaum.

Das, J. P. (1980). Planning: Theoretical considerations and empirical evidence. *Psychological Research, 41,* 141–151.

Das, J. P. (1994). Eastern views of intelligence. *Encyclopedia of Intelligence* (pp. 91–97). New York: MacMillan.

Das, J. P., & Dash, U. N. (1989). Schooling, literacy and cognitive development: A study in rural India. In C. K. Leong & B. S. Randhawa (Eds.), *Understanding literacy and cognition* (pp. 217–244). New York: Plenum.

Das, J. P., Kar, B. C., & Parrila, R. K. (1996). *Cognitive planning.* New Delhi: Sage.

Das, J. P., Kirby, J. R., & Jarman, R. F. (1975). Simultaneous and successive syntheses: An alternative model for cognitive abilities. *Psychological Bulletin, 82,* 87–103.

Das, J. P., Naglieri, J. A., & Kirby, J. R. (1994). *Assessment of cognitive processes: The PASS theory of intelligence.* Boston: Allyn & Bacon.

Das, J. P., & Thapa, K. (2000). Intelligence and cognitive processes. In J. Pandey (Ed.), *Psychology in India* (pp. 151–207). New Delhi: Sage.

Dash, U., & Mishra, H. C. (1989). Testing for the effects of schooling on memory in an ecocultural setting. *Psychology and Developing Societies, 1,* 153–163.

De Vijver, J. R., & Poortinga, H. (1991). Testing across cultures. In R. K. Hambleton & J. N. Zaal (Eds.), *Advances in educational and psychological testing: Theory and applications.* Boston: Kluwer.

Dwivedi, C. B., Mishra, R. K., & Chaturvedi, U. (1986). Orientation arousal and intentionality of processing differences in retention. *Psychological Studies, 31,* 103–107.

Gautam, S. B., & Singh, K. (1992). A study of certain personality correlates of intellectual giftedness among Navodaya Vidyalaya students of Himachal Pradesh. *Journal of Education and Psychology, 49,* 40–44.

Gupta, D., Khandelwal, S. K., Tandon, P. N., Maheswari, M. C., Mehta, V. S., Sundaram, K. R., Mahapatra, A. K., & Jain, S. (2000). The development and standardization of a comprehensive neuropsychological battery in Hindi (adult form). *Journal of Personality and Clinical Studies, 16,* 75–109.

Gupta, G. C. (1991). Cognitive science: Contemporary perspective. *Indian Journal of Current Psychological Research, 6,* 13–25.

Gupta, R., Mukherjee, M., & Chatterjee, S. (1993). A comparative study of the factors affecting academic achievement among four groups of adolescents. *Indian Journal of Applied Psychology, 30,* 30–38.

Gupta, S. K. (1985). Associative memory: Role of mnemonics in information processing and ordering recall. *Psycho Lingua, 15,* 89–94.

Gupta, S. M., & Chandradash, R. (1994). A study of demographic and cognitive correlates of creativity. *Journal of Educational Research and Extension, 30,* 164–173.

Gupta, U. (1989). The effects of cue-target uniqueness on immediate and delayed retention measured by free recall and recognition. *Psychological Studies, 34,* 93–96.

Harper, A. E., Jr. (1960). Recent advances in psychometry. *Silver Jubilee Volume of Vidhya Bhavan Society,* Udaipur.

Helode, R. D. (1985). Verbal learning and personality dimensions. *Psycho Lingua, 15,* 103–112.

Helode, R. D., & Sawade, S. D. (1985). Cognitive and non-cognitive correlates of verbal maze learning. *Journal of Psychological Researches, 29,* 46–54.

Jain, M. C. (1991). *Indian mental measurement handbook: Intelligence and aptitude tests.* New Delhi: NCERT.

Kulkarni, S. S., & Puhan, B. N. (1988). Psychological assessment: Its present and future trends. In J. Pandey (Ed.), *Psychology in India: The state-of-the-art* (Vol. 1, pp. 19–92). New Delhi: Sage.

Kumar, D., Malhotra, L., & Jerath, J. (1986). Speed and accuracy as a function of personality. *Psychologica Belgica, 26,* 227–233.

Kumar, K. (1991). Research in test and measurement: A trend report. In M. B. Buch (Ed.), *Fourth survey of research in education* (pp. 546–567). New Delhi: NCERT.

Kurian, G., & Sharma, N. K. (1988). Language and thought: A review of the mediational, cognitive, psycholinguistic, and neuropsychological perspectives and an attempted synthesis. *Psycho Lingua, 18,* 69–98.

Kurtz, B. E., Borkowski, J. G., & Deshmukh, K. (1988). Metamemory and learning in Maharashtrian children: Influences from home and school. *Journal of Genetic Psychology, 149,* 363–376.

Krishnamurti, J. (1973). *The awakening of intelligence.* New York: Harper & Row.

Lezak, M. D. (1995). *Neuropsychological assessment.* New York: Oxford University Press.

Luria, A. R. (1966). *Human brain and psychological processes.* New York: Harper & Row.

Mathur, P., & Das, J. P. (1997). Aspects of conceptual planning: A study on engineering students. In J. R. Isaac, S. Gupta, and M. Datta (Eds.), *Cognitive systems* (pp. 487–492). New Delhi: Tata McGraw-Hill.

McDermott, R. A. (Ed.). (1988). *The essential aurobindo.* Great Barrington, MA: Lindisfarne Press.

Mehta, J. (2001). Cognitive processes, self-perception, motivation, and behavior as factors of academic achievement. Unpublished doctoral thesis. Applied Psychology Department, University of Mumbai, India.

Mishra, R., Mohanty, N. & Nanda, S. (in preparation). Cognitive profiles in CAS of a clinical sample in India.

Mishra, R. C. & Gupta, V. (1988). Schooling, exposure and the skill for pictorial comprehension. *Indian Psychological Review*, 24, 29–34.

Mitchell, S. (1998). *Bhagavad Gita: A new translation*. New York: Harper Collins.

Mohan, J., & Bajaj, R. (1983). A study of intelligence and fluctuation of attention. *Indian Psychological Review*, 25, 38–42.

Mohan. J., & Jain, M. (1983). Intelligence and simple reaction time. *Asian Journal of Psychology and Education*, 11, 1–4.

Mohan, S. (1993). The national library of educational and psychological tests. *Psychological Studies*, 38, 157–159.

Mohanty, M. M. (1992). *Influence of schooling on classification, memory and reasoning abilities*. Unpublished doctoral dissertation, Utkal University, Bhubaneswar, India.

Mukherjee, B. N. (1993). Needed research in psychoeducational assessment in India. *Psychological Studies*, 38, 85–100.

Mukhopadhyay, P., & Dash, B. B. (1999). Cognitive style: Its relationship to intelligence and Locus of Control in children. *Social Science International*, 15, 81–85.

Naglieri, J. A., & Das, J. P. (1997). *Das-Naglieri cognitive assessment system*. Itasca, IL: Riverside.

Padhan, G. C. (1992). Value pattern of school students as a function of types of schools and levels of intelligence. *The Educational Review*, 98 (2), 133–138.

Panda, S. K., & Nath, K. S. (1992). Acculturation, intelligence and achievement: A cross-sectional study in India. *Perspectives in Education*, 8(2), 83–90.

Pandey, S. (1992). A study of interpersonal judgement with respect to social intelligence, sex, and discipline. *Perspectives in Psychological Researches*, 15, 23–25.

Pati, P., & Dash, A. D. (1990a). Interrelationships between incidental memory, nonverbal intelligence and Stroop scores. *Psycho Lingua*, 20, 27–31.

Pati, P., & Dash, A. D. (1990b). Effects of grade, sex and achievement levels on intelligence, incidental memory and Stroop scores. *Psychological Studies*, 35, 36–40.

Pershad, D. (1987). Arithmetic subtest of an intelligence scale: Measure of power or speed? *Journal of Psychological Researches*, 31, 26–29.

Radhakrishnan, S. (1948). *Bhagavadgita*. London: George Allen & Unwin.

Radhakrishnan, S. (1953) *The principal Upanishads*. (Chandogya Upanishad, Chapter 7, pp. 468–474). London: George Allen & Unwin.

RajaGopalan, M. (1995). An investigation of Piaget's formal research in science among a section of Indian school students. *Indian Educational Review*, 30, 20–25.

Rani, R., & Mehrotra, G. P. (1991). Validity of some structure of intellect abilities for predicting achievement in chemistry. *Journal of Psychological Researches*, 35, 70–75.

Rogoff, B. (1981). Schooling and the development of cognitive skills. In H. C. Triandis and A. Heron (Eds.), *Handbook of cross-cultural psychology*, (Vol. 4, pp. 233–294). Boston: Allyn & Bacon.

Saraswathi, T. S., & Dutta, R. (1987). *Developmental psychology in India, 1975–1986.* New Delhi: Sage.

Sen, A. (1991). Alternative to psychological testing. *Psychology and Developing Societies, 3* (2), 203–220.

Sen, A., Kurseja, M., & Chatterjee, S. (1988). Role of modality sensitization in dual task performance: An experimental investigation. *Indian Journal of Current Psychological Research, 3* (1), 22–28.

Sharma, R., & Bansal, I. (1991–92). A study of academic achievement and intelligence of extrovert and introvert adolescent girls. *Indian Psychological Review, 37,* 11–14.

Sharp, D., Cole, M., & Love, C. (1979). *Education and cognitive development: The evidence from experimental research.* (Monograph of the Society for Research in Child Development, 44, 1-2 serial no. 178). Chicago: Chicago University Press.

Shringy, R. K. (1976). *Philosophy of J. Krishnamurti: A systematic study.* New Delhi: Munshilal Manoharlal.

Singh, J., Kumar, P., Dwivedi, K., & Saxena, V. B. (1986). Behavioral toxicology: A developing field in industrial hygiene and occupational health hazard. *Journal of Personality and Clinical Studies, 2* (2), 109–116.

Singh, T., Siddiqui, A., & Srivastava, A. K. (1995). An exploration of children's conception of intelligence. *Journal of Indian Psychology, 13,* 47–55.

Sinha, D. (1983). Human assessment in the Indian context. In S. H. Irvine & J. W. Berry (Eds.), *Human assessment and cultural factors* (pp. 17–34). New York: Plenum Press.

Sri Aurobindo (1922). *Essays on Gita.* Pondicherry: Sri Aurobindo Ashram.

Sri Aurobindo (1939). *Life divine.* Calcutta: Arya Publishing House.

Srivastava, A. K., & Misra, G. (1996). Changing perspectives on understanding intelligence: An appraisal. *Indian Psychological Abstracts and Reviews, 3.* New Delhi: Sage.

Srivastava, A. K., & Mishra, G. (1999). Social representation of intelligence in the Indian folk tradition: An analysis of Hindi proverbs. *Journal of Indian Psychology, 17,* 29–38.

Srivastava, A. K., Tripathi, A. M., & Misra, G. (1996). The status of intelligence testing in India: A preliminary analysis. *Indian Educational Review, 31,* 1–11.

Srivastava, S. (1992). Sex-role adoption of Indian children: Effects of age, sex, socio-economic status, intelligence, and creativity. *Indian Journal of Applied Psychology, 30* (1), 41–51.

Srivastava, S. (1993). Social class and intelligence. *Perspectives in Psychological Researches, 16* (1 & 2), 117–118.

Srivastava, S., & Misra, G. (2000). *Culture and conceptualization of intelligence.* New Delhi: National Council of Ecuational Research and Training.

Sternberg, R. J. (1990). *Metaphors of mind: Conceptions of the nature of intelligence.* Cambridge: Cambridge University Press.

Sudhir, M. A., & Muraledharan-Pillai, P. G. (1987). Science achievement in relation to intelligence and socio-economic status: A study of secondary school students in Aizwal. *Indian Journal of Psychometry and Education, 18*(1), 37–44.

Tanwar, U., & Kumar, D. (1986). An experimental study of distractor and probe techniques in short term memory as a function of extraversion and levels of intelligence. *Journal of Psychological Researches, 30* (2), 105–116.

Tripathi, S. R., Bhattacharya, S. K., Chattopadhya, P., & Kashyap, S. K. (1989). Neuro-behavioral disturbances in workers engaged in high-pressure spray painting. *Journal of Human Ergology, 18*(2), 191–198.

Vygotsky, L. (1978). *Mind in society*. Cambridge, MA: Harvard University Press.

Wagner, D. A., & Spratt, J. E. (1987). Cognitive consequences of contracting pedagogies: The effects of Quoranic preschooling in Morocco. *Child Development, 58*, 1207–1219.

Yenagi, G. V. (1993). Comparative study of intelligence of urban and rural children. *Indian Psychological Review, 40, 7–9*.

Zimmer, H. (1951). *Philosophies of India*. London: Routledge & Kagan Paul.

10

Japanese Conception of and Research on Human Intelligence

Tatsuya Sato, Hiroshi Namiki, Juko Ando,
and Giyoo Hatano

It is very hard to describe in a comprehensive way how intelligence
has been treated in Japanese psychology and related areas in just a short
chapter. We limit ourselves to three topics that highlight the contribution
of Japanese psychology to our understanding of human intelligence, after briefly reviewing the Japanese history of intelligence research: (1) the
development of indigenous intelligence tests, (2) the interaction between
heredity and environment in intelligence, and (3) how "intelligence" is
viewed in the Japanese culture.

INTELLIGENCE RESEARCH IN JAPAN: A HISTORICAL REVIEW

This review covers mainly the period of the 1860s to 1960s, but we will
mention very briefly how education was pursued in the period preceding the Meiji Restoration. There was a fixed social stratification system
in the Edo Era (age of feudalism), with no mobility. However, education was taken seriously in each stratum. Toward the end of the Edo
Era, there were nearly 300 fief schools (*hanko*) in the country, and although no accurate statistics are available, several times that number
of private academies (*shijuku*) existed (Amano, 1990). Children in the
samurai stratum (the ruling class of warriors) usually were given moral
education, rooted in the Chinese Confucian classics, at the fief schools.

Author names are ordered in terms of the sections they primarily contributed; that is, Sato
reviewed the Japanese history; Namiki discussed indigenous intelligence tests; Ando,
behavior genetic studies; and Hatano, cultural views. The last author was responsible for
the final makeup.

People in other strata learned the "three Rs" at private academies. Generally speaking, education was structured to preserve the shogunate ruling system. Only at the end of the Edo Era were innovative private academies established; these attracted ambitious students and offered foreign languages and modern, technical knowledge. However, no nationwide examination system (like the Chinese *keju*) existed in premodern Japan (Amano, 1990). Needless to say, there was no intellectual tradition of psychology during the feudalism era in Japan.

The Meiji Restoration, actualized in 1868, was a joint product of two different movements: one toward modernization of the nation and the other toward restoration of the imperial rule. Ultimately, the drive for modernization smashed the unsophisticated restoration movement. As the fixed social stratification system was destroyed, the new government was confronted with the task of finding and appointing talented people. The government thus struggled to establish a new educational system, similar to the one used in modernized Western countries. It should be noted that in this pursuit an American system was adopted for teacher training. As a result, there has been a close relationship between education (teacher training particularly) and psychology in Japan and in the United States. The Ministry of Education (*Mombusho*) published the first book of Shinrigaku (psychology) in 1875. The book was a translation of Haven's *Mental Philosophy* (1869 version) by Amane Nishi. Nishi was one of the great enlightenment thinkers in the early Meiji Era, who believed that psychology was basically immutable, not changeable like fashion. That is, Nishi's psychology was not modern psychology consisting of empirical laws but a metaphysical system (Motoyama, 1997).

In 1888, modern psychology was transplanted to Japan by Yuzero Motora. He was born into a *samurai* family in 1858, 10 years before the Meiji Restoration. He studied at Doshisha English School, a private school run by Joh Neesima. After running a private school called the Tokyo Anglo-Japanese School, Motora went to the United States to study philosophy and psychology. He studied psychology at Johns Hopkins University under G. Stanley Hall and came back to Japan with a Ph.D. He was requested to teach psychophysics at the Imperial University (now the University of Tokyo) in 1888, and he took the chair of professor of psychology there in 1890.

Motora had interests in the theory of attention, consciousness, and the practice of cultivation, and he worked to devise training methods for developing the attention of school pupils. His methods were applied to mentally retarded pupils (or pupils with learning difficulties) in elementary school (Motora, 1911). According to him, most of the children with poor school achievement were not mentally retarded but suffered from attentional problems (Ohyama, Sato, & Suzuki, 2002). This work represented one of the few innovative ideas in Japan about the training of disabled children.

Motora had many students who distinguished themselves. Some of them went abroad and studied psychology under the supervision of prominent psychologists. Matataro Matsumoto was among them. He first studied psychology under Motora and then went to the United States. After earning a Ph.D. at Yale University under G. T. Ladd and E. W. Scripture, he went to Leipzig and studied experimental psychology under W. Wundt. Matsumoto was appointed as a professor at the Higher Normal College (now Tsukuba University) after returning to Japan in 1900, and he was the first professor of professional educational psychology in Japan. In 1906 Matsumoto moved to Kyoto Imperial University (now Kyoto University). In 1913, after Motora's death (1912) he returned to Tokyo as a professor at the Tokyo Imperial University. Matsumoto was interested in both experimental psychology and applied psychology, including intellectual functions, and he published a book of more than 1,100 pages on the Psychology of Intelligence. Matsumoto, like Motora, promoted the institutionalization of psychology in Japan and influenced many students, some of whom studied topics related to intelligence. For example, K. Masuda and M.Takagi, who both studied with Matsumoto in the department of psychology at the Tokyo Imperial University, studied animal intelligence.

The next period, starting in 1908, can be characterized by the acceptance of mental tests, including, among others, the Binet-Simon test. As the school enrollment ratio increased (up to 90% at the beginning of the 20th century), Japanese elementary schools, like those in other Westernized countries, had many problems to solve, such as how to deal with dropout pupils and how to provide special education for disabled pupils. An interest in understanding pupils' intelligence levels arose, and the significance of intelligence measurement at school was appreciated. Thus, the Binet-type mental test was transplanted quickly. K. Miyake was one of the first scholars to introduce the Binet-Simon test to Japan, which he did in 1908. After studying medicine at the Tokyo Imperial University, he went on to study psychiatry in Vienna and Munich. In Munich he studied under E. Kraepelin.

Binet-type mental tests had to be adapted and refined in Japan by professional psychologists, in terms of their constituent items because their literally translated versions did not work. Y. Kubo contributed greatly to this enterprise. He studied psychology at the Tokyo Imperial University under Motora, then studied at Clark University, where Hall was the president. Kubo worked hard to construct the Japanese version of the Binet-Simon test after he returned to Japan. He also translated group mental tests and compiled and standardized the National Intelligence Test (1918).

In the Taisho Era, which began in 1912, a number of mental tests were developed, standardized, used widely in schools and industries, and sometimes, later in this period, abused. After the Japanese Empire experienced three big successive wars (the Sino-Japanese War, the Russo-Japanese War, and World War I), liberal ideas and an intellectual atmosphere arose, with which the newly growing urban middle class was sympathetic. They produced the Taisho Free Education movement, which emphasized education for the "whole person" and took the concept of individuality seriously. The urban middle-class people's aspiration for higher education also produced an "examination hell." Students had to study extremely hard, and as a result, the detrimental effects of studying hard just for an examination were noted. Because educators believed that intelligence tests could scientifically measure innate intellectual ability, these tests were often used to mitigate these detrimental effects in selecting applicants.

The U.S. Army test was introduced after World War I. Both verbal and non-verbal tests derived from the army test were constructed and widely used. Intelligence tests were also used in non-educational settings, such as industry or the military. For example, air force applicants were selected and classified by a test battery including intelligence test items. As for the theoretical study of tests, Yataro Okabe (1923) published *Educational Measurement*, which was the forerunner of systematic studies of psychological testing (Yoda & Hidano, 1959).

The Taisho Era ended and the Showa Era began in 1926. In the early Showa Era, during which nationalism prevailed, intelligence testing was used to demonstrate the ethnic superiority of the Japanese as well as to identify able soldiers. A notable achievement was by H. Suzuki, who standardized the Stanford-Binet Scale on more than 10,000 participants. Suzuki had been an elementary school teacher, and this may have influenced the development of the close relationship between psychological testing and education. K. Tanaka conducted a comparative study of the intelligence of various Asian people using non-verbal group intelligence tests. He found that the Japanese people were the most intelligent, just as American psychologists found Americans to be the most intelligent. Tanaka was a student of Matsumoto. He wrote a book on the theoretical study of tests in 1926 and completed the Revised Scale of the Stanford-Binet test (1937 version) in 1941. Both Suzuki and Tanaka spent their lifetimes studying and improving intelligence tests.

The national government in this period, especially as World War II approached, minimized the scientific viewpoint in education. For example, the concept of individuality was completely ignored under the ultra-nationalistic system, and the use of tests in the educational field became less and less frequent during wartime.

Japan's eugenics movement was not institutionalized until 1924, with the establishment of the Japanese Eugenics Society. But the movement dated back to 1881, with the introduction to Japan of Francis Galton's ideas by Yukichi Fukuzawa. Fukuzawa was a Japanese scholar (Tukuba & Suzuki, 1967). Many scholars, including psychologists, were interested in the idea of eugenics. Galton's *Heredity Genius* (1869) was translated by Tsuruko Haraguchi, who was the first Japanese woman to receive a Ph.D. (1913). Haraguchi studied at Columbia University, supervised by E. R. Thorndike, because in those days, women could not attend Japanese universities.

During the period of the Allied occupation, after Japan's defeat in World War II in 1945, the Japanese educational system was reformed under the recommendation of the U.S. Education Mission. In this context, educational psychology was highlighted to make the Japanese educational system democratic and scientific. These American influences revived the interest in measurement, evaluation, and testing in Japanese education. In individual testing, Binet-type intelligence tests were widely used. H. Minami and others completed the standardization of the Wechsler-Bellevue Intelligence scale in 1950; H. Kodama and F. Shinagwa standardized the Wechsler Intelligence Scale Children (WISC) in 1954 and the Wechsler Adult Intelligence Scale (WAIS) in 1958. A number of group intelligence tests of various kinds were devised (translated or standardized) so that every child could take an intelligence test once or twice during elementary school and/or junior high school years (Yoda & Hidano, 1959).

The recommendation of the U.S. Education Mission was to administer the Scholastic Aptitude Test (SAT) for the selection of applicants for university- and college-level education. But the SAT, introduced in 1947, did not last long. Each university made light of the SAT and began to rely on its own system of entrance examinations. The SAT was abolished finally in 1954, due to the opposition of high school teachers and the general public. An underlying factor was that the SAT (or the idea of innate ability) was not compatible with the Japanese people's "belief-in-effort," as will be discussed later.

To conclude, throughout the period reviewed, the nation as a whole, psychology in general, and intelligence research in particular tried hard to catch up to the Western models but produced few unique alternative models or ideas.

DEVELOPMENT OF INDIGENOUS INTELLIGENCE TESTS

As reviewed in the preceding section, almost all popular intelligence tests were developed originally in Europe and the United States, translated into Japanese, and standardized on the Japanese population. Only a few intelligence tests have been developed by Japanese psychologists. We will describe three of them in this section.

Early Innovative Attempts

R. Osaka and A. Umemoto of Kyoto University constructed an intelligence test for group administration in 1953. The test was named the Kyoto University (Kyodai) NX intelligence test. There are several versions of the NX test for different age ranges of testees, and an SX version is available for highly intelligent persons over 15 years old (Osaka & Umemoto, 1973). For example, NX9-15 (age range from 9 to 15 years old) is composed of 12 subtests: paper folding and punching, sentence completion, figure decomposition, reconstruction of scrambled sentences, basic calculations, and so on. The authors indicate that 4 out of the 12 subtests were developed originally by them. Individual profiles can be obtained in terms of deviation scores on the subtests. In addition, based on the results of the factor analysis of the subtests, each testee can be given scores on those factors, namely, spatial, verbal, quantitative reasoning, memory, and verbal fluency. This test is still used in Japan today. Sano (1974) compared the intelligence scores on the NX 9-15 test of the 4th- and 5th-grade pupils at the same elementary schools in the Kyoto area in 1954, 1963, and 1972. He found that the deviation scores of intelligence, obtained by using the 1954 scoring manual, increased by 11 points between 1954 and 1972 in both grades, and that the difference was larger between 1954 and 1963 than between 1963 and 1972. He attributed this increase to the rapid reconstruction of the educational environment in Japan after World War II.

T. Indow and F. Samejima of Keio University developed a test for reasoning ability based on Lord's test theory (Indow & Samejima, 1962; Lord, 1952). The test was called the LIS measurement scale for non-verbal reasoning. It was composed of 30 items, and was homogeneous in the sense that all items shared one common factor. Test homogeneity is a strict prerequisite for scaling in terms of Lord's item response theory. The authors calculated two parameters, item difficulty and discriminating power, for each item based on the item's characteristic function, and estimated reasoning ability by the test characteristic curve, using a method of maximum likelihood. The word *non-verbal* did not mean a beta-type test, but rather that the score did not depend heavily on verbal ability. It was a type of power test, and testees were allowed a sufficient time to solve items. The items were ingenious and unique and included various kinds of reasoning problems (figural, logical, verbal, mathematical, etc.). The test was theoretically and technically the most advanced one available at that time. Indow wrote in the foreword to the test manual (Indow & Samejima, 1962) that Lord himself acknowledged the test as the very first constructed precisely on his theory. The test was, however, not accepted widely in Japan, probably because a test to measure a single pure factor, reasoning ability, was not very useful in practical settings, and to our regret, the test is out of print today.

Applying Models of Working Memory to Intelligence Testing

Since the beginning of the 1980s, Namiki has been interested in the notion of working memory capacity, especially Robbie Case's version, and has tried to use it in practical applications. A notable product from his extensive research over the past decade is the development, in collaboration with neurologists, of a neuropsychological test for diagnosing senile dementia. According to Baddeley et al. (1986), the performance of patients with Alzheimer's-type dementia declines drastically when performing a dual task of a digit span test and a psychomotor task, even when their performance on each task given singly is nearly perfect. This result and many other findings show that dementia, especially of the Alzheimer's type, is related deeply to a decrease in working memory capacity (Namiki, 1993). Generally speaking, intelligence test scores have a high predictive validity for complex and compound criteria, such as achievement at school or success in life, but cannot predict the performance of a particular person on a specific task. For the diagnosis of some particular cognitive deficits in certain types of patients, the theory of working memory may be very helpful, and might represent a break-through for traditional research on intelligence. Thus, Namiki tried to develop a new diagnostic test for dementia in terms of working memory and to integrate a psychometric scaling model with an analysis based on working memory theory (Namiki et al., 2002).

Twelve candidate sub-tests, including experimental tasks used in his previous developmental studies as well as newly developed ones, were administered to dementia patients of various etiological types. When these tasks were administered to a group of normal elderly participants, they responded correctly to nearly all of them. Namiki examined the factor pattern of the 12 sub-tests obtained from the patient group, their difficulty level, feasibility, the communicability of instructions, and so on, and finally decided to select five of them, four of which were developed originally by his research team. They are as follows: hierarchical classification, recall and reproduction of the number of objects, grouping of Kanji, a labyrinth test with a solution rule, and the digit span test. A sample item from the third task is shown in Figure 10.1 (Namiki, 1999). Five similar-looking *kanji* (Chinese characters used in Japanese) are presented, and the tester asks the testee to point out one *kanji* that does not belong to the group (that is, an oddity test). The meaning of the five *kanji*, from the left, are pine, cedar, peach, village, and cherry. Therefore, the second one from the right should be pointed out.

The ability to recognize and read *kanji* is generally not strongly influenced by aging or brain damage, and is usually intact in patients even at later stages of dementia; this is probably because knowledge of *kanji* is an aspect of typical crystallized intelligence, G_c, which has been over-learned since childhood, and because most *kanji* have a hieroglyphic trait or semantic meaning, completely different from phonetic symbols. However, even a patient who can read these *kanji* correctly does not always succeed in the task of pointing out the odd character. This discrepancy between performance in reading and in grouping can be explained in terms of the shortage of working memory capacity. The task of grouping is much more demanding of working memory. It requires,

FIGURE 10.1. Grouping of *Kanji* sub-test

among other things, simultaneously abstracting a common dimension from the members, keeping it in mind, and examining each member on this common dimension, over a short period of time, and is not simply a matter of retrieving the meaning of a *kanji* from long-term memory storage.

Eight scores can be obtained from these five sub-tests. The result of factor analysis of these scores by the principal factor method showed that this test was a typical homogeneous test. Thus item response theory was applied to the test scores using the two-parameter logistic function model. Each task was broken down into subroutines, and their difficulty was calculated and value of maximum working memory demand was estimated, following Case's (1992) method (Yonekura et al., 1997). The correlation coefficient between values of the maximum demand and difficulties estimated by the logistic function model for 30 subroutines (i.e., sub-tasks included in each test item) was high ($r = 0.77$). In addition, the factor loadings of the eight scores on the first factor completely corresponded in order to their values of the maximum demand of working memory. The common factor, therefore, could be interpreted as the factor of working memory capacity. When the administration of the whole test is difficult, as is often the case with patients, item response theory helps us estimate their scores from a smaller set of tasks. Thanks to this flexibility of testing, the practical utility of the test is high. The construction of this test for diagnosing dementia nicely corroborates Sternberg's (1980) assertion that the traditional studies of intelligence based on psychometric methods and recent cognitive approaches to intelligence should be complementary.

INTERACTION BETWEEN HEREDITY AND ENVIRONMENT IN INTELLIGENCE

The Nature–Nurture Issue

One of the most controversial issues in psychology is the nature–nurture (heredity and environment) debate of intelligence. The Burt affair, the Jensen affair, and the *Bell Curve* affair seem to provide us with an endless, and often fruitless, debate that is often more ideological than scientific. Unlike the politically charged Western approach to this issue, Japanese psychology has approached this issue apparently apolitically.

Since the beginning of the history of psychology in Japan, the issue of the heredity of intelligence has been a major focus of inquiry. We can find a notable twin study in the very first volume of *The Japanese Journal of Psychology*. T. Obonai (1926) conducted research on more than 100 pairs of twins living in Tokyo, reporting the similarities of physical traits, learning abilities, and intelligence as assessed with the Tokyo City National Intelligence Scale. Although the distinction between monozygotic (MZ) and dizygotic (DZ) twins had not been established at that time, he demonstrated the existence of these two kinds of twins, coming up with the correlation coefficient of 0.86 for 68 pairs of "extremely similar twins" (probably MZ) and 0.69 for 13 pairs of "twins whose facial features are as similar as those of ordinary siblings" (probably DZ). These figures showed there was a moderate amount of genetic contribution as well as a substantial "shared environmental" effect (corresponding to the sum of the environmental effects that make family members similar), to use current behavioral genetic terminology. The standard form of twin study, which assesses the similarities of the two types of twins whose zygosity is diagnosed by a proper scientific procedure, was first conducted by Inoue and Miyazawa (1984). For 90 pairs of MZ and 24 pairs of DZ pairs from 13 to 14 years old, they found high correlations in intelligence, as measured by the Noken Intelligence Test, for both types of twins (0.72 for MZ, 0.77 for DZ), showing no genetic variance. The twins used in Inoue and Miyazawa's study were applicants to the junior high school attached to the Faculty of Letters at the University of Tokyo. This high school was established to conduct studies on twins in educational settings, and in fact attracted many twins. This unique high school investigated twins' physical features, physiological traits, and personality, as well as intelligence.

Sagara, Takuma, and Morikawa (1956) conducted research on the intelligence of twins who applied to this twin high school, finding substantial genetic effects ($r = 0.50$ for 30 MZ pairs, 0.07 for 11 DZ pairs) on IQ measured by the WISC. However, the results from another intelligence test (the Koga Intelligence Test), using a larger pool of twins (53 MZ pairs and 13 DZ pairs), provided a high DZ correlation (for MZ, $r = 0.74$; for DZ, $r = 0.65$). Takuma (1968) offered a more comprehensive comparison of twin similarities using various kinds of intelligence tests (the Todai AS, Ushijima, New Tanaka B, Koga, Kyodai NX and Noken Tests). He showed a consistent tendency toward higher correlations for MZ (0.61–0.83) than for DZ (0.24–0.68) twins. His results also indicated that the family environment contributed substantially, because the DZ correlation was more than half of the MZ correlation (e.g., 0.78 vs. 0.68 for the Noken Test). (*Note*: the quantitative genetic theory predicts that

the DZ correlation becomes half of the MZ correlation when additive
genetic effects are the only cause of the twin similarity, and that the DZ
correlation becomes more than half of the MZ correlation when shared
(familial) environmental effects are substantial.)

Ohira (1953), using a different group of twins, consisting of 50 MZ
pairs and 14 DZ pairs from 6 to 12 years of age, found a higher DZ correlation (0.71) than had been estimated by the simple additive genetic
model calculated from the MZ correlation (0.90), indicating a shared environmental contribution. In more recent research by Ando (1993), who
used twins from the same high school, the correlation coefficient was
0.47 for 86 male MZ pairs, 0.59 for 11 male DZ pairs, 0.60 for 94 female
MZ pairs, and 0.44 for female DZ pairs at 12 years of age. Ando (1996)
also showed a high correlation in intelligence (0.80) for 15 pairs of 12-
year-old DZ twins, which was comparable to that of 19 MZ pairs (0.80)
of the same age, indicating no genetic contribution. Thus the Japanese
samples tended to show a more substantial amount of shared environmental contribution to intelligence than have the Western samples (the
averaged figures of twin correlations for the latter are 0.86 for MZ vs.
0.60 for DZ; see Bouchard & McGue, 1981).

There are two possible reasons for this discrepancy. One is that the
twins in the studies conducted in Japan were younger (less than 12 years
old) than in the Western studies, because the twin research in Japan was
conducted mostly in junior high schools. It is a well-established finding
in behavioral genetic literature that shared environmental effects contribute substantially to the development of intelligence when children
are young (less than 20 years old; McGue et al., 1993). Ando (1993) found
an elevation in the genetic contribution with no shared environmental
effect for boys at 15 years of age in the "twin high school" ($r = 0.74$ for
MZ vs. $r = 0.11$ for DZ). Ando, Ono, and Wright (2001) also reported a
substantial genetic effect without any effect of shared environment for a
larger pool of adolescent and adult twins (mean age $= 19.9$ years; sample
size: 87 MZ pairs vs. 62 DZ pairs; intraclass correlations: 0.68 for MZ vs.
0.34 for DZ for spatial ability and 0.66 for MZ vs. 0.22 for DZ for verbal
ability, as measured by the composite scores of subscales of Kyodai NX).
A second reason could be that shared environmental effects are actually
more substantial in Japan than in the Western cultures; that is, family coherence and educational efforts tend to be emphasized in Japan,
and therefore, the effect of family environment could make the intellectual performance of family members more similar than in Western
society.

Constancy of IQ

A naive hereditarian view of intelligence is the *consistency theory*, that is, being hereditary means being consistent, stable, and unchangeable. According to this naive theory, the levels of intelligence within persons are believed to stay constant across all ages and there is no developmental change throughout one's life. This deterministic view of heredity sometimes leads to the following false conclusion: "An unstable trait is not genetic but environmental." This view is wrong because recent findings from human behavioral genetics show that genes contribute not only to stability but also to change in psychological development (Plomin et al., 2000). For example, identical twins who share exactly the same genome sets show similar developmental trajectories and synchronized alterations in intelligence (Wilson, 1983). However, during the period when the naive consistency theory of intelligence was very popular, the anti-hereditarian camp wanted to cite longitudinal research that showed developmental fluctuations of intelligence to emphasize their environmentalist view.

It is embarrassing for us to have to cite Kano's excellent longitudinal studies of intelligence (Kano, 1960) in this context. Kano measured the intelligence of more than 700 schoolchildren during 10 successive years (the first group contained 306 individuals investigated from 1946 to 1954, and the second contained 418 from 1947 to 1955). The children were tested in April every year with the Suzuki-Binet Intelligence Test, and their IQ scores were measured. One of his major findings was that IQ fluctuated throughout these years. Table 10.1 shows the results of retests at intervals of 1 to 8 years (for example, an interval year of one means the test was conducted over two years like 6 to 7, 7 to 8, and so on). These

TABLE 10.1. *Fluctuations of IQ Scores When Tested with an Interval of 1–8 Years*

Fluctuation (points)	Intervals of Retests (years)							
	1	2	3	4	5	6	7	8
±0–5	66.8%	52.3	50.3	50.2	50.8	43.3	42.3	23.0
±6–10	25.0	30.3	29.8	27.8	28.1	28.1	26.5	15.9
±11–15	6.5	12.8	12.1	13.5	12.0	18.1	15.9	9.5
±16–20	1.2	3.4	5.6	4.5	4.9	4.8	6.8	16.7
±21–	0.7	1.2	2.1	3.1	4.1	5.7	8.3	34.9
n	1,256	1,043	808	598	416	266	132	126

Source: Based on Kano, 1960.

results indicate that IQ scores fluctuate more over longer intervals. For example, in the seven-year (2–7) interval noted, the scores of 68.8% of children stayed within 10 IQ points (either increase or decrease) but of 8.3% fluctuated by 21 points. Kano also measured the difference between individuals' maximum and minimum score through these years and found that 20.2% of the IQ scores stayed within 10 points, whereas 20.1% fluctuated by more than 21 points, although the correlations of the IQ scores between different ages were quite high ($r = 0.8$–0.9).

Kano believed that these fluctuations in intelligence were attributable to the regular periodic variation of development. He compared these intelligence data with physical parameters such as height and weight. Through his research, he found that development of children's intelligence shadowed their physical development (changes are large for children from 6 to 9 and small between ages 10 and 11). Kano also reported that IQ differences depended on a person's social status. The differences in average IQ scores between the upper (actually middle), and lower social class children were about 20 points in each year and showed no marked variation over the nine years that he conducted his study. However, when he compared the amount of the IQ change from the first school year to the second, he found some differences between these two SES groups. Although some of the upper-class children gained over 30 points in IQ in this period, a greater proportion (48%) gained less than 10 points from the initial scores, measured when they entered school. In contrast, many of the lower-class children (40%) gained more than 21 to 30 points, with a total proportion of greater than 10-point gainers of 65.7%. The increase in the IQ scores of the lower-class children was relatively larger than that of the upper class. It seems that the mental development of the lower-class children was more strongly influenced by schooling than was that of the upper-class children.

Statistically Sophisticated Analyses
Human behavioral genetics has developed dramatically in the past two decades and has become widely accepted in scientific psychology. One of the reasons for this rapid progress is the development of sophisticated statistical techniques, especially structural equation modeling, to analyze various and complicated kinship data sets under the quantitative genetic model (Neale & Cardon, 1992). The strength of this technique is its capability to test various hypotheses and deal with multivariate structures. The recent advances in human behavioral genetics have been introduced into Japan.

Ando et al. (2001) investigated the genetic structure of working memory (WM) and intelligence (cognitive ability) with 236 pairs of young adult twins. In this study, the storage and executive functions operating in both a spatial and verbal WM span task were measured by the dual task paradigm of working memory (Shah & Miyake, 1996). In 155 (87 MZ, 62 DZ) of these pairs, cognitive ability scores from the Kyodai NX were also obtained. The phenotypic correlations between WM and cognitive ability were substantial ($r = 0.26-0.44$). Individual differences in WM storage and executive functions were found to be significantly influenced by genes with heritability estimates that were all moderately high (43–49%), and estimates for cognitive ability were comparable to previous studies (65%). A large part of the genetic variance observed in storage and executive functions in both spatial and verbal modalities was due to a common genetic factor that accounts for 11–43% of the variance. Additional genetic variance in WM (7–30%) was due to modality-specific factors (spatial and verbal) and a storage-specific factor that may be particularly important for the verbal modality. In the reduced sample from which intelligence scores were obtained, this common genetic factor accounted for 64% and 26% of the variance in spatial and verbal cognitive ability, respectively. None of the variance in cognitive ability was accounted for by the modality- and storage-specific genetic factors.

Muraishi and Toyoda (1998) applied the genetic factor analysis to scholastic achievement scores of 125 pairs of twins from the twin high school and combined their data with data from 703 non-twin students to stabilize the covariance structure in consideration of classical test theory. They found no genetic effects for mathematics or Japanese, but found additive genetic effects and significant shared environmental effects for social studies.

GE Interactions

Ando (1996) conducted a co-twin control study to show genotype–environment interactions in an educational setting. Nineteen pairs of MZ twins and 12 pairs of DZ twins were divided into two different classes that were taught English using different methods, that is, the communicative approach (CA) and the grammatical approach (GA). The twins were all 6th-graders who had never had any formal English lessons before, and they were taught for a total of 7 hours over 8 days. GA has been the traditional teaching style of English in Japan, whereby grammatical rules are explained to students in Japanese.

The co-twin control method provides ideal homogeneous experimental groups because MZ twins have very similar aptitudes. If any difference in performance between these two experimental treatments in MZ participants is found, it means that the teaching method is a significant factor in developing their linguistic abilities, regardless of the participants' genetic disposition. If a larger extent of similarity is found in MZ than in DZ pairs under different experimental conditions, one can conclude that genetic factors play an important role, regardless of the different approaches to teaching. Furthermore, it is possible to find an interaction between participants' genetic dispositions and the experimental conditions, which is called the GE (genotype–environment) interaction. In this educational experiment, all three of these effects were identified. As for the experimental main effect, that is, the effect of the teaching methods, large mean differences between the two approaches were indicated. For grammatical ability, GA was significantly better than CA, and for communicative abilities and communicative motivation, CA was better. As for genetic effects, significant genetic contributions to the learning outcomes were also found. For almost all aspects of learning outcomes, the similarity of the MZ pairs exceeded that of the DZ pairs, indicating a genetic effect.

The most interesting finding of this experiment was that there were significant interactions between learners' genetic disposition and these learning styles; that is, for genetically high verbal ability learners, GA was more beneficial for acquiring grammatical skills. This interaction pattern is a kind of ATI (aptitude treatment interaction) at a genetic level. The GE interaction refers to the fact that the effects of genes are different depending upon the environment, or that the same genotypes show different phenotypes under different environments. In this experiment, identical twins who shared the same genotypes showed different learning outcomes under GA and CA.

Another interesting GE interactional phenomenon could be found at the cultural level. Twin studies on scholastic achievement scores conducted in Japan have consistently shown a *low* genetic influence on arithmetic and mathematical abilities. Iwashita (1956) reported the intersibling differences in academic scores for 268 pairs of MZ and 67 pairs of DZ twins who applied to the twin high school, finding that the difference was significantly larger in arithmetic and mathematics than in the other academic subjects. Soejima (1972) analyzed scholastic achievement data from a population-based twin sample of 6- to 14-year-olds in the Saga prefecture, and found that, at the junior high school level, the mathematics marks tend to be influenced more strongly by the environment.

Asaka (1978) also reported lower heritability of mathematics performance from the data of the twin high school in 1971 and 1972. Ando's
(1996) small twin sample showed a larger similarity for DZ (0.85) than
that for MZ (0.56) twins in mathematics, although there were substantial
genetic effects for Japanese and science. Finally, Muraishi and Toyoda
(1998) also reported no substantial genetic contribution to mathematics
performance, using a recent twin sample from the twin high school. No
such differences in heritability among subjects have been reported from
the United States and Sweden (Loehlin & Nichols, 1976; Husen, 1959),
although a German report (Frischeisen-Koehler, 1930) also indicated a
lower heritability in mathematics.

This discrepancy may be owing to differences in the educational culture of mathematics from country to country. One can speculate that
the Japanese culture has led to the development of various kinds of
arithmetic tools such as the abacus, multiplication table, and the Ku-
mon style of learning. These subject-specific mental tools are available
in the society, but their accessibility depends on the family environment.
People who have an opportunity to acquire these subject-specific mental tools could develop their arithmetic or mathematical abilities, and
therefore, a substantial contribution of shared environment could be
found in Japan.

HOW IS "INTELLIGENCE" VIEWED IN THE JAPANESE CULTURE?

"No psychological topic is of greater interest to the general public, and
to the discipline of psychology as a whole, than intelligence" (Gardner,
Kornhaber, & Wake, 1996, p. vii). We are not sure whether this statement is agreeable to most American psychologists, but if "laypeople
argue at length about who is intelligent, how to become smarter, and
what difference IQ makes" in the United States, this mentality is very
different from the Japanese mentality. The Japanese (except for psychologists and test-favoring educators) seldom refer explicitly to one's own
or another person's general and stable ability. Even when they compare
people in terms of intelligence, aptitude, or talent, they do not verbalize
their judgments. Instead, they often discuss who is diligent, works hard,
and so forth, on academic and occupational tasks. The dimension that
is considered critical and/or appropriate for describing people's task
performance may vary from culture to culture.

Of course, the Japanese have a notion of being smart or intelligent. For
example, Azuma and Kashiwagi (1987) asked college students to think
of an intelligent person they knew and rate whether each of 67 properties

fit that person. The students did the ratings without difficulty. The authors found three major factors from the ratings, that is, active social competence, processing efficiency, and receptive social competence. It should be noted, however, that none of these factors is considered to be innate. Japanese people try to manage without measuring or using for description any capabilities that do not reflect the amount of effort.

The Japanese may be characterized by what we shall term *belief-in-effort* (Hatano, 1982; Holloway, 1988); that is, an assumption of the supreme importance of effort as a determinant of intellectual achievement. This is in sharp contrast to the belief-in-ability that American people are typically committed to: Americans are particularly concerned with whether their achievement is due to ability (See Nicholls, 1979). Americans tend to regard effort as meaningful only insofar as one is smart or talented enough in the field, whereas Japanese people think that effort makes a difference everywhere in intellectual achievement (even when one lacks ability). Belief-in-effort implies that one can necessarily succeed in academic and occupational domains if he or she exerts enough effort, and that if one does not succeed, it is only because he or she has not tried hard enough. Intelligence as an ability that is domain-general and stable if not innate is thus not a popular notion in the daily life of Japanese people because the emphasis on intelligence is not compatible with their belief-in-effort. How Japanese belief-in-effort was produced and has been maintained historically is an issue beyond this chapter; we would like to point out, however, that Japanese children are seldom allowed in school to choose domains or tasks they are good at, and that most employees have to try hard to do assigned jobs successfully because mobility has been low until quite recently. In such a society it is almost impossible for people to give up belief-in-effort without becoming fatalists (Hatano & Inagaki, 1998).

Attributions of Success or Failure

Japanese people's belief-in-effort in intellectual achievements is clearly revealed in studies of the attribution of success or failure. Kitayama, Takagi, and Matsumoto (1995) concluded, based on their review of those studies, that Japanese people do not show a self-enhancing bias (i.e., a tendency to attribute success to one's own ability and failure to other factors than the ability), that has repeatedly been observed in the United States When an artificial intellectual task is used and the success or failure is experimentally manipulated, Japanese participants often attribute their success to the task characteristic, good luck, or another situational factor, and their failure to a lack of ability/effort. When an academic achievement or test performance in real life is the target, they most often attribute their success or failure to effort. For example, Miyamoto (1985) found that Japanese children attributed their hypothetical success in math much less often to ability, and their hypothetical failure more often to lack of effort and ability, than do their American counterparts.

Furthermore, Heine et al. (2001) recently found that, whereas American college students who had received failure feedback persisted less on a follow-up task than did those who had received success feedback, Japanese students who had received failure feedback persisted more on the follow-up task than did those who had received success feedback. The authors interpreted this tendency of the Japanese to increase effort in response to failure as due to their conception of self as improvable by expending more effort. The present authors are not prepared to accept such a domain-general interpretation of cross-cultural differences, but the response that the failure induces in this experimental situation certainly differs between Americans and Japanese.

Effort-Dependent Optimism

Japanese belief-in-effort may be extended to non-intellectual situations, if they are perceived as a challenge or the target of endeavor. Thus, the Japanese may overestimate the malleability of negative mental and physical properties. Nakashima, Inagaki, and Lockhart (2002) examined whether young Japanese children would reveal the optimism that was observed by Lockhart et al. (1997). They asked 5-year-olds, 6-year-olds, 3rd- and 4th-graders, and adults whether types of negative traits – physical–structural (e.g., being short), physical–functional (e.g., poor eyesight), psychological (e.g., being mean), and genetic (e.g., a disliked eye color) – that a hypothetical child possessed would change when he or she became an adult and an elderly, if he or she strongly wished for that change. They found that the 5-year-olds were more optimistic than the older participants, but unlike their American counterparts, the 6-year-olds showed no difference from the older elementary schoolers or college students in the extent of optimism. This result suggests that among Japanese children naive, global optimism disappears earlier than among American children.

However, they also found that Japanese college students often assume that negative traits can be changed by sustained effort. For example, 7 of 24 college students predicted that a 5-year-old child who was poor at learning things but hoped to be smart could become smarter than his or her peers at age 21. All of them used the term *effort* in their justification of the prediction. Twelve other students predicted that the child would be as smart as his or her peers, and 7 of them also referred to effort. The experimenter did not say what the hypothetical child did, but the college students inferred that he or she must try hard to achieve the desired goal. Similarly, 5 of the 24 students predicted that a child who was a slow runner would be able to run faster than his or her peers at maturity; 4 of these students mentioned effort and the remaining student, intensive training. Only 7 students replied that a slow-running child would become a slow-running adult. It is not a silly idea for Japanese that effort can change many negative traits (including non-intellectual ones) into positive characteristics. In other words, they are committed to effort-dependent optimism.

Distribution of the Fruits of Labor

Studies on fairness or equity of distribution have also shown the status of belief-in-effort. For example, Oye and Hatano (2002) showed that, although there are large individual differences, some Japanese people take it as fair if the distribution of an outcome is equal among members sharing the status or role or if it is proportional to the effort spent, but as not fair if it is proportional to ability. In one of the studies, they asked college students how the outcome of collaborative enterprises (e.g., income from a collectively run orchard) should be divided. When the students were asked to offer the best rationale for distribution by dividing 10 points, they gave on average 2.6, 3.7, and 3.7 to equality (give an equal amount to every participant), effort (give an amount proportional to the participant's effort), and ability (give an amount proportional to the participant's proposed ideas), respectively.

Social and Educational Policies

Many Japanese people believe that intellectual measures of academic and occupational achievements should reflect the amount of effort spent, at least to some extent. This corollary of the belief-in-effort may explain why the SAT introduced by the U.S. Education Mission is no longer used for university admission in Japan – it is considered that selecting applicants by innate capabilities is undesirable from an educational point of view. Many who were concerned disliked the SAT, especially because the SAT was assumed to represent innate capabilities and was used to eliminate applicants who failed to score at a certain level on it. According to Japanese lay educational philosophy, this is a bad practice that discourages students who are diagnosed as lacking capabilities, their parents, and educators from continuing teaching or learning in this domain.

However, this does not mean that Japanese people do not select candidates according to their general ability. In reality, performance in math or foreign language is used almost as a substitute for the SAT. These subjects are usually taught in Japan as an exercise for analyzing a sequence of symbols by applying a set of rules or assembling the sequence from symbols. The belief-in-effort does not necessarily deny that there are individual differences in the abilities people are endowed with genetically. Most Japanese are not empiricists in the sense of believing that abilities are products of rich early experience and training in the target domain only. They are reluctant to select candidates using measures that apparently cannot be changed by the candidates' effort.

The belief-in-effort implies that everyone can achieve a very high level of performance in any domain, if he or she engages in exercise or deliberate practice for an extended period of time. If someone cannot perform well after this amount of effort, educators or parents must be blamed, because this means that either the training provided by the educators was ineffective or the early experience arranged by the parents was insufficient. The failure to achieve highly must be the fault of students, educators, or parents.

These social implications may be undesirable. Belief-in-effort may lead to overemphasizing the responsibility of the learners and their parents or teachers for not achieving well. It may result in initial good performances of a majority of learners, because more time tends to be devoted to an area in which students are initially poor. However, belief-in-effort inevitably induces strong stress on the learning and teaching or parenting individuals, and some guilt when achieving less well than others. This is in fact happening in the contemporary Japanese society: Students study hard, achieve at high levels, yet dislike academic subjects (Hatano & Inagaki, 1998), the worst case of which is exemplified by examination hell.

References

Amano, I. (1990). *Education and examination in modern Japan* (W. K. Cummings & F. Cummings, Trans.). Tokyo: University of Tokyo Press.

Ando, J., Ono, Y., & M. J. Wright (2001). Genetic structure of spatial and verbal working memory. *Behavior Genetics.*

Ando, J. (1993). Twin study of intelligence and personality in Japanese high school students. *Proceedings of Behavior Genetics Association 23rd Annual Meeting, 12.*

Ando, J. (1996). Genetic effects upon instruction/learning processes: A comparative study of instructional methods of English by the cotwin control method. *The Japanese Journal of Educational Psychology, 44,* 223–233 (in Japanese).

Asaka, A. (1978). Scholastic achievement of twins. *Heredity, 32,* 27–34 (in Japanese).

Azuma, H., & Kashiwagi, K. (1987). Descriptors for an intelligent person: A Japanese study. *Japanese Psychological Research, 29,* 17–26.

Baddeley, A. D., Ligie, R., Bressi, S., Dellasala, S., & Spinnler, H. (1986). Dementia and working memory. *Quarterly Journal of Experimental Psychology, 38A,* 603–618.

Bouchard, T. J., Jr., & McGue, M. (1981). Familial studies of intelligence: A review. *Science, 212,* 1055–1059.

Case, R. (1992). Neo-Piagetion theories of child development, In R. J. Sternberg & C. A. Berg (Eds.), *Intellectual Development* (pp. 161–196). New York: Cambridge University Press.

Frisheisen-Koehler, I. (1930). Untersuchungen an schulzeugnissen von zwillingen [Investigations of the school report cards of twins]. *Zeitschrift fur Angewandte Psychologie, 37,* 385–416.

Gardner, H., Kornhaber, M. L., & Wake, W. K. (1996). *Intelligence: Multiple perspectives.* Orlando, FL: Harcourt Brace.

Hatano, G. (1982). Should parents be teachers too? A Japanese view. *Dokkyo University Bulletin of Liberal Arts, 17,* 54–72.

Hatano, G., & Inagaki, K. (1998). Cultural contexts of schooling revisited: A review of the learning gap from a cultural psychology perspective. In S. G. Paris & H. M. Wellman (Eds.), *Global prospects for education* (pp. 79–104). Washington, DC: American Psychological Association.

Heine, S. J., Kitayama, S., Lehman, D. R., Takata, T., Ide, E., Leung, C., & Matsumoto, H. (2001). Divergent consequences of success and failure in Japan and North America: An investigation of self-improving motivation and malleable selves. *Journal of Personality and Social Psychology. 81,* 599–615.

Holloway, S. D. (1988). Concept of ability and effort in Japan and the United States. *Review of Educational Research, 58,* 327–345.

Husen, T. (1959). *Psychological twin research: A methodological study.* Stockholm: Almqvist & Wiksell.

Indow T., & Samejima, F. (1962). *Manual of LIS measurement scale for reasoning: Non-verbal*. Tokyo: Nihon-Bunka-kagakusha (in Japanese).

Inouye, E., & Miyazawa, O. (1953). A study on intelligence by twin method. In Y. Uchimura (Ed.), *Studies on twins* (Vol. 1). Tokyo: Japanese Society for the Promotion of Science (in Japanese).

Iwashita, T. (1956). On paired discrepancy of scholastic achievement. In Y. Uchimura (Ed.), *Studies on twins* (Vol. 2). Tokyo: Japanese Society for the Promotion of Science (in Japanese).

Kano, H. (1960). *The longitudinal study on development of mental abilities*. Tokyo: Seikatsu Kagaku Kyokai (in Japanese).

Kitayama, S., Takagi, H., & Matsumoto, H. (1995). Causal attribution of success and failure: Cultural psychology of the Japanese self. *Japanese Psychological Review, 38*, 247–280 (in Japanese).

Lockhart, K., Stegall, S., Roberts, K., & Yip, T. (1997). Unlearned optimism: Children's beliefs about the stability of negative traits. Poster presented at the Biennial meeting of Society for Research in Child Development, Washington, DC.

Loehlin, J. C., & Nichols, R. C. (1976). *Heredity, environment, and personality*. Austin: University of Texas Press.

Lord, F. M. (1952). A theory of test scores. *Psychometric Monographs*, No. 7

McGue, M., Bouchard, T. J. Jr., Iacono, W. G., & Lykken, D. T. (1993). Behavioral genetics of cognitive ability: A life-span perspective. In R. Plomin & G. E. McClearn (Eds.), *Nature, nurture, and psychology* (pp. 59–76). Washington, DC: American Psychological Association.

Miyamoto, M. (1985). Parents' and children's beliefs and children's achievement and development. In R. Diaz-Guerrero (Ed.), *Cross-cultural and national studies in social psychology* (pp. 209–223). North-Holland: Elsevier Science.

Motora, Y. (1911). Ein experiment zur einubung von aufmerksamkeit [An experiment on the practice of attentiveness]. *Zeitschrift fur Kinderforschung, 16*, 214–225.

Motoyama, Y. (1997). *Proliferating talent* (G. M. Wilson, Trans.). Honolulu: University of Hawaii Press.

Muraishi, Y., & Toyoda, H. (1998). Analysis of standardized achievement test by classical test theory and genetic factor analysis models. *Japanese Journal of Educational Psychology, 46*, 395–402 (in Japanese).

Nakashima, N., Inagaki, K., & Lockhart, K. (2002). *Young children's optimism: How do Japanese children think about the stability of negative traits over time?* Poster presented at International Society for Study of Behavioural Development meeting, Ottawa.

Namiki, H. (1993). To what degree is the qualitative and quantitative diagnosis of dementia possible?: From the standpoint of psychology. *Journal of Adult Diseases, 23*, 4, 61–62 (in Japanese).

Namiki, H. (1999). Aging and cognitive functions in the case of Kanji processing: Development of a neuropsychological test for senile dementia based on the theory of Working Memory. In *Proceedings of the 5th meeting of the German-Japanese Society for Social Sciences*. Tokyo: Waseda University Press.

Namiki, H., Shinohara, Y., Yamamoto, M., & Yonekura, Y. (2002). A neuro-psychological test (T-K-W Test) for dementia based on working memory theory and item-response theory: Its development and construction. *Psychiatria et Neurologia Japonica, 104*, 8, 690–709 (in Japanese).

Neale, M. C., & Cardon, L. R. (1992). *Methodology for genetic studies on twins and families.* Boston: Kluwer.

Nicholls, J. G. (1979). Quality and equality in intellectual development: The role of motivation in education. *American Psychologist, 34*, 1071–1084.

Obonai, T. (1926). Study of mental inheritance by twins. *Japanese Journal of Psychology, 1*, 1–63 (in Japanese).

Ohira, K. (1953). A study of the degree of physical maturation, intelligence and proficiency in the Japanese language by twins. *Japanese Journal of Psychology, 24*, 79–82 (in Japanese).

Ohyama, T., Sato, T., & Suzuki, Y. (2002). Shaping of scientific psychology in Japan. *International Journal of Psychology, 36.*

Osaka, R., & Umemoto, A. (1973). Shintei Ktodai NX15 (New version Kyoto University NX-15) (2nd ed.). Tokyo: Taisei-shuppan (in Japanese).

Oye, M., & Hatano, G. (2002). Ability-based, effort-based and equal distribution of fruits of labor. Poster to be presented at International Congress of Applied Psychology, Singapore.

Plomin, R., DeFries, J. C., McClearn, G. E., & McGuffin, P. (2000). *Behavioral Genetics* (4th ed.). New York: Freeman & Co.

Sagara, M., Takuma, T., & Morikawa, M. (1956). A study of intelligence by twin method. In Y. Uchimura (Ed.), *Studies on twins* (Vol. 2). Tokyo: Japanese Society for the Promotion of Science (in Japanese).

Sano, T. (1974). Difference of intellectual abilities between the times. *Japanese Journal of Educational Psychology, 22*, 2, 42–46 (in Japanese).

Shah, P., and Miyake, A. (1996). The separability of working memory resources for spatial thinking and language processing: An individual differences approach. *Journal of Experimental Psychology: General, 125*, 4–27.

Soejima, Y. (1972). The effect of heredity on school marks: By twin-control method. *Japanese Journal of Psychology, 43*, 68–75 (in Japanese).

Sternberg, R. J. (1980). Factor theories of intelligence are all right almost. *Educational Researcher, 9–8*, 6–13.

Takuma, T. (1968). An experiment on hereditary influence on intelligence by twin study method. *Japanese Journal of Educational Psychology, 17*, 237–240 (in Japanese).

Tukuba, H., & Suzuki, Z. (1967). The Reaction of Yukichi Fukuzawa to Eugenics. *Igakushi Kenkyu (Historical Study of Medicine), 24*, 1225–1229.

Wilson, R. S. (1983). The Louisville twin study: Developmental synchronies in behavior. *Child Development, 54*, 298–316.

Yoda, A., & Hidano, T. (1959). Development of educational psychology in Japan. *Psychologia, 2*, 137–149.

Yonekura, Y., Fukai, E., Nakamura, S., & Namiki, H. (1997). Construction and valiclation of a neuropsychological diagnosis test for senile dementid based on working memory theory. *Proceedings of 39th Annual convention of the Japanese Association of Educational Psychology*, 363 (in Japanese).

11

Diligence Makes People Smart

Chinese Perspectives of Intelligence

Jiannong Shi

INTRODUCTION

In an impressive comparative study on mathematics achievements of primary school students between the United States and China, Professor Harold Stevenson of the University of Michigan and his colleagues from the Institute of Psychology, Chinese Academy of Sciences, obtained some interesting findings (Stevenson & Stigler, 1992). One of them is that the mathematics test scores of Chinese students were much higher than the scores of American students, however, the mean level of satisfaction of Chinese parents was much lower than that of American parents. In this case, are American parents overly optimistic? Or are Chinese parents too insatiate? Is this because of the differences of cultures or because of the differences of education systems? We all know that the education system in China is quite different from the education system in the United States or in other Western countries. But when we consider the following example, the educational system seems not to be the reason, at least not the main reason.

I visited a mathematically talented class when I was at the University of Michigan in 2001. There were about 20 students in this special class. But 17 of them were Chinese (from Hong Kong, Taiwan, and mainland China). In this case, all the students are in the same classroom with

The preparation of this article is supported by Natural Science Foundation of China (grant No. 39700045) and the President's Foundation of Institute of Psychology, Chinese Academy of Sciences. The author thanks Dr. Shin-ying Lee, who offered valuable information about U.S. education. The author also thanks the copyeditor, who spent time correcting the English.

the same teacher, and, of course, with the same educational system. But what does it mean that the most mathematically talented students are Chinese? Does it mean that Chinese students are naturally good at mathematics? Or does it mean that Chinese students are more intelligent genetically? The answer to both questions is "no!" because there is no biological or genetic superiority of Chinese to other people. But the Chinese culture is quite different from the cultures of the Western world.

In this chapter, philosophical attitudes about intelligence are presented and discussed from the perspective of Chinese traditional culture, as well as are the history of the study of intelligence, the tools of measuring human intelligence, and recent developments in the field of human intelligence in China.

INTELLIGENCE IN CONFUCIANISM

Confucianism is generally seen as the representative of traditional Chinese culture. Before I explain how Confucianism plays its role on people's intrinsic attitudes on human intelligence, I would like to present three stories underlining two Chinese idioms. From these idioms, we can find the implicit theory of intelligence of the Chinese people.

Story 1

This story has been told for more than 2,000 years since the Warring States Period (475–221 B.C.). It was said (see SWSP, 2001) that a man named Su Qin lived in Luoyang (now a city in Henan province) and studied very hard. Since he studied very hard every day until very late in the night, he felt sleepy and fell asleep frequently when he was studying, especially around midnight. In order not to fall asleep when he was sleepy during his studying, he put an awl at hand and stung himself in the thigh. He was awakened by the great pain and could continue to read. Some years later, he became a very famous politician. He held the position of premier of the union of Qi, Chu, Wei, Zhao, Yan, and Han (six countries during the age of Warring States Period). (Yuan & Shen, 1981, p. 656; Li & Lu, 1986, p. 957).

Story 2

This story is about a person named Sun Jing in the Han Dynasty (202–206 B.C.). Sun Jing was from Xin Du (now Ji County in Hebei province).

This story was written in Han Shu (the history of Han Dynasty). Like Su Qin, Sun Jing studied very hard. Learning or reading books was the most important thing for him in his life. Neighbors called him "Mr. Close-Door" because he usually closed himself at home, alone, and read books quietly. He persisted in studying no matter how tired he was. Sometimes, he was too tired to read a book. He was angry with himself when he could not help but fall into a doze during the time when he was studying. To force himself not to fall asleep when he was learning, he tied his hair with rope and it attached the rope to a girder. In this case, his head was lifted up, and he would be awakened because of the pain in the scalp if he nodded off when he felt sleepy during his learning. Ten years later, Sun Jing was a great scholar in Han Dynasty (Yuan & Shen, 1981, p. 656; Li & Lu, 1986, p. 957; Zhang, 2001).

These two stories were combined into a Chinese idiom, *xuan liang chi gu* (to hang one's head on the girder and to sting one's thigh with an awl), which symbolizes the spirit of studying hard.

Story 3

In the Jin Dynasty (265–420), there was a young man named Kuang Heng (cf. Ge Hong's [283–363] *Anecdotes of Western Capital*, Vol. 2), who was born into a very poor family. His family was so poor that he did not have enough money to buy books. He had to work in a landlord's home every day for nothing but the books he borrowed and brought back home in the evening. However, his family was too poor to buy even a candle. He could not read books without light. His neighbor was rich enough to have candles in the evening. One evening, he was home and found that some light came in through a small gap in the wall between his neighbor and him. It sparked him. He thought that if the gap were big enough then he could have enough light for reading books. He made the gap a little bit bigger to borrow enough light for his reading (Li & Lu, 1986, pp. 1095–1096). This is the underlying story of another Chinese idiom *zao bi tou guang* (making a hole on the wall to borrow lights).

These stories have been told from generation to generation for hundreds of years in China. The examples of these stories, and the meanings of these idioms, have been planted in the souls of the Chinese. They become the habits of the Chinese people's behavior, the styles of the Chinese people's thinking, and the guidelines of the Chinese people's social activities.

Confucius (551–479 B.C.) and Mencius (371–289 B.C.) were two representatives of Confucianism. Mencius indicated in *Mencius*, "*xue bu yan, zhi ye*" (intelligence means never being tired of learning). In other words, an intelligent person is never tired of learning. People are encouraged to study hard to be intelligent. Besides the endeavor or great efforts (hard studying, hard working, etc.) emphasized, Mencius thought that persistence was also important. He told a story about Yi Qiu, a famous chess master in the country. Yi Qiu was asked to teach two people to learn to play chess. One of them listened carefully and did as Yi Qiu said. But the other one was thinking about shooting an arrow at a bird flying overhead while Yi Qiu was speaking. The results for the two people were obviously different, though they both learned to play chess from the same teacher (Mencius, 2001).

People may argue that the theme of Confucianism also proposed by Confucius is *ren* (benevolence) (Yang, 2001). Yes, the main thought of Confucianism is *ren yi dao de* (kindheartedness, loyalty, justice, and morality or benevolence). But how people can be *ren*? According to Confucius, "knowledge is a key to achieving benevolence. To be benevolent requires one to control oneself so as to behave in accordance with a knowledge of rightness." (Yang & Sternberg, 1997, p. 105). And knowledge can only be acquired through learning. In fact, Confucius himself was a person who enjoyed learning and was never too old to learn. Hence, an intelligent person is, as summarized by Yang and Sternberg (1997), according to Confucianism, a person who expends a great deal of time and effort in learning, and enjoys learning with a high degree of enthusiasm.

In the school of Confucianism, Xun Zi (325–238 B.C.) was another important ancient Chinese philosopher who emphasized the importance of learning in one's intelligence: *Yu bu zhuo, bu cheng qi. Ren bu xue, bu zhi dao.* (Jade cannot become an article if it is not carved. Man cannot know the principle if he does not learn.) (Dai & Dai, 2001). According to Xun Zi, learning is the most important thing for an individual to be intelligent and to live in the world. *Xun Zi* is a collection of the works of Xun Zi. There are 32 articles in *Xun Zi*. *Quan Xue* (Encouraging Learning) was listed at the very beginning. Xun Zi wrote in *Quan Xue* that he could not understand something even after a whole day's thinking, but he could know it soon after he learned it. For learning or studying, Xun Zi emphasized the importance of "accumulation." He argued: *Bu ji kui bu, wu yi zhi qian li; bu ji xiao liu, wu yi cheng da hai. Qi ji yi yue, bu neng shi bu; nu ma shi jia, gong zai bu she. Qi er she zhi, xiu mu bu zhe; qi er bu she, jin shi ke lou*. It means that no one can arrive at a destination 1,000 miles away if he does not go step by step. There is not a sea if there are not many small streams. A horse cannot jump over *shi bu* (*bu* is a length unit in the Qin Dynasty in ancient China. One *bu* is about 2.67 meters.). A weaker horse can reach the destination 10 *jia* away (*jia* is another length unit in ancient China. One *jia* stands for the distance that a carriage can run in a day.) because it persists in running. You cannot break a rotten piece of wood if you try but give up immediately. But you can carve iron and stone if you persist in working hard for a long time (Xun Zi, 2001).

People can find the influences of the thought of Confucianism even from the class schedules of schools in China. I visited several U.S. schools in Ann Arbor, Michigan, when I was there as a visiting scholar. I found that the class schedules of American primary schools were quite different from school to school. My friend, Shin-ying Lee, who was a developmental psychologist in University of Michigan, told me, "Elementary school has no fixed class schedule in America. It is pretty much up to each teacher how he or she wants to schedule the school day. The only fixed schedule would be classes that are not taught by homeroom teachers, such as art, music, PE (physical education), or computer." But in China, each primary school has a fixed class schedule even for children as young as 6 years old. Normally, children in primary school have to take from 7 to 9 classes a day from 7:15 or 7:30 a.m. to 4:30 or 5:00 p.m., five days a week from Monday to Friday: mathematics including arithmetic and geometry, Chinese, English, computer, fine arts, music, PE, calligraphy, and natural history.

INTELLIGENCE TESTS

Tests in Ancient China

There was a folk custom written in Yan Zhitui's *Yan Shi Jia Xun – Feng Cao Pian* (Yan's Family Rules – Piece of Conduct) (Yan Zhitui, 531–591 B.C., a famous philosopher and educator in ancient China) called *shi er* (child prediction) (Yan, 2001) in South China in the old ages. According to the folk custom, when a child was 1 year old, he or she would be tested by placing stationery objects, such as writing brushes and paper; sewing items, such as threads and needles; foods; and cosmetics before him or her. People thought that the first object the child tried to grasp could tell whether he or she would be avaricious or disinterested, intelligent or not intelligent (Yang, 1994; Shi & Zha, 2000). For example, it was written in Chapter Two of one of the four most famous classic Chinese novels *Hong Lou Meng* (Dream of the Red Chamber or Story of a Stone) written by Cao Xueqin (1715–1763) that Jia Baoyu (one of the main characters) was tested by his father with the method of *shi er* when he was 1 year old. Baoyu was exposed to many different things and asked to grasp one from them. He reached for nothing but cosmetics. It made his father angry and sad because his father thought: "He will be a person who is fond of alcohol and women" (Cao & Gao, 2001).

Shi er is only a folk custom in ancient China, but it indicates that Chinese people think that a person can be studied through observation. In fact, the observation method was used to study human behavior very early in China. Liu Shao (220?–280?) argued in his book *Ren Wu Zhi* (*Records of People*) that people can learn a person's personality traits through observing the manner of a person's perception and responses (cf. Lin, 1980). According to Liu Shao, the most important way to know a person is to listen to what he or she says and to watch how he or she behaves. He wrote in his book, "You can know one is kind or not through listening what one says, and know one is intelligent or not through observing how he answer other's questions or react to others."

Zhu Geliang (181–234) suggested seven methods of observation in his book, *Xin Shu* (Book of Mind) to study one's inner world. The seven methods are: (1) to learn one's ambition by asking him or her "right"' or "wrong" questions, (2) to learn one's flexibility of response by asking him or her to get to the bottom of things, (3) to learn one's knowledge by asking for strategies, (4) to learn one's braveness by telling him or her misfortune, (5) to learn one's disposition by giving him or her alcohol or wine, (6) to learn one's honesty by exposing him or her before benefit, and (7) to learn one's quality by giving him or her expectation (cf. Lin, 1980, p. 76).

Besides the observation methods, "psychological" tests were used to study human intelligence in ancient China. One of the most famous and important tests is the tangram. It was said that the tangram was first developed in the Song Dynasty (Lin, 1980). It is considered the earliest psychological test in the world. The other kind of "psychological" test used in ancient China is *jiu lian huan* (nine linked rings). Tangram and *jiu lian huan* were designed to test one's intelligence, especially one's flexibility of thinking, because there were many alternative correct answers.

Many kinds of psychological tests have been developed during the long history of China, but they were used as entertainment tools rather than the psychological tests in China after the Sui Dynasty. The official method of testing for governmental employment after the Western Han Dynasty was *ke ju*, in which candidates were tested with different subjects, and the few top people would be selected for governmental employment or appointment. The number of subjects was different from time to time. For example, there were two subjects in *ke ju* in 598 (early Sui Dynasty). One of them was *zhi xing xiu jin* (devotion, ambition, behavior, habit, accomplishment, and respectfulness), and the other was *qing ping gan ji* (fairness, justice, ability of doing things, and achievement). The number of subjects in *ke ju* was increased from 2 to 10 nine years later (in 607). The 10 subjects were (1) *xiao ti you wen* (well-known in filial piety,), (2) *de xing dun hou* (great virtue), (3) *jie yi ke cheng* (complimentary moral integrity), (4) *cao lv qing jie* (good and clean record in behavior), (5) *qiang yi zheng zhi* (fortitude and justice), (6) *zhi xian bu nao* (to execute a law uncompromisingly), (7) *xue ye you min* (excellent in learning), (8) *wen cai mei xiu* (good at writing), (9) *cai kan jiang lue* (high talent like a general), and (10) *lu li xiao zhuang* (strong with great arm force). In the Tang Dynasty, there were two kinds of *ke ju*, one normal and the other special. The normal one was held regularly every year, and the special one was temporarily held and conducted directly by the emperor according to the demands of the country at the time. From the Tang Dynasty to the Song Dynasty, the *ke ju* included five kinds of tests: (1) *kou shi* (oral test), (2) *tie jing* (a kind of closed test based on *Analects, Mencius, Great Learning, The Doctrine of the Mean*, and so on), (3) *mo yi* (a kind of question-and-answer test in which the questions and answers were exactly selected from Confucian classics), (4) *ce wen* (a kind of paper-and-pencil test in which the examinees were asked to answer questions about politics, economics, military affairs, and agriculture), and (5) *shi fu* (poem and essay, in which the examinees were asked to write a poem or an essay within a limited time) (EC, 1985).

As the theoretical presupposition of *ke ju* was, "intelligence is knowledge or ability of knowledge acquisition," the contents of *ke ju* heavily relied on knowledge or memory. The system of *ke ju* lasted for more than 1,300 years, even though the criticism on the validity of *ke ju* for the selection of governor increased as time went on. It was finally abolished in 1906, but its effects did not stop with its abolishment. In fact, people can find the shadow of its influence on Chinese people in the National Examination for College Enrollment (NECE) held in July every year. The NECE still is a test heavily based on knowledge, although its content and form are quite different from *ke ju*. The candidates have to study their textbooks very carefully and do numerous exercises to prepare for the NECE.

Modern Intelligence Test

The early 20th century was a glorious period for intelligence testing in the Western world. It was a very important period of time for the development of intelligence testing in China, too. Binet and Simon created the first standardized intelligence test in France in 1905 and revised it in 1911. L. Terman introduced the Binet-Simon Intelligence Test to the United States and revised it into the Stanford-Binet Intelligence Test in 1911. A Chinese psychologist, Fan Bingqing, introduced the Binet-Simon test in China in 1916 (See Song & Zhang, 1987, p. 3). People cannot tell which version of Binet-Simon test was introduced by Fan, but Fan is recognized for first introducing the intelligence test and modern ideas about intelligence and intelligence measurement into China. *The Measurement of the Mental Development of the Child* by Binet and Simon was translated into Chinese by Fei Peijie and published by the Commercial Press in 1922 (Binet & Simon, 1922). Terman's (Terman, 1924) book, *The Measurement of Intelligence*, was translated by Hua Chao and published by the Commercial Press in 1924. After the Binet-Simon and Stanford-Binet intelligence tests were introduced into China, a test storm blew across the country in the 1920s and 1930s.

During the 1920s to 1940s, Chinese psychologists not only translated several Western intelligence tests into Chinese, but they revised some of these tests into Chinese versions or developed some intelligence tests by themselves. For example, Lu Zhiwei (Lu, 1924) revised the Binet-Simon test into the Chinese-Binet Intelligence Test (CBIT), which was published by the Commercial Press in 1924. Wu Tianmin (Wu, 1936) made the second revision of CBIT and published it in 1936. Ai Wei and his colleagues (Ai, 1948) started to collect data for standardizing the Intelligence Test for Primary School Children (ITPSC) in 1926. It took them more than 20 years to collect data from different parts of China and create the test because of the Northern Expedition Army War, the Japanese invasion and the Anti-Japanese War, and the Civil War. It was very difficult for Ai and his colleagues to collect data from different places. Sometimes they had to spend one or two years traveling from one place to another. Finally, more than 30,000 subjects were tested, and the ITPSC test was published by the Commercial Press in 1948.

Chinese psychologists translated, revised, and developed some other intelligence or ability tests, such as the English Test, Group Intelligence Test, Daily Knowledge Test for Primary School Students, Arithmetic Word Problem Test for Primary School Students, Silent Reading Ability Tests (for Primary and Secondary School Students), Method of Intelligence Test (Chen, 1927), Measurement of Mental Development of Children (Fei, 1927), Mechanical Intelligence Test, Non-Verbal Intelligence Test, National Survey Test for Primary School Students, Career Intelligence Test (Zou, 1927), Intelligence Test for the Popular Schools in City (Lai, 1928), Five Item Test, American Army Intelligence Test, Merrill-Palmer Scale (Xiao, 1936), Public School Test in Cities, and Drawing A Person Test (Xiao, 1935), and so on during that period of time.[1]

Intelligence tests nearly disappeared during the 30 years following 1949 because of political reasons (the influence of the former Soviet Union and of the Cultural Revolution in mainland China (Song & Zhang, 1987, p. 10). The study of intelligence and intelligence tests was not revived until 1978 when China started its new policy of reformation and openness. Chinese psychologists began to revise and develop intelligence tests again. Some intelligence and ability tests that were revised or developed in mainland China after 1978 are summarized and listed in Table 11.1

Most of the intelligence tests used in China were revised from foreign tests, and although some of them, especially culture-relevant tests, were changed a lot in contents. A few intelligence tests were developed by Chinese psychologists themselves under the guidance of their own theories of intelligence. For example, Zha, a developmentalist from the Institute of Psychology, Chinese Academy of Sciences, and her colleagues think that memory, observation, analogy, and creative thinking, as well as non-intellectual personality traits, are the most important components in human intelligence. They developed the Cognitive Ability Test for Identifying Supernormal Children (CATISC), which includes short-term and long-term memory, numerical, verbal, and figural analog reasoning, observation, and creative thinking sub-tests. Meanwhile, they developed a questionnaire to investigate children's non-intellectual personality traits. The CATISC test is special because it includes creative thinking and non-intellectual personality traits, which

---

[1] The author did not find all of the tests listed here. Most of the tests listed here are cited from an advertisement on the back cover of the book, *Chinese-Binet Intelligence Test* (Lu, 1927).

TABLE 11.1. *Some Intelligence Tests Revised and/or Developed in Mainland China after 1978*

Name of Test	Developer	YOV*	Reviser	YRV*
Denver Developmental Screening Test (DDST)	Frankenburg & Dodds	1967	Song & Zhu et al.	1978
Chinese-Binet Intelligence Test (3rd Version)	Binet & Simon	1916	Wu	1980
Peabody Picture Vocabulary Test (PPVT)	L. M. Dunn	1965	Feng et al.	1980
Non-Verbal Intelligence Test	Wu	1980		
Wechsler Intelligence Scale for Children-Revised (WISC-R)	Wechsler	1974	Lin & Zhang et al.	1981
Wechsler Memory Scale (WMS)	Wechsler	1945	Gong et al.	1981
Wechsler Adult Intelligence Scale (WAIS)	Wechsler	1955	Gong et al.	1982
Wechsler Preschool and Primary Scale of Intelligence (WPPSI)	Wechsler	1967	Guo, Wang, & Song et al.	1983
Wechsler Preschool and Primary Scale of Intelligence (WPPSI)	Wechsler	1967	Gong et al.	1984
Clinical Memory Scale	Xu et al.	1984		
Goodenough-Harris Drawing Test	F. L. Goodenough & D. B. Harris	1963	Zhang	1986
Cognitive Ability Test for Identifying Supernormal Children (CATISC)	Zha	1986		
Mental Development Test for Infants	Fan	1988		
Chinese-Wechsler Intelligence Scale for Children (WISC-C)	Wechsler	1974	Gong & Cai	1993
Intelligent Intelligence Test System	He & Li et al.	1994		
Group Intelligence Test for Children	Wechsler	1974	Jin	1994
Chang-An Group Intelligence Test	Gong & Wang et al.	1996		
Snijders-Oomen Non-Verbal Intelligence Test	Snijders, Oomen	1989	Zhang & Gong et al	1997
Chinese Infant Intelligence Scale	Tang & Gong et al.	1998		
Group Intelligence Test for Army College Students	Liu & Miao et al.	2001		
Psychological Synthesized Scale for Children-Revised (PSSC-R)	?	?	Zhou & Fang	2001
Basic Cognitive Ability Test (BCAT)	Li & Liu	2001		

* YOV stands for year of original version; and YRV, for year of revised version.

are not included in conservative intelligence tests. The CATISC has two versions suitable for young and school-aged children. The version for young children is suitable for children from 3 to 6 years old, and the version for school-aged children is for children from 7 to 14 years old. (Zha, 1986, 1990, 1993; Shi & Xu, 1998; Shi & Zha, 2000). Another test is the Basic Cognitive Ability Test (BCAT), which was recently developed by a life-span developmentalist and colleagues from the Institute of Psychology (Li, Liu, & Li, 2001).The BCAT test was developed according to the life-span development theory. It is suitable for individuals from 10 to 90 years old. It is called a basic cognitive ability test because the processing time of some basic cognitive processes, such as recognition reaction time, mental arithmetic, mental rotation of Chinese characters, digital working memory, two-character-word recognition, three-digit-number recognition, and no-meaning geometric figures recognition are emphasized.

RECENT RESEARCH AND THEORIES OF INTELLIGENCE

Research

Most research on intelligence in the last two decades has been conducted on special samples, such as gifted children, abnormal children, and children with special diseases. Only a few studies were on common concepts of intelligence. Among them, the studies conducted by Zhang and Wu in Beijing and Yang and Sternberg in Taipei are representative (Zhang & Wu, 1994; Yang & Sternberg, 1997). Both were designed to investigate the common conception or implicit theory as indicated by Sternberg (1985) or the naive theory of intelligence of Chinese people. The research methods of the two studies are similar to the method used by Sternberg and his colleagues to study people's conception of intelligence in the United States in 1981 (Sternberg et al., 1981).

There are some differences between the results of studies conducted in Beijing and Taiwan. With subjects from Beijing in their study, Zhang and Wu (1994) found that there were three categories in Chinese people's conception of intelligence. The three categories are active-thinking, including logical thinking, the ability to accept new things, creativity, and ability of adaptation; processing characteristics, including curiosity, insight, memory, imagination, and self-confidence; and non-intellectual characteristics, including energy, sense of humor, independence, expressiveness, and dexterity in operation. With subjects from Taiwan in their study, Yang and Sternberg found that five factors existed in Chinese people's conception of intelligence. The five factors are (1) general cognitive ability, (2) interpersonal intelligence, (3) intrapersonal intelligence, (4) intellectual self-promotion, and (5) intellectual self-effacement (Yang & Sternberg, 1997).

It is obvious that people from Taiwan emphasize more interpersonal and intrapersonal factors in intelligence conception than do people from Beijing. The reasons for such differences seem complicated. Intrapersonal factors were neglected by people from Beijing because Confucianism was strictly criticized or beaten down after 1949, especially during the time of the Cultural Revolution. However, Confucianism is enjoying a renaissance now in mainland China. Many classic books of Confucianism and books on Confucianism have been published.

Theories

Theories about human intelligence in China have a very long history, but they belong to the category of philosophy in ancient China. Modern theories of intelligence were developed in China in the early 20th century. The notion about intelligence came from the Western world. For example, when Binet-Simon's Intelligence Test was introduced into China, the Western notion about intelligence, "intelligence is learning ability," was imported, too. Meanwhile, Woodworth's concept of human intelligence made a great impact on Chinese psychology at that time. Woodworth (1925) suggested that intelligence is the wholeness of human innate mental constitution, including reflection, instinct, emotion, feeling (or affection), perception, and attention. According to Woodworth, the human being is an innately intelligent animal.

The mainstream of study methods of human intelligence during that period of time was psychometrics. Intelligence tests were widely used to investigate the distribution and development of intelligence of Chinese children. But some psychologists were interested in studying the intelligence of eminent individuals in the history of China with historiometrics. For example, with historiometrics Lin (1939) studied the intelligence and achievements of 34 eminent Chinese from the Tang and Song Dynasty. In his book, Lin (1939) mentioned Cox's study of 300 eminent geniuses born between 1450 and 1850, but he did not know Cox's work when he began his study. It is noteworthy that no names of scientists, technologists or mathematicians were listed in Lin's study, even though there were numerous scientists, technologists, and mathematicians who contributed a lot to the development of society in the history of China. It was not because of the bias of sample selection but because of the Chinese people's deep distrust of science and technology. It reflected that science and technology, as well as scientists and technologists, were not respected in periods of history in China. Furthermore, it reflected the Chinese people's theory of intelligence developed with the influence of culture. That was *xue er you ze shi* (study hard and good then be officer).

Study on human intelligence stopped for some 30 years during the time of 1949 to 1978, as previously mentioned. But it was revived in 1978. Since then, several intelligence theories have been introduced into China. A series called *References for Teaching Child Psychology*, edited by the famous child psychologist, Zhu Zhixian, was published in early 1980. The series includes six books. In two of them, *Basic Theories of the Psychology of Child Development* and *History of Child Psychology*, respected psychologists such as Alfred Binet, John Watson, Sigmund Freud, Henri P. H. Wallon, Leon S. Vygotsky, Jean Piaget, and J. S. Bruner, as well as their theories of intelligence, are included (Zhu, 1982a, 1982b). The theories of Piaget and Vygotsky have been widely introduced in China. Piaget's theory about children's cognitive development had a great impact on developmental psychology in China. In the late 1980s, Guilford's (1986) 3-D intelligence structure model was widespread in China. Meanwhile, Cattell's liquid-crystal theory of intelligence was introduced, too (Cattell, 1963; Baltes, 1986). In the 1990s, Gardner's (1983) multiple intelligences theory; Sternberg's (1988) triarchic theory of intelligence, practical intelligence theory (Sternberg & Wagner, 1986), and successful intelligence theory (Sternberg, 1996); and Das's (1994) PASS (Planning, Attention, Simultaneous, Successive) theory were introduced into China. It seems that Gardner's theory has had more impact on the Chinese educational world and Sternberg's theory has had more impact on the Chinese academic research world.

After 1978, a few Chinese psychologists devoted all their attention to intelligence study. They attempted to investigate the nature of intelligence theoretically and practically (Wu, 1980; Lin, 1991). Wu Tianmin was one of these psychologists. She indicated that the intelligence test itself is useless for understanding the nature of intelligence, although she was involved in revising and developing intelligence tests after the 1930s and was very famous in the field of intelligence measurement in China. She criticized the previous componential theories of intelligence and argued, "We can hardly expect that intelligence can be

explained with any theory of a bundle of abilities or a bundle of tiny frag-
ments, for intelligence is a unitary psychological phenomenon" (Wu,
1980, p. 265). She suggested that we should realize the nature of the
human mind in order to understand the nature of intelligence and indicated, "Psychological activities are the production or function of the
activities of nerve system, but after the psychological activities are activated they can control the next step's neuron activities" (Wu, 1980,
p. 261). From the perspective of neuropsychology, she defined human intelligence as a coordinating reflection of the activities of the neurons
that are characterized by intention, wideness, deepness, and flexibility.
And the intentional psychological activities are the results of certain
cortical activities and interactions with corresponding cortical activities
(Wu, 1980).

No matter how Wu criticized the componential theories, some
Chinese psychologists thought that human intelligence consisted of several abilities. Zhu Zhixian was one of these componential theorists. According to Zhu, intelligence is composed of different abilities, such as observation, memory, thinking, and imagination. The core of intelligence
is abstract thinking ability. (Zhu, 1989). His student, Lin Chongde, put
two extra components, language and practical skill, into the structure
of intelligence (Lin & Xin, 1996).

As a developmentalist, Liu Fan studied intelligence from the perspective of cognitive psychology. He constructed a cognitive model of
intelligence (see Figure 11.1). He suggested in his model that perception,

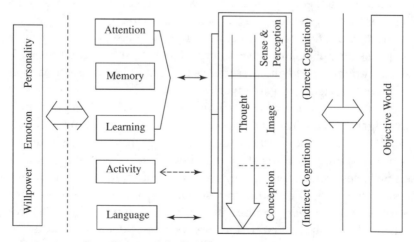

FIGURE 11.1. Cognitive model of intelligence (Liu, 1998).

image, and conception were three main components of cognition. Perception is direct cognition, and image and conception are indirect cognitions. Thinking is a very complicated mental process. All cognitive activities are related to thinking or belong to the category of thinking except the perception of neonates. Hence, thinking runs throughout the whole cognitive process. Attention, memory, and learning are different facets of cognition. Actions and language are not only closely related to cognition, but they are also the way in which cognition reflects the real world. Language is related mainly to conception, but emotion, willingness, and personality traits work as control factors to cognition (Liu, 1998).

Rather than from the perspective of psychology, Shi and Xu looked at the nature of intelligence from the perspectives of biology, physics, and chemistry (Xu & Shi, 1992; Shi & Xu, 1999). The fact that the mind is the function of the brain's or nerve system's activity is not doubted. To keep the brain or nerve system alive and active, energy is essential. In fact, the brain will die without energy, and, of course, the function of the brain will disappear. Any action of an object needs energy or has potential, and the action of the brain is not an exception. According to the conservation law of energy, energy will never be lost but changes from one form to another. Some parts of energy that an individual obtained from his or her surroundings are transmitted into bio-energy for the growth of the body. Some parts are used for the actions of the brain or nervous system. We know that the energy consumed in the action of the brain, such as for electrical signals along neurons and chemical reactions between synapses, will not be lost but will be changed or transmitted. The problem intriguing researchers is, "Where does it go?" Shi and Xu assumed that it is transmitted into "mental energy" (Xu & Shi, 1992). Mental energy is the energy used especially for mental activities. They further argued that mental energy is the potential of intelligence. There are two forms of intelligence: One is implicit or invisible and happens in the brain. The other one is explicit or visible and can be observed. The implicit one is the base of the explicit one. And the explicit one is always less than the implicit one, except in an ideal condition where the explicit one is equal to the implicit one. As there is not an ideal condition for human beings to live in the real world, the full potential of one's intelligence is not properly measured, at least until now. What we mostly measured or discussed are explicit forms of intelligence expressed in different ways in the practical world. As energy can be accumulated, mental energy can be accumulated, too. Then it is assumed that intelligence can be accumulated. Consequently, achievement in any aspect or field is not the result of intelligence but the result of intelligence accumulation.

This theory was employed to explain the relationship between intelligence and creativity (Shi, 1995). Shi suggested that some individuals with high IQs did not have high creative achievement not because they did not have creativity but because their intelligence is not expressed in the "proper" or expected way or because their intelligence is not accumulated enough to fulfill the creative work that is expected.

CONCLUSION

In summary, Chinese people's conception of intelligence can be illustrated with four Chinese idioms.

1. *Qin neng bu zhuo*. This idiom means that *diligence* makes people intelligent or smart. It emphasizes the importance of one's effort or endeavor. In other words, the endeavor is one component in the structure of intelligence.
2. *You zhi zhe, shi jing cheng*. Where there is a will, there is a way. Human willingness is emphasized extremely. The willingness here can be looked at as intrinsic motivation. So, intrinsic motivation is looked at as another component of intelligence in a Confucian perspective of intelligence.
3. *San ge chou pi jiang, sai guo zhu ge liang*. Two heads are better than one. It indicates that the intelligence of different people can be put together and can be accumulated. Combined with the first idiom, Chinese people think that not only can the intelligence of a single individual can be accumulated, but intelligence of different people can be accumulated, too.
4. *San bai liu shi hang, hang hang chu zhuang yuan*. Where there is an occupation, there is a number one scholar. It indicates there are many possibilities for people to be successful. Or it indicates that human intelligence can be expressed in a variety of ways. This includes the multiple meaning of human intelligence.

References

Ai, W. (1948). *Ability test for elementary school children*, pp. 2–3. Shanghai: Commercial Press (in Chinese).

Baltes, P. (1986). Life-span developmental psychology (F. Liu, trans.). *Developments in Psychology, 3*, 1–15.

Binet, A., & Simon, Th. (1922). *The measurement of the mental development of the child* (translated into Chinese by Fei Pei Jie). Shanghai: Commercial Press.

Cao, X., & Gao, E. (2001). *Dream of the red chamber*. In Chinese classic books series (multimedia version). Beijing: Beijing Yinguan Electronic Publishing (in Chinese).

Cattell, R. B. (1963). Theory of fluid and crystal intelligence: A critical experiment. *Journal of Educational Psychology, 54*, 1–22.

Chen, H. (1927). *Method of intelligence test*. Shanghai: Commercial Press (in Chinese).

Dai, D., & Dai, S. (2001). *Manners – Notes of learning*, Vol. 16. In Chinese classic books series (multimedia version). Beijing: Beijing Yinguan Electronic Publishing (in Chinese).

Das, J. P. (1994). *Assessment of cognitive processes.*Boston: Allyn & Bacon.

EC (Encyclopaedia of China) (1985). *Encyclopaedia of China*, pp. 202–206. Beijing: Publishing House of Encyclopaedia of China (in Chinese).

Fan, C. (Ed.). (1988). *Manual of mental growth test for infants*. Beijing: Tuanjie Publishing House (in Chinese).

Fei, P. J. (1927). *Measurement of mental development of children*. Shanghai: Commercial Press (in Chinese).

Gardner, H. (1983). *Frames of mind – The theory of multiple intelligences*. New York: Basic Books.

Ge, H. (283–363). *Anecdote of Western Capital*, Vol. 2. See Li, Y., & Lu, D. (Eds.) (1988). *Dictionary of Chinese idiom*, p. 1095. Chengdu: Sichuan Dictionary Publishing House (in Chinese).

Gong, J., Wang, X., Wang, J., Cai, T., Wang, Q., & Gong, Y. (1996). Changsha-Anshan group intelligence tests (C-AGIT) – Norms for middle school students in Changsha city. *Chinese Journal of Clinical Psychology, 4*(4), 197–201 (in Chinese).

Gong, Y., & Cai, T. (1993). *Manual of C-WISC*. Changsha: Hunan Map Publishing House (in Chinese).

Guilford, J. P. (1986). *Creative talents, their nature, uses and development*. New York: Bearly Limited.

He, J., Li, G., & Li, J. (1994). Design and implementation of an intelligent intelligence test system. *Journal of South China Normal University* (Natural Science Edition), *3*, 71–77 (in Chinese).

Lai, C. S. (1928). *Intelligence test for the popular schools in city*. Shanghai: National Association of Mass Education Movement (in Chinese).

Li, D., Liu, C., & Li, G. (2001). The construction of "basic cognitive capacity test" and its standardization. *Acata Psychologica Sinica, 33*(5), 453–460 (in Chinese).

Li, Y., & Lu, D. (Eds.). (1986). *Literary quotation of Chinese idiom.* Chengdu: Sichuan Dictionary Publishing House (in Chinese).

Lin, C. T. (1939). *A historiometric study of thirty four eminent Chinese*. Shanghai: Commercial Press (in Chinese).

Lin, C. T. (1980). A sketch on the methods of mental testing in ancient China. *Acta Psychologica Sinica, 1*, 75–80 (in Chinese).

Lin, C., & Xin, T. (1996). *Cultivation of intelligence*. Hangzhou: Zhejiang People's Publishing House (in Chinese).

Lin, C. T. (1991). Intelligence. In *Encyclopaedia of China – Psychology* (multimedia version). Beijing: Publishing House of Encyclopaedia of China (in Chinese).

Liu, F. (1998). On issues of cognitive development. In M. Zhu & Z. Xu (Eds.), *Selected collection of Liu Fan psychology*. (pp. 109–127). Beijing: Economic Press of China (in Chinese).

Liu, X., & Miao, D., Wang, G., An, C., Pan, C., Wang, W., & Li, X. (2001). Reliability and validity of group intelligence test for army college students. *Journal of Fourth Mil. Med. University*, 22(19), 1821–1824 (in Chinese).

Lu, Z. (1924). *Chinese-Binet intelligence test*. Shanghai: Commercial Press (in Chinese).

Mencius. (2001). *Mencius*, Vol. 9. In Chinese classic books series (multimedia version). Beijing: Beijing Yinguan Electronic Publishing (in Chinese).

Shi, J. (1995). A system model of creativity. *Developments in Psychology*, 5, 1–5 (in Chinese).

Shi, J., & Xu, F.(1998). The developmental trends and issues of study on supernormal children in China. *ACTA PSYCHOLOGICA SINICA*, 1998(3), 298–305 (in Chinese).

Shi, J., & Xu, F. (1999). *Discovering gifted children*. Beijing: China Esperanto Publishing House (in Chinese).

Shi, J., & Zha, Z. (2000). Psychological research on and education of gifted and talented children in China. In K. Heller, F. Moenks, R. Sternberg, & R. Subotnik (Eds.), *International handbook of research and development of giftedness and talent* (2nd ed., (pp. 757–764).Oxford: Pergamon Press.

Song, W., & Zhang, Y. (1987). *Psychology measurement*. Beijing: Science Press (in Chinese).

Sternberg, R. J. (1985). Implicit theories of intelligence, creativity, and wisdom. *Journal of Personality and Social Psychology, 49*, 607–627.

Sternberg, R. J. (1988). *The triarchic mind: A new theory of human intelligence*. New York: Viking.

Sternberg, R. J. (1996). *Successful intelligence*. New York: Simon & Schuster.

Sternberg, R. J., & Wagner, R. K. (Eds.). (1986). *Practical intelligence - Nature and origins of competence in the everyday world*. New York: Cambridge University Press.

Sternberg, R. J., Conway, B. E., Ketron, J. L., & Bernstein, M. (1981). People's conceptions of Intelligence. *Journal of Personality and Social Psychology, 41*(1), 37–55.

Stevenson, H. W., & Stigler, J. W. (1992). *Learning gap*. New York: Simon & Schuster.

SWSP (Strategies of the Warring States Period, Vol. 1, Strategies of Qin) (2001). In Chinese classic books series (multimedia version). Beijing: Beijing Yinguan Electronic Publishing (in Chinese).

Tang, Q., Gong, Y., Dai, X., Chen, M., & Cai, T. (1998). Development of intelligence scale for Chinese young children: II validity study. *Chinese Journal of Clinical Psychology, 6*(2), 76–84 (in Chinese).

Terman, L. M. (1924). *The measurement of intelligence* (Hua Chao trans.). Shanghai: Commercial Press.

Woodworth, R. S. (1925). *Psychology: A study of mental life*. New York: Columbia University Press (X. C. Xie, trans.)

Wu, T. M. (1936). *Second revision of Chinese-Binet intelligence test*. Shanghai: Commercial Press (in Chinese).

Wu, T. M. (1980). The nature of intelligence. *Acata Psychologica Sinica, 3*, 259–266 (in Chinese).

Xiao, X. (1936). *The Merrill-Palmer Scale* revised by Xiao Rong. Shanghai: Commercial Press (in Chinese).

Xiao, X. (1935). Revision of Drawing a Person Test. *Chinese Educational World, 23*(6), 59–68 (in Chinese).

Xu, F., & Shi, J. (1992). *Development of fetus and its education*. Beijing: Corresponding University of Institute of Psychology, Chinese Academy of Sciences (in Chinese).

Xun, Zi. (2001). Xun Zi, Vol. 1. In Chinese classic books series (multimedia version). Beijing: Beijing Yinguan Electronic Publishing (in Chinese).

Yan, Z. (2001). Yan's family rules – Piece of conduct. In Chinese classic books series (multimedia version). Beijing: Beijing Yinguan Electronic Publishing (in Chinese).

Yang, X. (1994). *The history of Chinese psychological thought*. Nanchang: Jiangxi Education Publishing House.

Yang, S.-Y. (2001). Conceptions of wisdom among Taiwanese Chinese. *Journal of Cross-Cultural Psychology. 32*(6), 662–680.

Yang, S.-Y., & Sternberg, R. J. (1997). Taiwanese Chinese people's conceptions of intelligence. *Intelligence, 25*(1), 21–36.

Yuan, L., & Shen, T. (Eds.). (1981). *Literary quotation of Chinese idiom*. Shenyang: Liaoning People's Publishing House (in Chinese).

Zha, Z. (1986). *Manual of cognitive ability test for identifying supernormal children*. Beijing: Institute of Psychology, Chinese Academy of Sciences (in Chinese).

Zha, Z. (1990). Study on gifted and talented children in China for ten years. *Acta Psychologica Sinica, 2*, 115–118 (in Chinese).

Zha, Z. (1993). *Psychology of supernormal children*. Beijing: People's Publishing House.

Zhang, H., & Wu, Z. (1994). A survey of the Beijing public's views on intelligence. *Psychological Science, 17*(2), 65–81, 127 (in Chinese).

Zhang, H., Gong, W., Sun, Y., & Tian, X. (1997). Revising Snijders-Oomen Nonverbal Intelligence Test–Revision in China. *Psychological Science, 20*(2), 97–103 (120) (in Chinese).

Zhang, J. (1986). *Manual of drawing a person test*. Beijing: Beijing Institute of Pediatrics (in Chinese).

Zhang, Q. (Ed.). (2001). *Comprehensive collection of stories of Chinese idiom*. Nanjing: Jiangsu People's Publishing House (in Chinese).

Zhu, Z. (Ed.). (1989). *Dictionary of psychology*. Beijing: Beijing Normal University Press (in Chinese).

Zhu, Z. (Ed.). (1982a). *Essays on the history of child psychology*. Beijing: Beijing Normal University Press (in Chinese).

Zhu, Z. (Ed.). (1982b). *Basic theories of child psychological development*. Beijing: Beijing Normal University Press (in Chinese).

Zou, S. (1927). *Career intelligence test*. Shanghai: Commercial Press (in Chinese).

12

Similar Thoughts under Different Stars

Conceptions of Intelligence in Australia

Lazar Stankov

To understand the development of psychology in Australia, one needs to be cognizant of the political and social history of this country.[1] The most salient aspects relate to its geography and cultural links to the "old world." It is usually assumed that Australia was discovered by Captain James Cook and first settled by the British upon the arrival of the First Fleet of eight ships in 1788. This fleet brought convicts from England, because the American War of Independence had signaled the need to seek a new penal colony for the Empire. To this day, some citizens of Australia think of themselves either as descendants of "convicts" or "squatters" (free settlers). The six colonies that were formed during the 1800s were united in 1901 despite "the tyranny of distance." (The island-continent is approximately the size of Europe or the continental United States, and its total population today is comparable to that of California.) Independence did not diminish Australia's attachment to the "mother country England" and its king and, when World War I started, many young Australians enlisted to be sent to fight at Gallipoli in Turkey, and later on, to France. The early European inhabitants of Australia behaved in a way that was similar to those of other colonizing powers. For example, since the very beginning of settlement, the Aborigines were denied the right to ownership of land, and in fact, these native Australians were not given a democratic right to vote until a referendum that was

---

[1] The first part of the title of this chapter is a paraphrase of the motto of the University of Sydney, which reads, *"Sidere mens eadem mutato."* Note, however, that there exist somewhat different literal interpretations of this motto.

I am grateful to Stanton Bongers for his help in working on this chapter.

held as recently as 1967. British influence remained strong until the beginning of World War II when Americans became the main anti-Japanese fighting force in the Pacific. Since that time, American and British influences on the way of life in Australia have been about equal. The influx of non-English-speaking migrants from Europe immediately after the war is nowadays seen as instrumental in generating the cosmopolitan and multicultural feel of contemporary urban centers and, perhaps, in diminishing British influence.

Being a relatively small country in terms of the size of its population, the use of English language was a blessing for the development of any branch of science, including psychology. Textbooks written by the distant "cousins" living in the northern hemisphere were available, and the first course on mental tests and the psychology of mental deficiency (later called *psychometrics*) was introduced at the University of Sydney in 1924. O'Neil (1987) points out that although Australian psychologists have not generated any important wide-ranging theories analogous to psychoanalysis, Gestalt theory, or behaviorism, their concern with the patterns of individual differences in abilities and intelligence has led to significant contributions to psychometric assessment and statistical analysis. These contributions were technically sound and "sometimes quite ingenious." Australian work provided evidence that has confirmed, added to, or corrected related overseas findings. This is a fair assessment of the overall contribution of Australians to psychology.

The existence of a shared language and small local market in psychology has also contributed to the tendency of Australians to publish their best products overseas – in America or Britain. A few of them also settled and made their mark on psychology in these countries.

Because Australia is the largest country in the South Pacific that has traditional ties with other nations in the region, the developments in psychology here have affected other countries as well. Particularly strong was the influence on Papua New Guinea and (somewhat less) on New Zealand. This review will focus on the situation in Australia since these other countries, being smaller, have less developed psychological services.[2]

---

[2] It is necessary to mention here the work of New Zealand political scientist and philosopher J. Flynn. His contribution to psychology and research on intelligence is important since it has documented significant generational increases in IQ scores, especially since the end of World War II (see Dickens & Flynn, 2001). It is difficult to reconcile such massive changes with the biological explanations of individual and group differences in intelligence.

DEFINITIONS AND THEORIES OF INTELLIGENCE

Given the developments just described, it is perhaps of little surprise that no unique theory of intelligence emerged in Australia. However, practical demands and the scientific interests of those in teaching positions have affected the overall landscape of research in intelligence in this country. Three broad theoretical stances in studies of intelligence in Australia can be discerned. These are:

Traditional Psychometric

Because several prominent early Australian "pilgrims" received their degrees in England, some under the supervision of Spearman, the psychometric tradition has been rather strong. Earlier in the last century, around 25% of all psychological publications were devoted to human abilities, more than to any other area in psychology. General factor theory, however, is not the dominant view. This is because practical needs related to strong vocational guidance services, schooling demands, and the armed forces have embraced the multiple aptitude test batteries that were influenced by the Thurstone's theory of primary mental abilities. Similar to the situation elsewhere, both camps – multiple intelligences and general factor theory – are represented about equally in Australia today.

Cross-Cultural and Developmental

One of the earliest attempts to study intelligence of indigenous people was carried out in Australia by Porteus in 1914 (Porteus, 1965). Some researchers showed similar interests in Aboriginal cognition later on last century. Their approach was to apply traditional psychometric tests of intelligence to Aborigines. The outcome reinforced the prevailing view of severe deficit. A good review of this work is provided by Klich (1988). Perhaps to move away from the emphasis on deficit, a group of researchers employed Piagetian tasks in studies of Aboriginal cognition. Others became interested in studying cognitive processes of Asian societies, frequently with the emphasis on psycholinguistic aspects of cognition (D. Keats, 1979).

This work in cross-cultural psychology has crystallized the position that "When research is conducted, respect for indigenous perceptions of priority social needs, construction of social issues, and methods of social inquiry can only be achieved if indigenous people are doing it or if they are in meaningful partnership with non-indigenous researchers who are doing it." (Davidson, 1998, p. 49). In other words, intelligence should not only be studied "in context" but also with the co-ownership of the research problems and procedures by the people who are being studied.

Biological

This approach is relatively new in Australian psychology, with its origins dating back to the 1970s. Its main emphasis today is on the use of inspection time that is sometimes treated as *the* measure of intelligence. It also employs electroencephalography (EEG) and visual imaging techniques. Some recent work based on a considerable amount of data from samples of twins looks at the genetic determination of elementary cognitive components of fluid intelligence. This approach is based on the belief that full understanding of psychological phenomena can be achieved through the study of lower-order processes that are physiological and physical in character. The position is decidedly reductionist.

There is a tension between proponents of cross-cultural view, who tend to subscribe to the social constructivist position, and those taking a biological stance, who claim that what they do is the only "true scientific" approach in psychology (Butler, 1998; Bates & Stough, 2000; Stankov, 1998, 2000). For the most part, again, the debate is not uniquely Australian but reflects existing tensions between these opposing positions elsewhere. Within the Australian context, however, the direct influence of the cross-cultural approach to the study of intelligence appears to have diminished over the past two decades.

HISTORY

According to the account of Porteus (1965), he was taken to the mission station in South Australia in 1915 where he administered Porteus Maze Test to 28 Aboriginal children. Prior to this event, he used the same test, consisting of increasingly more complex paper-and-pencil mazes, to assess the abilities of "mental defectives" in the city of Melbourne. The test was supposed to measure foresight, planning, and sustained attention, which were not adequately sampled by the Binet scale. The outcome produced a mean mental age of 9 years and 9 months for Aboriginal children whose mean chronological age was 10 years and 2 months. Thus, the average IQ was about 96 – unusually good for a racial group that was in his experience universally considered to be among the least intelligent of mankind. Later on, he tested the hypothesis that Aborigines perform equally well as non-Aboriginal high school students on tests of spatial abilities. Paradoxically, until the very end of his life Porteus retained his belief in "biologically determined inferiority" of Aborigines even though he advocated high belief in Aboriginal "social intelligence" that is evidenced in achievements in artistic, inventive, and general living skills.

A student of Spearman, G. E. Phillips, published the first revision of the Binet scale in Australia in 1924. His revision was based on a sample of 3,346 Sydney schoolchildren from 5 to 14 years of age, and it was generally regarded as work of a high quality. Another important development in the history of research in intelligence in Australia took place in 1930, with the formation of the Australian Council for Educational Research (ACER). This institution, particularly under the leadership of K. S. Cunningham, also placed great emphasis on normative studies of intelligence (Connell, 1980). Many people who worked within the ACER provided psychological services to the Australian Armed Forces during World War II and subsequently became involved in rehabilitation and vocational guidance services. Of course, the work of psychologists within the military continued in a significant way with the Australian Army Psychology Corps being a uniformed service and other branches of the Armed Forces employing civilians.

Although a large amount of work was carried out in the mainstream psychometric tradition in Australia, there have been two developments that either have made impact beyond the "fatal shore" of Australia or are unique to this country and therefore should be underscored. First, there has been significant work in statistical aspects of psychometrics, with J. Keats' (1951) early development of the statistical theory of objective test scores and McDonald's work on non-linear factor analysis and structural equation modeling procedures (McDonald, 1964, 1978). Second, the Queensland Test (McElwain & Kearney, 1970) was an important attempt to develop a measure that can be used with tribal Aborigines, non-English speakers, and the deaf. The test employs a "performance" mode of presentation and can be given using vernacular instructions and mime. Scores on this test have shown high correlation with the degree of acculturation to white society, and therefore separate norms were developed for tribal, fringe-dwelling, and urban-dwelling

Aborigines. This, of course, underscores the role of environment in cognitive abilities.

CURRENT RESEARCH

Although research into the intelligence of Aborigines was prominent in the past, contemporary work in this area has all but ceased. The reasons for this situation are not entirely clear – perhaps interest in the topic has evaporated, or there might have been a subtle political pressure to stop this kind of research. Those interested in working with Aborigines have shifted the emphasis to the examination of social conditions and value systems within the indigenous societies (see Fogarty & White, 1994).

The most significant current research efforts can be classified with respect to three main lines of inquiry: (1) the role of mental speed and inspection time in intelligence, (2) research broadly guided by the theory of fluid and crystallized intelligence, and (3) intelligence studies with developmental overtones. Curiously, although these different topics have been associated with different laboratories, there has been a tendency toward cross-fertilization, and the three areas, for the most part, now represent differences in emphasis.

AUSTRALIAN RESEARCH LINKING MENTAL SPEED TO INTELLIGENCE

The measurement of inspection time (IT) started in the early 1970s after a Cambridge graduate, D. Vickers, took a teaching position at the University of Adelaide. He developed a theoretical rationale for IT and the procedures for its measurement. These were first described in a paper that also reported three experiments from the just completed doctoral thesis by his student Ted Nettelbeck (Vickers, Nettelbeck, & Wilson, 1972). This procedure involves the presentation of a couple of unequal-length vertical lines joined on top by a horizontal line. This stimulus is followed quickly by a mask. The time period between the stimulus and mask is varied and IT "score" is the smallest time interval for a correct detection of the line that is shorter. The first report of the correlation between IT and intelligence was published by Nettelbeck and Lally (1976). This initial work was followed by over 90 articles, and an entire issue of the journal *Intelligence* in 2001 was devoted to the same topic to acknowledge 25 years of this line of research. Some, including this writer, were surprised by the amount of attention devoted to IT. After all, this is a perceptual task, and there have been many perceptual tasks (e.g., field-dependence measures, perceptual illusions, critical flicker frequency) that have been correlated with intelligence and have produced comparable correlations. In the most recent analysis by Grudnik and Kranzler (2001), the average correlation between IT and IQ is −.30, which becomes −.51 when corrected for the presumed artifactual effects.

Perhaps the reason for IT's popularity derives from the fact that, at the time of its first appearance in 1970s, there was a renewal of interest in the role of mental speed in intelligence, with A. Jensen being the prime mover. Because the original interpretation of the findings with IT emphasized a speed component, IT and reaction time data based on Hick's paradigm were used jointly in support of this interpretation. It appears that enthusiasm for IT-IQ research was more pronounced among the British aficionados of IT (e.g., C. Brand and I. Deary). In contrast, Australians seem to have been divided. A couple of them (T. Bates and C. Stough) seem to share the same amount of enthusiasm as the British (see, e.g., Stough et al., 2001). But Nettelbeck (2001), who remains the main figure in IT research, has always been cautious and thoughtful in his interpretation. Thus, his most recent "personal interpretation" of the correlation between inspection time and psychometric abilities points out that evidence does not support earlier claims that IT estimates the speed of a single process. Rather, "IT is probably sensitive both to focussed attentional capacities . . . and to decision processes, ongoing beyond mask onset, that monitor responding." Furthermore, he points out that in a young adult group, IT is correlated with the G_s (broad speediness) function, and, in the case of visual IT, to broad visualization (G_v) abilities. Contrary to the common assumption, in this group IT is not related to fluid intelligence (G_f).

As already indicated, IT is not the only measure of mental speed. There are several other well-known measures, including simple and choice reaction time, speed of test taking, perceptual speed, movement time, and the like. Australian researchers have looked at these as well. It is interesting that Brody (2001) ends his commentary on IT studies with the following comment: "It is still possible that multivariate research on information-processing skills will converge on a model that is isomorphic with the hierarchical model of psychometric indices of abilities. There may be several independent information-processing abilities that are correlated leading to a single ability (or a smaller subset of abilities) at a more general level of analysis. It might even be possible to align this model with the hierarchical model of psychometric abilities" (p. 540). He fails to cite, and therefore appears unaware, that Australian researchers have done exactly that by pointing to the factorially complex structure of mental speed. An entire recent issue of *Learning and Individual Differences* consists of a single paper containing precisely that information (Roberts & Stankov, 1999). This latter study did not include IT measures, and therefore it was impossible to ascertain the validity Brody's last speculation that, "It is still possible that we may come to believe that inspection time is an index of a singular information processing ability that plays a fundamental role in the development of intelligence." Maybe – but Roberts & Stankov's data point out that it is decision time calculated from several measures of mental speed that has *the* central role in linking mental speed to intelligence. For a long period of time, much of the work on IT was univariate, not multivariate. Unfortunately, as Brody implies in his commentary, interpretations prompted by univariate research have been the rule, and even today some writings on IT, particularly by the ardent supporters of biological interpretations of intelligence, sound like the author(s) believe that it is synonymous with intelligence. Furthermore, Stankov and Roberts (1997) argue that speed, however measured, although important in the structure of abilities, is not *the* basic process of intelligence, and Nettlebeck (2001) seems to concur with the spirit of this assessment.

Over the past several years, the Australian Research Council has provided resources for research into the genetics of intelligence. This work took advantage of the existence of the well-documented Twin Registry that was set up by Dr. Nick Martin in Brisbane, Queensland. The studies employed adolescent twin pairs who were given a computerized test of intelligence akin to Wechsler's scales and several elementary cognitive tasks, including measures of inspection time. Studies based on this research program are starting to appear in the literature (see Luciano et al., 2001). Curiously, the initial findings indicate that heritability estimates for inspection time measures are smaller than those for intelligence itself. If mental speed and inspection time are "basic" – that is, they reflect processes that are closer to physical aspects of the organism than IQ measures – one would expect that heritability estimates of inspection time will be higher than heritability of IQ. If replicated, this finding will indicate a need for further elaboration of the IQ-IT relationship and perhaps undermine current emphasis on the study of role of elementary cognitive tasks in intelligence.

AUSTRALIAN VARIATIONS ON THE THEORY OF FLUID AND
CRYSTALLIZED INTELLIGENCE

An active group of researchers in intelligence exists at the University
of Sydney. This group is influenced by the American, not British, psychometric tradition and has its immediate origins in Cattell and Horn's
ideas about fluid (G_f) and crystallized (G_c) abilities. There are four lines
of inquiry that set this work apart from the rest of research within this
theory of intelligence. These are:

The Role of Capacity Constructs in G_f

It is often claimed that G_f is perhaps the most important, some would
say quintessential, aspect of intelligence. It is also clear that *working
memory* is an important (but not necessarily the only relevant) aspect
of G_f (Kyllonen & Christal, 1990). Probably the earliest recorded factor
that was interpreted as a measure of working memory was the Temporal
Tracking factor, derived initially from research in the auditory domain
(Stankov & Horn, 1980). Tests that require keeping in mind, say, three
elements (e.g., letters, words, icons, or tones) and keeping track of how
many times each element appears in a sequential repeated presentation
of the same three elements – the so-called Mental Counting Tests – are
good measures of working memory.

   In our work (see Stankov, 1999), tasks that require an increasing number of mental steps to reach the solution to a problem are increasingly
more difficult, in the sense that fewer people can provide the correct answer to a problem. Importantly, they also show a systematic increase in
correlation between measures of performance on such tasks and measures of intelligence. The Swaps Test is a good example. In that test,
participants are shown three elements (e.g., icons, letters). The task is
to carry out pairwise mental permutations (swaps) of the elements. The
number of permutations vary from one to four. The answer consists in
choosing the alternative that depicts the order resulting from the series
of swaps. This task accords with the assumption that complex tests of
fluid reasoning require a larger number of mental operations than simple tasks (Stankov, 1999). However, this description of crucial processes
also suggests that the source of individual differences in fluid intelligence may not always depend on "capacity limitation," since memory demand is not high in the Swaps Test. In addition to the findings
with working memory, capacity limitations are also indicated by the

outcomes of competing tasks studies in which two cognitive tests are performed simultaneously.

Sensory/Perceptual Processes Within the Structure of Abilities

Abilities related to sensory modalities other than vision are poorly understood. The work in this area is partly motivated by a need to chart all important areas of cognition and partly by a hope that new psychometric abilities unique to a particular modality will be discovered. It is not motivated by the biological considerations that seem to be at the core of recent work on "elementary cognitive tasks." Three recent studies examined the structure of tactile, kinaesthetic, and olfactory abilities.

Tactile/Kinesthetic Abilities
Two studies of tactile/kinesthetic abilities have been carried out over the past several years. In the first study (Roberts et al., 1997) marker tests of G_f, G_c, and G_v were given together with several measures from the Halstead-Reitan Neuropsychological Test Battery and other measures of tactile and kinesthetic sensory and perceptual processes. An interesting finding emanating from this research was that complex Halstead-Reitan tasks could not be separated from broad visualization (Gv: see Pallier, Roberts, & Stankov, 2000). In other words, the processes involved in complex tactile and kinesthetic tasks seem to activate spatial visualization abilities during their performance. In the second study, two factors – one in the tactile and another in the kinesthetic domain – were found (Stankov, Seizova-Cajic, & Roberts, 2001). Tactile abilities require processing that depends on fine discrimination of pressure on the skin. Kinesthetic abilities involve the awareness of (passive) movements of upper limbs and the ability to visually recognize path that individuals follow while blindfolded.

What the Nose Knows?
The olfactory sensory modality appears to have remained largely uninvestigated. Evidence from within experimental cognitive psychology suggests that olfactory memory is distinct from memory in other sensory modalities. In a study by Danthiir et al. (2001), participants were tested with a battery of 12 psychometric tests, four putative cognitive olfactory tasks, and one olfactory discrimination measure. Results indicate the possible existence of an olfactory memory factor (OM), which is structurally independent of the established higher-order abilities

(G_f and G_v, G_c, and short-term acquisition and retrieval [SAR]), and un-related to simple olfactory sensitivity. The OM factor is defined by the olfactory tasks, all of which have a strong memory component. Impor-tantly, the tests defining this factor contain elements of memory systems that are ordinarily seen as separate – that is, short-term and long-term memory measures. In other words, Olfactory Memory appears unusual in the sense that it blurs the distinction between long-term and short-term memory.

Metacognitive Aspects of Intelligence

Self-confidence is measured by asking participants taking psychological tests to state, on a percentage scale, how sure they are that their answers to individual test items are correct. The average of confidence ratings over all items in the test is the self-confidence score. There is a good reason for expanding research into the area of self-confidence, which lies outside the traditional cognitive realm. Namely, it has been claimed that the difference between a confidence score and the actual percentage of correctly solved items provides information about metacognitive trait of self-monitoring. Typically, people tend to be overconfident – that is, their average confidence over all items is greater than the percentage of correctly solved items. The role of metacognition in intelligence is poorly understood at this stage.

There are two further reasons for the continued use of confidence ratings. First, the reliability of confidence ratings is high, certainly higher than the reliability of the accuracy scores from the same test, and only slightly lower than reliability of speed measures. A relatively stable characteristic is obviously being measured by the confidence ratings. Second, we have accumulated a considerable body of factor-analytic evidence suggesting that self-confidence is a replicable and well-defined trait, independent from other personality traits and also independent from measures of accuracy (Kleitman & Stankov, 2001; Stankov, 1999). In other words, self-confidence is a general trait that can be measured by whatever particular cognitive test is employed; both perceptual and general knowledge tasks tap the same self-confidence trait.

Emotional Intelligence

There is currently considerable popular interest in the construct of emo-tional intelligence. The findings of Davies, Stankov, and Roberts (1998) indicated that the existence of emotional intelligence is difficult to substantiate for two reasons that have to do with the measurement of the construct. These are: (1) questionnaire measures of emotional intelligence seem to be closely related to factors captured by existing personality questionnaires and (2) objective measures have employed consensual scoring procedures that seem to have poor reliability. Emotion Perception may be the only aspect of emotional intelligence that has a chance of becoming an established trait in future. This has mainly to do with the possibility of having an objective criterion for judging whether the observation of particular expression of emotion is correct. A recent book on the topic (Matthews, Zeidner, & Roberts, 2002) is in general agreement with this assessment. It is possible that some new measures of emotional intelligence, which employ verbal material, may possess more adequate measurement properties. However, it is still unclear whether these new measures define factors that are distinct from the primary abilities of G_c and, indeed, from well-established personality traits.

INTELLIGENCE WITHIN DEVELOPMENTAL FRAMEWORK

Some Australian researchers interested in human development, both child and lifespan, have more than casual interest in cognitive abilities and intelligence. It is therefore necessary to outline here some of the main outcomes of this cross-fertilization between developmental psychology and intelligence.

Thus, the only recent theory of intelligence proposed by an Australian psychologist, the theory of minimal cognitive architecture (Anderson, 1992) has been implemented mainly in his work with children. The theory postulates the existence of two routes of knowledge acquisition. The first route is through thought – a knowledge acquisition algorithm that can be generated through two specific processors. They are either visual or verbal/propositional. These two specific processors are sources of individual differences that are uncorrelated in the population. Although this means that, in theory, somebody may be very good in spatial thinking and bad in verbal/propositional, they are correlated in practice. This is because the observed ability served by a specific processor is constrained by the speed of a basic processing mechanism. This constraint on speed is the basis for general intelligence. One of the principal lines of evidence is the correlation between relatively simple reaction time (or IT) tasks and knowledge-rich intelligence test performance. This route establishes the fact that Anderson is the proponent of the g factor theory of intelligence and that speed is the underlying basic process. This is similar to other positions, especially that of A. Jensen's. The second route for acquiring knowledge is through "dedicated information-processing modules." Examples include perception of three-dimensional space, phonological encoding, syntactic parsing, and the like. These are mostly innate although some can be acquired through experience. The common features of these modules are that they operate automatically and independently of thought (i.e., the first route) and are unconstrained by the speed of the basic processing mechanism and are, therefore, unrelated to differences in IQ. The primary cause of developmental change is the maturation and acquisition of modules, establishing that "individual differences and cognitive development represent two independent dimensions of intelligence."

Stripped of jargon, the theory of minimal cognitive architecture postulates the existence of two kinds of abilities – g and group factors, some of which are not identified within the typical psychometric framework. Expressed in these terms, the theory does not appear to be very original from the psychometric point of view. Furthermore, to this day there seems to be relatively little empirical support for aspects of the theory that are perhaps unique (e.g., the role of the constraint on speed). Nevertheless, the theory has been employed successfully to account for findings with savants, and mentally retarded, autistic, and other types of children that show cognitive impairment.

Another important body of work within the area of child development that is leaving its mark on the study of human intelligence arises from studies of Halford and his associates (see Halford, Wilson, & Phillips, 1998a, 1998b). In spite of the apparent continuity of this program of research, it is convenient to divide it into two periods. Thus, during the 1980s the emphasis was largely on capacity limitations as assessed by the dual task methodology. Although the main focus was on young children, much of the logic of these studies had its parallels in contemporary studies of adult intelligence. The impact of the work on capacity limitations on the mainstream studies of intelligence was therefore limited. However, since the early 1990s, the effort of this group has been directed toward the development of the relational complexity theory. According to this theory, the complexity of the cognitive process depends on the number of interacting variables that must be represented in parallel to implement that process. These researchers have developed a set of rules, notational system, and language that provides for a systematic gradation of complexity of different cognitive tasks, and the usefulness of this approach for mainstream intelligence research is already becoming apparent.

Birney (2002) employed relational complexity theory in the analysis of three experimental cognitive tasks (Sentence Comprehension, Knight-Knave, and his newly developed Latin Square task). As it happened, the Knight-Knave task was not quite amenable to unequivocal complexity analysis. All three experimental tasks were then correlated with a battery of psychometric tests measuring broad abilities of the theory of fluid and crystallized intelligence. The results indicate that at least for one of the tasks (Sentence Comprehension) more complex versions show higher correlations with fluid intelligence measures. It was somewhat disappointing that Latin Square task did not show the same trend – different levels of complexity had the same level of high correlation, not increase, with Gf. This last finding needs to be replicated, because Latin Square task has many unique design features that make it quite interesting from the point of view of processing demands. Overall, Birney's (2002) work clearly demonstrates the usefulness of relational complexity metric for the study of individual differences in cognitive abilities and intelligence.

In the area of lifespan and cognitive aging, two groups of Australian psychologists are doing work that is on par with similar research anywhere in the world. One group is located at the Australian National University in Canberra, and it specializes in epidemiological studies that may be helpful in reaching policy decisions. The second group is located in South Australia, and its main emphasis is on changes in memory processes with age. Among many issues addressed by these groups of investigators, a recently reported study examined the evidence for the existence of a common factor that may be responsible for age-related deterioration in cognitive processes (Christensen et al., 2001). On the basis of the results of structural equation modeling procedures, the authors argue that although a common factor model can be fitted to the data, the evidence is weak that it represents a single common cause. This finding, of course, has a direct bearing on theories of intelligence, because "common cause" in the lifespan literature typically comes down to the effect of processing speed and the general slowing hypothesis. It also implies the existence of a strong general factor. The Christensen et al. (2001) result, therefore, questions both these assumptions.

Another issue is the relative roles of mental speed and working memory in the aging of fluid intelligence. Anstey (1999) reported a study that addressed this question with the outcome that is, in effect, complementary to the Christensen et al. (2001) finding. She provided evidence that both are important, but the effect of slowing is somewhat stronger than the effect of reduction in working memory capacity.

CURRENT TECHNIQUES OF ASSESSMENT

The assessment techniques depend largely on practical considerations and the area of application. In clinical areas and school counseling, individual testing often utilizing the Wechsler scales is the most common. Large-scale testing programs based on group tests of abilities that were used for vocational guidance ceased in the early 1970s. The Defence Force Psychology Organisation within the military relies on traditional paper-and-pencil tests that were developed during the World War II. These tests have undergone some revision but, apart from some being adopted for computer administration and scoring, remain essentially unchanged. It is generally accepted that the predictive validity of these tests is satisfactory.

The Individual Differences Laboratory at the University of Sydney introduced computerized testing for research purposes in Australia in the early 1980s. It is planned to meet military needs related to the screening of applicants for pilot training with the Australian Basic Abilities Tests (AUSBAT) that are currently being validated for this purpose (Bongers, 2001). However, a major development in computerized and internet delivery has been motivated by a pronounced increase in demand for personnel selection and screening within organizational settings, including government agencies. Several new test batteries, mostly based on the G_f/G_c theory, have appeared on the market, including Stankov's Tests of Cognitive Abilities (STOCA, Stankov & Dolph, 2000) and the Omnibus Screening Protocol (OSP) developed by Roberts (2001). As yet, these tests do not utilize the full range of options for test delivery available through technological advancements over the past two decades – they are in essence the translations of the traditional paper-and-pencil tests. Nevertheless, they provide additional information that was not available in the past. Routinely, computerized tests provide traditional accuracy and speed of test-taking information. They also provide scores that inform about the trait of self-confidence and self-monitoring. These latter scores are useful for predicting performance on jobs that require interaction with public and at least some forms of risk-taking (i.e., speeding through the lights in a driving simulator). Further work on the predictive validity of self-confidence scores is needed.

Current work on computerized testing in Australia is heading in three directions. First, there is a trend toward a full utilization of new technology in the development of test items, including the dynamic aspects of presentation, colored photographic material, and auditory stimulation. New jobs, particularly in information technology, will require skills that are likely to be different from those that are tapped by current tests of intelligence. For example, the skills needed for work in call centers or for Web design are absent from the repertoire of measures of cognitive abilities in use today.

Second, there is a trend to revisit the work on competing tasks and divided attention that was popular in the 1980s. These areas were seen as relevant for a small number of jobs in the past – usually high-workload jobs of pilots and people in managerial positions. There can be little doubt that the number of jobs that have similar demand characteristics has significantly increased in recent years. Also, competing tasks are known to be good measures of fluid intelligence and general cognitive ability and, because they are usually more difficult than single tests, may provide enough fidelity to discriminate among high-ability groups. Most contemporary IQ tests have poor discriminatory power within the group of top achievers.

Third, there is a trend toward an increased use of simulations in testing. Their main advantage is considerable face validity, which is of importance to the typical users of psychological services who are not trained in psychometrics. The best known are flying and driving simulators – specially constructed physical environments that approximate realistic conditions. They are expensive and unlikely to be employed in the way today's tests are used. Another class of simulations derives from the educational efforts to teach particular subject matter to university students, often as tutorial exercises. Much of the recent work has been carried out with business simulation games that describe a particular environment – for example, be a manager of a furniture factory – and person's performance is followed over a simulated period of half a year. In this type of simulation, the complexity of the task may be considerable, and although some of the original work showed low correlations between simulations and cognitive test performances, more careful analyses and attempts at replication have shown moderate correlations. Simulated business games can be used as testing devices for personnel selection purposes. There is a need for further work to establish their psychometric properties and especially their predictive validity. They can also be extremely time-consuming, and questions may be raised about the economic advantages of their use in place of tests that are typically shorter and more efficient of time. Given these considerations, simulated business games may be appropriate for the selection of personnel for particular industries; they cannot be thought of as measures of general ability.

CONCLUSIONS

Australian work in the area of human intelligence should be seen as a part of the broader effort similar to that happening elsewhere, particularly in Britain and North America. Given that fewer people are working in the field, it is natural that some aspects of research are attracting more attention than the others. The quality of the work in those areas of focus is comparable to anything being done elsewhere in the world.

Work in the psychometric, biological, and developmental traditions is proceeding with some vigor, but studies of cognitive abilities of Australian aborigines has been reduced, if not extinguished. Historically, this latter area did attract considerable interest among Australian psychologists. Cross-cultural psychologists today are often turning their attention to Asian countries on the Pacific Rim. Two areas of activity stand out: studies of the role of mental speed and, in particular, inspection time and studies conceived from within the framework of the psychometric theory of fluid and crystallized intelligence. Australians are among the world leaders in research on IT. Several themes emerge in work within G_f and G_c theory: the role of different sensory modalities within the structure of abilities, the role of speed and capacity in fluid intelligence, and metacognitive and non-ability influences on intelligence. Somewhat less focused and perhaps more eclectic are studies of intelligence undertaken by those whose primary interest is in cognitive development.

With respect to the measurement of intelligence, some interesting new procedures and techniques are being tried out at the moment. These include the study of the metacognitive trait of self-confidence and self-monitoring. Attempts are also being made to broaden the nature of computerized testing by incorporating new stimuli, competing tasks, and various forms of business simulation games into the testing programs.

References

Anderson, M. (1992). *Intelligence and development*. Oxford: Blackwell.

Anstey, K. (1999). Construct overlap in resource theories of memory aging [commentary]. *Gerontology, 45*, 348–350.

Bates, T. C., & Stough, C. (2000). Intelligence arguments and Australian psychology: A reply to Stankov and an alternative view. *Australian Psychologist, 35*, (1), 68–72.

Bongers, S. (2001, November). The Australian Basic Abilities Tests (AUSBAT). Paper presented at the 3rd International Spearman Seminar. Sydney, Australia.

Birney, D. P. (2002). *The measurement of task complexity and cognitive ability: Relational complexity in adult reasoning*. Unpublished doctoral dessertation, The University of Queensland, Brisbane, Australia.

Brody, N. (2001). Inspection time: Past, present, and future. *Intelligence, 29*, 537–542.

Butler, P. V. (1998). Psychology as history, and the biological renaissance: A brief review of the science and politics of psychological determinism. *Australian Psychologist, 33*, (1), 40–46.

Christensen, H., Mackinnon, A., Korten, A., Jorm, A. F., & Hofer, S. (2001, November). No common cause for the common cause factor. Paper presented at the 3rd International Spearman Seminar. Sydney, Australia.

Connell, W. F. (1980). *The Australian Council for Educational Research, 1930–1980*. Hawthorn, Vic: Australian Council for Educational Research.

Danthiir, V., Roberts, R. D., Pallier, G., & Stankov, L. (2001). What the nose knows: Olfaction and cognitive abilities. *Intelligence, 29*, 337–366.

Davies, M., Stankov, L., & Roberts, R. (1998). Emotional intelligence: In search of an elusive construct. *Journal of Personality and Social Psychology, 75*, 989–1015.

Davidson, G. (1998). In pursuit of social responsibility in psychology: A comment on Butler (1998). *Australian Psychologist, 33*, 47–49.

Dickens, W. T., & Flynn, J. R. (2001) Heritability estimates versus large environmental effects: The IQ paradox resolved. *Psychological Review, 108*(2), 346–369.

Fogarty, G. J., & White, C. (1994). Differences between values of Australian Aboriginal and non-Aboriginal students. *Journal of Cross-Cultural Psychology, 25*, 394–408.

Grudnik, J. L., & Kranzler, J. H. (2001). Meta-analysis of the relationship between intelligence and inspection time. *Intelligence, 29*, 523–535.

Halford, G. S., Wilson, W. H., & Phillips, S. (1998a). Processing capacity defined by relational complexity: Implications for comparative, developmental, and cognitive psychology. *Behavioral and Brain Sciences, 21*, 803–831.

Halford, G. S., Wilson, W. H., & Phillips, S. (1998b). Relational complexity metric is effective when assessments are based on actual processes. *Behavioral and Brain Sciences, 21*, 848–864.

Keats, D. M. (1979). Cross-cultural studies in cognitive development and language in Malaysia and Australia. *Educational Research and Perspectives, 6*, 46–63.

Keats, J. A. (1951). *A statistical theory of objective test scores*. Melbourne: Australian Council for Educational Research.

Kleitman, S., & Stankov, L. (2001). Ecological and person-driven aspects of metacognitive processes in test-taking. *Applied Cognitive Psychology, 15*, 321–341.

Klich, L. Z. (1988). Aboriginal cognition and psychological nescience. In S. H. Irvine & J. W. Berry (Eds.), *Human abilities in cultural context* (pp. 427–452). Cambridge: Cambridge University Press.

Kyllonen, P. C., & Christal, R. E. (1990). Reasoning ability is (little more than) working memory capacity?! *Intelligence, 12*, 389–433.

Luciano, M., Smith, G. A., Wright, M. J., Geffen, G. M., Geffen, L. B., & Martin, N., (2001). On the heritability of inspection time and its correlation with IQ: Twin study. *Intelligence, 29*, 443–458.

Matthews, G., Zeidner, M., & Roberts, R. D. (2002). *Emotional intelligence: Science and myth*. Cambridge, MA: MIT Press.

McDonald, R. P. (1964). *Nonlinear factor analysis*. (Psychometric Monograph, No. 15).

McDonald, R. P. (1978). A simple comprehensive model for the analysis of co-variance structures. *British Journal of Mathematical and Statistical Psychology, 31*, 161–183.

McElwain, D. W., & Kearney, G. (1970). *The Queensland Test*. Melbourne: Australian Council for Educational Research.

Nettelbeck, T. (2001). Correlation between inspection time and psychometric abilities: A personal interpretation. *Intelligence, 29*, 459–474.

Nettelbeck, T., & Lally, M. (1976). Inspection time and measured intelligence. *British Journal of Psychology, 67*, 17–22.

O'Neil, W. M. (1987). *A century of psychology in Australia*. Sydney: Sydney University Press.

Pallier, G., Roberts, R., & Stankov, L. (2000). Biological vs. Psychometric Intelligence: Halstead's (1947) distinction re-visited. *Archives of Clinical Neuropsychology. 15*, (3), 205–226.

Phillips, G. E. (1924). *The measurement of of general ability*. Sydney: Angus and Robertson.

Porteus, S. D. (1965). *Porteus Maze Tests: Fifty years of application*. Palo Alto, CA: Pacific Books.

Roberts, R. D. (2001). *Omnibus Screening Protocol (OSP). Status report*. Sydney: The RightPeople.

Roberts, R. D., & Stankov, L. (1999) Individual differences in speed of mental processing and human cognitive abilities: Towards a taxonomic model. *Learning and Individual Differences, 11*, (1), 1–120.

Roberts, R. D., Stankov, L., Pallier, G., & Dolph, B. (1997). Charting the cognitive sphere: Tactile/kinesthetic performance within the structure of intelligence. *Intelligence, 25*, 111–148.

Stankov, L. (1998). Intelligence arguments and Australian psychology. *Australian Psychologist, 33*, 53–57.

Stankov, L. (1999). Complexity, metacognition, and fluid intelligence. *Intelligence, 27*, 1–23.

Stankov, L. (2000). Intelligence debates & some Australian confusions. *Australian Psychologist, 35*, 73–76.

Stankov, L., & Dolph, B. (2000). *Some experiences with Stankov's Tests of Cognitive Abilities* (STOCA). Paper presented at the Industrial and Organizational Psychology Conference in Brisbane.

Stankov, L., & Horn, J. L. (1980). Human abilities revealed through auditory tests. *Journal of Educational Psychology, 72* 19–42.

Stankov, L., & Roberts, R. D. (1997). Mental speed is not *the* "basic" process of intelligence. *Personality and Individual Differences, 22*, (1), 69–84.

Stankov, L., Seizova-Cajic, T., & Roberts, R. D., (2001). Tactile and kinesthetic perceptual processes within the taxonomy of human abilities. *Intelligence, 29*, 1–29.

Stough, C., Thompson, J. C., Bates, T. C., & Nathan, P. J. (2001). Examining neurochemical determinants of inspection time: Development of a biological model. *Intelligence, 29*, 511–522.

Vickers, D., Nettelbeck, T., & Wilson, R. J. (1972). Perceptual indices of performance: The measurement of "inspection time" and "noise" in the visual system. *Perception, 1*, 263–295.

13

Being Intelligent with Zimbabweans

A Historical and Contemporary View

Elias Mpofu

Conceptions of intelligence and associated practices vary widely across societies and are influenced by the unique socio-cultural histories of those societies. For example, differences in perspectives on intelligence between nations or communities have been linked to differences in (1) cultural beliefs about human abilities (Cole, 1998; Serpell & Boykin, 1994, 2000), (2) availability and accessibility of formal education to the general public (Oslon, 1984), (3) the social and economic goals that people in different nations or communities seek to achieve (Serpell & Boykin, 1994; Vernon, 1969; Whyte, 1998;), (4) level of industrialization (or development) of nations or communities and the values underpinning the achieved or aspired developmental statuses (Azuma, 1984; Serpell, 2000; Vernon, 1969), and (5) the availability of human and material resources for the study of intelligence (Mpofu & Nyanungo, 1998). These differences in socio-cultural contexts are important for an understanding of the psychology of human intelligence across nations. For example, developed countries with their more complex socio-technical systems may place a higher premium or value on technical and bureaucratic efficiency than do developing countries, which tend to have simpler socio-technical systems (Serpell, 2000).

This chapter presents an overview of perspectives and research on intelligence in modern Zimbabwe as well as related practices. To begin with, I present a brief outline on the historical and demographic context of Zimbabwe as background to subsequent discussion. The historical and demographic summary is followed by a discussion of definitions and theories of intelligence in Zimbabwe. In doing so, I refer to the results of a survey on definitions of intelligence by Zimbabwean college students and from the perspective of implicit theories of intelligence. Second, historical and current research on intelligence in the country is discussed. Comparisons with theory, research, and assessment in other parts of Africa and the developing and developed world are also considered where appropriate.

THE CONTEXT OF THE PSYCHOLOGY OF INTELLIGENCE IN ZIMBABWE

Zimbabwe is a multicultural, southern African country with a population of about 11 million people (95% Blacks; 5% Asians, Whites, and others), and with a total area of 150,873 square miles (390,759 km²). Eighty percent of the population is from the Shona cultural or language group, and 15% are from a Ndebele cultural or language background. Eighty percent of the population lives in rural areas, and 20% live in the cities. Therefore, the country's economic base is largely agricultural, although mining, tourism, and manufacturing are also significant sectors of the economy. The average farmer in the country is primarily engaged in subsistence farming, although the practice of market-oriented farming has increased substantially in the last 20 years.

Zimbabwe was a British colony for 90 years until 1980. Its colonial legacy includes a White population of about 100,000 (or 1% of the population). As a result of historical–colonial precedent, 80% of the national economy is owned by Whites. Thus, though a numerical minority, Zimbabwean Whites are an economic majority. The Anglophone values they represent are both maligned and envied by a significant majority of the national population. For example, the curricula of Zimbabwean schools espouse White middle-class values of competition and individualism rather than the traditional, native African values of cooperativeness and collective well-being (Mandaza, 1986; Zvogbo, 1994). Mandaza (1986), for example, observed that the post-independence Zimbabwe education system promoted and sustained the colonial class structure by maintaining a schooling system based on social class and privilege. Furthermore, the ruling African elite classes actively encourage educational achievement in the Western sense as a means of "giving their next generation a competitive advantage for higher education and professional employment" (Kasfir, 1983, p. 591).

Zimbabwe shares borders with five countries: Botswana, Mozambique, Namibia, South Africa, and Zambia. Although Zimbabwe shares substantially similar precolonial and colonial histories with most of its southern African neighbors, it is relatively more industrialized than most of its neighbors and has a basic level of literacy among the general population in excess of 85%. As an example of the availability and accessibility of basic formal education to the general population, about 92% of children (2,334,477) ages 6 to 12 years old attended primary (elementary) school in 2001, whereas 60% (863, 636) of teenagers were enrolled in the country's high schools (Ministry of Education, Sport & Culture, 2001).

About 60% of the population comprises children and teenagers (Zimbabwe Central Statistical Office, 1992). Thus, the average Zimbabwean is Black, young, literate, and of a rural background. The cultural context for understanding intelligence in Zimbabwe is multicultural, with potentially competing influences from indigenous African and White, Anglophone cultures. Quite apparently, too, perspectives on intelligence in Zimbabwe reflect the country's cultural diversity.

DEFINING INTELLIGENCE: A ZIMBABWEAN PERSPECTIVE

Developing countries like Zimbabwe have multilayered definitions of intelligence: traditional–indigenous and modern. As discussed more fully later, Zimbabwean traditional or indigenous conceptions of intelligence tend to regard intelligence as expertise in interpersonal relationships and success with everyday activities. In other words, practical or functional ability within a social context and for the benefit of the collective defines intelligence from a Zimbabwean, traditional–indigenous perspective. By contrast, modern Zimbabwean views of intelligence consider it an individual's ability on cognitive or academic kind of tasks that is presumed to measure intelligence. Zimbabwean traditional–indigenous definitions and perspectives of intelligence are considered next, followed by modern definitions and perspectives.

Zimbabwean Traditional–Indigenous Definitions of Intelligence

Zimbabwean indigenous conceptions of intelligence are represented by the vernacular terms *njere* (Shona) and *ukaliphile* (Ndebele). These terms refer to deliberate, socially responsible, positively public-spirited, and altruistic behavior (Chimhundu, 2001; Hadebe, 2001; Irvine, 1988; Mpofu, 1993). *Njere* and *ukaliphile* also mean being wise. The definition of intelligence as socially motivated, discreet, and benevolent thought and behavior has also been noted by researchers on intelligence among the

Baganda of Uganda (Wober, 1974; Whyte, 1998), the Chewa of Zambia (Serpell, 1977), the Luo of Kenya (Sternberg et al., 2001), and the Shona of Zimbabwe (Irvine, 1966, 1969, 1988) and may be applicable to a majority of indigenous cultural–language communities across sub–Saharan Africa.

Indigenous Zimbabweans consider a person to be intelligent to the extent that he or she identifies with and seeks to achieve goals that benefit the collective. The collective could be family, kinship, or proximal or immediate community. In rural Zimbabwe, the family, kinship and community share a significant overlap in that the community is often made up of members of the extended family or part of the kinship. Similarly, among Zimbabweans resident in urban areas, intelligent behavior may be regarded as that which benefits primarily the family and kinsfolk or extended family from the rural home areas (*kumusha* or *ekhaya*). Thus, native Zimbabweans have historically associated purposive social behavior or action for communal benefit with intelligence.

Task participation, task accomplishment, and resource allocation are three areas that are central to considerations of intelligence among indigenous Zimbabweans. With regard to task participation, a person who readily volunteers to help others with a task is regarded as intelligent. The significance of a helping orientation is communicated by the Shona proverb, "*Chara chimwe hachitsvanyi inda*" ("One thumb cannot kill a louse"), which meants that a person's contribution is expected for the success of all. In the realm of ideas, the ideas of the collective are regarded to be superior to those of a single person. The Shona proverb, "*Zano ndega akapisa jira*" ("The one who thinks he or she is the fountain of knowledge burnt his or her blanket"), is consistent with the notion that true intelligence is the product of the collective and individuals are expected to contribute to it. Thus, there is the expectation that anyone carrying out a task is supposed to be helped to achieve it. The onus is on the person who is carrying out the task to decline the assistance. Assistance can still be offered regardless. Social etiquette demands that the person performing a task should decline help a number of times before he or she accepts it, and that the person offering to help should also make several overtures to help, and that help should rather be given than not given.

Task accomplishment is also collective rather than individual in intent so that even if an individual performed the task, its achievement is presumed to be of benefit to others. It is not expected of someone to admit that a task was over-taxing since that could imply that one was not willing to put in his or her bit for others' benefit. Thus, someone performing an arduous task is routinely saluted, *"Vasevenzi!"* and *"Vashumi!"* (Shona), or *"Basebenzi!"* (Ndebele) ("Workers!" or "Those at work!") and is supposed to respond by trivializing the significance of the task to him or herself, for example, *"Haa-i, vanoiteiko!"* (Shona), or *"Okwangapi!"* (Ndebele) ("Ooh, we aren't doing much"), or acknowledging participation, for example, *"Ndivo vano"* (Shona), *"Yikholokhu imbambanga-mandla"* (Ndebele) ("Yes, we are"). The plural terms used in the salutation and responses acknowledge the social significance of the task and that the participating individual is merely fulfilling an expected social role.

Indigenous Zimbabweans would regard a person to be intelligent if that individual could be relied on if sent to carry out tasks on behalf of significant others who may be immediate family, extended family, and/or members of the community. The Shona words *kutumika* (one who could be sent) and *munyayi* (the stand in) refer to qualities of social responsibility, sensitivity, and decorum. Serpell (1993a) reported that the quality of being relied upon on errands was an important signifier of intelligence among the Chewa of Zambia. Thus, the capacity to act on behalf of others is a highly regarded personal attribute in several African communities.

The way one disposes of personal resources is important to defining intelligence among indigenous Zimbabweans. In this connection, an intelligent person is one who shares his or her resources with others. The Shona proverb, *chawawana idya nehama mutogwa une hanganwa*, (anything you find, share with a relative because a stranger is forgetful) expresses the significance of service to family and kinship in considerations of intelligence among Zimbabweans. The word *stranger* (*mutogwa*) includes all people who are not related by blood or marriage. Friends are regarded as valued social partners who, nonetheless, may not be entirely relied on. They are more akin to strangers rather than family or kinsfolk. Thus, socially oriented behavior that benefits the general public may be less credited with intelligence for a number of reasons. First, the individual may be regarded as carrying out functions that are within the purview of a delegated or constitutional authority (e.g., the city council or other statutory bodies) at the expense of servicing the needs of the family or kinsfolk. Second, the general public may comprise people from different language or cultural groups and/or parts of the country and are least likely to be family or relations. They are likely to fall within the category of strangers or people who are susceptible to forgetfulness by convenience. Expending personal resources on one's urban community may be regarded as evidence of diminished social judgement. The practice of socially responsible behavior for the benefit of the collective is a benchmark against which intelligent action is judged by contemporary Zimbabweans.

In a pilot survey involving 49 Zimbabwean college students of a Shona cultural background (males = 18, females = 31), I sought to establish how members of their culture of origin define intelligence. The students were also asked to describe the behaviors that members of their culture of origin would consider to be indicative of superior intelligence and inferior intelligence. The students, who were undergraduate counseling psychology majors with a distance education university (mean age = 36.37, SD = 6.41 years), were from a cross section of Zimbabwean society: housewives/homemakers, policemen, nurses, social workers, members of religious orders, administrators, and teachers. Seventeen of the students resided in rural areas, and 32 in urban centers. Previous studies with Zimbabwean participants with formal education (Irvine, 1972; Mpofu, 1994a) have attested to "the existence side by side, in highly educated African students of two systems of causation": indigenous and modern (Irvine, 1972, p. 99). Thus, the students could reasonably be expected to report reliably on conceptions of intelligence by members of their cultures of origin since they share a worldview with that culture.

The students' narrative responses were analyzed thematically so that terms, phrases, or sentences with a similar meaning were clustered together. For example, statements like "Ability to express views in a responsible manner" and "Listening to other people's views and analyzing them positively" were considered to be thematically connected to being "considerate." "Respect for other people's opinions" and "Tolerance of other people's views" could be regarded as falling under the theme "considerateness" or "respectful." For that reason, "considerate" and "respectful" were clustered together (see Table 13.1). A description of an intelligent person as "One who comprehends things expected of older people," "Someone who acts above his/her age," and "Being cultured in actions and words" were regarded as exemplifying the theme of "Maturity." "Social and economic contributions to society," "Being able to solve everyday problems," "Productive use of skills," and "Successful farmer" were clustered under the theme "Successful." Definitions that referred to a number of themes were multiply scored by theme. For example, one definition that was presented was "They think intelligence

TABLE 13.1. *Thematic Descriptor Terms for Intelligence and Associated Behaviors among the Shona Cultural/Language Group.*[1]

Defining terms	*n*	%	Behavioral Descriptors	
			Superior Intelligence	Inferior Intelligence
Considerate, responsible, sociable, respectful, reliable	9	12	Tolerant, sharing, sociable, looks after self and others, can be sent	Carefree, unreliable
Harmonious, helpful, cooperatives, collectivistic, exemplary	14	19	Resolving differences through negotiation; sacrificing for the sake of harmony; seeking, promoting, and maintaining harmony	Poor interpersonal relationships, quarrelsome, uncommunicative, pugilistic
Humbleness, patient	4	5	Exercises restraint, takes his or her time	Impulsive, conceited, proud
Adaptive, creative, innovative, original, clever, spontaneous	3	4	Proactive, innovative, observant, quick with solutions, mischievous to draw attention	Lacks initiative, submissive, uncurious, placid
Successful, planful, solution focused	16	22	Renowned expert, rich, productive, success with day-to-day tasks, successful in a trade or occupation	Dependent, wasteful, disorganized; living in low-cost housing; regularly unemployed
Analytical, logical, rational	4	5	Unbiased, rational, unemotional, poised	irrational, impulsive, daft
Educated, academic, skilled	16	22	High grades at school; College educated; Holds many college diplomas	Poor school grades, no college education, illiterate despite opportunity, gullible
Fertile (able to bear many children) (1%)	1	1		
Mature	3	4	Is called upon by others, knows and identifies with his or her culture	Infantile, ignorant of culture
Wise	1	1		

(continued)

TABLE 13.1 *(continued)*

Defining terms	n	%	Behavioral Descriptors	
			Superior Intelligence	Inferior Intelligence
Individualistic	2	3		
Grooming	1	1		Poor grooming
			Exhibits supernatural powers	
				Single older male (difficulties finding partner)
				Practicing witchcraft
				A woman marrying someone not of her class
	74	100		

[1] *Note:* Percentages denote the frequency of statements for each thematic cluster.

is coupled with education and being dressed smartly, and at the same time showing respect for others." This definition was scored under themes "Educated," "Grooming," and "Respectful." Space limitations preclude a detailed description of how each of the thematic terms and clusters in the Table was derived. An interrater agreement index of .86 was observed for the thematic analysis procedure.

Table 13.1 presents the results of analysis for definition of intelligence and behaviors indicative of superior intelligence and inferior intelligence by people of one's culture of origin.

As can be seen from Table 13.1, about 30% of the responses given by the students defined intelligence in terms of social competence (i.e., categories a, b, c, i, k, l). Thus, results of this survey confirm the earlier observation that indigenous Zimbabweans, like other cultural groups native to sub-Saharan Africa, place a high premium on competence in interpersonal relations in defining intelligence. Of interest is that most definitions of intelligence given by the students fell within the thematic category "successful" (23%). The students were of the view that in their culture of origin, a person would be considered intelligent if he or she were successful materially, in terms of coping with the demands of everyday life. It would seem that indigenous Zimbabweans have a high regard for practical intelligence (Sternberg, 1981, 1999). Practical intelligence has been defined as "the ability to apply various kinds of adaptation for the purposes of adaptation to, shaping of, and selection of environments" (Sternberg, 1999, p. 352). Another noteworthy finding was that 22% of the definitions of intelligence referred to success in school and or college as important to perceptions of intelligence among the Shona. In fact, the students regarded level of formal education as second only to being successful as a criterion of intelligence among the Shona. Competence in interpersonal relations came third (i.e., after successful and educated: see Table 13.1). Studies by Sternberg et al. (2001) among the Luo of Kenya also identified school success as an aspect of intelligence among that African cultural group. However, Grigorenko et al. (2001) also found that academic success was not correlated with perceptions of intelligence in children by adults among the Luo. The findings of this survey may be explained in that Zimbabwean Shona may perceive a more direct connection between school achievement and success in life than the Luo of Kenya. Therefore, indigenous Zimbabweans may give greater consideration to academic success in defining intelligence vis-à-vis the Luo of Kenya.

Modern Definitions of Intelligence in Zimbabwe

As previously indicated, modern definitions of intelligence among Zimbabweans equate it with the ability to score highly on decontextualized, academic kinds of tasks that require the demonstration of ability in the following areas: verbal, numerical, spatial, memory, analogical. The prototypical tasks and procedures for determining an individual's intelligence are those represented on intelligence scales that were developed in or after the practice in Western countries. Modern Zimbabwean views on intelligence regard its assessment as leading to the selection or diagnosis of individuals based on personal attributes, their placement in programs or interventions that are led by social or economic agencies (e.g., industry, rehabilitation clinics, schools, government services, and vocational training centers), for the purpose of maximizing the development and utilization of manpower by the formal economic sector.

In the survey referred to earlier, Zimbabwean students of a Shona cultural background were asked to define intelligence from their own personal points of view. As previously noted, the students had a significant level of formal education and experience with employment in the formal sector. Therefore, they could reasonably be expected to be modern in outlook or to present a personal view of intelligence consistent with that of Zimbabweans with a modern worldview.

TABLE 13.2. *Personal Views on Intelligence and Ideal Intelligent Person by Zimbabwean College Students*

	Frequency (%)	
Descriptor by Category	Personal View	Ideal Intelligent Person
(a) Rate and speed in solution finding	8 (10)	1 (2)
(b) Ability to adapt to and manipulate the environment	11 (13)	4 (7)
(c) Rational, analytical, logical, unemotional	11 (13)	5 (9)
(d) Successfully plan and carry out activities	17 (20)	5 (9)
(e) Mature	4 (5)	4 (7)
(f) Innovative, creative, spontaneous, clever	4 (5)	7 (12)
(g) Educated	8 (10)	6 (10)
(h) Aptitude	4 (5)	1 (2)
(i) Remembering what one learned previously	3 (4)	2 (3)
(j) Expressive or linguistic ability	4 (5)	–
(k) That which is tested by an intelligence test	1 (1)	–
(l) Psychiatric status	1 (1)	–
(m) Individualistic, hedonistic	0	2 (3)
(n) Harmonious, collectivictic, helpful	–	5 (9)
(o) Confident, courageous	–	2 (3)
(p) Other (not classifiable)	3 (4)	2 (3)
(q) Missing cases (non-response)	4 (5)	12 (21)
TOTALS	83 (100)	58 (100)

The students' responses by category are summarized in Table 13.2. In arriving at the categorization, a thematic approach was used so that responses common to a theme were clustered together. For example, responses that referred to intelligence as "Fastness/quickness of understanding," "Someone who is clever and who always gets the right answer in a short period of time," and "Rate and speed at which one thinks and reacts to different situations" were counted under the theme "Rate and speed in solution finding." Examples of other thematically similar definitions that were given were "Being able to manipulate the environment to the fullest," "It is one's ability to adapt to and to manipulate the environment," "Knowledge of what to do, when to do it, how to do it, and with what knowledge of how to survive and make things or people work for you" and "Ability to understand and make the best positive use of available resources in the best way and the best time." These and similar others were scored under the general theme "Ability to adapt and to manipulate the environment." The rest of the thematic categorizations were determined similarly. An inter-rater agreement index of.94 was observed for the scoring procedure just described.

Three things are apparent from Table 13.2. First, 20% of definitions of intelligence by Zimbabwean college students regarded being successful as important to their personal views of intelligence. In this regard, the students' view of intelligence was consistent with their perception of how intelligence is regarded by members of their culture of origin. Successful or practical intelligence (Irvine, 1988; Sternberg, 1999) appears to be important to definitions of intelligence both from an indigenous Zimbabwean and modern Zimbabwean perspective. Second, 13% of definitions of intelligence by the students considered it to be the ability to adapt to and manipulate the environment. The definition of intelligence as adaptation to and manipulation of the environment is widely endorsed by experts in the field of human intelligence (Sternberg, 1999) and represents a modern view of intelligence. Similarly, personal definitions of intelligence by the students that referred to indicators such as rational, logical thinking (13%), rate and speed of responding (10%), memory for previous learning (4%), expressive ability (5%), and performance on an intelligence test (1%) were also consistent with a modern perspective. Third, it is noteworthy that the students' personal definitions of intelligence tended to disregard the social or interpersonal aspects, which they considered important to definitions of intelligence in their culture of origin.

Students were also asked to give their definitions of the ideal intelligent person. Responses were scored thematically as with previous questions. Students considered their ideal intelligent person to be educated (10%) and successful (9%) (see Table 13.2). This orientation was similar to that of their culture of origin. However, the students' views on their ideal intelligent person were closer to their personal views on intelligence than to those of members of their culture of origin. The students tended not to respond to the question on their ideal intelligent person, which may have compromised the adequacy with which the related themes were captured.

THEORIES ON THE MULTILAYERED NATURE OF INTELLIGENCE AMONG ZIMBABWEANS

No formal theories or explicit theories on conceptions of intelligence by indigenous Zimbabweans or natives to sub-Saharan Africa have been proposed. The definitions and behavioral descriptors of intelligence by Zimbabwean students and members of other native African cultures as previously discussed are essentially their implicit theories of intelligence. Sternberg (1985) defined implicit theories of intelligence as those that reside in people's minds and are the basis on which they make judgmental decisions on their own and other people's intelligence. The implicit theories on intelligence by Zimbabweans may later be the basis for proposing formal theories. On the basis of studies of implicit theories of intelligence Irvine (1988), Wober (1974), Sternberg et al. (2001) derived models on the structure of the intellect of members of a number of the native African cultures. These studies are the subject of discussion later in this chapter. Theories have been distinguished from models (Chapains, 1963; Lazarus, 1993; Patterson & Watkins, 1996). According to Lazarus (1993), a theory seeks to "answer the question why and how certain processes arise, are maintained, can be modified, or are extinguished, and to make predictions therefrom" (p. 675). Models are conceptually looser that theories and less comprehensive (Chapains, 1963). Additional research is required before a theory of intellect applicable to Zimbabweans or native Africans is proposed.

In this section, I attempt to explain the existence of multilayered views of intelligence among Zimbabweans. The discussion presented here should be considered together with that in a previous section on the context of the psychology of intelligence in Zimbabwe because the themes are elaborated in a continuation of the previous discussion. Specifically, I address issues pertaining to the (1) social emphasis in culture of origin definitions of intelligence by Zimbabweans and (2) influence of the British colonial heritage and modernity on the psychology of intelligence in Zimbabwe.

The social emphasis on the notion of intelligence among indigenous Zimbabweans can be better understood if cognizance is taken of the centrality of humanness, spiritualism, and kinship of the value systems of most African communities (Bourdillon, 1987). In the first instance, an important yardstick for appropriateness of behavior is whether it meets the criteria of humanness as in *hunhu* (Shona), *ubuntu* (Nguni/Ndebele), or *ubotho* (Sotho). Second, indigenous African religions emphasize communality and at the same time provide a vital interpretive framework for experience. Among the Shona, for example, the occasion of seeing a certain species of snake (e.g., a python) in the veld communicates a spiritual message (blessings and possible possession) from kinsfolk dead or alive (Mpofu, 1993). A high value is therefore placed by many African communities on the perceived inseparability of the person, the world in which he lives, and the cosmos as representing the most total experience of being (Serpell & Boykin, 1994).

As previously mentioned, the modern conceptions of intelligence by the Zimbabwean students are those that reflect a significant influence from the country's British colonial heritage and membership in the global, modern international community. As an example of the influence of the British colonial heritage, the first university in the country, the University of Rhodesia (now the University of Zimbabwe) opened in 1957 and was an affiliate of the University of London. The psychology curriculum at the University of Rhodesia was similar to that offered at the University of London. To date, there has been little change in the psychology courses offered at the University of Zimbabwe and other institutions of higher learning in Zimbabwe. The teaching of psychology and other social sciences in the country is still at the translation and modeling stage of the development of psychology in non-Western countries (Mpofu et al. 1997), which Azuma (1984) defined as characterized by attempts to apply Western psychological concepts and technologies, often with little or no adaptation. Mpofu et al. (1997) attributed the low level of development of psychology in Zimbabwe and other countries in sub-Saharan Africa to the training of African psychologists in or by Western countries, which in the majority of cases was deficient in cultural responsiveness. Not surprisingly, some Zimbabweans would associate intelligence with performance on academic kinds of tasks, as would be the case by mainstream psychology in Western countries. Mpofu et al. (1997), in view of the limitations imposed by Western psychology on the development of local or indigenous psychologies, recommended the formation of an international psychology institute "which would prepare . . . psychologists from across the globe [and] help provide advanced preparation that is more responsive to cultural diversity" (p. 399).

HISTORY OF RESEARCH ON INTELLIGENCE IN ZIMBABWE AND SUB-SAHARAN AFRICA

Research on intelligence in Zimbabwe and sub-Saharan Africa has a relatively short history. This limitation may be reflective of the lower demand for expertise on intelligence and human mental abilities by the largely rural, agricultural economy of the country and sub-region. The lower investment in research on intelligence was also due to the very limited number of psychologists in the sub-Saharan region (Mpofu & Khan, 1996; Mpofu et al., 1997). The historical research on intelligence in Zimbabwe shares many conceptual and methodological commonalities with that of a number of countries in the sub-Saharan region. Therefore, in subsequent discussion, I discuss a selection of studies on intelligence carried out in a number of countries in sub-Saharan Africa with a view to giving a broader view of the research on the psychology of intelligence in the sub-region and highlighting the research issues that have been historically pertinent. Thus, the studies that are discussed have been selected for their conceptual and methodological representativeness of studies on intelligence in sub-Saharan Africa.

The historical research on intelligence in Zimbabwe and sub-Saharan Africa was characterized by a focus on two contrasting themes: unraveling conceptions of intelligence indigenous to native African cultures and determining the transportability of Western ability constructs to sub-Saharan Africa. Studies on conceptions of intelligence by native Zimbabweans or sub-Saharan Africans have generally followed an ethnographic approach with the aim of explicating indigenous people's implicit understanding of intelligence. This approach contrasts with that of a psychometric approach to the study of intelligence in Zimbabwe and sub-Saharan Africa, whose goal was to test the applicability of Western conceptions of intelligence with native Africans. In this regard, studies on conceptions of intelligence of the Shona of Zimbabwe (Irvine, 1969, 1970, 1988), the Baganda and Batoro of Uganda (Wober, 1974), and the Chewa of Zambia (Serpell, 1977) are historically the most significant. Equally historically significant are studies on the development of taxonomic structure in Senegalese children (Greenfield, Reich, & Oliver, 1966) and Liberian peasant farmers (Glick, 1975).

Unraveling Indigenous Conceptions of Intelligence in Zimbabwe and Sub-Saharan Africa

Irvine (1970, 1988) investigated the meaning of wisdom and foolishness among the Shona. In pursuit of that goal, he studied a compilation of Shona proverbs that were judged to be related to wisdom and foolishness. Irvine held the assumption that proverbs captured central and survival-related meanings among traditional communities. Following a thematic analysis of the proverbs, Irvine (1988) concluded that dispositional intelligence (*ungwaru*), instrumental knowledge, and social intelligence (*uchenjeri*) and higher-order trait dispositions characterized intellect among the Shona. Dispositional intelligence among the Shona was associated with being logical, rational, skeptical, and cautious, and having respect for evidence, foresight, vigilance, and alertness. It could be from both learning and endowment, individualistic in orientation, and also apply to animals (as in *"Imbwa yako yakangwara"*–"Your dog is clever"). For the Shona, instrumental knowledge was that concerned with learning from others necessary information for survival. It included listening to and heeding the advice of the elders (*kuteerera vakuru*), strategies for task accomplishment, and practice. Social intelligence comprised the techniques for social effectiveness or influence within the group or collective (e.g., negotiation, openness, persuasiveness, being discreet, and respect for elders). Higher-order traits associated with intelligence that could be discerned from the proverbs included a sense of responsibility, willingness to take the initiative, humility, patience, and persistence. The root word *ngwa* in *ungwaru* refers to general mental energy, vigilance, and prudence (Chimhundu, 2001) and has been considered to have the same meaning as the general ability factor g in psychometric approaches to the study of intelligence (Irvine & Berry, 1988).

Wober (1974) interviewed Ugandan adults, students, and teachers from the Baganda and Batoro cultural communities to determine their views on intelligence. Questions were presented to the Baganda and Batoro adults in their native languages with the help of native speakers. The adults could answer in their native languages. Students and teachers were questioned in English and responded in the same language. Wober then used the terms these informants used to construct a scale for mapping intellect among the sample of Ugandans. Adults from the Baganda and Batoro communities perceived intelligence as largely to do with public-spirited behavior, as well as being cautious and patient. The minor differences between the Baganda and Batoro in their views of intelligence arose largely from difficulties with instrument translation into their respective native languages. Ugandan students and teachers had views on intelligence that differed from those of Baganda and Batoro adults in that the students' and teachers' views were more cognitivistic and individualistic. Their views were influenced by their exposure to Western culture through schooling.

Serpell (1977, 1993a, 1993b) investigated conceptions of intelligence among a Chewa community in rural eastern Zambia. Chewa is a widely spoken language in Zambia, Malawi, and Northwestern Mozambique.

To tap into Chewa notions of intelligence, Serpell asked 61 Chewa adults without any formal schooling to nominate from among a group of children familiar to them ($N = 41$) the children who were likely to succeed in carrying out ecologically valid tasks (looking after a pot of fire, being sent on an errand) or interpreting a riddle. The adults were also asked to give reasons why they selected a particular child for a given task. Serpell also interviewed some of the then-children as adults more than two decades later to establish their views of intelligence. These younger adults were asked to nominate peers who best represented Chewa terms for intelligence and to give reasons for their choices. A thematic analysis of the Chewa adults' responses revealed that intelligence among the Chewa was best represented by the words *nzelu* (wisdom), *chenjela* (aptitude) and *tumilika* (responsibility). *Nzelu* and *chenjela* refer to the cognitive aspect of intelligence among the Chewa, whereas *tumilika* represents the aspect of social responsibility. The Chewa notion of *nzelu* also includes a significant aspect of social responsibility. In that sense, *nzelu* was different and broader than the standard Western concept of intelligence, which emphasizes only the cognitive aspect. *Chenjela* includes personal qualities such as cleverness and being cunning and quick-witted. *Tumilika* refers to being obedient, trustworthy (*khulupilika*), cooperative, reliable, and observant.

Greenfield et al. (1966) studied the development of classification ability among Senegalese (Wolof) children in comparison to Anglo-American and French children. Among the key findings of their study was that the Senegalese children achieved superordinate classification ability at an older age than Anglo-American and French children. The Senegalese children also preferred enactive communication (e.g., pointing) rather than verbalization. Senegalese children from urban areas demonstrated a higher and faster grasp of classification ability than their rural counterparts. Greenfield et al. (1966) ascribed the lower development of classification ability among the Senegalese children to differences in levels of acculturation to modern information representation systems between urban and rural Senegalese children, and between Western counterparts. Glick (1975) studied classification ability among Liberian Kpelle farmers and observed a higher preference for instrumental (i.e., use-oriented) as opposed to abstract classification. Classification ability among the Liberian Kpelle farmers could be explained by the fact that functional classification skills may be more salient to survival in a subsistence economy than abstract classification skills. The studies by Greenfield et al. (1966), Glick (1975) and others (e.g., Berry et al., 1986) highlighted the significance of the cultural-environmental context to the development of human abilities.

Psychometric Approach to the Study of Intelligence in Zimbabwe and Sub-Saharan Africa

Irvine used a psychometric approach to study intelligence (e.g., Irvine, 1969). In related studies, he administered intelligence tests (e.g., Raven's Progressive Matrices) to many groups of students of a Shona background ($N = 1,651$) and correlated performance on the tests with demographic variables commonly believed to "explain" differences in ability in Western societies (e.g., social class, gender, school quality, family size, birth position). Irvine observed that differences in performance on ability tests among the Shona did not vary by these demographic variables. The lack of reliable variation in the performance of indigenous Africans on Western ability tests by demographic differences has been a robust finding (Irvine, 1988; Kendall, Verster, & Mollendorf, 1988), although largely ignored by mainstream research on intelligence (Irvine, 1988).

Irvine's studies (1969, 1970, 1988) also led him to the conclusion that the intellect of the Shona was well represented by domains of intellectual functioning identified with people of a Western culture, such as inductive reasoning, verbal knowledge, number operations, and speed of symbol recognition. His findings were consistent with those of Latif (1980) and Makanza (1988), who observed that the performance of Zimbabwean students on the Weschler Intelligence Scale–Revised (WISC-R) was structurally similar to that of students in North America and England. Latif (1980) carried out a study to determine whether the factor structure of the WISC-R could be replicated with the Zimbabwean students. His study showed that the performance of Zimbabwean students on the WISC-R replicated the four-factor structure as derived from studies of the test in Western countries: general ability, verbal ability, numerical ability, and freedom from distractibility. Rogers and Macguire (1990) carried out a pilot study on developing Zimbabwean norms for the WISC-R. They sampled about 800 students with a satisfactory command of spoken and written English as judged by a team of Zimbabwean educational psychologists. Among their key findings was that Zimbabwean students' performance on the WISC-R was similar to that of students in Western countries, although the Zimbabwean students scored relatively lower than same age North

American students. Makanza's (1988) study established that the WISC-R profiles of Zimbabwean students with learning disabilities were similar to those of North American students. Mpofu and Nyanungo (1998) surveyed practicing psychologists in Zimbabwe on their use of measures of intelligence developed in Western countries. They observed that up to 92% of the psychologists used one or more measures of intelligence that were developed in Western countries, particularly with children with a reasonable grasp of the English language. The psychologists also assumed the validity of the Western ability tests for educational placement purposes.

A few observations are in order with regard to studies on the psychometric studies on the intellect of Zimbabwean students as presented above. First, the participants of the studies were Zimbabweans with a reasonably high level of schooling and fluency in English – hence the participants were unrepresentative of Zimbabwean children in general. The studies were also carried out exclusively with students in Zimbabwean primary (elementary) schools, which also limits the extent to which they can be generalized to Zimbabweans in general. Nonetheless, there seems to be some tentative evidence that the structure of mental abilities as represented on Western measures of intelligence may have some limited applicability to Zimbabwean students with a good grasp of English.

The historical research on the psychology of intelligence in Zimbabwe and sub-Saharan Africa has been rather fragmented or piecemeal in approach (Kendall et al., 1988; Irvine, 1988). It has also not addressed the association between indigenous conceptions of intelligence and objective criteria like performance in school and other settings.

CURRENT RESEARCH ON INTELLIGENCE IN ZIMBABWE AND SUB-SAHARAN AFRICA

Current research on intelligence in Zimbabwe and sub-Saharan Africa is characterized by continuity with previous research, scaling down of other areas of research, and a focus on preferred strategies for problem solving within ecological niches. For example, continuity has been maintained with the research by Irvine, Wober, and Serpell on indigenous conceptions of intelligence (e.g., Grigorenko, 2001; Sternberg et al., 2001). There has been a decline in psychometric studies on the transportability of Western tests of intelligence to sub-Saharan Africa. Psychometric-oriented studies that seek to relate indigenous notions of intelligence to objective external criteria (e.g., school achievement: Grigorenko et al., 2001; Serpell, 1993b; Sternberg et al., 2001), and the development of measures of intelligence that are indigenous to Africa are relatively new but promising.

Current Studies on Indigenous Conceptions of Intelligence

Grigorenko et al.'s (2001) ethnographic study of conceptions of intelligence among the Luo of rural Kenya established they had a multilayered view of intelligence: *rieko, luoro, winjo,* and *paro. Rieko* refers to smartness, knowledge, ability, skill, competence, and power and was closest to the conventional Western notion of intelligence. However, *rieko* was also defined by the context of performance. For example, the Luo refer to ability in school settings as *rieko mar skul* (knowledge acquired in school). School-related *rieko* was differentiated from the White-man–type technical expertise, or *rieko mzungu,* and so on. *Rieko* is also likely to be ascribed to the older members of the community. Individuals who had too much *reiko* were likely to be naughty. *Luoro* is a personal quality characterized by respect of and care for others. It also encompasses considerateness, obedience, and a willingness to share. Luoro is very similar to *musoro* among the Shona, as previously defined. *Winjo* refers to understanding and comprehension with appropriate deference to adults, elders, or authority figures. *Paro* refers to personal qualities such as innovativeness, creativity, and ability to think and follow through with ideas. *Rieko* and *paro* could be classified as representing the cognitive dimension of intelligence, and *luoro* and *winjo,* the component of social intelligence.

The studies by Mpofu seek to determine whether there has been a value shift in indigenous conceptions of intelligence by the younger generation of Zimbabweans because of the wider availability of formal education to the native population in the 20 years since independence from Britain. The findings by Mpofu on personal and culture of origin conceptions of intelligence (which are outlined in the section on Traditional and Modern Definitions of Intelligence) suggest that there may be a value shift in conceptions of intelligence among Zimbabweans from a primary orientation toward social intelligence to a cognitive kind of intelligence. Previous research on conceptions of intelligence by native Zimbabweans (e.g., Irvine, 1972, 1988) and other cultural groups indigenous to sub-Saharan Africa (e.g., Wober, 1974; Serpell, 1977) observed a primary orientation toward social intelligence. These and similar studies used as participants what would now be the older generation of Africans. For example, for the greater part of the period of Irvine's studies "the great majority of Shona people were by no means secure in skills of literacy" (1988, p. 166). With the current high level of literacy and modernity trend in Zimbabwe, it is likely that latter-day Zimbabwean adults may hold and communicate to their children cognitivistic conceptions of intelligence.

CURRENT PSYCHOMETRIC STUDIES ON INTELLIGENCE
IN ZIMBABWE AND SUB-SAHARAN AFRICA

The renorming or localization of imported tests of intelligence is no longer a priority area of research in Zimbabwe (Mpofu & Nyanungo, 1998). This is partly because of the lack of resources for the high costs that kind of enterprise may involve. The shift in emphasis away from research on the localization of individually administered foreign ability tests is also due to the realization of the fact that the tests are largely inapplicable to the average Zimbabwean (Mpofu & Nyanungo, 1998). The very low psychologist-to-client ratio of about 1:110,000 in the country reduces the chances that an individually administered intelligence test would be used with a client – thus putting into question the wisdom of spending a lot of resources on an instrument that would be used by only a tiny minority of the population (Kwadzanai Nyanungo, chief educational psychologist, Zimbabwe Public Services, personal communication, December 4, 2001). However, some continuity with the historical psychometric approach to the study of intelligence in Zimbabwe is evident in studies on bias of imported tests of ability (e.g., Mpofu, 1994c; Mpofu & Watkins, 1994). Mpofu and Watkins investigated racial bias in performance of Zimbabwean Black and White children on the British Ability Scales Similarities sub-test. The test is a measure of taxonomic classification (categorization ability) in children. No racial bias was observed. In a follow-up study, Mpofu (1994c) examined possible racial bias between Zimbabwean urban and rural children on the same measure. Test bias was observed in favor of urban children. I interpreted that finding in terms of the greater exposure to referent items on the measure and familiarity with individualized testing procedures of Zimbabwean urban children.

The development and standardization of the *Panga Muntu* (Make a Person) Test, by Kathuria and Serpell (1999), represents a pychometric approach to the study of intelligence with native Zambians. The

Panga Muntu Test is a language-reduced test of intelligence in which children are asked to make human like figures from clay (plasticine). The children's figures are then scored for representation of human physical characteristics. A maximum score of 25 is possible on the test. An interrater reliability of.89 was observed for the scoring procedure. The *Panga Muntu* Test was standardized on 3,231 primary school age children across Zambia. Among the key findings by Kathuria and Serpell on the *Panga Muntu* Test were that (1) performance on the test was uncorrelated with teacher's ratings of children's ability or children's human figure drawings using the regular school medium of pencil and paper, and (2) the test is particularly appropriate in cultural settings where children are familiar with manipulation of the medium of clay. Serpell and others (1993a; 2000) concluded that the tasks that reliably measured intelligence among rural African children were unrelated to the activities of schooling.

Sternberg et al. (2001) developed a Test of Tacit Knowledge for Natural Herbal Medicines with the Luo of a rural Kenyan community. Tacit knowledge was defined as that which is acquired through incidental or informal observational learning. Tacit knowledge is regarded as a kind of practical intelligence. In this connection, the Test of Tacit Knowledge for Natural Herbal Medicines measured children's knowledge of common illnesses in the community and their treatment, and so it was a test of practical intelligence among Luo children. The children could reasonably be expected to have learned about common illnesses in their community and related herbal treatment regimens through various levels of informal learning. In developing the Test of Tacit Knowledge for Natural Herbal Medicines, Sternberg et al. had 85 Luo children respond to 22 stories that required them to identify well-known illnesses in the community and indigenous herbal treatments for the illnesses. For some of the stories, the children were told the name of an illness and asked to identify an appropriate herbal treatment. Children's responses were scored quantitatively. An internal consistency reliability of.60 was observed for the test. The children's performance on the Test of Tacit Knowledge for Natural Herbal Medicines was then correlated with their performance on measures of academic intelligence (e.g., Raven's Progressive Matrices, Math, English attainment tests). Children's performance on the Test of Tacit Knowledge for Natural Herbal Medicines was uncorrelated with their performance on the academic ability measures. In a related study with the Luo of Kenya, Grigorenko et al. (2001) ratings of children's abilities by Luo adults were unrelated to those by peers and teachers. In fact, parents' views on intelligence were different from those of teachers. The findings by Sternberg et al. were consistent with those by Serpell (1993a), Wober (1974), and others that among rural African communities, ecologically valid measures of intelligence were unrelated to the activities of schooling.

Information Processing and Process-Oriented Studies

Process-oriented research on intelligence in Zimbabwe has built on previous research by Greenfield et al. (1966) and Glick (1975), to which reference has been made previously. The studies have focused on examining the nature and developing of ecologically valid or preferred strategies for categorizing stimuli (e.g., Mpofu, 1993, 1994b, 1995, 2001). I investigated the development of and preference for abstract and instrumental taxonomic strategies among Zimbabwean school children with regard to race, social class, and gender. Among my key findings were that (1) younger, lower-class, Black children tended to use functional rather than abstract interpretive strategies in responding to verbally presented class inclusion tasks (Mpofu, 1994b); (2) Zimbabwean children achieved reliable taxonomic classification at an age significantly higher than predicted of children by Piaget; (3) schooling rather than age explained a greater proportion of differences in children's use of taxonomic interpretive strategies (Mpofu, 1993); and (4) children who tended to use abstract categorization strategies had significantly higher scores on measures of ability used in Zimbabwean schools (Mpofu, 1995). In a 5-year longitudinal study, the results supporting a linear schooling versus age-related effect on preferred type of interpretive strategy were replicated (Mpofu & van de Vijver, 2000). Ongoing research in this domain is investigating the effect of verbal facilitation on Zimbabwean children's use of functional and abstract class inclusion strategies. The students are presented tasks in (1) two modes of presentation (verbal and pictorial) and three conditions of verbal cueing (none, category cueing, exemplar plus category and (2) two language conditions (primary and secondary) and the three conditions of verbal cueing (Mpofu, 2001). The findings inform on language context as an environmental press in the development of taxonomic structure in children.

With few exceptions (e.g., Mpofu & van de Vijver, 2000; Serpell, 1993; Sternberg et al., 2001), current studies on intelligence in Zimbabwe and sub-Saharan Africa have not yet achieved the status of a sustained or programmatic research effort. As previously observed, this is partly due to the very small number of psychologists in the sub-region, and that research on HIV/AIDS is regarded as a greater national priority for the governments of the region's countries. HIV/AIDS prevalence rates in a majority of the countries in sub-Saharan Africa are in the region of 1:4, the highest in the world. Research on intelligence has to compete for resources for HIV/AIDS research. There has been no research carried out in Zimbabwe that has sought to link HIV/AIDS infection with aspects of intelligence, although that linkage would add relevance to research on intelligence in the country and draw more resources toward research in that area.

SUMMARY AND CONCLUSION

The status of the psychology of intelligence in a country is influenced by its unique socio-cultural history. In the case of Zimbabwe, the country's indigenous and British colonial cultural histories and the modernity trend among the population influence conceptions of intelligence. As a consequence of this diverse cultural heritage, there are multilayered conceptions of intelligence in the country. These may be described as falling within two major categories: traditional–indigenous and modern. Traditional–indigenous conceptions of intelligence place a higher value on the social aspects of intelligence. By contrast, modern conceptions of intelligence emphasize its cognitivistic characteristics. A pilot study on views of Zimbabwean college students revealed that they had personal views of intelligence that could be described as modern. Their definitions of their ideal intelligent person recognized both the social and cognitive aspects – although more representative of a modern view of intelligence. The students' views of conceptions of intelligence in their culture of origin indicated that their community of origin had a social competence view of intelligence. Being successful and educated are respected indicators of intelligence in Zimbabwe. There appears to be a value shift in conceptions of intelligence by adults in contemporary Zimbabwe from a traditional–indigenous perspective toward a modern cognitivistic–adaptationist orientation. The high levels of literacy in the general population and the modernity trend may explain the shift.

In Zimbabwe, theory development in the area of intelligence is still in its infancy. It is best described as at the implicit theory stage. The work of Irvine is credited with much of the knowledge on Zimbabwean implicit theories of intelligence. Research on intelligence in Zimbabwe has followed both an implicit theory and explicit theory (psychometric) approach. In recent times, there has been a shift from psychometric oriented studies toward examination of the development of competencies in eco-cultural niches. This research effort is likely to support the development of explicit theories of intelligence relevant to Zimbabwe. The findings of the research on intelligence indicate substantial similarities with those of studies that have been carried out in other parts of Africa and equally significant differences with commonly held assumptions on intelligence in Western societies.

Overall research output in the area of intelligence has been limited by the lower development of expertise in the psychology of intelligence, as well as the lower number of psychologists in the sub-region. The research opportunities in the psychology of intelligence are also surpassed by those in HIV/AIDS. The need for research on containment and treatment of HIV/AIDS is regarded a greater national priority in Zimbabwe and a majority of countries in sub-Saharan Africa. The sub-region has the highest prevalence of HIV/AIDS in the world. The very minute number of psychologists in Zimbabwe and sub-Saharan Africa with a research orientation further constrains the research output. The few psychologists with a research orientation choose to be involved with HIV/AIDS research. It is possible to boost the research effort in the area of intelligence in Zimbabwe by linking it with ongoing research on HIV/AIDS. An applied research orientation is likely to enhance the status of the psychology of intelligence in the country.

References

Azuma, H. (1984). Psychology in a non-Western country. *International Journal of Psychology, 19,* 45–55.

Berry, J. W., van de Koppe, J. M. H., Annis, R. C., Senechal, C., Bahuchet, S., Sforza-Cavali, L. L., & Witkin, H. A. (1986). *On the edge of the forest: Cultural adaptation and cogntive development in central Africa.* Location: Swets, North America.

Bourdillon, M. F. C. (1987). *The Shona peoples: An ethnography of the contemporary shona.* Gwetu, Zimbabwe: Mambo Press.

Chapains, A. (1963). Men, machines, and models. *American Psychologist, 16,* 116–131.

Chimhundu, H. (Ed.). (2001). *Dura manzwi guru rechiShona.* Harare: College Press.

Cole, M. (1998). Cognitive development, culture and schooling. In M. Cole, *Cultural psychology: A once and future discipline* (pp. 69–97). Cambridge, MA: Harvard University Press.

Glick, J. (1975). Cognitive development in cross-cultural perspective. In F. D. Horowitz (Ed.)., *Review of child development research* (Vol. 4., pp. 595–648). Chicago, IL: Chicago University Press.

Greenfield, P. M., Reich, I. C., & Oliver, R. R. (1966). On culture and cognition. In J. S. Bruner, R. R. Oliver, P. M. Greenfield, J. R. Hornesby, H. J. Kenney, M. Maccoby, N. Modiano, F. A. Mosher, D. R. Oslon, M. C. Potter, L. C. Reich, and A. M. Sonstroem (Eds.), *Studies in cognitive growth* (pp. 270–318). New York: Wiley.

Grigorenko, E. L., Geissler, P. W., Prince, R., Okatcha, F., Nokes, C., Kenny, D. A., Bundy, D. A., & Sternberg, R. J. (2001). The organization of Luo conceptions of intelligence: A study of implicit theories in a Kenyan village. *International Journal of Behavioral Development, 25, 367–378.*

Hadebe, S. (Ed.). (2001). *Isichamazwi.* Harare: College Press.

Irvine, S. H. (1966). Towards a rationale for testing abilities and attainment in Africa. *British Journal of Educational Psychology, 36,* 24–32.

Irvine, S. H. (1969). The factor analysis of African abilities and attainments: Constructs across cultures. *Psychological Bulletin, 71,* 20–32.

Irvine, S. H. (1970). Affect and construct: A cross-cultural check on theories of intelligence. *Journal of Social Psychology, 80,* 23–30.

Irvine, S. H. (1972). The African contribution to new thinking about intelligence. In S. H. Irvine & J. T. Sanders (Eds.), *Cultural adaptation within modern Africa* (pp. 97–102). New York: Teachers College Press.

Irvine, S. H. (1988). Constructing the intellect of the Shona: A taxonomic approach. In J. W. Berry, S. H. Irvine, & E. B. Hunt (Eds.), *Indigenous cognition functioning in a cultural context* (pp. 156–176). Dordrecht: Martinus Nijhoff.

Irvine, S. H., & Berry, J. W. (1988). The abilities of mankind: A revaluation. In S. H. Irvine & J. W. Berry (Eds.), *Human abilities in cultural context* (pp. 3–59). New York: Cambridge University Press.

Kasfir, N. (1983). Introduction: Relating state to class in Africa. *Journal of Commonwealth and Comparative Politics, 21,* 3–8.

Kathuria, R., & Serpell, R. (1999). Standardization of the Panga Muntu Test – a nonverbal cognitive test developed in Zambia. *Journal of Negro Education, 67,* 228–241.

Kendall, I. M., Verster, M. A., & Von Mollendorf, J. W. (1988). Test performance of blacks in Southern Africa. In S. H. Irvine & J. W. Berry (Eds.), *Human abilities in cultural context* (pp. 299–339). New York: Cambridge University Press.

Latif (1980). *Performance of Zimbabwean students on the WISC-R.* Unpublished manuscript.

Lazarus, A. A. (1993). Theory, subjectivity and bias: Can there be a future? *Psychotherapy, 30,* 674–677.

Makanza, M. (1988). *A comparative study of pupils' profiles on the WISC-R.* Unpublished masters thesis, University of Zimbabwe Location.

Mandaza, I. (1986). *Zimbabwe: The political economy of transition.* Dakar: Codresia.

Ministry of Education, Sport, and Culture (2001). Report on the national budget. Harare, Zimbabwe: Author.

Mpofu, E. (1993). The context of mental testing and implications for psychoeducational practice in modern Zimbabwe. In W. Su. (Ed.)., *Proceedings of the second Afro-Asian psychological conference* (pp. 17–25). Beijing: University of Peking Press.

Mpofu, E. (1994a). Exploring the self-concept in an African culture. *Journal of Genetic Psychology, 155,* 341–354.

Mpofu, E. (1994b). Children's interpretive strategies for class inclusion tasks. *British Journal of Educational Psychology, 64,* 77–89.

Mpofu, E. (1994c). The British Ability Scales Similarities sub-test's content and construct bias for a sample of Zimbabwean school children: A replication and extension study. *Zimbabwe Journal of Educational Research, 7,* 89–113.

Mpofu, E. (1995). Antecedents of children's performance on class inclusion tests: Some Zimbabwean evidence. *International Journal of Psychology, 30,* 19–34.

Mpofu, E. (2001) *Verbal facilitation effects on class inclusion response salience Zimbabwean children.* Unpublished manuscript.

Mpofu, E., & Khan, N. (1996). Regulations for psychological licensure in Zimbabwe: Procedures, problems and prospects. *World Psychology, 31,* 211–226.

Mpofu, E., & Nyanungo, K. R. L. (1998). Educational and psychological testing in Zimbabwean schools: Past, present and future. *European Journal of Psychological Assessment, 14,* 71–90.

Mpofu, E., & van de Vijver, F. (2000). Taxonomic structure in early to middle childhood: A longitudinal study with a sample of Zimbabwean children. *International Journal of Behavioral Development, 24,* 204–212.

Mpofu, E., & Watkins, D. A. (1994). The Similarities subtest of the British Ability Scales: Content and construct bias for a sample of Zimbabwe school children. *Educational and Psychological Measurement, 54,* 728–733.

Mpofu, E., Zindi, F., Oakland, T., & Peresuh, M. (1997). School psychological practices in East and Southern Africa. *Journal of Special Education, 31,* 387–402.

Oslon, A. R. (1984). Intelligence and literacy: The relationships between intelligence and the technologies of representation and communication. In R. J. Sternberg & R. K. Wagner (Eds.), *Practical intelligence.* Location: Cambridge University Press.

Patterson, C. H., & Watkins, C. E., Jr. (1996). *Theories of psychotherapy* (5th ed.). New York: Harper Collins.

Rogers, T., & Macguire, T. (1990). *Short course: Test norming and equating in urban areas in Zimbabwe.* Harare, Zimbabwe: June 24 – July 5.

Serpell, R. (1977). Estimates of intelligence in a rural community in eastern Zambia. In F. M. Okatcha (Ed.)., *Modern psychology and cultural adaptation* (pp. 179–216). Nairobi; Kenya Swahili Language Consultants and Publishers.

Serpell, R. (1988). Childhood disability in the sociocultural context: Assessment and information needs for effective services. In P. R. Dasen, J. W. Berry, & N. Sartorius (Eds.)., *Health and cross-cultural psychology: Toward applications* (pp. 256–276). Newbury Park: Sage.

Serpell, R. (1993a). Wanzelu ndani? A Chewa perspective on child development and intelligence. In *The significance of schooling: Life-journeys in an African society* (pp. 24–71). Cambridge: Cambridge University Press.

Serpell, R. (1993b). Interface between sociocultural and psychological aspects of cognition. In E. Forman, N. Minick, & A. Stone (Eds.), *Contexts for learning: Sociocultural dynamics in children's development* (pp. 357–368). New York: Oxford University Press.

Serpell, R. (2000). Intelligence and culture. In R. Sternberg (Ed.)., *Handbook of intelligence* (pp. 549–576). Cambridge University Press.

Serpell, R. & Boykin, A. W. (1994). Cultural dimensions of cognition: A multiplex, dynamic system of constraints and possibilities. In R. J. Sternberg (Ed.)., *Thinking and problem solving* (pp. 369–408). New York: Academic Press.

Sternberg, R. J. (1981). People's conceptions of intelligence. *Journal of Personality and Social Psychology, 41,* 37–35.

Sternberg, R. J. (1985). Implicit theories of intelligence, creativity and wisdom. *Journal of Personality and Social Psychology, 49,* 607–627.

Sternberg, R. J. (1998). A balance theory of wisdom. *Review of General Psychology, 2,* 347–365.

Sternberg, R. J. (1999). The theory of successful intelligence. *Review of General Psychology, 3,* 292–375.

Sternberg, R. J., Conway, B. E., Ketron, J. L., & Bernstein, M. (1991). Peoples conceptions of intelligence. *Journal of Personality and Social Psychology, 41,* 37–55.

Sternberg, R. J., Nokes, C., Geissler, P. W., Prince, R., Okatcha, F., Bundy, D. A., Grigorenko, E. L. (2001). The relationship between academic and practical intelligence: A case study in Kenya. *Intelligence, 29,* 401–418.

Vernon, P. E. (1969). Intelligence and cultural environment. London: Methuen.

Watkins, D., Akande, A., & Mpofu, E. (1996). Assessing self-esteem: An African perspective. *Personality and Individual Differences, 20,* 163–169.

Whyte, S. R. (1998). Slow cookers and madman: Competencies of heart and head in rural Uganda. In R. Jenkins (Ed.), *Questions of competence* (pp. 153–175). Cambridge: Cambridge University Press.

Wober, M. (1974). Towards an understanding of the Kiganda concept of intelligence. In J. W. Berry & P. R. Dasen (Eds.), *Culture and cognition: Readings in cross-cultural psychology* (pp. 261–280). London: Methuen.

Zimbabwe Central Statistical Office (1992). *National census data.* Harare, Zikmbabwe: Author.

Zimbabwe Central Statistical (1992). *Population Census.* Harare, Zimbabwe: Author.

Zvobgo, R. J. (1994). *Colonialism and education in Zimbabwe.* Harare: Sapes Books.

14

Intelligence Research in Latin America

Ricardo Rosas

INTRODUCTION

How do we explore a territory for which there are no maps available? This difficulty, faced by Spanish and Portuguese conquerors attempting to explore and dominate Latin America during the 16th century, is similar to that faced by the author of this chapter in finding out what has been researched in the region on the topic of intelligence. Where does this difficulty lie? On one side, in the insufficient development of the discipline in the region, and on the other, closely related to the former, in the scarce development of means of scientific communication that could contribute to the dissemination of the work being carried out.

Latin America includes 25 countries and two associated states. It counts only three psychology journals indexed in the Institute for Scientific Information (ISI) (*Revista Latinoamericana de Psicología*, *Revista Mexicana de Psicología*, *Revista Interamericana de Psicología*) and one non-indexed but recently included in PsycInfo (*Revista Psykhe*). Most of the countries in the region have begun to offer psychology as a major in their universities only within the last three decades (Toro & Villegas, 2001). Only Mexico, Brazil, and Chile have Ph.D. psychology programs that are competitive at an international level, all of them developed very recently. In other words, there is not a consolidated development of the discipline in the region, and there are not enough means of scientific dissemination. Therefore, it shouldn't be surprising that a subdiscipline

I acknowledge the contribution of Camilo Bertin, who helped to gather the information needed to write this chapter and María Rosa Lissi, who translated it into English.

such as the study of intelligence shows an incipient development, although as I attempt to demonstrate in this chapter, it includes some innovative studies and auspicious perspectives.

The method employed to gather the information needed to elaborate this chapter was as follows: first, an e-mail message was sent to all those registered for the 18th Congress of the Interamerican Psychological Society (SIP), whose work was related to the topic of intelligence, asking them to answer a short questionnaire regarding intelligence definitions and assessment techniques most frequently used in their own countries, as well as information about local publications or research work in the area. At the same time, a review was carried out of the four mainstream psychology journals published in the region, which were mentioned previously. Books and documents recommended by experts from the region were also reviewed.[1]

INTELLIGENCE DEFINITIONS AND THEORIES IN THE REGION

In Latin America, definitions and theories of intelligence are, like in the rest of the world, strongly determined by the assessment instruments used for diagnostic or research purposes. With a few exceptions, approaches to the topic of intelligence appear highly interwoven with the issue of its evaluation. Table 14.1 summarizes information about the main studies carried out in the region, grouped in five large categories: instrument standardization studies, cognitive enrichment studies, studies about prediction based on intellectual variables, studies characterizing populations on the basis of intellectual variables, and studies about conceptions of intelligence. Except for the last group of studies, which deals with implicit and explicit conceptions about intelligence and its evaluation, the rest adhere to the intelligence models that support the instruments chosen to assess it.

As it can be seen in Table 14.1, most of the studies use instruments developed in Europe or the United States. The only exception is the study carried out by Bralic (1981), who uses a psychomotor development scale created and standardized in Chile, which in any case is based in Lezine and Bradley's scales. To our knowledge, there are no instruments for

---

[1] Considering that a very significant portion of research work in the region is carried out by undergraduate students as part of their theses, which are not published, it is highly likely that the information included here leaves out an important part of the knowledge actually produced in the region in the topic of intelligence. I apologize in advance to the reader and the potential authors for this omission, which is completely involuntary.

TABLE 14.1. *Latin American Intelligence Studies*

Category	Publi- cations	Authors	Instruments or Conception of Intelligence
Standardizations, adaptations, and statistic analyses of the instrument	15	Adriasola et al. (1976)	WISC-R
		Backhoff-Escudero (1996)	MPR
		Bannen & Silva (1983)	WAIS-R
		Berreta et al. (1969)	GATB
		Calderón et al. (1980)	WISC-R
		Campazo et al. (1962)	WISC
		Cañas et al. (1978)	WISC-R
		Carroll et al. (1995)	EIWN-P-PR (adapted WISC-R)
		Cayssials & Perez (2001)	WISC-III
		Ivanovic et al. (2000)	RPMT, Goodenough, Language and Math tests
		Kalawski & Losada (1969)	Goodenough
		Padilla et al. (1982)	WISC-R, Bender Gestalt, student grades and teacher comments
		Paine (1978)	Verbal Scale of the WISC
		Rosas (1996)	BIST (Berlin Model, Jäger)
		Altez (1997)	Thorndike, Cattell
Cognitive enrichment	6	Alvarez et al. (1994)	Program based on Feuerstein. RPMT, Cattell
		Bralic (1981)	WISC, Basic Skills Test (Chilean)
		Herrnstein et al. (1986) & Walsh (1981)	OLSAT, Cattell, and General Abilities Test, besides an Oral Reasoning Test (non-standardized)
		Montenegro et al. (1978)	EEDP, Test based on Piaget's theory, Denver Test

(continued)

TABLE 14.1 *(continued)*

Category	Publi-cations	Authors	Instruments or Conception of Intelligence
		Rodríguez et al. (1985)	Curriculum based on descriptive theories of childhood development and Piaget's genetic theory. Stanford-Binet and TEPSI.
Prediction studies	3	Ivanovic et al. (1989)	RPMT, Language and Math tests
		Rosas (1992)	BIST (Berlin Model, Jäger)
		Varela (1977)	Guilford's Model. Questionnaire for the supervisor regarding intellectual capabilities of the employer to carry out the task.
Characterization studies	4	Donovan et al. (1983)	RPMT, WISC-R
		Gazmuri et al. (1978)	Goodenough, WISC, Language and Math tests and teacher appreciation
		Ivanovic & Marambio (1989)	Language and Math tests (PAA and SIMCE)
		Sans (1982)	WISC
Studies about Conceptions of Intelligence	2	Kaplan (1997) Rosas & Simonetti (1986)	

the assessment of intelligence in the region, developed on the basis of original conceptualizations.

Most standardization studies are related to Wechsler's scales, three of them of the children's scales and only one of the scales for adults. It is surprising to find out that standardization studies of Wechsler's scales are only reported in Argentina, Chile, Mexico, and Puerto Rico. This information contrasts strongly with personal communications to the author, in the sense that in all the region's countries some of the Wechler's scales are used as standard procedures to measure intelligence. The norms used in these cases are often those of the Spaniard version, or are even taken directly from the U.S. version. The great diversity and cultural specificity of the region's countries do not allow support of the use of foreign norms, and therefore the lack of research and development of properly standarized versions is amazing, considering the characteristics of each of the countries in the region. Regarding the rest of the standardization studies, they include other instruments that are widely known in the United States or some European countries: General Ability Test Battery (GATB), Raven, Cattell, Thorndike, and Goodenough. It is also possible to observe the standardization of an instrument with the purpose of testing an intelligence model (Rosas, 1996). Summarizing from those studies involving the creation and standardization of instruments, it is already possible to conclude that scientific conceptualization of intelligence is strongly influenced by the discourse of developed countries, and just as in the latter, theorization is strongly determined by instrumentation.

Cognitive enrichment studies carried out in the region show little variation with regard to construct definition and the instruments utilized. From the six studies reported, one adheres to the theorization and instrumentation of Feuerstein's Instrumental Enrichment Program (Alvarez, Santos, & Lebrón, 1994), two to the Intelligence Development program carried out in Venezuela during the 1970s by Herrnstein and Machado (Herrnstein et al., 1986; Walsh, 1981) and three to the early stimulation program of Montenegro et al. in Chile (Bralic, 1981; Montenegro et al., 1978; Rodríguez et al., 1985).

Feuerstein's instrumental enrichment program adheres to a conceptualization of cognitive deficit as a consequence of cultural deprivation. The program aims to stimulate the acquisition of higher cognitive structures, through mediated exposure to problem solving tasks involving analogical thought. The effects test is carried out basically through "culture-fair" tests, such as Raven's or Catell's tests.

The Intelligence Development Project of Herrnstein and Machado is not formally ascribed to any intelligence theory: "In fact, the Venezuelan program is not based on the theories of any particular school or individual. The approach is highly eclectic, using multiple methodologies" (Walsh, 1981, p. 640). Its results are assessed through the use of translated instruments (not developed in Venezuela) that were created in the United States.

Last, the early stimulation program developed by Montenegro and his colleagues holds to a classic conceptualization of intelligence at the time of evaluating its impact, although for process evaluation it rather adheres to models of cognitive functions, which are operationalized in psychomotor development tests.

We count three studies regarding prediction based on intelligence tests. Varela (1977) uses tests derived from Guilford's intellectual structure model to predict success in a variety of occupations. Ivanovic et al. (1989) study the relation of intelligence measured by Raven's Progressive Matrixes Test (RPMT), with anthropometric measures and school performance. Rosas (1992) uses the Berlin Intelligence Structure Test (BIST) to predict academic performance in university students. In these three studies the intelligence conceptualization is strongly determined by assessment techniques. In the case of the study by Ivanovic et al., there is not an explicit definition of intelligence offered, but it is assumed that this is reflected in the RPMT. In the cases of Varela and Rosas, there is explicit adherence to neofactorial models of intelligence dimensions proposed, respectively, by Guilford (1967) and Jäger (1982).

The six studies of population characterization show a similar picture. Four studies use the WISC, one uses Goodenough's test, one uses the RPMT, another uses the Chilean SAT (Scholastic Aptitude Test), and the other uses a test based on Piagetian cognitive tasks for the assessment of sensory-motor intelligence.

In summary, if we take as an indicator of the definition and theorization regarding intelligence the instruments utilized to measure it, it becomes clear that the studies in the region reproduce theories and methods from those countries with greater academic development. In the following section we come back to the most relevant results of some of the studies presented here, and we also offer a more detailed explanation of the results of those studies included in the table that have not been mentioned here. Until this point, presenting the studies has served the purpose of illustrating implicit theories of intelligence that are being employed in the region, based on the instruments utilized in the studies reviewed.

MAIN STUDIES IN THE REGION IN THIS AREA

Studies of Poverty and Intelligence

One of the major problems in Latin America is the high proportion of its population who live in poverty conditions. One of the most important and recurrent topics of interest with regard to intelligence in the region has been, therefore, characterizing this population in terms of intellectual variables, basically with the purpose of providing support for the investment in educational or stimulation programs targeting this population. One of the pioneer studies of this kind was carried out by Llanos in a sample of Peruvian children (1974, cited in Montenegro, 1989). In a sample of approximately 300 children between the ages of 6 and 7, he found highly significant differences in IQ distribution measured through the Wechsler Intelligence Scale for Children (WISC), between children of middle-high socioeconomic (SE) level and children of middle-low SE level, with clear and significant advantages for the former group. These results are consistent with those found in the normative sample of the same test standardized in Chile (Adriasola et al., 1976; Calderón et al., 1980; Cañas et al., 1978) and in a study carried out with 100 students in Buenos Aires City (Sans, 1982).

Gazmuri, Milicic, and Schmidt (1978), on their part, in a study about the prevalence of intellectual retardation associated to school achievement, assessed 918 children from the first elementary school grades in Santiago, Chile, from high and low SE levels. They used Goodenough's Test and the WISC and found significant differences in the performance of children based on their SE level. Prevalence of intellectual retardation was estimated to be 8%, which is represented almost completely by children in the low SE level.

A study more focused on children living in poverty was carried out in Chile by Donovan et al. (1983), who evaluated, through Raven's Progressive Matrixes Test, a total of 5,009 children between the ages of 6 and 14 from dysfunctional home environments and at high social risk. The average achievement attained by the children was percentile 31, equivalent to an IQ estimated by Wechsler of approximately 93, corresponding to the lower boundary of the normal range.

In a very original and provocative study, Haeussler (1981) presents evidence that there are no differences in intellectual performance of children from different SE levels. In fact, sensory-motor intelligence (assessed through a standardized instrument of Piagetian tasks, Haeussler, 1981) was assessed in 177 Chilean infants between 4 and 13 months of age from two SE groups (middle-high and low). The instrument applied comprises 4 scales: (1) use of means to achieve ends, (2) object notion construction, (3) causality notion development, and (4) construction of spatial relations. It was observed that before the acquisition of language and under certain conditions (such as absence of malnutrition, adequate obstetric conditions, and presence of the mother a half day at home), there are no differences in the intellectual development of infants from different SE backgrounds. This study's importance lies in the fact that it contributes to opening a perspective in the search for childhood psychological development risk factors that are more specific than SE background, which are prenatal and perinatal aspects and a certain environmental stability for the child. It also provides evidence in support of the hypothesis according to which before the emergence of language there are no differences in the intellectual development of children based on SE level, as long as the conditions for a normal biological development are given.

With regard to cognitive stimulation studies in the region, the most widely known is the Intelligence Development Project from Venezuela (Herrnstein et al., 1986; Walsh, 1981). This project, which will not be presented in detail here because it is the most easily accessible for those readers who are English speakers, had as its purpose to develop higher cognitive abilities in children from social risk areas who were attending 7th grade. The intervention involved exposure to 54 lessons tending to increment and stimulate six areas considered as keys for intelligence development: (1) reasoning fundaments, (2) language comprehension, (3) verbal reasoning, (4) problem solving, (5) decision making, and (6) inventive behavior.

An experimental group of 436 students and a control group of 432 students, from classes that were matched in both experimental conditions, participated in the study.

Regarding the issue that concerns us, the intervention's results measured through intelligence tests (using the Otis-Lennon School Ability Test, OLSAT; Culture-Fair Intelligence Test, Cattell; General Abilities Tests, GAT, all with norms from the United States), it was found that students in the experimental group scored significantly higher in all tests, although only marginally in Cattell. The d value or score in the GAT was 0.35, which indicates that an average student would move from percentile 50 to 64 by taking the course. From the four subtests of Cattell, only the increment for the visual series was significantly higher for the experimental group than for the control group. In GAT, the increment was significantly higher for the experimental group in seven of the eight subtests. The exemption was the numeric series, in which the experimental group achieved scores marginally higher than those of the control group. It is not yet clear why there was no observed improvement in the performance in two of Cattell's subtests, concretely: classification and rule inference, which have objectives that are coincident with central aspects of the course.

In the area of early stimulation, one of the most important programs carried out in the region was initiated at the beginning of the 1970s in

Chile (Montenegro et al., 1978). The program was targeted to infants between 0 and 24 months of age from low SE backgrounds, and it aimed to significantly improve the children's psychic development, increase the mothers' efficacy as agents for the children's stimulation, demonstrate that the proposed model was feasible of being implemented in the National Health Service, and propose a procedure for massive implementation of the program.

The program included two basic activities: educating the mothers and assessing the children's psychomotor development. To carry out the first activity the mothers received 24 stimulation manuals, one for each month of age. These manuals explain, in a simple and didactic manner, activities to be carried out with the children to foster their development. In addition, half-hour home visits were implemented, to deliver the curriculum in a more motivating way than in the manuals. The second activity was carried out using a standardized psychomotor development scale.

The sample for the program's pilot evaluation sample included 159 families of low SE background. In this sample, premature children or those presenting morbid antecedents related to pregnancy or delivery were not excluded. The sample was randomly assigned to three experimental groups and a control group.

Stimulation Group 1 (SG1): a group composed of 41 children of both genders, who received a stimulation curriculum from their birth until they were 24 months old. These children's mothers received an instruction manual monthly and were visited periodically. The children's psychomotor development was evaluated monthly.

Stimulation Group 2 (SG2): a group composed of 40 children of both genders, who were incorporated into the stimulation curriculum from their 4th month of age and received it until they were 24 months old.

Stimulation Group 3 (SG3): 43 children of both genders, who received home visits with information regarding their physical health until they turned 14 months old and were exposed to the same treatment received by SG1. They received the stimulation curriculum for 10 months.

Control Group 1 (CG1): 43 children of both genders, who had their psychomotor development evaluated every three months.

Control Group 2 (CG2): sample used for the standardization of the Psychomotor Development Evaluation Scale, from a high SE background ($N = 300$).

The achievements of the participating children were assessed using the *Escala de Evaluación del Desarrollo Psychomotor: 0–24 meses* (EEDP)

(Psychomotor Development Evaluation Scale: 0–24 months), with Piagetian tests to measure intelligence development between ages 0 and 2, and with Denver's Test with U.S. norms to conduct a follow-up evaluation after 36 months.

The results showed clear advantages for experimental group (EG) stimulation 1 over the rest of the experimental groups and control group 1. SG3 was compared with CG1, to see if the home visits per se had effects on the children's psychological development. The data show that periodic contact between mothers and health personnel, through home visits with physical development as their only content, did not have perceptible effects on children's psychological development.

With regard to children's age at the beginning of the intervention, it was determined that starting application of the curriculum at 4 months produced an immediate and maintained increment on the developmental coefficients (DC), which, from the time the curriculum was implemented became homologous to those of children stimulated from birth.

When the curriculum began to be implemented at 15 months, it did not produce a significant increment in DC in the short term, although a tendency to approach the DC of the SG1 was observed. This finding led researchers to think that if the stimulation period of SG3 would have been longer and similar to that of the other groups, the children could have reached DC equivalent to those of children in the SG1.

When the children were 36 months old, a follow-up study was carried out using Denver's Test, and there were not significant differences between SG1 and CG1; however, there were differences between SG1 and SG3, favoring the former. This superiority does not reflect higher achievement in all areas measured by the test, but only in the coordination area and social area (not in the motor development area and language area).

A follow-up of this study was carried out six years later by Bralic (1981), attempting to include all the children from SG1, SG3, and CG1 who had completed the program. They were able to locate 85% of them (EG1: 26, EG3: 25, CG1: 27).

The WISC was used to assess intellectual ability, and a Basic Skills Test was used to measure visual-motor coordination, sound discrimination, and comprehensive language. Vineland's Maturity Scale (with original norms) was also incorporated, as well as a questionnaire about child behavior to observe possible behavioral disorders.

The results show there are not statistically significant differences in any of the tests. There were not observed differences in the psychological

TABLE 14.2. *Standardization of Instruments in Latin America*

Instrument	Latin American Country Where It Has Been Standardized
WISC	Brazil (1978), Chile (1962)
WISC-R	Mexico (1982), Chile (1976–1980) Puerto Rico (1995)
WISC-III	Argentina (2001)
WAIS-R	Chile (1983)
CATTELL	Peru (1997)
GATB	Chile (1969)
GOODENOUGH	Chile (1969)
RPMT	Mexico (1996), Chile (2000)
BIST	Chile (1996)
THORNDIKE	Peru (1997)

development of children who did receive early stimulation compared with those that did not receive it, especially on the WISC and the Basic Skills Test. It should be highlighted, in any case, that SG1 and CG1 performance on the WISC is similar to what is expected for middle-class children, which suggests some sort of Hawthorne effect in this study.

Instrument Standardization Studies

Table 14.2 provides a summary of instrument standardization carried out in Latin America. As it can be seen in the table, most studies are about Wechsler's Scales, in their different versions, with a predominance of standardization studies of the children's scales.

Regarding the WISC, we count studies from Argentina, Brazil, Chile, Mexico, and Puerto Rico. The original WISC has been adapted and standardized in Brazil and Chile. Paine and García (1974) report standardization of the test's verbal scale in a sample of 242 children of ages 7, 10, and 13. Subsequently, Paine (1978) reports that the factorial structure of the WISC's verbal scale in Brazil is similar to that of the verbal scale used in the United States.

In Chile, the WISC was adapted, translated from the original English, and administered to a sample of 1,000 children between the ages of 6 and 15 to determine the norms (Campazo et al., 1962).

Regarding the Wechsler Intelligence Scale for Children–Revised (WISC-R), there are studies from Chile, Mexico, and Puerto Rico. In Chile, the standardization process was carried out in three stages (Adriasola et al., 1976; Calderón et al., 1980; Cañas et al., 1978). The first stage involved translating and adapting the test, which was evaluated in 390 children. Later, the test was administered to a sample of 720 children from the metropolitan area to obtain provisory norms, and, last, the test's final version was administered to 840 subjects, ages between 10 years and 16 years, 11 months, 30 days.

The WISC-R Mexican version was standardized using a sample of 1,100 students from Mexico's Federal District public schools, with ages ranging from 6 to 16 (Padilla, Roll, & Gomez-Palacio, 1982).

In Puerto Rico, Carroll, Herrans, and Rodríguez (1995) standardized the WISC-R, applying it to a sample of 200 children of ages between 6 and 16:11, stratified by age, gender, socioeconomic status, and area of residence (urban or rural). When contrasting the factorial structure of the test, the authors found two significant factors equivalent to the verbal and manual scales, and a distraction factor in five age levels.

With regard to the Wechsler Intelligence Scale for Children, 3rd Ed. (WISC-III), we only count a recent study carried out by Cayssials & Pérez (2001) in Buenos Aires, Argentina. Norms were obtained by administering the test to 717 children whose ages ranged from 6 to 16 years old.

Finally, with regard to the Wechsler Adult Intelligence Scale (WAIS), we only have infomation from a preliminar standardization of the Wechsler Adult Intelligence Scale–Revised (WAIS-R), carried out in Chile (Bannen & Silva, 1983). The test was translated from English, and then adapted and administered to 48 volunteers, categorized according to gender and SE level.

Regarding other intelligence scales, we count information from the following studies: Altez (1997) reports the standardization of Catell's culture-fair g factor intelligence test and Thorndike, Hagen, and Lorge's test. Both scales from Catell's test were standardized in samples of children from the metropolitan area in Lima, ranging in ages from 4 to 8 years for scale 1, and between 8 and 14 years of age for scale 2 (1,080 children were tested with scale 1, and 847, with scale 2). Standardization involved three SE levels and both genders.

Regarding Thorndike, Hagen, and Lorge's test, the sample used for the standardization comprised 600 children between 5 and 7:11 years old, from high, medium, and low SE backgrounds.

Berreta et al. (1969) translated and adapted the GATB in Chile. The test was administered to a sample of 345 workers, segmented according to occupational group, age, and years of schooling, and the norms obtained consider four age levels: from 15 to 19, from 20 to 24, from 25 to 30, and from 31 to 34 years old.

Kalawski and Losada (1969) standardized Goodenough's Test for Chilean children living in urban Santiago. For this purpose, they applied the test to 600 children, stratified according to 10 age levels (between 3 years, 6 months, and 13 years, 6 months), gender, and SE level.

Raven's Progressive Matrices Test has been standardized in Mexico (Backhoff-Escudero, 1996) and Chile (Ivanovic et al., 2000). Mexican norms come from a retrospective review of 10,771 records from the Universidad Autónoma de Baja California obtained after administering the test as a selection procedure to all students applying to the university from 1986 until 1990.

Chilean norms come from a study carried out between 1986 and 89 with 4,258 students segmented by grade, gender, type of school (public, subsidized, or private), and geographic area. The students' ages ranged from 5 years, 6 months, to 22 years, 1 month. The test's special scale was used with children between 5 and 11 years old.

The Berlin Intelligence Structure Test (BIST) was standardized by Rosas (1996). The BIST is an instrument based on the Berlin Intelligence Structure Model (BISM) proposed by Jäger (1982), which has a two-dimensional conception of intelligence (divided into processes and contents). The test is composed of 36 subtests, which simultaneously measure one of the four process factors (Speed, Short-Term Memory, Creativity, and Reasoning) and one of the three content factors (Verbal, Figural, and Numeric). The test was adapted, standardized, and subjected to structural analysis tests in a sample of 470 university students from 11 majors in the Pontificia Universidad Católica de Chile.

Studies About Teacher and Psychologists' Intelligence Conceptions

We found two studies in the region that analyze the intelligence problem from the actors that, in their professional practice, use or must use implicit or explicit conceptualizations of the construct.

Kaplan (1997) became interested in knowing teachers' representations of children's intelligence. In a study based on in-depth interviews of 34 elementary school teachers from Buenos Aires public schools, this author inquired into their conceptions of intelligence, both formal and popular (expressed in proverbs and popular sayings) and explored the importance given to intellectual variables as explicative factors of school failure.

The study's main results show that teachers differ greatly in their conceptions of intelligence. Innatist, environmental, and interactionist conceptions are observed, with a clear predominance of the first two. Varied definitions of intelligence are observed, both as general ability and as compound of specific abilities. When defining the characteristics of intelligent children, however, there is a generalized tendency to do it from their teaching practice, that is, intelligence is defined and situated in the school context. Thus, intelligent children are those characterized as disciplined and with good work habits, who are interested in learning and have some cognitive characteristics (speed, reasoning ability, learning ability), who are creative and – surprisingly – have certain social and family characteristics (well nourished, coming from well-constituted homes).

With regard to popular conceptions of intelligence and its incidence in school failure, Kaplan makes an interesting analysis of the "bad head" concept, very popular in southern Latin America. The teachers were asked the following question: "Some teachers have indicated that some children fail in school because their head is not fitted for studying. Have you faced a similar situation?" Surprisingly, 22 from 34 teachers agreed that the explanation "his head is not fitted for studying" was a correct explanation for school failure, with a higher frequency among those teachers working with children from middle-class homes.

In a study aiming to diagnose the objectives and methods used by Chilean psychologists to assess intellectual achievement in children between 6 and 17 years old, Rosas and Simonetti (1986) interviewed 98 professionals whose main occupational activity was to carry out this type of evaluation. The interview was focused on obtaining information about the instruments utilized, the assessment objectives, and the psychologists' intelligence conceptions when carrying out the evaluations.

The main results show that the objectives of intelligence assessment, as in most of the countries in the region, conform to administrative-legal reasons, specifically following state requirements, to make decisions regarding the type of education received by children. The instruments most widely used to carry out the evaluations are Wechsler's Scales, which are standardized in Chile, although in most of the cases (58%), they utilize abbreviated forms of the test. No uniform criteria were found for selecting subtests to be included in the abbreviated forms. Regarding intelligence conceptions handled by the professionals, it is surprising to realize that no clear correspondence was detected between the intelligence concept reported by the professionals in charge of the evaluations and the aspects assessed by the tests used by them. Specifically, the notion of intelligence as "adaptation capacity" predominates. However, when they are asked about the intellectual functions measured by the tests more frequently utilized by them, only 2% mention among them "adaptation capacity."

A last interesting result from this study is that most of the interviewees (55%) indicated not being completely satisfied with the available instruments. The main reason for this dissatisfaction is the sociocultural–regional bias of the existing tests – specially Wechsler's Scales – in spite of adaptations and standardizations. This aspect becomes highly relevant when considering that more than 90% of the children being evaluated live in areas characterized by poverty and extreme poverty. And therefore, they are specially harmed by an assessment carried out with instruments having a justification, structure, and stimuli that fits a different reality, which is foreign to theirs.

CONCLUSIONS

On Conceptualization and Theorization about Intelligence in the Region

As is clear from the review presented here, conceptualization and theorization about intelligence in the region is strongly determined by psychological instrumentation, with an acceptance, occasionally in a non-critical manner, of the values obtained through the tests as an unquestionable measure of intelligence. Considering that in most cases the instruments utilized lack adequate norms for those populations in which they are applied, this quite generalized practice is worrisome and reflects an insufficient preparation in the technical–methodological fundamentals that should be met by tests to be properly used and interpreted.

The exceptions to what we have just described are without doubt the intelligence stimulation studies carried out during the 1970s and 1980s in Chile (Montenegro et al., 1978) and in Venezuela (Herrnstein et al., 1986), from which, regrettably, there were no long-term follow-up longitudinal studies that could encourage their replication in other countries of the region. Although both programs had their origin and model in programs or ideas from the United States (the Head Start project in the case of Chile and the Harvard group in the case of Venezuela), there is no doubt regarding the fact that their implementation made possible the development of local technical capabilities that could not have been installed otherwise.

On the Decline of Interest in the Area of Intelligence in the Region

We have already mentioned the difficulties faced in accessing scientific information generated in the region, which can explain to a great extent that the information reported here is underestimated in terms of the amount of research in the area. As the discipline becomes more formally established in the region, based on the progressive development of internationally competitive doctoral programs, there is no doubt that this aspect will improve with the passage of time. However, in spite of the scarcity of existing information, the fact stands out that publications in the area of intelligence have suffered a strong decline during the last years. From the total of publications reviewed for this chapter, 72% are previous to 1990, and only 12.5% were published in the last five years.

On the Need of Basic Research About Intelligence in Latin America

The data just presented are especially worrisome if we take into account the great need to count on basic research on intelligence in Latin America, particularly research focused on having standardized instruments for each country in the region. This need becomes especially urgent, considering that in many countries of the region, psychologists and their technical instrumentation are trusted and have the responsibility of making decisions regarding the type of education, mainstreamed or special, that should be provided to the children. Rosas and Simonetti (1986) report that 34.7% of the total of evaluations done in Chile are carried out because of normative or legal requirements. And, in spite of that, more than 50% of the evaluations are conducted on the basis of instruments that have not been properly standardized for the population being evaluated.

Last, a shortage of studies that is particularly significant in the region is that of research on ethnic minorities. None of the studies reviewed makes reference to the Latin American indigenous population, which in some of the countries of the region is larger than 30%. This fact is especially relevant, considering that in some countries (e.g., Bolivia and Paraguay), the plans and programs for elementary education are developed taking into account minorities' linguistic and cultural peculiarities (Guaraníes, Quechuas, and Aymaras); however, there is no reference to objective instrumentation that allows the assessment of intelligence in these populations.

References

Adriasola, A., Ascencio, S., Bernales, M., Carrasco, C., Séller, A., Polanco, F., Salas, C. & Santelices, R. (1976). *Estandarización de la escala revisada de Wechsler para la medición de la inteligencia en los niños (WISC-R)* [Standardization of the revised Wechsler Intelligence Scale for Children (WISC-R)]. Memoria para optar al título de psicólogo, Escuela de Psicología, Pontificia Universidad Católica de Chile, Santiago, Chile.

Altez, I. (1997). *Estandarización de pruebas de aptitudes e inteligencia en niños: Thorndike y Cattell* [Standardization of tests for the assessment of aptitudes and intelligence in children: Thorndike and Cattell]. Lima: Unifé.

Alvarez, V., Santos, J., & Lebrón, F. (1994). Efectos del programa de enriquecimiento instrumental de Feuerstein sobre las habilidades cognoscitivas de una muestra de estudiantes puertorriqueños [Effects of Feuerstein's instrumental enrichment program on the cognitive abilities of a sample of Puerto Rican students]. *Revista Latinoamericana de Psicología, 26* (1), 51–68.

Backhoff-Escudero, E. (1996). Prueba de matrices progresivas de Raven: Normas de universitarios mexicanos [Raven Progressive Matrices Tests: Mexican norms for university students]. *Revista Mexicana de Psicología, 13* (1), 21–28.

Bannen, V., & Silva, M. (1983). *Adaptación y estandarización de la versión revisada de la escala de inteligencia de Wechsler para adultos (WAIS-R)* [Adaptation and standardization of the revised Wechsler Intelligence Scale for Adults (WAIS-R)]. Memoria para optar al título de psicólogo, Escuela de Psicología, Pontificia Universidad Católica de Chile, Santiago, Chile.

Berreta, I., Dennis, E., Manríquez, M., Martínez, F., Mateluna, I., Morales, A., Perea, M., Pérez, V., Quijada, P., Ruiz, A., & Vilchez, O. (1969). *Adaptación y estandarización de la batería general de test de aptitudes (GATB)* [Adaptation and standardization of the General Aptitude Test Battery]. Memoria para optar al título de psicólogo, Escuela de Psicología, Pontificia Universidad Católica de Chile, Santiago, Chile.

Bralic, S. (1981). Programa piloto de estimulación precoz: Seguimiento de los niños a los seis años de edad [Early stimulation pilot study: Follow-up study six years later]. Santiago: CEDEP.

Calderón, M., Castillo, M., Mandujano, L., Pérez, C., & Purcell, C. (1980). *Estandarización de la escala revisada de Wechsler para niños chilenos del área metropolitana* [Standardization of the revised Wechsler Intelligence Scale for Children (WISC-R) in a sample of Chilean children from Santiago]. Memoria para optar al título de psicólogo, Escuela de Psicología, Pontificia Universidad Católica de Chile, Santiago, Chile.

Campazzo, E., Cattani, M., Cousiño, M., Depetris, M., Elgueta, M., Favi, E., Japaz, O., Muñoz, M., Scagliotti, J., & Zerene, L. (1962). *Estandarización de la escala de Wechsler para la medición de la inteligencia en los niños (WISC)* [Standardization of the Wechsler Intelligence Scale for Children (WISC)]. Memoria para optar al título de psicólogo, Escuela de Psicología, Pontificia Universidad Católica de Chile, Santiago, Chile.

Cañas, M., Colzani, M., Domínguez, M., Jorquera, K., Orpinas, P., & Valdivieso, P. (1978). *Adaptación, análisis estadístico y construcción de normas de la escala revisada de inteligencia de Wechsler para niños entre 6 años o días y 9 años 11 meses 30 días (WISC-R)*. Memoria para optar al título de psicólogo [Adaptation, statistical analysis, and norm construction of the WISC-R for children between 6 years and 9 years, 11 months and 30 days]. Escuela de Psicología, Pontificia Universidad Católica de Chile, Santiago, Chile.

Carroll, J., Herrans, L., & Rodríguez, J. (1995). Análisis factorial de la EIWN-R de Puerto Rico, con niños de 11 niveles de edad, entre los 6 y 16 años [Factor analysis of the WISC-R of Puerto Rico with children of 11 age levels, between 6 and 16 years]. *Revista Latinoamericana de Psicología, 27* (2), 187–206.

Cayssials, A., & Pérez, M. (2001, Julio). *WISC-III: Normas regionales de la ciudad de Buenos Aires, Argentina* [WISC III: Regional norms for the city of Buenos Aires]. Poster presentado en el XXVIII Congreso Interamericano de Psicología, Santiago, Chile.

Donovan, L., Grove, B., Hidalgo, C., Rosas, R., Rosenblut, C., Simonetti, F., & Sziklai, G. (1983). *Evaluación del rendimiento intelectual de 5000 niños en situación de extrema pobreza* [Assessment of the intellectual performance of 5000 children in extreme poverty conditions]. Manuscrito no publicado. Universidad Católica de Chile, Santiago, Chile.

Gazmuri, V., Milicic, N., & Schmidt, S. (1978). Prevalencia de retardo mental y evaluación de rendimiento escolar en una muestra de 918 escolares [Prevalence of mental retardation and assessment of school performance in a sample of 918 students]. *Revista Chilena de Psicología, 1*, 57–64.

Guilford, J. (1967). *The nature of human intelligence*. New York: McGraw Hill.

Haeussler, I. (1981). Desarrollo intelectual del niño menor de dos años según nivel socioeconómico [Intellectual development of children up to 2 years, by SES]. *Revista Chilena de Psicología, 4* (2), 99–107.

Herrnstein, R., Nickerson, R., De Sánchez, M., & Swets, J. (1986). Teaching thinking skills. *American Psychologist, 4* (11), 1279–1289.

Ivanovic, R., Forno, H., Durán M. C., Hazbún, J., Castro, C., & Ivanovic, D. (2000). Estudio de la capacidad intelectual (test de matrices progresivas de Raven) en escolares chilenos de 5 a 18 años I. Antecedentes generales, normas y recomendaciones [Assessment of the intellectual capacity (RPMT) in Chilean students between 5 and 18 years. I. General background, norms and recommendations]. *Revista de Psicología General yAaplicada, 53* (1), 5–30.

Ivanovic, D., Ivanovic, R., Truffello, I., & Buitrón, C. (1989). Nutritional status and educational achievement of elementary first grade Chilean students. *Nutrition Reports International, 39* (1), 163–175.

Ivanovic, D., & Marambio, M. (1989). Nutrition and education. I. Educational achievement and anthropometric parameters of Chilean elementary and high school graduates. *Nutrition Reports International, 39* (5), 983–993.

Jäger, A. O. (1982). Mehrmodale klassifikation von intelligenztestleistungen. experimentell kontrollierte weiterentwicklung eines deskriptiven intelligenzstrukturmodells [Multimodal classification of intelligence test performance.

Experimental controlled advancement of a descriptive model of the structure of intelligence]. *Diagnostica, 28*, 195–226.

Kalawski, A., & Losada, J. (1969). *El test de inteligencia infantil de Goodenough en niños chilenos* [The Goodenough Intelligence Test in Chilean children]. Memoria para optar al Título de Psicólogo, Escuela de Psicología, Pontificia Universidad Católica de Chile, Santiago, Chile.

Kaplan, K. (1997). Inteligencia, escuela y sociedad. Las categorías del juicio magisterial sobre la inteligencia [Intelligence, school and society. The categories of the teachers judgment about intelligence]. *Propuesta Educativa, 16*, 24–32.

Montenegro, H. (1989). Programas de estimulación temprana en América Latina [Programs of early stimulation in Latin America]. *International Journal of Mental Health, 18* (3), 19–39.

Montenegro, H., Rodríguez, S., Lira, I., Haeussler, I., & Bralic, S. (1978). Programa piloto de estimulación precoz para niños de nivel socio-económico bajo entre 0 y 2 años [Pilot program of early stimulation for children of low SES between 0 and 2 years]. In Bralic, S., Haeussler, I., Lira, I., Montenegro, H. & Rodríguez, S. *Estimulación temprana*. Santiago: UNICEF/CEDEP.

Padilla, E., Roll, S., & Gomez-Palacio, M. (1982). The performance of Mexican children and adolescents on the WISC-R. *Revista Interamericana de Psicología. 16* (2), 122–128.

Paine, P., (1978). Escala verbal WISC: Análise fatorial de uma amostra brasileira [WISC Verbal Scale: factor analysis in a Brazilian sample]. *Revista Interamericana de Psicología, 12*, 165–169.

Paine, P., & García, V. (1974). A revision and standardization of the WISC-R verbal scale for use in Brazil. *Revista Interamericana de Psicología, 8*, 225–231.

Rodríguez, S., Edwards, M., Izquierdo, T., Seguel, X., & Haeussler, I. (1985). Programa piloto de estimulación para preescolares en extrema pobreza (PEPEP) [Pilot program of early stimulation for toddlers in extreme poverty conditions]. Documento N° 14. Santiago: CEDEP.

Rosas, R. (1992). Éxito académico universitario: Problemas de su definición, medición y predicción [University academic success: Problems in its definition, evaluation and prediction]. *Psykhe, 1*, 25–39.

Rosas, R. (1996). Replicación del modelo de estructura de inteligencia de Berlín en una muestra de estudiantes chilenos [Replication of the Berlin Intelligence Structure Model in a Chilean university students sample]. *Psykhe, 5* (1), 39–56.

Rosas, R., & Simonetti, F. (1986). Diagnóstico de los objetivos y métodos empleados en la evaluación del rendimiento intelectual en niños chilenos de 6 a 17 años [Diagnostic of the objectives and methods used in the assessment of the intellectual performance of Chilean children between 6 and 17 years]. *Revista Chilena de Psicología, 8* (2), 25–32.

Sans, M. C. (1982). Rendimiento intelectual de dos grupos de sujetos de diferente nivel socio-económico [Intellectual performance in two groups of different SES]. *Revista Latinoamericana de Psicología, 14* (2), 223–234.

Toro, J. P. & Villegas, J. (2001). *Problemas centrales para la formación académica y el entrenamiento profesionla del psicólogo en las américas* [Central problems in the

psychologist academic formation and professional training in the Americas].
Buenos Aires: SIP/JVE.

Varela, J. (1977). La validación de la predicción de éxito en las diversas ocupaciones usandos los test derivados del modelo de la estructura del intelecto de Guilford [Validation and prediction of success in different workplaces using tests derived from Guilford's intelligence structural model]. *Revista Interamericana de Psicología, 11* (1), 5–9.

Walsh, J. (1981). A plenipotentiary for human intelligence. *Science, 214* (6), 640–641.

15

North American Approaches to Intelligence

Robert J. Sternberg

WHY THEORIES OF INTELLIGENCE MATTER TO SOCIETY

WHY THEORIES OF INTELLIGENCE MATTER TO SOCIETY

Underlying every measurement of intelligence is a theory. The theory may be transparently obvious, or it may be hidden. It may be a formal explicit theory or an informal implicit one. But there is always a theory of some kind lurking beneath the test. And in the United States, at least, tests seem to be everywhere.

The Pervasiveness of Intelligence-Related Measurements

Students who apply to competitive independent schools in many locations, notably New York City, must present an impressive array of credentials. Among these credentials, for many of these schools, is a set of scores on either the Wechsler Preschool and Primary Scale of Intelligence – Revised (WPPSI-R) or the Stanford-Binet Intelligence Scale, 4th Ed. (Thorndike, Hagen, & Sattler, 1986). If the children are a bit older, they may take instead the Wechsler Intelligence Scale for Children, 3rd Ed. (WISC-III; Wechsler, 1991). The lower-level version of the Wechsler test is used only for very young children ages 3 to 7 $^1/_2$ years. The higher-level version of the Wechsler test is used for somewhat older children,

Preparation of this chapter was supported by Grant REC-9979843 from the National Science Foundation and by a government grant under the Javits Act Program (Grant No. R206R000001) as administered by the Office of Educational Research and Improvement, U.S. Department of Education. Grantees undertaking such projects are encouraged to freely express their professional judgment. This chapter, therefore, does not necessarily represent the positions or the policies of the U.S. government, and no official endorsement should be inferred.

ages 6 to 16 years, 11 months, of age. The Stanford-Binet test is used across a wider range of ages, from 2 years through adult.

Children applying to independent schools in other locations are likely to take either these or similar tests. The names may be different, and the constructs they are identified as measuring may be different – "intelligence," "intellectual abilities," "mental abilities," "scholastic aptitude," and so forth. But the tests will be highly correlated with each other, and ultimately, one will serve the schools' purposes about as well as another. These tests will henceforth be referred to as measuring "intelligence-related abilities" to group them together but to distinguish them from tests explicitly purported to measure "intelligence."

The need to take tests such as these will not end with primary school. For admission to independent schools in the United States, in general, regardless of level, the children may take the one of the Wechsler tests, the Stanford-Binet test, or some other intelligence test. More likely, they will take either the ERB (Educational Records Bureau) or the SSAT (Secondary School Admissions Test).

Of course, independent schools are supported by fees not tax dollars. But children attending public schools will be exposed to a similar regimen. At one time, these children would have been likely to take group intelligence (IQ) tests, which likely would have been used to track them or, at the very least, predict their future. Today, the students are less likely to take intelligence tests, unless they are being considered for special services, such as services for educable mentally retarded (EMR) children, learning-disabled (LD) children, or gifted children. If the children wish to go to a competitive college or university, they will likely take the SAT (an acronym that originally stood for Scholastic Aptitude Test, then for Scholastic Assessment Test, and now for nothing in particular) or the ACT (American College Test), the two most widely used tests used for college admissions. If their score is within the normal range of a particular college or university to which they apply for admission, the score may not much affect their admission prospects. But if their score is outside this range, it may be a crucial factor in determining acceptance, in the case of high scores, or rejection, in the case of low scores. These tests may be required whether the school is publicly or privately funded. The story still is not over.

If the individuals (now adults) wish to go on to further study, they will have to take tests of various kinds. These include the Graduate Record Examination (GRE) for graduate school, the Law School Admission Test (LSAT) for law, the Graduate Management Admission Test (GMAT) for business school, the Medical College Admission Test (MCAT) for medical school, and so forth. And the story of intelligence testing may not end with graduate-level study: Many kinds of occupational placements, especially in business, may require applicants to take intelligence tests as well.

This rather lengthy introduction to the everyday world of tests of intelligence-related abilities shows the extent to which such tests permeate U.S. society and some other contemporary societies as well. It is hard not to take such tests very seriously because they can be influential in or even determinative of a person's educational or even occupational fate.

The Societal System Created by Tests

Tests of intelligence-related skills matter for success in many cultures. People with higher test scores seem to be more successful in a variety of ways and those with lower test scores seem to be less successful (Herrnstein & Murray, 1994; Hunt, 1995). Why are scores on intelligence-related tests closely related to societal success? Consider two points of view.

According to Herrnstein and Murray (1994), Wigdor and Garner (1982), and others, conventional tests of intelligence account for about 10% of the variation, on average, in various kinds of real-world outcomes. This figure increases if one makes various corrections to it (e.g., for attenuation in measures or for restriction of range in particular samples). Although this percentage is not particularly large, it is not trivial either. Indeed, it is difficult to find any other kind of predictor that fares as well. Clearly, the tests have some value (Hunt, 1995; Schmidt & Hunter, 1981, 1998). They predict success in many jobs and predict success even better in schooling for jobs. Rankings of jobs by prestige usually show higher-prestige jobs associated with higher levels of intelligence-related skills. Theorists of intelligence differ as to why the tests have some success in prediction of job level and competency.

The discovery of an "invisible hand of nature"? Some theorists believe that the role of intelligence in society is along the lines of some kind of natural law. In their book, Herrnstein and Murray (1994) refer to an "invisible hand of nature" guiding events such that people with high IQs tend to rise toward the top socioeconomic strata of a society and people with low IQs tend to fall toward the bottom strata. Jensen (1970, 1998) has made related arguments, as have many others (see, e.g., [largely unfavorable] reviews by Gould, 1981; Lemann, 1999; Sacks, 1999; Zenderland, 1998). Herrnstein and Murray present data to support their argument, although many aspects of their data and their interpretations of these data are arguable (Fraser, 1995; Gould, 1995; Jacoby & Glauberman, 1995; Sternberg, 1995).

This point of view has a certain level of plausibility to it. First, more complex jobs almost certainly do require higher levels of intelligence-related skills. Presumably, lawyers need to do more complex mental tasks than do street cleaners. Second, reaching the complex jobs via the educational system almost certainly requires a higher level of mental performance than does reaching less complex jobs. Finally, there is at least some heritable component of intelligence (Plomin et al., 1997), so that nature must play some role in who gets what mental skills. Despite this plausibility, there is an alternative point of view, which is that U.S. society, to some extent, creates the correlation between test scores and job status by requiring tests of intelligence and related abilities for admission to the educational programs that provide access routes to more prestigious educational programs.

CLASSICAL THEORIES OF INTELLIGENCE AND THEIR CONTEMPORARY COUNTERPARTS

Implicit Theories

Implicit theories are people's conceptions of intelligence. Why even bother to study or report on implicit theories of intelligence? There are several reasons.

First, people's day-to-day interactions are far more likely to be affected by their implicit theories than by any explicit theories. In job interviews, admission interviews, and even daily conversations, people are continually judging each other's intelligence, based not on any formal explicit theories but on their own implicit theories of intelligence.

Second, implicit theories are of interest in their own right. Part of the study of psychology is seeking an understanding how people think, and given the importance of intelligence to society, learning how people think about intelligence is a worthy endeavor.

Third, implicit theories often serve as the basis for generating explicit theories. The formal explicit theories of many psychologists (and other scientists) had their origins in these individual's implicit theories.

How have psychologists conceived of intelligence? Almost none of these views are adequately expressed by Boring's (1923) operationistic view of intelligence as what intelligence tests test. For example, a symposium on experts' definitions of intelligence ("Intelligence and its Measurement: A Symposium," 1921) asked leading researchers how they conceptualized intelligence. Among those asked were leaders in the field such as E. L. Thorndike, L. M. Terman, L. L. Thurstone, and H. Woodrow. The researchers emphasized the importance of the ability to learn and the ability to adapt to the environment. These skills seem important. Are they the skills that play a major role in explicit theories of intelligence?

Explicit Theories

We consider here the three classical theories that today have the most influence: g theory, the theory of primary mental abilities, and the theory of fluid and crystallized abilities.

g Theory

Probably the most influential theory in the history of intelligence research is g theory, originally called two-factor theory, as proposed originally by Spearman (1904, 1927) but as carried forth by many modern theorists (whose work is summarized by Jensen, 1998, himself a g theorist).

Spearman (1904) noticed that tests purported to measure intelligence exhibit a *positive manifold* – they tend to intercorrelate positively with each other. He invented a technique he called *factor analysis,* which was designed to analyze these intercorrelations in order to identify the purported sources of individual differences underlying the observed patterns of test scores. His factor analyses revealed two types of factors (and hence the name "two-factor theory") – the general factor g, whose influence pervades all tests of mental abilities; and specific factors s, whose influence is limited to a single test.

g theory continues today in a more modern form. Indeed, a book published in the late 1990s was called *The* g *Factor* (Jensen, 1998). Jensen (1998, 2002) has defined g as a distillate of the common source of individual differences in all mental tests. He has proposed that underlying g are individual differences in the speed or efficiency of the neural processes that affect the kinds of behavior measured by mental-ability tests.

Jensen (1998) has built his argument in terms of converging operations that, to him, seem to indicate unequivocally the presence of some biologically based common source of variation in mental-test performance. For example, he has cited eight studies (as of 1998) using magnetic resonance imaging (MRI) that show a correlation between IQ and brain volume (p. 147). A number of other studies have shown correlations between aspects of spontaneously measured electroencephalogram (EEG) waves and IQ and between averaged evoked potentials (AEP) and IQ (pp. 152–157). Other studies using positron emission tomography (PET) scanning also have shown correlations with IQ (pp. 157–159), as have studies of peripheral nerve conduction velocity (pp. 159–160) and brain nerve conduction velocity (pp. 160–162). Some of these kinds of work are described in more detail later. A number of other American theorists also believe in *g* theory, and present a broad array of evidence in support of it (e.g., Detterman, 2002; Gottfredson, 2002; Kyllonen, 2002; Petrill, 2002).

Other kinds of work in North America have also suggested the viability of the general factor. One such kind of study is the heritability study (see Bouchard, 1997; Jensen, 1997, 1998; Petrill, 2002; Scarr, 1997). Such studies typically are designed to study identical twins separated at or near birth, to study identical versus fraternal twins, or to study adopted children (of known biological parentage) and biological children living in the same household. These kinds of studies enable investigators to separate, to some extent, genetic from environmental contributions to intelligence. Today it is recognized, however, that pure influences of genetics and environment are extremely difficult to disentangle (Sternberg & Grigorenko, 1997).

As mentioned earlier, the theory of general intelligence has been the longest-lasting and perhaps the most widely accepted in all of the psychological literature. The evidence is impressive, certainly more so than that garnered for any competing theory. Nevertheless, the available evidence need to lead one to at least some skepticism.

First, some theorists (e.g., Gardner, 1983, 1999a; Sternberg, 1997, 1999a; whose work is described later) suggest that a general factor is obtained in tests of intelligence because the tests are limited to a class of fairly academic and somewhat artificial tasks. They argue that the general factor disappears or at least is greatly weakened when a broader range of tasks is used.

Second, contrary to the claim of Jensen (1998), a general factor does tend to appear as a mathematical regularity when factorial solutions are left unrotated. Such a factor tends to be produced because the methods of both common-factor and principal-components analysis in widespread use today maximize the amount of variance they place in each successive factor, with the most possible variance going into the first factor. Thus, the first factor maximizes the loadings of variables on it.

Third, the sheer number of studies supporting a general factor does not necessarily engender support of the theory in proportion to the number of studies (Sternberg, 2000). The large majority of these studies tend to use a somewhat restricted range of tasks, situations in which intelligence is tested, and even participants.

The Theory of Primary Mental Abilities

Thurstone (1938) proposed a theory of primary mental abilities. Although this theory is not widely used today, the theory forms the basis of many contemporary theories, including two contemporary theories discussed later, those of Gardner (1983) and Carroll (1993). It is also the basis for many contemporary group tests of intelligence, which comprise items roughly of the types described in the following paragraph.

Thurstone (1938) analyzed the data from 56 different tests of mental abilities and concluded that, to the extent that there is a general factor of intelligence, it is unimportant and possibly epiphenomenal. From this point of view there are seven *primary mental abilities*:

1. *Verbal comprehension*. This factor involves a person's ability to understand verbal material. It is measured by tests such as vocabulary and reading comprehension.
2. *Verbal fluency*. This ability is involved in rapidly producing words, sentences, and other verbal material. It is measured by tests such as one that requires the examinee to produce as many words as possible beginning with a particular letter in a short amount of time.
3. *Number*. This ability is involved in rapid arithmetic computation and in solving simple arithmetic word problems.
4. *Perceptual speed*. This ability is involved in proofreading and in rapid recognition of letters and numbers. It is measured by tests such as ones requiring the crossing out of A's in a long string of letters or in tests requiring recognition of which of several pictures at the right is identical to the picture at the left.
5. *Inductive reasoning*. This ability requires generalization – reasoning from the specific to the general. It is measured by tests, such as letter series, number series, and word classifications, in which the examinee must indicate which of several words does not belong with the others.
6. *Spatial visualization*. This ability is involved in visualizing shapes, rotations of objects, and how pieces of a puzzle would fit together. An example of a test would be the presentation of a geometric form followed by several other geometric forms. Each of the forms

that follows the first one is either the same rotated by some rigid transformation or it is the mirror image of the first form in rotation. The examinee has to indicate which of the forms at the right is a rotated version of the form at the left, rather than a mirror image.

7. *Memory.* This ability is involved in remembering words, numbers, pictures, and assorted symbols.

Thurstone's theory today is not so often used in its original form, but it has served as a basis for many subsequent theories of intelligence, including hierarchical theories and modern theories such as Gardner's (1983, 1999a). Thus, to the extent that a theory is judged by its heuristic value, Thurstone's has been one of the most important to the field.

Fluid-Crystallized Ability Theory

The theory of fluid and crystallized abilities is one of a class of hierarchical theories of intelligence (Burt, 1949; Gustafsson, 1988; Jensen, 1970; Vernon, 1971), not all of which can be described here. The theory is still current. It was proposed by Cattell (1971) but now has been proposed in a contemporary and elaborated form by Horn (1994). Only the simple form is described here.

According to this theory, *fluid ability* (G_f) flexibility of thought and the ability to reason abstractly. It is measured by tests such as number series, abstract analogies, matrix problems, and the like. *Crystallized ability* (G_c), which is alleged to derive from fluid ability, is essentially the accumulation of knowledge and skills through the life course. It is measured by tests of vocabulary, reading comprehension, and general information. Sometimes a further distinction is made between fluid and crystallized abilities and a third ability, *visual ability* (G_v), which is the ability to mentally manipulate representations, such as those found in tests of spatial ability (as described previously for Thurstone's theory).

A number of contemporary tests of intelligence are based on this theory. One is the Test of *g*: Culture Fair (Cattell & Cattell, 1963), which seeks to capture general ability through tests of fluid abilities. Two other such tests are the Kaufman Adolescent and Adult Intelligence Test (KAIT; Kaufman & Kaufman, 1983) and the Woodcock-Johnson Tests of Cognitive Ability–Revised (Woodcock & Johnson, 1989) (see Daniel, 2000, for a review of these and other tests).

The theory of fluid and crystallized intelligence has been extremely influential in the psychological literature on intelligence. If one also includes visual ability (G_v), the theory seems to capture three of the most pervasive abilities constituting intelligence.

It is unclear whether crystallized ability really derives from or somehow springs out of fluid ability. Such a view seemed plausible when Cattell and many others could argue persuasively that tests of fluid ability are "culture-fair," and that fluid ability is largely unaffected by environmental factors. It now appears that both these views are erroneous. Fluid-ability tests often show greater differences between cultural groups than do crystallized ability tests, but more important, they are more susceptible to the Flynn effect (considered later) than are tests of crystallized abilities. This effect refers to secular increases in scores over time. If fluid-ability scores are increasing over time more rapidly than crystallized-ability scores, one can hardly argue that they are unaffected by enculturation or, most likely, by schooling. Indeed, Ceci (1991, 1996; Ceci & Williams, 1997) has suggested that schooling has a large effect upon measured intelligence of all kinds.

Third, it appears likely that there are other kinds of abilities beyond those specified by the theory of fluid and crystallized abilities. Some of the contemporary theories considered in the next section attempt to specify what these abilities might be.

CONTEMPORARY THEORIES OF INTELLIGENCE

Implicit Theories

Expert Views

Sixty-five years after the symposium in the *Journal of Educational Psychology* on intelligence, Sternberg and Detterman (1986) conducted a similar symposium, again asking experts their views on intelligence. Experts such as E. Butterfield, D. Detterman, E. Hunt, A. Jensen, and R. Sternberg gave their views. Learning and adaptive abilities retained their importance, and a new emphasis crept in – metacognition – or the ability to understand and control oneself. Of course, the name is new, but the idea is not, because long before that, Aristotle emphasized the importance for intelligence of knowing oneself.

The 1921 and 1986 symposia could be criticized for being overly Western in the composition of their contributors. In some cases, Western notions about intelligence are not shared by other cultures. For example, at the mental level, the Western emphasis on speed of mental processing (Sternberg et al., 1981) is not shared in many cultures. Other cultures may even be suspicious of the quality of work that is done very quickly. Indeed, other cultures emphasize depth rather than speed of processing.

They are not alone: Some prominent Canadian theorists have pointed out the importance of depth of processing for full command of material (e.g., Craik & Lockhart, 1972). Even L. L. Thurstone emphasized the importance of withholding a quick, instinctive response to human intelligence (1924).

Laypersons' Views
A set of factors was identified in a study of U.S. people's conceptions of intelligence by Sternberg et al. (1981). The factors uncovered by this study were (1) practical problem solving, (2) verbal ability, and (3) social competence – although in both cases, people's implicit theories of intelligence seem to go quite far beyond what conventional psychometric intelligence tests measure.

Explicit Theories

A Psychometric Theory
The psychometric approach to intelligence is among the oldest of approaches and dates back to Galton's (1883) psychophysical theory of intelligence in terms of psychophysical abilities (such as strength of hand grip or visual acuity) and later to Binet and Simon's (1916) theory of intelligence as judgment, involving adaptation to the environment, direction of one's efforts, and self-criticism.

Carroll (1993) has proposed a hierarchical model of intelligence, based on the factor analysis of more than 460 data sets obtained between 1927 and 1987. His analysis encompasses more than 130,000 people from diverse walks of life and even countries of origin (although non-English-speaking countries are poorly represented among his data sets). The model Carroll proposed, based on his monumental undertaking, is a hierarchy comprising three strata: Stratum I, which includes many narrow, specific abilities (e.g., spelling ability, speed of reasoning); Stratum II, which includes various group-factor abilities (e.g., fluid intelligence, involved in flexible thinking and seeing things in novel ways; and crystallized intelligence, the accumulated knowledge base); and Stratum III, which is just a single general intelligence, much like Spearman's (1904) general intelligence factor.

Of these strata, the most interesting is perhaps the middle stratum, which includes, in addition to fluid and crystallized abilities, learning and memory processes, visual perception, auditory perception, facile production of ideas (similar to verbal fluency), and speed (which includes both sheer speed of response and speed of accurate responding). Although Carroll does not break much new ground, in that many of the abilities in his model have been mentioned in other theories, he does masterfully integrate a large and diverse factor-analytic literature, thereby giving great authority to his model. At the same time, his meta-analysis assumes that conventional psychometric tests cover the entire domain of intelligence that needs to be covered by a theory of intelligence. Some theorists, discussed next, question this assumption.

Cognitive Theories

Cronbach (1957) called for a merging of the two disciplines of scientific psychology – the differential and experimental approaches. The idea is that the study of individual differences (differential psychology) and of cross-individual commonalities (experimental psychology) need not be separate disciplines. They can be merged.

Serious responses to Cronbach came in the 1970s, with cognitive approaches to intelligence attempting this merger. Two of the responses were the cognitive-correlates approach and the cognitive-components approach.

Hunt, Frost, and Lunneborg (1973; see also Hunt, Lunneborg, & Lewis, 1975) introduced the cognitive-correlates approach, whereby scores on laboratory cognitive tests were correlated with scores on psychometric intelligence tests. The theory underlying this work was that fairly simple components of information processing studied in the laboratory – such as the time to retrieve lexical information from long-term memory – could serve as a basis for understanding human intelligence. Intelligence tests, in this view, present complex problems whose solution nevertheless relies on fairly simple information processing. Thus, a participant in a cognitive study might be asked whether two letters, "A a," are identical in identity (answer: yes) or identical in case (answer: no). The tasks were directly out of the literature of experimental psychology, including the letter-comparison task, which is based on work by Posner and Mitchell (1967).

Sternberg (1977; see also Sternberg, 1983) introduced the cognitive-components approach, whereby performance on complex psychometric tasks was decomposed into elementary information-processing components. The underlying theory here was that intelligence comprises a series of component information processes. In contrast to the cognitive-correlates approach, however, the underlying components were seen as complex rather than as simple. For example, solving an analogy of the form A : B :: C : ? involves components such as encoding the terms, inferring the relation between A and B, applying this relation from C to ?, and so forth (see review by Lohman, 2000).

The cognitive approaches of Hunt and Sternberg are now primarily of historical interest. Both authors have expanded their conceptualizations of intelligence since this work. They were forced to do so. Neither approach yielded consistently high correlations between the tasks and task components and psychometric tests of intelligence used as criteria. Moreover, sometimes the components showing the highest correlations were the ones least expected to show them. Sternberg and Gardner (1983), for example, consistently found the regression constant component to have the highest correlations with psychometric test scores, leading them to wonder whether they had rediscovered through information-processing analysis the general factor that had been discovered through psychometric analysis. In the 1990s, cognitive and biological approaches (discussed next) began to merge (Vernon et al., 2000).

Biological Theories

An important approach to studying intelligence is to understand it in terms of the functioning of the brain, in particular, and of the nervous system, in general. Earlier theories relating the brain to intelligence tended to be global in nature, although not necessarily backed by strong empirical evidence. Because these earlier theories are still used in contemporary writings and, in the case of Halstead and Luria, form the bases for test batteries still in contemporary use, they are described here briefly.

EARLY BIOLOGICAL THEORIES. Halstead (1951) suggested that there are four biologically based abilities, which he called (1) the integrative field factor, (2) the abstraction factor, (3) the power factor, and (4) the directional factor. Halstead attributed all four of these abilities primarily to the functioning of the cortex of the frontal lobes.

More influential than Halstead has been Hebb (1949), a Canadian theorist who distinguished between two basic types of intelligence: Intelligence A and Intelligence B. Hebb's distinction is still used by some theorists today. According to Hebb, *Intelligence A* is innate potential; *Intelligence B* is the functioning of the brain as a result of the actual development that has occurred. These two basic types of intelligence should be distinguished from *Intelligence C*, or intelligence as measured by conventional psychometric tests of intelligence. Hebb also suggested that learning, an important basis of intelligence, is built up through cell assemblies, by which successively more and more complex connections among neurons are constructed as learning takes place.

A third biologically based theory is that of Luria (1973, 1980), which has had a major impact on two American tests of intelligence (Kaufman & Kaufman, 1973; Naglieri & Das, 1997). According to Luria, the brain comprises three main units with respect to intelligence: (1) a unit of arousal in the brain stem and midbrain structures; (2) a sensory-input unit in the temporal, parietal, and occipital lobes; and (3) an organization and planning unit in the frontal cortex. The more modern form of this theory is PASS theory (Das, Kirby, & Jarman, 1979; Naglieri & Das, 1990, 2001), which distinguishes among planning, attentional, successive processing, and simultaneous processing abilities. These latter two abilities are subsets of the sensory-input abilities referred to by Luria.

The early biological theories continue to have an influence on theories of intelligence. Oddly, their influence on contemporary psychometric work is substantially greater than their influence on contemporary biological work, which largely (although not wholly) has left these theories behind.

CONTEMPORARY BIOLOGICAL THEORIES. More recent theories have dealt with more specific aspects of brain or neural functioning. One contemporary biological theory is based on *speed of neuronal conduction*. For example, one theory has suggested that individual differences in nerve-conduction velocity is a basis for individual differences in intelligence (e.g., Reed & Jensen, 1992; Vernon & Mori, 1992). Two procedures have been used to measure conduction velocity, either centrally (in the brain) or peripherally (e.g., in the arm).

Reed and Jensen (1992) tested brain nerve conduction velocities via two medium-latency potentials, N70 and P100, which were evoked by pattern-reversal stimulation. Subjects saw a black and white checkerboard pattern in which the black squares would change to white and the white squares to black. Over many trials, responses to these changes were analyzed via electrodes attached to the scalp in four places. Correlations of derived latency measures with IQ were small (generally in the .1 to .2 range of absolute value), but were significant in some cases, suggesting at least a modest relation between the two kinds of measures.

Vernon and Mori (1992) reported on two studies investigating the relation between nerve-conduction velocity in the arm and IQ. In both studies, nerve-conduction velocity was measured in the median nerve of the arm by attaching electrodes to the arm. In the second study, conduction velocity from the wrist to the tip of the finger was also measured. Vernon and Mori found significant correlations with IQ in the .4 range, as well as somewhat smaller correlations (around $-.2$) with response-time measures. They interpreted their results as supporting the hypothesis of a relation between speed of information transmission in the peripheral nerves and intelligence. However, these results must be interpreted cautiously, as Wickett and Vernon (1994) later tried unsuccessfully to replicate these earlier results.

Other work has emphasized P300 as a measure of intelligence. Higher amplitudes of P300 are suggestive of higher levels of extraction of information from stimuli (Johnson, 1986, 1988) and also more rapid adjustment to novelty in stimuli (Donchin, Ritter, & McCallum, 1979). However, attempts to relate P300 and other measures of amplitudes of evoked potentials to scores on tests of intelligence have led to inconclusive results (Vernon et al., 2000). Indeed, the field has gotten a mixed reputation because so many successful attempts have later been met with failures to replicate.

There could be a number of reasons for the failures to replicate. One is almost certainly that there are just so many possible sites, potentials to measure, and ways of quantifying the data that the huge number of possible correlations creates a greater likelihood of Type 1 errors than would be the case for more typical cases of test-related measurements. Investigators using such methods therefore have to take special care to guard against Type 1 errors.

Another approach has been to study *glucose metabolism*. The underlying theory is that when a person processes information, there is more activity in a certain part of the brain. The better the person is at the behavioral activity, the less is the effort required by the brain. Some of the most interesting recent studies of glucose metabolism have been done by Richard Haier and his colleagues. For example, Haier et al. (1988) showed that cortical glucose metabolic rates as revealed by positron emission tomography (PET) scan analysis of subjects solving Raven Matrix problems were lower for more intelligent than for less intelligent subjects. These results suggest that the more intelligent participants needed to expend less effort than the less intelligent ones in order to solve the reasoning problems. A later study (Haier et al., 1992) showed a similar result for more versus less practiced performers playing the computer game of Tetris. In other words, smart people or intellectually expert people do not have to work as hard as less smart or intellectually expert people at a given problem.

What remains to be shown, however, is the causal direction of this finding. One could sensibly argue that the smart people expend less glucose (as a proxy for effort) because they are smart, rather than that people are smart because they expend less glucose. Or both high IQ and low glucose metabolism may be related to a third causal variable. In other words, we cannot always assume that the biological event is a cause (in the reductionistic sense). It may be, instead, an effect.

Another approach considers *brain size*. The theory is simply that larger brains are able to hold more neurons and, more importantly, more and more complex intersynaptic connections between neurons. Willerman et al. (1991) correlated brain size with Wechsler Adult Intelligence Scale–Revised (WAIS-R) IQs, controlling for body size. They found that IQ correlated .65 in men and .35 in women, with a correlation of .51 for both sexes combined. A follow-up analysis of the same 40 subjects suggested that, in men, a relatively larger left hemisphere better predicted WAIS-R verbal than it predicted nonverbal ability, whereas in women a larger left hemisphere predicted nonverbal ability better than it predicted verbal ability (Willerman et al., 1992). These brain-size correlations are suggestive, but it is difficult to say what they mean at this point.

Yet another approach that is at least partially biologically based is that of behavior genetics. A fairly complete review of this extensive literature is found in Sternberg and Grigorenko (1997). The basic idea is that it should be possible to disentangle genetic from environmental sources of variation in intelligence. Ultimately, one would hope to locate the genes responsible for intelligence (Plomin, McClearn, & Smith, 1994, 1995; Plomin & Neiderhiser, 1992; Plomin & Petrill, 1997). The literature is complex, but it appears that about half the total variance in IQ scores is accounted for by genetic factors (Loehlin, 1989). This figure may be an underestimate, because the variance includes error variance and because most studies of heritability have been with children, but we know that heritability of IQ is higher for adults than for children (Sternberg & Grigorenko, 1997). Also, some studies, such as the Texas Adoption Project (Loehlin, Horn, & Willerman, 1997), suggest higher estimates: .78 in the Texas Adoption Project and .75 in the Minnesota Study of Twins Reared Apart (Bouchard, 1997; Bouchard et al., 1990). At the same time, some researchers argue that effects of heredity and environment cannot be clearly and validly separated (Bronfenbrenner & Ceci, 1994; Wahlsten & Gottlieb, 1997). Perhaps, the direction for future research should be to figure out how heredity and environment work together to produce phenotypic intelligence (Scarr, 1997), concentrating especially on within-family environmental variation, which appears to be more important than between-family variation (Jensen, 1997). Such research requires, at the very least, very carefully prepared tests of intelligence, perhaps some of the newer tests described in the next section.

Systems Theories

Many contemporary theories of intelligence can be viewed as systems theories because they are more complex, in many respects, than past theories and attempt to deal with intelligence as a complex system.

THE THEORY OF MULTIPLE INTELLIGENCES (MI THEORY). Gardner (1983, 1993, 1999a, 1999b) proposed that there is no single, unified intelligence, but rather a set of relatively distinct, independent, and modular multiple intelligences. His theory of multiple intelligences (MI theory) originally proposed seven multiple intelligences: (1) linguistic, as used in reading a book or writing a poem; (2) logical-mathematical, as used in deriving a logical proof or solving a mathematical problem; (3) spatial, as used in fitting suitcases into the trunk of a car; (4) musical, as used in singing a song or composing a symphony; (5) bodily-kinesthetic, as used in dancing or playing football; (6) interpersonal, as used in understanding and interacting with other people; and (7) intrapersonal, as used in understanding oneself.

Recently, Gardner (1999a) has proposed one additional intelligence as a confirmed part of his theory – naturalist intelligence – the kind shown by people who are able to discern patterns in nature. Charles Darwin would be a notable example. Gardner has also suggested that there may be two other "candidate" intelligences: spiritual intelligence and existential intelligence. Spiritual intelligence involves a concern with cosmic or existential issues and the recognition of the spiritual as the achievement of a state of being. Existential intelligence involves a concern with ultimate issues. Gardner believes the evidence for these latter two intelligences to be less powerful than the evidence for the other eight intelligences. Whatever the evidence may be for the other eight, we agree that the evidence for these two new intelligences is speculative at this point.

Most activities involve some combination of these different intelligences. For example, dancing might involve both musical and bodily-kinesthetic intelligences. Reading a mathematical textbook might require both linguistic and logical-mathematical intelligences. Often it is hard to separate these intelligences in task performance.

In the past, factor analysis served as the major criterion for identifying abilities. Gardner (1983, 1999b) proposed a new set of criteria, including but not limited to factor analysis, for identifying the existence of a discrete kind of intelligence: (1) potential isolation by brain damage, in that the destruction or sparing of a discrete area of the brain may destroy or spare a particular kind of intelligent behavior; (2) the existence of exceptional individuals who demonstrate extraordinary ability (or deficit) in a particular kind of intelligent behavior; (3) an identifiable core operation or set of operations that are essential to performance of a particular kind of intelligent behavior; (4) a distinctive developmental history leading from novice to master, along with disparate levels of expert performance; (5) a distinctive evolutionary history, in which increases in intelligence may be plausibly associated with enhanced adaptation to the environment; (6) supportive evidence from cognitive-experimental research; (7) supportive evidence from psychometric tests; and (8) susceptibility to encoding in a symbol system.

Gardner (1993, 1995, 1997) has suggested that the multiple intelligences can be understood as bases not only for understanding intelligence, but for understanding other kinds of constructs as well, such as creativity and leadership. For example, Gardner has analyzed some of the great creative thinkers of the twentieth century in terms of their multiple intelligences, arguing that many of them were extraordinarily creative by virtue of extremely high levels of one of the intelligences. For example, Martha Graham was very high in bodily-kinesthetic intelligence; T. S. Eliot, in linguistic intelligence; and so forth.

The theory of multiple intelligences has proved to be enormously successful in capturing the attention both of the psychological public and of the public in general. Nevertheless, some caution must be observed before accepting the theory.

First, since the theory was proposed in 1983, there have been no published empirical tests of the theory as a whole. Given that a major goal of science is empirically to test theories, this fact is something of a disappointment but certainly suggests the need for such testing to occur.

Second, the theory has been justified by Gardner on the basis of post hoc reviews of various literatures. Although these reviews are persuasive, they are also highly selective. For example, there is virtually no overlap between the literatures reviewed by Gardner in his various books and the literatures reviewed by Carroll (1993) or Jensen (1998). This is not to say that his literature is "wrong" or that theirs is "right."

Rather, all literature reviews are selective and probably tend more to dwell on studies that support the proposed point of view. A difference between the literature reviewed by Gardner and that reviewed by Carroll and Jensen is that the literature Gardner reviews was not intended to test his theory of intelligence or anything like it. In contrast, the literatures reviewed by Carroll and Jensen largely comprise studies designed specifically to test psychometric theories of intelligence.

Third, even if one accepts Gardner's criteria for defining an intelligence, it is not clear whether the eight or ten intelligences proposed by Gardner are the only ones that would fit. For example, might there be a sexual intelligence? And are these intelligences really *intelligences*, per se, or are some of them better labeled *talents*? Obviously, the answer to this question is definitional, and hence there may be no ultimate answer at all.

Finally, there is a real need for psychometrically strong assessments of the various intelligences, because without such assessments, it will be difficult ever to validate the theory. Assessments exist (Gardner, Feldman, & Krechevsky, 1998), but they seem not to be psychometrically strong. Without strong assessments, the theory is likely to survive without, or because of, the lack of serious attempts at disconfirmation.

Since the theory was first proposed, a large number of educational interventions have arisen that are based on the theory, sometimes closely and other times less so (Gardner, 1993). Many of the programs are unevaluated, and evaluations of others of these programs seem still to be ongoing, so it is difficult to say at this point what the results will be. In one particularly careful evaluation of a well-conceived program in a large southern city, there were no significant gains in student achievement or changes in student self-concept as a result of an intervention program based on Gardner's (1983, 1999b) theory (Callahan, Tomlinson, & Plucker, 1997). There is no way of knowing whether these results are representative of such intervention programs, however.

SUCCESSFUL INTELLIGENCE. Sternberg (1997, 1999a, 1999b) has suggested that we may wish to pay less attention to conventional notions of intelligence and more to what he terms successful intelligence, or the ability to adapt to, shape, and select environments so as to accomplish one's goals and those of one's society and culture. A successfully intelligent person balances adaptation, shaping, and selection, doing each as necessary. The theory is motivated in part by repeated findings that conventional tests of intelligence and related tests do not predict meaningful criteria of success as well as they predict scores on other similar tests and school grades (e.g., Sternberg & Williams, 1997).

Successful intelligence involves an individual's discerning his or her pattern of strengths and weaknesses and then figuring out ways to capitalize upon the strengths and at the same time to compensate for or correct the weaknesses. People attain success, in part, in idiosyncratic ways that involve their finding how best to exploit their own patterns of strengths and weaknesses.

According to the proposed theory of human intelligence and its development (Sternberg, 1980, 1984, 1985, 1990, 1997, 1999a, 1999b), a common set of processes underlies all aspects of intelligence. These processes are hypothesized to be universal. For example, although the solutions to problems that are considered intelligent in one culture may be different from the solutions considered to be intelligent in another culture, the need to define problems and translate strategies to solve these problems exists in any culture.

Metacomponents, or executive processes, plan what to do, monitor things as they are being done, and evaluate things after they are done. Examples of metacomponents are recognizing the existence of a problem, defining the nature of the problem, deciding on a strategy for solving the problem, monitoring the solution of the problem, and evaluating the solution after the problem is solved.

Performance components execute the instructions of the metacomponents. For example, inference is used to decide how two stimuli are related, and application is used to apply what one has inferred (Sternberg, 1977). Other examples of performance components are comparison of stimuli, justification of a given response as adequate although not ideal, and actually making the response.

Knowledge-acquisition components are used to learn how to solve problems or simply to acquire declarative knowledge in the first place (Sternberg, 1985). Selective encoding is used to decide what information is relevant in the context of one's learning. Selective comparison is used to bring old information to bear on new problems. And selective combination is used to put together the selectively encoded and compared information into a single and sometimes insightful solution to a problem.

Although the same processes are used for all three aspects of intelligence universally, these processes are applied to different kinds of tasks and situations depending on whether a given problem requires analytical thinking, creative thinking, practical thinking, or a combination of these kinds of thinking. Data supporting the theory cannot be presented fully here but are summarized elsewhere (Sternberg, 1977; Sternberg, 1985; Sternberg et al., 2000).

Three broad abilities are important to successful intelligence: analytical, creative, and practical abilities.

Analytical abilities are required to analyze and evaluate the options available to oneself in life. They include things such as identifying the existence of a problem, defining the nature of the problem, setting up a strategy for solving the problem, and monitoring one's solution processes.

Creative abilities are required to generate problem-solving options in the first place. Creative individuals are ones who typically "buy low and sell high" in the world of ideas (Sternberg & Lubart, 1995, 1996): They are willing to generate ideas that, like stocks with low price-earnings ratios, are unpopular and perhaps even deprecated. Having convinced at least some people of the value of these ideas, they then sell high, meaning that they move on to the next unpopular idea. Research shows that these abilities are at least partially distinct from conventional IQ, and that they are moderately domain-specific, meaning that creativity in one domain (such as art) does not necessarily imply creativity in another (such as writing) (Sternberg & Lubart, 1995). Not all creative work is crowd-defying, of course. Some work is creative by virtue of extending existing paradigms (see Sternberg, 1999b; Sternberg, Kaufman, & Pretz, 2002).

Practical abilities are required to implement options and to make them work. Practical abilities are involved when intelligence is applied to real-world contexts. A key aspect of practical intelligence is the acquisition and use of tacit knowledge, which is knowledge of what one needs to know to succeed in a given environment that is not explicitly taught and that usually is not verbalized. Research shows several generalizations about tacit knowledge. First, it is acquired through mindful utilization of experience. What matters, however, is not the experience, per se, but how much one profits from it. Second, tacit knowledge is relatively domain-specific, although people who are likely to acquire it in one domain are likely to acquire it in another domain. Third, acquisition and utilization are relatively independent of conventional abilities. Fourth, tacit knowledge predicts criteria of job success about as well as and sometimes better than does IQ. Fifth, tacit knowledge predicts these criteria incrementally over IQ and other kinds of measures, such as of personality and of styles of learning and thinking (McClelland, 1973; Sternberg et al., 2000; Sternberg & Wagner, 1993; Sternberg et al., 1995).

The separation of practical intelligence from IQ has been shown in a number of different ways in a number of different studies (see Sternberg et al., 2000, for a review). Scribner (1984, 1986) showed that experienced assemblers in a milk-processing plant used complex strategies for combining partially filled cases in a manner that minimized the number of moves require to complete an order. Although the assemblers were the least educated workers in the plant, they were able to calculate in their heads quantities expressed in different base number systems, and they routinely outperformed the more highly educated white collar workers who substituted when the assemblers were absent. Scribner found that the order-filling performance of the assemblers was unrelated to measures of academic skills, including intelligence test scores, arithmetic test scores, and grades.

Ceci and Liker (1986) carried out a study of expert racetrack handicappers, and found that expert handicappers used a highly complex algorithm for predicting post time odds that involved interactions among seven kinds of information. Use of a complex interaction term in their implicit equation was unrelated to the handicappers' IQ.

In a series of studies, it has been shown that shoppers in California grocery stores were able to choose which of several products represented the best buy for them (Lave, Murtaugh, & de la Roche, 1984; Murtaugh, 1985). They were able to do so even though they did very poorly on the same kinds of problems when the problems were presented in the form of a paper-and-pencil arithmetic computation test. There is also evidence that practical intelligence can be taught (Gardner et al., 1994; Sternberg, Okagaki, & Jackson, 1990), at least in some degree. For example, middle-school children given a program for developing their practical intelligence for school (strategies for effective reading, writing, execution of homework, and taking of tests) improved more from pretest to post-test than did control students who received an alternative but irrelevant treatment.

None of these studies suggest that IQ is unimportant for school or job performance or other kinds of performance, and indeed, the evidence suggests to the contrary (Barrett & Depinet, 1991; Hunt, 1995; Hunter & Hunter, 1984; Schmidt & Hunter, 1981, 1993, 1998; Wigdor & Garner, 1982). What the studies do suggest, however, is that there are other aspects of intelligence that are relatively independent of IQ, and that are important as well. A multiple-abilities prediction model of school or job performance would probably be most satisfactory.

According to the theory of successful intelligence, children's multiple abilities are underutilized in educational institutions because teaching tends to value analytical (as well as memory) abilities at the expense of creative and practical abilities. Sternberg, Ferrari, Clinkenbeard, and Grigorenko (1996; Sternberg et al., 1999) designed an experiment in order to illustrate this point. They identified 199 high school students from around the United States who were strong in either analytical, creative, or practical abilities, or all three kinds of abilities, or none of the kinds of abilities. Students were then brought to Yale University to take a college-level psychology course that was taught in a way that emphasized either memory, analytical, creative, or practical abilities. Some students were matched, and others mismatched, to their own strength(s). All students were evaluated for memory-based, analytical, creative, and practical achievements.

Sternberg and his colleagues found that students whose instruction matched their pattern of abilities performed significantly better than did students who were mismatched. They also found that prediction of course performance was improved by taking into account creative and practical as well as analytical abilities.

In subsequent studies (Grigorenko, Jarvin, & Sternberg, 2002; Sternberg, Torff, & Grigorenko, 1998), students were taught subject matter in a variety of ways to compare instruction based on the theory of successful intelligence with other forms of instruction. For example, one set of studies compared such instruction with instruction based on critical thinking and instruction based on traditional, memory-based learning in social studies and science (Sternberg et al., 1998). Another study compared instruction based on successful intelligence to traditional instruction in reading (Grigorenko et al., 2002). Participants in these experiments ranged from middle-school to high-school level, and covered the range of socioeconomic levels from very low to very high. In general, instruction based on the theory of successful intelligence was superior to the other forms of instruction, even if tests of achievement measured only memory-based learning.

At a theoretical level, why should instruction based on the theory of successful intelligence be more effective than conventional or other forms of instruction? Five reasons have been proffered. First, instruction based on the theory of successful intelligence encourages students to capitalize on strengths. Second, it encourages them to correct or to compensate for weaknesses. Third, it enables them to encode material in three different ways, which, by increasing the number of retrieval routes to the information, facilitates memory retrieval later on. Fourth, it encourages elaborative rather than maintenance rehearsal, which results in more elaborated memory traces for the material. Fifth, it is more motivating to students because it typically renders the material more interesting than do conventional forms of presentation.

The theory of successful intelligence has been tested more extensively than many other contemporary theories of intelligence. Nevertheless, questions about it remain. For one thing, even some who might accept the existence of distinctive creative and practical abilities might argue that they represent psychological attributes distinct from intelligence. Second, the pervasiveness of the general factor in psychological investigations must make one wary of Type 1 errors in accepting the notion that the general factor is not truly general, but rather, applies primarily to academic kinds of tasks. Third, there is as yet no published test that measures the triarchic abilities, and the research-based tests clearly need further development. Without published tests, it will be difficult for laboratories other than those of the principal proponents of the theory adequately to put the theory to the test.

TRUE INTELLIGENCE. Perkins (1995) has proposed a theory of what he refers to as *true intelligence*, which he believes synthesizes classic views as well as new ones. According to Perkins, there are three basic aspects to intelligence: neural, experiential, and reflective.

Neural intelligence concerns what Perkins believes to be the fact that some people's neurological systems function better than do the neurological systems of others, running faster and with more precision. He mentions "more finely tuned voltages" and "more exquisitely adapted chemical catalysts" as well as a "better pattern of connecticity in the labyrinth of neurons" (Perkins, 1995, p. 97), although it is not entirely clear what any of these terms means. Perkins believes this aspect of intelligence to be largely genetically determined and unlearnable. This kind of intelligence seems to be somewhat similar to Cattell's (1971) idea of fluid intelligence.

The *experiential* aspect of intelligence is what has been learned from experience. It is the extent and organization of the knowledge base and thus is similar to Cattell's (1971) notion of crystallized intelligence.

The *reflective* aspect of intelligence refers to the role of strategies in memory and problem solving and appears to be similar to the construct of metacognition or cognitive monitoring (Brown & DeLoache, 1978; Flavell, 1981).

There have been no published empirical tests of the theory of true intelligence, so it is difficult to evaluate the theory at this time. Like Gardner's (1983) theory, Perkins's theory is based on literature review, and as previously noted, such literature reviews often tend to be selective and then interpreted in a way such as to maximize the fit of the theory to the available data.

THE BIOECOLOGICAL MODEL OF INTELLIGENCE. Ceci (1996) has proposed a bioecological model of intelligence, according to which multiple cognitive potentials, context, and knowledge all are essential bases of individual differences in performance. Each of the multiple cognitive potentials enables relationships to be discovered, thoughts to be monitored, and knowledge to be acquired within a given domain. Although these potentials are biologically based, their development is closely linked to environmental context, and hence it is difficult if not impossible cleanly to separate biological from environmental contributions to intelligence. Moreover, abilities may express themselves very differently in different contexts. For example, children given essentially the same task in the context of a video game and in the context of a laboratory cognitive task performed much better when the task was presented in the context of the video game.

The bioecological model appears in many ways to be more a framework than a theory. At some level, the theory must be right. Certainly, both biological and ecological factors contribute to the development and manifestation of intelligence. Perhaps what the theory needs most at this time are specific and clearly falsifiable predictions that would set it apart from other theories.

EMOTIONAL INTELLIGENCE. Emotional intelligence is the ability to perceive accurately, appraise, and express emotion; the ability to access and/or generate feelings when they facilitate thought; the ability to understand emotion and emotional knowledge; and the ability to regulate emotions to promote emotional and intellectual growth (Mayer & Salovey, 1993). The concept was introduced by Salovey and Mayer (Mayer & Salovey, 1993; Salovey & Mayer, 1990), and popularized and expanded upon by Goleman (1995).

There is some, although still tentative, evidence for the existence of emotional intelligence. For example, Mayer and Gehr (1996) found that emotional perception of characters in a variety of situations correlates with SAT scores, empathy, and emotional openness. Full convergent-discriminant validation of the construct, however, appears to be needed. The results to date are mixed, with some studies supportive (Mayer, Salovey, & Caruso, 2000) and others not (Davies, Stankov, & Roberts, 1998).

CONCLUSIONS

The study of intelligence has come far in about one century since Spearman (1904) published his seminal paper on general intelligence. Although there is no consensus as to what intelligence is or as to how to measure it, there are many viable alternatives. More research needs to distinguish among these alternatives rather than simply adducing evidence for any one of the alternatives.

Among the psychometric theories, Carroll's (1993) has achieved fairly widespread acclaim, perhaps because it is based on a meta-analysis of so much empirical work. Because of its complexity, however, it is likely to have less influence on measurement than simpler theories, such as the theory of fluid and crystallized abilities (Cattell, 1971; Horn, 1994). History suggests that very complicated theories (e.g., Guilford, 1967, 1982; Guilford & Hoepfner, 1971) tend not to have a long shelf life. In Guilford's case, however, it is more a compliment to than a criticism of his theory, because the demise of Guilford's theory is related to its falsifiability (Horn & Knapp, 1973), a property that not all modern theories have shown themselves to possess.

There are some questions that no existing theories of intelligence answer. Consider a few of these.

Challenges to Traditional Theories and Beliefs about Intelligence

Within recent years, several challenges have emerged from unexpected quarters to conventional theories and measures of intelligence. Consider two such challenges.

Dynamic Assessment

In dynamic assessment, individuals learn at the time of test (Sternberg & Grigorenko, 2002). If they answer an item incorrectly, they are given guided feedback to help them solve the item, until they either get it correct or until the examiner has run out of clues to give them.

The notion of dynamic testing appears to have originated with Vygotsky (1962, 1978), and was developed independently by Feuerstein and his colleagues (1985). Dynamic assessment is generally based on the notion that cognitive abilities are modifiable, and that there is some kind of zone of proximal development (Vygotsky, 1978), which represents the difference between actually developed ability and latent capacity. Dynamic assessments attempt to measure this zone of proximal development, or an analogue to it.

Dynamic assessment is cause both for celebration and for caution (Grigorenko & Sternberg, 1998). On the one hand, it represents a break from conventional psychometric notions of a more or less fixed level of intelligence. On the other hand, it is more a promissory note than a realized success. There is only one formally normed test available in the United States (Swanson, 1995). This test yields scores for working memory before and at various points during and after training, as well as scores for amount of improvement with intervention, number of hints that have been given, and a subjective evaluation by the examiner of the examinee's use of strategies.

Intelligence as Typical Performance

Traditionally, intelligence has been thought of as something to be conceptualized and measured in terms of maximum performance. The tests of intelligence have been maximum-performance tests, requiring examinees to work the hardest they can in order to maximize their scores. Ackerman (1994; Ackerman & Heggestad, 1997; Goff & Ackerman, 1992) has recently argued that typical-performance tests – which, like personality tests, do not require extensive intellectual effort – ought to supplement maximal-performance ones. On such tests, individuals might be asked to what extent statements like "I prefer my life to be filled with puzzles I must solve" or "I enjoy work that requires conscientious, exacting skills." A factor analysis of such tests yielded five factors: intellectual engagement, openness, conscientiousness, directed activity, and science/technology interest.

Ackerman's data suggest a weak relationship between his measures of typical performance and more conventional measures of maximum performance. What are most needed at this time are incremental validity studies that show that this theory provides significant incremental validity with respect to real-world task performance over the validity provided by available measures of intelligence. Because our intelligence so often is used in typical-performance settings (Sternberg et al., 1981), future theorists will need to cope with the challenge of typical performance, following Ackerman's lead.

References

Ackerman, P. (1994). Intelligence, attention, and learning: Maximal and typical performance. In D. K. Detterman (Ed.), *Current topics in human intelligence: Vol. 4. Theories of intelligence* (pp. 1–27). Norwood, NJ: Ablex.

Ackerman, P. L., & Heggestad, E. D. (1997). Intelligence, personality, and interests: Evidence for overlapping traits. *Psychological Bulletin, 121,* 219–245.

Barrett, G. V., & Depinet, R. L. (1991). A reconsideration of testing for competence rather than for intelligence. *American Psychologist, 46,* 1012–1024.

Binet, A., & Simon, T. (1916). *The development of intelligence in children.* Baltimore: Williams & Wilkins. (Original work published 1905.)

Boring, E. G. (1923, June 6). Intelligence as the tests test it. *New Republic,* 35–37.

Bouchard, T. J., Jr. (1997). IQ similarity in twins reared apart: Findings and responses to critics. In R. J. Sternberg & E. L. Grigorenko (Eds.), *Intelligence, heredity, and environment* (pp. 126–160). New York: Cambridge University Press.

Bouchard, T. J., Jr.,Lykken, D. T., McGue, M., Segal, N. L., & Tellegen, A. (1990). Sources of human psychological differences: The Minnesota study of twins reared apart. *Science, 250,* 223–228.

Bronfenbrenner, U., & Ceci, S. J. (1994). Nature-nurture reconceptualized in developmental perspective: A bioecological model. *Psychological Review, 101,* 568–586.

Brown, A. L., & DeLoache, J. S. (1978). Skills, plans, and self-regulation. In R. Siegler (Ed.), *Children's thinking: What develops?* Hillsdale, NJ: Erlbaum.

Burt, C. (1949). Alternative methods of factor analysis and their relations to Pearson's method of "principal axis." *British Journal of Psychology, Statistical Section, 2,* 98–121.

Callahan, C. M., Tomlinson, C. A., & Plucker, J., (1997). *Project START using a multiple intelligences model in identifying and promoting talent in high-risk students.* Storrs, CT: National Research Center on the Gifted and Talented, University of Connecticut Technical Report.

Carroll, J. B. (1993). *Human cognitive abilities: A survey of factor-analytic studies.* New York: Cambridge University Press.

Cattell, R. B. (1971). *Abilities: Their structure, growth and action.* Boston: Houghton Mifflin.

Cattell, R. B., & Cattell, A. K. (1963). *Test of g: Culture fair, scale 3.* Champaign, IL: Institute for Personality and Ability Testing.

Ceci, S. J. (1991). How much does schooling influence general intelligence and its cognitive components? A reassessment of the evidence. *Developmental Psychology, 27,* 703–722.

Ceci, S. J. (1996). *On intelligence . . . more or less* (expanded ed.). Cambridge, MA: Harvard University Press.

Ceci, S. J., & Liker, J. (1986). Academic and nonacademic intelligence: An experimental separation. In R. J. Sternberg & R. K. Wagner, (Eds.), *Practical intelligence: Nature and origins of competence in the everyday world* (pp. 119–142). New York: Cambridge University Press.

Ceci, S. J., & Williams, W. M. (1997). Schooling, intelligence, and income. *American Psychologist, 52*(10), 1051–1058.

Craik, F. I. M., & Lockhart R. S. (1972). Levels of processing: A framework for memory research. *Journal of Verbal Learning and Verbal Behavior, 11*, 671–684.

Cronbach, L. J. (1957). The two disciplines of scientific psychology. *American Psychologist, 12*, 671–684.

Daniel, M. H. (2000). Interpretation of intelligence test scores. In R. J. Sternberg (Ed.), *Handbook of intelligence*. New York: Cambridge University Press.

Das, J. P., Kirby, J. R., & Jarman, R. F. (1979). *Simultaneous and successive cognitive processes*. New York: Academic Press.

Davies, M., Stankov, L., & Roberts, R. D. (1998). Emotional intelligence: In search of an elusive construct. *Journal of Personality & Social Psychology, 75*, 989–1015.

Detterman, D. K. (2002). General intelligence: Cognitive and biological explanations. In R. J. Sternberg & E. L. Grigorenko (Eds.), *The general factor of intelligence: How general is it?* (pp. 223–244). Mahwah, NJ: Erlbaum.

Donchin, E., Ritter, W., & McCallum, W. C. (1979). Cognitive psychophysiology: The endogenous components of the ERP. In E. Callaway, P. Teuting, & S. H. Koslow (Eds.), *Event-related potentials in man* (pp. 349–441). San Diego: Academic Press.

Feuerstein, R., Rand, Y., Haywood, H. C., Hoffman, M., & Jensen, M. (1985). *The learning potential assessment device (LPAD). Examiners' Manual*. Hadassah – Wizo – Canada Research Institute, Jerusalem, Israel.

Flavell, J. H. (1981). Cognitive monitoring. In W. P. Dickson (Ed.), *Children's oral communication skills* (pp. 35–60). New York: Academic Press.

Fraser, S. (Ed.). (1995). *The bell curve wars: Race, intelligence and the future of America*. New York: Basic Books.

Galton, F. (1883). *Inquiry into human faculty and its development*. London: Macmillan.

Gardner, H. (1983). *Frames of mind: The theory of multiple intelligences*. New York: Basic Books.

Gardner, H. (1993). *Multiple intelligences: The theory in practice*. New York: Basic Books.

Gardner, H. (1995). *Leading minds*. New York: Basic Books.

Gardner, H. (1997). Six afterthoughts: Comments on "Varieties of intellectual talent." *Journal of Creative Behavior, 31*, 120–124.

Gardner, H. (1999a). *Intelligence reframed: Multiple intelligences for the 21st century*. New York: Basic Books.

Gardner, H. (1999b) Multiple approaches to understanding. In C. M. Reigeluth (Ed)., *Instructional-design theories and models: A new paradigm of instructional theory* (Vol. II, pp. 69–89). Mahwah, NJ: Erlbaum.

Gardner, H., Feldman, D., & Krechevsky, M. (Eds.). (1998). *Project Zero frameworks for early childhood education*. New York: Teachers College Press.

Gardner, H., Krechevsky, M., Sternberg, R. J, & Okagaki, L. (1994). Intelligence in context: Enhancing students' practical intelligence for school. In K. McGilly, (Ed.), *Classroom lessons: Integrating cognitive theory and classroom practice* (pp. 105–127). Cambridge, MA: MIT Press.

Goff, M., & Ackerman, P. L. (1992). Personality-intelligence relations: Assessment of typical intellectual engagement. *Journal of Educational Psychology, 84*, 537–552.

Gottfredson, L. S. (2002). *g:* Highly general and highly practical. In R. J. Sternberg & E. L. Grigorenko (Eds.), *The general factor of intelligence: How general is it?* (pp 331–380). Mahwah, NJ: Erlbaum.

Gould, S. J. (1981). *The mismeasure of man.* New York: Norton.

Gould, S. J. (1995). Curveball. In S. Fraser (Ed.), *The bell curve wars* (pp. 11–22). New York: Basic Books.

Grigorenko, E. L., Jarvin, L., & Sternberg, R. J. (2002). School-based tests of the triarchic theory of intelligence: Three settings, three samples, three syllabi. *Contemporary Educational Psychology, 27,* 167–208.

Grigorenko, E. L., & Sternberg, R. J. (1998). Dynamic testing. *Psychological Bulletin, 124,* 75–111.

Guilford, J. P. (1967). *The nature of human intelligence.* New York: McGraw-Hill.

Guilford, J. P. (1982). Is some creative thinking irrational? *Journal of Creative Behavior, 16,* 151–154.

Guilford, J. P., & Hoepfner, R. (1971). *The analysis of intelligence.* New York: McGraw-Hill.

Gustafsson J. E. (1988). Hierarchical models of the structure of cognitive abilities. In R. J. Sternberg (Ed.), *Advances in the psychology of human intelligence* (Vol. 4, pp. 35–71). Hillsdale, NJ: Erlbaum.

Haier, R. J., Nuechterlein, K. H., Hazlett, E., Wu, J. C., Pack, J., Browning, H. L., & Buchsbaum, M. S. (1988). Cortical glucose metabolic rate correlates of abstract reasoning and attention studied with positron emission tomography. *Intelligence, 12,* 199–217.

Haier, R. J., Siegel, B., Tang, C., Abel, L., & Buchsbaum, M. S. (1992). Intelligence and changes in regional cerebral glucose metabolic rate following learning. *Intelligence, 16,* 415–426.

Halstead, W. C. (1951). Biological intelligence. *Journal of Personality, 20,* 118–130.

Hebb, D. O. (1949). *The organization of behavior: A neuropsychological theory.* New York: Wiley.

Herrnstein, R. J., & Murray, C. (1994). *The bell curve.* New York: Free Press.

Horn, J. L. (1994). Theory of fluid and crystallized intelligence. In R. J. Sternberg (Ed.), *The encyclopedia of human intelligence* (Vol. 1, pp. 443–451). New York: Macmillan.

Horn, J. L., & Knapp, J. R. (1973). On the subjective character of the empirical base of Guilford's structure-of-intellect model. *Psychological Bulletin, 80,* 33–43.

Hunt, E. (1995). *Will we be smart enough? A cognitive analysis of the coming workforce.* New York: Russell Sage Foundation.

Hunt, E. B., Frost, N., & Lunneborg, C. (1973). Individual differences in cognition: A new approach to intelligence. In G. Bower (Ed.), *The psychology of learning and motivation* (Vol. 7, pp. 87–122). New York: Academic Press.

Hunt, E. B., Lunneborg, C., & Lewis, J. (1975). What does it mean to be high verbal? *Cognitive Psychology, 7,* 194–227.

Hunter, J. E., & Hunter, R. F. (1984). Validity and utility of alternative predictors of job performance. *Psychological Bulletin, 96,* 72–98.

Intelligence and its measurement: A symposium. (1921). *Journal of Educational Psychology, 12,* 123–147, 195–216, 271–275.

Jacoby, R. & Galuberman, N. (Eds.). (1995). *The bell curve debate*. New York: Times Books.

Jensen, A. R. (1970). Hierarchical theories of mental ability. In W. B. Dockrell (Ed.), *On intelligence* (pp. 119–90). Toronto: Ontario Institite for Studies in Education.

Jensen, A. R. (1997). The puzzle of nongenetic variance. R. J. Sternberg & E. L. Grigorenko (Eds.), *Intelligence, heredity, and environment* (pp. 42–88). New York: Cambridge University Press.

Jensen, A. R. (1998). *The g factor: The science of mental ability*. Westport, CT: Praeger/Greenwoood.

Jensen, A. R. (2002). Psychometric g: Definition and substantiation. In R. J. Sternberg & E. L. Grigorenko (Eds.), *General factor of intelligence: Fact or fiction* (pp. 39–54). Mahwah, NJ: Erlbaum.

Johnson, R., Jr. (1986). A triarchic model of P300 amplitude. *Psychophysiology*, 23, 367–384.

Johnson, R., Jr. (1988). The amplitude of the P300 component of the vent-related potential: Review and synthesis. In P. K. Ackles, J. R. Jennings, & M. G. H. Coles (Eds.), *Advances in psychophysiology: A research manual* (Vol. 3, pp. 69–138). Greenwich, CT: CAI Press.

Kaufman, A. S., & Kaufman, N. L. (1973) Sex differences on the McCarthy scales of children's abilities. *Journal of Clinical Psychology*, 29(3), 362–365.

Kaufman, A. S., & Kaufman, N. L. (1983). *Kaufman assessment battery for children: Interpretive manual*. Circle Pines, MN: American Guidance Service.

Kyllonen, P. C. (2002). g: Knowledge, speed, strategies, or working-memory capacity? A systems perspective. In R. J. Sternberg & E. L. Grigorenko (Eds.), *The general factor of intelligence: How general is it?* (pp. 415–446). Mahwah, NJ: Erlbaum.

Lave, J., Murtaugh, M., & de la Roche, O. (1984). The dialectic of arithmetic in grocery shopping. In B. Rogoff & J. Lace (Eds.), *Everyday cognition: Its development in social context* (pp. 67–94). Cambridge, MA: Harvard University Press.

Lemann, N. (1999). *The big test: The secret history of the American meritocracy*. New York: Farrar, Straus, & Giroux.

Loehlin, J. C. (1989). Partitioning environmental and genetic contributions to behavioral development. *American Psychologist*, 44, 1285–1292.

Loehlin, J. C., Horn, J. M., & Willerman, L. (1997). Heredity, environment, and IQ in the Texas adoption project. In R. J. Sternberg & E. L. Grigorenko (Eds.), *Intelligence, heredity, and environment* (pp. 105–125). New York: Cambridge University Press.

Lohman, D. F. (2000). Complex information processing and intelligence. In R. J. Sternberg (Ed.), *Handbook of intelligence* (pp. 285–340). New York: Cambridge University Press.

Luria, A. R. (1973). *The working brain*. New York: Basic Books.

Luria, A. R. (1980). *Higher cortical functions in man* (2nd ed., rev. & expanded). New York: Basic Books.

Mayer, J. D., & Gehr, G. (1996). Emotional intelligence and the identification of emotion. *Intelligence*, 22, 89–114.

Mayer, J. D., & Salovey, P. (1993). The intelligence of emotional intelligence. *Intelligence, 17,* 433–442.

Mayer, J. D., Salovey, P., & Caruso, D. (2000). Emotional intelligence. In R. J. Sternberg (Ed.), *Handbook of intelligence* (pp. 396–421). New York: Cambridge University Press.

McClelland, D. C. (1973). Testing for competence rather than for "intelligence." *American Psychologist, 28,* 1–14.

Murtaugh, M. (1985). The practice of arithmetic by American grocery shoppers. *Anthropology and Education Quarterly, 16,* 186–192.

Naglieri, J. A., & Das, J. P. (1990). Planning, attention, simultaneous, and successive cognitive processes as a model for intelligence. *Journal of Psychoeducational Assessment, 8,* 303–337.

Naglieri, J. A., & Das, J. P. (1997). *Cognitive Assessment System.* Itasca, IL: Riverside.

Naglieri, J. A., & Das, J. P. (2001). Practical implications of general intelligence and PASS cognitive processes. In R. J. Sternberg, & E. L. Grigorenko (Eds.), *The general factor intelligence: How general is it?* (pp. 55–86). Mahwah, NJ: Erlbaum.

Perkins, D. N. (1995) *Outsmarting IQ: The emerging science of learnable intelligence.* New York: Free Press.

Petrill, S. A. (2002). The case for general intelligence: A behavioral genetic perspective. In R. J. Sternberg & E. L. Grigorenko (Eds.), *General factor of intelligence: Fact or fiction.* Mahwah, NJ: Lawrence Erlbaum.

Plomin, R., DeFries, J. C., McClearn, G. E., & Rutter, M. (1997). *Behavioral genetics* (3rd ed.). New York: W. H. Freeman.

Plomin, R., McClearn, D. L., & Smith, D. L. (1994). DNA markers associated with high versus low IQ: The IQ QTL Project. *Behavior Genetics, 24,* 107–118.

Plomin, R., McClearn, D. L., & Smith, D. L. (1995). Allelic associations between 100 DNA markers and high versus low IQ. *Intelligence, 21,* 31–48.

Plomin, R., & Neiderhiser, J. M. (1992). Quantitative genetics, molecular genetics, and intelligence. *Intelligence, 15,* 369–387.

Plomin, R., & Petrill, S. A. (1997). Genetics and intelligence: What is new? *Intelligence, 24,* 53–78.

Posner, M. I., & Mitchell, R. F. (1967). Chronometric analysis of classification. *Psychological Review, 74,* 392–409.

Reed, T. E., & Jensen, A. R. (1992). Conduction velocity in a brain nerve pathway of normal adults correlates with intelligence level. *Intelligence, 16,* 259–272.

Sacks, P. (1999). *Standardized minds: The high price of America's testing culture and what we can do to change it.* Cambridge, MA: Perseus Books.

Salovey, P., & Mayer, J. D. (1990). Emotional intelligence. *Imagination, Cognition, and Personality, 9,* 185–211.

Scarr, S. (1997). Behavior-genetic and socialization theories of intelligence: Truce and reconciliation. In Sternberg, R. J., & Grigorenko, E. L. (Eds.), *Intelligence, heredity and environment* (pp. 3–41). New York: Cambridge University Press.

Schmidt, F. L., & Hunter, J. E. (1981). Employment testing: Old theories and new research findings. *American Psychologist, 36,* 1128–1137.

Schmidt, F. L., & Hunter, J. E. (1993). Tacit knowledge, practical intelligence, general mental ability, and job knowledge, *Current Directions in Psychological Science, 1*, 8–9.

Schmidt, F., & Hunter, J. (1998). The validity and utility of selection methods in personnel psychology: Practical and theoretical implications of 85 years of research findings. *Psychological Bulletin, 124*, 262–274.

Scribner, S. (1984). Studying working intelligence. In B. Rogoff & J. Lave (Eds.), *Everyday cognition: Its development in social context* (pp. 9–40). Cambridge, MA: Harvard University Press.

Scribner, S. (1986). Thinking in action: Some characteristics of practical thought. In R. J. Sternberg & R. K. Wagner (Eds.), *Practical intelligence: Nature and origins of competence in the everyday world* (pp. 13–30). New York: Cambridge University Press.

Spearman, C. (1904). "General intelligence," objectively determined and measured. *American Journal of Psychology, 15*(2), 201–293.

Spearman, C. (1927). *The abilities of man.* London: Macmillan.

Sternberg, R. J. (1977). *Intelligence, information processing, and analogical reasoning: The componential analysis of human abilities.* Hillsdale, NJ: Erlbaum.

Sternberg, R. J. (1980). Sketch of a componential subtheory of human intelligence. *Behavioral and Brain Sciences, 3*, 573–584.

Sternberg, R. J. (1983). Components of human intelligence. *Cognition, 15*, 1–48.

Sternberg, R. J. (1984). Toward a triarchic theory of human intelligence. *Behavioral and Brain Sciences, 7*, 269–287.

Sternberg, R. J. (1985). *Beyond IQ: A triarchic theory of human intelligence.* New York: Cambridge University Press.

Sternberg, R. J. (1990). *Metaphors of mind: Conceptions of the nature of intelligence.* New York: Cambridge University Press.

Sternberg, R. J. (1995). For whom the bell curve tolls: A review of *The bell curve. Psychological Science, 6*, 257–261.

Sternberg, R. J. (1997). *Successful intelligence.* New York: Plume.

Sternberg, R. J. (1999a). Human intelligence: A case study of how more and more research can lead us to know less and less about a psychological phenomenon, until finally we know much less than we did before we started doing research. In E. Tulving (Ed.), *Memory, consciousness, and the brain: The Tallinn conference* (pp. 363–373). Philadelphia: Psychology Press.

Sternberg, R. J. (1999b). A propulsion model of types of creative contributions. *Review of General Psychology, 3*, 83–100.

Sternberg, R. J. (2000). The ability is not general, and neither are the conclusions. *Behavioral and Brain Sciences, 23*(5), 697–698.

Sternberg, R. J., Conway, B. E., Ketron, J. L., & Bernstein, M. (1981). People's conceptions of intelligence. *Journal of Personality and Social Psychology, 41*, 37–55.

Sternberg, R. J., & Detterman, D. K. (1986). *What is intelligence?* Norwood, NJ: Ablex.

Sternberg, R. J., Ferrari, M., Clinkenbeard, P. R., & Grigorenko, E. L. (1996). Identification, instruction, and assessment of gifted children: A construct validation of a triarchic model. *Gifted Child Quarterly, 40*, 129–137.

Sternberg, R. J., Forsythe, G. B., Hedlund, J., Horvath, J., Snook, S. Williams, W. M. Wagner, R. K., Grigorenko, E. L. (2000). *Practical intelligence*. New York: Cambridge University Press.

Sternberg, R. J., & Gardner, M. K. (1983). Unities in inductive reasoning. *Journal of Experimental Psychology: General, 112,* 80–116.

Sternberg, R. J., & Grigorenko, E. L. (Eds.). (1997). *Intelligence, heredity, and environment*. New York: Cambridge University Press.

Sternberg, R. J., & Grigorenko, E. L. (2002). *Dynamic testing*. New York: Cambridge University Press.

Sternberg, R. J., Grigorenko, E. L., Ferrari, M., & Clinkenbeard, P. (1999). A triarchic analysis of an aptitude-treatment interaction. *European Journal of Psychological Assessment, 15,* 1–11.

Sternberg, R. J., Kaufman, J. C., & Pretz, J. E. (2002). *The creativity conundrum: A propulsion model of kinds of creative contributions*. New York: Psychology Press.

Sternberg, R. J., & Lubart, T. I. (1995). *Defying the crowd: Cultivating creativity in a culture of conformity*. New York: Free Press.

Sternberg, R. J., & Lubart, T. I. (1996). Investing in creativity. *American Psychologist, 51,* 677–688.

Sternberg, R. J., Okagaki, L., & Jackson, A. (1990). Practical intelligence for success in school. *Educational Leadership, 48,* 35–39.

Sternberg, R. J., Torff, B., & Grigorenko, E. L. (1998). Teaching triarchically improves school achievement. *Journal of Educational Psychology, 90,* 1–11.

Sternberg, R. J., & Wagner, R. K. (1993). The g-ocentric view of intelligence and job performance is wrong. *Current Directions in Psychological Science, 2,* 1–4.

Sternberg, R. J., Wagner, R. K., Williams, W. M., & Horvath, J. A. (1995). Testing common sense. *American Psychologist, 50,* 912–927.

Sternberg, R. J., & Williams, W. M. (1997). Does the Graduate Record Examination predict meaningful success in the graduate training of psychologists? A case study. *American Psychologist, 52,* 630–641.

Swanson, H. L. (1995). Effects of dynamic testing on the classification of learning disabilities: The predictive and discriminant validity of the Swanson Cognitive Processing Test. *Journal of Psychoeducational Assessment, 1,* 204–229.

Thorndike, R. L., Hagen, E. P., & Sattler, J. M. (1986). *Technical manual for the Stanford-Binet Intelligence Scale (4th ed.)*. Chicago: Riverside.

Thurstone, L. L. (1924). *The nature of intelligence*. New York: Harcourt Brace.

Thurstone, L. L. (1938). *Primary mental abilities*. Chicago, IL: University of Chicago Press.

Vernon, P. A., & Mori, M. (1992). Intelligence, reaction times, and peripheral nerve conduction velocity. *Intelligence, 8,* 273–288.

Vernon, P. A., Wickett, J. C., Bazana, P. G., & Stelmack, R. M. (2000). The neuropsychology and psycholophysiology of human intelligence. In R. J. Sternberg (Ed.), *Handbook of intelligence* (pp. 245–264). New York: Cambridge University Press.

Vernon, P. E. (1971). *The structure of human abilities*. London: Methuen.

Vygotsky, L. S. (1962). *Thought and language*. Cambridge, MA: MIT Press. (Original work published 1934)

Vygotsky, L. S. (1978). *Mind in society: The development of higher psychological processes*. Cambridge, MA: Harvard University Press.

Wahlsten, D., & Gottlieb, G. (1997). The invalid separation of effects of nature and nurture: Lessons from animal experimentation. In R. J. Sternberg & E. L. Grigorenko (Eds.), *Intelligence, heredity, and environment* (pp. 163–192). New York: Cambridge University Press.

Wechsler, D. (1991). *Manual for the Wechsler Intelligence Scales for Children (3rd. ed.)* (WISC-III). San Antonio, TX: Psychological Corporation.

Wickett J. C., & Vernon, P. A. (1994). Peripheral nerve conduction velocity, reaction time, and intelligence: An attempt to replicate Vernon and Mori. *Intelligence, 18*, 127–132.

Wigdor, A. K., & Garner, W. R. (Eds.). (1982). *Ability testing: Uses, consequences, and controversies*. Washington, DC: National Academy Press.

Willerman, L., Schultz, R., Rutledge, J. N., & Bigler, E. D. (1991). *In vivo* brain size and intelligence. *Intelligence, 15*, 223–228.

Willerman, L., Schultz, R., Rutledge, J. N., Bigler, E. D. (1992). Hemisphere size asymmetry predicts relative verbal and nonverbal intelligence differently in the sexes: An MRI study of structure function relations. *Intelligence, 16*, 315–328.

Woodcock, R. W., & Johnson, M. B. (1989). *Woodcock-Johnson Tests of Cognitive Ability (Rev.)*. Itasca, IL: Riverside.

Zenderland, L. (1998). *Measuring minds: Henry Goddard and the origins of American intelligence testing*. New York: Cambridge University Press.

16

Human Intelligence

From Local Models to Universal Theory

Andreas Demetriou and Timothy C. Papadopoulos

This book is unique in the sense that it provides a synopsis, that is, a comprehensive and concise picture of the history and current theory, research, and practice in the field of the psychology of intelligence all over the globe. To study the universal picture of the psychology of intelligence is a worthy task for at least two profound reasons: First, after more than a century, any single definition of intelligence may be still problematic; to study, therefore, the theoretical constructs relevant to the definition of intelligence around the globe appears to be an imperative task. Second, there has been significant progress in the study of intelligence, and the content of this book reflects this progress. For example, perhaps one of the most important advances we have made in recent years is to recognize that intelligence is not a unitary phenomenon but a complex set of functions dependent on many underlying processes. This advance alone brings up new debates.

Thus, this book is very practical for both epistemological and practical reasons. From the epistemological point of view, the book may be used to evaluate how the development of the field of intelligence spread from one country to another, influencing the relevant research accordingly. In fact, in the case of psychology students, this book may provide adequate information with regard to how a very strong theoretical and research tradition, which originated about a century ago in few of the European countries, such as France and Britain, was transferred and developed in other European countries and other continents. From the practical point of view, the book is very useful for the researcher, the teacher, and the student of psychology, because it accurately depicts the progress that has been made in the study of intelligence around the globe.

In this chapter we try to help the reader grasp the main threads underlying the development of theory, methods, and practices of the field across different countries. The aim is to show where a theory or method originated, what the main historical and cultural reasons underlying its origin are, how it spread and planted in other countries, and how, eventually, it contributed, if at all, to the further development of the field as a whole. Moreover, this chapter highlights what is commonly believed nowadays about the nature, the structure, development, and testing of intelligence.

The chapter is organized in three main sections. The first section attempts to summarize the whole volume and discuss the development of theories, methods, and practices in the various countries and parts of the world represented in the volume. The second section elaborates on a set of criteria that an overarching theory of intelligence would have to satisfy if it is going to be able to explain the organization and functioning of intelligence and direct the practice of testing and enrichment of it. Finally, the section part proposes a new theory about the architecture and development of intelligence that comes close to satisfying these criteria, and thus it may be used as a guiding framework for the construction of this overarching theory of intelligence that the field needs.

THE UNIVERSAL STATE OF THE ART IN THE SCIENCE OF HUMAN INTELLIGENCE

Theories and Models about Intelligence

Understanding human reason and intelligence is co-extensive with the very nature of human intelligence itself. That is, self-understanding is part of the adaptive tools that evolution implanted into the human mind so as to make it able to deal with its environment. Thus, theories or conceptions about the mind and intelligence abound in the long history of the human species (Donald, 1991; Mithen, 1996). However, the first formal models of human intelligence appeared in classical Greece. Plato's model of the origin of ideas and Aristotle's models of logic are the first attempts of human scholarship to explain where knowledge comes from and how humans make inferences to understand their environment and solve the problems the environment poses to them. However, the study of human intelligence as a scientific enterprise where ideas and theories are systematically stated and tested is an achievement of the 20th century. This achievement, naturally enough, appeared in three of the most powerful nations of Europe at the peak of their development, together with important achievements in many other sciences and fields of psychology. The turn of the 20th century was crucial for the psychology of intelligence.

Britain at the end of 19th century was a very fertile place for the birth of the science of intelligence. Darwin's theory of evolution, which was then already well known and at the center of scientific and intellectual discussions, together with the ideas of the empiricist philosophers, such as John Locke and David Hume, provided an excellent frame for inquiry into the origin and nature of human intelligence. Sir Francis Galton (1883), who is regarded as the father of experimental and differential psychology (Deary, this volume), attempted to understand human intelligence as the most advanced stage in the evolution of the species. Galton's work set the stage for Charles Spearman (1904), who advanced the first empirically based comprehensive, theory of intelligence.

This theory is still very strong in that its basic postulates are part of the currently most widely accepted theory of intelligence. This is the so-called two-factor theory, which postulates the existence of general intelligence or g, underlying all types of mental processing and specific variance that are associated with each specific test or problem. Later, Spearman recognized the operation of "group factors," that, is factors underlying performance on groups of tests similar to each other, such as verbal or mathematical tasks. We will see in the following pages that it is now generally accepted that the specialized or modular abilities co-exist with g. Therefore, the "theory of everything" in intelligence, if it is ever going to be such a theory, will have to include both provisions for general and specialized, or multiple, intelligences.

It may be noted here that the study of intelligence in Britain has always preserved the concerns of fundamental science. That is, its primary aim has been to understand the nature, composition, and functioning of the human mind rather than just to measure it. In fact, individual differences were taken as a means subservient to accessing the different components of intelligence. Thus, as a field, the psychology of intelligence in Britain has always remained close to experimental and cognitive psychology. In fact, Spearman himself attempted to analyze g into its fundamental underlying potentialities (such as the mental energy and space available for processing information) and elementary cognitive abilities (such as eduction of relations and correlates). These potentialities of g are still regarded as part of it. We will see here that the names may differ but the underlying mechanisms are more or less the same. For example, it is now believed that speed of processing and working memory are two important dimensions of g (Baddeley, 1990; Demetriou et al. 2002; Jensen, 1998; Kail, 1991; Kyllonen, 2002). Speed of processing may be taken as the modern term for mental energy; and working memory as the modern term for mental space. We will return to the question of the nature of intelligence later on.

The British concerns about the nature and structure of intelligence were taken up and developed extensively in the United States. Initially, there was a strong tendency in the United States to reject the construct of g and to emphasize the operation of specialized abilities or modules. Thurstone's (1938) theory of primary abilities is the first comprehensive and empirically robust model emphasizing the importance of different abilities or cognitive modules. In Thurstone's theory, these abilities are as follows: verbal comprehension, verbal fluency, number, perceptual speed, inductive reasoning, spatial visualization, and memory. Although not in use today in its original form, this theory has been an important building block for other modern theories emphasizing the modular nature of intelligence, such as Gardner's (1983) theory of multiple intelligences and the more comprehensive hierarchical theories to be discussed in this chapter.

The Cattell-Horn fluid-crystallized ability theory (Cattell, 1971) has been and still is influential. According to this theory, intelligence involves two fundamental dimensions. Fluid intelligence refers to general information processing and reasoning abilities that enable one to represent and process information so as to abstract relations and make inferences. Speed and control of processing, working memory, and Spearman's principles of cognition, are the components of fluid intelligence. Crystallized intelligence refers to knowledge and information possessed. It is considered to be the product of the functioning of fluid intelligence (see Sternberg, this volume).

It needs to be stressed, however, that the research and theorizing just summarized were never actually incompatible with g. Even Thurstone himself (Deary, this volume) was aware that general abilities were present in his multifactor models and that the strength of the various factors was, to a large extent, a function of the factor analytic method employed. Moreover, there has been extensive research throughout the century and all over the world (see mainly the chapters for Britain, North America, Germany, Israel, and Australia in this volume) about the nature of general abilities, their relation to more specialized or modular abilities, and their relation to more fundamental psycho-physiological and neurological measures of brain processes.

One currently accepted model of the structure of intelligence is the hierarchical model, which includes a hierarchy of three levels, or strata, comprising all of the dimensions or abilities identified by the various models summarized previously. Carroll (1993) analyzed systematically a very large amount of research on the structure of intelligence conducted during most of the 20th century and believes that this model is the closest approximation to the data. Moreover, modern confirmatory factor analysis provides strong mathematical support for the model (Carroll, 1993; Davidson & Downing, 2000; Gustafsson & Undheim, 1996; Jensen, 1998; Kaufman, 2000; Mackintosh, 1998).

The first level includes many narrow or medium task-specific abilities, such as reasoning in different contexts (e.g., mathematical, inductive, or classificatory reasoning), speed of processing in different contexts (e.g., speed of reasoning, speed of perceptual recognition, reaction time etc.), and different types of memory (e.g., memory span for words, numbers, and forms or locations). Thus, differences between abilities at this level reflect, to a considerable extent, the effect of contextual factors on the functioning and application of the various abilities. The second level includes a set of broad abilities or modules of thought and problem solving that enable thinking and problem solving in a particular type or domain of information and problems. Spatial, verbal, and numerical reasoning abilities, originally specified by Thurstone and so frequently identified by tests of intelligence, are examples of the abilities of this kind. The narrow or specific abilities or processes described previously are considered to emanate from these broad abilities. In other words, the narrow or medium-specific abilities mentioned previously are instantiations of these broad abilities in different contexts or conditions. Moreover, the fluid and crystallized intelligence of the Cattell-Horn model are located at this level. In general, abilities at this level are, by and large, distilled from their contextual effects and nuances. Thus, they must be described in reference to processes, mental operations, and principles organizing the mental operations in each of them. Finally, at the third level, there is *general intelligence,* or *g*.

According to Jensen (1998), *g* "is not fundamentally a psychological or behavioral variable, but a biological one" (p. 578). In other words,

It is wrong to regard *g* as a cognitive process, or as an operating principle of the mind, or as a design feature of the brain's neural circuitry. At the level of psychometrics, ideally, *g* may be thought of as a distillate of the common source of individual differences in all mental tests, completely stripped of their distinctive features of information content, skill, strategy, and the like. In this sense, *g* can be roughly likened to a computer's central processing unit. (Jensen, 1998, p. 74, emphasis in original)

Although not a psychological variable, *g* is directly indexed by some psychological functions because these functions reflect the efficiency of the brain to represent and process information. Speed of processing in its various manifestations, such as reaction time, inspection time, and choice time, is certainly a good index of *g*. More complex processes, such as selective or controlled attention and inhibition, are also good indexes of it (Das, Naglieri, & Kirby, 1994; Das & Papadopoulos, in press; Demetriou et al., 2002; Nigg, 2001; Stankov, this volume). Moreover, working memory, in both of its two main types of component processes, that is, executive processes underlying the transformation of information and storage capacity underlying the representation of information, do reflect *g* (Kyllonen, 2002). Gustafsson (1988) has shown that fluid intelligence is practically identical with *g*. Thus, both *g* and fluid intelligence include processes and functions that define processing efficiency and capacity (such as processing speed, selective attention, and working memory) (Jensen, 1998; Kyllonen, 2002), general inferential processes (such as induction and deduction) (Carroll, 1993), and even general self-awareness and self-regulation processes (Sternberg, 1985).

Therefore, each of the three types of models that have been influential during the 20th century are eventually found to be part of a widely accepted theory of the architecture of intelligence. These are Spearman's model, stressing the importance of *g*; the Cattell-Horn model, stressing the importance of the two main general aspects of intelligence, that is, its procedural and transformational aspect (i.e., fluid intelligence) and its declarative and conceptual aspect (i.e., crystallized intelligence); and Thurstone's model stressing the importance of domain-specific abilities or modules.

Modern research into the biological basis of intelligence provides clear support for this hierarchical model. That is, this research suggests that the various levels and dimensions of intelligence, which are included in the hierarchical model summarized here, appear to have their counterpart in the architecture or the functioning of the brain itself. Specifically, speed of processing is related to the connectivity between cells and different brain areas, efficiency of processing seems to be related to the rate of metabolism in the brain and selective attention, and working memory may be related to the coordination of functioning of several areas of the frontal lobe of the brain (Deary, this volume; Fernandez-Ballesteros, this volume; Li & Kunzmann, this volume; Sternberg, this volume). The condition of different modules or specialized abilities is clearly related to the condition of different specifically allocated areas of the brain, such as the occipital lobe for visual abilities and the temporal lobe for verbal abilities. Also, work on the genetic foundations of intelligence shows that different aspects of intelligence, such as *g* as compared to more specialized abilities, are related to different genes located at different parts of the DNA (Deary, this volume). Obviously, the integration of this research with psychological research proper is of paramount importance for the construction of the grand theory of intelligence in the future.

The contribution of other European countries to the understanding of intelligence has been very different from the Anglo-Saxon contribution summarized previously. That is, the contribution of the French- and the German-speaking world has been more developmentally oriented than that of the Anglo-Saxon world and more qualitative in nature.

France's greatest contribution to the psychology of intelligence (Lautrey & de Ribaupierre, this volume) came from Binet, who invented the first major test of intelligence. This contribution will be discussed in the next section. Another unique contribution of the Francophone world to the psychology of intelligence is the first comprehensive theory of cognitive development. This is the theory advanced by Piaget (1970), a French-speaking Swiss. It is not a coincidence that Piaget, a biologist with philosophical concerns about the origins, the phylogenetic evolution, and the ontogenetic development of intelligence, started his career as a researcher in Binet's laboratory. It may be noted, however, that Piaget never shared Binet's (or Spearman's, for that matter) concerns about individual differences. On the contrary, he was interested in the qualitative characteristics of intelligence at the successive phases of life. That is, he wanted to specify the kind and nature of understanding the child is capable of at different stages of development. In fact, Piaget's stages of cognitive development are supposed to describe the underlying general mechanisms of intelligence that characterize the "epistemic subject," that is, the kind of understanding that is common to all persons of a particular age. The lack of interest of Piaget in individual differences and of differential psychologists in the qualitative and developmental aspects of intelligence explain, to a large extent, why the two fields remained separate until very recently. However, Piaget's general mechanisms that are characteristic of the successive stages of cognitive development may reflect the general understanding and problem-solving capabilities emanating from g at the successive phases of life. We will return to this point later on when we will try to highlight how the integration of different traditions and approaches may be achieved.

In the German-speaking world in general and Germany in particular, the life-span perspective to the study of intelligence has been very strong (Li & Kunzmann, this volume). Moreover, this approach remained connected with a practical concern about the use of intelligence to cope efficiently with the multiple and complex demands of life at different phases of development from birth to death, rather than simply to solve problems. In this context, the British concerns about the nature and organization of elementary cognitive processes were not the primary concern in the German tradition. Rather, the primary interest was to specify the basic dimensions underlying the structuring of the individual's interaction with the actual world. In a similar vein, the French concerns about the measurement and specification of an individual's mental age were not a priority because the emphasis is on the specification of the particular coping mechanisms and strategies that characterize different phases of life. Thus, in the German tradition, the study of intelligence is characterized by its life-span orientation to the constitution and functioning of intelligence. As such, it is more practical than the British but also more molar and broader in perspective than the French-speaking tradition.

The currently dominant model in Germany is the dual-process theory of life-span intellectual development developed by Baltes and his colleagues (Li & Kunzmann, this volume). This model builds on the classic German life-span perspective and integrates postulates and evidence collected from the perspective of other models, such as the fluid-crystallized intelligence model already discussed here. According to this model, intelligence is analyzed into two broad categories of functions and processes, that is, cognitive mechanics and cognitive pragmatics. The cognitive mechanics refer to biology-based, information-processing primitives for memorizing, learning, and reasoning, implemented by the neurophysiological architecture of the mind. They are considered to grow fast and reach a steady state early in the years of adulthood and to start to decline from middle age onward. Cognitive pragmatics involve culture-based knowledge that is acquired through cultural learning and life-experiences. Its efficacy develops until well into old age and, ideally, leads to wisdom. Wisdom is defined as knowledge about important and difficult aspects of life meaning and conduct, and includes knowledge about life planning, life management, and life review. Wisdom helps the individual to place situations into broader contexts; to integrate one's own past, present, and future, and also one's own and others' needs; and to deal with life's uncertainties constructively (Li & Kunzmann, this volume).

Obviously, cognitive mechanics are close to fluid intelligence, and cognitive pragmatics, to crystallized intelligence. According to this theory, life-span development is the result of the dynamic interaction between the two types of processes. Several models were proposed to accommodate this interaction. One of these is the Model of Selection, Optimization, and Compensation. According to this model, optimal development requires the developing person to select his personal goals, optimize functioning in the selected goal domain, and compensate for losses in goal-relevant means. This model resembles very much the concept of successful intelligence as proposed by Sternberg (this volume).

The ex-Soviet Union's contribution to the study of intelligence is also unique and influential (Grigorenko, this volume). The uniqueness of this contribution comes from the sweeping changes that took place as a result of the 1917 Communist revolution, which eradicated the European-oriented tradition that was under formation until then and halted the interaction between pre-Communist Russian science and the rest of the world. The Communist regime imposed very strict constraints on what kind of psychology could be developed and practiced. This was because of the fact that psychology, like many other forms of activity, was put under the service of the creation of a new type of human being, the Soviet human being. Thus, on the one hand, testing was prohibited as a bourgeois type of activity, which was allegedly used as a justification for discrimination against individuals belonging to certain social classes. On the other hand, the main principle underlying acceptable scientific activity was the Marxist doctrine that the human psyche and behavior are socially determined. Under these conditions, no empirically based theory of intelligence could be formulated. However, several systems of ideas, rich in assumptions and intuitions about the phylogenetic and ontogenetic development of thinking and the impact of social forces on this development, were formulated during the Soviet years.

The most well known is Vygotsky's (1978) theory. In this theory emphasis is placed on processes such as interiorization and internalization, which help to translate the child's activity and interactions with others into internal thought skills and strategies. It is to be noted that

these theories were never actually tested under the strict specifications of
Western behavioral science. However, because of the fact that the dominant theories of intelligence underestimated the role of social factors
in the functioning and development of intelligence throughout at least
the first half the 20th century, these Soviet theories, Vygotsky's theory
in particular, did exert an influence on Western psychology when it
became known in the late 1960s through the 1980s. In fact, Vygotsky's
theory is still influential. That is, some of its basic postulates have been
integrated in some of the current developmental theories, such as Fischer's (Fischer & Bidell, 1998) theory of cognitive development, and
in some theories concerning social and cultural effects on intellectual
functioning (see Wertch, 1985). However, it needs to be stressed that a
satisfactory integration of this approach and theory with the psychometric theories advanced in the Anglo-Saxon world and the developmental
theories advanced in continental Europe is still far away.

The Testing of Intelligence

The development of the first theories of intelligence was motivated by
intellectual reasons, that is, the aim to explain how humans think, how
they understand the world, and how they adapt to it. Intelligence testing appeared (and still develops) for practical reasons. It aimed to enable educators and other decision makers to specify the intellectual and
thinking capabilities of persons either for the sake of the further enrichment and support of these capabilities or for the selection of persons for
various functions or activities. As early as 1575, Huarte, in Spain, proposed a theory of mental abilities and constructed a test based on it
that can be used for diagnostic and counceling purposes (Fernandez-
Ballesteros, this volume). However, the first proper test of intelligence
was developed by Binet much later, when the social and epistemological
conditions were ripe for this development (Binet & Simon, 1905/1916).
That is, the first test of intelligence was developed in France as a response
to the demands placed upon the educational system by the decision of
the French government to expand primary education so as to include all
children of primary school age. This test was developed as a means for
specifying the learning capabilities and special needs of low-achieving
students so that special attention could be given to the remediation of
those needs. This test was so successful that it is still in use, either in
its modern Stanford-Binet version, or as the background for other tests
that were constructed since then.

Why was the testing enterprise so successful? Do the various tests really measure intelligence? The answer is rather simple. The testing enterprise was successful because it measured intelligence, at least that part of it that is related to academic success. Thus, it is well suited to its purpose of predicting school performance and diagnosing learning difficulties and mental retardation. In fact, Binet's test, like many other tests that followed, are implicitly or explicitly directed to measuring most of the processes and abilities involved in the three-level-hierarchy just summarized. That is, they involve measures of speed of processing, or they time responses to the test items, so that speed does become a factor. They also involve items addressed to working memory or to short-term memory span. Moreover, they involve items addressed to verbal, numerical, and spatial reasoning and also to knowledge related to these domains. Thus, at one and the same time they address fluid and crystallized intelligence. In a sense, Binet's test paved the way for the multifactor theories of intelligence that appeared later rather than for the theory of his contemporaneous colleague Spearman (1904).

It may be worth noting here that Spearman, himself, often spoke in most unflattering terms about the stated intentions of IQ testers. He referred to IQ (Spearman, 1931, p. 402) as the "mere average of sub-tests picked up and put together without rhyme or reason." He decried this heterogeneous mixture of tests with the name intelligence and differentiated between "general ability," or *g*, and "ability in general." General ability, or *g*, refers to what is common between different tasks and it is reflected in the correlation between tasks. Ability in general reflects average performance on tests of different abilities and, although related with *g*, it does not necessarily coincide with it because it reflects performance over various realms rather than what is common between them (Jensen, 1999; Spearman, 1950). Thus, he warned that IQ tests may reflect ability in general rather than *g*, unless they include measures of *g* as such. Of the various tests, only the Raven's test was designed to directly test Spearman's principles of cognition, (that is, the apprehension of relations, the eduction of relations, and the eduction of correlates), which, according to Spearman, constitute an important part of *g*. Indeed, a vast amount of empirical research shows that this test does load on the factor standing for *g* or fluid intelligence (Jensen, 1998). It must be noted, however, that if the recent definition of *g* as a reflection of brain efficiency rather than as a psychological function is to be taken at face value, tests of intelligence must include tasks able to directly index this efficiency, such as tasks addressed to speed, inhibition, or working memory. In fact, recent research suggests that the relation of the Raven test with *g* is mediated by its dependence on those processes that index *g*, mainly working memory (Mackintosh, 1998).

Over the years, the development of the testing industry evolved, to a large extent, independently of the study of intelligence as such. This industry first flourished in a number of European nations and the United States and then flourished in other parts of the world, albeit less promisingly. In fact, the present volume attests to this. It can be seen that the vast majority of the countries around the world followed the same course to intelligence testing: Although Binet's test was adapted for use early enough in many countries, other, similarly successful tests in the country of their origin, such as the Weschler tests and other comparatively more modern tests such as the Kaufman's test, were also adapted gradually for use on a broader basis. In addition, in some countries new tests were constructed to meet specialized local needs, such as Feuerstein's dynamic testing in Israel (Zeidner, et al., this volume) or the Porteus Mazes test, which was constructed to test the intelligence of Australian Aboriginal people (Stankov, this volume). In some other countries, such as China (Shi, this volume) and Japan (Sato, Namiki, & Hatano, this volume), new tests were constructed on the basis of dominant models of intelligence or some combination of them. However, these tests have not gained any wide popularity.

A recent original contribution in the domain of testing is the idea and practice of dynamic testing. Dynamic testing was developed in Israel by Feuerstein, on the basis of the Vygotskyan notion of the *zone of proximal development* (see Grigorenko, this volume; Zeidner, Matthews, & Roberts, this volume), which suggests that children need support to demonstrate their full potential. Dynamic testing assumes that to measure one's intelligence we must specify the individual's learning potential by providing him with learning opportunities within the context of testing and examine how able this individual is to profit from these opportunities. Thus, dynamic testing capitalized directly on the ability to learn, which is supposed to be one of the most important components of intelligence. The original intention underlying the idea of dynamic testing was to provide an opportunity to individuals belonging to underprivileged and test-illiterate populations, such as the various groups returning to Israel for settlement from various developing parts of the world, to warm up during testing and show their actual intellectual potential. Nowadays, the method is gaining increasing popularity, because modern computer technology enables one to integrate learning environments into the testing process itself and systematically examine the person's ability to learn in various domains. Two recent books, one by Kozulin and Rand (2000) and another by Sternberg and Grigorenko (2002), exemplify the impact of Feuerstein's theory and methods in the training and assessment of intelligence and expand on the recent developments in dynamic testing.

The Nordic countries have contributed significantly to the development of methods for measuring intelligence and testing models of it (Carlstedt, Gustafsson, & Hautämaki, this volume). The emphasis on precision, which is sometimes viewed as characteristic of the Nordic cultures, may be the cultural background upon which these contributions flourished. That is, test constructors in Sweden and Denmark, driven by the model of primary mental abilities (Thurstone, 1938), have been quite prolific in developing their own intelligence tests. Their major contributions to the psychometric conceptions of intelligence could be reasonably summarized by the following developments:

1. The Rasch Model, developed by the Danish statistician Georg Rasch (1980). This is a measurement model that made it possible to determine the difficulty of items included in a test and the ability of the persons taking the test. This model proved very powerful in its potential to build fine-grained hierarchies of different levels of ability.
2. A wide range of new methods for factor analysis in multiple populations and a general method for analyzing relations among sets of variables. These methods generated a whole new family of structural-equation methods for analyzing the organization and relations between cognitive processes and abilities (Jöreskog, 1977).
3. Based on these methods, it has been possible to conduct large-scale research addressing the big questions of the nature and organization of intelligence. The robust structural models mentioned before (Gustafsson, 1988; Gustafsson & Undheim, 1996), which indicate that intelligence is a hierarchical edifice involving both modular and molar abilities and functions, could only be developed on the basis of these methods. Moreover, the integrated use of Rasch modeling and structural equation modeling will prove very useful in the future for the integration of psychometric with

developmental theories of intelligence and the construction of tests that would be able to reveal at the same time the person's IQ and developmental level (Demetriou et al., 2002).

Enriching Intelligence

Cognitive acceleration and intellectual enrichment have always been a social and political goal of utmost importance in the United States. The Head Start Program is probably the most massive attempt to boost the intellectual capabilities of children. It is well known that this program met with moderate success (Mackintosh, 1998). In recent years, the attempt to improve the intellectual functioning of children has been more theory-driven than when the Head Start Program was initiated in the 1960s. That is, attempts to boost intellectual development are based on theories that were invented as models able to explain the variability of everyday intellectual performance and direct success in each person's domain of talent or preference.

Gardner's (1983) theory of multiple intelligences proved particularly attractive to people in education because it provides a frame for the understanding and cultivation of talent in one domain of activity independently of other domains. In recent years, this theory has attracted wide interest among educators, and many programs have been developed to cultivate the intelligence of different students in each student's domain of talent. It needs to be noted, however, that according to Sternberg (this volume), the empirical basis of this theory is still very weak. For example, the psychometric properties of the various intelligences and their possible relations with general intelligence have never been systematically investigated. Thus, the effectiveness of programs designed within the context of this theory, if any, may be explained by reasons other than the ones assumed by the theory, such as the ubiquitous presence of a general factor, which is not recognized by the theory.

Sternberg (1985, this volume) has recently developed his triarchic theory into what he called the theory of successful intelligence (Sternberg, 1997). Successful intelligence is

"the ability to adapt to, shape, and select environments so as to accomplish one's goals and those of one's society and culture. A successfully intelligent person balances adaptation, shaping, and selection, doing each as necessary.... Successful intelligence involves an individual's discerning his or her pattern of strengths and weaknesses, and then figuring out ways to capitalize upon strengths and at the same time to compensate for or correct weaknesses."

(Sternberg, this volume). Successful intelligence involves, in addition to all of the processes mentioned previously in the context of other theories, analytical abilities (that is, abilities such as the identification and specification of the nature of a problem, required to analyze and evaluate the options available), creative abilities (that is, abilities such as the generation of new ideas, required to generate problem-solving options in the first place and produce new and attractive solutions), and practical abilities (that is, abilities, such as the acquisition and use of tacit knowledge required to implement options and make them work). Attention is drawn to the similarities between this model of successful intelligence and the Berlin Selection, Optimization, and Compensation Model, already summarized. That is, they both emphasize that, to be successful, one must be able to capitalize on one's strengths and compensate for one's weaknesses.

In many countries, such as Israel (Zeidner, Matthews, & Roberts, this volume), Turkey (Gulgoz & Kagitcibasi, this volume), and several countries in South America (Rosas, this volume), where large groups of the population are underprivileged and face problems in attending regular schools, several cognitive enrichment programs have been implemented. These programs, which were inspired by the Head Start Program in the United States, were only partially successful. That is, some progress is indeed observed but not at an impressive level. The lesson to be learned from these programs is that long periods of cultural and educational deprivation can not be canceled by short intervention programs, however well they are designed. Thus, boosting the intelligence of underprivileged populations requires permanently enriching their cultural and educational environment rather than trying to compensate for deprivation.

Implicit Theories about Intelligence

Sternberg (this volume; Sternberg et al., 1981) pioneered interest and research in implicit theories of intelligence. Implicit theories refer to what laypersons believe about intelligence. Although implicit theories may differ from explicit theories – that is, the theories advanced by psychology, such as the theories discussed so far – recording and understanding them is important for three reasons. First, implicit theories may direct people how to behave and use their intellectual abilities because they specify what is and what is not acceptable or intelligent in a particular social or cultural environment. Thus, they shape cognition, understanding, and problem solving. Second, implicit theories may influence the formation of explicit theories themselves, thereby shaping psychological research on intelligence. Third, implicit theories of intelligence may differ across social groups and cultures, thereby explaining social and cultural differences in intelligence, at least to a certain extent.

Findings suggest that implicit theories do have both similarities and differences from explicit theories. In the West, individuals differentiate among practical ability, verbal ability, and social competence (Sternberg et al., 1981). Moreover, in the Western conceptions of intelligence, terms such as *cognition, intelligence,* and *memory* are assumed to apply exclusively or primarily to the individual. In Eastern traditions, emphasis is placed on the social, historical, and spiritual aspects of everyday functioning, understanding, and problem solving.

In the Indian tradition (Baral & Das, this volume), reason, will, emotion, thinking, judgment, and decision all participate in intelligence. In fact, it is the harmony among all of these functions that is considered more important than any of them. This harmony is achieved through the unifying function of self-awareness and pure consciousness. Moreover, emphasis is placed on the relations of the person with the other. That is, the intelligent person is thought to be capable of knowing the intention of others, is polite, refrains from self-praise, shows initiative and interest in work, and lacks rigidity. Intelligence, therefore, with all its aspects, is not seen as a set of attributes and properties of the individual but as functions that may be carried out between individuals who are aware of themselves and of each other. Therefore, intellectual development is considered a product of social developmental forces. This means that higher mental functions, such as planning, have their origin in social life and are heavily shaped by the historically evolved tools and sign systems that mediate them (Das, Kar, & Parrila, 1996; Parrila, 1995).

The same is true for the Chinese (Shi, this volume) and Japanese (Sato, Namiki, & Hatano, this volume) conceptions of intelligence. In both of these cultures, effort is considered to be the most important factor in the acquisition of knowledge, skills, and in success in life. Literally, in these two cultures, the intelligent person is the one who is never tired of learning. Moreover, in the Chinese conception, emphasis is placed on kindness, loyalty, justice, morality, and benevolence.

On the same premises, in Zimbabwe and other African cultures (Mpofu, this volume), intelligence is generally regarded as expertise in interpersonal relationships and success with everyday activities. In other words, practical or functional ability within a social context and for the benefit of the collective is an important characteristic of intelligence. The ability to share one's own skills and knowledge with others, relatives in particular, is highly valued. In other African cultures, such as the Shona, to be logical, rational, skeptical, and have foresight, vigilance, and alertness is considered important. Among the Chewa, wisdom, aptitude, and responsibility are considered important.

It needs to be noted, however, that these traditional conceptions have not been taken in the countries of their origin as a basis for the development of theories and research about intelligence embedded into the local cultures. Indeed, in India, there have been calls for an Indian psychology of intelligence that would formulate its research agenda on the basis of their own tradition. However, not much has been achieved, in this regard, in terms of empirical studies conducted or theory building. On the contrary, the bulk of research in India (Baral & Das, this volume; Shi, this volume), as well as in China (Shi, this volume), Japan (Sato, Namiki, & Hatano, this volume), and Africa (Mpofu, this volume), draws upon the various dominant models developed in the west, such as the psychometric, the developmental, and the Vygotskian model as a basis for empirical research. Moreover, from very early on, the various established tests of intelligence, such as the Stanford-Binet, the Wechsler Intelligence Scale for Children (WISC), and the Wechsler Adult Intelligence Scale (WAIS), were adapted and standardized, and some research was conducted to test the factorial structure of intelligence as assumed by the theories advanced by the British and the American grand theories.

However, it needs also to be noted that modern implicit conceptions of intelligence in these non-Western cultures tend to diverge from their traditional priorities and come closer to the Western conceptions. That is, they have come to stress cognitive competence over social competence or practical ability. This is due to the globalization of the Western conceptions of the mind, the Western-type systems of education, which emphasize understanding and individual effort, and the Western professional-occupational lifestyle. Finally, it needs also to be stressed that the same dimensions (more or less reminiscent of the various dimensions mentioned in the three-stratum model) are found to underlie performance on tests of intelligence all over the world. Of course, the particular dimensions found depend upon the test used (Baral & Das, this volume; Mpofu, this volume; Sato, Namiki, & Hatano, this volume; Shi, this volume).

STRIVING FOR THE GRANT UNIVERSAL THEORY

The discussion of the chapters in this book makes it clear that the study of intelligence still has a long way to go before the various traditions and approaches can be integrated into a comprehensive theory that will be able to direct research and practice along the many dimensions that a complete theory of intelligence would have to accommodate. We suggest that the main dimensions to be accommodated by this theory are as follows:

The Architecture of Intelligence

That is, researchers in the field must agree on what the main processes, functions, and abilities that constitute human intelligence are and how they are organized. It has been noted previously that there is a convergence among traditions and approaches that human intelligence is a hierarchical edifice. Moreover, there is broad agreement that this hierarchy involves three main levels, namely, g, a set of broad domain-specific systems or modules, and many narrow skills, processes, and functions. Although this hierarchy appears to be a convenient approximation of a heuristically valuable theory, it still departs from a commonly acceptable or a fully empirically substantiated theory. Specifically, there is still no general agreement as to what is actually included in each of the three levels of the hierarchy.

That is, in Carroll's (1993) three-stratum model, fluid and crystallized intelligence are placed in the second level or stratum. However, these dimensions are, by definition, broader than all of the rest of the domain-specific systems of abilities, such as spatial and verbal reasoning. In fact, in line with this assumption, Gustafsson's (1988) model, which is based on large data sets and robust structural equation modeling, suggests that fluid intelligence is practically identical with g. Thus, fluid intelligence may not be needed as an independent dimension in the architecture of mind. Moreover, each of the systems and processes (such as spatial reasoning, verbal reasoning, working memory, etc.) involved at the various levels has its own micro-architecture, which may involve several dimensions or levels. It is accurate to say that it is only the aim and resolution of methods of analysis that constrain what and how many levels in the organization of a particular system or process may be seen.

Reaching an agreement on how to specify these architectures is not going to be an easy task. However, if it is ever going to be possible, we will have to decide on the conceptual and methodological criteria that must be applied. Obviously, an agreement on the criteria may prove even more difficult than their application. For example, is type of mental operation, type of relations in the environment, actual activity in the real world, content, or a symbol system more important for analyzing the organization of a particular domain or system of intelligence? There is no commonly accepted answer to this question, because the different theories are used to analyze intelligence according to a different set of criteria.

The Dynamic Relations Between the Various Systems and Levels of Intelligence

The theory of intelligence, if it is going to be complete, must also specify how the various systems and processes residing at a particular level interact with each other or with the systems and functions residing at the other levels. For example, how do the encoding, control, and storage processes interact to shape the state of a person's g? How does each of these processes interact with lower-level processes, such as cell interconnectivity, glucose metabolism, and nerve conduction velocity in the brain? How does each of them relate with higher-level processes, such as the mental operations or the inferential processes involved in each of the various specialized systems oriented to the environment (e.g., mental rotation in spatial reasoning or arithmetic operations in quantitative reasoning)?

It is a indeed true that recent developments in various fields have opened the way for considerable progress in answering questions just posed. For example, recent developments in neuroimaging technology give promise that we will be able to better understand the relations between brain functions and intelligence. Thus, research in the direction of the studies summarized by Deary (this volume) and Sternberg (this volume) will further highlight how different brain circuits relate to different intellectual functions. In the same vein, recent developments in structural equation modeling (Gustaffson, 1988) and dynamic systems modeling (van Geert, 1994) give promise that we will be able to map the relations between different systems, processes, and abilities more accurately than before. It is safe to anticipate that these methods will prove very useful in our attempt to uncover the composition and architecture of multi-dimensional and multi-level systems such as human intelligence. Research in the direction of the studies summarized by Carlstedt,

Gustafsson, and Hautamäki (this volume) highlights how this may be achieved. Ideally, the different methods that capture different constructional levels of the nature of human intelligence, such as the level of the genetic bases of intelligence, the level of the brain, and the functional level captured by various psychological and behavioral measures, should provide pictures of intelligence that are mutually consistent.

Intellectual Development and Change

All theories of intelligence, such as the classical theories of Spearman or Thurstone, and modern theories, such as the hierarchical theories of Carroll and Gustafsson or the practically oriented theories of Sternberg or Gardner, do not integrally involve provisions about development as such. That is, they do not specify the nature of intelligence at the different phases of life, nor do they specify what successful intelligence is at different phases of life. Obviously, the meaning of intellectual success is different at different phases of life. Moreover, these theories do not specify how intelligence or its priorities change with age. The concept of mental age, which is associated with psychometric theories of intelligence and the practice of mental testing, is a descriptive construct that does not convey much information about the actual intellectual qualities of different age levels. That is, this construct simply indicates what test items a person can solve relative to an age-related norm specifying what items can be solved at the successive years of life.

However, developmental theorists of intelligence, such as Piaget, never specified how their stages of intellectual development or the mechanisms of change they describe are related to the various constructs and dimensions of intelligence specified by psychometric theories of intelligence. It is indeed true that there have been attempts to integrate different traditions into a comprehensive theory. One such example is the Berlin dual-process model that was developed in Germany and summarized by Li and Kunzman (this volume). In this model, an attempt is made to specify how developmental changes in one aspect of intelligence (that is, fluid intelligence or cognitive mechanics) are related to developmental changes in another aspect (that is, crystallized intelligence or cognitive pragmatics). Moreover, this theory tries to explicate how life experiences shape, with time, the person's actual orientation and stance to different aspects of life, which lead to actual decision-making and problem-solving strategies and skills. The coming of wisdom in the middle and the latter years is an example of how changes internal and external to the individual are amalgamated into deep changes in the person's style of interfacing with life and the world. However, this theory falls short of a precise description of the various processes at different stages of life, the earlier phases in particular. Moreover, this theory does not provide a satisfactory explanation of how these transformations affect the condition of each of the various systems and dimensions of the mind described here, nor does it deal with changes in their dynamic relations along with the progression of age.

Another example comes from the so called neo-Piagetian theories of cognitive development. These theories, which appeared in the early 1970s and flourished in the 1980s and early 1990s (see Demetriou, 1988), have attempted to explain the development of thinking and problem solving along Piagetian and neo-Piagetian stages, regarding changes in processing capacity, practically taken as equivalent to working memory (Case, 1985, 1992; Halford, 1993; Pascual-Leone, 1970). In Spearman's terms, these theories attempted to explicate the developmental transformation of one aspect of general intelligence, that is, reasoning and inferential processes, referring to the transformation of another aspect of general intelligence, that is, mental energy and space.

The neo-Piagetian research program was a good attempt to relate two different approaches to the study of intelligence, that is, the developmental, which was rooted in the rationalist tradition of continental French-speaking Europe, and the psychometric and experimental, which was rooted in the British empiricist tradition. We must credit this research program with some exciting insights and fascinating findings about how different levels in the organization of the mind may be dynamically related. However, epistemologically speaking, this program seems to have come to the end of its scientifically generative cycle because it focused on the developmental relations of two of aspects of general intelligence and ignored its many others. Thus, the field is still in need of a comprehensive theory that would identify the basic dimensions, processes, and functions of human intelligence; map their organizations onto systems, modules, and levels; trace the development of each from the beginning to the end of life; and model the transformations of their dynamic interactions along with the progression of age.

The Social Aspects of Intelligence

The social aspects of intelligence may be approached from two complementary points of view. That is, from the point of the view of (1) the influences that may be exerted on intellectual functioning and development by social and cultural factors and (2) the implementation and use of intelligence in everyday life.

Insofar as the influence of social and cultural factors on intelligence is concerned, research was conducted from the point of view of all main traditions represented in this volume. That is, a large part of the research conducted all over the globe and summarized in this volume (Israel, Turkey, South America, India, Japan) was designed from the point of view of the psychometric tradition. That is, this research investigated how, if at all, various social and cultural factors, such as schooling and education in general, family composition and size, parents' education and profession, and family residence, influence various aspects of intelligence. These aspects are described by psychometric theory, that is, IQ, mental age, fluid and crystallized intelligence, and the various more specialized modules included in the various architectures, such as spatial reasoning, quantitative reasoning, and verbal reasoning. The general finding is that these effects are present in some degree.

Interesting research was also conducted from the point of view of the social and cultural tradition as it has developed in the former Soviet Union (see Grigorenko, this volume). This research was more explicative rather than descriptive. That is, it attempted to specify the effect of the mechanisms (sign mastery, interiorization, internalization, etc.) that are considered responsible for the transfer of social and cultural influences on the intellectual functioning of the individual (Wertch, 1985). However, it is to be noted that the various lines of research remained largely separate. That is, there is not as yet any systematic study of how the mechanisms specified by these social and cultural theories function as means for the transfer of social and cultural effects on each of the various dimensions and systems of intelligence, as specified by psychometric theories, and at the various phases of development, as specified by developmental theories. This is an important step that needs to be taken by future research and theory.

Construction of intelligence tests throughout the century remained close to their initial character and orientation, as conceived by Binet. That is, they have been constructed to tap intelligence through academically relevant test items so that they will be useful for educationally relevant decisions. As a result, the criticism grew strong over the years that theories of intelligence do not accommodate functioning in every day life and test scores cannot predict how well a person can deal with the problems posed by actual life. As a result, several theories have appeared that aimed to remedy this weakness by integrating into their premises concerns about more realistic and complex situations than school-like tasks. One of these theories is Coleman's theory of emotional intelligence (see Sternberg, this volume). This theory tries to become more realistic and broader than traditional theories of intelligence by embedding the cognitive aspects of intelligence into the broader context of personality and emotional functioning. Other theories are Sternberg's (this volume) theory of successful intelligence and the Berlin dual-process theory (Li & Kunzmann, this volume). Research in this direction is also conducted in Israel (Zeidner, Matthews, & Roberts, this volume). These theories attempt to specify how a person's personality, dispositions, and characteristics frame and channel how one's intelligence is to be efficiently used. However, this work on the intelligence–personality relations is, by and large, sketchy and piecemeal, as there is not as yet a theoretical framework that would explain in integrated way how personality and intelligence are dynamically interwoven in conditions of on-line everyday functioning. That is, it looks for relations between particular variables taken from theories of intelligence and theories of personality. It does not come from a theory where the relations between intelligence and personality are systematically specified in the context of an overarching conception of the person where his cognitive, emotional, and personality aspects are integrally considered. This theory is needed if progress is to be made.

A POSSIBLE FRAME FOR UNIFYING RESEARCH AND THEORY

The model developed by Demetriou and colleagues (Demetriou, 1998; Demetriou et al., 2002; Demetriou, Efklides, & Platsidou, 1993; Demetriou & Kazi, 2001) draws on all three traditions concerned with intelligence, that is, the psychometric, the experimental, and the developmental tradition, to describe and explain the architecture and development of the human mind and individual differences. Moreover, the model integrates concerns about the relations of intellectual development with the development of personality and the self and the influence of social factors on these relations. Thus, this model may be taken as a framework that might direct the integration of the research and theory on intelligence and development. This model was developed in Greece and Cyprus, and it may thus be taken as the Greek contribution to the study of human intelligence.

According to this model, the mind is organized into three hierarchical levels. The most basic of these levels involves general processes and functions that define the processing potentials available at a given time. Mental speed, control of processing, and working memory are the functions that define these potentials. The other two are knowing levels, in that they involve systems and functions underlying understanding and problem solving. One of them involves systems specializing in the representation and processing of the different aspects of the environment. Seven such systems were identified, that is, the systems of categorical, quantitative, causal, spatial, propositional, social thought, and the pictographic system. These systems are computationally, symbolically, and developmentally distinct from each other. The other knowing level involves processes directed and self-understanding, understanding of other minds, and self-regulation. Thus, the input to this level is information arising from the other two levels (sensations, feelings, and conceptions caused by mental activity), which is then used to guide their functioning (Demetriou et al., 1993, 2002; Demetriou & Valanides, 1998).

All of the systems and functions included in each of the three levels of the mental architecture change systematically with age. Insofar as processing capabilities are concerned, with age the mind becomes faster in recognizing and making meaning of information, more able to focus on goal-relevant information and ignore irrelevant information, and it can hold and operate on increasingly more units of information. In the environment-oriented systems, with development the person (1) can deal with increasingly more complex concepts and problems and (2) build increasingly more abstract and inclusive relations. Likewise, the mental maps and self-regulation strategies and skills involved in the self-oriented level, with age, become increasingly more accurate and focused in regard to the various processes, characteristics, and abilities of the individual to which they refer (Demetriou & Valanides, 1998).

In this model, both development as such and individual differences are due to the dynamic relations among the three levels of the architecture of the mind (Demetriou & Raftopoulos, 1999). That is, changes in the level of processing potentials open possibilities for the construction of more complex concepts and skills at the level of the environment- and the self-oriented systems. In psychometric terms, these changes are related to transformations in g that determine mental age. Changes in any of the environment-oriented systems enhance the knowledge base of intelligence and pave the way for changes in other environment-oriented systems. Changes in self-motoring and self-regulation strategies improve the handling of processing potentials and of the environment-oriented systems. Moreover, they affect interpersonal relations. In psychometric terms, these changes are related to implementation of the potentialities of each level of mental age into actual knowledge, abilities, and skills. Thus, they are related to individual differences in IQ (Demetriou et al., 1993, 2002).

Our research has also shown that the dynamic relations among the three levels of the mind are related to one's self-concept and personality. For example, we showed that processing efficiency is directly reflected in one's cognitive self-concept. That is, the faster one is in processing the more one believes that he is strong in learning and reasoning. In turn, one's cognitive self-concept participates directly in one's personality dispositions. For example, we showed that persons with a very positive cognitive self-concept are more open to experience than persons with a less positive self-concept. In turn, persons who are open to experience tend to prefer to be involved in activities, which require originality (Demetriou & Kazi, 2001).

In another set of studies, we investigated how persons represent each other's cognitive abilities and how mutual representations influence each other. We found that all domains and dimensions present in actual performance are also present in both self-representations and the representations persons hold about each other. This is an important finding because it indicates that the structures we describe are not merely latent constructs underlying individual behavior, but also have an interpersonal component that makes them shared or interpersonal constructs through which individuals can formulate and negotiate views and representations they hold about each other (Demetriou & Kazi, 2001).

Finally, a series of studies have shown that the architecture described by this theory is the same across human cultures. However, the rate of development may differ across cultures and social groups within the same culture, depending upon particular conditions and opportunities relevant to intellectual functioning and development. This finding suggests that the theory can be used as a system for the comparison of different cultures or groups of the population (Shayer, Demetriou, & Prevez, 1988).

CONCLUSIONS

This book as a whole suggests some interesting conclusions about the history and the development of theory, research, and practice in regard to human intelligence. These are as follows:

1. The appearance and development of psychometric theories of intelligence has, by and large, remained an Anglo-Saxon endeavor. All of these theories appeared in the United Kingdom and the United States in the first decades of the 20th century and are still developed mostly in these countries. Of course, significant research is indeed carried our in many other countries, such as the Scandinavian countries, Israel, and Germany. However, the bulk of the research conducted in most other countries is conducted to test and validate these theories rather than transform them or advance new ones.

2. The situation is more or less the same insofar as testing is concerned. That is, although the first test of intelligence was constructed in France, it is in the Anglo-Saxon nations where it flourished and then spread throughout the world. In a similar vein, although some tests were developed in several countries, the tests with universal use come from Britain (the Raven test) and the United States (the various versions of the Stanford-Binet and the Wechsler test). Thus, most of the research in other countries on test development aims to adapt and standardize these tests in the local environment rather than develop new ones.

3. Two other paradigms have dominated research on intelligence for some time. The first is the developmental paradigm that was initiated by Piaget. This paradigm was very influential for about three decades (i.e., from the 1960s to the 1980s). Its appeal, however, declined rapidly for reasons that go beyond the concerns of the present chapter. The other was the social–cultural paradigm that was initiated by Vygotsky and other Soviet psychologists. The appeal of this paradigm is still present, although it was never as strong as the appeal of the Piagetian paradigm. Both paradigms have evolved into what has come to be known as neo-Piagetian (see Demetriou, 1988) or neo-Vygotskyan (Wertch, 1985) models of development. However, it may be safely said that all of these models, having served their epistemological purposes, have come to the end of their epistemological cycle.

4. The future of the psychology of intelligence lies in its ability to break the boundaries of the various paradigms and build new

theories that would integrate the various models and traditions into an overarching theory that would be able to accommodate the architecture of intelligence, its development during the life-span, its biological and social–cultural aspects, and its use in different contexts by the real person. An example of one such model was given in this chapter. However, it is fully recognized that this model departs considerably from the model that would satisfy all of the criteria that this model of everything would have to satisfy. Moreover, new tests of intelligence are needed that would draw upon these kinds of integrative theories, so they would be able to provide information about general and specialized abilities, developmental states, and style of functioning.

5. To come close to this model, we need to coordinate both our methods and our resources all over the globe, because the history of the field (and science as a whole, for that matter) suggests that no method is sufficient to unravel all of the mysteries of complex phenomena. Thus, we need to coordinate our use of the various methods if we are to map the various aspects and levels of the architecture of human intelligence and grasp how they are connected. Specifically, we need to coordinate the maps of mental processes as revealed by neuroimaging methods with the architectures suggested by structural equations modeling and dynamic systems modeling. This coordination will highlight how the organization of neural processes in the brain correspond with the organization of functional (psychological) processes applied on problems. This kind of complex research requires the collaboration of researchers with different expertise and access to infrastructure. In fact, the people and infrastructure required for this kind of research may not even be located in the same country. Therefore, if research of this kind is to move forward, we will have to start thinking in terms of megascience projects that will pull together people and material means from different institutions and countries with the aim to work jointly on very complex questions of the science of intelligence. This policy, which has long been implemented in the natural sciences, and a few years ago in the biological sciences, is necessary if big progress is to be made in our field.

6. This policy of international cooperation must coexist with a policy that would allow local and national research to explore how intelligence develops and functions within particular social and cultural contexts. Human intelligence evolved to enable humans to cope with variation and diversity, and this should be reflected in

our research agenda. Thus, we encourage researchers from different countries to investigate more thoroughly and systematically their own implicit theories of intelligence, specify what is successful intelligence in their own social and cultural context, and investigate how these theories affect intellectual functioning as such. This approach may be the contribution of psychology to the preservation of diversity that exists in the world, that is, the preservation of different types of understanding that the diversity of human civilizations has produced over the millennia. All in all, we suggest that the globalization of research that is implied by megascience go hand in hand with research that is sensitive to lacal needs and particularities.

References

Baddeley, A. D. (1990). *Human memory: Theory and practice*. Hillsdale, NJ: Erlbaum.

Binet, A., & Simon, T. (1905/1916). *The development of intelligence in children*. Baltimore: Williams & Wilken.

Carroll, J. B. (1993). *Human cognitive abilities: A survey of factor-analytic studies*. New York: Cambridge University Press.

Case, R. (1985). *Intellectual development. Birth to adulthood*. New York: Academic Press.

Case, R. (1992). *The mind's staircase: Exploring the conceptual underpinnings of children's thought and knowledge*. Hillsdale, NJ: Erlbaum.

Cattell, R. B. (1971). *Abilities: Their structure, growth, and action*. Boston: Houghton Mifflin.

Davidson, J. E., & Downing, C. L. (2000). Contemporary models of intelligence. In R. J. Sternberg (Ed.), *Handbook of Intelligence* (pp. 34–49). Cambridge: Cambridge University Press.

Das, J. P., Kar, B. C., & Parrila, R. K. (1996). *Cognitive planning: The psychological basis of intelligent behavior*. New Delhi: Sage.

Das, J. P., Naglieri, J. A., & Kirby, J. R. (1994). *Assessment of cognitive processes: The PASS theory of intelligence*. Boston: Allyn & Bacon.

Das, J. P., & Papadopoulos, T. C. (in press). Behavioral inhibition and hyperactivity: A commentary from alternative perspectives. *European Journal of Special Needs Education*.

Demetriou, A. (Ed.) (1988). *Neo-Piagetian models of cognitive development: Towards an integration*: Amsterdam: North-Holland.

Demetriou, A. (1998). Nooplasis: 10 + 1 Postulates about the formation of mind. *Learning and Instruction: The Journal of the European Association for Research on Learning and Instruction*, 8, 271–287.

Demetriou, A., Christou, C., Spanoudis, G., & Platsidou, M. (2002). The development of mental processing: efficiency, working memory, and thinking.

Monographs of the Society for Research in Child Development, 67 (1, Serial No. 268).

Demetriou, A., Efklides, A., & Platsidou, M. (1993) The architecture and dynamics of developing mind: Experiential structuralism as a frame for unifying cognitive developmental theories. *Monographs of the Society for Research in Child Development, 58* (5–6, Serial No. 234).

Demetriou, A., & Kazi, S. (2001). *Unity and modularity in the mind and the self: Studies on the relationships between between self-awareness, personality, and intellectual development from childhood to adolescence.* London: Routledge.

Demetriou, A., & Raftopoulos, A. (1999). Modeling the developing mind: From structure to change. *Developmental Review, 19,* 319–368.

Demetriou, A., & Valanides, N. (1998). A three level of theory of the developing mind: Basic principles and implications for instruction and assessment. In R. J. Sternberg & W. M. Williams (Eds.), *Intelligence, instruction, and assessment* (pp. 149–199). Hillsdale, NJ: Erlbaum.

Donald, M. (1991). *Origins of the modern mind:* Cambridge, MA: Harvard University Press.

Fischer, K. W., & Bidell, T. R. (1998). Dynamic development of psychological structures in action and thought. In R. M. Lerner (Ed.), & W. Damon (Series Ed.), *Handbook of child psychology: Vol. 1. Theoretical models of human development* (5th ed., pp. 467–561). New York: Wiley.

Gardner, H. (1983). *Frames of mind. The theory of multiple intelligences.* New York: Basic Books.

Galton, F. (1883). *Inquiries into human faculty and its development.* New York: AMS Press.

Gustafsson, J. E. (1988). Hierarchical models of individual differences in cognitive abilities. In R. J. Sternberg (Ed.), *Advances in the psychology of human intelligence* (Vol 4, pp. 35–71). Hillsdale, NJ: Erlbaum.

Gustafsson, J. E., & Undheim, J. O. (1996). Individual differences in cognitive functions. In D. Berliner & R. C. Calfee (Eds.), *Handbook of educational psychology* (pp. 186–242). New York: Macmillan.

Halford, G. (1993). *Children's understanding: The development of mental models.* New York: Erlbaum.

Jensen, A. R. (1998). *The g factor: The science of mental ability.* New York: Praeger.

Jensen, A. R. (1999). *Galton's legacy to research on intelligence.* Paper presented at the Conference on Man and Society in the new Millennium, London.

Jöreskog, K. G. (1977). Structural equation models in the social sciences: Specification, estimation and testing. In P. R. Krishnaiah (Ed.), *Applications of statistics* (pp. 265–277). Amsterdam: North-Holland.

Kail, R. (1991). Developmental functions for speed of processing during childhood and adolescence. *Psychological Bulletin, 109,* 490–501.

Kaufman, A. S. (2000). Tests of intelligence. In R. J. Sternberg (Ed.), *Handbook of Intelligence* (pp. 445–476). Cambridge: Cambridge University Press.

Kozulin, A., & Rand, Y. (2000). *Experience of mediated learning: An impact of Feuerstein's theory in education and psychology.* Oxford: Pergamon Press.

Kyllonen, P. (2002). "g": Knowledge, speed, strategies, or working memory capacity? A systems perspective. In R. J. Sternberg & E. L. Grigorenko (Eds.),

The general factor of intelligence: How general is it (pp. 415–445). Mahwah, NJ: Erlbaum.

Mackintosh, N. J. (1998). *IQ and human intelligence.* Oxford: Oxford University Press.

Mithen, S. (1996). *The prehistory of the mind.* New York: Thames and Hudson.

Nigg, J. T. (2001). Is ADHD a disinhibitory disorder? *Psychological Bulletin, 127,* 571–598.

Parrila, R. K. (1995). Vygotskian views on language and planning in children. *School Psychology International, 16,* 167–183.

Pascual-Leone, J. (1970). A mathematical model for the transition rule in Piaget's development stages. *Acta Psychologica, 32,* 301–345.

Piaget, J. (1970). Piaget's theory. In P. H. Mussen (Ed.), *Carmichael's handbook of child development* (pp. 703–732). New York: Wiley.

Rasch, G. (1980). *Probabilistic models for some intelligence and attainment tests.* Chicago: University of Chicago Press.

Shayer, M., Demetriou, A., & Pervez, M. (1988). The structure and scaling of concrete operational thought: Three studies in four countries. *Genetic, Social, and General Psychology Monographs, 114,* 307–376.

Spearman, C. (1904). General intelligence, objectively determined and measured. *American Journal of Psychology, 15,* 201–293.

Spearman, C. (1927). *The abilities of man: Their nature and measurement.* New York: Macmillan.

Spearman, C. (1931). Our need of some science in place of the word "intelligence." *Journal of Educational Psychology, 22,* 401–410.

Sternberg, R. J. (1985). *Beyond IQ. A triarchic theory of human intelligence.* New York: Cambridge University Press.

Sternberg, R. J. (1997). Successful intelligence. New York: Plenum.

Sternberg, R. J., Conway, B. E., Ketron, J. L., & Bernstein, M. (1981). People's conceptions of intelligence. *Journal of Personality and Social Psychology, 41,* 37–55.

Sternberg, R. J., & Grigorenko, E. (2002). *Dynamic testing.* Cambridge: Cambridge University Press.

Thurstone, L. L. (1938) Primary mental abilities. *Psychometric Monographs, 1.*

van Geert, P. (1994). *Dynamic systems development: Change between complexity and chaos.* Hemel Hempstead: Harvester Wheatsheaf.

Vygotsky, L. V. (1978). *Thought and language.* Cambridge, MA: MIT Press.

Wertch, J. V. (1985). *Culture, communication, and cognitive development: Vygotskian perspectives.* Cambridge: Cambridge University Press.

Index